Building on the Past

Medieval and postmedieval essays in honour of Tom Beaumont James

EDITED BY
AMANDA RICHARDSON
AND MARK ALLEN

BAR BRITISH SERIES 662 | 2021

BAR
PUBLISHING

Published in 2021 by
BAR Publishing, Oxford

BAR British Series 662

Building on the Past

ISBN 978 1 4073 5781 2 paperback
ISBN 978 1 4073 5366 1 e-format

DOI https://doi.org/10.30861/9781407357812

A catalogue record for this book is available from the British Library

COVER IMAGE *View to great hall at Clarendon from kitchens (Tom James). Illustration: Reconstruction of 'knights in combat' group 1 Wessex tiles, c.1240-44, as found in the royal apartments (Sem Vine).*

BAR
PUBLISHING

BAR titles are available from:

BAR Publishing
122 Banbury Rd, Oxford, OX2 7BP, UK
EMAIL info@barpublishing.com
PHONE +44 (0)1865 310431
FAX +44 (0)1865 316916
www.barpublishing.com

Of Related Interest

Stories from the Edge
Creating Identities in Early Medieval Staffordshire
Matthew Blake

Oxford, BAR Publishing, 2020 BAR British Series **657**

Coin Hoarding in Medieval England and Wales, c.973-1544
Behaviours, motivations, and mentalités
Murray Andrews

Oxford, BAR Publishing, 2019 BAR British Series **651**

The Moneyers of England, 973–1086
Labour organisation in the Late Anglo-Saxon and Early Anglo-Norman English mints
Jeremy Piercy

Oxford, BAR Publishing, 2019 BAR British Series **650**

Inscribed Vervels
A corpus and discussion of late medieval and Renaissance hawking rings found in Britain
Michael J. Lewis and Ian Richardson

Oxford, BAR Publishing, 2019 BAR British Series **648**

Multi-period Occupation at Football Field, Worth Matravers, Dorset
Excavations 2006–2011
Lilian Ladle

Oxford, BAR Publishing, 2018 BAR British Series **643**

Industry and the Making of a Rural Landscape
Iron and pottery production at Churchills Farm, Hemyock, Devon
Edited by Chris Smart

Oxford, BAR Publishing, 2018 BAR British Series **636**

Fishing and Managing the Trent in the Medieval Period (7th–14th Century)
Excavations at Hemington Quarry (1998–2000), Castle Donington, UK
Lynden P. Cooper and Susan Ripper with contributions by Matt Beamish, Jennifer Browning, Nicholas J. Cooper, Robert Howard, Patrick Marsden, Angela Monckton, Anita Radini and Deborah Sawday

Oxford, BAR Publishing, 2017 BAR British Series **633**

Tom James in October 2020 (Photograph courtesy of Mary James).

Acknowledgements

A volume of essays honouring Tom James was never going to be an easy thing to complete. When we initially took on the task, around 2013, one of the first things to address was what sort of focus the book should have. Tom's interests are both broad and deep and we therefore cast our net wide. It says much about the regard in which Tom is held that almost everyone we contacted agreed to contribute an essay. We ended up with a vast array of topics that cover around two thousand years of archaeology and history. The genesis of the volume has been characterised by periods of intense activity followed by fallow times when other – often apparently lifechanging – matters took precedence, so the editors are, first and foremost, immensely grateful to the contributors for their forbearance and good humour while waiting for their papers to be published. We hope that the result pleases readers and especially Tom, but also those who have contributed essays.

Thanks are due to several people and organisations. Of those whose names appear in this volume, we would particularly like to thank Professors Elizabeth Stuart and Chris Given-Wilson, whose tributes relate to working and studying with Tom over a number of years. We hope that the warmth of their comments illustrates the enduring friendships that have formed with Tom. Mary South has helped with some of the editing and John Hare has also been a source of reassurance and advice; he has worked tirelessly to ensure that the volume stayed true to its original conception. The individual authors have thanked those who specifically helped with their research in their chapters, but we would like to acknowledge the help of staff at archives and libraries, who have aided the research which made this volume possible. A number of individuals and organisations are also acknowledged for granting permission for us to use images for which they hold the copyright. These are, Jeremy Ashbee (Figure 4.8); James Ayres (Figures 15.1–15.9); the Bodleian Library (Figure 13.2); the British Library Board (Figures 3.5, 3.16 and 4.6); the Trustees of the British Museum (Figures 3.1 and 3.7–3.14); Cambridge University Collection of Aerial Photography (Figure 13.1); David Cousins and The Salisbury Museum (Figure 14.1); George Eastman House, International Museum of Photography and Film (Figure 16.16); Bill Fergie (Figures 9.3 and 9.6); Alejandra Gutiérrez (Figure 3.2); John Hare (Figures 5.1–5.9); Historic England Archive (Figure 14.6); Historic Royal Palaces (Figures 4.1, 4.2, 4.3, 4.7 and 4.10); Carlos Lemos (Figures 4.4 and 4.5); Northamptonshire County Council (Figures 13.13–13.16); the Provost and Fellows to The Queen's College, Oxford (Figures 16.2–16.5 and 16.7); Edward Roberts (Figures 9.1 and 9.5); Jonathan Snowdon (Figures 9.2, 9.4 and 9.7); Mary South (Figures 3.3, 3.4 and 3.15); K. South (Figure 3.6); the Local Studies and Maritime Collection, Southampton City Council (Figures 16.1 and 16.15); Andrew Spicer (Figures 16.6, 16.8, 16.10–16.13 and 16.17); and John Steane (Figures 13.5–13.9, 13.11 and 13.12). In addition, we acknowledge Figure 4.9 is Crown Copyright (2019) and Figures 14.2–14.5 are available in the public domain on Wikimedia Commons. All other images are taken from publications that are out of copyright. We would also like to thank the staff at the library of the Institute of Historical Research, who went beyond what would be expected of them in finding some obscure page references during the Covid-19 pandemic and the four anonymous readers who looked at an initial draft of the whole volume.

A number of other people helped with the production of the volume. Sem Vine produced the cover illustration, which is a contemporary view of the remains at Clarendon from Tom James's archive. At the publishers, the editorial team has been most helpful, especially Dr Ruth Fisher and her predecessor Dr Jane Burkowski as well as Liam Barrett, David Davison, Matthew Hands and the editor-in-chief Jacqueline Senior. We also extend our gratitude to the University of Winchester, which provided financial support to help with publication and reproduction costs. In addition, we would like to acknowledge the Friends of Clarendon Palace for the support and friendship they have offered Tom, their Honorary President since 2013, in sometimes challenging times. Their flourishing membership and enthusiasm in keeping the palace site clear of weeds, as well as the conferences and lectures they have put on, are testament to Tom's inspirational love of medieval history and his determination to involve the public in historical and archaeological research.

We are also most grateful to Tom's wife Mary James, Virginia Jansen, Ryan Lavelle, John Oldfield, Caroline Palmer, Gill Rushton, Dick Selwood and Matthew Woollard for their help and advice over the course of the production of this volume.

The editors would also like to thank Jane and Ken, who have lost us for many evenings and weekends whilst we have grappled with editing, formatting, photographic permissions and writing. Most of all, however, we would like to thank Tom. Without his encouragement and guidance neither of us would have ended up where we are now, and we hope the scholarship in this volume is in some small way a note of thanks from all of us, and many generations of past undergraduate and postgraduate students, for his friendship and guidance over the years.

Mark Allen and Amanda Richardson
Eastleigh and Kings Worthy.
October 2020.

Contents

Tom James at the University of Winchester

Elizabeth Stuart

First Deputy Vice Chancellor, University of Winchester.

Academics want to be remembered for being academics, for their research, their publications, and their contribution to knowledge. They aspire to be fondly remembered by their students for exciting their passion for knowledge. Generally speaking, we do not particularly want to be remembered for our administration and management. Indeed, in some parts an academic with a reputation for being a good administrator or manager would be a highly suspect creature, a devil to be supped with only with the aid of a long spoon. However, the British university system relies on colleagues being willing to sacrifice some or all of their identities as academics in order to ensure that the sector continues to be managed by its own and is not taken over by those without any sensitivity to its values or mission.

To celebrate Tom James as a scholar and teacher, which is the point of this volume, is the right thing to do, but it would be amiss not to recognise with gratitude his willingness to take on other responsibilities at the University of Winchester. In 2005, I was appointed Director of Research and Knowledge Transfer with the task of ensuring that the institution obtained research degree awarding powers (RDAP). Tom was always going to play a vital role in that process because he was at that time the member of staff with the most research degree completions, including those of many of the contributors to this book. He was, however, willing to take on a much more onerous role in the process by becoming Chair of our Research Degrees Committee and becoming responsible for the management of research degrees in the institution. Between us, a theologian and a historian, we navigated the labyrinthine Quality Assurance Agency (QAA) processes and various obstacles and RDAP was awarded in 2008. We were more than ready because Tom had prepared Winchester regulations and processes even before the RDAP assessors touched down to inspect us. Working with the redoubtable Professor Pat Cryer who he brought to the University and with whom he assumed a kind of double-act that was a joy to behold, Tom sought to professionalise the role of research degree supervisor (one of the most unscrutinised roles in British higher education), writing a Postgraduate Certificate in Research Degree Supervision of which I am proud to have been the first graduate. As a result, we have a growing and thriving postgraduate research degree community at Winchester which owes much to the foundations laid by Tom. That Tom should have devoted the final years of his time at the University to academic management and administration shows a generosity of spirit and love for the institution which should not be overlooked or under-appreciated. Tom was as excellent a manager as he is an academic, and his award of MBE in June 2011 for services to Higher Education was richly deserved.

Tom James: An Appreciation

Chris Given-Wilson
University of St Andrews

I first met Tom James at a student rally. It was October 1967, and we had both arrived as undergraduates at St Andrews to find ourselves thrown into one of those triennial contests whereby, faced with a rather improbable list of candidates, Scottish students elect a rector to represent their interests to the university authorities. The candidates on this occasion were: Sean Connery; the West Indian cricketer Sir Learie Constantine; the ex-leader of the Liberals Jo Grimond; and Alexander Gibson, conductor of the Scottish National Orchestra. Tom supported Constantine (cricket has always been one of his passions), while I supported Gibson. Ranged on each side of the university quadrangle, four sets of over-excited students were chanting and waving placards at each other when a genial, slightly unkempt figure with a straggly moustache broke ranks, ambled across the grass and asked me if I came from Hampshire. Local connections have always mattered to Tom. As the son of a Winchester clergyman and the cousin of Colin James, the late bishop of Winchester, he was steeped from an early age in Hampshire history and traditions.

We soon became friends, especially once we discovered that we were both studying medieval history. Not that we saw a great deal of each other initially. I spent my first year in a university hall of residence, which all first-years had been informed that they had to do, and mixed largely with others in the same hall. Tom, characteristically, had returned the form on which we were meant to indicate our choices of residence with the boxes un-ticked and a note to the effect that under no circumstances would he stay in a university residence. Equally characteristically, he got away with it. Determined to be independent, he found a bedsit in the town and a similarly free-spirited circle of friends. Several of them were actors or singers, as a result of which he made occasional appearances in student dramatic productions and later joined the university's Renaissance group. Gregarious and outgoing by temperament, he made friends easily: someone once remarked he knew everyone from the Principal to the porters.

After we moved from undergraduate to postgraduate work, we saw much more of each other. In the early 1970s, postgraduates made up a far smaller proportion of students in British universities than nowadays. There were, I think no more than five or six of us writing doctoral theses in medieval history at St Andrews. Tom's thesis, which grew out of his roots, was supervised by Ann Kettle and entitled 'The Geographical Origins and Mobility of the Inhabitants of Southampton, 1400-1600'. Local history – which for him really meant the history of Hampshire and Wiltshire – has always been at the heart of his interests. Even before coming up to St Andrews he had taken part in the great programme of excavations in Winchester in the 1960s. It thus seemed almost preordained when, in 1976, shortly before completing his PhD, he was appointed as lecturer in history and archaeology at King Alfred's College (now the University of Winchester). This marked the start of a long and fruitful collaboration with Professor Colin Platt (University of Southampton), and in 1979 Tom became general editor of the Southampton Records Series, under whose imprint his 1983 collection, *Southampton Sources, 1086-1900*, was published.

Following correspondence in *The Times* on the occasion of Queen Elizabeth II's jubilee in 1977, Tom also embarked on a project which was to occupy him on and off for thirty years, the excavation of the royal palace and deer park at Clarendon, two miles east of Salisbury in Wiltshire. Clarendon was another collaborative enterprise, this time with Christopher Gerrard (University of Durham). It was a study of landscape as much as, indeed more than, a famous building. Although it was only during the medieval period that this 'grandest western royal residence in England' assumed national significance (it was here that Henry II presented Thomas Becket with the Constitutions of Clarendon in 1164, and here that Henry VI suffered his initial mental collapse in 1453) the aim of the project was, quite literally, to unearth the changing face of a landscape from prehistory to the present day. Established as a royal hunting-ground by Henry I, Clarendon park had grown by the fourteenth century to enclose more than 4,000 acres. Teamwork was thus of the essence, and teamwork is something Tom has always been good at. Experts on fish bones, dendrochronology and medieval floor tiles mingled with numismatists and even Danish bear specialists to provide as complete a history as possible of the site. Prehistoric and Roman remains were discovered and the ruins of the medieval palace consolidated (they are now open to visitors from the Clarendon Way). Many of those who helped by field-walking or sifting spoil heaps were undergraduates or volunteers, testimony to the enthusiasm aroused in the local community. The Clarendon project culminated in a sumptuous feast in the Great Hall in 2004 and the publication in 2007 of a monograph, *Clarendon: Landscape of Kings*, jointly authored with Christopher Gerrard.

The completion of this ground-breaking study is testimony not just to Tom's creative energy but also to his sense of responsibility. He believed strongly that, given the funding which such projects received (the excavations at Clarendon attracted a total of nearly £500,000), archaeologists had a duty to ensure that their work was properly written up and published. Tom was not the first to direct excavations at Clarendon. A team led by Tancred Borenius and John Charlton had worked there in the 1930s, and further digs followed in 1948, 1951, and for several seasons during the 1960s, led by Elizabeth Eames and John Musty. Interim reports had been issued, plans drawn up, some of the more notable finds catalogued and put on display, and brief articles published in archaeological and antiquarian journals, local newspapers, or magazines such as *The Field*. The first task was thus to collate and publish the findings of these earlier reports, and the result was the publication in 1988 of *Clarendon Palace: the History and Archaeology of a Medieval Palace and Hunting Lodge near Salisbury, Wiltshire*, co-authored with Annie Robinson. As its title indicates, this dealt almost exclusively with the medieval palace and hunting lodge, which had been the focus of the excavations between the 1930s and 1960s. It was the same desire to ensure that the fruits of archaeological investigation were made publicly available which motivated Tom, once Clarendon was finished, to collate and publish the reports on *The Perth High Street Archaeological Excavation 1975-1977* (2011), another collaborative venture. Before leaving St Andrews in 1976, Tom had acted as deputy director of the excavations at Perth, but the untimely death of the director, Nicholas Bogdan, meant that the findings had not been published.

Tom's passion for local history continued to inspire both his teaching and his research throughout his career at Winchester. His numerous publications included *The English Heritage Book of Winchester* (1997, with an expanded edition published as *Winchester From Prehistory to the Present* ten years later), *The Black Death in Wessex* (1998), *The Black Death in Hampshire* (1999), and *The 1871 Census for Winchester* (2006). Many of the two dozen or so students whom he successfully supervised at doctoral level at both Winchester and Southampton also worked on local projects, and most of them became lifelong friends. He was always in demand as a teacher, not only because of his knowledge and dedication, but also because he had a twinkle in his eye, a readiness to listen to what others had to say, and the laid-back demeanour of a man who is comfortable in his own skin. One former student recalls 'Tutorials with Tom' as follows: Once the unwary student accepted that it was normal to cautiously pick their way around, or over, Tom's floor filing system, remove another pile of papers, files and books from the one potentially available chair, momentarily wonder what to do with it, before being told, 'Put it on the floor', tutorials worked fine. Once coffee had been made, he would lower himself into a worn, saggy-bottomed, stuffing escaping, much loved and well-used old leather armchair which reposed in one corner. (How I wished I could have whisked that chair away and had it traditionally re-upholstered and restored to its original beauty). This was the signal for work to begin, although due to the 'open door' policy that Tom employed, there were often interruptions, with staff putting their heads round the door or students wanting to leave or collect a piece of work, or book. All were made welcome and rarely did they go away empty-handed with their mission unfulfilled. The fire escape provided me with my favourite memory of all. Going along one warm summer afternoon, Tom and I arrived more or less together outside his door. As usual he was loaded up with a pile of papers and, balancing these precariously on one hand, he unlocked the door. The 'floor filing' had got out of hand - there was just enough space for the door to open, nothing more. This was immediately filled by the paper pile Tom was carrying. 'What about the fire escape?' he said. 'OK', I replied. So out onto the warm steps of the fire escape we went, to sit and chat and work completely uninterrupted for the next hour and a half. The best tutorial ever!

If local history and archaeology were at the heart of Tom's research, he also saw them as a springboard to examine wider issues. It was his detailed work on Clarendon, for example, that made him aware of the need for a broader synthetic survey of medieval English palaces and led to his publication in 1990 of *The Palaces of Medieval England c. 1050-1550: Royalty, the Nobility, the Episcopate and their Residences from Edward the Confessor to Henry VIII*. (He was in fact well qualified to tackle this subject, for, as he could not resist pointing out in the preface, he was one of the few people in England who had relatives living in a palace – namely, Wolvesey Palace, the residence since the middle ages of the bishops of Winchester). Similarly, it was his doctoral work on Southampton's shifting population and his experience with the Perth High Street excavations that led to the compilation of a sourcebook entitled *The Urban Experience: English, Scottish and Welsh Towns, 1450-1700*, co-edited with Roger Richardson (1983). Research infused his teaching, and vice versa. It was his course at Winchester on the Hundred Years' War that inspired him to co-edit with John Simons the scurrilous Francophobic *Poems of Laurence Minot* (1989); his article on 'John of Eltham, History and Story: Abusive International Discourse in Late Medieval England, France and Scotland', in *Fourteenth-Century England II* (2002), reprised a similar theme on a neighbouring stage.

Tom's abiding interest in the Black Death (the subject of another course) led him in a different direction. It began with analysis of the manorial records which revealed so graphically the devastation caused by the Black Death in the southwest – especially on the well-documented estates of the bishopric of Winchester, which formed the evidential basis for a doctoral thesis which he supervised by Paula Arthur – and developed into a fascination with plague and its impact on society. His acknowledged expertise on the Black Death also led to media work: he acted as consultant on the pestilence for Melvyn Bragg's *2000 Years of Christianity* and Bettany Hughes's *Seven Ages of Britain*, which in turn led to the writing of a history of Britain to accompany the broadcast of *This Scepter'd Isle* (Radio 4, 1996). Tom has appeared at various times on BBC2, ITV, Channel 4, the Discovery Channel, the History Channel and Sky Atlantic.

These burgeoning commitments were undertaken against the background of a full family life. In 1978, Tom married Mary ('Muffie') Watson, a fellow St Andrews graduate whose equally busy career as a publisher led to spells working in Cheltenham, Oxford and, latterly, London.

With the birth of their sons, Edward, Richard and Alex, between 1985 and 1995, this inevitably entailed a good deal of synchronization to accommodate the demands of work and home, and in 1991 they moved to Cheltenham, from where Tom commuted to Winchester in term-time and worked mostly from home during the vacations. Throughout his sons' childhood, he was involved to the hilt with them, taking equal responsibility for their care, a relaxed and deeply affectionate parent, always alert to their differing needs. He also continued into his fifties to play cricket for the King Alfred's Staff team, one of the highlights of which was a biennial visit to Northumberland to fulfil a long-standing fixture. Sometimes this would be combined with a holiday to Ballater, where they stayed in a family house just yards from the Dee, a base for long walks in the Cairngorms.

A fluent and engaging speaker, Tom has always been in demand to give talks to local and regional historical and archaeological groups, as well as to national bodies such as the Society of Antiquaries and the British Archaeological Association. In 1986 he undertook a lecture tour of Australia which included papers at Sydney, Melbourne, Adelaide and Canberra. He has also lectured in Germany, France, the Netherlands and Russia, and on several occasions at the annual International Medieval Congresses at Leeds and Kalamazoo (Michigan), where he was a familiar figure not only in the lecture theatre but also at the dances with which these conferences traditionally end. Sometimes his visits to Kalamazoo would be preceded or followed by mini-holidays. In 1999, he and I spent the week before the conference in California, firstly in San Francisco and then at Yosemite National Park, where we climbed to the top of a mighty waterfall and, before retiring to our cabin for the night, were made to watch a video demonstrating the ability of the local black bears to break into almost anything if they smelt food – especially car-boots, even when locked.

Generally speaking, Tom's attitude towards cars is utilitarian – the interiors of those he drives generally resemble the 'floor filing' system in his office – but there is one significant exception to this rule. About thirty years ago, he acquired various parts of a vintage Rolls-Royce, including a chassis, bodywork panels and an engine, which have sat in his garage ever since awaiting assembly into a working model. Despite the acquisition in 2013 of another vintage Rolls-Royce (complete, but in pieces), so far reconstruction has not happened, but this does not stop him proudly showing them to visitors, and it would not be the first time he has confounded the sceptics. Meanwhile, the cars which he and Muffie actually drive are relegated to the forecourt.

Tom spent his whole teaching career at Winchester, where his gentle, convivial manner and strong collaborative ethos led to the formation of lasting friendships with staff and students. Within five years of arriving there, he was promoted to a senior lectureship, and in 2000 he became Professor of Regional Studies. He also involved himself fully in academic life, assuming a major role in the negotiations during the 1980s and 1990s whereby what had originally been the Diocesan Teacher Training College, founded in 1840, was eventually (in 2004) granted the right to award its own undergraduate degrees. A year later, King Alfred's College became the University of Winchester, and Tom was appointed as Chair of the Research Degrees Committee, entrusted with managing the process of acquiring research degree awarding powers for the university. These were granted in 2008, and Tom retired in the same year, being promptly appointed as Emeritus Professor of Archaeology and History. Yet he retains his links with the university, and published, in December 2015, *Winchester University: 175 Years of Higher Education*, written as part of the university's 175th anniversary celebrations. His love of local history continues to bear fruit, and in 2018 he published, with Jen Best, *Debt of Honour. Winchester City's First World War Dead*, detailing the stories of 459 men from Winchester who died in the Great War.

In 2011, Tom was appointed MBE for services to higher education, a fitting culmination to an outstanding career. The essays in this book represent a further tribute. Written by former students, colleagues, fellow historians and friends, they reflect his areas of expertise: the history of Winchester and Southampton, along with local history more generally; the Black Death, especially in Hampshire; buildings and the landscape, using both archaeological and documentary evidence; and the history of towns, with the emphasis on the people who lived in them. They are a mark of the esteem and affection in which he has always been held.

Contributors

Mark Allen is a Senior Lecturer in Modern History at the University of Winchester. He studied at the University of Hull in the early 1990s before completing a PhD at King Alfred's College in 2000 on the effects of the arrival of the Railways in Winchester, with Tom James as Director of Studies. He was a Research Officer at the University of Essex between 1996 and 1998 and has been teaching at Winchester since 1998. He specialises in nineteenth-century social and economic history, especially the development of census taking and post-medieval Winchester. Mark co-directs The Winchester Project with Tom James, which aims to trace the city's property history from 1550 to the present. He has published *The 1871 Census of Winchester* (2006) with Tom and contributed to *God and War: The Church of England and Armed Conflict in the Twentieth Century* (2012), looking at Winchester Clergy and the Boer War.

Paula Arthur studied English and History at King Alfred's College, Winchester before taking an MA in Medieval Studies at Birkbeck College, University of London. She then followed her MA by completing a PhD studying and translating the Bishop of Winchester's pipe rolls for the years 1348–9. She was awarded her PhD in September 2005. Paula has also published articles on the Black Death of 1348–9 in *The Hatcher Review* and the series *Fourteenth Century England*, as well as conducting presentations on the Black Death. She continues to work as an independent scholar furthering research into the Black Death whilst also working as a Financial Liabilities Underwriter in Lloyds of London. In her leisure time, Paula is restoring and researching a fourteenth-century hall house in West Essex.

Jeremy A. Ashbee is the head properties curator at English Heritage, where he is responsible for research to inform the conservation and presentation of the 420 monuments in the organisation's care. After studying archaeology at Cambridge and York universities, and working as a field archaeologist at units in Lincoln and Lancaster, he joined the curatorial department of Historic Royal Palaces in 1996, based at the Tower of London. He undertook researches into the history and development of the Tower, receiving his doctorate in 2006. He has published widely on medieval castles and palaces in England and Wales, including official guidebooks for the castles at Goodrich, Dunstanburgh, Rochester, Conwy, Beaumaris and Harlech.

James Ayres was for many years Director of the John Judkyn Memorial at Freshford Manor, Bath. This organisation circulated exhibitions, throughout Europe, on the social history of the USA and shared trustees with the American Museum at Bath into which it has now been incorporated. As an architectural historian the focus of Ayres's research has been on the empirical values of the building trades. This is not only reflected in his books listed in the bibliography for his paper in this volume but also in his founding of the Building of Bath Museum (since renamed the Bath Architecture Museum) and his Presidency of the Wiltshire Buildings Survey. His other publications include *The Artist's Craft* (Oxford: Paidon, 1985), *Two Hundred Years of English Naïve Art* (Alexandria, Virginia: Art Services International, U.S., 1996) and *Art, Artisans and Apprentices* (Oxford: Oxbow, 2014). He has worked with John Steane for the past 25 years, surveying and analysing listed buildings.

Cheryl Butler is a Fellow of the Royal Historical Society and the Royal Society of Arts; trustee of the Hampshire Archives Trust, and a member of the editorial board for the Southampton Records Series. Publications include three Southampton Records Series volumes on the *Southampton Mayors Book of Fines*; an oral history of Itchen Ferry Village; *Tudor Southampton: rioters, revellers and reformers*; and *Jane Austen and Southampton Spa*. She was winner of the BALH personal achievement award in 2014 and the City of Southampton award in 2018 for service to heritage. In 2010 she became an Honorary Fellow of the University of Winchester. In her working career she led on Culture, including heritage and tourism with Southampton and Eastleigh Councils. She has spoken at numerous national and international conferences raising the profile of Southampton and its rich archives and history.

Anne Curry is Emeritus Professor of Medieval History at the University of Southampton. She has been President of the Historical Association, a Vice President of the Royal Historical Society and a Trustee of the Royal Armouries and Chair of the Battlefield Trust. Her main research focus is on Anglo-French relations and military organisation, particularly Agincourt and the English occupation of Normandy. Her publications include *The Hundred Years War* (1993, 2003); *The Battle of Agincourt: Sources and Interpretations* (2000, 2015); *Great Battles. Agincourt* (2015); *Henry V* (2015); *Bosworth 1485; A Battlefield Rediscovered* (2013, with Glenn Foard) and *The Soldier in Later Medieval England* (2013, with Adrian Bell, Andy King and David Simpkin). She edited the *Parliament Rolls of Medieval England* for 1422–53, and co-directed www.medievalsoldier.org and www.gasconrolls.org. She has published around 90 articles in English and French, edited several collections, and features as a hologram in the Historial de Jeanne d'Arc in Rouen.

Christopher M. Gerrard is a Professor of Archaeology at the University of Durham. He has authored several books on later medieval archaeology including *Medieval Archaeology* (2003), *Interpreting the English Village* (with Mick Aston, 2013), and *Lost Lives, New Voices* (co-authored, 2018). In 2007 he co-authored *Clarendon. Landscape of Kings* with Tom James. His latest edited volume is *The Oxford Handbook of Later Medieval Archaeology in Britain* (with Alejandra Gutiérrez, 2018). Chris has conducted fieldwork in many different parts of Britain, notably at Shapwick (Somerset), Clarendon (Wiltshire) and now Auckland Castle (Co Durham). All these projects have benefited greatly from the involvement of local communities and volunteers. He has also worked in NE Spain for many years and published excavations and standing building recording projects there, including Templar, Hospitaller and monastic sites. His most recent writing is on natural disasters and their impact.

Chris Given-Wilson is Emeritus Professor of Medieval History at the University of St Andrews. He is the author or editor of eleven books, including *The Royal Household and the King's Affinity 1360–1413* (1986); *Chronicles: The Writing of History in Medieval England* (2004); and *Henry IV* (2016); as well as some thirty articles in historical journals. He was also general editor of *The Parliament Rolls of Medieval England 1275–1504* (16 volumes, 2005). He won the Alexander Prize of the Royal Historical Society in 1987, and *Henry IV* was shortlisted for the Wolfson History Prize in 2017. He was a councillor of the Royal Historical Society and has been a member of the History of Parliament Editorial Board since 2008. He is married with two children and four grandchildren and lives in St Andrews, Fife.

John Hare spent his career teaching history at a sixth form college at the other end of Winchester to the honorand. His digging began as a schoolboy, included Clarendon Palace long before Tom started the massive clear-up and publication, and ended in directing excavations at Battle Abbey. His published work has focussed on medieval economic and social history and its buildings. His books include a study of late medieval Wiltshire, co-authorship of a study of inland trade, and most recently a study of Basingstoke in the Middle Ages. He is a Visiting Research Fellow at the University of Winchester.

David A. Hinton is an Emeritus Professor of Archaeology, University of Southampton, where he was on the staff from 1973, after beginning his career in the Ashmolean Museum, Oxford. He has specialized in the medieval period; his books include *Gold and Gilt, Pots and Pins* (2006) and *Archaeology, Economy and Society* (1990). He co-edited the *Oxford Handbook of Anglo-Saxon Archaeology* (2011) and contributed to the companion volume on later medieval archaeology (2018). He was editor of the journal *Medieval Archaeology,* 1979–89, and President of the Royal Archaeological Institute, 2001–04.

Phil Marter is Senior Lecturer in the Archaeology of the Recent Past at the University of Winchester. He completed his PhD on the medieval pottery industry in England with the University of Southampton in 2005. This research developed an analysis of the changing fortunes of the medieval pottery industry through the use of a nationwide archaeological data set combined with digital GIS mapping work. An interest in landscape archaeology has continued to influence his research on the archaeology of the more recent past. His latest work includes the survey and excavation of the UK's largest WWI military transit camp at Morn Hill outside Winchester and a series of projects to examine Allied and German aviation crash sites from the 1939–45 Air War in the UK, Germany and France.

Susan K. Parkinson completed her master's and doctoral theses at Lancaster University and at the University of Southampton (1997–2004). Her initial work focussed on the Catholics of Winchester in the aftermath of the Reformation, but this research was soon extended to become a comparative study of Winchester and Southampton's responses to the Elizabethan Settlement of Religion. During this time, Tom James offered a tremendous amount of support and encouragement. Sue has taught history at the University of York, University of Hull and the Open University, and organised exhibitions in libraries and archives in Yorkshire. She also assisted with research and transcription on various historical projects, organised and published by the University of London, Roehampton University, University of Hertfordshire and University of Cambridge. In 2007, Tom invited Sue to present some of her PhD research at the University of Winchester, and this presentation forms the basis of her paper in this volume.

Amanda Richardson studied BA History with Archaeology at the now University of Winchester from 1995–8 before completing the MA in Medieval Culture at Southampton. In 1999 she returned to Winchester to read for a PhD on the medieval and early modern forest and park of Clarendon, Wiltshire, supervised by Tom James, Christopher Gerrard and Andrew Reynolds. Since 2004 she has taught at the University of Chichester, where she is programme leader for the BA (Hons) in Medieval and Early Modern History. Amanda's main research avenue is medieval forests and parks, although she has recently focused on the post-medieval cultural significance of deer and deer parks. She has also published extensively on social space, regarding both landscape and high-status buildings, and has recently completed historiographical entries on gender and space for *The Oxford Handbook of Later Medieval Archaeology in Britain* (2018) and the *Routledge Medieval Encyclopedia Online* (2019).

Edward Roberts read English Language and Literature at Magdalen College, Oxford. He took a master's degree in the Philosophy of Education at London University and taught that subject at King Alfred's College, Winchester, for 17 years. Tom James, then editor of *The Proceedings of the Hampshire Field Club and Archaeological Society*, encouraged him to write for publication. There followed several articles for *The Proceedings*, *Vernacular Architecture*, *the Archaeological Journal* and *Medieval*

Archaeology. At Tom's request he co-edited two volumes of the Southampton Records Series (XXIV and XXV). He co-authored *Medieval Hall Houses of the Winchester Area* (1988) and led a programme of dendrochronology that resulted in the dating of over 200 phases of timber-framed Hampshire buildings. This work culminated in the publication of the book *Hampshire Houses 1250-1700: their dating and Development,* (2003, second edition 2016). In 2004 he was elected a Fellow of the Society of Antiquaries.

Mary South has followed a varied career path, vacillating between her twin passions of science and history. Having worked in both industrial and NHS laboratories, she gained a degree in biology and ecology before becoming Head of Science in a girls' comprehensive school. She went on to gain a postgraduate Diploma in Local History from Portsmouth University. This led to work with the Southern Tourist Board, before she became Head of Education, at the Sir Harold Hillier Gardens and Arboretum. At the same time, she gained an MSc at London South Bank University. On retirement she investigated smallpox inoculation in Southampton for her PhD thesis from the University of Winchester. Mary is on the editorial boards of the Southampton Records Series and *Hampshire Papers*, and contributes to ongoing research at Clarendon Palace. She has written three books; *Titanic Threads* (2012); *The Southampton Book of Days* (2012) and *The Inoculation Book 1774–1783* (2014).

Andrew Spicer is Professor of Early Modern European History at Oxford Brookes University. His PhD, at the University of Southampton, was supervised by Alastair Duke and Tom James and was later published as *The French-speaking Reformed Community and their Church in Southampton, c. 1567–1616* (1997). Besides early modern immigration, his research focuses on the socio-cultural impact of the Reformation. His publications include *Calvinist Churches in Early Modern Europe* (2007). He co-edited *Society and Culture in the Huguenot World, c.1559–1685* (2002), *Sacred Space in Early Modern Europe* (2005), *Defining the Holy. Sacred Space in Medieval and Early Modern Europe* (2005), *Public Opinion and Changing Identities in the Early Modern Netherlands* (2006), *Ritual and Violence: Natalie Zemon Davis and Early Modern France* (2012), *The Place of the Social Margins, 1350–1750* (2016) and edited *Lutheran Churches in Early Modern Europe* (2012) and *Parish Churches in the Early Modern World* (2016).

John Steane was educated at Dulwich College and Magdalen College, Oxford, where he read Modern History. He taught in schools for 11 years becoming headmaster of Kettering Grammar School, 1964–76. At Oxford he was a student of W.G. Hoskins. During his time at Kettering he undertook research in landscape history, involving dozens of boys in surveys of fishponds, parks, gardens and excavations at the deserted settlement of Lyveden in Northamptonshire. He wrote *The Northamptonshire Landscape* (1974) and *Peopling Past Landscapes* with Brian Dix in 1978. He moved to Oxfordshire where he was County Archaeologist 1976–90, and he wrote *The Archaeology of Medieval England and Wales* (1985), *The Archaeology of the Medieval English Monarchy* (1993) and *The Archaeology of Power* (2001). He taught adult education classes for Oxford University for 30 years and worked for 25 years with James Ayres, recording 100 buildings and publishing *Traditional Buildings in the Oxford Region* (2013).

Elizabeth Stuart joined the University of Winchester in 1998 as a Professor of Christian Theology and Director of the Centre for the Study of Theology and Religion. She became Director of Research and Knowledge Transfer in 2005 before being appointed Pro-Vice-Chancellor (Academic) in August 2008, and then First Deputy Vice-Chancellor in January 2013. Prior to joining the University of Winchester, Professor Stuart taught Religious Studies and Theology at the University of Glamorgan and University College St Mark and St John. She is an internationally renowned scholar who has published widely on the theologies of sexuality and gender. She has been involved in various national initiatives relating to internationalisation and higher education, equality and diversity and the Research Excellence Framework and, most recently, degree classification.

Barbara Yorke taught early medieval history (and some archaeology) for many years as a colleague of Tom James's at King Alfred's College of Higher Education (subsequently the University of Winchester). She is currently Professor Emeritus of Early Medieval History at the University of Winchester and Honorary Professor of the Institute of Archaeology, University College, London. Major publications include *Kings and Kingdoms in Early Anglo-Saxon England* (1990), *Wessex in the Early Middle Ages* (1995), *Nunneries and the Anglo-Saxon Royal Houses* (2003), *The Conversion of Britain 600-800* (2006) and, edited with Jayne Carroll and Andrew Reynolds, *Power and Place in Europe in the First Millennium AD* (2019). She is currently a Vice-President of the Royal Archaeological Institute and was formerly on the council of The Society of Antiquaries of London.

Introduction

Amanda Richardson and Mark Allen

The papers delivered in this volume reflect a career that has been remarkable in its eclecticism. Building on his undergraduate and doctoral work on migration from 1400–1600 to and from Southampton, where he was born, Tom James moved into the new world of 'quantitative history' in his doctorate, at the University of St Andrews under the supervision of Ann Kettle. A post in the early 1970s with the exceptional scholar Colin Platt as a Social Science Research Council Research Fellow in Southampton University provided a basis for expanding Tom's historical horizons from 1066 to 1900 (published as *Southampton Sources*, 1983). The opportunity to work on Clarendon Palace arose through his connection with Platt – the nearest post-Conquest medieval archaeologist and historian in the region when questions were raised about the site's poor state in the Silver Jubilee year, 1977, notably in a letter from Tim Tatton Brown in *The Times*. Clarendon required a basic history of medieval palaces to provide some context, and over 40 years later Tom is still endeavouring to save the site and ensure its future, ably supported by academics as well as enthusiastic volunteers. As editor of several journals and newsletters including Hampshire Field Club, Southampton Records Series and *Hampshire Papers*, Tom encouraged others to publish their work on a then unfashionable area of study – royal, episcopal and noble residences, their landscapes and structures, as is so forcefully represented in some of the papers to follow.

The chapters in this volume cover around one and a half millennia, from the fifth to the nineteenth centuries, and are written by archaeologists, architectural historians, historians and heritage practitioners, some Tom James's long-standing colleagues, others his past students – and many of them both. Tom became a Professor of Regional Studies and is now Professor Emeritus in Archaeology and History, so it is fitting that the main focus of this work is the archaeology and history of the south of England, specifically Wessex (broadly Dorset, Hampshire and Wiltshire). Some chapters, however, centre on London, Oxfordshire and Suffolk and one transports us across the Channel to Lancastrian-occupied Normandy during the Hundred Years' War, a topic Tom taught for many years, and where Hampshire men played active roles. The thread that connects these disparate outputs is their capacity to inspire future generations of archaeologists, architectural historians and historians.

A number of different structures for this volume were attempted, but because Tom's interests have been so varied any sort of thematic arrangement ended up looking forced. It is therefore presented as a series of essays arranged broadly chronologically, stretching from the early medieval period to the nineteenth century. Yet even this has not been straightforward, as many authors cross into the modern period whilst exploring issues from earlier times. It is hoped, though, that a broad chronology has been maintained, and that it remains possible to discern Tom's main research avenues – the archaeology and history of Clarendon Palace and Park in Wiltshire; medieval buildings analysis, medieval palaces, and the history and archaeology of towns and urban life, especially Southampton and Winchester, as well as other of his academic interests; the socio-cultural impact of the Black Death, and of war and migration. This introduction addresses some of these themes.

Urban life, particularly the history and archaeology of Southampton and Winchester, has been prominent in Tom's academic output since his first works, and this is reflected in several of our papers. David Hinton commences the volume with his chapter on early medieval defences in southern England by referring to the recent excavations of a cemetery at St Mary's Stadium and how they have revised assumptions regarding the chronology of Hamwic's foundation. He cites the emerging power of Mercia as a factor behind West Saxon consolidation in the mid Saxon period (*c*.650–850) – for example East and West Wansdyke (Wiltshire and Somerset) were perhaps created to delineate West Saxon territory in the face of the Mercian threat. As well as the possible purpose of such linear earthworks, Hinton discusses the continuity of use of hillforts, Roman towns and fortifications, and the construction of the burhs, enclosures and precincts of the later mid-Saxon era, including those at Wareham and Wimborne (Dorset), and Winchester. Several theories are dissected, and Hinton concludes that despite claims for earlier defensive strategies and structures, a coherent 'military system' of defences only becomes apparent in the ninth century. Even then, whether defensive features like burhs were cohesively planned remains debatable.

Barbara Yorke then revisits links between the origins of Wessex and of Hamwic, a Saxon trading settlement on the west bank of the River Itchen which thrived in the eighth century, beginning with the St Mary's stadium excavations, which have pushed the settlement's possible origins back as far as the mid-to late-sixth century. Yorke concludes that although Hamwic undoubtedly resulted from rapid early eighth-century expansion, the earlier cemetery provides a context out of which the settlement developed. In particular she cites the strengthening of royal authority and a drive for emulation in the face of the rise Mercia from the late seventh century, concluding that Hamwic's foundation, almost certainly a result of the overlordship of King Ine of Wessex (d.725), may have been inspired by that of Lundenwic under Wulfhere of Mercia (d.675).

Four papers discuss Clarendon at various points in time, from the thirteenth to the nineteenth century. Mary South looks afresh at the circular pavement which occupied Henry III's chapel at the palace, in a lively discussion of its symbolism and its possible personal relevance for the king. Its design, influenced by an upsurge in interest in mathematics, science and astronomy in the late 1100s and early 1200s, is compared with contemporary rose windows, labyrinths, cosmological understandings of the four elements, Isidore's roti and the natural curves and spirals of Fibonacci. South argues that the pavement was intended to invoke feelings of peaceful spirituality. She also questions the accepted date of construction of 1244, preferring the late 1230s when Henry was feeling the need to marry and produce an heir – hence the incorporation of foliate designs which may represent the phases in a plant's lifecycle. Despite years of research, notably by Elizabeth Eames, this is therefore the first analysis of not how, but *why*, the pavement was made.

A 'tendency for seclusion' features in Jeremy Ashbee's paper on Edward I's water-gate at the Tower of London, more familiarly known as Traitor's Gate, built 1275–81. Ashbee surveys the building's form, function and interior details, suggesting a range of possible architectural models. Several conclusions emerge. Far from a structure conceived primarily according to military concerns, the building expressed royal identity, power and confidence in terms of pageantry, its external outward-facing façade made deliberately ornamental. Ashbee also notes the complexity of the layout of Edward I's apartments and of access routes into them, comparing contemporary structures including Leeds Castle in Kent, Winchester Castle in Hampshire, and Conwy Castle in Wales, all of which display a similar trend towards seclusion. He therefore concludes that separation was a fundamental element of royal residences as early as the thirteenth century.

The seclusion noted by Ashbee is also detected by John Hare (and, later on, by Edward Roberts) as he notes a marked shift in emphasis from communal to private spaces in the Bishop of Winchester's residences over time. Hare's work, among a few examples of buildings analysis in the volume, is another of Tom's interests, following on from Tom's seminal work, *The Palaces of Medieval England* (1990). Hare's chapter represents the first attempt to analyse the Episcopal residences of the bishopric of Winchester as a group. He sheds light on the bishops' significance, lordship and patronage by analysing the function and design of their buildings and how they changed over time between 1300 and 1500. As Hare points out, bishops' palaces are second only to royal residences in their extant documentation and structural remains. However, they differ in that the peculiarities of Episcopal life were inscribed in them; for example, in their large chapels and the absence of accommodation for wives and children. Wider links are also made – the decline of the Episcopal residence at Downton (Wiltshire) in the fourteenth century is compared with the parallel neglect of nearby Clarendon Palace, which accelerated after Edward III's reign, while the extravagant spending of later archbishops of Canterbury is also contrasted. Hare suggests that the comparatively less lavish expenditure by the bishops of Winchester on their residences by the fifteenth century perhaps resulted from distractions caused by their collegial foundations at Oxford.

Paula Arthur also uses the extensive records of the Bishops of Winchester, alongside other sources, to determine the impact of the Black Death of 1348–49 on the medieval fair of St Giles, held annually for up to sixteen days in Winchester, and at its height among the largest in Europe. She examines the fair's effects on the city's functioning, since the bishop and his bailiffs assumed total control of both commerce and municipal operations throughout its duration. Arthur concludes that the fair's decline was relatively steady from the mid-twelfth century, and that in the years immediately before the Black Death it had already assumed the characteristics of a regional, rather than an international, market. For this the numerous wars of the late thirteenth and fourteenth centuries were partly responsible, as was Winchester's declining status as a royal centre from the end of the reign of Henry III. Nevertheless, the sources show that the fair's takings reached record lows in 1348–49, when more stalls than ever before were unoccupied. The Black Death thus accelerated an already downward trend, and the fair's decline became irreversible from the early 1400s.

Winchester's post-Black Death commercial decline echoes that of many towns, with many industries, such as pottery manufacture, moving to rural locations. Phil Marter examines the plague's impact on countrywide ceramic production using data from his PhD, which formed the basis of English Heritage's National Database of Medieval Pottery Production Centres in England. While production of ceramics declined following the plague's onset, pottery manufacture was also transformed from a seasonal occupation to a fully-fledged industry by the fifteenth century. Marter examines the circumstances of this change, interrogating the evidence for the industry's post-plague decline from the fourteenth to the fifteenth centuries against developments in other craft industries. The data identify a drop of around 30 per cent in pottery production sites countrywide, with the central Southern region and the South-East particularly hard-hit, especially Berkshire, Hampshire, West Sussex and Wiltshire, which show a decline of around 50 per cent. Although this pattern may have resulted from increased opportunities for alternative work as much as from mortality, the value of using the supply and demand of such ubiquitous household items as ceramic vessels to track the Black Death's cataclysmic impact is clear.

Anne Curry's paper focuses on a topic familiar to Tom's final year undergraduates over many years, and one that features in much of his research: The Hundred Years' War. She discusses the complexities of the English occupation of Normandy of 1417–50, relating it to recent 'peace keeping' endeavours in Afghanistan and Iraq. Curry begins by highlighting issues in common between the fifteenth and the early twenty-first centuries, especially that men trained to fight all too often struggle with a peacekeeping role. She concludes that in the early fifteenth century there were strenuous efforts to ensure that English soldiers behaved courteously towards civilians, although results did not always match expectations. A key issue is whether the people of Normandy (and indeed the English nobility) saw English rule as 'occupation' given the comparable governmental and legal traditions, similar social structures, and a shared language of sorts, at least at the upper level. Curry highlights the prevalence of Anglo-Norman intermarriage, business partnerships and friendships and suggests that the enthusiastic welcome of Charles VII in 1450 was a standard civilian reaction to the arrival of thousands of armed troops, rather than evidence of a deep-seated enthusiasm for a return to French rule.

With Edward Roberts's contribution we return to Wessex. His work represents the first ever regional study, centring on Hampshire, of the architecture and plan-form of late-medieval inns. He tackles the thorny issue of distinguishing inns which evolved from private houses from those that were purpose-built, questioning longstanding assumptions such as the presence of first-floor galleries as evidence for the latter. A multiplicity of rooms can be a pointer, qualified by privacy indicators such as the number of locks and keys listed in inventories. In this way Roberts identifies the Angel at Andover and the George at Alton as 'undoubtedly' purpose-built, while the White Horse at Romsey and the George at Odiham are likely contenders due to their lockable rooms and patterns of access. Throughout the paper Roberts qualifies the 1961 typology of W.A. Pantin, whose hypothesis of two plan-form types (Courtyard or Gatehouse), he argues, has been misinterpreted by successive scholars. He ends with a call for other county-wide studies which might similarly extend Pantin's conclusions.

Cheryl Butler's piece, which weaves together academic and public history, discusses the HLF-funded 'People Project', inspired by Tom James's career-long aim to raise the profile of Southampton's history and heritage. Like Anne Curry, she evaluates the relationship between immigrant and indigenous communities as part of her paper. The project involved producing a searchable database of all surviving references to Southampton residents between 1485 and 1603. Highlights include the traceability through time of various families – one of which was implicated in one of the earliest recorded incidences of witchcraft before the mass trials of James I's reign – and the visibility of women, of whom at least 4,400 appear in the database. Indeed, the vitality of Southampton's records means that those on society's margins, including the disabled and the poor, are traceable. Butler sets out the challenges posed to endeavours such as the People Project, especially the frustrating gaps in the record. Yet she presents an inspiring example of a historical study which is relevant to both amateur and academic history, and which demonstrates the role played by individuals in the prominence of sixteenth-century towns on the national as well as the international stage.

In the second paper on Clarendon, Amanda Richardson considers issues of gender and space in the late-medieval and early-modern deer park, using two documents towards the beginning and end of the 1500s. The first, the Framlingham Park Game Roll (1515–19) relates to Framlingham Great Park in Suffolk and the second, George Penruddock's Ranger's Book (1572–5), to Clarendon Park in Wiltshire.[1] She considers licit and illicit hunting, gendered, spatial and temporal boundaries, and the involvement of royal women in hunting in the two parks. It is demonstrated that women, parks and the forms of hunting that took place within them were firmly linked in the sixteenth-century mindset. However, there is little solid evidence in either source to substantiate recent theories equating parks (and, by extension, their increasing internal compartments in the 1600s) with female space. Nevertheless men, whether poachers or gentlemen hunters, were often found in the more peripheral areas of the parks in question, raising questions concerning masculinity in flux during the late medieval/ early modern transition.

Sue Parkinson takes us back to Winchester in a study of the reception of the Elizabethan Religious Settlement (1559), for which, reportedly, neither the city's 'common' residents nor the 'better' sort were enthusiastic. She discusses the ways in which this 'stubbornness' manifested itself, focusing on recusancy, Catholic services, and the sympathetic lenience of prominent lay officials. Winchester appears to have been a significant centre for Catholicism at all social levels, with wives and widows particularly prominent in the records and in 1591 several young women were condemned to death for attending confession and Mass. But many men were similarly resistant to change. Most Winchester aldermen were less than enthusiastic in promoting conformity, while churchwardens allowed midsummer bonfires until 1569, routinely missed bishops' visitations and were slow to acquire new Bibles and exchange chalices for communion cups. Parkinson notes that this is only half the story, since her discussion concerns the laity and not the clergy. However, it is clear that Winchester's bishops found little active support in their endeavours to eradicate the old religion from the city.

The manifestation of religious ideas in a post-medieval city is evident also in John Steane's paper on the gardens at Wadham and Merton Colleges, Oxford, laid out *c.*1650 and sometime between 1643 and 1675 respectively. That is, Wadham's warden from 1648–59, who probably contributed to its garden's creation, was John Wilkins, later Bishop of Chichester and member of an intellectual circle which saw the Garden of Eden as a model for the ideal state. Steane outlines the garden's walks, its planning (roughly as at Merton's – four quadrants within a square),

[1] BL Add Ch 17745; Add Ch 16554; WSA 549/8. Papers of the Penruddocke Family of Compton Chamberlayne (1570–5), ff.7–23d.

its 'plum-pudding shaped' prospect mount, perhaps meant to invoke the mount of Olives, and water features, paths, pleached avenues and arbours. His discussion is aided by data from resistivity surveys funded by the colleges, which located several features of the gardens' layout. However, Steane also presents a wider discussion of ideas which coalesced in later seventeenth- and eighteenth-century garden planning such as the superiority of square plans, the eschewing of knot designs and the addition of serpentine paths and summer houses. For Merton College he discusses in particular the loss in 1996 of an avenue of limes – the only remnant of the formal garden's plan – which had survived since the eighteenth century, the felling of which yielded informative evidence of former management techniques.

The next two papers in the volume return to a focus on Clarendon. A biographical approach to place and material culture is employed by Chris Gerrard, who discusses the value and meaning bestowed on one object – a coronation medallion of William and Mary (1689) found at the site of the medieval palace. Gerrard uses wills and inventories, the palace site itself in the late seventeenth century and national narratives associated with it, to carry out a lively 'whodunnit'. He concludes that the medallion's most likely depositor was Henry Hyde, brother of Anne Hyde, first wife of James II. Henry was loyal to James, refusing to swear allegiance to William and Mary. He was also familiar with medieval history and is known to have visited Clarendon, so that the combination of artefact and place may have symbolised his loss of influence in royal circles after the overthrow of James II. Gerrard argues that the afterlife of medieval monuments should be seen as more than a narrative of decay, destructive tourism and vandalism, arguing that significant relationships between objects and people remain to be unpicked even in well-documented eras.

Henry Hyde – and possibly his penchant for depositing meaningful offerings – makes another appearance in James Ayres's chapter on Clarendon House (a mansion built *c.*1720 on the Clarendon Estate,), as the likely builder of a late-seventeenth-century lodge at its core in which horse bones seem deliberately to have been deposited. In the early 2000s the House was saved from seemingly terminal decline by its new owners, who wished it to become their family home, inviting Tom James, with Ayres, to produce a historical report. This work forms the basis of the paper, in which Ayres traces the building's evolution from the late-1680s Hyde lodge to the early nineteenth century, also comparing prominent contemporary buildings. Since these include the Duke of Beaufort's Swangrove on the Badminton estate and Sir Benjamin Bathurst's Cirencester Park (Gloucestershire), the great Conservatory at Chatsworth (Derbyshire) and even John Nash's 1825–30 work on Buckingham Palace, Ayres ably demonstrates the worth of rescuing from obscurity this Baroque masterpiece.

Cheryl Butler's People Project identified around 2,394 French speaking immigrants in sixteenth-century Southampton, and aspects of the lives of some of their successors are discussed in a further paper by Andrew Spicer. The French-Walloon community, established in the city in 1567, was granted use of the chapel of the medieval hospital of God's House, an association reinforced by the influx of Huguenot immigrants following Louis XIV's purges and the Revocation of the Edict of Nantes (1685). Spicer's focus, however, is the increased interest in the Huguenot diaspora in the nineteenth century, when the survival of French-speaking congregations came under threat. The relationship between God's House chapel and the French church is explored through the writings of various historians, related artistic and literary representations, and rich descriptions of the chapel's architectural detail. Spicer concludes that the history of the relationship between the French church and God's House was not dwelled upon, so that the bicentenary of the Revocation of the Edict of Nantes had a negligible impact on the congregation. However, this reflected the agency of the church and its ministers, who were more focused on the religious needs of French-speaking residents and visitors than on memorialising the past.

Tom is also the driving force behind the Winchester Project. This builds on Derek Keene's *Survey of Medieval Winchester* by using a variety of textual and visual sources to produce a plot by plot history of the post-medieval city. It has so far produced over half a dozen PhDs, mostly under Tom's supervision. The final paper in this volume on Winchester, by Mark Allen, derives from one of these projects.[2] It analyses the work of census enumerators between 1841 and 1901. The enumerators' books (CEBs) are frequently used by professional historians and genealogists, but few have considered how those who wrote them have influenced our understanding of the population, and our perceptions are largely based on contemporary views of their shortcomings. Allen expands the work he did with Tom James in 2006 in *The 1871 Census for Winchester*. He shows how, at least in the case of Winchester, most enumerators across the century were

[2] Other doctoral theses on the Winchester Project include Mark Allen, "A Railway Revolution? A census-based analysis of economic, social and topographical effects of the coming of the railways upon the city of Winchester, *c.*1830–*c.*1890," unpublished PhD thesis, King Alfred's College/University of Southampton, 1999; Justine Cooper, "Aspects of the development of Winchester's High Street 1550–2000, with special reference to the period after 1750," unpublished PhD thesis, King Alfred's College/University of Southampton, 2001; Peter Crossley, "Winchester Corporation 19th century leases: a review of financial aspects as a source of city building history," unpublished PhD thesis, King Alfred's College/University of Southampton, 2003; Christine Grover, "The suburban development of Winchester from *c.*1850 to 1912," unpublished PhD thesis, University of Winchester, 2008; Michael May, "Winchester houses and people *c.*1650–1710: A study based on probate inventory evidence," unpublished PhD thesis, King Alfred's College/University of Southampton, 1998; Karen Parker, "A comparison of Winchester and Southampton house inventories and furnishings from probate inventories 1447–1575," unpublished PhD thesis, University of Winchester, 2009; Craig Pinhorne, "An urban study of central Winchester applying GIS methodology to 20th century directory and complementary sources," unpublished PhD thesis, King Alfred's College/University of Southampton, 2001; Alex Turner, "Socio-economic aspects of non-local stone building in Winchester, 1500–1800," unpublished MPhil thesis, King Alfred's College/University of Southampton, 1993.

diligent men (no women were employed) who constituted part of a local network of often voluntary officials acting as, for example, Poor Law Guardians, rate collectors, school inspectors, surgeons, teachers or members of the Corporation. Their preoccupations sometimes shine through, for example during the 'moral panic' over the evils of drink and vice, which was manifested across the country in the 1850s. Despite plenty of evidence of confusion among enumerators in how to fill in around a dozen answers to straightforward questions, the evidence of the original CEBs, which are not normally made available to researchers, shows interventions in the originals to be rarer as the century wore on, and they tended towards clarification of material to be coded for publication, rather than correcting obvious discrepancies discovered by the registrars and superintendents who checked them.

The essays in this volume are framed by two appreciations of Tom James that reveal more than just an inspiring researcher and teacher. Chris Given-Wilson assesses Tom's life and career in a way that only a close friend can, affording us a glimpse the personality behind the distinguished academic celebrated throughout this volume. Also, Elizabeth Stuart highlights another side to Tom's academic life - as an administrator and manager willing to take on roles that may not have helped his personal profile, but certainly aided the development of the institution he served for over thirty years; King Alfred's College, later the University of Winchester.

The tributes to a warm and generous colleague, supervisor and friend that appear in the following pages testify to the vitality of many and varied forms of the study of the past.[3] They also demonstrate how the history – and indeed material culture – of any period can resonate with us in the modern world. This is the very essence of Tom James's *modus operandi* and this publication is delivered to him with great respect and profound gratitude.

Bibliography

Primary sources

British Library (BL)

Add Ch 16554: Certificate of tho keeper of Framlingham Park, of "dere slayne and dede of moreyn;" 1515-16. Framlingham Manor; Suffolk: Deer accounts of the parker: 1509-1520. Richard Chambyr, Parker of Framlingham Park: Deer accounts: 1509-1520.: Imperf.

Add Ch 17745: Framlingham Manor; Suffolk: Deer accounts of the parker: 1509-1520.Richard Chambyr, Parker of Framlingham Park: Deer accounts: 1509-1520.: Imperf.

Wiltshire and Swindon Archives (WSA)

549/8. Papers of the Penruddocke Family of Compton Chamberlayne (1570–5), ff.7–23d.

Unpublished theses

Arthur, Paula A. "The Impact of the Black Death on Seventeen Units of Account of The Bishopric of Winchester." Unpublished PhD Thesis, University College Winchester/University of Southampton, 2005.

Allen, Mark A. "A Railway Revolution? A census-based analysis of economic, social and topographical effects of the coming of the railways upon the city of Winchester, *c.*1830–*c.*1890." Unpublished PhD thesis, King Alfred's College/University of Southampton, 1999.

Brown, Richard A. "Bastard feudalism and the bishopric of Winchester, *c.*1280–1530." Unpublished PhD thesis, University College Winchester/University of Southampton, 2003.

Cooper, Justine M. "Aspects of the development of Winchester's High Street 1550–2000, with special reference to the period after 1750." Unpublished PhD thesis, King Alfred's College/University of Southampton, 2001.

Crossley, Peter A. "Winchester Corporation 19th century leases: a review of financial aspects as a source of city building history." Unpublished PhD thesis, King Alfred's College/University of Southampton, 2003.

Eastlake, Elizabeth. "Redressing the balance: Boxley 1146–1538: a lesser Cistercian house in southern England." Unpublished PhD thesis, University of Winchester, 2015.

Fairbrother, Louise. "Burgesses, Freemen and Strangers: The Organisation of Industry and Trade in Southampton, 1547 to 1603." Unpublished PhD thesis, University of Southampton, 2018.

Grover, Christine. "The suburban development of Winchester from *c.*1850 to 1912." Unpublished PhD thesis, University of Winchester/University of Southampton, 2008.

Haddlesey, Richard. "Building in fear?: a re-evaluation of late medieval joint chrono-typologies (*c.*1250-1530) in the light of recent dendrochronological investigations in Hampshire." Unpublished PhD thesis, University of Winchester, 2011.

Marter, Phil. "Medieval Pottery Production Centres in England, AD 850–1600." Unpublished PhD thesis, University of Winchester/University of Southampton, 2005.

May, Michael. "Winchester houses and people *c.*1650–1710: A study based on probate inventory evidence."

[3] As well as the theses on the Winchester Project already mentioned, Tom has been involved, either as Director of Studies or second supervisor, in a further 15 theses by Paula Arthur, Richard Brown, Elizabeth Eastlake, Richard Haddlesey, Phil Marter, Rebecca Oakes, Simon Philips, Jonathan Pitt, Amanda Richardson, Mary South, Andrew Spicer, Myrtle Ternstrom, Anne Thick, Cindy Wood and Roger Young. He also acted as an external advisor for the thesis of Louise Fairbrother. The full details of these works are given in the bibliography to this introduction.

Unpublished PhD thesis, King Alfred's College/ University of Southampton, 1998.

Oakes, Rebecca H.A. "Mortality and life expectancy: Winchester College and New College Oxford c.1393-c.1540." Unpublished PhD thesis, University of Winchester/University of Southampton, 2008.

Parker, Karen. "A comparison of Winchester and Southampton house inventories and furnishings from probate inventories 1447–1575." Unpublished PhD thesis, University of Winchester/University of Southampton, 2009.

Phillips, Simon, D. "The role of the prior of St John in late medieval England, *c*.1300–1540." Unpublished PhD thesis, University College Winchester/University of Southampton, 2005.

Pinhorne, Craig. "An urban study of central Winchester applying GIS methodology to 20th century directory and complementary sources." Unpublished PhD thesis, King Alfred's College/University of Southampton, 2001.

Pitt, Jonathan. "Wiltshire minster parochiae and West Saxon ecclesiastical organisation." Unpublished PhD thesis, King Alfred's College/University of Southampton, 1999.

Richardson, N. Amanda. "The forest, park and palace of Clarendon, *c*.1200–*c*.1650: reconstructing an actual, conceptual and documented Wiltshire landscape." Unpublished PhD thesis, King Alfred's College/ University of Southampton, 2003.

South, Mary L., "The Southampton smallpox inoculation campaigns of the eighteenth century." Unpublished PhD thesis, University of Winchester, 2010.

Spicer, Andrew. "The French-speaking Reformed community and their church in Southampton, 1567 – *c*.1620." Unpublished PhD thesis, University of Southampton, 1994.

Ternstrom, Myrtle. "Lundy: an analysis and comparative study of factors affecting the development of the island from 1577 to 1969, with a gazetteer of sites and monuments." Unpublished PhD thesis, Cheltenham and Gloucester College of Higher Education, 1999.

Thick, Anne. "The fifteenth-century stewards' books of Southampton." Unpublished PhD thesis, King Alfred's College/University of Southampton, 1997.

Turner, Alex. "Socio-economic aspects of non-local stone building in Winchester, 1500-1800." Unpublished MPhil thesis, King Alfred's College/University of Southampton, 1993.

Wood, Cindy. "Cage chantries and late medieval religion *c*.1366–1555." Unpublished PhD thesis, University of Winchester, 2010.

Young, Roger. "Aspects of a microhistory of Sparsholt Hampshire in the nineteenth century." Unpublished PhD thesis, University College Winchester/University of Southampton, 2005.

1

Early Medieval Defences in Southern England

David A. Hinton

University of Southampton

Abstract: No agreed pattern of 'military' provision and organisation in fifth- to eighth-century southern England has emerged, despite much recent debate and many new discoveries. The 'Burghal Hidage' texts seemingly provided for a coherent system, but are still open to different interpretations and dating. Later Anglo-Saxon developments include estate-owners' prestigious houses and the development of towns.

Key words: Burghal Hidage; forts; dykes; enclosures; beacons; towns

This contribution to a collection of essays presented to an old friend does not reflect any particular interest of his, except insofar as he has always been involved in studies that combine archaeological and historical evidence. We were colleagues for a while at the University of Southampton, and often met at King Alfred's College, subsequently the University of Winchester, where Tom Beaumont James was one of a small but very productive group of medievalists. He has worked in Scotland, which I have not, but both of us have had a southern, English, focus in most of our research, and my paper here concentrates on central southern England.

Tom's main work has been in the post-Norman Conquest period, but I want here to review some of the work done on the earlier, post-Roman period, much of it recent and some by his former colleagues. The issues raised include the extent to which formal arrangements for protecting people from raids and invasions were in place before the ninth century, and how they were operated thereafter, when documentary evidence permits glimpses of coherence. Questions that arise include the extent to which words and phrases in early written sources convey information about events that actually occurred, or describe situations in terms that can be reconciled with what is observable on or in the ground. To give an example, I have in the past more than once written that the mid Saxon port (*wic*) at Southampton, generally known as *Hamwic*, was probably founded by King Ine of Wessex, who reigned from 688 to 726,[1] because the earliest objects from the site seemed to fit into that time bracket, and Ine seemed the sort of dynamic king who would have wanted to promote an outlet for exports that would have brought in wine and other luxuries to sustain royal power. How much I regretted that assumption when the Stadium site cemetery brought to light both cremation urns and the inhumation graves of men with elaborate weaponry and of women with valuable costume jewellery, many of which clearly predate 688![2]

Roman forts and towns

To consider the physical works that may have been used for defensive purposes in southern England after the Roman legions withdrew – not necessarily finally in A.D. 410 as used to be thought – the starting-point needs perversely to be far to the north, and Hadrian's Wall. Much as the dating of this was misunderstood by Bede and other writers, its presence was well known in the Middle Ages, and recent excavation has shown one reason why. At some of the forts along it, notably at Birdoswald, there is now evidence of substantial post-Roman occupation, including timber buildings, with no obvious hiatus between use of the site by formally recruited soldiers from overseas adapting to new conditions, and occupation by relatively well-off people amongst whom may have been soldiers or their descendants able to make themselves into local leaders.[3] Such descendants might have been among the princes who according to the epic fought and mostly died at *Catraeth*, perhaps having ridden south down the old Roman road to Catterick, where there is much evidence that the fort at *Cataractonium* and the area around it remained a focal, later royal, centre.[4]

[1] Or 728, as one trouble with documents is that they often come in different versions: M. Swanton, (ed. and trans.), *The Anglo-Saxon Chronicles. New edition* (London: Phoenix Press, 2000), 42–43. All mentions of dates, battles and places below are not separately itemised if taken from this edition of the *Chronicles*.

[2] V. Birbeck, *The Origins of Mid-Saxon Southampton. Excavations at the Friends Provident St Mary's Stadium 1998–2000* (Salisbury: Wessex Archaeology, 2005). Mentioning this date does not imply agreement that all furnished Anglo-Saxon graves pre-date *c.* 680, as argued in J. Hines and A. Bayliss (eds), *Anglo-Saxon Graves and Grave-Goods of the 6th and 7th Centuries A.D.: a Chronological Framework* (Leeds: Society for Medieval Archaeology Monograph 33, 2013) against the conventional numismatic dating.

[3] A. Wilmott, "The late Roman frontier: a structural background," in *Finds from the Frontier*, eds R. Collins and L. Allason-Jones (York: Council for British Archaeology Research Report 162, 2010), 10–16, for a convenient summary.

[4] R. Cramp, "A lost pendant from near Catterick Bridge, Yorkshire," in *Early Medieval Art and Archaeology in the Northern World. Studies in honour of James Graham-Campbell* eds A. Reynolds and L. Webster (Leiden/Boston: Brill, 2013), 78–80.

Nothing comparable to Birdoswald or *Catraeth* exists either in poetry or in archaeology for the Roman forts in southern England. Sussex's Pevensey, the Roman *Anderitum*, has recently yielded sherds of Mediterranean pottery imported between the early/mid fifth century and late sixth/seventh century, by far the most easterly examples of exotica which in south-west Britain and in Wales are taken to have been associated with feasting, found at such high-status western sites as Tintagel, reaching Britain through the Straits of Gibraltar. The pottery found at Pevensey may have come through the Rhineland, however, and the late sixth-/seventh-century sherd in particular is therefore unlikely to demonstrate occupation of the fort by someone with western British connections.[5] In general, Sussex's archaeological record suggests a switch from 'British' to 'Anglo-Saxon' culture during the second half of the fifth century, which, perhaps fortuitously, accords with the account in the *Anglo-Saxon Chronicles* of Aelle's arrival in 477.[6] The Patching hoard, which contained several coins minted up to the 460s and imported from Gaul/Francia rather than from the Rhineland, seems to have been a treasure hoard but one that could have been owned by contestants on either side, assuming that there was indeed conflict.[7] Pevensey might well have been used as a base by someone seeking power over the area around it, and the imported pottery and the Patching hoard both suggest that fifth-/sixth-century connections between Sussex and the continent were stronger than used to be appreciated.[8]

In Hampshire, excavation of a part of the interior of the Roman fort at Portchester found no Mediterranean sherds; 'Portchester D' ware, a type of late Roman pottery, is now thought to have been made in the borders of Hampshire, Surrey and Sussex and to have stayed in production into the fifth century.[9] The post-hole building complexes excavated in the fort could be either 'British' or 'Anglo-Saxon', but its small sunken-featured buildings are still seen as more indicative of the latter, although the organic-tempered pottery in the fills of some of them is not now seen as so culturally distinctive.[10] The parallels that the late Martin Welch drew for the two fifth-century disc-brooches were Germanic rather than late Roman/British,[11] and there are none of the military or official belt fittings that many archaeologists associate with *laeti* or other soldiers brought in by British rulers to bolster their defences. Clearly the archaeology does not support any contention based on the record in the *Anglo-Saxon Chronicles* that a noble young Briton killed in 501 was associated with Portchester.[12] The scale of the excavations inevitably leaves open the possibility that evidence of Birdoswald-like features remains to be found, but at present direct 'continuity' is supported only by a well and a *Grubenhaus* that from the contents of their lower fills are argued to have been in use in the first half of the fifth century; use either by a British élite or by incoming adventurers is unproven.

Similar uncertainty hangs over another Roman fortification in Hampshire, at Bitterne on the River Itchen. This is often but quite probably erroneously taken to be *Clausentum*, a site listed in the Antonine Itinerary.[13] An unstratified disc-brooch found there is very similar to one of the two from Portchester.[14] Although recent work in and around the Bitterne fort has shown more post-Roman evidence, notably burials, their dating effectively excludes them from interpretation as fifth-century British or Germanic 'warriors'.[15] On the Isle of Wight, even whether a Roman fort at Carisbrooke existed is controversial, let alone its immediate post-Roman use, and there is no trace of any other such site on the island.[16]

Even the Mediterranean sherds at Pevensey, therefore, do not provide unequivocal evidence of higher status,

[5] J. Timby, "The pottery," in M.G. Fulford and S. Rippon, *Pevensey Castle, Sussex: Excavations in the Roman Fort and Norman Keep, 1991–95* (Salisbury: Wessex Archaeology Report 26, 2011), at 43–45 and 125.
[6] See discussion in M. Lyne, *Excavations at Pevensey Castle 1936 to 1984* (Oxford: British Archaeological Reports British Series 503, 2009), 122–23. 'Anglo-Saxon' material culture has to be taken as evidence of 'Germanic' *laeti* or some such military involvement if it is not to be taken as evidence of 'Anglo-Saxon' cultural influence.
[7] R. Abdy, "After Patching," in *Coinage and History in the North Sea World* c. *500–1250. Studies in honour of Marion Archibald*, eds B. Cook and G. Williams (Leiden/Boston: Brill, 2006), 76–83. Abdy notes the proximity of Highdown Hill to the find, and the late Roman and early Anglo-Saxon cemeteries close to it, but proximity is the only reason to make the case for a connection. See also essays in *The Archaeology of Sussex to AD 2000* ed. D. Rudling (Kings Lynn: Heritage Marketing and Publications, 2003). As well as coins, the hoard contained two gold rings, one of such purity as to suggest fairly direct import from a source in southern France or Spain, and a Germanic chape, so disparate mixing contributed to it. J. Gerrard, *The Ruin of Roman Britain. An archaeological perspective* (Cambridge: Cambridge University Press, 2013), 166–67, stresses similarities with other hoards from late Roman Britain, and sees the rings as in the Roman finger-ring wearing tradition, despite the size and purity of the larger.
[8] The 'Quoit Brooch Style' metalwork points in the same direction; it is not confined to Sussex, but is also found elsewhere in England, and in Francia: L. Webster, *Anglo-Saxon Art* (London: British Museum, Press, 2012), 52–55; B. Ager, "A late Roman buckle- or belt-plate in the British Museum, said to be from northern France," *Medieval Archaeology*, 40 (1996): 206–11.
[9] Lyne, *Excavations at Pevensey*, 98–99 and 111.
[10] B. Cunliffe, *Excavations at Portchester. Volume II: Saxon* (London: Society of Antiquaries of London, 1975); for the buildings, 16–21 and 52–55. Sunken-featured, though larger, buildings have been found on a few Romano-British sites, and chaff-tempered pottery is known outside the area of early 'Anglo-Saxon' influence, for instance in Gloucestershire, where it is thought to date from the fifth century onwards: J. Timby, "Pottery (Roman, pre- and post-Roman)," 125–62 in E. Price, *Frocester. A Romano-British settlement, its antecedents and successors. Volume 2, the finds* (Stonehouse: Gloucester and District Archaeological Research Group, 2000), 137–38.
[11] M. Welch, "The finds," 205–14 in Cunliffe, *Portchester II.*
[12] The record only says 'Portes mouth': Cunliffe, *Portchester II*, 301–02; see also B.A.E. Yorke, *Wessex in the Early Middle Ages*, Studies in the Early History of Britain (London/New York: Leicester University Press, 1995), 39, for the historical account.
[13] A.R. Rumble, "HAMTVN *alias* HAMWIC (Saxon Southampton): the place-name traditions and their significance," in P. Holdsworth, *Excavations in Melbourne Street 1971–6* (London: Council for British Archaeology Research Report 33, 1980), 18, note 3.
[14] Welch, "The Finds," 205.
[15] Dating and other problems of interpretation were reviewed by A. King, "Roman Bitterne in the third and fourth centuries," *Hampshire Field Club and Archaeological Society Newsletter*, new series 11 (1989): 19–20. For the recently discovered late seventh- to tenth-century burials, A.K. Cherryson, "'Such a resting-place …': Saxon Southampton and the development of churchyard burial," 54–72 in *Burial in Later Anglo-Saxon England,* c. *650–1100 AD* eds J. Buckberry and A. Cherryson (Oxford/Oakville: Oxbow Books, 2010), 57–60.
[16] C.J. Young, *Excavations at Carisbrooke Castle, Isle of Wight, 1921–1996* (Salisbury: Wessex Archaeology Report 18, 2000), 190.

'British', use of the Roman walled areas on the southern English coast. Inland, the perimeter walls of the major towns, Chichester, Silchester, Winchester and Dorset's Dorchester must have remained usable; such massive structures do not collapse readily, as indeed those at Pevensey and Portchester still show. Traffic continued to pass through Winchester's south entry even after the Roman gate collapsed – evidence of use of the intra-mural space, but not of an authority within, anxious to shore up its post-Roman dignity. Later, the entrance was deliberately blocked up, but by whom and precisely when is unclear.[17] Recent excavation of the Roman cemetery at Lankhills outside Winchester yielded no evidence of fifth-century burials indicative of well-to-do 'British' occupants,[18] but that of course could result from the cemetery falling into disuse altogether, with burial taking place elsewhere, rather than that people of higher status had ceased to exist. Smaller walled places inland could also have been used, Wiltshire's *Cunetio* being one possibility, but to demonstrate incontrovertibly that they were used for defence is a different matter, even if activity of some sort could be shown to have gone on inside them.[19] A defensive role for the extra-mural amphitheatre at Silchester was once suggested, but excavation showed no sign of it, despite evidence inside the city of fifth-century occupation, and the possibility of its subsequent continuation.[20]

Early medieval use of Roman enclosures by indigenous leaders for defensive purposes, or to create chieftains' eyries, has yet, therefore, to be positively demonstrated in central southern England. Other evidence of defensive provision is also elusive. The late Roman 'military' belt fittings in Grave 376 at Lankhills might have belonged to a hired soldier, but did not contain weapons and remain exceptional.[21] There are still no examples of burials like those near Dorchester-on-Thames, Oxfordshire, where there are weapons and belt fittings, and women's dress items, indicative of the early fifth century.[22] Metal-detected buckles and strap-ends in the Dorchester-on-Thames mode are seen by some as evidence of the presence either of transient 'mercenaries' or of *laeti* settled within the territory that they were brought in to protect. The density of these things varies; no great coherence emerges from their distributions in southern England,[23] and anyway some of the later types are found in women's graves, suggesting that they had made a gender transition and were no longer markers of soldierly aspiration.[24] In all these respects, therefore, the earliest post-Roman history of central southern England seems very different from that of other areas, possibly a reflection of the area's relative distance from marauding Picts, Irish slave-raiders, and pillagers from northern lands and the Low Countries, and that it was unthreatened by conquest or reconquest from Gaul.

Battles, hillforts and linear earthworks

Hillforts are often recorded as scenes of battles in the written sources. The entry in the *Anglo-Saxon Chronicles* for 552 tells of one fought at *Searo byrg*, which clearly refers to Old Sarum in Wiltshire. The *beran byrg* of 556 could be Wiltshire's Barbury Castle hillfort. Slightly different is the annal for 491 which records a siege, rather than a battle, at Pevensey, but that entry looks like a dualism with 477, which reduces its credibility. Similarly, the 552 record is open to question because it has a supposedly Anglo-Saxon king, Cynric, fighting against Britons, yet it was 'Anglo-Saxon' culture that dominated around Old Sarum by then, so the hint that Cynric was winning territory from the indigenous population may be misleading. A century later, a battle is said to have been fought by King Cenwalh in 652 at *bradanforde be aefna*; Bradford-on-Avon, Wiltshire, is overlooked by the hillfort known now as

[17] M. Biddle and B. Kjølbye-Biddle, "From *Venta* to *Wintanceastre*," 189–214 in *Pagans and Christians – from Antiquity to the Middle Ages. Papers in honour of Martin Henig presented on the occasion of his sixty-fifth birthday* ed. L. Gilmour (Oxford: British Archaeological Reports International Series 1610, 2007), 191–93.

[18] P. Booth *et al*, *The Late Roman Cemetery at Lankhills, Winchester. Excavations 2000–2005* (Oxford: Oxford Archaeology Monograph 10, 2010), 462.

[19] S. Laycock, *Britannia, the Failed State. Tribal conflict and the end of Roman Britain* (Stroud: History Press, 2008), 146, would see the reconstruction of *Cunetio* in *c.* 370 as the work of the Atrebates, but a resurgent tribe is unlikely to have had the ability to muster resources for masonry walls and towers. Gerrard, *Ruin of Roman Britain*, 52–55, notes that *Cunetio* is unique in Britain in being a small inland fort with added towers such as are known in Gaul and the Rhineland. He suggests that, as with towns, this should not be seen as evidence of external threat or internal insurrection, but as a late Roman prestige statement. Recent work has not revealed significant new dating evidence: R. Seager Smith and G. Wakeham, "Further investigation of the Roman small town of *Cunetio*: a *Time Team* evaluation," *Wiltshire Archaeological and Natural History Magazine*, 108 (2015): 79–88.

[20] M. Fulford, *The Silchester Amphitheatre. Excavations of 1979–85* (Britannia Monograph 10, 1989), 57–65 and 193; the post-holes of an aisled building and other features are attributed to the late eleventh/thirteenth centuries. For discussion of post-Roman use of the interior, M. Fulford, A. Clarke and H. Eckardt, *Life and Labour in Late Roman Silchester. Excavations in Insula IX since 1999* (Society for the Promotion of Roman Studies, 2006), 254–80. (The points made in the paragraph in the present paper relate only to defences, not to intra-mural occupation generally).

[21] J.C.N. Coulson, "Military equipment of the 'long' 4th century on Hadrian's Wall," 50–63 in *Finds from the Frontier*, eds Collins and Allason-Jones, 51 and 60.

[22] H. Hamerow, C. Ferguson and J. Naylor, "The Origins of Wessex Project," *Oxoniensia*, 78 (2013): 49–69; page 60 for an update on recent discoveries. Unfortunately for the southern English coastal district, the Wessex dynasty's origins are seen as lying in the Thames Valley, so the research project is limited geographically. There seem to be real differences, however, e.g. the Portable Antiquities Scheme database, searched Feb. 2014, only records four probable clipped ('reduced weight') siliquae for Hampshire, Dorset and Wiltshire, many fewer than the Project has in its zone.

[23] S. Laycock, "Buckles, belts and borders," *Current Archaeology*, 207 (May 2008), 12–19, map on page 18; there is a small knot of 'Dobunnic' buckles in N.E. Hampshire, and about three others in southern Wessex. Gerrard, *Ruin of Roman Britain*, 106 considers that to see these as the property of men available for active service is 'simplistic', and that they should be seen as part of a general shift towards more militaristic display. A search of the Portable Antiquities Scheme database, Feb. 2014, under 'Buckles' '400 to 600' produced no new central southern examples, although a very interesting fixed-plate Quoit Brooch Style buckle from the Isle of Wight, dated 425–75 by Frank Basford, has a frame that looks as though it has devolved from the late Roman series.

[24] Such transitions are not evidence of 'new' people, as penannular brooches were already making the gender switch in the late Roman period: Booth *et al.*, *Lankhills 2000–2005*, 285.

Budbury, which is quite likely to be the *Wirtgeornesbeorg* ('Vortigern's enclosure or fort') referred to by William of Malmesbury, writing in the early twelfth century.[25] That would imply another Saxon versus Briton encounter, but, apparently having access to a different source, Aethelward had earlier referred to it as 'civil war'.[26] Conflicting accounts like those throw doubt on the hillforts' actual use. Furthermore, they were prominent landmarks, often close to roads and road junctions, as is Old Sarum, or to river crossings, like Budbury, the name *bradanforde* implying that it was the control of the River Avon that mattered. Battles, or just skirmishes, may have taken place near, not at, them, when a raiding-party was met by an opposing force that was not necessarily based within the hillfort. Indeed, battles recorded in the *Chronicles* or elsewhere may never in fact have happened, as stories get told to explain places, and what could need explanation more than an ancient hillfort?[27] At any rate, none of the sites named in the *Chronicles* stands comparison with South Cadbury, Somerset, where the post-Roman timber-laced drystone wall makes 'fortification' a viable interpretation.[28]

For Dorset, Bruce Eagles and Catherine Mortimer drew attention to a couple of potentially fifth-century 'Anglo-Saxon' brooches and a spear-head from the slopes below Hod Hill, prompting them to suggest that there were 'mercenaries' there with womenfolk, but who did not establish a permanent Germanic presence; to the east, spearheads have come from another hillfort, Spetisbury Rings, and a single one from Badbury Rings,[29] many people's favourite for the location of the British victory at *Mons Badonicus* recorded by Gildas, who might have been writing in the sixth century, possibly about an event that had, or even had not, happened long before.[30] Christopher Sparey Green noted that the last phase of the Iron Age hillfort at Poundbury, Dorset, excavated in the 1930s, is effectively undated, and could therefore have been reoccupied by people whose predecessors had lived inside Dorchester and who were still using the area of the Romano-British cemetery outside it between the hillfort and the town.[31]

On the Isle of Wight, the claim of the Iron Age hillfort at Yaverland, overlooking Brading Harbour, to have had post-Roman use must be considered, though at present the only evidence is mid rather than early Anglo-Saxon, and has not included work on the defences.[32]

Hampshire's claimed battles were not at hillforts but on the coast where the immigrants supposedly landed, and at *cerdices ford*; this is almost certainly Charford on the River Avon, just downstream from which a quite remarkable Anglo-Saxon cemetery at The Shallows, Breamore, has been found recently.[33] The story of the battle might just possibly therefore be accounted for by a folk memory of a brief, unsuccessful land-taking episode by a special group of people, a story subsequently given credence and respect by being linked to the great Gewissan dynasty founder, King Cerdic.

A possible exception to the non-continuity of military functions of Roman works in southern England is Bokerley Dyke in north-west Dorset, an earth bank of different phases, cumulatively over three miles long; as its ditches are on its north side, it was presumably built by people to the south.[34] Effectively it remains undated, as a coin of Valens found by General Pitt-Rivers apparently in a ditch proves nothing other than that that feature was filled after *c.* 364, but does not therefore date the work to the late Roman period. Its line might perpetuate a prehistoric boundary between two tribes, but only makes sense in a late Roman context if it is accepted that authority broke

[25] D.A. Hinton, "Recent work at the chapel of St Laurence, Bradford-on-Avon, Wiltshire," *Archaeological Journal*, 166 (2009): 193–209, at page 194. P. Sims-Williams, "The settlement of England in Bede and the *Chronicle*," *Anglo-Saxon England*, 12 (1983): 1–41, at page 39 note 175 expressed scholarly caution over, but not outright rejection of, the attribution.

[26] Swanton trans. and ed., *Chronicles*, 28 note 5.

[27] For this point but in relation to later battles, see R. Lavelle, *Alfred's Wars. Sources and interpretations of Anglo-Saxon warfare in the viking age* (Woodbridge: Boydell Press, 2010), 265. Cf. Sims-Williams, "Settlement of England," 27 note 114: 'stories about battles at such sites may have arisen and been attached to more or less legendary heroic figures'; see 36–37 for his explanation of dualisms as resulting from application of the Dionysiac nineteen-year lunar cycle.

[28] L. Alcock, *Cadbury Castle, Somerset. The early medieval archaeology* (Cardiff: University of Wales Press, 1995). Whitsbury hillfort, for long in Wiltshire but in a salient which shows that it probably previously belonged, as it has done since 1895, within what is now Hampshire, has some evidence of late or post-Roman work on the defences, and part of an organic-tempered pot, but not really enough to lay claim to 'refurbishment', though that remains a possibility: A. Ellison and P. Rahtz, "Excavations at Whitsbury Castle Ditches, Hampshire, 1960," *Proceedings of the Hampshire Field Club and Archaeological Society*, 43 (1987): 63–81; see 72–75 and 79.

[29] B. Eagles and C. Mortimer, "Early Anglo-Saxon artefacts from Hod Hill, Dorset," *Antiquaries Journal*, 73 (1993): 132–40; M. Austin, "Rethinking Hardown Hill: our westernmost early Anglo-Saxon cemetery?" *Antiquaries Journal*, 94 (2014): 49–69.

[30] And at which neither he nor anyone else sensible would place King Arthur; see G. Halsall, *The Worlds of Arthur* (Oxford: Oxford University Press, 2013) for the most recent polemic. Sims-Williams, "Settlement of England," 39 note 174 pointed out that the Latin name of Badbury Rings was *Vindocladia*, 'Baddanburg' not occurring earlier than *c.* 900; I take this as a hint that any fifth- or sixth-century Gildasian reference to Badbury Rings would have been a derivative of the Latin name, which *Badonicus* clearly is not.

[31] C. Sparey Green, *Excavations at Poundbury. Volume I: The settlements* (Dorset Natural History and Archaeological Society Monograph 7, 1987), 153.

[32] R. Waller, "Archaeological resource assessment of the Isle of Wight: early medieval period," accessible on-line from Oxford Archaeology, Projects, Solent-Thames, County Resource Assessment, under the heading 'Settlement'.

[33] Partly excavated by 'Time Team' in 2001 as a result of an initiative by Sally Worrell of the Portable Antiquities Scheme, and of David Hopkins, Hampshire County Council Archaeologist. Double and triple burials, more stave-bound 'buckets' than the rest of southern England put together, a Byzantine 'pail' and a garnet-inlaid buckle are among the reasons to claim it as exceptional.

[34] Description and references in Royal Commission on Historical Monuments (England), *Historical Monuments in the County of Dorset. Volume V: East* (London: Her Majesty's Stationery Office, 1975), 55–56; H.C. Bowen and B.N. Eagles (eds), *The Archaeology of Bokerley Dyke* (London: Her Majesty's Stationery Office, 1990); B.N. Eagles, "Anglo-Saxon presence and culture in Wiltshire *c.* AD 450–*c.* 675," 199–233 in *Roman Wiltshire and After. Papers in honour of Ken Annable* ed. P. Ellis (Devizes: Wiltshire Archaeological and Natural History Society, 2001), 212–15 W. Putnam, *Roman Dorset* (Stroud: Tempus Publishing, 2007), 148–49.

down in the fourth century to such an extent that old feuds between the Iron Age *Durotriges* to the south and the *Belgae* to the north reasserted themselves. Views on this diverge; Roman authority probably resumed temporarily after *c.* 370, removing any reason to provide special measures after that date for the road from Salisbury to Dorchester that ran through the Dyke, which is not related to any known Roman provincial administrative divisions. It is possible that old tribal rivalries reopened in the fifth century,[35] but the Dyke makes better sense in a later fifth- and sixth-century context, when cemeteries showing Anglo-Saxon cultural influence cluster round the Salisbury area, only crossing the earthwork in the later sixth and seventh centuries.[36] The shire boundary followed the Dyke, which suggests that it was not wholly redundant when Dorset and Wiltshire were created, at a date itself uncertain, though perhaps as early as towards the end of the seventh century.[37] No record exists of its ever having served any other useful purpose subsequently. That Brittonic-speaking *Durnovarii* squared up to Germanic-speaking *Wylye-saetan* in the sixth century is a beguiling possibility, but has no further evidence to support it.[38]

All earthworks suffer from the problem presented by the late Roman coin at Bokerley Dyke; precise dating is almost impossible from artefacts found in ditches and banks, as material that was already old can get incorporated into the one and may subsequently slip down into the other as it fills from erosion, or may get thrown into it if the bank is deliberately levelled. Optically Stimulated Luminescence is a promising new dating technique for buried soils,[39] but it has not yet been applied in Wessex, leaving interpretation open not only of Bokerley Dyke.[40] A case in point is provided by the two linear banks, again with ditches on their north sides, known as West and East Wansdyke, which are linked by a Roman road.[41] West Wansdyke is in modern Somerset, as though confronting Gloucestershire across the River Avon; unlike Bokerley, the shire boundary does not run along it but uses the river instead, until it veers away to the north near Bath.[42] Wiltshire's East Wansdyke is even further south of the present shire boundaries between Gloucestershire and Berkshire, and in contrast to West Wansdyke it does not have any hillforts in its immediate proximity in the prominent length from the Roman road to Savernake Forest. The two dykes may not have been constructed at the same time, though knowledge of the one might have informed the decision to build the other. Uncertainty hangs even over their lengths, both West Wansdyke's extent westwards towards the Severn and East Wansdyke's eastwards into and beyond Savernake Forest; LiDAR survey has shown no trace of it in the woods.[43] Andrew Reynolds and Alex Langlands, however, have suggested that it ran on east of Savernake as far as Inkpen Beacon, along a less substantial dyke that links up to the hillfort at Chisbury, from which a dyke also extends southwards.[44]

Like Bokerley, East Wansdyke was investigated by General Pitt-Rivers, and taken by him to be Roman, but as its west end slightly overlies the Roman road that connects it to the West Wansdyke a post-Roman ascription can be justified. Furthermore, it is not followed by the shire boundary, nor even for any significant lengths by parish boundaries, so that it had until recently been taken to date to the fifth, sixth or possibly seventh century, before most estate and administrative divisions were formed. In a careful review of all the evidence, however, Reynolds and Langlands proposed that both dykes could be of the mid Saxon period, constructed by West Saxons to define their territory against the emerging power of Mercia, and

[35] Laycock, *Britannia, the Failed State*, 141–52, influenced by K.R. Dark, *Civitas to Kingdom: British Political Continuity 300–800* (Leicester: Leicester University Press, 1994). Gerrard, *Ruin of Roman Britain*, 205 *et seq.* gives good reasons to be sceptical about such long-term survival, however.

[36] As mapped originally by C. Taylor, *Dorset* (London: Hodder and Stoughton, 1970), 45: there is one grave with a sixth-century Anglo-Saxon button brooch, and a long string of beads; recent work by Bournemouth University in the area has found more graves, but not a different dating scenario: J. Gale, I. Hewitt and M. Russell, "Excavations at High Lea Farm, Hinton Martell, Dorset: a third interim report, on fieldwork undertaken during 2006–7," *Proceedings of the Dorset Natural History and Archaeological Society*, 129 (2008): 105–114, at page 112. S. Esmonde Cleary, who also favours a 'failed state' model that may have become evident in the fourth century, and certainly so in the fifth, but without recourse to tribal divisions, favours a later fifth-century date for Bokerley: "The ending(s) of Roman Britain," 13–29 in *The Oxford Handbook of Anglo-Saxon Archaeology*, eds H. Hamerow, D.A. Hinton and S. Crawford (Oxford: Oxford University Press, 2011), 23–24. Gerrard, *Ruin of Roman Britain*, does not mention Bokerley Dyke.

[37] B.A.E. Yorke, "Dorchester and the early shire centres of Wessex," *Proceedings of the Dorset Natural History and Archaeological Society*, 134 (2013): 106–12; see 106. Shire formation is discussed further below.

[38] *Durnovarii* is coined from the Roman name for Dorchester, *Durnovaria*, and to use it in the present context is to imply, quite probably falsely, that the place remained the focus of post-Roman authority. For the settlers of the River Wylye, see below.

[39] L. Hayes and T. Malim, "The date and nature of Wat's Dyke: a reassessment in the light of recent investigations at Gobowen, Shropshire," *Anglo-Saxon Studies in Archaeology and History*, 15 (2008): 147–79.

[40] N.J. Higham and M.J. Ryan, *The Anglo-Saxon World* (New Haven/London: Yale University Press, 2013), 53 for a useful map distinguishing between those 'probably' and 'possibly' in post-Roman use; within the study area, the latter includes the Silchester complex, the former only the three discussed in detail in the present paper.

[41] A. Reynolds and A. Langlands, "Social identities on the macro scale: a maximum view of Wansdyke," 13–44 in *People and Space in the Middle Ages, 300–1300*, Studies in the Early Middle Ages 15, eds W. Davies, G. Halsall and A. Reynolds (Turnhout: Brepols Publishing, 2006); 14–25 for physical details of the dykes; 31–32 for the name and possible relationship to *Woden's Barrow*/Adam's Grave and battle sites; and 33–37 for the political contexts.

[42] J.G.P. Erskine, "The West Wansdyke: an appraisal of the dating, dimensions and construction techniques in the light of excavated evidence," *Archaeological Journal*, 164 (2007): 80–108; dating summary (late Roman to seventh century): page 81; hillfort use: page 105. Gloucestershire was the territory of the Hwicce, and that people's influence may be shown by the boundaries of the see of Worcester: D. Hill, *An Atlas of Anglo-Saxon England* (Oxford: Basil Blackwell, 1981), page 81; it verged away from the river north of Bath, which is hard to reconcile with the line of Wansdyke if that is to be viewed as relating to a frontier. That the two dykes were separate constructions is also advocated by H. Whittock and M. Whittock, *The Anglo-Saxon Avon Valley Frontier. A river of two halves* (Fonthill Media, 2014), 46.

[43] B. Lennon, *Savernake Forest: Continuity and Change in a Wooded Landscape* (Oxford: British Archaeological Reports British Series 555, 2012), 117–18 and fig. 1.6.

[44] Reynolds and Langlands, "Social identities," 20–21. This 'extension' is accepted by J. Baker and S. Brookes, *Beyond the Burghal Hidage. Anglo-Saxon civil defence in the viking age* (Leiden/Boston: Brill, 2013), 219.

to control passage from frontier zones into the Wessex heartland.[45]

In a meticulous subsequent analysis, Bruce Eagles and Michael Allen accepted a mid Saxon date for East Wansdyke west of Savernake as one possibility, but have shown how little is definite. Pitt-Rivers may still be right that its primary phase at least, and at least in parts, is late Roman. It could be fifth- or sixth-century, or at any rate have been strengthened in the immediate post-Roman period, by 'British' indigenes against 'Anglo-Saxons' establishing themselves in the Upper Thames Valley – or by the Salisbury-based 'Anglo-Saxons' against now-established Oxford-area 'cousins'. And it could perpetuate a much earlier division, as types of Iron Age coins associated with tribal groups are found to the north and to the south of it, but do not intermingle.[46] Others who have written on it recently include Peter Fowler, who reviewed its progress through some woodland, fieldwork which led him to a date after *c.* 500, rather than late Roman or fifth-century, for that section.[47] As for the putative eastwards 'extension', others retain the traditional view that the Chisbury system is entirely prehistoric.[48]

Clearly it is not possible at present to be definitive about either of the two Wansdykes, the only certainty being that nothing less than well-organised polities could have arranged their construction. East Wansdyke from the Roman road to Savernake is some 10 miles long, much longer than Bokerley, and it may well be that it would not have been needed in the Roman period, nor possible to construct in turbulent fifth-century conditions. Is it, though, as late in date as Reynolds and Langlands tentatively concluded? They suggested that if King Ine of Wessex controlled Berkshire in the late 680s/690s, as his Streatley grant implies, and because one of his sub-kings named Cissa founded Abingdon Abbey at around the same time, he would not have needed East Wansdyke, and that it has a better context subsequently in the late eighth or early ninth century, after King Offa of Mercia had a great victory over Wessex at Bensington in 779.[49] That does not explain, however, why the Chisbury dykes are less substantial than the dyke west of Savernake, or why no dyke can be traced along the steep crest from Inkpen Beacon to east of Kingsclere in Hampshire, to deter Offa's Mercians from attacking Winchester.

An earlier date than post-779 might be preferred; the Abingdon Abbey charters are so doubtful that the attribution to Cissa cannot be sustained, and neither the Vale of the White Horse nor the downs between the Vale and the Kennet valley may ever have been in West Saxon hands.[50] The West Saxons' Wiltshire might therefore have been closer to undisputed Mercian-controlled territory (i.e. nowadays northern Berkshire), than was Hampshire (confronting southern Berkshire), so King Ine might have been more concerned about it. And perhaps with good reason. If the battle of 715 between Ine and Ceolred of Mercia actually happened, and happened at *wodnesbeorg*, as the *Chronicles* state, and if the barrow really is Adam's Grave just south of Wansdyke in Alton Priors parish, all of which are perfectly credible,[51] it becomes worth noting that the *Chronicles*, seemingly composed in Wessex, do not name a victor, a silence politically expedient if it was actually the Mercian king, as William of Malmesbury said; his source for that statement is unknown,[52] but in this case there seems no reason to doubt him. A Mercian success would help to explain why Bede, writing in the early 730s, could state that their King Aethelbald had 'all the southern kingdoms' subject to him.[53] That East Wansdyke existed by 715 but did not prevent Mercians passing through to Altons Priors, should be considered, and that after Ceolred's victory, King Ine was not in a position to risk his enemy's wrath by continuing with the construction. In other words, East Wansdyke was proscribed, not superfluous, and no later Wessex king felt confident enough to take up the challenge to complete it, nor to strengthen the Hampshire border even though southern Berkshire was disputed territory. In those circumstances it becomes even easier to understand why no West Saxon king is known to have visited Berkshire before the ninth century.[54]

Or is East Wansdyke later in date, as Reynolds and Langlands suggested, but unconnected to Offa's 779 victory at Bensington? Optically Stimulated Luminescence dating suggests that the linear defence work known as Wat's Dyke in the Welsh Marches was constructed at the very end of the eighth century or early in the ninth.[55] If

[45] Reynolds and Langlands, "Social identities," 26–37.

[46] B. Eagles and M.J. Allen, "A reconsideration of East Wansdyke: its construction and date – a preliminary note," 147–55, in *Studies in Early Anglo-Saxon Art and Archaeology: Papers in Honour of Martin G. Welch*, eds S. Brookes, S. Hamilton and A.J. Reynolds (Oxford: British Archaeological Reports British Series 527, 2011).

[47] P.J. Fowler, "Field archaeology in West Woods, Fyfield and West Overton, Wiltshire," *Wiltshire Archaeological and Natural History Magazine*, 104 (2011): 135–41; 141 for the dating.

[48] B. Lennon, "The Bedwyn Dyke: a revisionist view," *Wiltshire Archaeological and Natural History Magazine*, 103, (2010): 102–29.

[49] Reynolds and Langlands, "Social identities," 36–37. This is considered the best option by Baker and Brookes, *Beyond the Burghal Hidage*, 220.

[50] J. Blair, *Anglo-Saxon Oxfordshire* (Stroud: Alan Sutton Publishing, 1994), 54–55, 59–60, citing the work of Heather Edwards, *The Charters of the Early West Saxon Kingdom* (Oxford: British Archaeological Reports British Series 198, 1988), 177, who showed that the attribution to Cissa has 'no authentic tradition', and that what purport to be Abingdon's charters are filtered from those of a minster at Bradfield, near Reading. Both Mercians and West Saxons seem to have been involved in that church, so the southern part of Berkshire adjoining Hampshire may have been much more disputed territory than Reynolds and Langlands allowed. See also S.E. Kelly, *Charters of Abingdon Abbey, Part 1*, Anglo-Saxon Charters VII (Oxford: Oxford University Press, 2000), xxxvi–xix and cci–iii. These sources were noted by Baker and Brookes, *Beyond the Burghal Hidage*, 46, but they did not consider the implications for dating East Wansdyke differently from Reynolds and Langlands.

[51] Reynolds and Langlands, "Social identities," 31–32 for careful discussion.

[52] R.M. Thomson, *William of Malmesbury* Gesta Regum Anglorum. *The History of the English Kings, Volume II. General introduction and commentary* (Oxford: Clarendon Press, 1999), 61.

[53] B. Colgrave and R.A.B. Mynors, (eds) *Bede's Ecclesiastical History of the English People* (Oxford: Clarendon Press, 1969), 558–59.

[54] Hill, *Atlas of Anglo-Saxon England*, 83.

[55] Hayes and Malim, "Wat's Dyke," 174–75; ninth-century and later treaties do not seem to have involved constructing frontier lines, though cattle-raiding, in some areas at least, remained a problem: P. Wormald, *The Making of English Law: King Alfred to the Twelfth Century. Volume I, legislation and its limits* (Oxford: Blackwell, 1999), 381.

that can be believed, such defence lines were still regarded as useful in the early part of the reign of King Egbert of Wessex (802–39). When he became king, the Hwicce people, based in the West Midlands, crossed the Thames at Kempsford but were beaten back. At that stage the Hwiccians should have been subservient to Mercia, and yet there are three charters that seem to show eighth-century Mercian dominance within Wiltshire in the area south of Kempsford;[56] the implication must surely be either that that dominance had in 802 been recently lost to Wessex, and the Hwiccians were seeking to regain it for Mercia, or that they were acting independently, having seized the opportunity of King Offa's death in 794 to reject Mercian control. Either way, having had his bacon saved by Ealdorman Weohstan and the Wilsaetan, Egbert's reaction could have been to bolster his defences in that part of his kingdom, by building one or both Wansdykes against the resurgent Hwiccians. East Wansdyke is rather far south for that, however, and would have been better located on the north downs running between Barbury Castle to Liddington Castle, using the Ridgeway for communication; but with Mercians controlling the line from there eastwards, perhaps it was not regarded as feasible.[57]

These tissues of narrative threads show nothing other than that virtually any date can be argued for East Wansdyke based on the tenuous political information that has survived, and the uncertain record of charters. None fits so well that it precludes an undocumented period as still the best candidate for the East Wansdyke's construction, which leaves less need to explain why there is no dyke in north Hampshire. The matter is important, however, for more than narrative precision; even though unfinished and even if built in stages, the earthwork's ten-mile length took time and effort to construct, particularly if it was not merely a bank and ditch, but was revetted, like West Wansdyke, and timber-laced. Cutting and carting considerable amounts of timber would have added considerably to the person-power needed, and the communal effort required would have been greater than could be supplied locally; it must surely be envisaged that service labour could be brought in from a wide area. Whether this was already arranged on a shire basis is unknown, but it should be noted that the battle of Kempsford was fought by 'men of the Wylye' – this is surely more likely to mean that the name by 802 applied to the whole of Wiltshire, not that a band of warriors from the Wilton area in the south marched all the way north to fight the Hwiccians, without input from those who lived more locally.[58]

Burhs, enclosures, precincts and signalling systems

Little is recorded of King Egbert of Wessex after 802 until his success against the Mercians in 825 at the battle of Ellandun. Assuming that that victory gave him control of north Wiltshire up to the Thames, he would not thereafter have needed East Wansdyke, one reason why he might have left it unfinished, another being that by 825 defensive work requirements were changing. King Offa's charters show that obligations placed upon Mercian land-holders were increasingly formalised, with mandatory 'fortress-work'. The word used, *geweorc*, is not specific about whether these were linear or enclosure banks, but in Mercia at least there is growing evidence of focus on the latter, large defended places enclosed by banks and ditches, with timber revetting.[59] The precise meaning of the word *burh* (dative *byrig*) has been debated recently, Simon Draper arguing that it need not mean 'stronghold', but a weaker 'enclosure', subsequently 'manor'; in some cases it may relate to a mid Saxon church, as in Gloucestershire where Tetbury and Bibury are first recorded as Tetta's minster and Bebba's minster respectively.[60]

In Wessex, many 'minster' enclosures of the mid Saxon period seem likely to have been curvilinear ovals or near-circles, their lines sometimes preserved by lanes and property boundaries as at Lambourne, Berkshire,[61] rather than rectangular like Roman forts. Rectilinearity prevailed at Chalton and Cowdery's Down, both in Hampshire, where excavations have revealed the sort of stockades that might surround a high-status secular residence – enough to keep out animals and casual robbers, but not solid enough to hold against a determined attack by even

[56] Cited by Baker and Brookes, *Beyond the Burghal Hidage*, 216.

[57] Yorke, *Wessex*, 94–95 for Berkshire's transfer to Wessex, probably after Egbert's reign. The Wessex/Mercia battle at Ellendun, thought to be Wroughton, Wiltshire, in 825 may show that the Hwiccians had been put back in their place, and that even if East Wansdyke was patrolled, it was not relied upon for active defence, as Wroughton is well to its north.

[58] Erskine. "West Wansdyke," 89, 90 and 97. All this has implications for the formation of the large shires which have become the basis of modern counties, reviewed recently by B. Eagles, "'Small shires' and *regiones* in Hampshire and the formation of the shires of eastern Wessex," *Anglo-Saxon Studies in Archaeology and History*, 19 (2015): 122–52; even though smaller units predominated, the 802 battle seems to me to indicate that 'Wiltshire' existed at least as a federation by then. The labour required should be stressed, as published estimates do not seem to allow for timber, only for digging – usefully summarised by E. Grigg, "The early medieval dykes of Britain," in *Towns and Topography. Essays in memory of David Hill*, eds G.R. Owen-Crocker and S.D. Thompson (Oxford: Oxbow Books, 2014), 103–10; G Molyneaux, *The Formation of the English Kingdom in the Tenth Century* (Oxford: Oxford University Press, 2015), 86–91, in discussing the 'burhs', also seems to consider only the digging, although the Oxford defences were both timber-laced and timber-revetted – and even some of the turves seem to have been carted in: A. Dodd (ed.), *Oxford before the University. The late Saxon and Norman archaeology of the Thames crossing, the defences and the town*, Thames Valley Landscapes Monograph 17 (Oxford: Oxford University School of Archaeology, 2003), 143–46.

[59] The *trinoda necessitas*, the defences at Hereford and Tamworth, and the Kentish charters have been reviewed many times, e.g. N.P. Brooks, "The development of military obligations in eighth- and ninth-century England," in *England before the Conquest. Studies in primary sources presented to Dorothy Whitelock*, eds P. Clemoes and K. Hughes (Cambridge: Cambridge University Press, 1971), 69–84; Reynolds and Langlands, "Social identities," 40; Baker and Brookes, *Beyond the Burghal Hidage*, 49–52.

[60] S. Draper, "The significance of Old English *burh* in Anglo-Saxon England," *Anglo-Saxon Studies in Archaeology and History*, 15 (2008): 240–53.

[61] G.G. Astill, *Historic Towns in Berkshire; an Archaeological Appraisal* (Reading: Berkshire Archaeological Committee Publication 2, 1978), 37–41.

a small raiding party.[62] The episode of 757 at *Merantun* was at a 'stronghold' with a 'gate' that could be locked but which was not robust enough to be defended for very long. That it was named a *-tun* not a *-bury* is unlikely to be significant. The scene of the archer on the Franks Casket that is often used to illustrate the *Merantun* episode shows him at the gate of what looks like a palisade.[63] Such places were not strongly defended with earth banks and ditches. Nor apparently was the large new settlement on the Southampton peninsula, *Hamwic*; on at least part of its east side, it had a ditch not less than 1.4 metres deep and 3.5 metres wide, which probably had an internal bank. But the features had a short life, the ditch being infilled and the bank removed, so it was almost certainly not regarded as necessary for defence.[64] Nor, probably, was it continuous all round the occupation area; no similar ditch has been seen on the north side,[65] and those seen at the southern end are very different in size.[66]

One place with *-bury* in its name is Yatesbury, Wiltshire, where interesting fieldwork undertaken by Andrew Reynolds has revealed a place with three enclosures; one turned out to be a late medieval pond, the second surrounds the churchyard, while the third proved on excavation to be a late Roman ditch, redug in the Anglo-Saxon period and still a visible feature in the eighteenth century.[67] Close to the entrance to that third enclosure and partly incorporated in its bank are the remains of what proved to be a Bronze Age mound, that had been flattened off and had had a ditch dug around it, in which was a late Anglo-Saxon sherd, so it was open in the tenth/twelfth century. The top of the mound had been intensely burnt, to a depth of 0.3 metres, and the ditch had quantities of charcoal in its fill. Reynolds interpreted the mound as the site of a bonfire,[68] but bonfires do not usually cause such intense burning as to scorch the ground far below the surface, and to surround them with ditches is merely to make access to them more difficult.

Rejection of the interpretation of the mound at Yatesbury as the site of a bonfire has more than local significance, as it has been claimed to have been part of a mid Saxon signalling system of beacons, lit to warn neighbourhoods of raids, and intervisible so that whole kingdoms could be alerted. Yatesbury is not a particularly good location to choose as part of an effective chain, and none of the other suggested sites is within or close to an occupied area, but are in more prominent locations.[69] Did even they, however, exist? No direct documentary evidence hints at a beacon system, and maintaining them is not specifically said to be one of anybody's duties. Although there are plenty of 'Beacon Hills', none of those place-names is recorded in a pre-Norman document. Alternative words, such as *ād*, are too few and too ambivalent to imply a system. The parallel that has been drawn with fourteenth- and sixteenth-century systems are not necessarily valid, as by then fires could be lit using tar or pitch, derived from the resin of pine trees, imported from the Baltic; pine trees did not grow in Anglo-Saxon southern England.[70] Gorse, which burns and flares readily, does not grow in any reliable quantity on alkaline soils such as are found in the Wessex chalklands. Setting fire to damp wood in an emergency would have presented a challenge.

Considerable doubt must therefore be felt over the Anglo-Saxons' ability to create a viable beacon system, which removes one of the props in the theory that they had a grand 'military strategy', at least before the ninth century. Names like 'Toot Hill' have much earlier origins than do the 'Beacon Hill' names, and their meaning as

---

[62] Chalton: P.V. Addyman and D. Leigh, "The Anglo-Saxon village at Chalton, Hampshire: second interim report," *Medieval Archaeology*, 17 (1973): 1–25, pl. IIIA; Cowdery's Down: M. Millett, "Excavations at Cowdery's Down, Basingstoke, Hampshire, 1979–81," *Archaeological Journal*, 140 (1983): 151–279, at 209, figs 27–28 and pl. 10A. These examples seem to me enough to indicate that a ditch was not necessarily essential for somewhere with a stout palisade to be thought of as a *burh*, *contra* Draper, "Old English *burh*," 248 – which would make the identification of a distinct class of 'stronghold' by geophysics or excavation even more difficult. Wessex sites do not seem to have the outer perimeter ditches of the mid Saxon period discussed by H. Hamerow, *Rural Settlements and Society in Anglo-Saxon England* (Oxford: Oxford University Press, 2012), 78–83, but there are too few for this to be a definite distinction.
The rectilinearity of layout at Chalton is singular, but whether it conforms to the 'four-pole square grid-plan' that he advocates is not discussed by J. Blair, "Grid-planning in Anglo-Saxon settlements; the short perch and the four-perch module," *Anglo-Saxon Studies in Archaeology and History*, 18 (2013): 18–61. Blair's 'short rod' is of 4.6m; the very first building length listed by Addyman and Leigh, 10, is 13.8m, precisely three times 4.6m; the largest, at 28m, is within four centimetres of six 'short rods'; and the only others over 15m are both 23.0m, which is exactly five 'short rods'. Their widths, however, do not conform to multiples of 4.6m. I have not attempted to lay a four-pole grid over the site plan, as I am not sure that I would not find what I was looking for.

[63] The 'palisade' looks, however, suspiciously similar to the precinct wall shown around the Temple of Jerusalem in the *Codex Amiatinus* manuscript, which took its illustrative inspiration from Italian books not Anglo-Saxon observation: G. Henderson, *Vision and Image in Early Christian England* (Cambridge: Cambridge University Press, 1999), 112; L. Webster, *The Franks Casket* (London: British Museum, 2012).

[64] An outer ditch, arguably discontinuous and not very strong, was an early feature that was filled in before the ninth century: A.D. Morton, *Excavations at Hamwic, Volume 1. Excavations 1946–83 excluding Six Dials and Melbourne Street* (York: Council for British Archaeology Research Report 84, 1992), 30–31. P. Andrews (ed.), *Excavations at Hamwic Volume 2: Excavations at Six Dials* (York: Council for British Archaeology Research Report 109, 1997), 23–30. The *wic* at London had a very similar ditch on its north side: R. Cowie and L. Blackmore, Lundenwic. *Excavations in Middle Saxon London, 1987–2000* (London: Museum of London Archaeology Monograph 63, 2012), 65.

[65] B.E. Whitehead, "Archaeological investigations at Charlotte Place, Southampton," *Proceedings of the Hampshire Field Club and Archaeological Society*, 67, ii (2012): 317–22.

[66] N. Stoodley, "New light on the southern end of Hamwic: excavations at the Deanery by Southampton City Council Archaeological Unit and Wessex Archaeology," *Proceedings of the Hampshire Field Club and Archaeological Society*, 67ii (2012): 240–42.

[67] A. Reynolds and S. Brookes, "Anglo-Saxon civil defence in the localities: a case study of the Avebury region," 561–606 in A. Reynolds and L. Webster (eds), *Early Medieval Art and Archaeology in the Northern World. Studies in honour of James Graham-Campbell* (Leiden/Boston: Brill, 2013), at 569–76. 'Chaff-tempered' pottery suggests occupation in the sixth to eighth centuries (p. 572), which is why I have discussed the enclosure at this point.

[68] Reynolds and Brookes, "Anglo-Saxon civil defence," 572 and 575. The implication of the late Saxon sherd in the mound's ditch is discussed below.

[69] These views are developed by Baker and Brookes, *Beyond the Burghal Hidage*, 180–97. They consider that the system may have been in operation as early as the mid Saxon period: 386.

[70] D. Hooke, *Trees in Anglo-Saxon England. Literature, lore and landscape* (Woodbridge: Boydell Press, 2010), 275.

'look-outs' is not in doubt, but how regularly they were used is another matter. The numerous *weards* in charter boundaries might refer to guardians of flocks as often as to watchmen, although there does not seem to be overlap between *weard* and *hyrde* – shepherds are called 'herdsmen' not 'flockwards'.[71] On the continent, land-holders' responsibilities included keeping watch, but the 'three necessary duties' in English charters never mention that particular service; indeed, the only direct evidence for it appears to be in a single Kent charter regarded as dubious,[72] and even that has no mention of bonfires. If 'watch' was systematically kept it was probably by shepherds whose work took them to places where they could see approaching raiders as well as their flocks. But shepherds presumably carried horns, and warning notes could be sounded for humans as well as for livestock to hear, without recourse to lighting beacons.[73]

Also to be considered is the possibility of coastal watch – somehow word reached the shire leader of Dorset in the late eighth century that there were strangers on the coast to be challenged, but a messenger may have ridden to him, as there is no hint that he observed a warning beacon. Later stories about signalling across the Channel certainly do not suggest use of anything systematic, as they supposedly involved burning down houses.[74] Katherine Barker has recently argued that when the scholarly Abbot/Bishop Aldhelm wrote in the late-seventh or early-eighth century, he was describing an actual light-house on the south coast. She relies upon two separate sources for this, however, and the words and phrases from them that she selects do not bear the weight of her construction.[75]

Aldhelm was not the only ecclesiastical writer to write in terms that should not be taken too literally; the minster at Wimborne is described as within a substantial enclosure – *muris altis et firmis circumdatis* – but whether the 'high walls' were of stone, or of earth and timber, with or without an outer ditch, is not revealed, and the description is as likely as not to be allegorical, meaning that the walls were the protection provided by the Word of God.[76] Various possible precinct lines have been suggested from Wimborne's topography, but none has been discovered by excavation.[77]

That a minster church like Wimborne would have had some sort of boundary around it is very likely, and evidence of others has been sought. Near Yatesbury, for instance, which has only a small parish church, and no claim to have been a mid or late Saxon 'minster', is Avebury. In Domesday Book, one of Avebury's land-holders was an ecclesiastic, his two independently held hides being a mark of 'minster' status. How long that had pertained is not revealed in any earlier source, unfortunately, but sculpture and architectural features point to a pre-Conquest building.[78] Earthworks in fields to the west of the present village have been claimed as parts of early elliptical enclosures,[79] but they have not been excavated and as they lay in the meadows might be of any date and may have been for water control. Although the name may be 'stronghold [minster] on the Avon', possibly an early name for the River Kennet, it could also be 'stronghold [minster] of a man called Afa'.[80]

Vikings!

A more coherent 'military system' becomes apparent in the ninth century. What are undoubtedly 'strongholds' are the places listed in the series of documents that has long interested both historians and archaeologists and is known collectively as the 'Burghal Hidage'; after each named place is stated the numbers of 'hides' needed to maintain and defend it. Historians have identified two basic strands in the documents, which are not precisely the same in many instances, either about the number of hides each

[71] Baker and Brookes, *Beyond the Burghal Hidage*, present these words and names in detail; 'look-out points' have good visibility, but discussion of the viewsheds from some of the *weards* would have been welcome. Although there were shep- and cow-herds, there were probably also hay-ward(en)s, a role requiring less constant vigilance.

[72] Lavelle, *Alfred's Wars*, 244 discusses urban watch-duties recorded in eleventh-century Domesday Book. If authentic, a grant of 1066 to Westminster Abbey implies the same, as *weardwite* occurs in a list of Old English privileges: B. Thorpe, Diplomatarium Anglicum Aevi Saxonici. *A collection of English charters* (London: Macmillan, 1865), 411.

[73] I am not aware of any early documentation for horns other than Ine's Wessex law that a stranger had to blow one if travelling off-track; the same code mentions the penalty for loaning a horse to a fugitive, which implies that horse ownership even as early as the end of the seventh century was not exceptional, as does the reference to Welsh horsemen carrying the king's messages: D. Whitelock (ed.), *English Historical Documents* c. *500–1042* (London: Eyre Methuen, 1979), 401–02, clauses 20, 29 and 33. A system for getting even verbal messages carried directly to a recipient is likely to have been preferable to one relying on smoke signals.

[74] Baker and Brookes, *Beyond the Burghal Hidage*, 183–84.

[75] K. Barker, "*Aldhelmus episcopus*: the making and shiring of the Sherborne bishopric – Saxon, Briton and the Byzantine," *Proceedings of the Dorset Natural History and Archaeological Society*, 134 (2013): 113–27. On page 122, Barker switches between two texts; in the '*Carmen Rhythmicum*', *flammiger* refers to Lucifer, the Morning Star, not to a priest, and the tower mentioned at the end of the poem is the biblical Tower of Siloam (Luke XIII, 4), not part of the West Country church which lost its nave roof in a storm; in the other text, which is a riddle, a tall light-house is used to display the author's Latin learning, not to describe an actual structure on the south coast: see e.g. M. Lapidge, D.R. Howlett and K. Barker, "Aldhelm's *Carmen Rhythmicum*," 271–89 in *Aldhelm and Sherborne*, ed. K. Barker (Oxford: Oxbow Books, 2010).

[76] P.H. Coulstock, *The Collegiate Church of Wimborne Minster* (Woodbridge: Boydell Press, 1993), 60. That the fight at the king's residence at *Merantun*, recorded in the *Chronicles* for 757, took place at Dorset's Martin is stretching the name a long way, and the suggestion that an enclosure at Abbots Street Wood dates to the mid Saxon period is unsubstantiated; ibid. 61–65. Another near-by enclosure at Cowgrove, which Heywood Sumner took to be a Saxon meeting-place, may have been no more than an old clay-pit: Royal Commission on Historical Monuments, *Dorset South-East* (London: Her Majesty's Stationery Office, 1970), 53.

[77] P.J. Woodward, "Wimborne Minster, Dorset – excavations in the town centre 1975–80," *Proceedings of the Dorset Natural History and Archaeological Society*, 105 (1983): 57–74, at 57–58. For 'minster' enclosures generally, see J. Blair, *The Church in Anglo-Saxon Society* (Oxford: Oxford University Press, 2005), 196–98.

[78] Reynolds and Brookes, "Anglo-Saxon civil defence," 577–79. They tentatively date the northern enclosure to no later than the late ninth century, on the basis of sculptures in the church. The date of the minster's establishment could of course have been earlier than that.

[79] Reynolds and Brookes, "Anglo-Saxon civil defence," 577–79.

[80] A.D. Mills, *A Dictionary of British Place-Names*, First Edition revised (Oxford: Oxford University Press, 2011), 25.

place was supposed to be supported by, or all their names. One of the strands, known as 'version A', ends with a formula stating that each hide should send one man to the place to be defended; that four men were needed for each 'acre's breadth' (taken to mean a 'pole') of wall, which leads to the enticing prospect of finding ditches and banks of lengths that comply with the formula.[81]

Both the dating and the reasons for compilation remain controversial about the 'Burghal Hidage', and the accuracy of what it seems to tell us. In a series of papers and a book, Jeremy Haslam has argued that it was composed in a short 'window of opportunity' by King Alfred, soon after his great victory at the Battle of Edington in 878 gave him control not only of Wessex and Sussex, but also, in Haslam's view, of territory on the north side of the River Thames.[82] Others uphold the conventional view that the versions that have come down to us are compilations, with additions made in the early years of the tenth century to an 'original' created at some time in Alfred's reign, and that the Thames was a frontier.[83]

One aspect of debate concerns whether the formula in 'A' really allows the length of defences to be established, and for places to be identified as 'Burghal Hidage' forts on that basis. In Winchester's case, the formula allows a length of 9,900 feet from an assessment of 2,400 hides, and this is almost exactly the length of the Roman walls, most of which were presumably still standing. Not only does that seem to confirm the accuracy of the document, but it also shows that the 'acre's breadth' pole used in Winchester measured 16½ feet.[84] Haslam has called in question other claims that a fort's circuit fits the measurement that the 'Burghal Hidage' allows for, an argument which deserves more scrutiny.

The very first name in the 'Burghal Hidage', *Eorpeburnan*, has not survived into that of a modern place, and only its position at the start of a list that clearly follows a geographical order enables it to be located somewhere in East Sussex, probably near the shire boundary with Kent. What seemed a persuasive argument in favour of Rye, because there was a ditch there recorded in the mid nineteenth century as 1,337 feet long, which is exactly what the formula would prescribe from the 324 hides attributed to *Eorpeburnan* assuming a 16½-foot pole, has not won general favour, however.[85]

The other Sussex entries in the 'Burghal Hidage' present a range of comparable issues. Of Hastings nothing definite can be said other than that it was assessed for 500 hides, but no-one has seriously doubted that the fort was within the present town, or some adjacent part swept out into the sea.[86] The third in the list, Lewes, has different assessments in versions 'A' and 'B', and in this case the assumption that the fort was on the site of the present town has been challenged by a claim that it was actually a near-by Iron Age hillfort called The Caburn that was the original site. Excavations there only found Iron Age pottery in and under chalk dumps thought to derive from one of the ditches and taken to indicate a date 'during or after the Romano-British period', so the archaeology does not directly support the suggestion that this was the 'burh'.[87] Michael Holmes's work on the present town's topography gives no support to the view that The Caburn was a direct predecessor,[88] but the possibility cannot be altogether discounted. Sussex's next fort, Burpham, has a substantial earth bank across a promontory site, which is much too short to account for the length that 720 hides would allow it, but which would not be enough to provide for the entire circuit.[89] Chichester is mostly interesting for the implication of the reuse of the Roman walls there, but their length, 7,800 feet, is greater than the 6,187 feet that its 1,500 hides would allow; a full circuit might possibly have been thought unnecessary if the River Lavant provided a barrier.[90] Whatever the length, the *Chronicles* record that in 894 the *burgware* had a success against vikings, implying that the defences were effective by then.

The first Hampshire site is the old Roman fort at Portchester. Its standing walls are some 2,430 feet overall, while 500 hides provides for only 2,062 feet. If only its three land-facing sides are counted, the fit is little better, at 1,830 feet. Reconciliation can only be achieved by taking the ditch not the wall as the line measured, and even that sleight of hand depends on guessing exactly where the ditches met the sea. The late David Hill argued that the next 'Burghal Hidage' site, *Hamtun* with 150 hides attributed to it and therefore provision for 619 feet, was also an old Roman fort, the one at Bitterne. He cited an excavation report from the 1930s which showed the inner land ditch as 625 feet.[91] Unfortunately the length shown on the more

[81] D. Hill and A.A. Rumble (eds), *The Defence of Wessex. The Burghal Hidage and Anglo-Saxon fortifications* (Manchester/New York: Manchester University Press, 1996).

[82] J. Haslam, *Urban-Rural Connections in Domesday Book and Late Anglo-Saxon Royal Administration* (Oxford: British Archaeological Reports British Series 571, 2012), 119–22.

[83] For example, Baker and Brookes, *Beyond the Burghal Hidage*, 32–34.

[84] D. Hill, "Gazetteer of Burghal Hidage sites," in Hill and Rumble (eds), *Defence of Wessex*, 225–26.

[85] F. Kitchen, "The *Burghal Hidage*: towards the identification of *Eorpeburnan*," *Medieval Archaeology*, 28 (1984): 175–77. Castle Toll, Newenden, and somewhere near modern Grinstead, have also been mooted, but Hill's judgement that 'the matter remains opaque' (Hill, "Gazetteer," 202) remains true.

[86] Hill, "Gazetteer," 205–06.

[87] P. Drewett and S. Hamilton, "Marking time and making space: excavations and landscape studies at The Caburn hillfort, East Sussex, 1996–8," *Sussex Archaeological Collections*, 137 (1999): 7–37 at 28–29.

[88] M. Holmes, "The street plan of Lewes and the Burghal Hidage," *Sussex Archaeological Collections*, 148 (2010): 71–78.

[89] Hill, "Gazetteer," 195. Recent geophysical and other work by Scott Chaussée has revealed a few internal features not previously recorded, but no further dating evidence. That the promontory was a 'pre-English' fort, as Baker and Brookes, *Beyond the Burghal Hidage*, 100, is not substantiated.

[90] Hill, "Gazetteer," 196–97. A. Westman, *Chichester City Walls* (London: Museum of London Archaeology, 2012) at 62–65 attributes the discrepancy to marshland as well as the river, which changed course in the post-Roman period to flow through the eastern ditch, either from natural causes or as a deliberate measure to improve the defences.

[91] D. Hill, "The Burghal Hidage – Southampton," *Proceedings of the Hampshire Field Club and Archaeological Society*, 24 (1967), 59–61 and id., "Gazetteer," 217, accepted by Baker and Brookes, *Beyond the Burghal Hidage*, 397.

detailed map published subsequently shows it as some 770 feet, a difference caused by extending its putative length from a modern road to the postulated Roman river edge, which makes the 'fit' much less exact.[92] The 'burh' might not have been the Roman fort; as no enclosure within mid Saxon *Hamwic* is known,[93] the defended area may either have been the part of the 'Below Bar' settlement that succeeded the *wic*,[94] or a zone to its north, where a 'large ditch running east-west was 7.4m wide and at least 2.5m deep. The fill ... included finds dated to the late Saxon period'.[95]

The next entry in the 'Burghal Hidage' list is variously named *Tweneam/twouham* in the documents, subsequently usually rendered as Twynham, and now Christchurch. It was assessed for 470 hides in the 'A' version, 460 in 'B'. The former produces a length of 1,939 feet, the latter of 1,732 feet, both of which are, as Hill pointed out, much greater than the length across the promontory at the point where a double ditch and berm have been excavated.[96] The promontory is only some 1,200 feet from the River Avon to a fall of ground on the west, and Hill postulated that it had turned southwards on its west side, running for a short length before marshland at what is now Wick Lane rendered further extension unnecessary. Remains of a ditch have indeed been observed on that side.[97] In the 1980s, however, a bank and ditch were found on the east side also, so Haslam refuted Hill's analysis, arguing that the dating is all so imprecise that the north, east and west sides cannot be proven not to be co-eval, and that the overall original length would have been considerably greater even than 1,939 feet.

Interpretation of the Christchurch defences is made more difficult by the evidence that the north side had both an inner and an outer ditch, with no evidence of whether they were dug at the same time, or the outer one added later. Haslam argued that the west side also had double ditches, as he would place the earth bank to the east of the line suggested by other commentators.[98] The only long section on that side was a trench that could not be fully excavated because of wet weather and waterlogging.[99] All the excavations on the Christchurch defences have faced such difficulties, problems exacerbated by the high water-table, and on the east side by the Millstream, seemingly an artificial cut but of unknown date and possibly interfering with the remains of the defences.[100] Such dating evidence as currently exists, in the form of pottery found in the various excavations, is too imprecise to argue against Haslam's reinterpretation that the 'burh's' primary walls were longer than allowed for in the 'Burghal Hidage' formula. He suggested that the mid Saxon minster at the south end of the peninsula would have had some sort of enclosure, and that King Alfred extended it.[101] It could be argued that if the minster's perimeter were very extensive, Alfred might only have needed to add the 1,939 feet that the formula allows, but that is a desperate defence.

The site where the evidence is greatest, yet no more satisfactory, is Wareham, Dorset, the next 'Burghal Hidage' entry. This had strong royal connections, as King Beorhtric was buried there in 802 according to the entry in the *Chronicles* for 784. Writing in the late ninth century,[102] Asser said that it was a nunnery, and the convent was probably based in the large Anglo-Saxon church there that was nearly all demolished in 1841–42; recent redating of the Anglo-Saxon church at Brixworth, Northamptonshire, takes Wareham's into the late eighth or early ninth century, perhaps built by Beorhtric himself in emulation of what his patron King Offa of Mercia may have done at Brixworth.[103] In 876, a viking army entered Wareham, which in the 'Burghal Hidage' was assessed for 1,600 hides, which should provide for 6,600 feet. A bank still survives round three sides of Wareham, and the measurement along the top of it is around 5,900 feet, which leaves only some 700 feet, not nearly enough to cover the unbanked south side along the River Frome. In this case, the sleight of hand that used the ditch rather than the wall around Portchester cannot be applied, as the north side does not have a ditch, being on the crest of a steep slope. Baker and Brookes

[92] M. Aylwin Cotton and P.W. Gathercole, *Excavations at Clausentum, Southampton, 1951–1954* (London: Her Majesty's Stationery Office, 1958), fig. 1; the measurement refers to the inner ditch – the outer is even longer.

[93] An inner enclosure within the *wic* at London may have been a defence either by or against vikings: Cowie and Blackmore, Lundenwic, 211.

[94] Baker and Brookes, *Beyond the Burghal Hidage*, fig. 27.

[95] H. Kavanagh, "West Quay Shopping Centre," *Archaeology in Hampshire, Annual Report for 1998*, 49–50, at 50.

[96] D. Hill, "Sites X1 and X2 – Pound Lane," 22–27 in K.S. Jarvis, *Excavations in Christchurch 1969–80* (Dorset Natural History and Archaeological Society Monograph 5, 1983); Hill, "Gazetteer," 199. (Christchurch was in Hampshire until transferred to Dorset in 1974).

[97] Jarvis, *Excavations in Christchurch*, 31–32, site X5, Druitts Gardens.

[98] J. Haslam, "The development of Late-Saxon Christchurch, Dorset, and the Burghal Hidage," *Medieval Archaeology*, 53 (2009): 95–118.

[99] Jarvis, *Excavations in Christchurch*, trench X5, 31–32; Jarvis was not the excavator and had to rely on inadequate site records for his careful analysis.

[100] The northern end of the eastern side was excavated in the early 1980s: S.M. Davies, "Excavations at Christchurch, Dorset, 1981 to 1983," *Proceedings of the Dorset Natural History and Archaeological Society*, 105 (1983): 21–56. A more central zone was excavated in 2006: P. Reeve, J. Schuster and A.P. Fitzpatrick, "The eastern defences of the Saxon burh at Christchurch, Dorset: an archaeological evaluation at the King's Arms Hotel," *Proceedings of the Dorset Natural History and Archaeological Society*, 132 (2011): 127–30.

[101] Haslam, "Late-Saxon Christchurch," 107.

[102] A.P. Smyth, *Alfred the Great* (Oxford: Oxford University Press, 1995) would disagree.

[103] The redating of the very comparable church at Brixworth to the late eighth/mid ninth century is by D. Parsons and D. S. Sutherland, *The Anglo-Saxon Church of All Saints, Brixworth, Northamptonshire. Survey, excavation and analysis 1972–2010* (Oxford: Oxbow Books, 2013), 142–43 and 232, with a preference for the earlier part of the range. Wareham's St Mary could be very slightly later: 196–97. Blair, "Grid-planning," 24–26, notes that Brixworth's plan conforms to a 'short rod' of 4.6 m; using the plan in Royal Commission on Historical Monuments, *Dorset. Volume II, South-East part 2* (London: Royal Commission on Historical Monuments, 1970), 305, I calculate that the nave's internal length was 62 modern feet long, which works out at 18.9m, significantly close to four 'short rods' that would give 18.4m; the nave's width of 25 feet, 7.62m, is nowhere near to significance; but the overall internal width, assuming that porticuses existed on the south as well as the north sides, was 47 feet, 14.3m, which is only five centimetres adrift of three 'short rods' giving 13.8m. The eleventh-century Wareham St Martin has proportions that suggest use of the 'long' rod: D.A. Hinton, and C.J. Webster, "Excavations at the church of St Martin, Wareham, 1985–86, and 'minsters' in south-east Dorset," *Proceedings of the Dorset Natural History and Archaeological Society*, 109 (1987): 47–54, at 47.

rightly point out the difficulties in knowing exactly what all this means; they suggest a precinct around the church, and that that was what the vikings 'slipped into' in 876.[104] Asser pointed out that the site had natural strength except on the west side,[105] so it is conceivable that the fortification that he knew about ran only between the Rivers Frome and Piddle, possibly constructed by the vikings in the winter of 876, much like the one that they had constructed earlier between the Thames and the Kennet at Reading.[106] If that were the case, the 'Burghal Hidage' would imply that Wareham was strengthened further after 876.

All this shows that Haslam seems to be correct to have found no convincingly direct correlations in southern Wessex between the 'Burghal Hidage' formula and the forts' walls, except at Winchester.[107] Only one other place has such a high assessment, Wallingford, also with 2,400 hides. There, no Roman walls existed to be reused, and an earth bank and ditch surround three sides of the town, with the River Thames forming the fourth. Wallingford's circuit does not measure 9,900 feet, unlike Winchester, even when the river side is counted in; it is about 9,090 feet. Peter Huggins pointed out, however, that the 'fit' is as good as for Winchester – if the pole used was the 'northern' one of 15¼ feet.[108]

Haslam dismissed the significance of the shorter pole allowing a correlation between the Burghal Hidage and the defences at Wallingford,[109] and he has been supported by those working on the '*Burh* to Borough Research Project'. Their study of Wallingford postulates an early zone of urban planning in the south-east quadrant of the town, with tenements laid out using a pole of 16½ feet.[110] One problem with this is that what seems from its profile to have been a very substantial ditch, found inside the 'burh' area, and which would have extended under the line of St Mary's Street, calls in question what elements may be regarded as part of any early planned lay-out, as it had early pottery in its fill.[111] A further point is the research undertaken by John Blair, who has endorsed Huggins's argument in favour of a 'short pole'.[112]

Use of a 'short pole' at Wallingford would have implications for the compilation of the 'Burghal Hidage', for if two different pole lengths can be shown to have applied, it is more difficult to accept Haslam's argument that the list derives from a single administrative order made in 878–79. The traditional view that it is a compendium has been defended twice by Baker and Brookes, and again refuted by Haslam.[113] Much turns on Portchester, as the estate in which that fort lies was owned by the Bishop of Winchester in 904, when it was exchanged with the king. The implication is that the fort was therefore not on a

[104] Baker and Brookes, *Beyond the Burghal Hidage*, 396–97. The precinct has been sought but not found in excavation, e.g. *Proceedings of the Dorset Natural History and Archaeological Society*, 114 (1992), 238, 248 and 252; 115 (1993), 161–62; 116 (1994), 120–21. It would help if we had a better idea of the date of the causeways leading into the north and south sides of the town; the late Norman Field thought that he had found a Roman road, but what he saw was off the direct line: N.H. Field, "North causeway, Wareham, December 1988," *Proceedings of the Dorset Natural History and Archaeological Society*, 110 (1988): 152–54. That the north causeway was part of Morden parish, to the north, although bracketed by Wareham St Martin, is another oddity: Hinton and Webster, "St Martin, Wareham," 53; the opposite applies at Cricklade.

[105] S. Keynes and M. Lapidge, trans., *Alfred the Great. Asser's* Life of King Alfred *and other contemporary sources* (Harmondsworth: Penguin Books, 1983), 82 and 245, n. 87. They note that Asser used the word *castellum*, but that he was writing fifteen or so years after the vikings took Wareham, when the whole promontory might not have been fortified. Baker and Brookes, *Beyond the Burghal Hidage*, 396–97, may well be correct that they moved into the minster precinct, from which they would have had direct access to the river for their ships when those arrived – many to be wrecked off Swanage the following year.

[106] I advance this on the basis of no evidence, partly to give an opportunity to object to an unpublished proposal that the whole circuit was constructed by the vikings and that St Martin's Church was incorporated into it in the same way as was the church at Repton. Not only is the present building clearly later than the ninth century, but as Laurence Keen pointed out when the idea of a gate church was mooted some years ago, the building is set slightly behind the rampart and is not adjacent to the entry-point in the way that St Michael's is at Oxford: "The towns of Dorset," in *Anglo-Saxon Towns in Southern England*, ed. J. Haslam (Chichester: Phillimore, 1984), 239. That the defences on the north and east sides were added later could help to explain why St Martin's parish is almost entirely extra-mural and clearly taken from the *parochia* of St Mary, as was Holy Trinity parish also: ibid. 224–27. Holy Trinity and St Martin would therefore both post-date the first defence but pre-date the second, unlike St Peter and others which have only small intra-mural parishes; on that argument, the first two were planned to augment the 'new town', perhaps as early as the late ninth century, and the others were later testimony to its success.

[107] Now supported by Molyneaux, *Formation*, 88, who points out that the compiler may not have known anything about the reality of the 'burhs' other than Winchester; but his dismissal of arguments that a shorter rod or pole was used elsewhere ignores the very exact correlation for Wallingford, below.

[108] P.J. Huggins, "Anglo-Saxon timber building measurements: recent results," *Medieval Archaeology*, 35 (1991): 6–28, at 24–25.

[109] Haslam, "Late-Saxon Christchurch," 114.

[110] N. Christie and O. Creighton, *Transforming Townscapes. From burh to borough: the archaeology of Wallingford, AD 800–1400* (Society for Medieval Archaeology Monograph 32, 2013), 81.

[111] Christie and Creighton, *Transforming Townscapes*, 71–72, drew attention to the discoveries made in 2003, but did not show them on fig. 2.7 or elsewhere. J. Pine, "Medieval and later occupation at 51–53 St Mary's Street," in *Archaeological Investigations in Wallingford, Oxfordshire, 1992–2010* ed. S. Preston (Reading: Thames Valley Archaeological Services Monograph 10, 2012), 10–12 and 35–36 described the probable ditches. Circumstances for excavation were very unfavourable, but the auger-holes indicate that the east side of F117 – if indeed a ditch as its profile suggests – would have extended across at least most of the line of St Mary Street, and would have taken up the space that was to be used for the market. The dating is inevitably imprecise, but on page 11 it is said that 'the earliest pottery (from the lowest fills) was late Saxon Oxford ware' presumably type OXB ascribed by Paul Blinkhorn to the late-eighth to early-eleventh century (19); the ditch could therefore have been dug at any time in the early history of the town, but its upper layers contained pottery of eleventh-century and later types – which would probably have entered the lowest fills if the ditch had been dug subsequent to their introduction.

[112] Blair, "Grid-planning," 20; their chosen lengths are marginally different, but Blair accepts that variation of up to 8cm can be expected. Blair also endorses my argument of some years ago that in general the 'short rod' fits the northern 'burhs' a little better than those in the south of Wessex: D.A. Hinton, "The fortifications and their shires," 151–59 in *Defence of Wessex*, eds Hill and Rumble, 153–54.

[113] Initially in J. Baker and S. Brookes, "From frontier to border: the evolution of northern West Saxon territorial delineation in the ninth and tenth centuries," *Anglo-Saxon Studies in Archaeology and History*, 17 (2011): 108–23, at 116–18 and then in Baker and Brookes, *Beyond the Burghal Hidage*, 32–33 and 66, clearly written before they had had the opportunity of considering Haslam, *Urban-Rural Connections*, 22, 27 and 120. I would have added that Blair's recent 'Grid-plan' article favours the view that different measuring systems were used by Wessex and Mercia, with only a street length at Hamwic as an exception, 35–36; but I have argued above that the 'short rod' can also be seen in building lengths at Chalton, and in both length and width at Wareham (notes 62 and 103). The difference might therefore be in use of the 'four-pole grid'; analysis of the overall plan of Chalton might prove or disprove that.

royal estate until then, and some would argue that it would not have entered the 'Burghal Hidage' list until it was in royal ownership.[114] Haslam's view that no such ban would have existed is supported by uncertainty over direct royal ownership of other burghal sites,[115] especially since, like Wareham and Twynham, some were at the least associated with major ecclesiastical institutions which might have claimed to own the land on which they were built. In particular, Winchester itself has been cited, as Bishop Swithun was credited with building the south bridge,[116] and that might mean that he was actively re-establishing the city's infrastructure, and thus potentially its defences, immediately after the vikings had sacked it in 860[117] – an interpretation, of course, which does no favours to the argument that the 'Burghal Hidage' should be assigned specifically to 878–79.

One other point to be made about the controversy over the 'Burghal Hidage' dating goes back to the event of 802 when the Hwiccians crossed the Thames and were driven off by the *Wilsaetan.* The victory presumably brought that zone back into the shire,[118] and therefore the territory on which the 'burh' at Cricklade was constructed; Baker and Brookes have argued 'possibly that [Cricklade] was a later imposition on to an earlier system',[119] a plank in their argument that the assessments were not all drawn up at the same time. No very sound historical reason seems to exist for the Cricklade zone not being part of the Wiltshire calculations if they were drawn up at any time after 802, however, and the total of hides for the county, 4,800 according to the 'best' estimates, is exactly twice the 2,400 that Winchester and Wallingford suggest to have been important, which looks too precise to be coincidence.[120] Haslam's view that the Wiltshire assessments were unitary seems more likely to be correct, therefore, and, taken together with allowance for Portchester being included within the royal defensive measures before 904, favours an argument that for some counties at least the 'Burghal Hidage' was drawn up as a single document at a particular time in the ninth century, though not necessarily in 878–79 and not necessarily without further additions being made before the extant 'Burghal Hidage' documents were written.[121]

As for Cricklade's archaeology, it is a pity that the recent development of the north-east corner of the 'burh' was not used as an opportunity to get a proper look at the defences in that area. The single two-metre wide trench located a ditch, but was not extended far enough eastwards to see if there was a second, outer ditch. Westwards, a feature a few centimetres high was taken to be what remains of a rampart, overlain by a bank of some 1.25 metres in height, which contained 'eleventh-/twelfth-century sherds'. There seems to have been no berm between the outer face of that bank and the ditch – a ditch which was not excavated below one metre from the present ground surface and was not even augered.[122] If the published section is accurately recorded, it was quite steep-sided, and could have gone down another metre or so. If the earlier deposits really were all that remained of an 'Alfredian' bank, there was space for a berm between it and the ditch, but in that case the latter must have been cut back so that all trace of its original side was removed, as its cut-line is shown as starting from a higher level than the ground surface below the 'first' rampart. Nothing suggests that either bank was revetted, either with timber or with stone, and the report makes no mention of the sort of stone spreads seen at Christchurch and elsewhere. It seems quite possible that the first 'rampart' was no more than a marking-out line for what the sherds in the overlying bank show to have been a Norman or possibly later construction. In other words, this part of the Cricklade defences might not have existed until well after the 'Burghal Hidage' was written, which could help to explain the discrepancy between the hidage figures and the length of the four sides of the town.[123]

After Alfred

Whether 'burhs' were fully effective is a moot point; Chichester's walls seem to have held out in 894 against vikings, but an unfinished fortress somewhere in the Weald fell to them in 892 because it was only half-finished. Within Wessex, a salutary lesson against overstressing the 'Burghal Hidage' forts' importance is provided by what happened in 900, when Alfred's nephew Aethelwold contended for the throne against Edward, Alfred's son. The former seized both Wimborne and Twynham (Christchurch); his motive in entering Wimborne seems to have been to secure for himself one of the nuns, unnamed but probably a princess who would have given his claim further legitimacy if he married her. Edward camped at Badbury Rings, not a Burghal Hidage 'burh' but close to

[114] Baker and Brookes, *Beyond the Burghal Hidage*, who review the history of the conflicting theories and themselves favour the view that 904 would be the earliest date for Portchester to have been a 'Burghal Hidage' 'burh': 32, 83 and 397.

[115] J. Haslam, "King Alfred and the vikings: strategies and tactics 876–888 AD," *Anglo-Saxon Studies in Archaeology and History*, 13 (2005): 144.

[116] Our honorand, Thomas Beaumont James, can be credited here: *English Heritage Book of Winchester* (London: B. T. Batsford/English Heritage, 1997), 44.

[117] M. Biddle, "The study of Winchester: archaeology and history in a British town, 1961–1983," *Proceedings of the British Academy*, 69 (1983): 120–22, pointed out that the terms used could indicate that the defences were already in service.

[118] Yorke, *Wessex*, 64.

[119] Baker and Brookes, *Beyond the Burghal Hidage*, 265.

[120] Hinton, "The fortifications," 151–52.

[121] Haslam, *Urban-Rural Connections*, 19–20 and 24–26. Haslam argued that it is possible to establish precisely which hundreds had to send men to each 'burh', on the assumption that each one was supported by its own territory and that men could not be switched from one to another. Although they did not mean the precise figures to be taken too seriously, Reynolds and Langlands, "Social identities," 41, pointed out that on the "Burghal Hidage" assessments, men from several different shires would have been needed to construct East Wansdyke; if they could have been brought together in whatever earlier period that work was done, the same could surely have been achieved by King Alfred and his successors.

[122] T. Longman, "Excavations at Abingdon Court Farm, Cricklade, Wiltshire, 2000–1," *Wiltshire Archaeological and Natural History Magazine*, 106 (2013): 167–203, at 180–81. The main bank is context 507, the ditch sides 520. If safety regulations constrained the depth of ditch dug, the upper layers on either side of the section should have been cleared back.

[123] Hill, "Gazetteer," 199–200 for a summary.

Wimborne, which he attacked. Aethelwold barricaded the gates there and vowed to hold out, but instead he 'stole away'. Whether Edward in fact caught him unawares and he had no choice but to make a show of resistance before escaping is not clear, but no-one seems to have blamed him for his behaviour; that he slipped away suggests that his exit was not blocked, and although it is recorded that he was pursued on horseback, he must have had access to at least one ship, because he joined the vikings in Northumbria. Why did he not pull back to Twynham and defy Edward there – could it be that its defences were still inadequate?

A coherent sequence through all the various Christchurch section drawings, photographs and plans is nearly impossible, and the different phases of construction that must have taken place as ditches were dug, banks piled up and stone walls added cannot be sorted out in a way that would reveal their condition at any one date. Serious issue can really only be taken with Haslam's interpretation of the final phases, when the defences were destroyed. He asserted that on the west side, on site X5, 'stones ...were tipped into the open ditch ...', but this is not demonstrable from the section drawings, which show that the ditch was not completely excavated, and had many more stones over the top of it than in its uppermost layer.[124] Another trench on the west side, X7, had a probably defensive ditch filled with 'fine silty sand', again contrary to what Haslam says.[125] On the north side, Haslam cited trench X1 as another example, but the published section of the ditch there seems to be shown as not having stones in it. The other ditches on the north side also had loamy fills.[126] These results were mirrored in the early 1980s work, where again only the uppermost ditch layers contained stone rubble;[127] in W37, nothing but 'chipped fragments of heathstone were found'[128]– if anything, more indicative of a wall's construction than of its demolition. On the east side, there was indeed a substantial amount of rubble within a ditch, 120, in site W10. This was not the primary ditch, however, but seemingly a recut of an earlier one, 123, which did not have rubble in it.[129] Haslam's claim that the Anglo-Saxon stone wall was razed in a single operation on all three sides of the defences, at a time when the perimeter ditches were still a formidable obstacle, is not therefore supported by data from the ditches on the west and north. His further conclusion that the infilling took place in the early eleventh century scarcely allows sufficient time for a primary ditch, even if of the 870s, to have silted up so much that it had had to be recut at least once before the order came to destroy it all.[130] Demolition of the north wall could have taken place when it became desirable to add the northern suburb into the borough; on the east, it may simply have not been worth maintaining as water-courses encroached on it for mill leats.

The destruction of Twynham's defences has some consequences, as Haslam saw it as a consequence of an unrecorded demand made by King Cnut in the early eleventh century, after the 'second viking wars' and the replacement of Ethelred the Unready's dynasty with the Danish one, that all the 'burhs' were to be slighted. Removal of the best case study throws doubt on the others, where excavation has been even more limited, and questions the contention that Cnut saw the extant 'burhs' as challenges to his authority. It is a great pity that more work was not done at Cricklade in the north-east corner, as the 'eleventh-/twelfth-century' sherds in the bank seem to put it in the second viking period at the very earliest, and it could as well be some fairly inadequate twelfth-century civil war work.[131]

The 'second' viking wars of course saw use and reuse of many defended places, most of them more substantial than Wimborne, for instance, seems to have been. Reuse of Old Sarum because Wilton was unsafe is a classic example of the apparent limitation of the 'Alfredian' 'burhs'.[132] Much less is heard of the smaller defensible places, such as residences, being attacked, which partly explains why so many of the place-names that end in *bury* are not attested until the late eleventh-century Domesday Book. Consequently, as with Yatesbury and Avebury, the ages of the names cannot be measured; it can only be said that the names persisted even though the word was coming to signify 'town' as well as 'manor'. That Avebury had early elliptical defences has been questioned above, but the contention that it was subsequently defended by a rectilinear enclosure and was a 'failed town' can also be questioned. A ditch excavated at one end of a house property proved to be large for a mere boundary, at 1.5 metres in depth and 3.5 in width,[133] not dissimilar to some

[124] Haslam, "Late-Saxon Christchurch," 101; compare Jarvis, *Excavations in Christchurch*, 1983, 30–32.

[125] Haslam, "Late Saxon Christchurch," 101; Jarvis, *Excavations in Christchurch*, 32–33.

[126] Site X1: Hill, "Pound Lane," fig. 4, layer 16; X2: ibid. 26–27, fig. 5, layers 2–5 and 10; X15: Jarvis, *Excavations in Christchurch*, 51 and pl. 12; watching brief by Paul Aitken, 37 and pl. 10.

[127] Davies, "Excavations at Christchurch," 25–26.

[128] P.A. Yeoman, "The 1982 excavation: site W37, 14 High Street," in Davies, "Excavations at Christchurch," 46.

[129] Davies, "Excavations at Christchurch," 28–30.

[130] Haslam, "Late Saxon Christchurch," 104.

[131] Longman, "Abingdon Court, Cricklade," 181. Note that the bank has become 'late' eleventh- or twelfth-century by 182. The quantities of sherds found in it, and their fabrics, are not revealed in the pottery report, 185–87.

[132] Lavelle, *Alfred's Wars*, 235–63.

[133] J. Pollard and A. Reynolds, *Avebury: the Biography of a Landscape* (Stroud: Tempus Publishing, 2002), 206–07. There is also a much shallower outer ditch, that may or may not be co-eval. A report on geophysical work undertaken in the Recreation Ground on the south side of the village claims to have 'identified…the line of the bank and ditch of the late Saxon settlement', but does not give dimensions or mention the possible outer ditch: *Wiltshire Archaeological and Natural History Magazine*, 108 (2015): 215. The precise route of the *herepath* which Reynolds argued in an earlier paper to have passed through Avebury from Yatesbury cannot be mapped with enough precision to show whether it used a crossing on the High Street line or the more northern route: A.J. Reynolds, "Avebury, Yatesbury and the archaeology of communications," *Papers from the Institute of Archaeology*, 6 (1995): 21–30.

Since this paper was drafted, Alex Langlands has proposed that a late Saxon 'burh' rather like that postulated for Avebury may have been located in fields south of Old Sarum: "Placing the burh in *Searobyrg*;

of those at Christchurch mentioned above, for instance. But its internal bank is suggested to have been only half a metre in height – and, as there was no berm between the bank and the ditch, seems unlikely to have been any higher or it would have slumped forward and slid into the ditch, taking with it the fence on top indicated by two post-holes. Compared to the known 'burhs', the provision at Avebury looks ineffective as a defence, and the ditch's size may be a factor of water in the low-lying meadows, and the need to carry it off quickly. The notion that it was part of the perimeter of a 'failed town' would be more convincing if the present main street led directly to a causeway and a crossing of the River Kennet, but none is indicated on maps or by surviving earthworks, including those shown on recent LiDAR survey.

The interior of the present-day village at Avebury has not been investigated, so what sort of manor-house or manor-houses were there is not known. At near-by Yatesbury, Reynolds's work has revealed the circular enclosure within the present village discussed above. This might well have developed into a thegn's residence. In Domesday Book, Yatesbury was a five-hide estate, and therefore exactly the sort of place where a thegn was expected to have a *burh-geat* and a *bel-hus*, presumably meaning a bell-tower.[134] Reuse of the enclosure would have been logical, and would not imply that a perimeter ditch was the norm. It could account for the name Yatesbury, Old English *geat burh*, the first element giving the modern 'gate' or 'gap'. That term occurs in many Anglo-Saxon sources, including some which imply that the 'gate' was a feature of an enclosure. *Geat-burh* is not certainly known as a place-name, however, as even 'Yatesbury' is first recorded, in Domesday Book, as *etesberie,* which could derive from an owner's name, 'Stronghold of a man called Gēat'.[135]

If 'Yates' really derives from 'gap' or 'gate', one reason why it was viewed as such a distinctive feature could be accounted for by the excavations. The interpretation of the Bronze Age mound as an Anglo-Saxon beacon site has been questioned above; an alternative is that it served as the base of a timber tower, which would have been made more conspicuous by being on the mound, and by having a ditch dug around it. The likelihood is that if any such tower existed, it would have been late rather than mid Saxon, which is consistent with the sherd in the ditch. A timber building – of some sort, not necessarily a tall tower, of course – might, if burnt down, whether by accident or hostile design, have produced the degree of burning observed on the summit and the quantity of charred timber and charcoal in the ditch.

Several quite tall but narrow late Saxon stone towers are known, such as the originally free-standing tower at St Michael's, Oxford, which is close enough to a gate into the town to suggest that it was an integral part of the enclosure's entrance. A stone-footed tower in the secular late Saxon residence has been traced at what was probably another five-hide estate at Portchester; those foundations may well have supported a timber superstructure rather than a stone one.[136] The post-holes excavated at Bishopstone, Sussex, suggest a timber superstructure, which Gabor Thomas argues to have been a tower;[137] existence of timber towers is substantiated by skeuomorphs in stonework, notably Earl's Barton. All these except probably Bishopstone had some sort of ecclesiastical use, even Portchester's having burials around it, but some may not have had such use when first built. Bishopstone had post-holes in each corner, and unless some were found at Yatesbury it must be assumed that any structure on the mound there was built on ground cills. Such 'surface-laid' buildings are known from at least the tenth century in London,[138] and apparently in Hampshire at Bishops Waltham,[139] although it has to be admitted that they were not observed at the more extensively excavated thegns' house sites in the county,

rethinking the urban topography of early medieval Salisbury," *Wiltshire Archaeological and Natural History Magazine*, 107 (2014), 91–105. As he says (97), this needs more fieldwork investigation, but preliminary doubts include the sheer size of the suggested lay-out, which makes it as big as Winchester; that instead of straddling an existing through-route, it would have had the Port Way running along the edge of the ditch on the east side, unlike any other 'burh'; and a LiDAR image shows a long linear feature north of the axial lane that has no obvious relationship with the suggested plan, though is of course undated.

134 For *burh-geat* and Anglo-Saxon social conventions, see M. Gardiner, "Late Saxon settlements," 198–217 in *Oxford Handbook*, eds Hamerow, Hinton and Crawford, 199–200 (including a caveat about too literal interpretations), and A. Williams, *The World before Domesday* (London: Continuum UK, 2008), 67 and 90–104; Bishopstone: G. Thomas, *The Later Anglo-Saxon Settlement at Bishopstone; a Downland Manor in the Making* (York: Council for British Archaeology Research Report 163, 2010), 61–33, 192–93 and 195–97, Structure W (which had a cellar, unlike any others known); Baker and Brookes, *Beyond the Burghal Hidage*, 110–17 (they reject Reynolds's *geat-burh* interpretation of Yatesbury, without saying why, and suggest instead that the name refers to a gap in the Wansdyke (116–17, n. 70); as Wansdyke is at least six kilometres from Yatesbury and is not directly connected to it by any of the very many roads and paths mapped on page 253, that seems unlikely); Domesday Book , in which 'Alwey held [Yatesbury] before 1066; it paid tax for five hides': C. and F. Thorn (eds), *Domesday Book. 6: Wiltshire* (Chichester: Phillimore, 1979), entry 54, 1.

135 Mills, *Dictionary of Place-Names*, 516.

136 In Domesday Book, it is recorded that three freemen had held three manors, with an overall total of five hides, suggesting a recent estate division, with one perhaps having the '*hallam*' with attached fishery: J. Munby (ed.), *Domesday Book. 4: Hampshire* (Chichester: Phillimore, 1982), entry 35.4; this 'hall' was very possibly the excavated complex: Cunliffe 1975, 49–52, 60 and 303 (it is worth noting here that Michael Hare showed that the 'Watergate' arch is more probably early Norman than Anglo-Saxon: "The Watergate at Portchester and the Anglo-Saxon porch at Titchfield," *Proceedings of the Hampshire Field Club and Archaeological Society*, 40 (1984): 71–80). Williams, however, *Before Domesday*, 89, suggests that the excavation could be of a royal reeve's house, as 'another part' of the royal manor of Wymering was in Portchester: Munby, ed., *Hampshire*, entries 1.9 and 1.11. For a recent review of the stone towers, see M. Shapland, "St Mary's Church, Broughton, Lincolnshire: a thegnly tower-nave in the late Anglo-Saxon landscape," *Archaeological Journal*, 165 (2008): 471–519, esp. 501–02.

137 Thomas, *Bishopstone*, 61–63, 192–93 and 195–97.

138 V. Horsman, Christine Milne and Gustav Milne, *Aspects of Saxo-Norman London: I. Building and street development near Billingsgate and Cheapside* (London and Middlesex Archaeological Society Special Paper 11, 1988), 66–71. See also Hamerow, *Rural Settlements*, 27 and 53.

139 M. Gardiner, "Vernacular buildings and the development of the later medieval domestic plan in England," *Medieval Archaeology*, 44 (2000): 159–81, at 170–72. (By coincidence, this paper is immediately followed by one written by Tom Beaumont James and Edward Roberts, on Winchester.)

Portchester and Netherton.[140] Post-Conquest mottes had post-hole towers, so far as is known, but those mounds were new and unstable.[141] They were also quite high, just as their ditches were generally deeper than those known at thegns' residences where they existed, at Netherton for example.[142]

Another very small hint that an existing mound might have been used in late Saxon Yatesbury is that two other examples of reuse are known, both also in the Kennet valley. One is Silbury Hill, where evidence of possibly military occupation has been found.[143] The other is the mound at Marlborough, very recently shown to have been prehistoric, not Norman, though used as a motte in the Norman period, and possibly earlier as a vantage-point.[144] Far from conclusive though this is, a local tradition of using pre-existing earthworks could perhaps be indicated, as *Merleberge* is recorded in Domesday Book, and contains Old English *beorge*, 'mound' or 'hill'. Although the first element could be 'place where gentians grow', a personal name Maerla is equally possible; albeit that that name is otherwise unknown, it could refer as might Avebury and Yatesbury to a personally owned stronghold.[145] Marlborough presents another problem, however, as it is not by any means certain when the mound first functioned as a defensive point; unsurprisingly, it has not yielded evidence like that at Silbury for late Anglo-Saxon use, and although it became the motte of a royal castle of some importance, that may only be a twelfth-century development; William the Conqueror imprisoned a bishop somewhere in Marlborough, and transferred the mint from Bedwyn to it – but both those could indicate that the embryonic town was regarded as defensible, not that a castle already existed.[146]

To take the discussion of early medieval defences in southern England further would involve entering the world of castles, of Anarchy under Stephen and Matilda, and of retrenchment under Henry II – on, in fact, into that better-documented world which has been Tom Beaumont James's strong-hold.

Postscript

Since the completion of this paper, a wide-ranging and stimulating book by John Blair has been published.[147] His discussions of enclosures throw light on many of the issues discussed above, but his suggestion about the places in southern England named Burton is particularly germane.[148] Blair argued that a 'Burton' was not 'a defensive site in itself' but was supplementary to a more important place 'at a distance of two to four miles',[149] noting the proximity of the name to four of the Wessex places listed in the 'Burghal Hidage': Malmesbury, Wareham, Axbridge and Twynham/Christchurch.[150] The last of those is the only one with a nearby Burton that is recorded in Domesday Book, and is therefore the only one certainly with late Saxon origins. As Blair noted, the Burton near Malmesbury has been investigated by geophysics and LiDAR, but the evidence is consistent with twelfth-century 'Anarchy' siegeworks;[151] late Saxon use might have been too vestigial to be traced, although it was identified at Silbury Hill.[152] The Burton closest to Axbridge is in Compton Bishop parish, so any ancient link has been lost; the early nineteenth-century Ordnance Survey map spelled the name 'Bourton', and a modern lane is 'Bournton', so derivation from *bourne*, stream, seems a viable alternative. The Wareham example is presumably represented by West Burton and East Burton; the latter is closer to the town, but is about five miles away, too far to be significant. Furthermore, the names are not recorded until the thirteenth century, and are in Winfrith Newburgh parish, Newburgh being the family that owned the estate from the twelfth century, and perhaps therefore the origin of the farm names.[153]

Blair rightly did not include Burton [Bradstock], which is close to both of the two possible 'Burghal Hidage' west Dorset sites, Bridport or Bredy hillfort. It is in Domesday,

[140] Portchester: Cunliffe, *Portchester II*; Netherton: J.R. Fairbrother, *Faccombe Netherton: Excavations of a Saxon and Medieval Manorial Complex* (London: British Museum Occasional Paper 74, 1990), 128–32; buildings without post-holes start there in the twelfth century. On page 87, Fairbrother gave good reasons for thinking that the first-phase flint-walled structure at Netherton was not the base for a timber building at ground level. At both sites, and at Bishopstone, posts set in shallow trenches were much more frequently found, but those involved deeper groundworks. The reconstruction on the front cover of Thomas, *Bishopstone*, has a circular thatched structure around the central tower, which protrudes above it by only a single storey – an appearance not wholly unlike that of a single-storey timber structure atop the grassy mound at Yatesbury?

[141] J.R. Kenyon, *Medieval Fortifications* (Leicester/London: Leicester University Press, 1990), 9–23.

[142] Fairbrother, *Faccombe Netherton*, 65–67 and 231: 'not intended as a defensive measure, but to impress and deter entry except through the prescribed ways'.

[143] Reynolds and Brookes, "Anglo-Saxon civil defence," 584–86; J. Leary, D. Field and G. Campbell, *Silbury Hill. The largest prehistoric mound in Europe* (London: English Heritage, 2013), 289–304. That good intervisibility could be achieved from the summit is undoubted, but page 298 records that no remains of bonfires were noted in the excavations. It might be objected that the top of the mound was flattened off for the eleventh-century defence-work, removing any trace of an earlier beacon; but the cone of the hill would have had to be removed before a bonfire could have been constructed upon it.

[144] Baker and Brookes, *Beyond the Burghal Hidage*, 237.

[145] Mills, *Dictionary of Place-names*, 318. The name is truncated on Norman coins. For a full discussion, see Baker and Brookes, *Beyond the Burghal Hidage*, 237, note 12.

[146] J. Haslam, *Wiltshire Towns. The archaeological potential* (Devizes: Wiltshire Natural History and Archaeological Society, 1976), 41 for details. That Marlborough was an early tenth-century 'planned urban fortified centre' has been postulated: Reynolds and Brookes, "Anglo-Saxon civil defence," 581, but the case would be better if the name derived from *burh* not *beorge*, and if Domesday had listed it as a borough instead of merely attributing the 'earl's third penny' to it. The present-day urban area has as much mid Saxon evidence of occupation as of late: Baker and Brookes, *Beyond the Burghal Hidage*, 237.

[147] J. Blair, *Building Anglo-Saxon England* (Princeton/Oxford: Princeton University Press, 2018).

[148] See note 60 above.

[149] Blair, *Building*, 199.

[150] Blair, *Building*, 235 n 11.

[151] D. W. Wright, M. Fradley and O. Creighton, "The ringwork at Cam's Hill, near Malmesbury: archaeological investigation and landscape assessment," *Wiltshire Natural History and Archaeological Magazine*, 108 (2015): 105–18.

[152] See note 143 above.

[153] A. D. Mills, *Dorset Place-Names. Their Origins and Meanings* (Wimborne: Roy Gasson Associates, 1986), 47–48 for this and the following Dorset examples.

but as *Bridetone*, becoming *Brytton* and *Bertone* before becoming Burton. That example shows that place-names were fluid, and must throw doubt upon the early antecedents claimed for those that have so many possible derivations other than from *burh*, [*ge-*] *bur-tun* being another. Blair gave another possible case as High and Low Burton west of the Roman defences at Dorchester, but like the Winfrith Newburgh examples they are also only recorded for the first time in the thirteenth century, and seem likely to have been named from Poundbury hillfort to which they are closer than to the *ceastre*. Finally, Blair postulated a 'chain of eight *burh-tunas* ... to protect the West Saxon royal heartland', but they are all minor places, not all 'Burton' on the early map, with one, Boreham outside Warminster, being especially questionable; even if originally a *burh* name, it is closer to Scratchbury hillfort than to Warminster.[154]

Bibliography

Abdy, R. "After Patching." In *Coinage and History in the North Sea World* c. *500–1250. Studies in honour of Marion Archibald*, edited by B. Cook and G. Williams, 76–98. Leiden/Boston: Brill, 2006.

Addyman P.V. and D. Leigh. "The Anglo-Saxon village at Chalton, Hampshire: second interim report." *Medieval Archaeology*, 17 (1973): 1–25.

Ager, B. "A late Roman buckle- or belt-plate in the British Museum, said to be from northern France." *Medieval Archaeology*, 40 (1996): 206–11.

Alcock, L. *Cadbury Castle, Somerset. The early medieval archaeology.* Cardiff: University of Wales Press, 1995.

Andrews, P., ed. *Excavations at Hamwic Volume 2: Excavations at Six Dials.* York: Council for British Archaeology Research Report 109, 1997.

Astill, G.G. *Historic Towns in Berkshire; an Archaeological Appraisal.* Reading: Berkshire Archaeological Committee Publication 2, 1978.

Austin, M. "Rethinking Hardown Hill: our westernmost early Anglo-Saxon cemetery?" *Antiquaries Journal*, 94 (2014): 49–69.

Baker, J. and S. Brookes. "From frontier to border: the evolution of northern West Saxon territorial delineation in the ninth and tenth centuries." *Anglo-Saxon Studies in Archaeology and History*, 17 (2011): 108–23.

Baker, J. and S. Brookes. *Beyond the Burghal Hidage. Anglo-Saxon civil defence in the viking age.* Leiden/Boston: Brill, 2013.

Barker, K., ed. *Aldhelm and Sherborne.* Oxford: Oxbow Books, 2010.

Barker, K. "*Aldhelmus episcopus*: the making and shiring of the Sherborne bishopric – Saxon, Briton and the Byzantine." *Proceedings of the Dorset Natural History and Archaeological Society*, 134 (2013): 113–27.

Biddle, M. and B. Kjølbye-Biddle. "From *Venta* to *Wintanceastre*." In *Pagans and Christians – from Antiquity to the Middle Ages. Papers in honour of Martin Henig presented on the occasion of his sixty-fifth birthday* edited by L. Gilmour, 189–214. Oxford: British Archaeological Reports International Series 1610, 2007.

Biddle, M. "The study of Winchester: archaeology and history in a British town, 1961–1983." *Proceedings of the British Academy*, 69 (1983): 93–136.

Birbeck, V. *The Origins of Mid-Saxon Southampton. Excavations at the Friends Provident St Mary's Stadium 1998–2000.* Salisbury: Wessex Archaeology, 2005.

Blair, J. "Grid-planning in Anglo-Saxon settlements; the short perch and the four-perch module." *Anglo-Saxon Studies in Archaeology and History*, 18 (2013): 18–61.

Blair, J. *Anglo-Saxon Oxfordshire.* Stroud: Alan Sutton Publishing, 1994.

Blair, J. *The Church in Anglo-Saxon Society.* Oxford: Oxford University Press, 2005.

Blair, J. *Building Anglo-Saxon England.* Princeton/Oxford: Princeton University Press, 2018.

Booth, P., A. Simmonds, A. Boyle, S. Clough, H.E.M. Cool and D. Poore. *The Late Roman Cemetery at Lankhills, Winchester. Excavations 2000–2005.* Oxford: Oxford Archaeology Monograph 10, 2010.

Bowen, H.C. and B.N. Eagles, eds. *The Archaeology of Bokerley Dyke.* London: Her Majesty's Stationery Office, 1990.

Brookes, S., S. Hamilton, A. and Reynolds, eds. *Studies in Early Anglo-Saxon Art and Archaeology: Papers in Honour of Martin G. Welch.* Oxford: British Archaeological Reports British Series 527, 2011.

Brooks, N.P. "The development of military obligations in eighth- and ninth-century England." In *England before the Conquest. Studies in primary sources presented to Dorothy Whitelock*, edited by P. Clemoes and K. Hughes, 69–84. Cambridge: Cambridge University Press, 1971.

Buckberry, J. and A. Cherryson, eds. *Burial in Later Anglo-Saxon England,* c.*650–1100 AD.* Oxford/Oakville: Oxbow Books, 2010.

Cherryson, A.K. "'Such a resting-place ...': Saxon Southampton and the development of churchyard burial." In *Burial in Later Anglo-Saxon England,* c. *650–1100 AD*, edited by J. Buckberry and A. Cherryson, 54–72. Oxford/Oakville: Oxbow Books, 2010.

Christie, N. and O. Creighton. *Transforming Townscapes. From burh to borough: the archaeology of Wallingford, AD 800–1400.* Society for Medieval Archaeology Monograph 32, 2013.

[154] Blair, *Building*, 224, mapped in fig. 60.

Clemoes, P. and K. Hughes, eds. *England before the Conquest. Studies in primary sources presented to Dorothy Whitelock.* Cambridge: Cambridge University Press, 1971.

Colgrave, B. and R.A.B. Mynors, eds. *Bede's Ecclesiastical History of the English People.* Oxford: Clarendon Press, 1969.

Collins, R. and L. Allason-Jones, eds. *Finds from the Frontier.* York: Council for British Archaeology Research Report 162, 2010.

Cook, B., and G. Williams, eds. *Coinage and History in the North Sea World* c. *500–1250. Studies in honour of Marion Archibald.* Leiden/Boston: Brill, 2006.

Cotton M. Aylwin and P.W. Gathercole. *Excavations at Clausentum, Southampton, 1951–1954.* London: Her Majesty's Stationery Office, 1958.

Coulson, J.C.N. "Military equipment of the "long" 4th century on Hadrian's Wall." In *Finds from the Frontier* edited by R. Collins and L. Allason-Jones, 50–63. York: Council for British Archaeology Research Report 162, 2010.

Coulstock, P.H. *The Collegiate Church of Wimborne Minster* (Woodbridge: Boydell Press, 1993).

Cowie, R. and Blackmore, L. Lundenwic. *Excavations in Middle Saxon London, 1987–2000* (London: Museum of London Archaeology Monograph 63, 2012).

Cramp, R. "A lost pendant from near Catterick Bridge, Yorkshire." In *Early Medieval Art and Archaeology in the Northern World. Studies in honour of James Graham-Campbell* edited by A. Reynolds and L. Webster, 73–85. Leiden/Boston: Brill, 2013.

Cunliffe, B. *Excavations at Portchester. Volume II: Saxon.* London: Society of Antiquaries of London, 1975.

Dark, K.R. Civitas *to Kingdom: British Political Continuity 300–800.* Leicester: Leicester University Press, 1994.

Davies, S.M. "Excavations at Christchurch, Dorset, 1981 to 1983." *Proceedings of the Dorset Natural History and Archaeological Society*, 105 (1983): 21–56.

Davies, W., G. Halsall and A.J. Reynolds, eds. *People and Space in the Middle Ages, 300–1300*, Studies in the Early Middle Ages 15. Turnhout: Brepols Publishing, 2006.

Dodd, A., ed. *Oxford before the University. The late Saxon and Norman archaeology of the Thames crossing, the defences and the town*, Thames Valley Landscapes Monograph 17. Oxford: Oxford University School of Archaeology, 2003.

Draper, S. "The significance of Old English *burh* in Anglo-Saxon England." *Anglo-Saxon Studies in Archaeology and History*, 15 (2008): 240–53.

Drewett, P. and S. Hamilton. "Marking time and making space: excavations and landscape studies at The Caburn hillfort, East Sussex, 1996–8." *Sussex Archaeological Collections*, 137 (1999), 7–37.

Eagles, B. and M.J. Allen. "A reconsideration of East Wansdyke: its construction and date – a preliminary note." In *Studies in Early Anglo-Saxon Art and Archaeology: Papers in Honour of Martin G. Welch* edited by S. Brookes, S. Hamilton and A.J. Reynolds, 147–55. Oxford: British Archaeological Reports British Series 527, 2011.

Eagles, B. and C. Mortimer. "Early Anglo-Saxon artefacts from Hod Hill, Dorset." *Antiquaries Journal*, 73 (1993): 132–40.

Eagles, B.N. "'Small shires' and *regiones* in Hampshire and the formation of the shires of eastern Wessex." *Anglo-Saxon Studies in Archaeology and History*, 19 (2015): 122–52.

Eagles, B.N. "Anglo-Saxon presence and culture in Wiltshire *c.* AD 450 – *c.* 675." In *Roman Wiltshire and After. Papers in honour of Ken Annable*, edited by P. Ellis, 199–233. Devizes: Wiltshire Archaeological and Natural History Society, 2001.

Edwards, H. *The Charters of the Early West Saxon Kingdom.* Oxford: British Archaeological Reports British Series 198, 1988.

Ellis, P., ed. *Roman Wiltshire and After. Papers in honour of Ken Annable.* Devizes: Wiltshire Archaeological and Natural History Society, 2001.

Ellison, A. and P. Rahtz. "Excavations at Whitsbury Castle Ditches, Hampshire, 1960." *Proceedings of the Hampshire Field Club and Archaeological Society*, 43 (1987): 63–81.

Erskine, J.G.P. "The West Wansdyke: an appraisal of the dating, dimensions and construction techniques in the light of excavated evidence." *Archaeological Journal*, 164 (2007): 80–108.

Esmonde Cleary, S. "The ending(s) of Roman Britain." In *The Oxford Handbook of Anglo-Saxon Archaeology*, edited by H. Hamerow, D.A. Hinton and S. Crawford, 13–29. Oxford: Oxford University Press, 2011.

Fairbrother, J.R. *Faccombe Netherton: Excavations of a Saxon and Medieval Manorial Complex.* London: British Museum Occasional Paper 74, 1990.

Field, N.H. "North causeway, Wareham, December 1988." *Proceedings of the Dorset Natural History and Archaeological Society*, 110 (1988): 152–54.

Fowler, P.J. "Field archaeology in West Woods, Fyfield and West Overton, Wiltshire." *Wiltshire Archaeological and Natural History Magazine*, 104 (2011).

Fulford, M., A. Clarke, and H. Eckardt. *Life and Labour in Late Roman Silchester. Excavations in Insula IX since 1999.* Society for the Promotion of Roman Studies, 2006.

Fulford, M. *The Silchester Amphitheatre. Excavations of 1979–85.* Britannia Monograph 10, 1989.

Fulford, M.G. and S. Rippon. *Pevensey Castle, Sussex: Excavations in the Roman Fort and Norman Keep, 1991–95.* Salisbury: Wessex Archaeology Report 26, 2011.

Gale, J., I. Hewitt and M. Russell. "Excavations at High Lea Farm, Hinton Martell, Dorset: a third interim report, on fieldwork undertaken during 2006–7." *Proceedings of the Dorset Natural History and Archaeological Society*, 129 (2008): 105–114.

Gardiner, M. "Late Saxon settlements." In *The Oxford Handbook of Anglo-Saxon Archaeology*, edited by H. Hamerow, D.A. Hinton and S. Crawford, 198–217. Oxford: Oxford University Press, 2011.

Gardiner, M. "Vernacular buildings and the development of the later medieval domestic plan in England." *Medieval Archaeology*, 44 (2000): 159–81.

Gerrard, J. *The Ruin of Roman Britain. An archaeological perspective.* Cambridge: Cambridge University Press, 2013.

Gilmour, L., ed. *Pagans and Christians – from Antiquity to the Middle Ages. Papers in honour of Martin Henig presented on the occasion of his sixty-fifth birthday.* Oxford: British Archaeological Reports International Series 1610, 2007.

Grigg, E. "The early medieval dykes of Britain." In *Towns and Topography. Essays in memory of David Hill* edited by G.R. Owen-Crocker and S.D. Thompson, 103–10. Oxford: Oxbow Books, 2014.

Halsall, G. *The Worlds of Arthur.* Oxford: Oxford University Press, 2013.

Hamerow, H., C. Ferguson and J. Naylor. "The Origins of Wessex Project." *Oxoniensia*, 78 (2013): 49–69.

Hamerow, H., D.A. Hinton and S. Crawford, eds. *The Oxford Handbook of Anglo-Saxon Archaeology.* Oxford: Oxford University Press, 2011.

Hamerow, H. *Rural Settlements and Society in Anglo-Saxon England.* Oxford: Oxford University Press, 2012.

Hare, M. "The Watergate at Portchester and the Anglo-Saxon porch at Titchfield." *Proceedings of the Hampshire Field Club and Archaeological Society*, 40 (1984): 71–80.

Haslam, J., ed. *Anglo-Saxon Towns in Southern England.* Chichester: Phillimore, 1984.

Haslam, J. "King Alfred and the vikings: strategies and tactics 876–888 AD." *Anglo-Saxon Studies in Archaeology and History*, 13 (2005): 122–54.

Haslam, J. "The development of Late-Saxon Christchurch, Dorset, and the Burghal Hidage." *Medieval Archaeology*, 53 (2009): 95–118.

Haslam, J. *Urban-Rural Connections in Domesday Book and Late Anglo-Saxon Royal Administration.* Oxford: British Archaeological Reports British Series 571, 2012.

Haslam, J. *Wiltshire Towns. The archaeological potential.* Devizes: Wiltshire Natural History and Archaeological Society, 1976.

Hayes L. and T. Malim. "The date and nature of Wat's Dyke: a reassessment in the light of recent investigations at Gobowen, Shropshire." *Anglo-Saxon Studies in Archaeology and History*, 15 (2008): 147–79.

Henderson, G. *Vision and Image in Early Christian England.* Cambridge: Cambridge University Press, 1999.

Higham N.J. and M.J. Ryan. *The Anglo-Saxon World.* New Haven/London: Yale University Press, 2013.

Hill, D. and A.A. Rumble, eds. *The Defence of Wessex. The Burghal Hidage and Anglo-Saxon fortifications.* Manchester/New York: Manchester University Press, 1996.

Hill, D. "Gazetteer of Burghal Hidage sites." In *The Defence of Wessex. The Burghal Hidage and Anglo-Saxon fortifications* edited by D. Hill, and A.A. Rumble, 189–231. Manchester/New York: Manchester University Press, 1996.

Hill, D. "Sites X1 and X2 – Pound Lane." In *Excavations in Christchurch 1969–80*, by K.S. Jarvis, 22–27. Dorset Natural History and Archaeological Society Monograph 5, 1983.

Hill, D. "The Burghal Hidage – Southampton." *Proceedings of the Hampshire Field Club and Archaeological Society*, 24 (1967): 59–61.

Hill, D. *An Atlas of Anglo-Saxon England.* Oxford: Basil Blackwell, 1981.

Hines J. and A. Bayliss, eds. *Anglo-Saxon Graves and Grave-Goods of the 6th and 7th Centuries A.D.: a Chronological Framework.* Leeds: Society for Medieval Archaeology Monograph 33, 2013.

Hinton, D.A. and C.J. Webster. "Excavations at the church of St Martin, Wareham, 1985–86, and "minsters" in south-east Dorset." *Proceedings of the Dorset Natural History and Archaeological Society*, 109 (1987): 47–54.

Hinton, D.A. "Recent work at the chapel of St Laurence, Bradford-on-Avon, Wiltshire." *Archaeological Journal*, 166 (2009): 193–209.

Holdsworth, P. *Excavations in Melbourne Street 1971–6.* London: Council for British Archaeology Research Report 33, 1980.

Holmes, M. "The street plan of Lewes and the Burghal Hidage." *Sussex Archaeological Collections*, 148 (2010): 71–78.

Hooke, D. *Trees in Anglo-Saxon England. Literature, lore and landscape.* Woodbridge: Boydell Press, 2010.

Horsman, V., Christine Milne and Gustav Milne, *Aspects of Saxo-Norman London: I. Building and street development near Billingsgate and Cheapside.* London and Middlesex Archaeological Society Special Paper 11, 1988.

Huggins, P.J. "Anglo-Saxon timber building measurements: recent results." *Medieval Archaeology*, 35 (1991): 6–28.

James, T.B. *English Heritage Book of Winchester.* London: B. T. Batsford/English Heritage, 1997.

Kavanagh, H. "West Quay Shopping Centre." *Archaeology in Hampshire, Annual Report for 1998*, 49–50.

Keen, L. "The towns of Dorset." In *Anglo-Saxon Towns in Southern England*, edited by J. Haslam, 203–48. Chichester: Phillimore, 1984.

Kelly, S.E. *Charters of Abingdon Abbey, Part 1*, Anglo-Saxon Charters VII. Oxford: Oxford University Press, 2000.

Kenyon, J.R. *Medieval Fortifications.* Leicester/London: Leicester University Press, 1990.

Keynes, S., and M. Lapidge, trans. *Alfred the Great. Asser's* Life of King Alfred *and other contemporary sources.* Harmondsworth: Penguin Books, 1983.

King, A. "Roman Bitterne in the third and fourth centuries." *Hampshire Field Club and Archaeological Society Newsletter*, new series 11 (1989): 19–20.

Kitchen, F. "The *Burghal Hidage*: towards the identification of *Eorpeburnan*." *Medieval Archaeology*, 28 (1984): 175–77.

Langlands, A. "Placing the burh in *Searobyrg*; rethinking the urban topography of early medieval Salisbury." *Wiltshire Archaeological and Natural History Magazine*, 107 (2014): 91–105.

Lapidge, M., D.R. Howlett, and K. Barker. "Aldhelm's *Carmen Rhythmicum*." In *Aldhelm and Sherborne*, edited by K. Barker, 271–89. Oxford: Oxbow Books, 2010.

Lavelle, R. *Alfred's Wars. Sources and interpretations of Anglo-Saxon warfare in the viking age.* Woodbridge: Boydell Press, 2010.

Laycock, S. "Buckles, belts and borders." *Current Archaeology*, 207 (May 2008): 12–19.

Laycock, S. *Britannia, the Failed State. Tribal conflict and the end of Roman Britain.* Stroud: History Press, 2008.

Leary, J., D. Field and G. Campbell. *Silbury Hill. The largest prehistoric mound in Europe.* London: English Heritage, 2013.

Lennon, B. "The Bedwyn Dyke: a revisionist view." *Wiltshire Archaeological and Natural History Magazine*, 103, (2010): 102–29.

Lennon, B. *Savernake Forest: Continuity and Change in a Wooded Landscape.* Oxford: British Archaeological Reports British Series 555, 2012.

Longman, T. "Excavations at Abingdon Court Farm, Cricklade, Wiltshire, 2000–1." *Wiltshire Archaeological and Natural History Magazine*, 106 (2013): 167–203.

Lyne, M. *Excavations at Pevensey Castle 1936 to 1984.* Oxford: British Archaeological Reports British Series 503, 2009.

Millett, M. "Excavations at Cowdery's Down, Basingstoke, Hampshire, 1979–81." *Archaeological Journal*, 140 (1983): 151–279.

Mills, A.D. *Dorset Place-Names. Their Origins and Meanings.* Wimborne: Roy Gasson Associates, 1986.

Mills, A.D. *A Dictionary of British Place-Names*, First Edition revised. Oxford: Oxford University Press, 2011.

Molyneaux, G. *The Formation of the English Kingdom in the Tenth Century.* Oxford: Oxford University Press, 2015.

Morton, A.D. *Excavations at Hamwic, Volume 1. Excavations 1946–83 excluding Six Dials and Melbourne Street.* York: Council for British Archaeology Research Report 84, 1992.

Munby, J., ed. *Domesday Book. 4: Hampshire.* Chichester: Phillimore, 1982.

Owen-Crocker, G.R. and S.D. Thompson, eds. *Towns and Topography. Essays in memory of David Hill.* Oxford: Oxbow Books, 2014.

Parsons D., and D.S. Sutherland. *The Anglo-Saxon Church of All Saints, Brixworth, Northamptonshire. Survey, excavation and analysis 1972–2010.* Oxford: Oxbow Books, 2013.

Pine, J. "Medieval and later occupation at 51–53 St Mary's Street." In *Archaeological Investigations in Wallingford, Oxfordshire, 1992–2010*, edited by S. Preston, 9–37. Reading: Thames Valley Archaeological Services Monograph 10, 2012).

Pollard, J. and A.J. Reynolds. *Avebury: the Biography of a Landscape.* Stroud: Tempus Publishing, 2002.

Preston, S., ed. *Archaeological Investigations in Wallingford, Oxfordshire, 1992–2010.* Reading: Thames Valley Archaeological Services Monograph 10, 2012.

Price, E. *Frocester. A Romano-British settlement, its antecedents and successors. Volume 2, the finds.* Stonehouse: Gloucester and District Archaeological Research Group, 2000.

Putnam, W. *Roman Dorset.* Stroud: Tempus Publishing, 2007.

Reeve, P., J. Schuster, and A.P. Fitzpatrick. "The eastern defences of the Saxon burh at Christchurch, Dorset: an archaeological evaluation at the King's Arms Hotel." *Proceedings of the Dorset Natural History and Archaeological Society*, 132 (2011): 127–30.

Reynolds, A.J. and S. Brookes. "Anglo-Saxon civil defence in the localities: a case study of the Avebury region." In *Early Medieval Art and Archaeology in the Northern World. Studies in honour of James Graham-Campbell*, edited by A. Reynolds and L. Webster, 561–606 Leiden/Boston: Brill, 2013.

Reynolds, A.J. and A. Langlands. "Social identities on the macro scale: a maximum view of Wansdyke." In *People and Space in the Middle Ages, 300–1300*, Studies in the Early Middle Ages 15, edited by W. Davies, G. Halsall and A. Reynolds, 13–44. Turnhout: Brepols Publishing, 2006.

Reynolds, A.J. "Avebury, Yatesbury and the archaeology of communications." *Papers from the Institute of Archaeology*, 6 (1995): 21–30.

Reynolds, A.J., and L. Webster, eds. *Early Medieval Art and Archaeology in the Northern World. Studies in honour of James Graham-Campbell.* Leiden/Boston: Brill, 2013.

Royal Commission on Historical Monuments (England). *Historical Monuments in the County of Dorset. Volume V: East.* London: Her Majesty's Stationery Office, 1975.

Royal Commission on Historical Monuments. *Dorset South-East.* London: Her Majesty's Stationery Office, 1970.

Royal Commission on Historical Monuments. *Dorset. Volume II, South-East part 2.* London: Royal Commission on Historical Monuments, 1970.

Rudling, D., ed. *The Archaeology of Sussex to AD 2000.* Kings Lynn: Heritage Marketing and Publications, 2003.

Rumble, A.R. "HAMTVN *alias* HAMWIC (Saxon Southampton): the place-name traditions and their significance." In *Excavations in Melbourne Street 1971–6* by P. Holdsworth, 7–19. London: Council for British Archaeology Research Report 33, 1980.

Seager Smith, R. and G. Wakeham. "Further investigation of the Roman small town of *Cunetio*: a *Time Team* evaluation." *Wiltshire Archaeological and Natural History Magazine*, 108 (2015): 79–88.

Shapland, M. "St Mary's Church, Broughton, Lincolnshire: a thegnly tower-nave in the late Anglo-Saxon landscape." *Archaeological Journal*, 165 (2008): 471–519.

Sims-Williams, P. "The settlement of England in Bede and the *Chronicle*." *Anglo-Saxon England*, 12 (1983): 1–41.

Smyth, A.P. *Alfred the Great.* Oxford: Oxford University Press, 1995.

Sparey Green, C. *Excavations at Poundbury. Volume I: The settlements.* Dorset Natural History and Archaeological Society Monograph 7, 1987.

Stoodley, N. "New light on the southern end of Hamwic: excavations at the Deanery by Southampton City Council Archaeological Unit and Wessex Archaeology." *Proceedings of the Hampshire Field Club and Archaeological Society*, 67ii (2012): 240–42.

Swanton, M., ed. and trans. *The Anglo-Saxon Chronicles. New edition.* London: Phoenix Press, 2000.

Taylor, C. *Dorset.* London: Hodder and Stoughton, 1970.

Thomas, G. *The Later Anglo-Saxon Settlement at Bishopstone; a Downland Manor in the Making.* York: Council for British Archaeology Research Report 163, 2010.

Thomson, R.M. *William of Malmesbury* Gesta Regum Anglorum. *The History of the English Kings, Volume II. General introduction and commentary.* Oxford: Clarendon Press, 1999.

Thorn, C. and F. Thorn, eds. *Domesday Book. 6: Wiltshire.* Chichester: Phillimore, 1979.

Thorpe, B. Diplomatarium Anglicum Aevi Saxonici. *A collection of English charters.* London: Macmillan, 1865.

Timby, J. "Pottery (Roman, pre- and post-Roman)." In *Frocester. A Romano-British settlement, its antecedents and successors. Volume 2, the finds*, by E. Price, 125–62. Stonehouse: Gloucester and District Archaeological Research Group, 2000.

Timby, J. "The pottery." In *Pevensey Castle, Sussex: Excavations in the Roman Fort and Norman Keep, 1991–95*, by M.G. Fulford and S. Rippon, 39–52. Salisbury: Wessex Archaeology Report 26, 2011.

Waller, R. "Archaeological resource assessment of the Isle of Wight: early medieval period," accessible on-line from Oxford Archaeology: https://oxfordarchaeology.com/images/pdfs/Solent_Thames/County_resource_assessments/Early_Medieval_IOW.pdf accessed July 2020.

Webster, L. *Anglo-Saxon Art.* London: British Museum, Press, 2012.

Webster, L. *The Franks Casket.* London: British Museum, 2012.

Welch, M. "The finds." In *Excavations at Portchester. Volume II: Saxon.* By B. Cunliffe, 205–14. London: Society of Antiquaries of London, 1975.

Westman, A. *Chichester City Walls.* London: Museum of London Archaeology, 2012.

Whitehead, B.E. "Archaeological investigations at Charlotte Place, Southampton." *Proceedings of the Hampshire Field Club and Archaeological Society*, 67ii (2012): 317–22.

Whitelock, D., ed. *English Historical Documents* c. *500–1042.* London: Eyre Methuen, 1979.

Whittock, H. and M. Whittock. *The Anglo-Saxon Avon Valley Frontier. A river of two halves.* Fonthill Media, 2014.

Williams, A. *The World before Domesday.* London: Continuum UK, 2008.

Wilmott, A. "The late Roman frontier: a structural background." In *Finds from the Frontier*, edited by R. Collins and L. Allason-Jones, 10–16. York: Council for British Archaeology Research Report 162, 2010.

Woodward, P.J. "Wimborne Minster, Dorset – excavations in the town centre 1975–80." *Proceedings of the Dorset Natural History and Archaeological Society*, 105 (1983): 57–74.

Wormald, P. *The Making of English Law: King Alfred to the Twelfth Century. Volume I, legislation and its limits.* Oxford: Blackwell, 1999.

Wright, D. W., M. Fradley and O. Creighton. "The ringwork at Cam's Hill, near Malmesbury: archaeological investigation and landscape assessment," *Wiltshire Natural History and Archaeological Magazine*, 108 (2015): 105–18.

Yeoman, P.A. "The 1982 excavation: site W37, 14 High Street." In S.M. Davies, "Excavations at Christchurch, Dorset, 1981 to 1983." *Proceedings of the Dorset Natural History and Archaeological Society*, 105 (1983): 46–50.

Yorke, B.A.E. "Dorchester and the early shire centres of Wessex." *Proceedings of the Dorset Natural History and Archaeological Society*, 134 (2013): 106–12.

Yorke, B.A.E. *Wessex in the Early Middle Ages*, Studies in the Early History of Britain. London/New York: Leicester University Press, 1995.

Young, C.J. *Excavations at Carisbrooke Castle, Isle of Wight, 1921–1996.* Salisbury: Wessex Archaeology Report 18, 2000.

2

Hamwic and the Origins of Wessex Revisited

Barbara Yorke

University of Winchester

Abstract: Tom James and I shared an interest in combining historical and archaeological evidence, and joined together to teach various undergraduate courses on the history and archaeology of medieval Winchester and Southampton. Tom was much more of an expert on the archaeology of Southampton than I was as he had worked on various aspects of the medieval town for his PhD. From necessity I began to study the fascinating evidence for Saxon Southampton, especially for its Middle Anglo-Saxon emporium of Hamwic. In 1989 I published a re-assessment of the origins of Wessex, stressing the significance of the foundation of Hamwic within the Jutish provinces of southern Hampshire and the Isle of Wight for the developing kingdom. Since writing that paper, further excavations, especially on the St Mary's stadium site, have suggested earlier, and possibly rather different origins for Hamwic, than were anticipated in 1989. Since that date much has been written also more generally on early Anglo-Saxon emporia and trade and how they might relate to kingdom formation, especially in the light of new excavations in England and adjoining areas of Europe, and from the recording of finds under the Portable Antiquities Scheme. It therefore seems timely to return to the question of Hamwic and the origins of Wessex to review my original suggestions in the light of subsequent studies. Although some revisions are in order, the more recent evidence only serves to reinforce the importance to the aspiring kings of Wessex of the annexation of southern Hampshire and Wight. Their actions can be seen as part of political and economic realignment within the seventh century, and help to demonstrate how control and exploitation of economic resources was at the heart of the development of Middle Saxon kingship.

Key words: Anglo-Saxons; Jutes; trade; towns; wics; coins; warfare; kingship; Solent; Southampton

Tom James and I worked together for more years than we both may care to calculate at King Alfred's College, subsequently the University of Winchester. Among the courses that we shared was one on the history and archaeology of Winchester and Southampton. One of the highlights of the course was a regular trip to Southampton to view current excavations, mostly on the site of Hamwic. I was very grateful to this course for making me attempt to get grips with the archaeology of the two towns, and some of this material found its way into my publications. In 1989 I published a paper on the origins of Wessex which explored some of the implications of the apparent coincidence of the foundation of Hamwic and of the kingdom of the West Saxons (as opposed to that of the Gewisse).[1] Since then there has been the important excavation on the St Mary's Stadium site in Southampton which has added a new dimension to the question of the town's Anglo-Saxon origins.[2] There has also been much new work on other emporia and trading centres, and on many aspects of the sixth and seventh centuries which are relevant to the origins of Anglo-Saxon kingdoms and their claimed identities. I have therefore wanted to revisit the question of the links between the origins of Hamwic and Wessex, and this seemed an appropriate opportunity to do so. Although this is not a period on which our honorand himself has worked, Southampton, trade, and the places associated with kings are all topics which Tom has explored to great effect in his own publications, or those which he has helped others to make, and so I hope this will be an appropriate offering in a book of essays in his honour.

The Jutes of Hampshire and the Isle of Wight

In his description of the *adventus* of the Anglo-Saxons in the *Historia Ecclesiastica* I, 15, Bede made the celebrated statement that:

> They came from three very powerful Germanic tribes, the Saxons, Angles and Jutes. The people of Kent and the inhabitants of the Isle of Wight are of Jutish origin and also those opposite the Isle of Wight, that part of the kingdom of Wessex which is still today called the nation of the Jutes.[3]

[1] B.A.E. Yorke, "The Jutes of Hampshire and Wight and the origins of Wessex," in *The Origins of Anglo-Saxon Kingdoms*, ed. S. Bassett (London: Leicester University Press, 1989), 84–96.

[2] V. Birbeck, *The Origins of Mid-Saxon Southampton. Excavations at the Friends Provident St Mary's Stadium 1998–2000* (Salisbury: Wessex Archaeology, 2005).

[3] B. Colgrave, and R.A.B. Mynors, *Bede's Ecclesiastical History of the English People* (Oxford: Oxford University Press, 1969), 50–51.

It was not Bede's intention to dwell on the pre-conversion history of the Anglo-Saxons, and this account is a gross simplification and foreshortening of complex developments over many decades. Although different opinions exist on the significance of the three *nationes* of Angles, Saxons and Jutes, it is probably safe to say that they are groupings which were made after the period of settlement within different geographical areas of Britain rather than simple migrations *en masse* of peoples from corresponding areas of northern Europe. They fit with patterns of ethnogenesis found in other parts of Europe in the post-Roman period whereby new significant groupings of people often adopted names of peoples that already existed, and with whom they might have some association, presumably as a form of validation.[4] While not all authorities might endorse this, a case can be made for the Angles and Saxons as peoples whose leading families habitually associated together and shared some community of interest so that each area developed a distinctive dialect of Old English and women from families of a certain status adopted distinctive costumes.[5] The Saxons were concentrated initially in the Thames valley and areas to its south, and the Angles in eastern areas of England. But the south of England was not the sole preserve of the Saxon people as there were also the two areas to which Bede assigned a Jutish identity.

The issue of the possible Jutish origins of Kent has received much attention in recent years and there is now a much clearer understanding of what it might mean. A detailed study by Pernille Kruse has established that the early burial traditions of early medieval Kent differed from those of Jutland.[6] However, it is also the case that many high status objects in use in eastern Kent in the fifth and sixth century, such as D-bracteates and silver relief brooches, strongly suggest Jutish connections, and that these continued to be active over a much longer period than that of initial settlement.[7] Other material can be more readily classified as 'North Sea coastal zone' and early pottery forms have been characterised as 'Jutish-Frisian'.[8] At the same time there is much evidence for the presence of Frankish material, particularly as a way of signalling high status in burials. Women's dress by the sixth-century was showing a strong influence from Merovingian fashions and incorporated Merovingian dress accessories though with some detail of the costume such as tablet-weaves coming from southern Scandinavian traditions.[9] Some of the same material culture occurs on the Isle of Wight, with a rich female burial from Chessell Down being particularly notable for its close parallels with Kentish examples.[10] There has been an increasing number of finds, particularly from metal detection, that suggest affinities between the material culture of Kent and that of the Isle of Wight and southern Hampshire.[11] Studies of female costume assemblages in southern Hampshire (and including the Appledown cemetery just over the border in West Sussex) have established that there was a distinctive style which was a more muted version of the Kentish/Jutish costume also worn on the Isle of Wight.[12] It was significantly different from the Saxon styles of northern Hampshire cemeteries such as Andover and Alton. The conclusions from the archaeological evidence are ably summed up by Andrew Richardson:

> During the second half of the fifth century east Kent, as well as the Isle of Wight and perhaps the more general areas around the Solent and the mouth of the Thames, came under control of an elite group who were able and keen to demonstrate a Jutlandic or North Sea coastal zone identity, a group that also had a strong affinity to Frankish or proto-Frankish material culture. This identity does seem to have been distinct from Saxon or Anglian identities being celebrated and adopted elsewhere across Lowland Britain during the same period.[13]

Such archaeological evidence provides important support for a reality behind Bede's indication of a common identity shared between Kent, the Isle of Wight and southern Hampshire that lasted into his own lifetime (d. 735). The names Wihtgisl and Wecta that appear in the genealogy of the Kentish kings given by Bede [I, 15][14] are derived from the Latin name of the Isle of Wight, *Vecta*, and are suggestive of a desire to demonstrate a connection between the rulers of Kent and the royal house of Wight, one of whose founders, as depicted in the *Anglo-Saxon Chronicle*, Wihtgar bore a comparable name.[15] Some

[4] W. Pohl, "Ethnic names and identities in the British Isles: a comparative perspective," in *The Anglo-Saxons from the Migration Period to the Eighth Century. An Ethnographic Perspective*, ed. J. Hines (Woodbridge: Boydell Press, 1997), 7–31.

[5] J. Hines, "The becoming of the English: identity, material culture and language in early Anglo-Saxon England," *Anglo-Saxon Studies in Archaeology and History* 7 (1994): 49–59.

[6] P. Kruse, *Jutes in Kent? On the Jutish Nature of Kent, Southern Hampshire and the Isle of Wight* (Oldenburg: Probleme der Kütenforschung im südlichen Nordseegebiet Band 31, 2007).

[7] C. Behr, "The origins of kingship in early medieval Kent," *Early Medieval Europe* 9 (2000): 25–52.

[8] A. F. Richardson, "'What came before': the kingdom of Kent to 800," in *Early Medieval Kent 800–1220*, ed. S. Sweetinburgh (Woodbridge: Boydell Press and Kent County Council, 2016), 21–41.

[9] P. Walton Rogers, *Cloth and Clothing in Early Anglo-Saxon England AD 450–700*, CBA Research Report 145 (York: Council for British Archaeology, 2007), 189–93.

[10] C. Arnold, *The Anglo-Saxon Cemeteries of the Isle of Wight* (London: British Museum Publications, 1982), especially 27–30.

[11] K. Ulmschneider, "Markets around the Solent: Unravelling a 'Productive' Site on the Isle of Wight," in *Markets in Early Medieval Europe. Trading and 'Productive' Sites, 650–850* eds T. Pestell and K. Ulmschneider (Macclesfield: Windgather Press, 2003), 73–83; B. Eagles, *From Roman Civitas to Anglo-Saxon Shire. The Formation of Wessex* (Oxford: Oxbow Books, 2018), 117-28. (I am very grateful to Bruce Eagles for making this paper available to me in advance of publication).

[12] Walton Rogers, *Cloth and Clothing*, 196–98; N. Stoodley, "The origins of Hamwic and its central role in the seventh century as revealed by recent archaeological discoveries," in *Central Places in the Migration and the Merovingian Periods. Papers from the 52nd Sachsensymposion, Lund August 2001* eds B. Hårdh and L. Larsson (Lund: Almqvist and Wiksell International, 2003), 317–31; N. Stoodley, "Costume groups in Hampshire and their bearing on the question of Jutish settlement in the fifth to seventh centuries AD," in *The Land of the English Kin. Studies in Wessex and Anglo-Saxon England in Honour of Professor Barbara Yorke*, eds A. Langlands and R. Lavelle (Leiden: Brill, 2020), 70-94.

[13] Richardson, "What came before," 30–31.

[14] Colgrave, and Mynors, *Bede's Ecclesiastical History*, 50–51.

[15] P. Sims-Williams, "The settlement of England in Bede and the 'Chronicle'," *Anglo-Saxon England* 12 (1983): 1–41; B.A.E. Yorke,

sort of political alliance may be indicated, just as it can be suspected there was one between the rulers of Kent and one of the branches of the Frankish house that was marked by the marriage of prince Æthelbert of Kent to the Frankish princess Bertha c.580.[16]

But how should this community of interest be interpreted? Kent and the Solent areas were not, of course, contiguous, but features they had in common included good natural harbours and the shortest crossing-places between southern England and northern Francia. In fact, one can see parallels for the safe-harbourage provided by the Solent between the Isle of Wight and southern Hampshire and that of the Wantsum Channel between the Isle of Thanet and mainland Kent around which many of its most prestigious early medieval sites were situated.[17] It has come to seem increasingly likely that it was involvement in trade with mainland Europe that united these areas and can account for their early prosperity. Although Francia was an important market, these areas were part of a much wider North Sea trading zone. Luxury goods from Francia have often dominated the discussion of early trading relations and were undoubtedly important for demonstrating status.[18] But we now have a much better understanding of the trade in bulk goods that underpinned this prosperity and of trade-routes in southern England that linked with Kent and the Solent.[19] It is in the context of this background that the recent excavations at St Mary's Stadium, Southampton need to be viewed and the subsequent development of Hamwic interpreted.

The Origins of Hamwic

After the major excavations of a substantial portion of the north-western part of the Anglo-Saxon settlement of Six Dials in Southampton, Phil Andrews felt able to make the following pronouncement about Hamwic's likely date of foundation:

> On the present evidence, it is likely that occupation in the settlement began around 700, in the reign of King Ine of Wessex (688–726), and nothing points unequivocally to a 7th-century origin.[20]

However, subsequent excavations of what is now St Mary's Stadium, Southampton, on the north-east side of Hamwic overlooking the river Itchen, have modified that conclusion. Excavation under the future western stand revealed part of a mixed-rite cemetery of 18 cremations and 26 inhumations in 25 graves, many with grave-goods.[21] Two burials excavated at nearby Melbourne Street in 1975 (SOU 20) are seen as outliers of the group.[22] The St Mary's Stadium burials are quite distinct from those of cemeteries excavated previously within Hamwic which had not produced any cremations, and where even a single item with a burial was the exception rather than the rule.[23] Radio-carbon dates from the cremations gave a date range from late sixth to ninth century, though it has been considered unlikely that any in fact dated after 700. Most of the datable artefacts included as grave-goods fell in the range from the mid- to late-seventh century, though possibly some could date as late as the early eighth century. This includes a burial (Grave 4202) with two series B sceattas, and an impression of a third, with a likely date range of c.685–90.[24] Although the proportion of burials with grave-goods (80 per cent) was judged high for Hampshire, most were conventional and unspectacular.[25] What was exceptional, especially in Hampshire, was the high percentage of burials with weapons (42 per cent). Four individual burials included seaxes, and there were two more seaxes from an unusual double burial (Grave 3520). Chris Scull has argued that some of the burials with seaxes may be of men of continental origin.[26] The richest of these burials (Grave 3549) also included a continental belt-set and a sheath or scabbard with unusual belt-fittings, both of which are closely paralleled in Grave 1306 (also with a seax) from the Buttermarket cemetery, Ipswich, dated by Scull to AD 630/40–660/70. Also notable from St Mary's Stadium are two female burials which included, respectively, a Frisian gold pendant (Grave 4202), and a gold-and-garnet pendant (Grave 5508) that was probably made by a Frisian craftsman.[27]

"The Jutes of Hampshire and Wight."

16 I.N. Wood, *The Merovingian North Sea* (Alingsås: Occasional Papers on Medieval Topics I, 1983); N. Brooks, "The creation and early structure of the kingdom of Kent," in *The Origins of Anglo-Saxon Kingdoms*, ed. S. Bassett (London: Leicester University Press, 1989), 55–74.

17 A.F. Richardson pers. comm.

18 M. Welch, "Anglo-Saxon Kent to AD 800," in *The Archaeology of Kent to AD 800*, ed. J.H. Williams (Woodbridge: Boydell Press for Kent County Council, 2007), 189–251.

19 S. Harrington and M. Welch, *The Early Anglo-Saxon Kingdoms of Southern Britain AD 450–650. Beneath the Tribal Hidage* (Oxford: Oxbow Books, 2014).

20 P. Andrews, *Excavations at Hamwic Volume 2; Excavations at Six Dials*. Southampton Archaeology Monographs 7 (York: Council for British Archaeology, 1997), 252; see also A. Morton, *Excavations at Hamwic Volume I: Excavations 1946–83, excluding Six Dials and Melbourne Street*. Southampton Archaeology Monographs 5. (York: Council for British Archaeology, 1992), 26–29.

21 Birbeck, *The Origins of Mid-Saxon Southampton*, 11–81.

22 P. Holdsworth, *Excavations at Melbourne Street, Southampton, 1971–76*. Southampton Archaeology Monographs 1. (London: Council for British Archaeology, 1980), 39; Birbeck, *The Origins of Mid-Saxon Southampton*, 5–6.

23 N. Stoodley, "Burial practice in seventh-century Hampshire: St Mary's Stadium in context," in *Burial in Later Anglo-Saxon England c650–1100 AD*, eds J. Buckberry and A. Cherryson (Oxford: Oxbow books 2010), 38–53.

24 D.M. Metcalf, "Coins," in *The Origins of Mid-Saxon Southampton. Excavations at the Friends Provident St Mary's Stadium 1998–2000*, V. Birbeck (Salisbury: Wessex Archaeology, 2005), 130–36. However, the dating of the introduction of the sceatta coinage is currently under review and the date range may be up to 20 years earlier.

25 N. Stoodley, "The early cemetery and its place within southern England," in *The Origins of Mid-Saxon Southampton. Excavations at the Friends Provident St Mary's Stadium 1998–2000*, V. Birbeck (Salisbury: Wessex Archaeology, 2005), 75–81; Stoodley, "Burial practice in seventh-century Hampshire."

26 C. Scull, "Foreign identities in burials at the seventh-century English *emporia*," in *Studies in Early Anglo-Saxon Art and Archaeology: Papers in Honour on Martin G. Welch*, British Archaeological Reports British Series 527, eds S. Brookes, S. Harrington and A. Reynolds (Oxford: BAR Publishing, 2011), 82–87.

27 D. Hinton, "Gold pendants," in *The Origins of Mid-Saxon Southampton. Excavations at the Friends Provident St Mary's Stadium 1998–2000*, V. Birbeck, (Salisbury: Wessex Archaeology, 2005), 64–67; Scull, "Foreign identities," 84.

The higher than average number (especially by this date) of weapon burials not only suggest status and continental affiliations, but are a distinctive feature of the contemporary phases of other sites that have a role in facilitating or supervising trade. These include burials from the early phases of the emporia of Ipswich and London,[28] and from Kentish cemeteries at Sarre and Dover Buckland in Kent, both probably associated with important ports.[29] One can also note that the sixth-century cemetery at Breamore on the Hampshire Avon was also characterised by an exceptional number of weapon burials as well as Byzantine and other imports,[30] and a concentration of weapon burials was also a feature of a cemetery of similar, or slightly late date, at Christchurch (Twynam) on the mouth of the Avon.[31] The burials are not specifically signalling a 'Jutish' identity, but can be seen as a common feature of the Jutish provinces as well as of other areas where foreign trade was significant. Kings themselves were not necessarily directly involved in establishing or directing these early trade networks, but they may well have levied fees, or payment in kind, for the right to trade, as seems to be recorded in the early Kentish lawcodes (on terms that echo those of trading clauses in later Anglo-Saxon laws).[32]

The St Mary's Stadium cemetery makes explicit what was only hinted at before, namely that the future Hamwic site was occupied in the seventh century, perhaps stretching back into the sixth century as well. However, what is generally taken to typify the emporium of Hamwic, that is a densely-occupied trading and craft centre, remains a development largely of the eighth century. Indeed, there was a rapid spread of structures and artefacts typical of the emporium phase over the whole of the Stadium site, completely over-laying the cemetery within a generation of its last use (though with less density than on the Six Dials site).[33] The settlement area of the inhabitants buried in the cemetery has yet to be located making it hard to know at what point it became involved in trade and so exercised some of the functions of the eighth-century emporium.

The hypothetical pre-Hamwic settlement may have been only one of several early Saxon trading places along the Solent. Hugeburh writing of events in the early 720s describes her brother Willibald picking up a ship bound for Rouen at Hamblemouth, that is at the mouth of the river Hamble, further east along the Solent. She seems in different works to describe both Hamwic and Hamblemouth as a *mercimonium* which she defines as 'a place where goods were sold' (*loca venalia*).[34] Coins (admittedly mostly ninth century) have been found from Eling Creek to the west of Hamwic, in addition to major trading activities across the Solent on the Isle of Wight in the vicinity of Carisbrooke on the Medina river.[35] Each river valley draining into the Solent may have had its own out-port at its mouth to serve the needs of inhabitants and estates along its banks.[36] However, the peninsula between the rivers Itchen and Test, the *hamm* that gave its name to Hamwic,[37] was particularly well placed to dominate the needs of the region. The Itchen valley was also one of the most productive and well-settled agricultural areas with a series of findspots of early eighth-century sceattas.[38] That is presumably why we find close to the River Itchen the wealthy graves of St Mary's Stadium with their continental connections; they may have been exercising some sort of supervisory role within the region in the seventh century.[39] This site has been suggested as a candidate for the location of Hamtun, a place of royal administration in the eighth century which gave its name to the shire, as well as to the estate which contained the settlement.[40] In contrast to Six Dials, in the eighth century the Stadium site appears to have been less densely occupied and less involved with industrial activities. It adjoined the part of the settlement (SOU 47) that continued to be occupied when the main commercial focus switched to the Test side of the peninsula, and from which higher status finds are said to have come (though such finds were unfortunately made in the nineteenth century and are poorly recorded).

The cemetery at St Mary's Stadium must have begun in the Jutish phase of the settlement's history. In the second half of the seventh century, it received some notably richer burials with continental connections at a time when some of the characteristics of eighth-century Hamwic and Hamtun may already have been present. This was a significant period when the Jutish alliance was broken up and Wessex and Mercia vied for control of the Solent region. Exactly when and how the West Saxons established control of southern Hampshire has to be understood before the St Mary's Stadium cemetery can be contextualised further.

---

[28] Scull, "Foreign identities."

[29] N. Stoodley, "The early cemetery and its place within southern England," 81.

[30] D. Hinton and S. Worrell, "An early Anglo-Saxon cemetery and archaeological survey at Breamore, Hampshire, 1999–2006," *Archaeological Journal* 174 (2017): 68–145.

[31] K.S. Jarvis, *Excavations in Christchurch 1969–1980*, Dorset Natural History and Archaeological Society Monograph 5 (Dorchester: DNHAS, 1983).

[32] N. Middleton, "Early medieval port customs, tolls and controls on foreign trade," *Early Medieval Europe* 3 (2005): 313–58.

[33] Birbeck, *The Origins of Mid-Saxon Southampton*, 82–139.

[34] A. Morton, "Hamwic in its context," in *Anglo-Saxon Trading Centres. Beyond the Emporia*, ed. M. Anderton (Glasgow: Cruithne Press, 1999), 48–62.

[35] Ulmschneider, "Markets around the Solent."

[36] Stoodley, "The origins of Hamwic"; Birbeck, *The Origins of Mid-Saxon Southampton*, 190–4.

[37] A. Rumble, "Hamtun alias Hamwic (Saxon Southampton): the place-name traditions and their significance," in *Excavations at Melbourne Street, Southampton, 1971–76* Southampton Archaeology Monographs 1, P. Holdsworth (London: Council for British Archaeology, 1980), 7–20.

[38] K. Ulmschneider, *Markets, Minsters, and Metal-detectors: the Archaeology of Middle Saxon Lincolnshire and Hampshire Compared.* British Archaeological Reports British Series 307. (Oxford: BAR Publishing, 2000), 152–60; M. Biddle, and B. Kjølbye-Biddle, "Winchester from *Venta* to *Wintancæstir*," in *Pagans and Christians – from Antiquity to the Middle Ages. Papers in Honour of Martin Henig*, British Archaeological Reports, International Series 1610, ed. L. Gilmour (Oxford: BAR Publishing, 2007), 189–214.

[39] Stoodley, "The origins of Hamwic."

[40] Rumble, "Hamtun alias Hamwic"; Morton, *Excavations at Hamwic Volume I*, 28–29; Birbeck, *The Origins of Mid-Saxon Southampton*, 190–204.

The Origins of the Kingdom of the West Saxons

It was apparently only after the spectacular achievements of King Caedwalla (685–8) that the titles 'King of the Saxons' and, eventually, 'King of the West Saxons' began to be used.[41] Before his reign, Bede refers instead to his predecessors as kings of the Gewisse (*gens Geuissorum*). As Bede described the foundation in 634 of a bishopric for the Gewisse at Dorchester-on-Thames [III,7][42], it is usually assumed that their territory was based in the upper Thames, one of the areas of the country with a significant concentration of early Anglo-Saxon cemeteries and what appears to be a series of royal halls at Sutton Courtenay.[43] It is not clear whether the settlers of the upper Thames originally had significant links with other areas to their south that were culturally Saxon. It is possible that Saxon groups in northern Hampshire and southern Wiltshire, in the vicinity of Salisbury and the Avon valley, could have developed independently.[44] The *Anglo-Saxon Chronicle* annals for the late sixth century, which are the first ones to have any historical credibility, depict West Saxon battles in Wiltshire. The late sixth and early seventh centuries are the time when other major kingdoms were formed and began to expand their territories, and, irrespective of whatever arrangements may have existed, the Gewissan kings seem to have consolidated control in central southern England in this period.

It is difficult to be certain where the boundary lay in modern Hampshire between the Jutish and Saxon areas, and, of course, it may never have been firmly delineated and could have been subject to change and interaction. Nick Stoodley's study of female burial assemblages brings out the contrast between the northern Hampshire cemeteries such as Alton and Andover and those such as Droxford and Appledown (Sussex, but close to the later Hampshire/Sussex border).[45] His analysis of the Worthy Park cemetery at King's Worthy (on the river Itchen, just to the north of Winchester) could place it with the Jutish areas of the south, rather than the Saxon areas of the north. It is therefore possible that in the sixth century Winchester lay close to the border between Saxon and Jutish areas of influence. In probably 663 a new Gewissan bishopric was established in Winchester[46] which provides a *terminus antequem* for Gewissan expansion into the Winchester area.[47]

The Gewissan kings probably had to centre their interests further south because of the rising power of Mercia under the great warrior kings Penda (d. 655) and his son Wulfhere (658–75). Their expansion of Mercian power in all directions included ambitions to take over the Thames valley. In 645 the Gewissan king Cenwalh was expelled by Penda and was in exile for three years; [48] it is not clear whether Penda directly controlled Gewissan territory in his absence, but that is a possible inference. In 648 Cenwalh was back on the throne and placed his kinsman Cuthred in control of a territory based on Ashdown, the Berkshire Downs.[49] Ashdown was 'harried' by Penda's son Wulfhere in 661 and Cuthred died.[50] The creation of a new Gewissan bishopric in Winchester at about this time may have been because the Dorchester-on-Thames area was no longer under their control. But even their influence in what became Hampshire was circumscribed by Mercian ambitions. In 661 Wulfhere also established overlordship over the Isle of Wight, and delegated supervision of it and the Jutish province of the Meonware in southern Hampshire to his ally King Æthelwalh of the South Saxons.[51] Wulfhere, it would appear, was determined on making Mercia the main power in southern England, and this included breaking up the Jutish alliance of Kent and the Solent region, as well as building up London as a trading centre and focus of Mercian commercial interests.[52] The Gewissan leaders may have been hard-pressed even to keep control of Winchester and its surrounding area, and this conflict may provide the background to archaeological evidence for possible refortification in the city through blocking entry at the Roman south gate.[53] Around the middle of the 660s, only a few years after its foundation, the Winchester see was suspended, and its bishop Wine instead purchased the see of London from Wulfhere.[54] It is, therefore, possible that Wulfhere had control of Winchester at this time, but, if so, it had apparently become a Gewissan city again by 670 when Leuthere was appointed bishop by King Cenwalh.[55]

The balance of power was not decisively tipped in favour of the Gewisse until 685 when the exiled Gewissan prince Caedwalla launched his claim to the throne by attacking King Æthelwalh of the South Saxons and temporarily took over his kingdom.[56] In spite of being driven out by South Saxon ealdormen, the conquest seems to have given

[41] H.E. Walker, "Bede and the Gewissae: the political evolution of the heptarchy and their nomenclature," *Cambridge Historical Journal* 12, (1956).

[42] Colgrave, and Mynors, *Bede's Ecclesiastical History*, 232–33.

[43] N. Brennan and H. Hamerow, "An Anglo-Saxon great hall complex at Sutton Courtenay/Drayton, Oxfordshire: a royal centre of early Wessex?," *Archaeological Journal* 172 (2015): 325–50.

[44] B. Eagles, "Anglo-Saxon presence and culture in Wiltshire," in *Roman Wiltshire and After: Papers in Honour of Kenneth Annable*, ed. P. Ellis (Devizes: Wiltshire Archaeological and Natural History Society, 2001), 199–233.

[45] Stoodley, "The origins of Hamwic"; Stoodley, "Costume groups in Hampshire."

[46] Colgrave, and Mynors, *Bede's Ecclesiastical History*, 232–37; D. Whitelock, with D.C. Douglas, and S.I. Tucker, *The Anglo-Saxon Chronicle. A Revised Translation* (London: Eyre and Spottiswoode, 1965), 21.

[47] B.A.E. Yorke, "The foundation of Old Minster and the status of Winchester in the seventh and eighth centuries," *Proceedings of the Hampshire Field Club and Archaeological Society* 38, (1982): 75–83.

[48] Colgrave, and Mynors, *Bede's Ecclesiastical History*, 232–37.

[49] Whitelock et al. *The Anglo-Saxon Chronicle*, 17.

[50] Whitelock et al. *The Anglo-Saxon Chronicle*, 21.

[51] Whitelock et al. *The Anglo-Saxon Chronicle*, 21; Colgrave, and Mynors, *Bede's Ecclesiastical History*, 370–77.

[52] J.R. Maddicott, "London and Droitwich, c.650–750: trade, industry and the rise of Mercia," *Anglo-Saxon England* 35 (2005), 7–58; R. Cowie, and L. Blackmore *Lundenwic. Excavations in Middle Saxon London, 1987–2000*. Museum of London Archaeology Monograph 63 (London: Museum of London, 2012), 107–08.

[53] M. Biddle. "Excavations at Winchester, 1971. Tenth and Final Interim Report, Part I," *Antiquaries Journal*, 55, (1975): 109–12.

[54] Colgrave, and Mynors, *Bede's Ecclesiastical History*, 234–35.

[55] Colgrave, and Mynors, *Bede's Ecclesiastical History*, 236–37. B.A.E. Yorke, "Competition for the Solent and seventh-century politics," in *The Middle Ages Revisited. Studies in the Archaeology and History of Medieval Southern England Presented to Professor David A. Hinton*, ed. B. Jervis (Oxford: Archaeopress, 2018), 35-44.

[56] Colgrave, and Mynors, *Bede's Ecclesiastical History*, 380–85.

Caedwalla a sufficient launch pad to establish himself as king of the Gewisse, after which one of his priorities seems to have been to take control of the Isle of Wight, and he attempted to take Kent also. In other words, he may have followed a similar approach to Wulfhere in neutralising a former Jutish confederation in order to advance his own interests. Caedwalla was king for only three years, and it was his successor Ine (688–725) who consolidated his successes, including, it would appear, the development of Hamwic as the main emporium on the Solent.

It would seem that the Gewisse were in control of much of the Hampshire side of the Solent, however, especially in the area immediately to the west of Southampton before the accession of Caedwalla. The best support for this contention comes from evidence for the series of minsters established in the river valleys that drain into the Solent.[57] They may well have been set up to support the Gewissan take-over of the area, rather than simply being a result of it. When Caedwalla took the Isle of Wight, two princes of its royal house fled across the Solent to the New Forest, but were captured and condemned to death. Abbot Cynebert of a minster in Redbridge (perhaps actually based at Eling) intervened to allow the princes to be baptised before their execution.[58] We do not know when Cynebert founded his minster, but the evidence discussed above makes it unlikely that there could have been a Gewissan foundation there before 670 when the Winchester see was re-established. The new bishop was the Leuthere, a Frank whose uncle Agilbert had been bishop in Dorchester-on-Thames previously (c.650–c.660). Bede describes Leuthere as 'governing the whole see of the Gewisse with industry and moderation', and he seems to have worked closely with Theodore, the reforming archbishop of Canterbury.[59] The establishment of systems of pastoral care can therefore be expected to have been one of his priorities.

It is probably to the same period between 670 and 685 that we can date the foundation of the neighbouring minster at Nursling. Its abbot Wynbert was an important associate of Bishop Leuthere and appears to have been the notary (in the Frankish fashion) of some of the charters of his episcopate.[60] Wynbert was clearly well-educated in Latin, and it would be interesting to know where he and Cynebert had been trained and had been living prior to the creation of the Solent minsters. One can speculate that they could have come from the former Gewissan see at Dorchester-on-Thames, and moved to Winchester on its cessation. However, Wynbert who seems to have worked closely with Leuthere could possibly have left Wessex with the latter's uncle Agilbert when he went home to Francia, and then subsequently returned to Wessex with Leuthere. Nursling was where Boniface 'the apostle of Germany' was trained. His Anglo-Saxon name was Wynfrith. The shared first name-element and the fact that Wynfrith/Boniface was expected to succeed Wynbert as abbot of Nursling may suggest that they were related.[61] Other relations of Boniface, the family of the nun Hugeburh who provided us with the earliest reference to Hamwic, are found in association with the minster of Bishop's Waltham, nine miles north-east of Southampton, in the early eighth century. Immediately south of Bishop's Waltham, on the east bank of the river Hamble, is the parish of Titchfield. The lower portions of the western tower of its church (formerly a two-storey porch) and adjoining areas of nave have been dated to the late seventh or early eighth centuries,[62] and so suggests foundation within the same period.

There is therefore (for the period) relatively good evidence for a series of minster churches founded in the river valleys of the Hampshire Solent as part of a consolidated campaign, beginning in the 670s. This naturally leads to the issue of whether the minster church of Hamwic/Hamtun was founded as part of the same programme. There is no early written evidence for the minster of St Mary's, Southampton which was the mother church of medieval Southampton where its inhabitants had to be buried, in spite of the inconvenience of it being on the site of the Middle Saxon emporium.[63] There has been no excavation of the Middle Saxon church itself which might be expected to lie under its Victorian successor, but burials have been excavated which may have been part of its graveyard. Radio-carbon dating has only been able to establish that the churchyard was likely to have been in use before the decline of Hamwic in the ninth century.[64] Burials at the Cook Street cemetery (500m to the south of St Mary's) may date from the late seventh or eighth century.[65] They might possibly provide support for the foundation of St Mary's in this period if Moreton's suggestion of a south-west minster enclave in this corner of Hamwic is accepted.

We can turn now to the question of how the burials on the site of St Mary's Stadium may be related to these events. As we have seen this cemetery is likely to have come into use in the period when the Solent was part of a Jutish

[57] P.H. Hase, "The mother churches of Hampshire," in *Minsters and Parish Churches. The Local Church in Transition 950–1200*. Oxford University Committee for Archaeology Monograph 17, ed. J. Blair (Oxford: Oxbow Books, 1988), 45–66.

[58] Colgrave, and Mynors, *Bede's Ecclesiastical History*, 382–5 [IV, 16]; Hase, "The mother churches of Hampshire," 45.

[59] Colgrave, and Mynors, *Bede's Ecclesiastical History*, 236–37 [III, 7].

[60] H. Edwards, *The Charters of the Early West Saxon Kingdom* (Oxford: British Archaeological Reports, (British Series) 1988), 12–13; S. Kelly, *Charters of Shaftesbury Abbey*. Anglo-Saxon Charters V. (London: British Academy, 1996), 7–8.

[61] B.A.E. Yorke, "The insular background to Boniface's continental career," in *Bonifatius-Leben und Nachwirkedn. Die Gestaltung des christlichen Europa im Frühmittelalter* Quellen und Abhandlungen no. 121, eds F. Felten, J. Jarnut and L. von Padberg (Mainz: Gesellschaft für mittelrheinische Kirchengesischte, 2007), 23–38.

[62] M.J. Hare "The Anglo-Saxon church of St Peter, Titchfield," *Proceedings of the Hampshire Field Club and Archaeological Society*, 32 (1976): 5–48.

[63] Morton, *Excavations at Hamwic Volume I*, 50–51.

[64] A. Cherryson, "'Such a resting-place as is necessary for us in God's sight and fitting in the eyes of the world'; Saxon Southampton and the development of church-yard burial," in *Burial in Later Anglo-Saxon England c650–1100 AD*, eds J. Buckberry and A. Cherryson (Oxford: Oxbow Books, 2010), 54–72.

[65] D. Garner, "A Middle Saxon cemetery at Cook Street, Southampton (SOU 823)," *Proceedings of the Hampshire Field Club and Archaeological Society*, 56 (2001): 170–91.

confederation. However, its most striking burials, the male warrior burials and the female burials with gold jewellery, can only be dated, with greatest likelihood, to the latter part of the seventh century. This was the very period when control of the Solent was being contested between the Mercian and Gewissan kings, and so the burial of well-armed individuals could have had an appropriate context in events of the time. Possibly the unusual double burial of two young warriors with seaxes (grave 3520) could be of two individuals who had died in armed combat (though not enough of the bodies survived to show any significant injuries).[66] However, as we have seen there were well-armed burials from the early stages of other Anglo-Saxon trading centres,[67] so those at St Mary's stadium need not be related to a specific event. In the context of the complicated politics in southern England in the late seventh century such individuals could have been seen as neutral. Even if the St Mary's stadium group had begun working with Jutish or Mercian leaders, it would probably have been possible for them to switch their allegiance to the Gewisse if both parties wanted it.

One can draw a possible analogy with the involvement of the Northumbrian bishop Wilfrid in the events of southern England in the 680s. Wilfrid had a somewhat chequered relationship with the Northumbrian kings and spent several periods in exile, usually under the protection of Mercian kings who were as much involved in warfare against Northumbria as with the southern kingdoms.[68] In the 680s Wilfrid arrived among the South Saxons when they were in alliance with Wulfhere of Mercia and in effect acted as their bishop, including baptising people and establishing a church in the province.[69] According to the *Anglo-Saxon Chronicle* (*sub anno* 661) Wilfrid was also responsible for beginning the conversion of the Isle of Wight.[70] However, in spite of a 'treaty of peace' Wilfrid had entered into with King Æthelwalh of the South Saxons,[71] when the king was attacked and killed by Caedwalla, Wilfrid was able to switch his allegiance to the latter instead, and received generous gifts from him in Sussex and the Isle of Wight.[72] It served the mutual interests of Caedwalla and Wilfrid to form a new alliance,[73] and something similar could have brought the putative traders of the St Mary's Stadium and the Gewissan kings together, irrespective of any previous political alignments.

Hamwic and the Origins of the West Saxon Kingdom

It appears to be in the context of the reigns of Caedwalla (685–88) and Ine (688–725) that the titles 'king of the Saxons', and ultimately 'king of the West Saxons', replaced that of 'king of the Gewisse'.[74] These kings were no longer just kings of their original people the Gewisse, but had incorporated other Saxon areas, the Jutish areas of Hampshire and the Isle of Wight and major parts of the British provinces to the west, as well as exercising a more intermittent overlordship of other areas in the south. Their achievements matched those of King Wulfhere of Mercia (658–75) in the south, and so it is not surprising to find similar strategies operating in both kingdoms in order to capitalise on their successes. The foundation of wics is one example of such a strategy. The rapid growth of Hamwic, which the archaeological evidence suggests must have fallen in the reign of Ine, parallels the impressive expansion of Lundenwic (London) that can be dated to the reign of Wulfhere, from a combination of written and archaeological evidence.[75] It might not be too fanciful to suggest that the development of Lundenwic was a direct inspiration for the foundation of Hamwic. It is a common pattern in the early history of Anglo-Saxon kingship to find an innovation in one kingdom, such as conversion to Christianity or the adoption of coinage, being taken up soon after in other kingdoms. Wics may be another example of the more powerful kings intervening to encourage new initiatives that enabled them to strengthen and exploit their positions.

When Richard Hodges first expounded his influential theory on the development of the emporia/wics, he suggested that they represented a royal initiative to kick-start trade.[76] Since he wrote, far more has been discovered, particularly through the Portable Antiquities Scheme, about the active trade networks of the sixth and early seventh centuries that fuelled the economic growth of 'the long eighth century'.[77] Wics can now be seen as attempts by kings to get a slice of action that was already taking place.[78] John Maddicott has demonstrated how the growth of London fits with the exploitation by Mercian kings of natural resources such as salt, timber and metal

[66] Birbeck, *The Origins of Mid-Saxon Southampton*, 30–31; Stoodley, "The early cemetery and its place within southern England," 78–81.

[67] Stoodley, "Burial practice in seventh-century Hampshire"; Scull, "Foreign identities."

[68] D.P. Kirby, "Northumbria in the time of Wilfrid," in *Saint Wilfrid at Hexham*, ed. D.P. Kirby (Newcastle upon Tyne: Oriel Press 1974), 1–34; R. Sharpe, "King Ceadwalla and Bishop Wilfrid," in *Cities, Saints and Communities in Early Medieval Europe. Essays in Honour of Alan T. Thacker*, eds S. DeGregorio and P. Kershaw (Turnhout: Brepols, 2020), 195–222.

[69] B. Colgrave, *The Life of Bishop Wilfrid by Eddius Stephanus* (Cambridge: Cambridge University Press, 1927), 80–85; Colgrave, and Mynors, *Bede's Ecclesiastical History*, 370–77 [IV, 13].

[70] Whitelock et al. *The Anglo-Saxon Chronicle*, 21.

[71] Colgrave, *The Life of Bishop Wilfrid*, 82–83.

[72] Colgrave, *The Life of Bishop Wilfrid*, 84–85; Colgrave, and Mynors, *Bede's Ecclesiastical History*, 380–85 [IV, 15–16].

[73] N. Higham, "Bishop Wilfrid in southern England: a review of his political objectives," *Studien zur Sachsenforschung* 13 (1999); Sharpe, "King Ceadwalla and Bishop Wilfrid."

[74] Walker, "Bede and the Gewissae."

[75] Maddicott, "London and Droitwich," 8–16; Cowie, and Blackmore, *Lundenwic*, 106–10.

[76] R. Hodges, *Dark Age Economics: The Origins of Towns and Trade AD 600–1000* (London: Duckworth, 1982).

[77] I.L. Hansen, and C. Wickham, (eds) *The Long Eighth Century* (Leiden: Brill, 2000); T. Pestell and K. Ulmschneider, (eds) *Markets in Early Medieval Europe. Trading and 'Productive' Sites, 650–850* (Macclesfield: Windgather Press, 2003); Harrington and Welch, *Early Anglo-Saxon Kingdoms*.

[78] M. Anderton, (ed.) *Anglo-Saxon Trading Centres. Beyond the Emporia*. (Glasgow: Cruithne Press, 1999); G. Astill, "General survey 600–1300," in *Cambridge Urban History of Britain. Volume I 600–1540* ed. D.M. Palliser (Cambridge: Cambridge University Press, 2000), 27–50; D. Hill, and R. Cowie, (eds) *Wics. The Early Mediaeval Trading Centres of Northern Europe* (Sheffield: Sheffield Academic Press, 2001).

ores in their kingdom.[79] 'Power is an accumulation and use of resources' as Ulf Näsman argued in a study of the forces behind the development of early medieval kingship in Denmark.[80] Wessex may not have been as fortunate in its natural resources as Mercia, but the rapid expansion of Wessex, especially into the British west, would have brought all sorts of booty and surpluses into royal hands which they would have wanted to dispose of profitably.

There are a number of grounds for identifying a royal authority behind the growth of wics in the late seventh and eighth centuries, a grouping that includes not just Lundenwic and Hamwic, but also Ipswich, York and various sites in Kent. Characteristics, known particularly through excavation of the first four places, include rapid growth, perhaps implying deliberate resettling from the countryside; planned settlement with such features as regular resurfacing of roads; and organised food supplies that may imply stocking through the royal tributary system.[81] All such features are to be found at Hamwic which by the early eighth century had become the most densely populated settlement in Wessex. The likelihood of West Saxon kings moving individuals around between areas under their control is alluded to by Bede in his description of Caedwalla's conquest of the Isle of Wight: '[he] endeavoured to wipe out the natives by merciless slaughter and to replace them by inhabitants from his own kingdom' [IV, 16].[82] One hopes that the scale of slaughter may be exaggerated, but – and this is not really much better – there were more profitable ways to shift a population, namely through the slave-trade, one of the types of trading Bede knew took place through Lundenwic [IV 22].[83] Possibly another alternative would have been to resettle craftsmen and labourers within Hamwic. The industrial quarter of Six Dials is characterised by organised and uniform low-order housing and a somewhat monotonous diet featuring rather elderly animals.[84] The exact status of the inhabitants of Six Dials is hard to know, but the type of varied social mix of later medieval towns is not apparent, and the emporia were not so much embryonic towns as a distinctive type of Middle Saxon site concerned with trade and production.[85] As on rural sites, it is likely that not all of those working and living in wics would have been of free status, or were there by choice.

Although it is likely that royal authority lay behind the rapid growth of wics, the nature of royal involvement requires some clarification. An analogy could be drawn with the spread of the church in the conversion period of the seventh century. Missionaries needed the support of royal authority to operate within kingdoms, and the early Kentish law codes show how the church there was integrated into the Anglo-Saxon legal structure.[86] The land on which the first churches were founded was donated by kings, and kings expected to be able to appoint or remove bishops if they so desired. If we substitute traders for churchmen, we may reach a better understanding of how places like Hamwic came into being. Royal support and authority were needed, but it was probably specialist traders who encouraged them to provide it and were responsible for the details and the day-to-day running. It is quite possible that the traders of the St Mary's Stadium cemetery (if they may so be interpreted) were involved in the creation of Hamwic. It has been suggested that there may have been a trader's enclave in the south-east corner of Hamwic (i.e. including the area of St Mary's Stadium), but larger scale excavation is needed to develop the hypothesis of difference between that area and that of Six Dials in the north-west.[87] Protection of traders also occurs in the earliest lawcodes,[88] and the only identical chapter in the contemporary lawcodes of Ine and King Wihtred of Kent (690–725) concerns arrangements for traders moving through the countryside.[89] Rory Naismith has suggested from his analysis of early mints and minters that the prime instigators of the coinage were members of the trading community operating in cooperation with kings.[90] Hamwic had its own prolific secondary sceatta coinage (Series H, type 49). Its apparently limited circulation, with very few finds outside the settlement itself, seems to underline the artificial creation of Hamwic and the difference between it and later medieval towns.[91]

Kings would have received various advantages through supporting the development of wics. They would have somewhere to dispose of surpluses and raw materials, both from their estates and from the payments they took in kind from those of others, and to acquire in exchange cash or imported items. In addition, as a series of Kentish and Mercian charters demonstrate, their representatives could collect tolls from ships using wics, and they probably took profits from other activities that took place within them.[92] Local noble families and the minsters they supported no doubt also made use of the facilities of Hamwic. The

[79] Maddicott, "London and Droitwich."

[80] U. Näsman, "Exchange and politics: eighth century to early ninth century in Denmark," in *The Long Eighth Century*, eds I.L. Hansen, and C. Wickham, (Leiden: Brill, 2000) 35–68.

[81] Astill, "General survey 600–1300"; Hill, and Cowie, *Wics.*

[82] Colgrave, and Mynors, *Bede's Ecclesiastical History*, 382–3.

[83] Colgrave, and Mynors, *Bede's Ecclesiastical History*, 400–5.

[84] J. Bourdillon, "Countryside and town: the animal resources of Saxon Southampton," in *Anglo-Saxon Settlements* ed. D. Hooke (Oxford: Basil Blackwell, 1988), 176–96; Andrews, *Excavations at Hamwic: Volume 2*, 242–5.

[85] D. Hinton, "Metalwork and the emporia," in *Anglo-Saxon Trading Centres. Beyond the Emporia*, ed. M. Anderton (Glasgow: Cruithne Press, 1999); Astill, "General survey 600–1300"; Hill, and Cowie, *Wics.*

[86] L. Oliver, *The Beginnings of English Law* (Toronto: Toronto University Press, 2002).

[87] Morton, *Excavations at Hamwic Volume I*, 67–68; Birbeck, *The Origins of Mid-Saxon Southampton*, 203–34.

[88] S. Kelly, "Trading privileges from 8th-century England," *Early Medieval Europe* 1, (1992): 3–28.

[89] Oliver, *The Beginnings of English Law*, 179–80.

[90] R Naismith, *Money and Power in Southern England. The Southern English Kingdoms, 757–865* (Cambridge: Cambridge University Press, 2012), 87–96.

[91] D.M. Metcalf, "The Coins," in *Southampton Finds, Volume 1: The Coins and Pottery from Hamwic*, Southampton Archaeology Monographs 4, ed. P. Andrews (Southampton: Southampton City Museums 1988), 17–59; B. Palmer, "The hinterlands of three southern English *emporia*: some common themes," in *Markets in Early Medieval Europe. Trading and 'Productive' Sites, 650–850*, eds T. Pestell and K. Ulmschneider, (Macclesfield: Windgather Press, 2003), 48–61.

[92] Kelly, "Trading privileges."

minsters bordering the Solent may have had their own outports for various functions that may, like Hamwic, have had their origins in more *ad hoc* arrangements before the eighth century. Hamblemouth could have been utilised by minsters at Bishops Waltham and Titchfield as well as other estates in the Hamble valley, while Eling creek (where there have been Middle Saxon coin finds) could have served the lower Test valley including the minsters at Redbridge and Nursling.[93] However, the minsters may still for some purposes have made, or been obliged to make, use of Hamwic itself, just as many of the minsters of Kent and the London area made use of London, while also having their own small outports.[94]

Wics may have been deliberate creations, but ultimately would stand or fall on their success as commercial centres, though fluctuating political fortunes of their royal protectors might be relevant as well. Hamwic's long term commercial viability seems to have been limited and within a century or so of its foundation it was in decline. Of course, the general instability in the North Sea trading zone as a result of viking raids must bear a lot of the blame, and other Middle Saxon wics also suffered major setbacks.[95] But it has also been suspected that Hamwic was never supported by fully developed commercial links with a rural hinterland in the way that characterised later medieval towns.[96] It may have been less well-served for transportation of bulk goods by river than the other wics.[97] The limited circulation of its sceatta coinage may well be indicative of the problem, and, unlike the other southern wics, Hamwic produced at best a very limited penny coinage in the late eighth century. This was a period when Offa of Mercia (757–96), a ruler much interested in trade and commercial profits, dominated southern England. Part of northern Wessex was taken over by him, and West Saxon kings may have had to pay him tribute for part of his reign at least.[98] There may have been fewer royal surpluses to process through Hamwic, initiating a period of crisis and decline from which it never fully recovered. Only three pennies in the name of King Beorhtric (786–802) are known, and these were probably produced after Offa's death.[99] His successor King Ecgbert of Wessex (802–39) managed to extend West Saxon control over most of southern England outside Mercia. But although there was some revival of, it is presumed, the Hamwic mint, most of his coinage was produced in Kentish mints,[100] suggesting that Hamwic's commercial activity was of limited significance by the early ninth century.

[93] Ulmschneider, "Markets around the Solent."

[94] Cowie, and Blackmore, *Lundenwic*, 94–103.

[95] Astill, "General survey 600–1300," 33–37; Cowie, and Blackmore, *Lundenwic*, 110–13.

[96] Hinton, "Metalwork and the emporia."

[97] Palmer, "The hinterlands of three southern English *emporia*."

[98] B.A.E. Yorke, *Wessex in the Early Middle Ages* (London: Leicester University Press, 1995), 61–64.

[99] Naismith, *Money and Power in Southern England*, 120.

[100] R.H.M. Dolley, "The location of the pre-Ælfredian mint(s) of Wessex," *Proceedings of the Hampshire Field Club and Archaeological Society*, 27 (1970), 57–61; Naismith, *Money and Power in Southern England*, 106–07.

Conclusion

The St Mary's Stadium excavations do not alter the conclusion that the emporium of Hamwic was the result of rapid expansion in the early eighth century. Its cemetery though does provide a context out of which the emporium could have developed, and one that further links Hamwic with the other emporia sites, especially in southern England. Competition between Mercia and Wessex for domination of England south of the Thames may explain some of the features of the cemetery, and a context for the reordering of the links with Kent that had been significant in the area prior to the end of the seventh century when both areas were part of a Jutish confederation. The foundation of Hamwic still seems best explained as a direct result of the overlordship of King Ine of Wessex in southern England. It can be suggested that conscious emulation of the development of Lundenwic under Wulfhere of Mercia lay behind the rapid growth of Hamwic in the early eighth century. Ine may have wished not only to maximise profits from his newly acquired territories, but also to establish more state-like structures to underpin his regime. But it seems to have been a false dawn and Hamwic was unable to sustain its early promise particularly in the unsettled conditions in southern England and its overseas trading areas in the late eighth and ninth centuries. However, when more settled conditions returned a new site was opened up on the Test side of the peninsula which rejuvenated many of the earlier links and became the medieval town of Southampton.

Acknowledgements

The author is very grateful to Nick Stoodley for reading an earlier draft of this paper and making many useful suggestions.

Bibliography

Anderton, M., ed. *Anglo-Saxon Trading Centres. Beyond the Emporia*. Glasgow: Cruithne Press, 1999.

Andrews, P. *Excavations at Hamwic Volume 2: Excavations at Six Dials*. Southampton Archaeology Monographs 7. York: Council for British Archaeology, 1997.

Andrews, P., ed. *Southampton Finds, Volume 1: The Coins and Pottery from Hamwic*, Southampton Archaeology Monographs 4. Southampton: Southampton City Museums 1988.

Arnold, C. *The Anglo-Saxon Cemeteries of the Isle of Wight*. London: British Museum Publications, 1982.

Astill, G. "General survey 600–1300." In *Cambridge Urban History of Britain. Volume I 600–1540*, edited by D.M. Palliser, 27–50. Cambridge: Cambridge University Press, 2000.

Bassett, S., ed. *The Origins of Anglo-Saxon Kingdoms*. London: Leicester University Press, 1989.

Behr. C. "The origins of kingship in early medieval Kent." *Early Medieval Europe* 9 (2000): 25–52.

Biddle, M., and B. Kjølbye-Biddle. "Winchester from *Venta* to *Wintancœstir.*" In *Pagans and Christians – from Antiquity to the Middle Ages. Papers in Honour of Martin Henig.* British Archaeological Reports, International Series 1610, edited by L. Gilmour, 189–214. Oxford: BAR Publishing, 2007.

Biddle. M. "Excavations at Winchester, 1971. Tenth and Final Interim Report, Part I." *Antiquaries Journal*, 55 (1975): 96–126

Birbeck, V. *The Origins of Mid-Saxon Southampton. Excavations at the Friends Provident St Mary's Stadium 1998–2000.* Salisbury: Wessex Archaeology, 2005.

Blair, J., ed. *Minsters and Parish Churches. The Local Church in Transition 950–1200.* Oxford University Committee for Archaeology Monograph 17. Oxford: Oxbow Books, 1988.

Bourdillon, J. "Countryside and town: the animal resources of Saxon Southampton." In *Anglo-Saxon Settlements*, edited by D. Hooke, 176–96. Oxford: Basil Blackwell, 1988.

Brennan, N., and H. Hamerow. "An Anglo-Saxon great hall complex at Sutton Courtenay/Drayton, Oxfordshire: a royal centre of early Wesssex?" *Archaeological Journal* 172 (2015): 325–50.

Brookes, S., S. Harrington and A. Reynolds, eds. *Studies in Early Anglo-Saxon Art and Archaeology: Papers in Honour on Martin G. Welch.* British Archaeological Reports British Series 527. Oxford: BAR Publishing, 2011.

Brooks, N. "The creation and early structure of the kingdom of Kent." In *The Origins of Anglo-Saxon Kingdoms*, edited by S. Bassett, 55–74. London: Leicester University Press, 1989.

Buckberry, J., and A. Cherryson, eds. *Burial in Later Anglo-Saxon England c650–1100 AD.* Oxford: Oxbow Books, 2010.

Cherryson, A. "'Such a resting-place as is necessary for us in God's sight and fitting in the eyes of the world': Saxon Southampton and the development of church- yard burial." In *Burial in Later Anglo-Saxon England c650–1100 AD*, edited by J. Buckberry and A. Cherryson, 54–72. Oxford: Oxbow Books, 2010.

Colgrave, B. *The Life of Bishop Wilfrid by Eddius Stephanus.* Cambridge: Cambridge University Press, 1927.

Colgrave, B., and R.A.B. Mynors. *Bede's Ecclesiastical History of the English People.* Oxford: Oxford University Press, 1969.

Cowie, R., and L. Blackmore. *Lundenwic. Excavations in Middle Saxon London, 1987–2000.* Museum of London Archaeology Monograph 63. London: Museum of London, 2012.

DeGregorio, S. and P. Kershaw, eds. *Cities, Saints and Communities in Early Medieval Europe. Essays in Honour of Alan T. Thacker.* Turnhout: Brepols, 2020.

Dolley, R.H.M. "The location of the pre-Ælfredian mint(s) of Wessex." *Proceedings of the Hampshire Field Club and Archaeological Society*, 27 (1970): 57–61.

Eagles, B. "Anglo-Saxon presence and culture in Wiltshire." In *Roman Wiltshire and After: Papers in Honour of Kenneth Annable*, edited by P. Ellis, 199–233. Devizes: Wiltshire Archaeological and Natural History Society, 2001.

Eagles, B. *From Roman Civitas to Anglo-Saxon Shire. The Formation of Wessex.* Oxford: Oxbow Books, 2018, 117–28.

Edwards, H. *The Charters of the Early West Saxon Kingdom.* Oxford: British Archaeological Reports, (British Series), 1988.

Ellis, P., ed. *Roman Wiltshire and After: Papers in Honour of Kenneth Annable.* Devizes: Wiltshire Archaeological and Natural History Society, 2001.

Felten, F., F. and J. Jarnut and L. von Padberg, eds. *Bonifatius-Leben und Nachwirkedn. Die Gestaltung des christlichen Europa im Frühmittelalter* Quellen und Abhandlungen no. 121. Mainz: Gesellschaft für mittelrheinische Kirchengesischte, 2007.

Garner, D, "A Middle Saxon cemetery at Cook Street, Southampton (SOU 823)." *Proceedings of the Hampshire Field Club and Archaeological Society*, 56 (2001): 170–91.

Gilmour, L., ed. *Pagans and Christians – from Antiquity to the Middle Ages. Papers in Honour of Martin Henig.* British Archaeological Reports, International Series 1610. Oxford: BAR Publishing, 2007.

Hansen, I.L. and C. Wickham, eds. *The Long Eighth Century.* Leiden: Brill, 2000.

Hårdh, B. and L. Larsson, eds. *Central Places in the Migration and the Merovingian Periods. Papers from the 52nd Sachsensymposion, Lund August 2001.* Lund: Almqvist and Wiksell International, 2003.

Hare M.J. "The Anglo-Saxon church of St Peter, Titchfield." *Proceedings of the Hampshire Field Club and Archaeological Society*, 32 (1976): 5–48.

Harrington, S., and M. Welch. *The Early Anglo-Saxon Kingdoms of Southern Britain AD 450–650. Beneath the Tribal Hidage.* Oxford: Oxbow Books, 2014.

Hase, P.H. "The mother churches of Hampshire." In *Minsters and Parish Churches. The Local Church in Transition 950–1200.* Oxford University Committee for Archaeology Monograph 17, edited by J. Blair, 45–66. Oxford: Oxbow Books, 1988.

Higham, N. "Bishop Wilfrid in southern England: a review of his political objectives." *Studien zur Sachsenforschung* 13 (1999): 207–17.

Hill, D., and R. Cowie, eds. *Wics. The Early Mediaeval Trading Centres of Northern Europe.* Sheffield: Sheffield Academic Press, 2001.

Hines, J. "The becoming of the English: identity, material culture and language in early Anglo-Saxon England." *Anglo-Saxon Studies in Archaeology and History*, 7 (1994): 49–59.

Hines, J., ed. *The Anglo-Saxons from the Migration Period to the Eighth Century. An Ethnographic Perspective.* Woodbridge: Boydell Press, 1997.

Hinton, D. "Gold pendants." In *The Origins of Mid-Saxon Southampton. Excavations at the Friends Provident St Mary's Stadium 1998–2000*, edited by V. Birbeck, 64–7. Salisbury: Wessex Archaeology, 2005.

Hinton, D. "Metalwork and the emporia." In *Anglo-Saxon Trading Centres. Beyond the Emporia*, edited by M. Anderton, 24–31. Glasgow: Cruithne Press, 1999.

Hinton, D. and S. Worrell. "An early Anglo-Saxon cemetery and archaeological survey at Breamore, Hampshire, 1999–2006." *Archaeological Journal* 174 (2017): 68–145.

Hodges, R. *Dark Age Economics: The Origins of Towns and Trade AD 600–1000.* London: Duckworth, 1982.

Holdsworth, P. *Excavations at Melbourne Street, Southampton, 1971–76.* Southampton Archaeology Monographs 1. London: Council for British Archaeology, 1980.

Holdsworth, P. *Excavations at Melbourne Street, Southampton, 1971–76.* Southampton Archaeology Monographs 1. London: Council for British Archaeology, 1980.

Hooke, D., ed. *Anglo-Saxon Settlements.* Oxford: Basil Blackwell, 1988.

Jarvis, K.S. *Excavations in Christchurch 1969–1980.* Dorset Natural History and Archaeological Society Monograph 5. Dorchester: DNHAS, 1983.

Kelly, S. "Trading privileges from 8th-century England." *Early Medieval Europe* 1 (1992): 3–28.

Kelly, S. *Charters of Shaftesbury Abbey.* Anglo-Saxon Charters V. London: British Academy, 1996.

Kirby, D.P. "Northumbria in the time of Wilfrid." In *Saint Wilfrid at Hexham*, edited by D.P. Kirby, 1–34. Newcastle upon Tyne: Oriel Press 1974.

Kirby, D.P., ed. *Saint Wilfrid at Hexham.* Newcastle upon Tyne: Oriel Press 1974.

Kruse, P. *Jutes in Kent? On the Jutish Nature of Kent, Southern Hampshire and the Isle of Wight.* Oldenburg: Probleme der Kütenforschung im südlichen Nordseegebiet Band 31, 2007.

Maddicott, J.R. "London and Droitwich, c.650–750: trade, industry and the rise of Mercia." *Anglo-Saxon England* 35 (2005): 7–58.

Metcalf, D.M. "Coins." In *The Origins of Mid-Saxon Southampton. Excavations at the Friends Provident St Mary's Stadium 1998–2000*, by V. Birbeck, 55–6. Salisbury: Wessex Archaeology, 2005.

Metcalf, D.M. "The Coins." In *Southampton Finds, Volume 1: The Coins and Pottery from Hamwic*, Southampton Archaeology Monographs 4, edited by P. Andrews, 17–59. Southampton: Southampton City Museums 1988.

Middleton, N. "Early medieval port customs, tolls and controls on foreign trade." *Early Medieval Europe* 3 (2005): 313–58.

Morton, A. "Hamwic in its context." In *Anglo-Saxon Trading Centres. Beyond the Emporia* edited by M. Anderton, 48–62. Glasgow: Cruithne Press, 1999.

Morton, A. *Excavations at Hamwic Volume I: Excavations 1946–83, excluding Six Dials and Melbourne Street.* Southampton Archaeology Monographs 5. York: Council for British Archaeology, 1992.

Naismith, R. *Money and Power in Southern England. The Southern English Kingdoms, 757–865.* Cambridge: Cambridge University Press, 2012.

Näsman, U. "Exchange and politics: eighth century to early ninth century in Denmark." In *The Long Eighth Century*, edited by I.L. Hansen, and C. Wickham, 35–68. Leiden: Brill, 2000.

Oliver, L. *The Beginnings of English Law.* Toronto: Toronto University Press, 2002.

Palliser, D.M., ed. *Cambridge Urban History of Britain. Volume I. 600–1540.* Cambridge: Cambridge University Press, 2000.

Palmer, B. "The hinterlands of three southern English *emporia*: some common themes." In *Markets in Early Medieval Europe. Trading and 'Productive' Sites, 650–850*, edited by T. Pestell and K. Ulmschneider, 48–61. Macclesfield: Windgather Press, 2003.

Pestell, T. and K. Ulmschneider, eds. *Markets in Early Medieval Europe. Trading and 'Productive' Sites, 650–850.* Macclesfield: Windgather Press, 2003.

Pohl, W. "Ethnic names and identities in the British Isles: a comparative perspective." In *The Anglo-Saxons from the Migration Period to the Eighth Century. An Ethnographic Perspective*, edited by J. Hines, 7–31. Woodbridge: Boydell Press, 1997.

Richardson, A.F. "'What came before': the kingdom of Kent to 800." In *Early Medieval Kent 800–1200*, edited by S. Sweetinburgh, 21–41. Woodbridge: Boydell Press and Kent County Council, 2016.

Richardson, A.F. "The Third Way: thoughts on non-Saxon identity south of the Thames AD 450–600." In *Studies in Early Anglo-Saxon Art and Archaeology: Papers in Honour on Martin G. Welch.* British Archaeological Reports British Series 527, edited by S. Brookes, S. Harrington and A. Reynolds, 72–81. Oxford: BAR Publishing, 2011.

Rumble, A. "Hamtun alias Hamwic (Saxon Southampton): the place-name traditions and their significance." In *Excavations at Melbourne Street, Southampton, 1971–76.* Southampton Archaeology Monographs 1, by P. Holdsworth, 7–20. London: Council for British Archaeology, 1980.

Scull, C. 'Foreign identities in burials at the seventh-century English *emporia*', in S. Brookes, S. Harrington and A. Reynolds (eds) *Studies in Early Anglo-Saxon Art and Archaeology: Papers in Honour on Martin G. Welch* British Archaeological Reports British Series 527 (Oxford: BAR Publishing, 2011) ,82–7.

Sharpe, R. "King Ceadwalla and Bishop Wilfrid." In *Cities, Saints and Communities in Early Medieval Europe. Essays in Honour of Alan T. Thacker*, edited by S. DeGregorio and P. Kershaw, 195–222. Turnhout: Brepols, 2020.

Sims-Williams, P. "The settlement of England in Bede and the 'Chronicle.'" *Anglo-Saxon England* 12 (1983): 1–41.

Stoodley, N. "Burial practice in seventh-century Hampshire: St Mary's Stadium in context." In *Burial in Later Anglo-Saxon England c650–1100 AD*, edited by J. Buckberry and A. Cherryson, 38–53. Oxford: Oxbow books 2010.

Stoodley, N. "Costume groups in Hampshire and their bearing on the question of Jutish settlement in the fifth to seventh centuries AD." In *The Land of the English Kin. Studies in Wessex and Anglo-Saxon England in Honour of Professor Barbara Yorke*, edited by A. Langlands and R. Lavelle, 70–94. Leiden: Brill, 2020.

Stoodley, N. "The early cemetery and its place within southern England." In *The Origins of Mid-Saxon Southampton. Excavations at the Friends Provident St Mary's Stadium 1998–2000* by V. Birbeck, 75–81. Salisbury: Wessex Archaeology, 2005.

Stoodley, N. "The origins of Hamwic and its central role in the seventh century as revealed by recent archaeological discoveries." In *Central Places in the Migration and the Merovingian Periods. Papers from the 52nd Sachsensymposion, Lund August 2001*, edited by B. Hårdh and L. Larsson, 317–31. Lund: Almqvist and Wiksell International, 2003.

Sweetinburgh, S., ed. *Early Medieval Kent 800–1200.* Woodbridge: Boydell Press and Kent County Council, 2016.

Ulmschneider, K. "Markets around the Solent: Unravelling a 'Productive' Site on the Isle of Wight." In *Markets in Early Medieval Europe. Trading and 'Productive' Sites, 650–850*, edited by T. Pestell and K. Ulmschneider, 73–83. Macclesfield: Windgather Press, 2003.

Ulmschneider, K. *Markets, Minsters, and Metal-detectors: the Archaeology of Middle Saxon Lincolnshire and Hampshire Compared.* British Archaeological Reports British Series 307. Oxford: BAR Publishing, 2000.

Walker, H.E. "Bede and the Gewissae: the political evolution of the heptarchy and their nomenclature." *Cambridge Historical Journal* 12, (1956): 174–86.

Walton Rogers, P. *Cloth and Clothing in Early Anglo-Saxon England AD 450–700.* CBA Research Report 145. York: Council for British Archaeology, 2007.

Welch, M. "Anglo-Saxon Kent to AD 800." In *The Archaeology of Kent to AD 800*, edited by J.H. Williams, 189–251. Woodbridge: Boydell Press for Kent county Council, 2007.

Whitelock D. with Douglas, D.C. and Tucker, S.I. *The Anglo-Saxon Chronicle. A Revised Translation.* London: Eyre and Spottiswoode, 1965.

Williams, J.H., ed. *The Archaeology of Kent to AD 800.* Woodbridge: Boydell Press for Kent county Council, 2007.

Wood, I.N. *The Merovingian North Sea.* Alingsås: Occasional Papers on Medieval Topics I, 1983.

Yorke, B.A.E. "The foundation of Old Minster and the status of Winchester in the seventh and eighth centuries." *Proceedings of the Hampshire Field Club and Archaeological Society* 38, (1982): 75–83.

Yorke, B.A.E. "The insular background to Boniface's continental career." In *Bonifatius-Leben und Nachwirkedn. Die Gestaltung des christlichen Europa im Frühmittelalter* Quellen und Abhandlungen no. 121, edited by F. Felten, J. Jarnut and L. von Padberg, 23–38. Mainz: Gesellschaft für mittelrheinische Kirchengesischte, 2007.

Yorke, B.A.E. "Competition for the Solent and seventh-century politics." In *The Middle Ages Revisited. Studies in the Archaeology and History of Medieval Southern England Presented to Professor David A. Hinton*, edited by B. Jervis, 35–44. Oxford: Archaeopress, 2018.

Yorke, B.A.E. "The Jutes of Hampshire and Wight and the origins of Wessex." In *The Origins of Anglo-Saxon Kingdoms*, edited by S. Bassett, 84–96. London: Leicester University Press, 1989.

Yorke, B.A.E. *Wessex in the Early Middle Ages.* London: Leicester University Press, 1995.

3

A Different Perspective on the Thirteenth-Century King's Chapel Pavement at Clarendon Palace

Mary South

University of Winchester

Abstract: Clarendon Palace is renowned for its decorated floor tiles. In particular the large circular pavement that adorned the floor of Henry III's chapel, has been the source of considerable discussion regarding its structure, manufacturing technique and date. This paper, however, offers a new perspective by considering the role of the pavement in Henry III's chapel as a meditational tool. Analysis of its overall design, and each individual tile design, places the circular pavement firmly within the context of medieval cosmological and ecclesiastical understanding of the period. At the same time, it provided Henry with references to some of his favourite themes and his own progress through life. This fusion of ideas and concepts makes the King's chapel pavement a significant part of the medieval renaissance then taking place.

Key words: Clarendon Palace; circular pavement; meditational tool; Henry III; Elias of Dereham

Introduction

When the Clarendon Palace site was excavated by Tancred Borenius in the 1930s, quantities of inlaid medieval tiles and their pavements were some of the most significant finds. Since then, together with an associated tile kiln, they have been the subject of considerable investigation and speculation. This has continued since their removal and reassembly at the British Museum, in the mid 1960s, by Elizabeth Eames. The date of the circular pavement from the King's Chapel has been the source of much debate due to the ambiguity of the associated documentation, from the 1230s and 1240s. This issue will be considered in this paper with regard to the date's relevance for the significance of the pavement, and its location in Henry III's own chapel.

Little, if anything, has been done to consider whether the circular pavement had any relevant underlying symbolism for Henry III, with his liking for such themes as the Tree of Jesse, and the Wheel of Fortune.[1] Initially such concepts appear to be totally alien to the design of the pavement, but this paper will attempt to show that this idea should be reconsidered.

The Design

Probably Eames's most significant contribution to understanding the structure and, therefore, the overall design of the pavement was her identification of construction marks on the backs of the green tiles forming the successive series of circular bands.[2] Assuming these to be correct it then follows that there was a particular sequence for each decorated tile within the pavement. Once the green bands were fixed, the sizes of the rows between ensured the patterned tiles were assembled in the correct sequence. That there is a correct order is immediately apparent to the viewer; there is a cohesiveness and overall balance to the design, apparently unlike anything seen in comparable circular pavements elsewhere. (See Figure 3.1) Apart from the King's Chapel pavement, other circular pavements give an impression of tile carpets comprising 'busy' overall patterns, with little clear design or cohesion, appearing instead to have been constructed on the whim of either the tilers or the patron.[3]

During the twelfth and early thirteenth centuries there was an upsurge in mathematics and science, with concepts and ideas being brought back to England via the writings of various European scholars. Amongst these, Adelard of Bath (*c.*1080–1150) was a key figure in the development of the scientific movement in England during the twelfth century, culminating in the work of Robert Grosseteste (d.1253) in the early thirteenth century.[4] Adelard introduced

[1] Tancred Borenius, "The Cycle of Images in the Palaces and Castles of Henry III," *Journal of the Warburg and Courtauld Institutes* 6 (1943): 40–50.

[2] Tom Beaumont James and Anne M. Robinson, *Clarendon Palace: the history and archaeology of a medieval palace and hunting lodge near Salisbury, Wiltshire*, Reports of the Research Committee of the Society of Antiquaries of London 45 (London: Society of Antiquaries and Thames and Hudson, 1988), 139–40.

[3] Christopher Norton, "Thirteenth-century Tile Pavements in Anjou," in *Anjou, Medieval Art, Architecture and Archaeology*, ed. John McNeill and Daniel Prigent, British Archaeological Association Conference Transactions 26 (Routledge: Leeds, 2003), 210–27; Elizabeth Eames, *English Medieval Tiles* (London: British Museum Press, 1985), 50–54; Elizabeth Eames, *English Tilers* (London: British Museum Press, 1992), *passim*.

[4] Charles Burnett, "Bath, Adelard of (*b.* in or before 1080? *d.* in or after 1150)," *Oxford Dictionary of National Biography* (2004), accessed 14 July, 2018, http://www.oxforddnb.com/view/article/163.

Figure 3.1: The reconstructed segment of the Clarendon pavement in the British Museum. Courtesy of the Trustees of the British Museum.

the system of Arabic numerals into England, and wrote various versions of Euclid's *Elements*, forming the basis of standard mathematical texts. Another influential figure was John of Tynemouth (*fl.* early thirteenth century) who not only updated Adelard's *Euclid*, but also produced an advanced work, based on Archimedes' calculations, relating to the volumes and surfaces of cones, cylinders and spheres. His work was widely disseminated and referred to by Grosseteste, Roger Bacon, and Gerard de Bruxelles amongst others, well into the fourteenth century.[5] There is a strong possibility that this man, John of Tynemouth, was the same person versed in canonical law who, before his death in 1221, was part of Hubert Walter's household during the late 1190s.[6]

Since these men either studied or travelled in Europe it seems impossible that with their interest and skill in mathematics, they would not have come into contact with Leonardo Fibonacci (*c.*1170–*c.*1240) at Pisa, and/or his work. Fibonacci was considered to be the greatest mathematician of the age and the aesthetics of his discoveries still engage and fascinate today. Among the derivatives of his work on numerical sequencing is the beautiful logarithmic spiral, also known as *spira mirabilis*.[7] The mathematician Jakob Bernoulli (1654–1705) was so entranced by the spiral that he asked for it to be engraved on his tombstone.[8]

Running through these mathematical developments, from the time of Pythagoras and Euclid, was the notion of perfect proportions and the *Golden Section*, or *Divine Proportion*, which was exemplified in Greek art and architecture. The Parthenon is the most famous example, the length, breadth and height of which are in the proportions/ratios of the golden section.[9] Linked to Fibonacci's sequence work

[5] Wilbur R. Knorr, "Tynemouth, John of (*fl.* early 13th cent.)," *Oxford Dictionary of National Biography* (2004), accessed 14 July, 2018, http://www.oxforddnb.com/view/article/52685.

[6] Knorr, "Tynemouth, John."

[7] H.E. Huntley, *The Divine Proportion: a study in mathematical beauty* (New York: Dover Books, 1970) 156–76; D'Arcy Thompson, *On Growth and Form* (Cambridge: Cambridge University Press, 1969), 172–88; Mary Carruthers, *The Experience of Beauty in the Middle Ages* (Oxford University Press, Oxford, 2013), 195–96.

[8] Huntley, *The Divine Proportion*, 168.

[9] Huntley, *The Divine Proportion*, 63.

(known as the Fibonacci numbers) and the logarithmic spiral, this is the proportion for an aesthetically pleasing appearance and balance, which has the ascribed value of *phi* (ϕ). Crudely described this is a proportion of approximately two thirds between two related units of measurement, but usually given a value of 1.618 or the related 0.618, according to how the ratio is expressed. Like π, it has the fascination of leading to an apparently endless calculation.[10] Foster points out that classical masons approximated the golden section/proportion by using lengths of 12 and 17 Roman feet to give a proportion of 0.67, or two thirds.[11] Fibonacci's numbers and the related spiral can be found in numerous places in nature; the spiral of a snail's shell, the uncurling fern frond and the breaking waves on a beach, all reflect to a greater or lesser degree, either in part or in full, the aesthetics of geometric curves and proportions. Eames appears to have appreciated the aesthetic appeal of the individual tile designs of the circular pavement, when she referred to their 'beautiful curves'.[12]

There were, however, other considerations for design and interpretation during the medieval period. These were related to the cosmological understanding and visual interpretation of the various levels of being, ranging from the four basic elements of earth, fire, water and air, to the angelic host and the Holy Trinity. Isidore of Seville (560–636) was one of the earliest scholars who tried to explain geographical and cosmological theories in an easily understood format. He used a series of concentric circles (*rotae*) in his attempts to harmonise the contemporary understanding of the world, the heavens, classical and biblical knowledge. One recurring theme was the relationship of the cosmos to the world, and the four elements. The elements became symbolically represented in various ways; most significantly as a simple world map with an inferno within the earth, the great sea surrounding the world and the four winds of the air (eight or 12 winds were also used) issuing from the various compass points. These links between the cosmos and elements were important since they were believed to be responsible for ruling various aspects of people's lives, as well as their temperaments, and the qualities of plants suitable for use as food or medicine.

These circular formats were applied to a variety of teaching situations and the 'wheels of Isidore' became used in monastic schools as visual memory devices, which the students were expected to familiarise themselves with and remember – hence 'learning by rote'.[13] The roti, sometimes called 'rose' diagrams, continued to be used as a visual means of explanation for the great cycles of the stars, sun, moon, winds, seasons, and the life of man, for several hundred years and continued to be widely employed during the scientific and mathematical renaissance referred to above.[14]

Huntley expresses some of the reasons for the aesthetic appeal of geometry and, by inference, how that may have influenced the use of roti:

> There is a sensuous pleasure to be derived from geometry. One of the gentle satisfactions enjoyed by all our ancestors, which must have left its mark on the unconscious mind, is the smooth sweep of the eye along the many quiet curves found in Nature. The smoothness of their contours is associated with the ease and comfort of the eye's muscular effort. Jagged and jerky lines have been shown by psychologists to produce an opposite mental effect. The curves that the human gaze has followed for a million years include the sea horizon, the skyline of the rolling downs, the rainbow, the meteor track, the parabola of the waterfall, the slingshot and the arrow, the arcs traced in the sky by the sun and the crescent moon, the flight of a bird and many others.
>
> Such purely sensuous pleasure is an ingredient of the aesthetic joy found in the geometry of the circle, the ellipse and other conic sections . . .[15]

Thus, the concentric circles of the King's Chapel pavement may be likened to Isidore's roti, but there are other aspects to its appeal as well. The designs comprise a series of stylised plants using the natural curves and spirals of Fibonacci, helping to induce the feeling of serenity referred to by Huntley. Carruthers has found that trees and roti were symbols commonly used for meditation, in the monastic tradition, moreover these cohesive artistic designs (such as the King's Chapel pavement) were intended to lead the viewer on, in a series of meditational steps.[16] If these ideas are accepted together with Norton's finding that these circular pavements were sited in liturgically significant areas, then the Clarendon pavement's design may have been intended not only as an impressive novelty, as stated by Eames, but as a means of invoking a feeling of peaceful spirituality and meditation in the viewer as well.[17]

Circular pavements can be compared with the great rose windows, with their wheel like traceries, which were being incorporated into medieval cathedrals and monasteries at this time. Many of these windows demonstrate the

[10] Huntley, *The Divine Proportion*, 23–57.

[11] Richard Foster, "The Context and Fabric of the Westminster Abbey Sanctuary Pavement," in *Westminster Abbey: the cosmati pavements*, ed. Lindy Grant and Richard Mortimer (Andover: Ashgate, 2002), 55.

[12] Elizabeth Eames, "Further Notes on a Thirteenth-Century Tiled Pavement from the King's Chapel, Clarendon Palace," *Journal of the Archaeological Association* 35, 3rd series (1972): 73.

[13] Naomi Reed Kline, *Maps of Medieval Thought* (Woodbridge: the Boydell Press, 2001), 13–20; Mary Carruthers, *The Book of Memory: a Study of Memory in Medieval Culture* (Cambridge: Cambridge University Press, 2009), 330–31.

[14] Some roti, known as volvelles, were constructed with the circles rotating around one another, producing something akin to an analogue computer. The Persian polymath Al-Biruni is usually credited with their invention. A. Vibert Douglas, "Al-Biruni, Persian Scholar, 973–1048," *Royal Astronomical Society of Canada Journal* 67 (1973): 209–11.

[15] Huntley, *The Divine Proportion*, 86.

[16] Mary Carruthers, *The Craft of Thought: meditation, rhetoric and the making of images, 400–1200* (Cambridge: Cambridge University Press, 2000), 200; Carruthers, *The Experience of Beauty*, 54.

[17] James and Robinson, *Clarendon Palace*, 152.

importance of mathematical proportion and their links to the wind rose by their division into eight or 12 sections.[18] Other themes between different features could be linked through the mathematics of the buildings.

A definite mathematical link has been shown to exist between the west rose window in Chartres cathedral and the labyrinth in the floor below, matching them in size and position as well as linking their represented themes of the Last Judgement and each individual's journey through life to attain paradise.[19] The labyrinth dates from *c.*1200 whilst the rose window dates from 1215, indicating that the window was sited in the west wall with the intention of matching the size and position of the labyrinth.

Apart from the obvious physical similarity to the *rotae* and rose windows, are any potentially mathematical proportions exhibited by the design of the Clarendon pavement? Are there any indications that mathematics played any part in the design? Eames pointed out that although the individual tile designs did not appear to be particularly imaginative, great care was taken in their execution. Each design is well drawn and symmetrical about a central axis, with the 'beautiful curves', as previously suggested, attributable to logarithmic spirals.[20] Figure 3.1 conveys an impression of expansion and dominance centred around tiles six and seven (below, Figures 3.12 and 3.13).[21] This is confirmed by comparing the heights of the decorated tiles in each concentric ring excluding the debated tile 1 of the innermost circle, as shown in Table 3.1.

The difference in size is confirmed by the measurements shown in Table 3.1 with tiles six and seven being significantly taller than any other tiles, number six being marginally the largest of all. Comparison of the ratio between the total heights of all eight decorated tiles and their dividing green bands, with the total heights of the first five tiles and their dividing green tiles gives 1797:1116 = 0.62 i.e. the value of *phi*, the mathematical ratio employed by architects and artists to provide a pleasing aesthetic balance to their work.

It seems very probable that the green bands themselves are a key element in understanding the pavement and these initial measurements, and calculations, are just the first clue. The green bands divide the pavement into nine concentric circles, excluding the inscription. Such a division can be reasonably linked to the earth-centred astronomy of the period, which proposed that the visible planets (including the sun and moon) moved around the earth, within a series of concentric spheres.[22] An eighth sphere carried the fixed stars on its inner visible surface and the outermost ninth sphere, or *primum mobile*, provided the force, or energy, to drive the entire system. The circular 2D representation of such a 3D system had, of necessity, to be a cross-section. So the possibility now exists that the nine green bands themselves represent an aspect of medieval systems of belief and understanding.[23] If the green bands represent the spheres around the earth with only the inner surface visible from the earth then the upper white border on the decorated tiles forms a 'lining' to each green ring which can be construed as a reference to the inside of each sphere/ring. Similarly the ninth, and last, green ring is provided with both a white inner and a white outer border.[24] Was this to mark it out as being the *primum mobile* of the whole system producing not only an influence on all the other spheres within itself, but also everything that lay beyond?

As already seen, the calculation comparing the radii of the circles containing tiles six and nine (see the solid white radii in Figure 3.2) including the green bands, gives a result of 0.62 the value of *phi*.[25] Therefore there is an overall balanced and cohesive design to the pavement, with tiles six and seven playing a significant role within that design. When a third calculation applied *phi* (using 0.62 as its value) to the overall radius of the pavement, this falls towards the top of tile six (see broken white line radius in Figure 3.2).

Viewing the computer-generated diagram of the pavement reconstruction, by Alejandra Gutiérrez (Figure 3.2), the significance of tile six becomes even clearer. Its bold uncluttered decoration immediately attracts the eye, particularly being set in its key position linked to *phi*. This focal point of the Golden Section was used for significant features, usually in classically constructed architecture or art. Assuming that this is the case and the location of the sixth tile is significant, two questions arise – why should the location of the tiles, and by inference their sequence, be important? Who would/could have designed it?

Is there a purpose to the pavement's design?

Helen Dow made the case for the actual circular shape of rose windows as having a number of Christian meanings for the medieval viewer. The first was the eye of God, denoting an omnipresent deity, the second was a representation of the word of God, which could be linked to some of the images contained within the window. This latter symbolism had connotations linked to the earlier Wheel of Fortune.[26] Her final suggestion is

[18] Helen J. Dow, "The Rose Window," *Journal of the Warburg and Courtauld Institutes* 20 (1957): 258–60.

[19] Malcolm Miller, *Chartres Cathedral* (Andover: Pitkin Publishing, 1996), 18.

[20] Eames, "Further Notes," 73.

[21] Numbering starts from the centre, excluding the uncertainly identified central area. See James and Robinson, *Clarendon Palace*, 141. The first tile band is, therefore, the only cursive pattern in the pavement, comprising a series of linked spirals.

[22] In a similar way to the impression received by a viewer in a planetarium.

[23] Dante (1265–1321) used a similar format of concentric rings in his *Divine Comedy*, taking his travellers through various levels of existence in hell, purgatory and paradise.

[24] The outer border is provided by the lower white border on the lettered tiles.

[25] Foster, "The Westminster Abbey Sanctuary Pavement," 55.

[26] Boethius in the sixth century first suggested the concept of Fortuna's Wheel, but it does not appear to have been visually represented until the eleventh century. Ernst Kitzinger, "World Map and Fortune's Wheel: a medieval mosaic floor in Turin," *Proceedings of the American Philosophical Society* 117, no. 5 (1973): 362.

Table 3.1

Tile number	Height in ⅓ scale drawing	Height calculated from ⅓ scale drawing	Height recorded in British Museum catalogue
2	32 mm	96 mm	96 mm
3	45 mm	135 mm	138 mm
4	40 mm	120 mm	121 mm
5	41 mm	123 mm	122 mm
6	59 mm	177 mm	177 mm
7	58 mm	174 mm	174 mm
8	54 mm	162 mm	162 mm
9	38 mm	114 mm	114 mm
Single green tile			77 mm *(measured by author)*

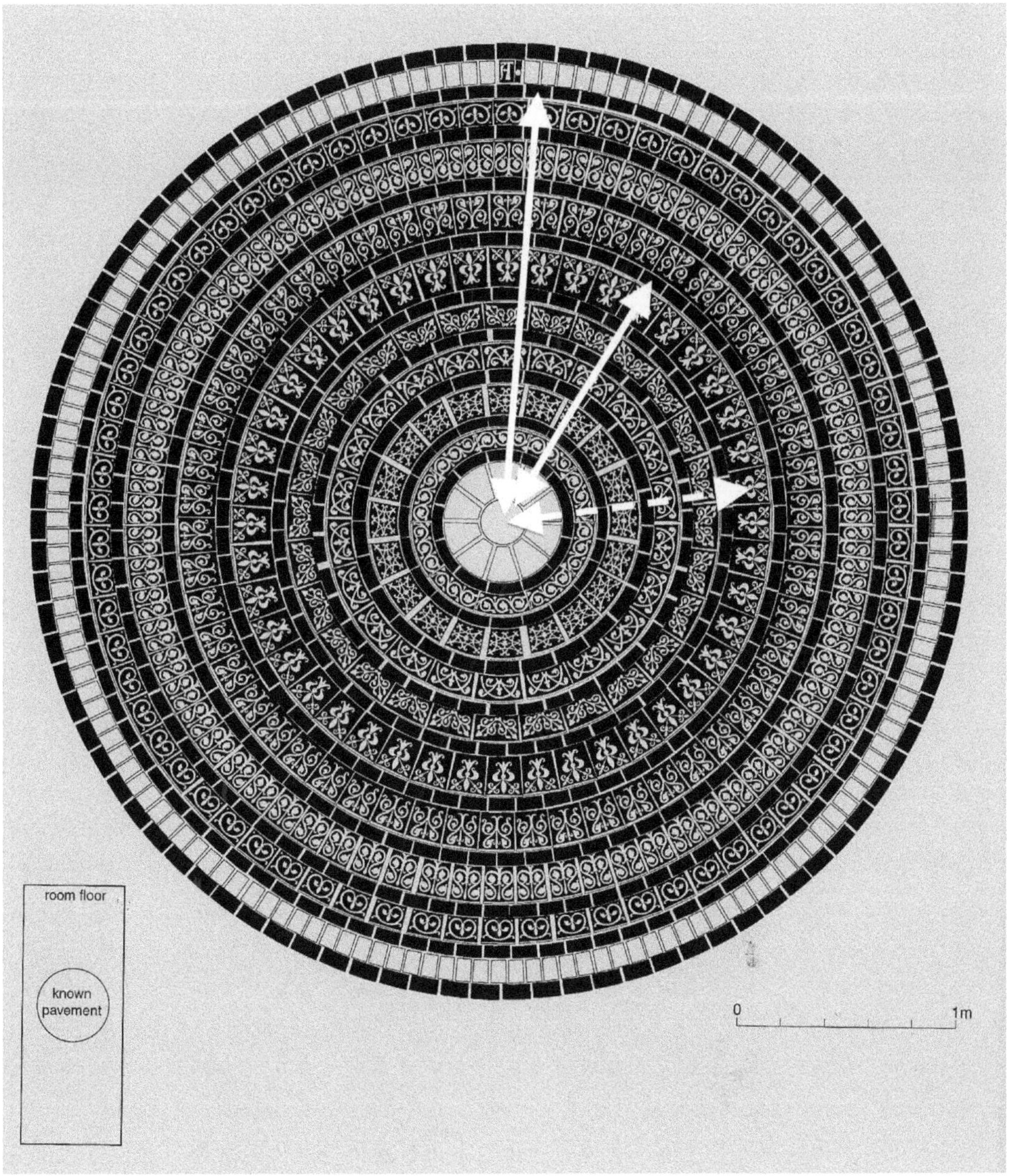

Figure 3.2: Reconstruction of the circular pavement showing the radii used in calculations. Figure: Alejandra Gutiérrez, with radii added by M. South.

the use of small oculi, which may or may not have been glazed windows, but could have been simply small round recesses, as 'guards' to doorways. This, she suggests, is related to the all-seeing God who will see you on your way through the door into a potentially unknown future. Although apparently coming from a Christian perspective, Dow does make the link between earlier imagery and how it was overlain by Christian interpretations.[27] The suggested link with the Wheel of Fortune is more fully explored by Kline, as is the circle itself, the two ultimately becoming conflated into ideas of human life and the Day of Judgement.[28]

Henry III's liking for Fortune's Wheel may have arisen from these other interpretations associated with the wheel's imagery. He requested it should be painted at Winchester Castle in 1235–36, and at Clarendon in 1247. Even more popular was the Tree of Jesse, which had been commissioned for the Queen's apartments at Windsor, in 1236, the year of their marriage; been embroidered on a cope which Henry offered to St Peter's church at Westminster in 1245; painted in the hall at Clarendon in 1247, and finally added to the Painted Chamber at Westminster in 1259.[29] Whether by intention or common usage, Watson believed that the Jesse Tree ultimately became conflated with the Tree of Life by the thirteenth century; an evolution already taking place by the late twelfth century as shown by the tympani over the church doors at Dymock (Figure 3.3) and St Mary's Kempley, in Gloucestershire, both dating from the 1190s.[30] Coincidentally Michell points out that in Hebrew mysticism the number calculated for the Tree of Life is 1,625, which seems to bear a curious similarity to the value of *phi*, 1.618.[31] Henry III's enthusiasm for the Tree of Jesse/Life would make the use of a symbolic tree and its lifecycle an acceptable theme, for the circular pavement, in his private chapel.

At the same time Fortune's Wheel was changing its dynamic to become linked not only with the changing fortunes of an individual's life circumstances, but also the stages of development and decline throughout life. Thus, there were four main phases; the learning and attainment achieved in childhood and adolescence towards the goal of full manhood and strength, followed by waning powers, and eventually decrepitude and death, at the end of the cycle. By the late thirteenth century and early fourteenth century this had developed into a wheel with Christ's head at the hub and as many as 10 different ages of man, representing an individual's life – including death and burial as two separate stages. St Mary's Church at Kempley shows a fourteenth-century depiction of such a design (Figure 3.4), which is almost identical to another in the De Lisle Psalter held in the British Library (Figure 3.5).[32]

The overlaying of the earlier Fortune's Wheel with a Christian meaning appears to have had little influence on the continuing concept of an individual's progress through life, apart from the inclusion of his progress into the eternal realms after death.

However, floor decoration was problematic because representations of the Holy Family or saints were only acceptable on walls, windows and ceilings, having been banned from floors in 427 C.E., by the Byzantine emperor Theodosius II, for fear of their defilement by the passage of feet. In the twelfth century St Bernard of Clairvaux protested forcefully about images of saints and angels being ground underfoot and spat upon.[33]

Church designers, therefore, were presented with the problem of trying to produce church interiors conveying a message, or series of messages, whilst ignoring one of the largest surfaces at their disposal. Therefore, it became more usual to adorn floors with images representing country life, the world of nature, and/or the zodiac, as being sufficiently neutral to be acceptable. A medieval floor in St Salvadore Church, Turin, dating to the second half of the twelfth century, appears to demonstrate how a circular design in front of the altar could incorporate not only a world map (another of Henry III's artistic choices), but also Fortune's Wheel and a wind rose showing the characteristics of the eight principal winds.[34] Within many of these various roti the central position was occupied by the world, frequently using the T-O format developed by Isidore of Seville. The O was the Great Ocean encircling the world, while the T represented the Great Sea that divided the known continents from one another (Figure 3.6).[35]

The concentric circles of the Clarendon pavement can be equated with the similar circles of the teaching roti, and can be shown, like some other roti, to correspond with the number of concentric spheres believed to make up the universe. At the same time the 'safe' images of stylised plants were acceptable as suitable designs for a floor within a liturgical setting, but was that all they represented? This writer suggests that it was not, and the overall composition represented some of the themes that Henry III had ordered not only for Clarendon Palace, but other royal buildings as well.

[27] Dow, "The Rose Window," 248–97.
[28] Kline, *Maps of Medieval Thought*, 10–48.
[29] James and Robinson, *Clarendon Palace*, 13–16; Borenius, "Cycle of Images," 47, 49; *Calendar of Liberate Rolls* [CLR] 1240–1245 (London: HMSO, 1930), 20 March 1245, 294.
[30] Arthur Watson, *The Early Iconography of the Tree of Jesse* (Oxford: Oxford University Press, 1934), 52–54; Kline, *Maps of Medieval Thought*, 74.
[31] John Michell, *The Dimensions of Paradise: Sacred Geometry, Ancient Science and the Heavenly Order on Earth* (Rochester: Inner Traditions, 2008), 204.
[32] British Library (BL) MS Arundel 83 II, f.126v, c.1310.
[33] Kitzinger, "World Map and Fortune's Wheel," 344–45, 356, 358; Christopher Norton, "The Luxury Pavement in England before Westminster," in *Westminster Abbey: the cosmati Pavements*, ed. Lindy Grant and Richard Mortimer (Andover: Ashgate, 2002), 17.
[34] Borenius, "Cycle of Images," 46, 49; Kitzinger, "World Map and Fortune's Wheel," 354–55. Henry III's inclusion of the 12 months of the year as another motif again underlines his interest in the cyclical aspects of life.
[35] Kline, *Maps of Medieval Thought*, 13–18.

Figure 3.3: Tympanum at Dymock church representing the Tree of Life. Photograph: M. South.

Figure 3.4: Wheel of life in St Mary's church at Kempley showing 10 stages in the life of man. Photograph: M. South.

Figure 3.5: De Lisle psalter, Ten Ages of Man with the four stages from Fortune's Wheel, in the outside corners. British Library Board. C13385–26. Arundel 83, f.126v.

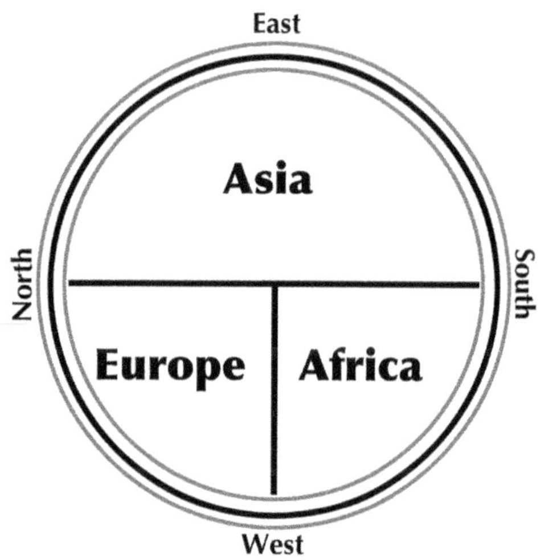

Figure 3.6: Diagrammatic representation of the T-O world map of Isidore of Seville. Figure: K. South.

The tile decorations and their potential symbolism

The loss of the two central tile designs of the pavement is unfortunate as these could be the key for interpreting the whole composition. It may be reasonable, however, to assume that there was a central circular tile, which could have represented the earth. The designs for each tile radiating from the centre will be discussed individually. Although the numbering sequence includes the debated first tile, this will not be considered here.

Tile 2

This is the only cursive pattern in the pavement (Figure 3.7). By using a creeping, twining plant stem, the design creates an impression of a series of waves, entirely encircling the two unknown central tile designs. Is this a symbolic reference to the Great Ocean surrounding

Figure 3.7 Tile 2 of the King's Chapel Pavement. Courtesy of the Trustees of the British Museum.

the earth, or perhaps 'Water' as one of the four classical elements? If it is assumed that the central round tile was 'Earth' itself, as one of the classical elements then the possibility exists that Tile 2, with its cursive pattern, does represent both 'Water' and the Great Ocean.

Tile 3

Figure 3.8, together with tile 4 (Figure 3.9), appears to be one of the designs exclusive to the Clarendon site with no replicas or derivatives apparently extant elsewhere at present.[36] The open pattern initially appears to have no particular significance. However, the inclusion of the central marker joined to the curves around it, terminating in eight points towards the periphery of each tile is suggestive of some of the eight wind compass designs already noted, albeit contained within a distorted rectangle rather than within a circle. If this should be the case – and it must be a conjectural supposition – the difficulty of making such a complex tile stamp, which had little or no versatility, would almost certainly preclude its subsequent inclusion in a tiler's sample book. Its significance exists in the specific production for this pavement, suggesting it had a particular meaning within this context. This writer suggests there are two linked interpretations for this design one being the representation of the eight winds or 'Air', the fourth element. There is, however, a second possibly more relevant interpretation of this tile design, as a simplified depiction of Hugh de St Victor's (1096–1141) ekphrasis of the Ark. He envisaged Noah's Ark as a central square with cross arms dividing an outer series of squares (similar to the concentric circles of a windrose) into four quadrants containing the winds. Hugh, however, does not stop there; his is a three-dimensional depiction. He imagines the Ark to be covered, as if by a cloth, and now the central square is pulled upwards into a column, drawing the cloth upwards with it, whilst remaining attached to the periphery. This central column sprung from the Ark now signifies the

[36] Russel suggests that itinerant tilers carried a sample book of designs, to show prospective customers. The 'samples' may have comprised the actual stamps and this pattern is so complex and fragile to produce, with little opportunity for integration with other patterns at other sites. i.e. it loses its relevance when taken out of context; therefore, there was little incentive to reproduce the necessary stamp for its replication. The same can be argued for Tile 4, which can neither be used as part of a two or four tile design, nor as a cursive pattern. Andy Russel, "Report on the Medieval Floor Tiles," in *Romsey Abbey: Report on the Excavations 1973–1991*, ed. I.R. Scott (Stroud: Sutton Publishing, 1996), 122–42.

Figure 3.8 Tile 3 of the King's Chapel Pavement. Courtesy of the Trustees of the British Museum.

Figure 3.9 Tile 4 of the King's Chapel Pavement. Courtesy of the Trustees of the British Museum.

Tree of Life, with a kaleidoscope of images appearing on the surface of the cloth. The whole being intended as a meditational tool.[37]

Tile 4

Comparison with the tympanum from Dymock (see Figure 3.3) leaves little doubt that this tile is intended to represent the Tree of Life. As such, then, it is reasonable to expect it to be associated with a representation of a life cycle, akin to the Wheel of Fortune. In the monastic tradition of the time, images of trees and the associated symbolism with the Tree of Life, were also used to invoke a state of meditation in the viewer. Thus, these two tiles (3 and 4) are intended as aids towards a state of meditation and introspection by using themes from both the monastic and more secular traditions.

Tile 5

From this point onward there is a subtle change in the tile designs and their relationship with each other in the sequence. It is apparent that they represent the life history of one tree, or an individual. Therefore, viewed in terms of a plant's life cycle, as represented on the pavement, this tile (Figure 3.10) can be seen as either a stylised version of the first two leaves produced, by a dicotyledon seed as it germinates and breaks through the soil, or as the joining together of two individuals prior to the production of the next generation.

Tile 6

Figure 3.11 is the tile that falls within the significant mathematical proportion examined previously. Here is a strong and vigorous plant at the peak of its growing powers, producing new strong branches. It is this point of intersection which appears (from the crude estimations

Figure 3.10 Tile 5 of the King's Chapel Pavement. Courtesy of the Trustees of the British Museum.

Figure 3.11 Tile 6 of the King's Chapel Pavement. Courtesy of the Trustees of the British Museum.

[37] Carruthers, *The Book of Memory*, 293–302.

previously noted) to represent the most accurate value for *phi*, potentially the most significant point of the pavement's overall design.

Tile 7

Here the plant has reached full maturity, still actively growing, as shown by the central growing point with its new small leaves (Figure 3.12). The tree is spreading its branches wide, not only continuing to uncurl new leaves, but possibly beginning to bear fruit on the topmost branches.

Figure 3.12 Tile 7 of the King's Chapel Pavement. Courtesy of the Trustees of the British Museum.

Tile 8

The plant has undergone a subtle change (Figure 3.13), the growing tip is no longer producing young leaves and the branches are no longer spreading outwards, but instead are turned inwards, laden with fruit. The plant has come to the end of its natural life cycle, the days of expansion are over, but it has had a rich and productive life.

Figure 3.13 Tile 8 of the King's Chapel Pavement. Courtesy of the Trustees of the British Museum.

Tile 9

Now begins a new phase. A seed promises a new life beyond the old one, with a stylised cross section of a seed (Figure 3.14), showing the new young plant within. The concept of a new beginning is underlined by the two small dots at the bottom of the tile; two small oculi acting as guardians for all those passing through a doorway into a potentially unknown future.[38]

From the forgoing sections it can be seen that the design of the King's Chapel pavement may not have been intended solely as a decorative addition to the chapel. It had the potential not only to remind spectators of the great cosmic forces that shaped their lives, but also reinforced some of Henry III's favourite themes, with a possible reminder to the king of his own mortality. Moreover it exemplified some of his own ambitions; to produce sons to carry on his lineage (are these the strong branches produced at the *phi* point of tile 6?); to extend his realm (the strongly spreading branches of the tree in tile 7); to have a long and fruitful reign (the fruit laden tree of tile 8) and lastly to pass safely into eternity and a new life (the seed and oculi in tile 9). Hugh de St Victor proposed that there was a Scale of Being when the human soul continued to strive and develop through different levels of understanding during the afterlife.[39]

While the role of the tree's life cycle can be seen to be directly applicable to the king, the designs of tiles 3 and 4 are reminders to him to reflect on the significance of the next five tiles i.e. the life cycle, and to consider his own life in the light of it. Henry was not averse to such symbolic abstract designs or esoteric concepts. The Cosmati pavement set before the altar in Westminster Abbey, in 1268, was intended as a depiction of the universe, the *primum mobile*, and provided a calculation to predict how many years before its end.[40] In a similar manner his grandfather, Henry II (1133–89), had an image

[38] Dow, "The Rose Window," 258–60.

[39] Kline, *Maps of Medieval Thought*, 46; 48 n70.

[40] David Carpenter, "Westminster Abbey and the Cosmati Pavements in Politics," in *Westminster Abbey: the cosmati pavements*, ed. Lindy Grant and Richard Mortimer (Andover: Ashgate, 2002), 37–42.

Figure 3.14 Tile 9 of the King's Chapel Pavement. Courtesy of the Trustees of the British Museum.

of an eagle being attacked by its four young painted on a wall in Winchester Castle. The imagery was understood only by the king himself, but when asked, he explained to his courtiers that it was symbolic of his sons' mutiny.[41] Therefore any symbolism represented by the King's Chapel circular pavement may have been appreciated only by Henry III, and the designer.[42]

Carpenter has said that to comprehend the role of mathematics and geometry in the Cosmati pavement, it is also necessary to understand, or at least be aware of, the politics of the time. The role of number patterns was intended not only for esoteric reasons but political power as well, using cosmic patterns and movements as augurs of the future.[43] In other words the question, 'Why was the pavement created?' needs to be answered. While the 'how?' question has received considerable investigation, 'why?' has received very little attention. If such questions should be asked of the Cosmati pavement, then it seems equally important that these same criteria are applied to the Clarendon pavement. It becomes apparent, however, that before 'why' can be considered, the question 'when' must first be addressed, which is one of the most vexed questions relating to the palace.

Dating the Pavement

Norton has extensively researched circular pavements, both in Britain and on the Continent, and considers that England has some of the finest examples pre-dating the 1268 Westminster pavement. He states that the 1240s workshop, probably originating at Clarendon, was the first of a number of similar tiling workshops in England and France, plausibly developing from a common prototype in Normandy.[44] Mostly such pavements were constructed from the two-colour inlaid tiles as seen at Clarendon. Norton and Eames agree on the technique used to produce the tiles, which used a thick white clay paste firmly pressed into a deeply stamped design on each tile. Later versions of the technique used thinner tiles, shallower impressions and a clay 'slip' rather than a clay paste.[45] The thick clay inlay method would have been both painstaking and time consuming.

Reference has already been made to the symmetry of each tile design and their related proportions, within the pavement's design. Such considerations indicate a substantial mathematical ability on the part of the designer. They also underline the care and time taken to produce each tile, not forgetting the importance of the task, being both a royal commission and a religious one, or the novelty of the technique. It is usually understood that the technique was developed in Normandy and arrived in England fully developed. Norton considers that both English and Angevin circular pavements developed from an as yet unknown early French pavement, with Normandy acting as a distribution centre disseminating the technique farther afield, in a similar fashion as the exchanges that were taking place with methods for stained glass decoration.[46] Using his detailed knowledge of the methods employed in England and France, Norton has now come to the conclusion that the Clarendon pavement, probably predates that at Cunault, which is the most similar circular pavement found so far.[47]

Using the evidence from the waster tiles found in it when excavated, Eames deduced that the kiln from the Clarendon site was the one used to fire the tiles for the King's circular pavement.[48] Although this agrees with the kiln's decommissioning in 1244, when it was overbuilt during the construction of the salsary, Norton's conclusions contradict this idea, placing the date of the pavement in the 1230s.[49] It may be that the wasters support Eames's hypothesis for two other circular pavements on the site.[50]

Previously the chapel circular pavement has been dated to the later date of 1244, solely on the strength of an order by the king for 'a pavement of tiles in the King's own chapel and the gallery and the latter to be wainscotted'.[51] However, examination of the small insertion, in Figure 3.2, shows that the circular pavement only occupies approximately

[41] Borenius, "Cycle of Images," 41.

[42] Roger Rosewell, *Medieval Wall Paintings* (Boydell, Woodbridge, 2011), 182–91.

[43] Carpenter, "Westminster Abbey," 42–44.

[44] Norton, "Tile Pavements in Anjou," 227.

[45] Christopher Norton, "The Origins of Two-Colour Tiles in France and in England," in *Terres Cuites Architecturales au Moyen Age,* ed. D. Deroeux, Mémoires de la Commission Départementales d'Histoire et d'Archéologie du Pas-de-Calais 22 (Arras, 1986), 289. James and Robinson, *Clarendon Palace*, 147–52.

[46] Norton, "Two-colour Tiles," 291; Meredith Parsons-Lillich, review of *Early Stained Glass of Canterbury Cathedral c.1175–1220, by* Madeline H. Cariness, *Speculum* 54 (1979), 557.

[47] Norton, "Tile Pavements in Anjou," 227; C. Norton, pers. comm.

[48] Elizabeth Eames, "A Thirteenth-Century Tiled Pavement from the King's Chapel, Clarendon Palace," *Journal of the Archaeological Association* 26, 3rd series (1963): 42.

[49] CLR 1240–45 (London: HMSO, 1930), 223–24.

[50] James and Robinson, 143.

[51] See note 46 above; Eames, "Thirteenth-Century Pavement," 41.

25 per cent of the total chapel floor area. Therefore, the 'pavement of tiles' could refer to another section of the same floor, or even to one of the other chapels on site.[52] Moreover, as shown above, the 1244 order also included a tiled floor for the gallery of the chapel as well as the construction of the salsary, with the removal of the tile kiln. Therefore, it is suggested that the 1244 date can no longer be ascribed to the construction of the circular pavement with any certainty.

By considering the date that the kiln was built, an alternative earlier date is reached for the pavement. Henry III made an order for an 'oven' (*furnum*) to be built in the court/courtyard at Clarendon in June 1237.[53] Before the kiln was overbuilt in 1244, it was situated in the courtyard, and considerable care had been exercised in the preparation of the site for the kiln, with neither time nor expense being spared to ensure the ground was properly prepared.[54] The use of the term '*furnus*' or '*furnum*' (usually translated as 'oven') by the king seems to indicate that he understood this to be a different process from the more usual lime kilns. A lime kiln was referred to as '*rogum*', literally a 'funeral pyre'. Although both used a burning process the two techniques were very different. Pottery and tiles were baked in an oven, but lime was made by building a pile of alternate limestone and wood or charcoal before setting fire to it, so producing the lime used to make mortar.

Henry, with his personal interest in his properties, almost certainly would have been aware of the differences between the two kiln types. This is exemplified in his directions for what appear to be three lime kilns employed in the extensive work ordered in 1244 at Clarendon, including the construction of the salsary and kitchen, when he gave instructions about the lime produced.[55] Therefore, it is suggested that in December 1237, when he gave an order for a roof over his 'oven', he was not referring to a bakery, as has frequently been assumed, but the tile kiln in the courtyard, which was exposed to the severe storms, prolonged rain and high temperatures of 1236–37.[56] The weather seems to have caused damage to several of the roofs at the palace site, if the numbers of roofing repairs can be used as confirmation.[57]

The king possibly had every right to be concerned about the kiln during the winter; tile kilns were not constructed with permanent roofs, the tiles needed to be loaded through the top of the kiln and then a temporary roof made to cover these during the firing.[58] Therefore, an unroofed kiln would be vulnerable to winter weather damage. Extreme wet weather could cause the fabric to become saturated, which would delay use of the kiln in the following spring. The fact that some voussoirs were still plastic when the kiln was removed to the British Museum may indicate that this was an ongoing problem throughout the life of the kiln, and that temperature control may have been unusually difficult on the site.[59] Moreover the existing drain, which appears to have been on the same level as the tile kiln, would have been discharging water from higher up the site, into the area surrounding the kiln, further compounding the damp problems. The water flow, however, from the drain across that section of the courtyard may have been regulated in order to produce an area of ground comprising a chalk/clay mixture suitable to use for drawing out a design, in a similar manner as on a mason's tracing floor.[60] Eames has suggested that wooden templates were cut from a pattern, laid on the flattened tile clay and cut round to produce the required size and shape for each tile.[61] The usual right-angled 'tile formers' would have been useless for this design with the angled sides needed for each tile. Instead the tilers would have needed a full-sized drawn pattern of the pavement to produce either the wooden templates, or the tiles themselves. This would have been necessary to provide them with the correct dimensions to construct each circle of the pavement. Therefore, it seems reasonable to suggest that such a drawing/diagram would have been near the kiln, to prevent any undue distortion of the tiles caused by transportation around the site, while in their unfired state. It is likely, however, that the drawn plan would only have represented a portion of the pavement, perhaps just one quarter of the intended circular arrangement.

During the careful preparation of the kiln site, the ground had been cut into the natural chalk to a depth of approximately one metre (three feet), estimated by the present author from the existing remains of the salsary.[62] Such an arrangement would probably have facilitated loading the kiln, with tilers able to stand on the chalk banks so produced. Unfortunately, these enclosing banks

[52] Tom Beaumont James, and Christopher Gerrard, *Clarendon: Landscape of Kings* (Macclesfield: Windgather Press, 2007), 5. Richardson speaks of similar confusion between the various lodges within the forest, any one of which could be referred to as the 'king's lodge'. Amanda Richardson, *The Forest, Park and Palace of Clarendon c.1200–1650. reconstructing an actual, conceptual and documented Wiltshire landscape*, British Archaeological Reports British Series, 387 (Oxford: BAR Publishing, 2005), ch 3.

[53] CLR 1226–40 (London: HMSO, 1964), 277; Thomas Hudson Turner, *Some Account of Domestic Architecture in England from the Conquest to the End of the Thirteenth Century* (Oxford, 1851), 184. Norton has suggested that it was unlikely this '*furnus*' was the kiln responsible for producing the pavement tiles, although he gives no reason. Following a site visit in 2017 he now accepts that the furnus was the tile kiln excavated and removed in the 1960s. Christopher Norton, "The Decorative Pavements of Salisbury Cathedral and Old Sarum," in *Medieval Art and Architecture at Salisbury Cathedral*, ed. Laurence Keen and Thomas Cocke (London: Routledge, 1996), 103, n.7.

[54] James and Robinson, *Clarendon Palace*, 138.

[55] *Calendar of Close Rolls* [CCR] 1242–47 (London: HMSO, 1916), 168, 198.

[56] "Historical Weather Events," Booty Meteorological Information Source, accessed 15 July, 2018, http://booty.org.uk/booty.weather/climate/1200_1299.htm.

[57] CLR 1226–40, 304.

[58] James and Robinson, *Clarendon Palace*, 131–34.

[59] Peter C. van Geersdale, and Sandra Davison, "The Thirteenth-Century Tile Kiln from Clarendon Palace: its removal and reconstruction for exhibition," *Studies in Conservation* 20 (1975): 159.

[60] This may not be entirely incompatible with the 1930s excavators' suggestion that there might have been both a chalk floor and a subsequent cement floor in this area prior to the building of the salsary. James and Robinson, *Clarendon Palace*, 90.

[61] Eames, *English Tilers*, 11, James and Robinson, *Clarendon Palace*, 139, 157.

[62] James and Robinson, *Clarendon Palace*, 138.

would have increased the retention of moisture within their boundaries, further increasing the potential damp problems of the kiln's structure.

Construction of the King's Chapel took place from 1236, during a period of relative stability in the country, when Henry III was forging and consolidating various political alliances and truces, including the marriages of his two eligible sisters.[63] Apparently thoughts of dynasty and the continuity of life were at the forefront of his mind at this period, especially his own need to provide an heir for his kingdom, and in 1236 he married the thirteen-year old Eleanor of Provence, with their first son, Edward, being born three years later.

As previously noted, Eames showed that the order of the tiles in the pavement was governed by each successive circle of green tiles, and this author has suggested that by controlling the sequence of tile patterns a significant overall design based on the life history of a plant, probably a tree, is produced. Such a theme would be entirely compatible with the king's personal preoccupations with the continuation of the royal dynasty at this time. The significant positioning of the new branches in the Tile 6 design, representing the most accurate value for *phi*, confirms not only the role of the pavement design, but also the importance to Henry III of producing strong heirs/offshoots.[64] In 1246, after the birth of his second son Edmund, he had the story of St Margaret of Antioch, the patron saint of pregnancy and childbirth, painted in his upper chamber, demonstrating his continuing concern for the royal line.[65]

Drawing on the documentary evidence it is possible to produce a chronology for building the chapel and its related kilns, and by inference the making of the pavement. There are several references to wood ordered for 'a certain kiln' when the term used is '*rogum*' suggesting a lime kiln.[66] These agree with a finishing date for the chapel of early 1237, when Henry III ordered the expenses to be paid on 3 January, and a week later on 10 January 1237, he ordered the finishing touches to be completed.[67] It was not until 15 June 1237 that the courtyard oven, '*furnus*', was ordered to be made.[68] It has already been recorded that this was undertaken with great care, so it is unlikely that any firings took place that year, hence the king's concern, on 24 December 1237, that it should be covered during the winter.[69] Therefore, from this evidence the most likely firing period to produce tiles would be 1238, which is compatible with Norton's suggested earlier date for the pavement.

Two pieces of indirect evidence from 1243 seem to show that Henry was pleased with the concept of large circles in his buildings. On 24 April that year he ordered a round window, thirty feet in circumference (9.5 feet diameter), to be made in the hall at Dublin Castle. From the suggested size, this would of necessity have been a rose window. In the following November he ordered new wainscotting at Windsor Castle 'with boards radiated and coloured so that nothing might be found reprehensible in that wainscot'.[70] Assuming that the chapel pavement was the first of such large circular decorations in the royal residences (not forgetting there may have been others at Clarendon palace as well), this evidence indicates that their concept had considerable appeal to Henry, and that the chapel pavement had been completed sometime before 1243.

However, the production of such a pavement would have required an individual with considerable mathematical, artistic and practical skills. The most likely candidate is Elias of Dereham, who was already involved with the construction of the King's Chapel. But did he have the necessary skills and background for such a complex piece of mathematical artistry?

Elias of Dereham (*c.*1165–1245)

There has been considerable debate about Elias of Dereham's true capabilities, mainly due to the ambiguity of Matthew Paris's references to him.[71] Mostly this discussion has centred on whether Elias was an artistic craftsman or a designer only; even his generally accepted role, as architect of Salisbury Cathedral, has been called into question by some.[72] That debate lies outside the scope of this paper, but it should be noted that Carruthers has found that artefacts ranging from diagrams and pictures, through to the architecture of a building, were all considered to be *aide-memoires* in the act of meditation, and therefore craftsmen, artists and designers were held in equal esteem as the producers of these artefacts.[73] In the light of this, there is no ambiguity in Matthew Paris's description of Elias. In the context of this paper, however, more significant are the factors which may have influenced his potential as a designer for the King's Chapel pavement. Eames considered that he had to be the creator

[63] Huw W. Ridgeway, "Henry III (1207–1272)," *Oxford Dictionary of National Biography* (2004), accessed 15 July, 2018, http://www.oxforddnb.com/view/article/12950.

[64] See above.

[65] Borenius, "Cycle of Images," 47. The cult of St Margaret was very popular at this period, despite her having been declared apocryphal in 494 C.E. She was finally suppressed in 1969. Her legend was originally included in *The Golden Legend* (1275), which became a medieval bestseller. It is likely that her story grew out of the turmoil within the early Christian church during the fourth century. Michael Gaddis, *There is no Crime for Those Who Have Christ* (Berkeley: University of California Press, 2005), 29–102.

[66] CCR 1231–1234, 29 July 1234, 486; CCR 1234–1237, 18 June 1236, 279.

[67] CLR 1226–1240 (London: HMSO, 1916) 3 January 1237, 10 January 1237, 251.

[68] CLR 1226–1240, 277.

[69] CLR 1226–1240, 304.

[70] CLR 1242–1247, 23; 24, 136; Turner, *Some Account of Domestic Architecture*, 259–60.

[71] Adrian Hastings, *Elias of Dereham: architect of Salisbury Cathedral* (Much Wenlock: R.H. Smith and Associates, 1997), 11.

[72] Nicholas Vincent, "Dereham, Elias of (*d.*1245)," *Oxford Dictionary of National Biography* (2004), accessed 15 July, 2018, http://www.oxforddnb.com/view/article/37391.

[73] Carruthers, *The Craft of Thought*, 18–22, 199, 232; Carruthers, *The Book of Memory*, 332; Rosewell, *Medieval Wall Paintings*, 182–85.

of both the circular pavement, and the Queen's Chamber pavement, apparently unaware that Elias died in 1245 and therefore could not have been responsible for work in Queen Eleanor's apartments in 1251–52.[74] The Queen's Pavement lacks the flair and overall design of the circular pavement and is more likely to have been composed as a pattern by the tilers themselves.

Elias's early life is uncertain, but it is known that in 1188, he was one of the signatories on the foundation charter for Hubert Walter's new Premonstratensian Abbey in the two men's home village of West Dereham, in Norfolk (Figure 3.15).[75] Elias became part of Archbishop Hubert's coterie during the 1190s, which also included John of Tynemouth, the lawyer, potential mathematician and geometer previously mentioned. From his various administrative duties associated with the archbishop's properties, Elias must already have had, or developed, a logical and probably analytical approach to running Hubert Walter's affairs. This continued throughout his life in all his dealings with the estates of the bishops and the Church, and indicates considerable mathematical ability.

If, as Hastings suggests, Elias studied in Paris he was certain to have been aware of, and possibly visited, some of the great buildings that were being constructed during the approximate period 1180–95, when feasibly he would have been at the incipient University, or its forerunner the Abbey school at St Victor.[76] Whether he attended the early University or the Abbey school, he was certain to have been aware of Hugh de St Victor's theological and mystical teachings. During his time as head of the Abbey school Hugh had been highly influential in building its reputation.

Elias's time on the Continent did not end then, either. After Hubert's death in 1205, Elias became acquainted with Stephen Langton, Archbishop of Canterbury, and during the interdict when Langton had gone to the Continent, Elias seems to have joined Langton's *familia* in France *c.*1209. After their return in 1213, Elias was involved with the political situation between King John and the barons, which produced the Great Charter and the ensuing debacle with the dauphin Louis of France's claim to the English throne.[77] This resulted in Elias's banishment to France again in 1217, this time with Simon Langton, Stephen's brother. Altogether Elias probably spent about 12 years of his life in France and, plausibly, a period in Italy travelling to Rome although there is no evidence that he reached the city.[78]

During these extended periods spent in France it seems reasonable to suggest that Elias would have had opportunities to see some of the developing cathedral architecture there, in particular the labyrinth and rose windows at Chartres Cathedral, observing not only their artistic beauty but their inbuilt mathematical symmetry as well. His interest in such concepts is clearly demonstrated in two wind rose diagrams credited to him, by Matthew Paris. Although one is incomplete, the second bears a striking similarity to the design for the circular pavement at Clarendon (Figure 3.16).[79]

Harvey points out that Elias's influence can be seen in the proportions of Salisbury Cathedral, which are based on strict mathematical principles.[80] His application of mathematics to the chapel design is exemplified by the footprint of the ground floor of the chapel building, the Antioch Chamber beneath the King's Chapel, where the length is twice the breadth (32feet x 16 feet). It should be noted that the overall measurements for the chapel building are 50 feet x 20 feet, such dimensions appearing to be compatible with the architectural fashion for tall thin buildings which was becoming established at this period.[81] However, it may also be worth noting that the length of the Antioch Chamber (approximately 32 feet) harks back to the two thirds formula when compared with the overall length (50 feet) of the whole building.[82]

Elias was pardoned by the pope and returned from Europe to Stephen Langton's household in 1219, not, apparently, to take up his previous position but instead to design and oversee, with his friend Walter of Colchester, the production of a shrine for Thomas Becket at Canterbury.[83] From this time onward Elias became more involved with artistic and architectural projects for Henry III, including Winchester Castle, Salisbury Cathedral and Clarendon Palace.[84] His time appears to have been spent dealing with the finances, overseeing and co-ordinating the many and various activities linked to these tasks.[85] However, he did suggest to Henry that the hall at Winchester could be lightened by inserting two small windows and painting the wainscoting green.[86] It may be significant that much of the

[74] Eames, *Medieval Tiles*, 48–50; Elizabeth Eames, "A Decorated Tile Pavement from the Queen's Chamber, Clarendon, Wiltshire, dated 1250–1252," *British Museum Quarterly* 22 (1960): 34–37.

[75] Hastings, *Elias*, 4.

[76] Hastings, *Elias*, 4–6; Kathleen Major, "The 'Familia' of Archbishop Stephen Langton," *English Historical Review* 192 (1933): 545; Bernard McGinn, *The Growth of Mysticism* (New York: Herder and Herder, 1994), 365.

[77] Hastings, *Elias*, 6–8.

[78] Hastings, *Elias*, 24; Major, "The 'Familia' of Archbishop Stephen Langton," 541.

[79] Hastings, *Elias*, 28, n. 46.

[80] John Harvey and Arthur Oswald, English Medieval Architects: a biographical dictionary down to 1550 (Gloucester: Sutton, 1984), 82.

[81] Henry III's obvious admiration for Louis IX's Sainte-Chapelle in Paris may have stemmed from his appreciation of his own Clarendon chapel, but now seen as taken to its ultimate refinement. The Sainte-Chapelle was consecrated in 1248, so is unlikely to have influenced the Clarendon chapel which had been completed for some years. James and Robinson, *Clarendon Palace*, 9.

[82] It is tempting to suggest that the upper storey King's Chapel could be arranged along similar lines, with the body of the Chapel occupying two-thirds of the floor and the gallery the other third. However, there is no evidence to support this suggestion.

[83] Hastings, *Elias*, 9–10; Major, "The 'Familia' of Archbishop Stephen Langton," 544. Was this to mark the fiftieth anniversary of Becket's death?

[84] Hastings, *Elias*, 24.

[85] Josiah C. Russell, "The Many-Sided Career of Master Elias of Dereham," *Speculum* 5, no. 4 (1930): 381–82; Major, "The 'Familia' of Archbishop Stephen Langton," 545; Hastings, *Elias*, 12–13.

[86] CLR 1226–1240, 202–03.

Figure 3.15. St Andrew's church West Dereham possibly dates from Saxon period, but the first written record is in the 1246 Tax Roll. Photograph: M South.

wainscoting at Clarendon was also ordered by the king to be painted green. The trust placed in Elias's abilities and integrity is summed up by a quote from St Osmund's register that 'the Bishop at that time had confidence in no one else'.[87] Clearly Elias was a talented man whose abilities were not only practical and administrative but artistic as well, even if this was only as a talented and respected amateur.[88]

Elias's involvement with the King's Chapel at Clarendon is well documented, but apart from various orders of trees and fuel for 'a certain kiln', there is little to link him directly with the pavement. Nonetheless, drawing together these various strands of Elias's character and the external influences he had encountered mathematically, artistically and culturally, it seems plausible that he was responsible for the design of the circular pavement. The presence of the construction marks on the tiles making up the green bands suggest that the designer was unlikely to be the tiler who assembled the pavement; i.e. the two were separate. The designer would not need always to be present when the pavement was put together as long as the tilers followed the construction marks. Indeed, Elias was also engaged with the building of Salisbury Cathedral at this period, so would not always be able to spend large amounts of time at Clarendon. Therefore, the tilers would have to be able to produce the pavement with less supervision than might be expected, hence the construction marks. Perhaps there is also another slight clue in Henry's gift of a fallow buck from Merdon Park to Elias in 1236.[89] Was this a token of appreciation for receipt of a special commission – the design of a pavement to adorn the King's Chapel, based on some of Henry's favourite themes, but also very relevant to his personal life? Alternatively, it could equally have been a gift of appreciation for the work done on the building of the chapel itself.

Conclusions

The circular tile pavement in the King's Chapel at Clarendon was designed during a period of English and

[87] Hastings, *Elias*, 13; Major, "The 'Familia' of Archbishop Stephen Langton," 545; Russell, "The Many-Sided Career," 382; A. Hamilton Thompson, "Master Elias of Dereham and the King's Works," *Archaeological Journal* 98 (1941): 1–35, 11.

[88] Harvey and Oswald, *English Medieval Architects*, 82.

[89] Edward Roberts, "The Bishop of Winchester's Deer Parks in Hampshire 1200–1400," *Proceedings of the Hampshire Field Club and Archaeological Society*, 44 (1988): 72.

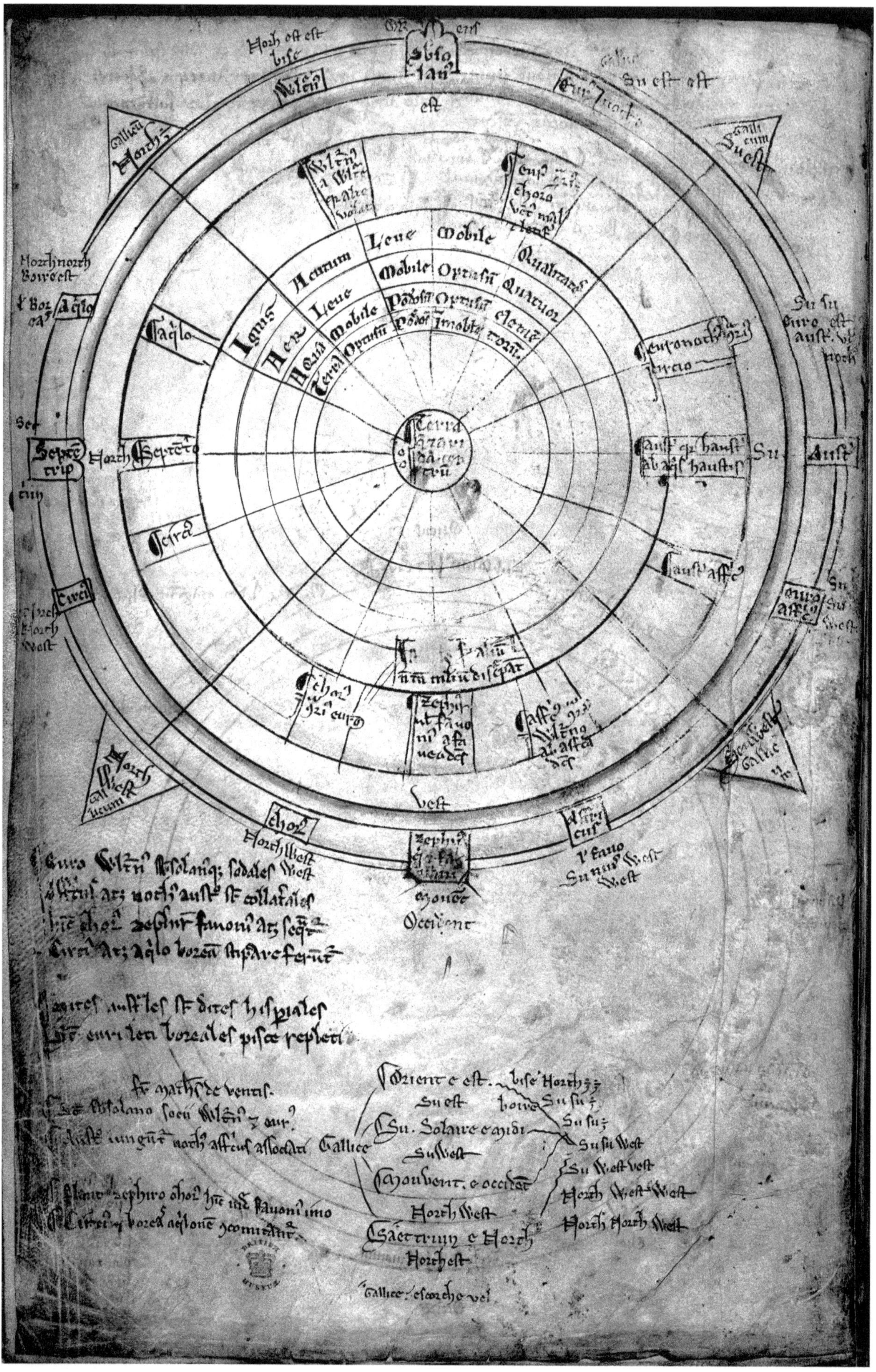

Figure 3.16 Wind rose credited to Elias of Dereham. British Library Board. BL Cotton MS Nero D.I, f.185v.

European intellectual renaissance, including techniques for the development of personal meditation and introspection. This coincided with an era of relative stability in Europe, when Henry III was able to turn his thoughts towards his personal life and marriage. All these factors would plausibly have had an influence on the development of the pavement's overall design.

The pavement demonstrates a cohesion between mathematical beauty, artistic aesthetics, and various symbolic themes of the period; the structure of the universe, the four classical elements, the Ark, Tree of Life/Tree of Jesse and more indirectly, Fortune's Wheel. Moreover, these themes have been woven together in such a way to make them relevant to Henry III's own situation, when thoughts of his need to marry and produce an heir were gaining importance in his life. In addition, its use of meditational images such as trees, roti, and Hugh de St Victor's Ark ekphrasis, the circular pavement of the King's Chapel can be seen to be a powerful tool for furthering spiritual advancement in the viewer. This appears to be in agreement with Norton's finding that circular pavements were located at liturgically significant points. Moreover, it has been shown that the builder of the King's Chapel, Elias of Dereham, was a man who possessed the necessary insights, background, experience and ability to produce such a design.

Pushing the date for the production of the pavement back from the early 1240s to 1238, by linking it to the earliest date for the tile kiln to be in use, means that it just pre-dates the Cunault pavement in France, and may even have had some influence on the latter. Taking its structure with its overall balanced design, linked to the development of mathematical concepts during the period, and the two men, Henry III and Elias of Dereham, responsible for its creation, then the Clarendon circular pavement can be viewed as a significant part of the English medieval renaissance.

Bibliography

Unpublished primary sources

British Library (BL)

BL MS Arundel 83 II. De Lisle Psalter, *c.*1310.

BL Cotton MS Nero DI. Matthew Paris, Liber Additamentorum, 1250-9.

Published primary sources

Calendar of Close Rolls [*CCR*] 1231–1234. London: HMSO, 1905.

CCR 1234–1237. London: HMSO, 1908.

CCR 1242–1247. London: HMSO, 1916.

Calendar of Liberate Rolls [*CLR*] 1226–1240. London: HMSO, 1916.

CLR 1240–1245. London: HMSO, 1930.

CLR 1242–1247. London: HMSO, 1916.

Secondary sources

Beaumont James, Tom, and Christopher Gerrard. *Clarendon: Landscape of Kings*. Macclesfield: Windgather Press, 2007.

Booty Meteorological Information Source. "Historical Weather Events." Accessed 15 July, 2018. http://booty.org.uk/booty.weather/climate/1200_1299.htm.

Borenius, Tancred. "The Cycle of Images in the Palaces and Castles of Henry III." *Journal of the Warburg and Courtauld Institutes* 6 (1943): 40–50.

Burnett, Charles. "Bath, Adelard of (*b.* in or before 1080? *d.* in or after 1150)." *Oxford Dictionary of National Biography* (2004). Accessed 14 July, 2018. http://www.oxforddnb.com/view/article/163.

Carpenter, David. "Westminster Abbey and the Cosmati Pavements in Politics." In *Westminster Abbey: the cosmati pavements*, edited by Lindy Grant and Richard Mortimer, 37–42. Andover: Ashgate, 2002.

Carruthers, Mary. *The Craft of Thought: meditation, rhetoric and the making of images, 400–1200*. Cambridge: Cambridge University Press, 2000.

Carruthers, Mary. *The Book of Memory: a Study of Memory in Medieval Culture*. Cambridge: Cambridge University Press, 2009.

Carruthers, Mary. *The Experience of Beauty in the Middle Ages*. Oxford University Press, Oxford, 2013.

Douglas, A. Vibert. "Al-Biruni, Persian Scholar, 973–1048." *Royal Astronomical Society of Canada Journal* 67 (1973): 209–11.

Dow, Helen J. "The Rose Window." *Journal of the Warburg and Courtauld Institutes* 20 (1957): 248–97.

Eames, Elizabeth. "A Decorated Tile Pavement from the Queen's Chamber, Clarendon, Wiltshire, dated 1250–1252." *British Museum Quarterly* 22 (1960): 34–37.

Eames, Elizabeth. "A Thirteenth-Century Tiled Pavement from the King's Chapel, Clarendon Palace." *Journal of the Archaeological Association* 26, 3rd series (1963): 40–50.

Eames, Elizabeth. "Further Notes on a Thirteenth-Century Tiled Pavement from the King's Chapel, Clarendon Palace." *Journal of the Archaeological Association* 35, 3rd series (1972): 71–5.

Eames, Elizabeth. *English Medieval Tiles*. London: British Museum Press, 1985.

Eames, Elizabeth. *English Tilers*. London: British Museum Press, 1992.

Foster, Richard. "The Context and Fabric of the Westminster Abbey Sanctuary Pavement." In *Westminster Abbey: the cosmati pavements*, edited by Lindy Grant and Richard Mortimer, 49–91. Andover: Ashgate, 2002.

Gaddis, Michael. *There is no Crime for Those Who Have Christ*. Berkeley: University of California Press, 2005.

Hamilton Thompson, A. "Master Elias of Dereham and the King's Works." *Archaeological Journal* 98 (1941): 1–35.

Harvey, John, and Arthur Oswald. *English Medieval Architects: a biographical dictionary down to 1550*. Gloucester: Sutton, 1984.

Hastings, Adrian. *Elias of Dereham: architect of Salisbury Cathedral*. Much Wenlock: R.H. Smith and Associates, 1997.

Hudson Turner, Thomas. *Some Account of Domestic Architecture in England from the Conquest to the End of the Thirteenth Century*. Oxford, 1851.

Huntley, H.E. *The Divine Proportion: a study in mathematical beauty*. New York: Dover Books, 1970.

James, Tom Beaumont, and Anne M. Robinson. *Clarendon Palace: the history and archaeology of a medieval palace and hunting lodge near Salisbury, Wiltshire*, Reports of the Research Committee of the Society of Antiquaries of London 45. London: Society of Antiquaries and Thames and Hudson, 1988.

Kitzinger, Ernst. "World Map and Fortune's Wheel: a medieval mosaic floor in Turin." *Proceedings of the American Philosophical Society* 117, no. 5 (1973): 344–73

Knorr, Wilbur R. "Tynemouth, John of (*fl.* early 13th cent.)." *Oxford Dictionary of National Biography* (2004). Accessed 14 July 2018, http://www.oxforddnb.com/view/article/52685.

Major, Kathleen. "The 'Familia' of Archbishop Stephen Langton." *English Historical Review* 192 (1933): 529–553.

McGinn, Bernard. *The Growth of Mysticism*. New York: Herder and Herder, 1994.

Michell, John. *The Dimensions of Paradise: Sacred Geometry, Ancient Science and the Heavenly Order on Earth*. Rochester: Inner Traditions, 2008.

Miller, Malcolm. *Chartres Cathedral*. Andover: Pitkin Publishing, 1996.

Norton, Christopher. "The Origins of Two-Colour Tiles in France and in England." In *Terres Cuites Architecturales au Moyen Age, edited by D.* Deroeux, Mémoires de la Commission Départementales d'Histoire et d'Archéologie du Pas-de-Calais 22, 256–93. Arras, 1986.

Norton, Christopher. "The Decorative Pavements of Salisbury Cathedral and Old Sarum." In *Medieval Art and Architecture at Salisbury Cathedral*, edited by Laurence Keen and Thomas Cocke, 90–105. London: Routledge, 1996.

Norton, Christopher. "The Luxury Pavement in England before Westminster." In *Westminster Abbey: the cosmati Pavements*, edited by Lindy Grant and Richard Mortimer, 7–27. Aldershot: Ashgate, 2002.

Norton, Christopher. "Thirteenth-century Tile Pavements in Anjou." In *Anjou, Medieval Art, Architecture and Archaeology*, edited by John McNeill and Daniel Prigent, British Archaeological Association Conference Transactions 26, 210–27. Routledge: Leeds, 2003.

Parsons-Lillich, Meredith. Review of *Early Stained Glass of Canterbury Cathedral c.1175–1220, by* Madeline H. Cariness (Princeton: Princeton University Press, 1977), *Speculum* 54, 555–9 (1979).

Reed Kline, Naomi. *Maps of Medieval Thought*. Woodbridge: the Boydell Press, 2001.

Richardson, Amanda. *The Forest, Park and Palace of Clarendon c.1200—1650: reconstructing an actual, conceptual and documented Wiltshire landscape*, British Archaeological Reports British Series, 387. Oxford: BAR Publishing, 2005.

Ridgeway, Huw W. "Henry III (1207–1272)." *Oxford Dictionary of National Biography* (2004). Accessed 15 July, 2018. http://www.oxforddnb.com/view/article/12950.

Roberts, Edward. "The Bishop of Winchester's Deer Parks in Hampshire 1200–1400." *Proceedings of the Hampshire Field Club and Archaeological Society*, 44 (1988): 68–86.

Rosewell, Roger. *Medieval Wall Paintings*. Woodbridge: Boydell, 2011.

Russel, Andy. "Report on the Medieval Floor Tiles." In *Romsey Abbey: Report on the Excavations 1973–1991*, edited by I.R. Scott, Hampshire Field Club Monograph 8, 122–42. Stroud: Sutton Publishing, 1996.

Russell, Josiah C. "The Many-Sided Career of Master Elias of Dereham." *Speculum* 5, no. 4 (1930): 378-87.

Thompson, D'Arcy. *On Growth and Form*. Cambridge: Cambridge University Press, 1969.

van Geersdale, Peter C., and Davison, Sandra. "The Thirteenth-Century Tile Kiln from Clarendon Palace: its removal and reconstruction for exhibition." *Studies in Conservation* 20 (1975): 158-168.

Vincent, Nicholas. "Dereham, Elias of (*d.*1245)." *Oxford Dictionary of National Biography* (2004). Accessed 15 July, 2018. http://www.oxforddnb.com/view/article/37391.

Watson, Arthur. *The Early Iconography of the Tree of Jesse*. Oxford: Oxford University Press, 1934.

4

King Edward I and the Water-Gate at the Tower of London

Jeremy A. Ashbee

English Heritage

Abstract: St Thomas's Tower at the Tower of London, also known as the 'Traitors' Gate', was built between 1275 and 1281, as part of the expansion of the fortress ordered by King Edward I (1272–1307). Known through most of the Middle Ages as 'le watergate', its primary function was to allow people and provisions to enter and leave the fortress by boat, through a gate opening directly onto the river Thames. Above the gate, the building contained a suite of accommodation, often claimed as the apartment of the king himself; these rooms, first shown to the public in 1993 have been re-presented by Historic Royal Palaces, re-opening in 2006. Drawing on an archaeological examination in the early 1990s and more recent documentary research, this article discusses the original configuration of the apartment, the architectural models on which the tower was based, and its place in the evolving royal lodgings at the Tower of London. The evidence from the Tower and comparable royal sites suggests that the planning of royal palaces in the thirteenth century allowed for greater complexity than has hitherto been recognised, and that far from being modern concepts, seclusion and possibly even privacy were valued attributes in the royal residences of the Plantagenet kings.

Key words: Tower of London; castle; palace; hall; chamber; gatehouse; King Edward I

Introduction

At the death of Henry III on 16 November 1272, the Tower of London bore little resemblance to the castle he had inherited 56 years before. Its land area had almost doubled, with expansion towards the north and east, enclosing the former parish church of St Peter ad Vincula and breaking out eastwards beyond the limits of the Roman city. The castle was now ringed by a high stone curtain wall with D-shaped mural towers spaced at regular intervals along its north and east sides. On the western side, facing the city of London, an attempt was made to create an imposing and strongly-fortified gateway, which unfortunately collapsed in 1240, and was never rebuilt.[1] A water-filled ditch ran around the three landward sides of the castle.

Just as at Henry III's other houses and castles, the king had spent large amounts of time and money at the Tower in rebuilding and redecorating his own apartments, here located on the fourth side, then fronting directly onto the river Thames to the south. Henry's reign witnessed the building or rebuilding of all principal elements of the palace: the great hall, the chamber blocks, two large round residential towers (the Wakefield and Lanthorn Towers), the kitchens and parts of the eastern range. In most cases, the buildings themselves survived throughout the Tower's use as a royal residence, and in the case of the Wakefield Tower, down to the present. In other cases, some of the fabric was replaced in later-medieval and Tudor re-buildings but the overall plan of the royal lodgings remained unchanged. Many of the best-known events in the Tower's history, such as the celebrations before the coronations of all kings and queens from the late fourteenth to the mid-seventeenth century, the imprisonment and trial of Anne Boleyn and the confinement of the future Elizabeth I took place in these thirteenth-century buildings.

During the reign of Henry's son Edward I, an important addition was made to the Tower's building stock in the area of the palace. The building also survives today and is now officially known as St Thomas's Tower (see Figure 4.1), though has achieved wider notoriety under the name 'Traitors' Gate'. These names first appear in documents of the sixteenth and seventeenth centuries respectively,[2] and throughout the Middle Ages, the building was known by the utilitarian name '*le Watergate*'.[3] This describes the building's primary function perfectly; it provided a direct entrance into the castle from the river Thames, through which persons and provisions could be brought into the Tower by boat.

Above the gateway on an upper level were residential chambers. Here too, despite a reconstruction in 1532 and

[1] Henry R. Luard (ed.), *Matthaei Parisiensis Monachi Sancti Albani Chronica Majora* vol. 3, Rolls Series (London: Longman, 1876), 80.

[2] For example, The National Archives (TNA) E101 474/12, f3v of *c.*1532; Sir Bernard de Gomme's scheme for adding artillery bastions to the Tower *c.*1666, in Geoffrey Parnell's *The Tower of London*, (London: Batsford, 1993), fig. 57.

[3] The term is usually written as masculine until the 1330s, when *la* begins to predominate. Interpreting this feminisation as an offset to a new militaristic designation of the building would be far-fetched.

Figure 4.1: General view of the Tower of London from the south. Saint Thomas's Tower stands in the left foreground. Since the mid-fourteenth century, a stone wharf has run across the frontage of the building, with a bridge leading to the watergate. Courtesy of Historic Royal Palaces.

a drastic restoration by Anthony Salvin in the 1860s, they still retain substantial fabric from the medieval building. Until the 1990s, the tower was still occupied by one of the fortress's officers and archaeological examination was impossible, but the building has since been vacated, recorded, re-presented and is now open to the public.[4] It is now possible to compare the substantial documentary material from the first construction with new archaeological findings.

News of his accession reached the lord Edward in Sicily, where he was recuperating from the Crusade, but he made a leisurely return through Europe and did not land in England until August 1274.[5] In the meantime, it seems likely that little new work had been carried out at the Tower. Correspondence between Robert Burnell and Walter de Merton, clearly from this period, mentions only maintenance and urges particular care for 'the garden in which my lord takes the greatest pleasure,[6] giving no hint of the building works which the Tower would immediately undergo.[7]

During the first decade of his reign, Edward converted his father's castle into what is substantially the Tower we see today: a concentric fortress with two curtain walls, a deep moat around the perimeter (water-filled until 1843) and two complex entrance gateways including that at the south-west corner, containing two large gatehouses, three drawbridges and a barbican. Though certainly not without precedents in England or Wales, being pre-figured almost a century earlier at Dover or Château Gaillard and only a few years before by the magnificent castle built by Gilbert de Clare at Caerphilly, these works completely altered the appearance and function of the Tower of London. Some idea of the finished effect is given in the description of two Irish friars in 1324: 'and at the edge of this city as you go towards the sea is the most famous and impregnable castle, encircled with two walls, yawning ditches full to the

[4] The first published assessment of this archaeological examination is given in Simon Thurley, "Royal Lodgings at the Tower of London 1216–1327," *Architectural History* 38 (1995): 36–57.

[5] Henry T. Riley (ed.), *Chronica Monasterii S Albani Wilelmi Rishanger, quondam Monachi S Albani et quorundam anonymorum Chronica et Annales Regnantibus Henrico Tertio et Edwardo Primo*, vol. 3 (London: Public Record Office, 1865), 78; Henry R. Luard (ed.), *Flores Historiarum*, vol. 3 (London: HMSO 1890), 43. For the expenses of Edward's journeys through Europe, see TNA, E352/70 rot 2 and E101 350/8.

[6] TNA, SC1 7/46.

[7] Note that the authors of *History of the King's Works* [hereafter *HKW*] postulated that the second curtain had been planned during Henry III's lifetime; Reginald Allen Brown, Howard M. Colvin and Arnold J. Taylor, *HKW*, vol. 2 (London: HMSO, 1963), 722. A factor which may favour this hypothesis is the re-assignment of Master Robert of Beverley from Westminster Abbey to the Tower as early as February 1272: *Calendar of Liberate Rolls, 1267–72* (London: HMSO, 1964), 205. See also Peter Curnow, "Some Observations on the Planning and Construction of the West Curtain at the Tower of London," in *Mélanges d'Archéologie et d'Histoire Médiévales: en l'honneur du Doyen Michel de Bouard* (Geneva: Droz, 1982), 65–74.

brim with water, and every possible device of warfare'.[8] In their execution, the works involved not merely the construction of new masonry walls, but the partial infilling of Henry III's moat and the excavation of another outside it, and most dramatically, the complete reconstruction of the north bank of the river Thames. It naturally entailed an enormous programme of earth-moving to create a new foreshore further to the south of the earlier line, and it was on this newly reclaimed ground that the water-gate was to be built.

Edward I's creation of the new outer ward along the south side (now 'Water Lane') had the effect of leaving Henry III's riverside buildings literally high and dry.[9] There was obviously a clear functional requirement for a river-gate on the new shore-line, to replace Henry III's redundant water-gates, the Bloody Tower and the postern under the great chamber block. This is the building now known as St Thomas's Tower.

The form of the building

The external fabric of St Thomas's Tower (see Figure 4.2) and the archaeological discoveries within the building of the 1990s have each been discussed in print and no detailed description is necessary. However, several detailed points require amplification where they have consequences for reconstructing the building in its late thirteenth-century form.

The evidence of the surviving building has several important limitations for the study of its medieval design. The present timber-framed lodgings over the water-gate and basin are not those of Edward I but a rebuilding carried out in 1532 by James Nedeham, Henry VIII's master-carpenter, before which the medieval timber-framed lodgings were completely dismantled.[10] As a consequence, the volumes of the present rooms do not reflect those of their medieval predecessors. For example, it is clear from the relationship between the timber-framed building and the stone structure of the tower that Edward I's timber lodgings were jettied out northwards over the basin, as the present rooms are not.[11] Nevertheless, despite alterations to the windows and fireplaces, and the almost total re-facing of the exterior by Salvin in the 1860s,[12] the stone screen walls of the west, south and east faces are substantially medieval, at least inside the building. They retain evidence for fireplaces in both the east and west portions of the tower on the first floor, rere-arches for original windows, possible garderobes at both levels, as well as the basic shape of the building standing today: an open-backed basin and dock flanked by archers' galleries, behind a broad flat façade with slender corner turrets facing out into the river. These turrets contain, at both lower and upper levels, hexagonal rooms vaulted with simple chamfered ribs, springing from columnar shafts with moulded capitals and bases. The capitals, all either mutilated or restored in the nineteenth century, are all roughly of the 'three-unit scroll' type typical of the late-thirteenth century; a similarity to other royal works, such as Robert of Beverley's nave at Westminster Abbey, or the chapel in *la Gloriete* at Leeds Castle is likely.[13] These mouldings offer the only potential for detailed stylistic analysis of medieval fabric in the building.

Certain 'lost' elements of the thirteenth-century plan can be recovered by examination of this stone structure. The mural galleries of the lower level contain some evidence for blocked arrow-loops; for example one in the eastern wall of the western gallery is partly cut away by a post-medieval sluice. The width of the opening for the 'Traitors' Gate' remains unaltered (see Figure 4.3), with implications for the layout of the upper rooms; the partitions in the room over the gate must have allowed clearance for its portcullis to rise and fall. The documented 'chamber' and 'hall', described below, were either of equal sizes to either side of a central portcullis room, or else the portcullis was located towards one end of a larger room, with a smaller chamber partitioned-off beyond. Parallels exist for both layouts in contemporary gatehouse architecture.[14]

The positions of several medieval doorways can also be confirmed, and access arrangements reconstructed, at least in outline (see Figures 4.4 and 4.5). There is convincing evidence that the chambers over the basin could be entered from three points: two surviving at the eastern end, either across the bridge from the first floor of the Wakefield Tower or up the spiral staircase from Water Lane. The third entrance, the present main door to the building at its western end has been more altered and its presence as part of the medieval plan rests on medieval documentary and pictorial evidence. In July 1348, Thomas de Northyne provided oaks to rebuild the stairs (also called *oriolum*, a form of covered stairway) of 'the lord king's wardrobe over the water-gate in the Tower', most plausibly in this position.[15] A probable staircase here is shown in both the Orleans Manuscript (as a red brick structure) and

[8] Mario Esposito (ed.), *Scriptores Latini Hiberniae volume four. Itinerarium Symeonis Semeonis Ab Hybernia ad Terram Sanctam* (Dublin: Dublin Institute for Advanced Studies, 1960), 26.
[9] Simon Thurley, *The Royal Palaces of Tudor England* (London: Yale University Press, 1993), 5.
[10] TNA, SP1/70 fol. 112 and E101 474/12 m3r, m4r; Bodleian Library, MS Rawlinson D. 775 fol. 202–1111.
[11] This is clearest in the east room, where the Tudor north wall cuts across the opening of a medieval window in the east wall; Thurley, "Royal Lodgings," especially p.48. Jettying had certainly become part of the London timber-framing tradition by the mid-13th century: John Schofield, *Medieval London Houses* (London: Yale University Press, 1995), 147.
[12] TNA, Work 14/2/1 and 14/2/2.
[13] See Richard K. Morris, "The Development of Later Gothic Mouldings in England, *c.*1250–1400: Part II," *Architectural History* 22 (1979), fig. 16T. There is also similarity to mouldings from other Edward I buildings at the Tower, especially the polygonal capitals of the Byward and Middle Towers; one of the original mouldings (discarded) was recovered from the west arm of the moat adjacent to these towers in the summer of 1996; Graham Keevill, *The Tower of London Moat: archaeological excavations 1995–9* (Oxford: English Heritage, 2004), 102–05.
[14] The symmetrical layout can be seen at Tonbridge, Caerphilly and Beaumaris; Harlech and the Burgess Gate at Denbigh show one larger and one smaller room.
[15] TNA, E101 471/1 m1.

Figure 4.2: Saint Thomas's Tower from the south-east. Courtesy of Historic Royal Palaces.

Figure 4.3: Interior of the rear basin of Saint Thomas's Tower. The timber-framed building on the first floor is a rebuilding of 1532, but the arch that supports it, the stone walling and the main watergate arch (left) are substantially of the late thirteenth century. Courtesy of Historic Royal Palaces.

Wyngaerde's panorama. The possibility that from the first design, the tower could be entered at its west end from Water Lane is useful in identifying the documented 'hall' and 'chamber' within the building.

Previous discussions of the disposition of rooms inside the building have generally involved placing the hall to the east and the chamber to the west.[16] This is based on the presence of a possible garderobe in the western room and on the accepted model that the principal access into the building was *via* the Wakefield Tower, leading first into the eastern room and thence into the more private space to the west. With independent access from the other direction, the western room would have been no more 'private' than the eastern. Most suggestive is the tiny chapel in the turret adjoining the east room, clearly identified by its Purbeck marble *piscina* and *lavabo*.[17] Domestic chapels and oratories appear by convention to have been placed close to chambers more often than halls.[18] The eastern

[16] Parnell, *Tower of London*, 39–40; Thurley, "Royal Lodgings," 48–51.
[17] This also accords with the documentary references to a 'small chapel above the water' and to a 'hermitage' beside the king's chamber, possibly used by '*un poure chapeleyn nostre synur le Roy ffrere Geffrey le Eremyte de la Tour de Londres*'; TNA, C47/3/47 m1 and SC1 30/87.
[18] The clearest documentation comes from the reign of Henry III: *HKW*, 497–98, 675, 758, 808–09, 862, 914, 1013. This placing also holds true for some castles of Edward I's reign, such as Chepstow (Marten's Tower); at others, including Harlech (gatehouse), Goodrich (a largely missing structure over the north range lobby) and the inner ward at Conwy, this is still probable but less certain. The clearest examples

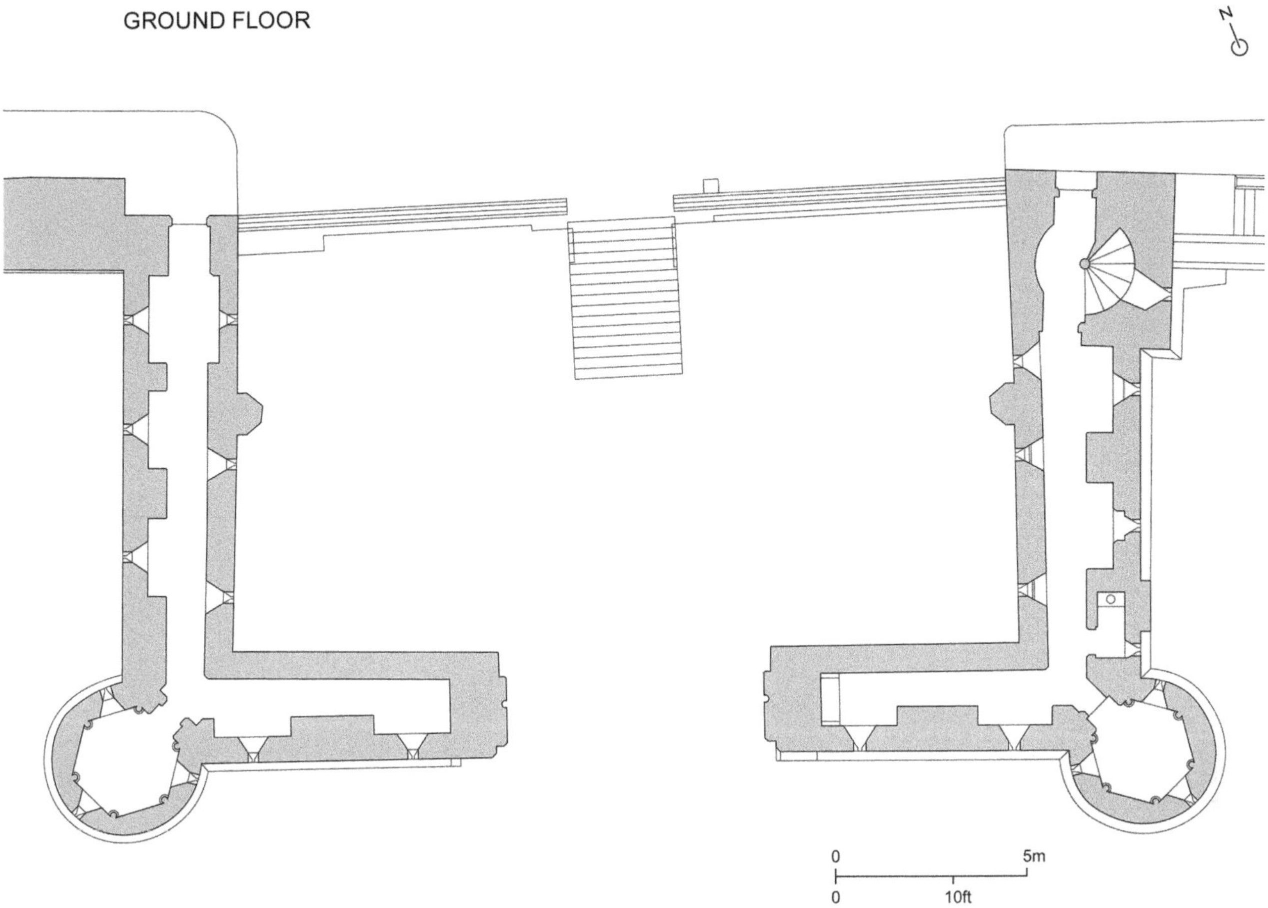

Figure 4.4: Reconstructed ground-floor plan of Saint Thomas's Tower, showing the original form of the building, with a mural passage running around three sides of the water-filled basin. Plan by Carlos Lemos.

room therefore has the better claim to have served as the chamber.

Details of the building mentioned in documentary sources

From 1275 until 1281, the Pipe Rolls and the 'foreign rolls' appended to them describe in some detail the construction of St Thomas's Tower under a variety of names: 'the hall with the chamber above the gate over the water',[19] 'the great chamber facing the river Thames',[20] 'the new hall over the water' and 'the house/building over the water'.[21] Several important pieces of information are missing. Though two viewers of the works, Robert of Beverley and 'Brother John of the Order of St Thomas of Acre', are cited by name, there is no hint at the individual author of the building's design, and these two are never mentioned directly in connection with St Thomas's Tower.[22]

The documents are also silent about important architectural elements, including the basin under the tower, the archers' galleries in its flanks and the supporting arch on its north face, some 62 feet wide and by any standards, an impressive piece of engineering; there are no references to garderobes, one possible mention of a fireplace and little information concerning interior decorations or furnishing. Were it not for the remarkable survival of parts of the building a reconstruction would be impossible, though none of the documentary references contradicts what we can see from the standing fabric, or can reconstruct using historic plans and depictions.

Just as in the present structure, the building described in the Pipe Rolls contained three turrets (on the north-east, south-east and south-west corners) and was built in stone, though with timber-framing 'facing the castle'.[23] It was roofed in

of chapels adjoining halls are Caerphilly and Kidwelly, both in South Wales, from their size more likely to have served for congregational than private domestic worship. The same argument may also hold true for Beaumaris and for the outer ward at Conwy, according to Arnold Taylor's final interpretation; Arnold J. Taylor, "The Town and Castle of Conwy: preservation and interpretation," *Antiquaries Journal* 75 (1995): 339–63, especially 346 and 349.

[19] TNA, E372/120 rot 22.

[20] TNA, E372/121 rot 22.

[21] TNA, C47/3/47.

[22] For the career of Robert of Beverley, see *HKW*, 206–07; Paul Binski, *Westminster Abbey and the Plantagenets: kingship and the representation of power 1200–1400* (London: Yale University Press, 1995), 29–33.

[23] TNA, E372/121 rot 22.

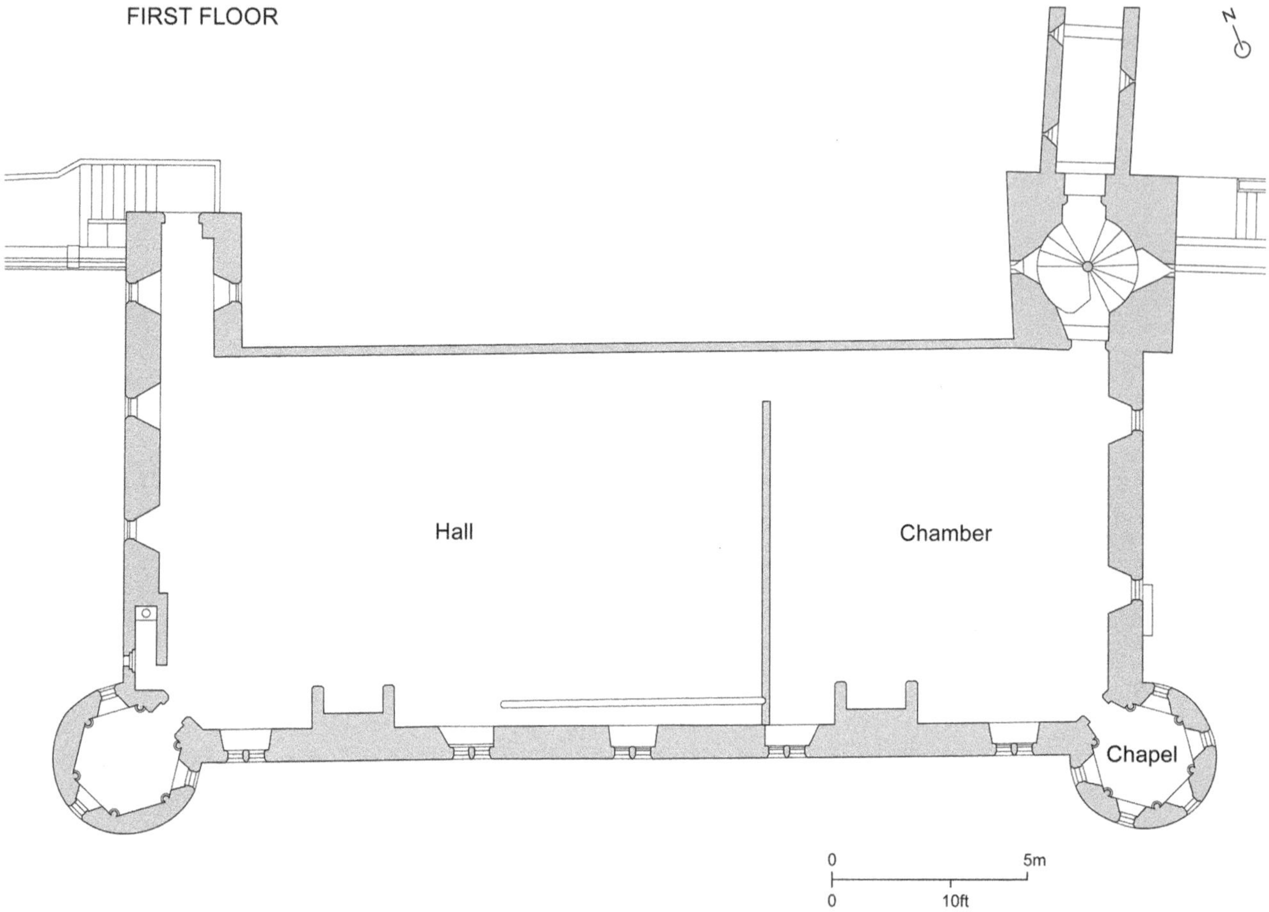

Figure 4.5: Reconstructed first-floor plan of Saint Thomas's Tower, showing the original form of the building. The hall lay to the west, the chamber to the east, served by a small chapel in the south-east turret. Plan by Carlos Lemos.

lead, almost certainly a low-pitched roof, over a ceiling of pine boards.[24] It had a surprisingly high number of windows; the roll for 1276–77 mentions 34 'moving windows' (*fenestre currentes*), and the position of this entry in the middle of an account for carpentry leaves little doubt that this refers to wooden shutters.[25] Some of these 34 were individual lights within traceried windows, examples of which can be seen in the 'Orleans Manuscript' (see Figure 4.6), Wyngaerde's panorama and in Hollar's riverside elevation.[26] At least some of the windows were strengthened with heavy ironmongery, some of it covered with tin.[27]

Another remarkable external feature was polychrome external statuary, indicated in a payment for 'painting in colours the figures of stone mounted over the great chamber facing the Thames'.[28] While some writers have interpreted these as statues affixed to the south elevation,[29] it may be better to reconstruct them as decoration on the merlons of the crenellated parapet, as in slightly later castles such as Chepstow and Caernarfon, the chapter house and nave of York Minster and the gatehouse of St Augustine's, Canterbury.[30] Sadly no evidence survives as to what they represented, but there can be no doubt that they were intended to be visible to a non-royal audience on the river Thames. They identify St Thomas's Tower as a building of 'show', outside the conventional utilitarian model for the mainstream of castle architecture.

Internally, the rooms were equally fine, though details are less plentiful. Several windows were evidently fitted with figural stained glass, though it appears that others were not; since these were also glazed, they must have contained either clear glass or *grisaille*. At least one of the rooms had a tiled floor.[31] The individual rooms were defined by timber partitions, of which there were clearly several; their configuration cannot now be reconstructed,

[24] TNA, E372/121 rot 22.

[25] TNA, E372/121 rot 22.

[26] The medieval windows probably survived largely intact until 1735: TNA, Work 31/78.

[27] TNA, E372/121 rot 22. Simon Thurley has highlighted the presence of apparently gilded window-bars in the Orleans Manuscript; "Royal Lodgings," 48.

[28] TNA, E372/121 rot 22.

[29] For example, Reginald Allen Brown, "Architectural History and Development," in *The Tower of London: Its buildings and institutions*, ed. John Charlton (London: HMSO, 1978), 38–54, especially 42.

[30] Rick Turner *et al.* "The New or Marten's Tower," in *Chepstow Castle: Its history and buildings*, ed. Rick Turner and Andy Johnson (Little Logaston: Logaston Press, 2006), 151–66; Charles Kightly, *A Royal Palace in Wales: Caernarfon* (Cardiff: CADW, 1991), 5; 9. Professor Paul Crossley (pers. comm.) kindly pointed out the single figure on the parapet at St Augustine's, a building with numerous points of comparison to St Thomas's Tower.

[31] TNA, E372/121 rot 22.

Figure 4.6: Illustration of the Tower of London, c. 1480, sometimes called the 'Orleans Manuscript', showing the buildings of the royal residence facing the River Thames. Saint Thomas's Tower is shown with its original traceried windows. The British Library Board, BL MS Royal 16F II fol. 73r.

beyond the fact that they must have left a clear space in the centre of the building for the portcullis of the water-gate to occupy when raised. The 'great chamber' contained four large tables; otherwise, with the exception of a problematic reference to a royal bed (discussed below) there is nothing about furniture.[32] It is tempting to interpret the silence of the Pipe Rolls about either wall-painting or wainscoting as evidence for wall-hangings, which Matthew Paris lampooned as a bizarre Spanish affectation originating with Edward's queen, Eleanor of Castile. Her first lodgings in London, which Henry III had thoughtfully decorated in a manner suggested by the Spanish 'after the custom of their homeland', appeared to the English 'like a temple' (or a mosque), and reduced them to laughter.[33]

[32] TNA, C47/3/47.

[33] Henry R. Luard (ed.), *Chronica Majora*, vol. 5 (London: Longman, 1880), 513–14; Nicola Coldstream, *The Decorated Style* (London: British Museum Press, 1994), 73. Thomas Tolley, "Eleanor of Castile and the 'Spanish Style' in England," in *England in the Thirteenth Century: Proceedings of the 1989 Harlaxton symposium*, ed. W. Mark Ormrod (Stamford: Paul Watkins, 1991), 167–92.

The function of the building

The first reference in the Pipe Rolls to St Thomas's Tower speaks of 'a hall with a chamber', the vocabulary of domestic architecture. While variations in terminology can be detected as the works progressed and were completed (references later appear for a 'small chapel over the water' and 'hall' is increasingly replaced by 'great chamber'), the tower was always considered as accommodation and clearly grand accommodation at that. The question of exactly whose lodgings remains debatable.

The favourite candidate for living in St Thomas's Tower is Edward I himself (see Figure 4.7 for a reconstruction of his chamber).[34] Unfortunately conclusive proof of this, such as reference to 'the king's chamber over the Water-Gate', is presently lacking, and Arnold Taylor urged caution over this assumption.[35] It may be claimed that an entry in the 1280–81 Pipe Roll for 'heightening the turret/s next to the king's chamber and the hermitage' refers to St Thomas's Tower, particularly as the first part of the same entry is certainly concerned with building its roof.[36] An undated document mentions 'a bed for the king's use' in the middle of a series of references to 'the new hall over the water' and could refer to St Thomas's Tower.[37] The building clearly did stand adjacent to the king's lodgings of Henry III's reign and probably communicated with them from the outset, *via* a walk-way across Water Lane to the Wakefield Tower.[38] Moreover, such a prominent and visible location in the centre of the Tower's river frontage certainly conveys high status. Favouring the counter-argument is that Edward I retained at least one other 'king's chamber' elsewhere in the fortress, whose tiled roof was repaired in the early 1280s.[39] This document cannot refer to St Thomas's Tower, which has always been roofed in lead, though interestingly also disqualifies Henry III's great chamber, likewise lead-roofed.[40]

In considering whether St Thomas's Tower was built for Edward himself, it must be admitted that any such debate is largely academic. After December 1280, when St Thomas's Tower was still unfinished, he avoided staying at the Tower of London for nine and a half years, and in the 1290s he is thought to have lived there for no more than 15 days in total.[41] In his absence, the king was represented by the constable of the Tower, a figure who exercised the royal authority by proxy over the city and who, fourteenth-century documents confirm, was to be treated as the king during royal absences.[42] It is at least possible, if not likely, that the constable used St Thomas's Tower; certainly there is evidence from later periods of a connexion between the constable and the royal lodgings.[43] For the entire period in which St Thomas's Tower was under construction, this office was held by Antony Bek, Edward's companion on Crusade who would later, as Bishop of Durham, himself become an architectural patron of note. Bek spent much time away from the Tower with the king but his successors, notably Ralph of Sandwich, resided there on a more regular basis.[44] The constable's exercise of royal authority over the city and particularly the River Thames was a matter of some importance and controversy in the late thirteenth century, and St Thomas's Tower, with its fine views over the river, may have had a critical role to play.

The design suggests that the builders realised even during construction that St Thomas's Tower would mostly be used by the constable or someone outside the royal family. Two wooden drawbars sealed the door between St Thomas's Tower and the bridge leading to the Wakefield Tower and the rest of the palace, but were set on the 'bridge' side of the door rather than inside the tower.[45] These made it impossible to prevent entry into St Thomas's Tower from the palace: rather, the bars sealed the palace against entry from St Thomas's Tower, probably because Edward I wanted to ensure that the ceremonial and administrative activities of the rest of the palace could carry on uninterrupted by whoever was using the water-gate rooms.

With its hall, chapel and chamber, the water-gate contained all the main rooms of an important house. Though it lacked a kitchen, it could otherwise function independently of the main palace, already containing great and small halls of its own, chambers and numerous chapels.

The architectural models for the building

Since the publication of the *History of the King's Works*, it has been claimed that the design of St Thomas's Tower was based on a late twelfth-century gateway outside the east gate of the Louvre, piercing the city wall of Paris.[46] Research

[34] Parnell, 38–40; Thurley, "Royal Lodgings," 47–51.

[35] Simon Thurley, pers. comm; Historic Royal Palaces archive, Hampton Court Palace.

[36] TNA, E372/125 rot comp 125.

[37] TNA, C 47/3/47 m1–m3; see David A. Carpenter, *The Reign of Henry III* (London: Hambledon Press, 1996), 19–218, n.54 for Carpenter's cautious reception of this evidence.

[38] The first documentary reference to this walkway (*alura*) only occurs in the 1320s: TNA, E101 469/7 m8 etc.

[39] TNA, E101 467/9 m4.

[40] TNA, C54/63 m9.

[41] The place of the Tower in Edward I's itinerary is discussed in Carpenter, *The Reign of Henry III*, appendix 2.

[42] *Calendar of the Charter Rolls of Henry III and Edward I, 1257–1300* (London, 1906), 478; Henry T. Riley (ed.), *Munimenta Gildhalle Londoniensis*, vol. 2 part 1 (London: Longman *et al.*, 1860), 150.

[43] For example, references from the reign of Henry IV to 'the king's oratory' and 'king's great chamber' within the constable's ward; TNA, E101 502/23 m2; 502/25 m2.

[44] Bek's deputy was allotted a house for himself and his household in 1278, though it should be noted that St Thomas's Tower itself would not yet have been habitable. Constance M. Fraser, *A History of Antony Bek, Bishop of Durham, 1283–1311* (Oxford: Clarendon Press, 1957), 13, 21, 233–36. Awkwardly, there are exactly contemporary Patent Rolls naming another individual, Giles of Audenarde, both as constable and sub-constable. It is uncertain whether this represents the clerks' confusion or fluidity over the actual exercise of delegated authority.

[45] George Clark examined St Thomas's Tower soon after Salvin's restoration but before the reconstruction of the 'Salvin Bridge' linking it to the Wakefield Tower: he interpreted the sockets as original medieval features. George T. Clark, "Some Particulars Concerning the Military Architecture of the Tower of London," in *Old London* (London: John Murray, 1867), 11–189, especially 84.

[46] *HKW*, 719–20. The authors cite Adolphe Berty, *Topographie Historique du Vieux Paris* (Paris: Imprimerie Impériale, 1866), 148. This

Figure 4.7: Interior of the eastern room of Saint Thomas's Tower with replica furniture and decoration representing the 'King's Chamber' during the reign of King Edward I. Courtesy of Historic Royal Palaces.

by Mary Whiteley has recently demonstrated that this detail of the ground plan originated no earlier than a 1928 reconstructed plan by Louis Hautecoeur; no historic plan or depiction shows it, though nineteenth-century conjectural reconstructions by Viollet-le-Duc and Hoffbauer arguably inspired the feature.[47] No archaeological excavation has ever been carried out in this area of the *Cour Carée* and modern scholars reconstructing the Louvre have assumed that this form of the building is an invention, rather than a historic feature.

More supportable parallels for St Thomas's Tower can be found in British structures dating to the years immediately around its construction. Since the building was designed to serve as a gatehouse, albeit water-borne, it might be expected that St Thomas's Tower would pre-figure the spectacular land gateways for which later Edwardian castles are renowned, or resemble the contemporary land gates at the Tower itself, the Byward and Middle Towers. Comparison with several of these, including Aberystwyth, Rhuddlan, Harlech, Beaumaris and the Byward and Middle Towers, shows that there are important differences in form, particularly the absence of large drum towers flanking the entrance passageway. At St Thomas's Tower, these are replaced by a broad flat façade with thin corner-turrets, three-quarters engaged and facing away from the gate. Certainly this kind of structure imposed less weight on the made-up ground than a traditional 'large-drum' gatehouse would have done, and there are strong suggestions from the accounts that the engineers were indeed anxious about subsidence during construction.[48] The idea that a lightweight structure was militarily more permissible on

reads '[the east gate of the Louvre] *était precédé d'un bâtiment carré, sorte de barbecane ou tête de pont, en bordure sur la rue d'Autriche, et dont la profondeur égalait celle de l'espace compris entre la rue et la fossé*'. Neither of Berty's reconstructed plans gives any authority for reconstructing this building to a plan similar to St Thomas's Tower. Ibid., facing 126 and 128.

[47] Louis Hautecoeur, *Le Louvre et les Tuileries* (Paris, 1928), fig. 1. I am very grateful to Mary Whiteley (pers. comm.) for generously sharing the results of her research into this myth of the Louvre. For a sequence of historic plans and depictions showing the development of the Louvre, see Maurice Berry and Michel Fleury (eds), *L'Enceinte et le Louvre de Philippe Auguste* (Paris: Délégation à l'action artistique de la Ville de Paris, 1988), 137–205, particularly 191; 201.

[48] In particular, TNA, E372/120 rot 22 mentions the purchase of iron for cramps (*grapas*) to tie the stone walls together. While the ashlar masonry of St Thomas's Tower is lead-jointed and may well contain iron cramps hidden in the coursing, it is interesting that some iron staples can be seen added to the outer surfaces. Some of these are clearly post-medieval, but a localised area at the foot of the south-west turret contains several which could be of thirteenth-century date.

the river-side because the threat of waterborne attack was minimal is not convincing; in 1267, something akin to a naval battle had taken place on the Thames in front of the Tower, and Edward was presumably aware that the water-gate was as vulnerable as any other part of the castle.[49] More probable is that this different design was intended to convey a different impression.

The most striking visual similarities are with gatehouses at Tonbridge and Caerphilly castles (the Inner East Gate), built by the de Clare earls of Gloucester (see Figures 4.8 and 4.9).[50] These gatehouses are now dated to the 1250s and the 1260s–early 1270s respectively, pre-dating St Thomas's Tower, and in both, the original elevations have survived in a remarkably complete condition; only the restored plate tracery with quatrefoils at Caerphilly differs from the original design.[51] Moreover, inside the buildings, it is clear that both of them were fitted up to serve as residential apartments, with fireplaces, window-seats, garderobes and at Caerphilly a possible oratory. By 1373, the uppermost room in the gatehouse at Caerphilly was designated as the constable's hall, a use to which it may have been put at an earlier date.[52] Though both gatehouses contain three storeys and are as a result slightly taller and narrower in proportions, the same flat façades, thin corner turrets (containing spiral staircases, a detail not copied in the Tower of London) and traceried upper windows can be seen. Making allowances for the wharf which now obscures the foot of St Thomas's Tower and makes it appear unnaturally short, the similarity to these two buildings is remarkable. Unexpectedly, however, it is the elevations facing *inwards* into the courtyards at Tonbridge and Caerphilly that St Thomas's Tower most closely resembles.[53]

The hypothesis is that the façade of St Thomas's Tower was designed to resemble the rear face of a conventional gateway, based on examples built in the previous decades by Richard and Gilbert de Clare, one of the most powerful families in England and one with which Edward I was well-acquainted.[54] Edward had certainly seen the building at Tonbridge himself; on his return to England as king in 1274, he was entertained for several days in Tonbridge Castle before continuing his journey towards London.[55] From later in his own reign, the gatehouses at Harlech and Beaumaris contain similar elevations, but once again, on the inward faces.[56] St Thomas's Tower, with this type of elevation on the outside, was therefore a gatehouse turned inside-out.

It seems that Edward I wished the external elevation of his water-gate to be something other than purely military. Certainly it contains some defensive features, such as the narrow gallery in the thickness of the wall at ground level, from which arrow-loops open both outward to the river and inward to the basin underneath the main rooms. By contrast, the presence of large traceried windows in the upper façade seems more in keeping with sophisticated living than with the defensive paranoia often implicitly attributed to the builders of castles. Edward I's chambers over the water-gate were equipped with opening windows, affording fine views over the river and down towards London Bridge, in the manner of the rooms named *Gloriette* at Leeds, Corfe and Chepstow (that at Corfe Castle had acquired this name by 1280 and Leeds by 1301–02; that at Chepstow intriguingly pre-dates Edward I's reign, being already in existence in 1271),[57] or with Bishop Robert Burnell's new castellated house of the 1280s at Acton Burnell.[58]

The medieval history of the building after Edward I

Though the reign of Edward I's successor, Edward II, produced relatively few surviving works accounts, it is easy to trace the decline in the fortunes of St Thomas's Tower over the first half of the fourteenth century. The use of individual rooms in the fortress was always fluid and it is clear that by the 1320s, Edward II had switched his attention away from St Thomas's Tower to the eastern end of the housing complex. From 1327 at the latest, the king's chamber was established in or beside the Lanthorn Tower and with interruptions, it was to remain here until the sixteenth century. St Thomas's Tower continued to serve for a time as a chamber, this time for the younger Hugh Despenser, who established himself as Edward II's favourite after Piers Gaveston's execution in 1312. The fact that Despenser's name was used in 1324–26 to designate the room need not necessarily imply that this was an arrangement of any great permanence, although he does seem to have made himself at home: the same

[49] Luard, *Flores Historiarum*, vol. 3, 16.

[50] Derek Renn, "Tonbridge and Some Other Gatehouses," in *Collectanea Historica: Essays in Memory of Stuart Rigold*, ed. Alec Detsicas (Maidstone: Kent Archaeological Society, 1981), 93–103; Royal Commission on the Ancient and Historical Monuments of Wales (RCAHMW), *Glamorgan: Later Castles* (Aberystwyth: RCAHMW, 2000), 51–104; Tonbridge and Malling Borough Council, *Tonbridge Castle* (Tonbridge, 1992).

[51] Investigations at Caerphilly in the late 19th century recovered fragments of plate tracery with roundels similar to those at Tonbridge; Bute Collection, 714B fo 331, surveys of Caerphilly Castle by William Frame. I am very grateful to Peter Humphries, Rick Turner and the late Richard Avent for arranging access to this archive, then on loan to Cadw, and for discussing the material at Caerphilly.

[52] RCAHMW, *Glamorgan*, 71.

[53] This point was made by Alexander Hamilton Thompson in *Military Architecture in England during the Middle Ages* (Oxford: Oxford University Press, 1912), 277, n. 2.

[54] Treatments of the de Clare gatehouses currently see them as innovative, in advance of the royal works. This may be true, but the extremely poor rate of survival of documented royal gatehouses built for Henry III, raises the suspicion that they conformed to a much wider tradition, now mostly lost.

[55] Luard, *Flores Historiarum*, vol. 3, 43.

[56] Though only low walls survive, something similar can plausibly be reconstructed at Aberystwyth; certainly the rear elevation of the gatehouse incorporated round corner turrets.

[57] Jeremy Ashbee, "'The Chamber called *Gloriette*': living at leisure in thirteenth and fourteenth-century castles," *Journal of the British Archaeological Association* 157 (2004): 17–40. I am grateful to Rick Turner and David Robinson for first bringing the Chepstow evidence to my attention.

[58] Jeffrey West, "Acton Burnell Castle, Shropshire: a re-interpretation," in *Collectanea Historica: essays in memory of Stuart Rigold*, ed. Alec Detsicas (Maidstone: Kent Archaeological Society, 1981), 85–92.

Figure 4.8: South elevation of the gatehouse at Tonbridge Castle, Kent, facing into the courtyard, with traceried windows lighting the second floor and rounded turrets covering the salient angles. Photograph: the author.

account states that he had ordered the Tower's carpenters to enlarge the table in the Great Hall.[59]

Also in 1324, the accounts record the construction of a walkway (*alura*) connecting St Thomas's Tower to the Wakefield Tower, then occupied by the king's wardrobe. It is unclear whether this was a stone passage, in the manner of the Victorian bridge which presently links the two buildings, or a timber structure, but it certainly ran above a gateway in a stone cross-wall that formed a barrier across Water Lane. Most architectural historians have assumed that a connection of some sort was made between the two towers when St Thomas's Tower was first built 40 years previously, in order to provide access from the royal chambers into the rest of the house and the Great Hall without needing to descend to ground level. This is likely, although the cross-wall must have been carefully designed to allow clearance at ground-level for the door at the foot of the north-east turret of St Thomas's Tower; this provides the only independent access into the eastern archers' gallery around the basin and must have been an original feature.

An account of 1348 implies that there was a second means of access into St Thomas's Tower, by means of a covered external staircase, a common meaning of the Latin *oriolum*. The account states that the carpenter made the stairs *de novo*, meaning either the replacement of existing stairs or their recent manufacture possibly for the first time.[60] Given the importance of knowing the direction or directions from which St Thomas's Tower was originally entered, it is frustrating that the document is so inconclusive. However, access at the west end (from Water Lane, as at present) was certainly a feature at the end of the Middle Ages. The Orleans manuscript and Wyngaerde's panorama both show what appears to be a brick staircase running up from Water Lane on the west side of St Thomas's Tower.

On 25 June 1336, Robert of St Albans received sixpence for 200 nails to strengthen and repair 'the boards on which to place the king's weapons in the chamber over *le watergate*'. This shows that the space had been annexed and fitted with shelving by the Privy Wardrobe, the branch of the wardrobe responsible for the logistics of military provisioning, and is further supported by references a

[59] TNA, E101 469/7 m8.

[60] TNA, E101 471/1 m1.

Figure 4.9: West elevation of the inner east gatehouse at Caerphilly Castle, Glamorgan. As at Tonbridge, the similarity to the outward-facing elevation of Saint Thomas's Tower is striking. Crown copyright (2019) Wales.

decade later to 'the lord king's wardrobe over the water-gate' and the installation there of 'rails from which to hang the lord king's crossbows'.[61] This repository, the 'chamber of the Privy Wardrobe hanging over the water',[62] was the space looted during the revolt of 1381, and by then firmly established as a place for armament storage.[63] It seems most likely that no person of rank lived over the water-gate again until the 1530s.[64]

Conclusions

The investigation of St Thomas's Tower has called into question the working model in which the building formed an extension to Henry III's palace. Its traditional interpretation as Edward I's own chamber, while still overwhelmingly likely, cannot be proved, but contemporary documents show that the tower was originally colourful and ostentatious, possibly internally, and certainly to an outside observer on the Thames. In a new reconstruction of its appearance, and particularly in a hypothesis of the prototypes on which it was based, St Thomas's Tower seems less plausible as a 'military' castle building and more a creation of pageantry and illusion. A building of this character is only understandable as an expression of the royal identity.

The interpretation of St Thomas's Tower given above flies in the face of several potent mythologies: of Edward I as the archetypal warrior-king in the mould of Judas Maccabeus,[65] of his castles as 'the culmination of the advancing techniques in medieval military architecture',[66] or specifically of the Traitors' Gate as 'perhaps the

[61] TNA, E101 471/1 m1 and m5.

[62] TNA, E101 397/18 m1.

[63] TNA, E101 400/10 m2.

[64] British Library (BL), Rawlinson MS D 775, fol. 206 etc; '*And also in the lathyng dawbyng and pargiting of iiii particions wth in the same (Saynt Thomas Tower) for the transposing of the said Tower into ii lodgynges for the Erle of Oxfford and thother for the lord Chaumberlayin*'. I am grateful to Dr Claire Gapper (pers. comm.) for discussing this reference in connection with the use of gypsum plaster at the Tower.

[65] Michael Prestwich, *Edward I* (London: Methuen, 1988), 358 and *passim*.

[66] Reginald A. Brown, *English Castles* (London: Batsford, 1976), 100.

most tragical gateway anywhere to be found'.[67] The reconstructed building which emerges, with its painted statues, 34 opening windows, comparatively few arrow-loops and single portcullis was doubtless an oddity in the context of the rest of the Tower of London, otherwise a most formidable castle. Rather than a military redoubt, it seems to be a show-palace, a structure of ostentation which verges on the frivolous.

St Thomas's Tower was attached to the Wakefield Tower, almost certainly from its original construction, and thus communicated indirectly with the body of the royal lodgings: the great hall and other chambers. What is most remarkable for its period is the complexity of the layout. As shown above, St Thomas's Tower could be entered directly from Water Lane at two points, but this openness and accessibility is in marked contrast to the building's remote situation in relation to the rest of the palace. A hypothetical visitor in the Great Hall wishing to enter the royal chamber would need to pass into a river-side gallery, through the rectangular chamber-block built by Henry III, thence through the upper room of the round Wakefield Tower with its private royal chapel, and finally along the walk-way across Water Lane, into St Thomas's Tower itself. Parallels for this type of separation can be found in some of Edward's other castles: at Leeds, where the block called *la Gloriete* contained important royal chambers and could be isolated from the 'public' areas of the castle by a drawbridge,[68] Winchester, where a fortified enclosure known as 'donjon' (*dunione* or *dongone*) at the castle's south end contained a hall duplicating the surviving great hall in the outer ward,[69] and most obviously today at Conwy, where the inner royal lodgings were enclosed in an eastern ward with its own private access from the sea.[70] It would be unwise to suggest that this tendency towards seclusion was an innovation of Edward I's period: just as good a case can be made for his father, for whom the donjon enclosure at Winchester was first built,[71] or even his grandfather, King John (1199–1216), whose fine residential chamber-block at Corfe Castle, lying within the area known to Edward I as 'the upper donjon', was built as early as 1201 in relatively inaccessible space at the top of the hill, the innermost of at least three baileys.[72] Nevertheless, the fact that Edward's masons adopted such a design when building castles from scratch, as at Leeds or Conwy, certainly suggests that he valued the social effects of physical separation of his own space from the body of the castles. Such a layout provides strong support for the notion that, far from being an invention of the modern, or late-medieval world, 'privacy' was recognisable in royal circles in the thirteenth century.[73]

There were further benefits in placing such a building in this position, projecting physically into the river at the entrance to the pool of London. In the king's absence, it may well have functioned as a residence and vantage-point for the constable, the king's agent. The period of its construction witnessed a great expansion of merchant shipping on the Thames, with the construction of large numbers of wharves along the north foreshore, immediately upstream from the Tower.[74] The extraction of dues from incoming vessels was a major source of revenue for the constable, a right which the Londoners vocally contested and which the constables just as often abused, culminating in 1321 when Constable John de Cromwell was indicted as a pirate.[75]

St Thomas's Tower also provided a reminder of the king's power and confidence in a location where few could miss it, by means of an architectural flourish. Recent scholarship has begun to re-assess the visual message of Edward I's castle architecture, invoking Imperial Roman prototypes and Welsh mythology at Caernarfon Castle, *chanson de geste* literature at Corfe and Leeds, and so on.[76] Possibly the architectural connection with Tonbridge and Caerphilly was specific; Edward I was intentionally appropriating and de-naturing the architecture of Gilbert de Clare, an over-mighty subject with whom Edward's personal relationship had often been difficult, and whose new castles were becoming more regal than the royal works. St Thomas's Tower reversed the usual design of a castle gatehouse, placing the most elegant façade on the outside, allowing the occupants a good view over the Thames and affording those on the river a glimpse of royal architecture at its most luxurious (see Figure 4.10). The display of the gatehouse's 'soft underbelly' to the Thames may also have broadcast more widely Edward's refusal to be cowed by the city of London, a perennial thorn in his father's side. The character of this elevation's architecture, its materials and its external use of polychromy, sets it aside from the other buildings of the fortress at any time of its history. The new tower provided a perfect counterpoint to the Tower's new royal barges, with their painted dragon-heads;[77] it would not be excessive to see all this as pageantry. The contrast between the garish building and the grim reputation under which the 'Traitors' Gate' now labours, is one of many ironies in the Tower of London's mythology.

---

[67] Charles G. Harper, *The Tower of London: fortress, palace and prison* (London: Chapman and Hall, 1909), 56.

[68] TNA, E372/147 rot 16d; Charles Wykeham Martin, *The History and Description of Leeds Castle, Kent* (Westminster: Martin Nichols and sons, 1869), 41–42; 43.

[69] TNA, E101 491/17 m3–m5. M3 mentions 16 wooden *columpnas*, though in view of the large number and tiny cost (3 s collectively), they must be small vertical members within the roof, not aisle-posts. M4 specifically allocates the hall in the *dunione* to the king.

[70] Taylor, "The Town and Castle of Conwy"; Jeremy Ashbee, "The Royal Apartments in the Inner Ward at Conwy Castle," *Archaeologia Cambrensis* 153 (2006): 51–72.

[71] For example, TNA, C62/42, m4 (1266); C62 45 m4 (1269).

[72] TNA, E101/460/27 rot 3 m1; *HKW*, 617.

[73] For a discussion of the evolution of privacy, see Diana Webb, *Privacy and Solitude in the Middle Ages* (London: Hambledon Continuum, 2007), especially 47–59 and 97–117.

[74] John Schofield, *The Building of London from the Conquest to the Great Fire* (London: British Museum with The Museum of London, 1993), 64.

[75] For example, TNA, E101/4/10 m1, E101 4/25 (accounts of Ralph de Sandwich, constable of the Tower); Henry T. Riley (ed.), *Munimenta Gildhalle Londoniensis*, vol. 2 part 1, Rolls Series (London: Longman *et al.*, 1860), 407.

[76] Ashbee, "The Chamber called Gloriette"; Taylor, *The Welsh Castles of Edward I*, 78–79; *Conwy Castle* (Cardiff: Cadw,1998), 15.

[77] For example, TNA, E403/28 m3; E101 467/9, m8 and m9.

Figure 4.10. Reconstruction by Ivan Lapper showing an aerial view over the complex of royal buildings in the Tower of London, c. 1330, with Saint Thomas's Tower bottom left. Courtesy of Historic Royal Palaces.

Acknowledgements

Like many others, I owe Tom James several enormous debts, but one above all: the "Chapman's Homer" experience of first reading *The Palaces of Medieval England*. The immediate circumstance of this was my writing of a 'grey literature' report, mercifully long forgotten, on the management of several types of ancient monument, including medieval palaces. Tom's *Palaces* did not only contain all the information needed for the task in hand, although it certainly did that, but several of its lessons have had much more lasting impact. Tom gave a masterly demonstration that it is possible (and laudable) to work in several different disciplines without compromising in any of them, that there are wonderful insights to be gained from abrupt changes in scale (from the international power-politics of the Angevin empire to the excavated evidence that hedgehog and badger were on the menu at Kennington Palace), and of course, it was written in an urbane and elegant style that I soon learned to be entirely characteristic of the man himself. Above all, Tom opened my eyes to the delights of a period and a field that I knew much less well than I should, and which, two decades later, have lost none of their appeal. In gratitude for this, and for his friendship, voluminous information always generously given, and constantly sage counsel, I offer this paper.

Bibliography

Unpublished primary sources

The National Archives (TNA)

C47/3/47. Account of materials for the Tower of London, 1276–78.

C62/42 m4. Chancery: Liberate Rolls, 1266.

C62 45 m4. Chancery: Liberate Rolls, 1269.

E101/4/10 m1. Account of Ralph de Sandwico, constable of the Tower of London, 13–34 Edw I.

E101 4/25. Account of Ralph de Sandwico, constable of the Tower of London, 17–29 Edw I.

E101 350/8. Wardrobe account of Philip de Wilueby, 57 Hen III to 7 Edw I.

E101 397/18 m1. Particulars of the account of Richard Ravenser of expenses for the anniversaries of queens Isabel and Philippa, 48 Edw III.

E101 400/10 m2. Account of John de Haytfeld, clerk of the privy wardrobe at the Tower of London, 2 to 5 Rich II.

E101/460/27 rot 3 m1. Accounts of Richard de Bosco, constable of Corfe Castle, of works, 8 to 14 Edw I.

E101 467/9, mm8, 9. Particulars of diverse works at the Tower of London, 9 to 12 Edw I.

E101 469/7 m8. Account of William Chaillou, clerk of the works at Westminster and the Tower of London, 17 to 19 Edw II.

E101 471/1 m1; m.5. Particulars of the account of Thomas de Stapelford, clerk of the works at Westminster and the Tower of London, 22 Edw III.

E101 474/12, f3v; m3r; m4r. Account book of works at the Tower of London, 24 Hen VIII.

E101 491/17 m3–m5. Account of works at Winchester castle, 17 Edw I.

E101 502/23 m2. Account of works, 2 and 3 Hen IV.

E101 502/25 m2. Counter-roll of John Saperton, controller of works, at diverse places, 4 to 6 Hen IV.

E352/70 rot 2. Exchequer: Pipe Office: Chancellor's Rolls, 1276–77.

E372/120 rot 22. Exchequer: Pipe Office: Pipe Rolls, 1275–76.

E372/121 rot 22. Exchequer: Pipe Office: Pipe Rolls, 1276–77.

E372/147 rot 16d. Exchequer: Pipe Office: Pipe Rolls, 1301–02.

E403/28 m3. Exchequer of Receipt: Issue Rolls and Registers, 3 Edw I.

SC1 7/46. Robert Burnel to Walter de Merton, chancellor: for the Tower of London to be put in order, 1274.

SC1 30/87. Ancient Correspondence of the Chancery and the Exchequer, 1274–1307.

SP1/70 fol. 112. State Papers, Henry VIII, 1532.

Work 14/2/1. Tower of London. Fittings up of St. Thomas's Tower as a residence for the Keeper of the Crown Jewels etc., 1852–69.

Work 14/2/2. Tower of London. Restoration of St. Thomas's Tower, 1862–66.

Work 31/78. Tower of London: Traitors' Tower. Plans and sections, showing infirmary, 1735.

Bodleian Library (BL)

MS Rawlinson D. 775 fol. 202-1111. Pay-books of James Nedam, surveyor of... the King's manors.., 1532–43.

Published primary sources

Calendar of Liberate Rolls, 1267–72 (London: HMSO, 1964).

Esposito, Mario, ed. *Scriptores Latini Hiberniae volume four. Itinerarium symeonis semeonis ab Hybernia ad Terram Sanctam*. Dublin: Dublin Institute for Advanced Studies, 1960.

Luard, Henry R., ed. *Matthaei Parisiensis Monachi Sancti Albani Chronica Majora*, vol. 3, Rolls Series. London: Longman, 1876.

Luard, Henry R., ed. *Chronica Majora*, vol. 5. London: Longman, 1880.

Luard, Henry R., ed. *Flores Historiarum*, vol. 3. London: HMSO 1890.

Riley, Henry T., ed. *Munimenta Gildhalle Londoniensis*, vol. 2 part 1. London: Longman *et al.*, 1860.

Riley, Henry T., ed. *Chronica Monasterii S Albani Wilelmi Rishanger, quondam Monachi S Albani et quorundam anonymorum Chronica et Annales Regnantibus Henrico Tertio et Edwardo Primo,* vol. 3. London: Public Record Office, 1865.

Secondary sources

Ashbee, Jeremy. "'The Chamber called *Gloriette*': living at leisure in thirteenth and fourteenth-century castles," *Journal of the British Archaeological Association* 157 (2004): 17–40.

Ashbee, Jeremy. "The Royal Apartments in the Inner Ward at Conwy Castle," *Archaeologia Cambrensis* 153 (2006): 51–72.

Berry, Maurice and Michel Fleury, eds. *L'Enceinte et le Louvre de Philippe Auguste*. Paris: Délégation à l'action artistique de la Ville de Paris, 1988.

Berty, Adolphe. *Topographie Historique du Vieux Paris*. Paris: Imprimerie Impériale, 1866.

Binski, Paul. *Westminster Abbey and the Plantagenets: kingship and the representation of power 1200-1400.* London: Yale University Press, 1995.

Brown, Reginald Allen. "Architectural History and Development." In *The Tower of London: Its buildings and institutions*, edited by John Charlton, 38–54. London: HMSO, 1978.

Brown, Reginald Allen. *English Castles.* London: Batsford, 1976.

Brown, Reginald Allen, Howard M. Colvin and Arnold J. Taylor. *History of the Kings Works*, vol. 2. London: HMSO, 1963.

Carpenter, David A. *The Reign of Henry III.* London: Hambledon Press, 1996.

Clark, George T. "Some Particulars Concerning the Military Architecture of the Tower of London." In *Old London*, 11–189. London: John Murray, 1867.

Coldstream, Nicola. *The Decorated Style.* London: British Museum Press, 1994.

Curnow, Peter. "Some Observations on the Planning and Construction of the West Curtain at the Tower of London." In *Mélanges d'Archéologie et d'Histoire Médiévales: en l'honneur du Doyen Michel de Bouard,* 65–74. Geneva: Droz, 1982.

Fraser, Constance M. *A History of Antony Bek, Bishop of Durham, 1283–1311.* Oxford: Clarendon Press, 1957.

Hamilton Thompson, Alexander. *Military Architecture in England during the Middle Ages.* Oxford: Oxford University Press, 1912.

Harper, Charles G. *The Tower of London: fortress, palace and prison.* London: Chapman and Hall, 1909.

Hautecoeur, Louis. *Le Louvre et les Tuileries.* Paris, 1928.

Keevill, Graham. *The Tower of London Moat: archaeological excavations 1995–99.* Oxford: English Heritage, 2004.

Kightly, Charles. *A Royal Palace in Wales: Caernarfon.* Cardiff: CADW, 1991.

Morris, Richard K. "The Development of Later Gothic Mouldings in England, *c.*1250–1400: Part II," *Architectural History* 22 (1979): 1–48.

Parnell, Geoffrey. *The Tower of London.* London: Batsford, 1993.

Prestwich, Michael. *Edward I.* London: Methuen, 1988.

Renn, Derek. "Tonbridge and Some Other Gatehouses." In *Collectanea Historica: Essays in Memory of Stuart Rigold*, edited by Alec Detsicas, 93–103. Maidstone: Kent Archaeological Society, 1981.

Royal Commission on the Ancient and Historical Monuments of Wales, *Glamorgan: Later Castles.* Aberystwyth: RCAHMW, 2000.

Schofield, John. *The Building of London from the Conquest to the Great Fire.* London: British Museum with The Museum of London, 1993.

Schofield, John. *Medieval London Houses.* London: Yale University Press, 1995.

Taylor, Arnold J. "The Town and Castle of Conwy: preservation and interpretation," *Antiquaries Journal* 75 (1995): 339–63.

Thurley, Simon. *The Royal Palaces of Tudor England.* London: Yale University Press, 1993.

Thurley, Simon. "Royal Lodgings at the Tower of London 1216–1327," *Architectural History* 38 (1995): 36–57.

Tolley, Thomas. "Eleanor of Castile and the 'Spanish Style' in England." In *England in the Thirteenth Century: Proceedings of the 1989 Harlaxton symposium*, edited by W. Mark Ormrod, 167–92. Stamford: Paul Watkins, 1991.

Tonbridge and Malling Borough Council, *Tonbridge Castle.* Tonbridge, 1992.

Turner, Rick, *et al.* "The New or Marten's Tower." In *Chepstow Castle: Its history and buildings*, edited by Rick Turner and Andy Johnson, 151–66. Little Logaston: Logaston Press, 2006.

Webb, Diana. *Privacy and Solitude in the Middle Ages.* London: Hambledon Continuum, 2007.

West, Jeffrey. "Acton Burnell Castle, Shropshire: a re-interpretation." In *Collectanea Historica: essays in memory of Stuart Rigold,* edited by Alec Detsicas, 85–92. Maidstone: Kent Archaeological Society, 1981.

5

The Palaces and Residential Buildings of the Medieval Bishops of Winchester, *c.*1300–*c.*1500

John Hare

University of Winchester.

Abstract: This paper examines the diverse functions of different episcopal houses of the Bishops of Winchester, and the changing nature of what was expected of such residences at different times. The Bishops of Winchester were the richest in England and were frequently key members of the royal court, itself of supreme importance in architectural patronage. The bishopric houses, of which there were many, survive relatively well, and are extremely well documented. While not seeking to be comprehensive, this paper brings together the archaeology of the buildings and their documentation, published work by others, together with unpublished work by the author. This approach enables the distinctive examination of the houses of a whole episcopal estate.

Key words: Winchester; palaces; residences; housing; medieval; bishops; diocese; architecture

Introduction

Like their contemporaries, whether kings or noblemen, medieval bishops needed to display their importance, lordship and patronage through their buildings. Winchester was the richest bishopric in the country, but its holders were also frequently major royal administrators or ministers, and these roles generated further sources of income.[1] A succession of bishops such as des Roches, Wykeham and Beaufort dominated the politics of their times.[2] Moreover, they were close to the Crown and the royal court, so that these bishops were well aware of, and involved in, the changes in court life and buildings, and they employed some of the leading architects of the age. Wykeham, for example, used the court architects Wynford, Yevele and Herland on his residences.[3] The ecclesiastical foundations of the bishops, such as those of bishop des Roches at Netley and Titchfield abbeys, or of Wykeham's New College, Oxford and Winchester College are well known, but their episcopal residences less so. These bishops were rich and were great builders, and their residences offer two further advantages for study. They are probably second only to the royal houses in the range and coverage of their documentation. Moreover, while much is lost or in ruins, there remain fragments that may be linked to the documentation itself.

Traditionally the episcopal palaces and residences have been treated as studies of individual houses, usually of that at the centre of the diocese.[4] By contrast, this paper deliberately seeks to examine all the episcopal houses on a single but particularly well documented estate. As elsewhere, official documents were copied into registers from the thirteenth century onwards and the bishop's itineraries can be compiled from these. Such itineraries provide an incomplete record of their movements but can in part indicate the relative importance of particular residences. For Winchester, we also possess the bishopric pipe rolls, which incorporate the enrolled versions of the individual manorial accounts copied up at Wolvesey Palace, in Winchester, and which record money spent on the episcopal residences and other manorial buildings. These documents are remarkable both in the fullness of their survival and how early they begin. From 1208/09 onwards, there is an account for most manors and for most years.[5] They offer a huge and often neglected source of information about the bishopric residences. They have their

[1] On the bishops and their estates see Mark Page, *The Medieval Bishops of Winchester: estate, archive and administration* (Winchester: Hampshire County Council, 2002).

[2] The dates of the main bishops are listed in Table 5.1.

[3] John Hare, "The Architectural Patronage of Two Late Medieval Bishops: Edington, Wykeham and the rebuilding of Winchester Cathedral nave," *Antiquaries Journal* 92 (2012): 299, 301.

[4] But for a notable exception on a national level, see Michael W. Thompson, *Medieval Bishops Houses in England and Wales* (Aldershot: Ashgate, 1998). Individual houses are considered in Anthony Emery, *Greater Medieval Houses of England and Wales* including the bishopric of Winchester houses in vol. 3 (Cambridge: Cambridge University Press, 2006), 430–34, 333–39 and in David Rollason, ed., *Princes of the Church: bishops and their palaces*, Medieval Archaeology Monograph 39 (Abingdon: Routledge, 2017). On palaces in general see Tom Beaumont James, *The Palaces of Medieval England* (London: Seaby, 1990).

[5] On introductions to the pipe rolls, Richard H. Britnell, "The Winchester Pipe Rolls and their Historians," in *The Winchester Pipe Rolls and Medieval English Society*, ed. Richard H. Britnell (Woodbridge: the Boydell Press, 2003): Jan Z. Titow, *English Rural Society* (London: George Allen and Unwin, 1969); Four of these are in print: Hubert Hall (ed.), *The Pipe Roll for the Bishopric of Winchester, 1208–9* (London: King and Son, 1903) (hereafter *Pipe Roll, 1209*); Neville R. Holt (ed.), *The Pipe Roll of the Bishopric of Winchester, 1210–11* (Manchester: Manchester University Press, 1964) (hereafter *Pipe Roll, 1211*); Mark Page (ed.), *The Pipe Roll of the Bishopric of Winchester, 1301–2* (Winchester: Hampshire County Council, 1996) (hereafter *Pipe Roll, 1302)*; Mark Page (ed), *The Pipe Roll of the Bishopric of Winchester, 1409–10* (Winchester: Hampshire County Council, 1999) (hereafter *Pipe Roll, 1410*). The last two are in translation.

Table 5.1: Some bishops of Winchester referred to in the text.

		Building changes referred to
Henry of Blois	1129–71	Wolvesey, Southwark, Farnham, Waltham
Peter des Roches	1205–38	Wolvesey, Southwark, Farnham, Waltham
William Raleigh	1244–50	Esher
John of Pontoise	1282–1304	
Henry Woodlock	1305–16	
John Sandale	1316–19	
John Stratford	1324–33	
Adam Orleton	1334–45	Farnham
William Edington	1346–66	Sutton, Marwell, Farnham, Highclere
William Wykeham	1367–1404	Wolvesey, Southwark, Waltham, Highclere, Esher, Farnham, Downton
Henry Beaufort	1405–47	Wolvesey, Southwark, Waltham, Marwell, Meon
William Waynflete	1447–86	Esher, Farnham
Thomas Langton	1493–1501	Waltham, Marwell, Esher
Richard Fox	1501–28	Esher
Thomas Wolsey	1529–30	

problems. There are missing rolls, often at an infuriating time in relation to a building programme. The fullness of the record varies – sometimes providing a great deal of detail and at other times merely giving a total sum spent on the building campaign. Moreover, the absence of a record of building cannot be taken as evidence that nothing was being done. When Cardinal Beaufort rebuilt the chapel at Bishop's Waltham, he accounted for the buildings on a lost separate account answerable to his central treasury and not through the manorial accountant. Incidental references in the manorial accounts show that the chapel was being built, but they are tantalisingly brief. Something similar occurred at Esher under Bishop Waynflete, with work under Langton at Marwell, and it was probably the case with Beaufort's new chapel at Wolvesey.[6] Despite all their difficulties and frustrations this is a remarkable source that enables us to learn so much about the chronology of the bishops' building activities. But the mass of the data brings its own problems of selection, and this study cannot hope to be comprehensive. In addition to the documentary sources the diocese retains a relatively good survival of ruins and remains, especially Wolvesey (Winchester), Farnham, Esher, Bishop's Waltham, East Meon, Taunton and Southwark, supplemented by the evidence of archaeological excavations. This essay is not comprehensive and is built on, and seeks to integrate, the earlier work of others and myself on individual residences, supplemented by examples from other houses. But it should contribute to the wider study of episcopal residences.

Numbers and trends

In 1301–02 the estate comprised 56 manors, each of which would probably have had a manor house with hall and chamber, and which would serve as the headquarters of local agricultural production and represent episcopal lordship, even when the lord had given up direct agriculture.[7] But we need to distinguish between such small manor houses fulfilling this limited role and the episcopal residences where the bishops and their household could stay, as well as welcome visiting guests and their households. This can in part be done from the documentation. A hall and a chamber would have been required on any manor, but a chapel, or the various communal rooms of the household (the chambers of the esquires, of the knights, of the clerks or of the monks), suggests the presence of an episcopal residence. In addition, its importance may have been reflected in the provision of those things needed by the elite: the fresh fish of fishponds or the hunting of park and chase.[8] It should also be noted that some of the residences would not have occurred in the published pipe

[6] John N. Hare, "Bishop's Waltham Palace, Hampshire: William of Wykeham, Henry Beaufort and the transformation of a medieval episcopal palace," *Archaeological Journal* 145 (1988): 223, 233–34: at Esher in the years 1464–67 the pipe rolls record no buildings but explain this because they were recorded on the cofferer's account which does not survive (Edward Roberts, pers. comm.).

[7] Page, *Medieval Bishops*, 5–6.

[8] Edward Roberts, "The Bishop of Winchester's Fishponds, 1159–1400: their development, function and management," *Proceedings of the Hampshire Field Club and Archaeological Society* 42 (1986): 67; Edward Roberts, "The Bishop of Winchester's Deer Parks in Hampshire, 1200–1400', *Proceedings of the Hampshire Field Club and Archaeological Society* 44 (1988): 73.

rolls. North Waltham does not, but in 1298, its buildings included a chapel, lord's chamber and a knights' chamber.[9] The episcopal itineraries provide an indication of places where the bishops stayed, but their evidence needs to be examined in conjunction with the other evidence.

In the early fourteenth century there were about 23 such episcopal residences, representing a sizeable number of the 56 manors. This was a similar number to a century before, although in the intervening period a few changes had occurred. Most importantly, Esher was acquired in the thirteenth century, and became a major residence. During the fourteenth and fifteenth centuries, the bishops, like royalty and nobility, reduced the number of the residences that they used.[10] Royal houses were reduced from 24–25 in the early fourteenth century to about 9–10 under the Yorkists, and the number of residences of the bishop of Worcester fell from 15 in the fourteenth century to six in the sixteenth century.[11] The bishopric of Winchester showed a similar substantial decline from about 23 to about six main residences still frequented by the bishops. This was not a sign of economic problems rather of the higher expectation of what a great lord's residence should provide: for the lord, his household and his guests. Investment was now concentrated on few houses where the lords stayed for longer. The bishops' itineraries (Table 5.2) show this focus on many fewer places, and a group of residences which had previously been significant lesser residences now dropped out of regular episcopal circulation, as with Bitterne, Fareham, Brightwell, Downton, Witney, and Overton, although they may have remained in use by the bishop's officials and household and guests. Bitterne had seen its bishop quite commonly in the thirteenth and early fourteenth century but not apparently in the late fourteenth and fifteenth century. It was recorded as having a tower in 1302 and the ruins of substantial buildings are suggested by Leland who in the 1540s commented 'the bishops used to have a castle here, ruins still surviving'.[12] By contrast, William of Wykeham stayed in only seven main residences: Southwark, Bishop's Waltham, Esher, Farnham, Highclere, Wolvesey and Marwell, carrying out extensive alterations at most of these (Table 5.2). By the time of William Waynflete (1447–86), Highclere and Marwell had ceased to see regular episcopal visits, although Marwell probably later made a comeback. The episcopal itineraries probably exaggerate the changes, although this does not mean that other residences ceased to operate. The bishop might still need them as foci for the gentry of the neighbourhood and to maintain his influence over a wider area. Thus bishops had rarely stayed at East Meon since the episcopate of Henry Woodlock (1305–16), but Wykeham invested heavily spending over £110 in 1395–97 on a grand new hall and chamber block, and subsequently Beaufort also spent over £100 on buildings in 1438/39 and 1440/41, spending on a probable gatehouse and on his own private accommodation.[13] Occasionally, materials from the buildings were disposed of and recycled, suggesting declining use. Slates were taken from Bishop's Sutton to Bishop's Waltham in 1427 and ashlar was being mined from the buildings of Merdon for Wolvesey in 1441/42.[14] It should also be remembered that the use of individual houses could be affected by the decisions of individual bishops: Orleton spent his time increasingly at Farnham from 1339 and Wykeham at Bishop's Waltham from 1390s.[15] Woodlock, the only cathedral monk to become bishop showed a very distinctive pattern of habitation. His most frequently used house was Marwell, and his lack of a role in royal government was reflected in Southwark, usually the most commonly used residence, being only third in importance. He seems to have spent very little time at Wolvesey, and his monastic past was reflected in the presence of a number of monks' chambers, as at Wargrave and Sutton, reflecting hospitality to his former brethren.[16]

Hierarchy and function

The large number of residences possessed by the bishop naturally led to some being more important than the others, and to various houses possessing different functions: residential, administrative and political. They were an essential part of the patterns of influence, patronage and bureaucracy, maintained in part through display, feasting, hunting, and gathering, reflected in the association of park, fishponds and residences.[17] With the exception of a brief period in the Anarchy of the twelfth century when a group of castles were created, the episcopal palaces were residential rather than military.[18] Subsequently only Taunton, Farnham and Wolvesey seem to have retained a military role, were regularly referred to as castles, or show evidence of military preparations and stores.[19]

Wolvesey Palace, in Winchester, was very much the administrative headquarters of the estate and the diocese. Here was the treasury to where the estate revenues came. The wool from the estates was brought to a wool store

[9] HRO: 11M59/B1/54.

[10] Emery, *Greater Medieval Houses,* vol.3, 29.

[11] Reginald Allen Brown, Howard M. Colvin and Arnold J. Taylor, *The History of the Kings Works* [hereafter *HKW*], vol. 1 (London: HMSO, 1963), 243, usefully summarised in the maps in James, *Palaces of Medieval England,* 165; Christopher Dyer, *Standards of Living in the Late Middle Ages* (Cambridge: Cambridge University Press, 1989), 100; Christopher M. Woolgar, *The Great Household in Late Medieval England* (London: Yale University Press, 1999) 46–47.

[12] John Chandler (ed.), *John Leland's Itinerary* (Stroud: Sutton, 1993), 206.

[13] Edward Roberts, "William of Wykeham's House at East Meon, Hants," *Archaeological Journal* 150 (1993): 466, 473–75.

[14] HRO: 11M59/BW55; Martin Biddle, *Wolvesey: the Old Bishop's Palace, Winchester* (London: English Heritage, 1986).

[15] Roy M. Haines, *The Church and Politics in Fourteenth-Century England: the career of Adam Orleton c.1275–1345* (Cambridge: Cambridge University Press, 1978), 64–65.

[16] HRO: 11M59/B1/4 m29r; 97M97/A33.

[17] Roberts, "The Bishop of Winchester's Fishponds," 67.

[18] Martin Biddle (ed.), *Winchester in the Early Middle Ages* (Oxford: Clarendon Press, 1976), 315; Hare, "Why so many?," 196–99.

[19] On preparations in 1264/65, 1268/72, 1270/71 see Nicholas Vincent, "The Politics of Church and State as Reflected in the Winchester Pipe Rolls, 1208–80," in Britnell, *Winchester Pipe Rolls,* 176, 9; and on stores in 1302, *Pipe Roll, 1301–2,* 15, 218; on Taunton, see Arthur W. Vivian-Neal and Harold St. George Gray, "Materials for the History of Taunton Castle," *Somersetshire Archaeological and Natural History Society Proceedings,* 86 (1940): 49–52, 63.

Table 5.2: Episcopal Residences.

	Episcopal residential days			
	1282–1319	**1346–66**	**1367–1404**	**1447–86**
Hampshire residences				
Bishop's Sutton	33	12	3	3
Bishop's Waltham	55	81	352	317
Bitterne	61	3	4	0
Fareham	50	1	0	0
Highclere	109	78	150	2
Marwell	228	14	55	6
Wolvesey	166	25	684	499
Other Hants houses (E. Meon, Hambledon, Merdon,* N. Waltham, Overton	43	16	4	1
Surrey residences				
Farnham	112	209	256	65
Esher	148	213	343	250
Southwark	404	1126	774	853
Residences outside Hampshire and Surrey				
Downton	24	5	7	0
Taunton	14	0	0	3
Wargrave	25	59	6	0
Witney	37	4	2	3
Others: Brightwell, Harwell, Ivinghoe, Wycombe	26	1	1	1
Total	21	17	15	12
Adjusted total	23	18	17	12

* Edington's register does not include Merdon, but includes Hursley, the parish in which the manor house lay. I have placed the Hursley figures under Merdon.

Such figures must be treated with caution. They depend on the bishop's presence and on him doing official work recorded in the register. How long would he have stayed at the house beyond the day that was recorded? His visits may have been missed out or shortened.
Source: Figures for Hampshire taken from Roberts, "William of Wykeham's House." Non-Hampshire and Edington figures newly calculated. Itineraries published in Cecil Deedes (ed.), *Registrum Johannis de Pontissara* (Canterbury and York Society, 1924); Arthur W. Goodman (ed.), *Registrum Henrici Woodlock* (Canterbury and York Society, 1940); Francis J. Baigent (ed.), *The Registers of John of Sandale and Rigauld de Asserio* (Winchester: Hampshire Record Society, 1897); Stanley F. Hockey (ed.), *The Register of William Edington Bishop of Winchester*, Part 1 (Winchester: Hampshire County Council, 1986); Thomas F. Kirby (ed.), *Wykeham's Register*, 2 vols (London: Simpkin and co., 1896, 1899); Virginia Davis, *William Waynflete, Bishop and Educationalist* (Woodbridge: the Boydell Press, 1993), 159–74. See also Roy M. Haines (ed.), *Register of John de Stratford, Bishop of Winchester 1323–1333*, vol. 1 (Woking: Surrey Record Society, 2010). For a fuller table see Hare "Why so many?" 212.

here. Its bureaucratic role was aptly reflected in this being the home of the records of the estate and above all of the Pipe Rolls of the bishopric with their invaluable record of the building works. Wolvesey's buildings were large and complex with at least 38 rooms on the ground floor and 6 internal courts.[20] Together with Southwark, it was the only one of the residences which might be described as urban. Its administrative role may have been both an attraction, and an encouragement for the bishop to go to one of the easily accessible rural retreats. In the thirteenth century it seems to have been the most actively used residence under des Roches and Pontoise, and saw the major rebuilding of its great hall.[21] This may have reflected both the bishop's own perception of his own importance and the greater presence of the royal court and its building, in the city and the area around, as in the magnificent new hall built

[20] Biddle, *Wolvesey*, 14.

[21] Biddle, *Wolvesey*, 32–36.

in Winchester Castle in 1222–35.[22] Wolvesey declined in importance in the fourteenth century until William of Wykeham remodelled the private wing in the early years of his episcopate. Subsequently, he was much concerned with the cathedral, his new college just outside the city and the running of the diocese. From the fourteenth century, royalty tended to stay at Wolvesey when visiting Winchester, as did Richard II, and later Queen Mary. This palace retained its importance under Waynflete (Table 5.2).

Southwark had been acquired by Henry of Blois in the twelfth century at a time when the growing importance of London in government meant that such a base became essential. It provided easy access to the court and for those bishops who held major ministerial responsibilities: they had easy access by river boat both to Westminster, where government was increasingly centred, and to other royal residences along the river. Southwark had a role to play in the running of the estates particularly when agricultural produce was being brought to the London market. It was immensely important and from the early fourteenth century it was the most frequently used of the bishop's residences.[23]

Esher was the only new residence to be acquired after the end of the twelfth century. Peter des Roches (1205–38) had bought the manor from the abbey of Croix St Leuffroy as part of the endowment for his new monastery at Netley in about 1235.[24] A successor as bishop, William de Raleigh (1244–50), persuaded the abbot to sell it back in 1245.[25] His concern to acquire this property suggests that he wanted it for a particular reason and this was probably as a residential site near to London. By 1257/58, in addition to the hall, lord's chamber, kitchen and bakehouse, there were already chambers for the knights and for clerks.[26] A new chapel was built in 1267/68, and other improvements were subsequently made, with a royal visit in 1290.[27] Soon afterwards, under de Sandale, it had become the fourth most frequently recorded residence on the estate. Expansion occurred and in 1331, Bishop Stratford was given royal permission to move a pathway in order to enlarge his dwelling-house here.[28] Esher was a well-located site, a country residence but near to Southwark and London, with access by road and water. It was also close to Windsor, another frequent and increasingly important base for the royal court. Here was clearly something more important than a stopping point on the way to London.

Farnham was the third of the bishop's eastern group of residences. It served a variety of roles including, unusually, that of a castle. It was a stopping-point on the route to London from the west, and it was reasonably close to London and to Windsor. Farnham was an important place for visitors whether in the lists on the early thirteenth century accounts or in the recorded visits of royalty, from John to Mary.[29] It was much stayed in by the bishops, although less than at Esher, and bishops like Wykeham and Waynflete spent heavily here.

As major ministers and royal advisors, the bishops needed ready access to the king, who was itinerant but increasingly present in London and the Thames valley. This was reflected by the bishops' preponderant presence in Southwark, Esher and Farnham (Table 5.2). But coping with the peripatetic court provided opportunities and the need for other houses. The bishops could track the court and have ready access to the king.[30] Downton was outside the diocese but was extremely important while neighbouring Clarendon was one of the major royal centres in the country during the later twelfth century and above all under Henry III. 'Through his personal interest he [Henry III] elevated the buildings at Clarendon to a state only marginally less magnificent than that of the prime palace of the realm at Westminster'.[31] From Downton, bishop des Roches could intervene in the world of national politics as with establishing a settlement between the earl of Salisbury and the Poitevin courtier Peter de Maulay at Downton in 1218.[32] Significantly, Downton was the second most recorded residence of his episcopate. But it was little used by the bishops in the fourteenth century, and its decline reflected that of Clarendon as a royal residence. Clarendon retained some importance for Edward III, until his last recorded visit in 1371.[33] Interestingly, Edward was there in the summer of 1370, when Wykeham was at Downton, paid a visit to Clarendon and probably made significant decisions on the future layout of the manor.[34] But thereafter episcopal visits were extremely rare. The buildings were maintained, but for a lesser role, with £68 being spent in 1467, including a complete new roof on the great chamber.[35] We know little of the residence at Wargrave (Berks), but it was evidently important in the fourteenth century under Stratford and Edington, when it

[22] Brown, Colvin and Taylor, *HKW*, vol. 2 (London: HMSO, 1963), 858–59; 912–17, 730–31, 735–37.

[23] On Southwark see Martha Carlin, "The Reconstruction of Winchester House," *London Topographical Record* 25 (1985): 35–57; Derek Seeley, Christopher Phillpotts and Mark Samuel, *Winchester Palace: excavations at the Southwark residence of the bishops of Winchester*, Museum of London Archaeology (MoLA) Monograph 31 (London: MoLA, 2006).

[24] Cecil A.F. Meekings, "The Early Years of Netley Abbey," reprinted in C.A.F. Meekings, *Studies in Thirteenth-Century Justice and Administration* (London: Bloomsbury Academic, 1981), ch xvii, 6.

[25] Meekings, "Netley Abbey," ch xvii, 12.

[26] HRO: 11M59/B1/28.

[27] D. Stone, pers. comm.

[28] J Kestell Floyer, "The Ancient Manor House of the Bishopric of Winchester at Esher," *Proceedings of the Society of Antiquaries* 2nd series, 32 (1919–20): 72; D. Stone, pers. comm.

[29] Etienne Robo, *Medieval Farnham: everyday life in an episcopal manor* (Farnham: E W Langham, 1939), 169–70.

[30] For the later example of Wolsey tracking his king see Simon Thurley, "The Domestic Building Works of Cardinal Wolsey," in *Cardinal Wolsey: church, state and art*, ed. Steven J. Gunn and Peter G. Lindley (Cambridge: Cambridge University Press, 1991), 87. His country houses were used 'for entertaining the king in person but they were used as bases for tracking the king when he went on progress' (87).

[31] Tom Beaumont James and Anne M. Robinson, *Clarendon Palace: the history and archaeology of a medieval palace and hunting lodge near Salisbury, Wiltshire*, Reports of the Research Committee of the Society of Antiquaries of London 45 (London: Society of Antiquaries and Thames and Hudson, 1988), 8–10.

[32] Vincent, "The Politics of Church and State," 158.

[33] James and Robinson, *Clarendon Palace*, 40.

[34] Kirby, *Wykeham's Register*, vol. 2, 621. The following year the demesne buildings were moved. HRO: 11M59/B1/123.

[35] 'According to the form of the roof of the hall of the rectory', HRO: 11M59/B1/199.

would have benefitted from its proximity to Windsor (Table 5.2) and its facilities are reflected by Edington staying there for at least a fortnight, as in 1365.[36] Highclere would have offered access to the royal palace at Woodstock.

Bishop's Waltham was the most important of the rural retreats in the western part of the diocese with a less complex function than Farnham in the east: it was not a journey stop on the way to London, and after the thirteenth century the royal court had migrated from Wessex. Bishop's Waltham had been sufficiently rebuilt by Henry of Blois to be able to hold royal councils in 1182 and 1194.[37] It was important in the thirteenth century and Henry III paid several and sometimes extended visits here.[38] Bishop's Waltham was already one of the better used episcopal residences in Hampshire before Wykeham's great rebuilding. Wykeham and his successor Beaufort transformed the palace, and its subsequent importance is reflected in the itineraries (Table 5.2), where it became by far and away the most heavily used rural residence in Hampshire, and remained a place of great importance until the seventeenth century.[39]

Marwell lay just outside Winchester, within the manor of Twyford, and may have served as a rural retreat outside the town. Might this have led to less formal work being done and recorded here, rather than at neighbouring Wolvesey and thus an underestimate of its use? Although very little survives of the palace building, it would seem to have been the creation of Henry de Blois in the twelfth century. His importance was marked out by his foundation of a college of four priests and the construction of a church.[40] The latter was later described as a church rather than a chapel and the cloisters may have been associated with this. The church was big enough to hold large scale ordinations.[41] The importance of this house may have been reflected in the magnificent two sets of double fish ponds.[42] Already in 1208–11, the accounts show a painted chamber, with the painter paid for over half a year, chambers, high chamber and cloister, as well as wine brought in.[43] Henry III was a regular visitor here, suggesting the importance of the buildings.[44] For a brief moment under Henry Woodlock, who came from nearby, Marwell was the most frequently used episcopal residences although it is unclear whether this should be explained as the positive remembrance of childhood elsewhere in the neighbourhood or a monk's dislike of Wolvesey. The bishops would still spend heavily on these buildings, as did Beaufort and Langton.

Highclere was another major rural residence, although also offering a place within striking distance of the royal court at Woodstock, and of Oxford. It was already visited by Peter des Roches and possessed a hall, chapel and chamber, and gradually acquired further buildings for the household. In the 1240s, it acquired rooms for the knights and clerks, an almonry, wine cellar, larder and salsary. By the 1270s, there were additional chambers for the esquires, the steward and for the bailiff and a long chamber. Its period of greatest importance lay in the fourteenth century from Woodlock to Wykeham. Edington had made alterations particularly to the agricultural demesne complex, but it was Wykeham who began the major transformation of the residential buildings. In 1370/71, he spent £314 with the main change being a new hall, with buttery and pantry and a room overhead at the hall's lower end.[45] It ceased to see new building in the fifteenth century, when episcopal visits were also rare.[46]

Bishop's Sutton was another important rural mansion whose usage declined in the fifteenth century. It had been acquired by Henry of Blois,[47] and was one of the more important residences under des Roches, serving as both a stopping point on the way to London and as an important country house. Here des Roches spent the Christmas feast in 1211 and it already possessed a clerks' chamber in 1209.[48] Its early importance is also reflected in the great fishpond at Alresford. Bishops continued to invest in its buildings during the fourteenth century, with £395 being spent there in the four years 1355–58 with £32 in 1360 and £38 in 1362.[49] It had a chapel and a lord's study. The emphasis in the buildings work given to a new chamber, with glazed windows and fireplace, and for improving the arrangements at the service end, around the bakehouse, brewhouse and kitchen, confirm that Bishop's Sutton was more than merely a temporary stopping off point.

Finally, there was a group of lesser residences, which were evidently designed to cater for the visit of the household, but which the bishops themselves seem rarely, or infrequently, to have visited. But their officials or representatives would have used them. A good example is provided by East Meon, which, with the exception of the episcopate of Henry Woodlock, rarely saw a documented visit of the bishop. Yet it had seen a royal visit in 1211/12. Moreover, a century later there were buildings in which Woodlock could stay, and it possessed a glazed heated bishop's chamber, chapel, and hall for the clerks, with fishpond and park.[50] Moreover, Wykeham evidently thought it worth spending heavily on a new grand hall and chamber block at a cost of about £110, a programme planned since

[36] Haines, *Register of John de Stratford, passim;* Hockey, *The Register of William Edington* vol.1, xxvi.
[37] Hare, "Why so many?," 197; John Hare, *Bishops Waltham Palace* (London: English Heritage, 1987).
[38] The National Archives (TNA), Anon., *Itinerary of Henry III: 1215–1272*, unpublished typescript.
[39] Hare, "Why so many?," 197–98.
[40] Michael J. Franklin (ed.), *English Episcopal Acta, VIII: Winchester 1070–1204* (Oxford: Oxford University Press, 1993), 55–56.
[41] HRO: 11M59 B1/108; HRO: 11M59 B1/110.
[42] Roberts, "The Bishop of Winchester's Fishponds," 126; 134; 137; C. Currie, "Earthworks in Fisher's Pond and Hassock's Wood," *Newsletter of Hampshire Field Club*, 9 (1988): 15–16.
[43] *Pipe Roll, 1209*, 53; *Pipe Roll, 1211,* 13.
[44] TNA, *Itinerary of Henry III.*

[45] Christopher J. Phillpotts, "Plague and Reconstruction: Bishops Edington and Wykeham at Highclere, 1346–1404," in *Fourteenth Century England 1*, ed. Nigel Saul (Woodbridge: The Boydell Press, 2000), 116–17, 122–25, 127.
[46] Phillpotts, "Plague and Reconstruction," 128.
[47] Page, William (ed.), *The Victoria History [VCH] of Hampshire and the Isle of Wight*, vol. 3 (London: VCH, 1908), 42.
[48] *Pipe Roll 1209*, 42.
[49] HRO: 11M59/B1/107–10, 112, 114.
[50] Roberts, "William of Wykeham's House," 460, 475, 479.

1385 and virtually all carried out in 1395/96.[51] This was an important area of the bishopric estates and with its adjoining great park provided an opportunity for episcopal patronage and display, as documented in the thirteenth century. Its value would be still recognisable to Wykeham, for whom his suffragans or stewards would display his authority, eminence and patronage. Further substantial alterations were made under Beaufort. He visited it in 1438 and 1440/41 but episcopal visits in the fifteenth century were rare.[52] Some houses, like Fareham and Bitterne, had often been visited in the thirteenth century, but ceased to see episcopal use thereafter. Their position close to the ports of Portsmouth/ Portchester and Southampton respectively would have enhanced their importance, and they would have lost out in the changing relationship of England with Europe. Merdon, with the exception of a period under Edington, also declined. It had a range of buildings, a hall and bishop's chamber with undercroft, a chapel, a tower and a clerks' chamber and an extensive park beyond, and was occasionally visited by the bishop.[53] Hambledon was a later development as an episcopal residence, but never seems to have quite made the change from a local manor house. It does not provide any hint of a greater role in 1209 or 1211. The first reference to its park was in 1251–53, and although it hosted a visit from Henry III in 1231/32, it never became a regular place for episcopal visits, and these had probably ceased by the time of Waynflete or possibly Wykeham. In the fifteenth century the main accommodation seems to have been of the steward rather than of the bishop.[54] Overton was another minor residences which had possessed a range of buildings with pretensions: a stone chimney in 1257, a new garderobe in 1283, a bishop's chamber roofed in lead in 1285 and a knight's chamber in 1278.[55] There was a clerks' chamber in 1488/89 and the bishop spent nearly £42 on a new hall and chamber block in 1505–07, although not for episcopal visits. [56] It is important to emphasise that the role of the episcopal country house went beyond merely a residence, and that house and park equally represented an element of good lordship within the surrounding county.[57]

Most of the houses were within the diocese, particularly those which were in frequent use. But some others needed to be maintained. Taunton remained an important castle and residence in the early thirteenth century, although it was rarely visited by the bishops thereafter. It remained defensible in the later Middle Ages, withstood a three day siege in 1451, was repaired on the eve of the Armada, and played a military role in 1644–45.[58] Waynflete visited it early in his episcopate and then seems to have spent several months there in 1460, but this was probably the result of royal banishment rather than of any desire to see a neglected house.[59] Later, Bishop Langton founded a school in its outer court, a reflection of diminished use as a residence, and in 1495/96 spent £226 on the new schoolhouse, as well as other works done about this time.[60] Nevertheless it should be emphasised that Taunton castle was the headquarters of the largest manorial complex on the estate and the bishop would have been expected to maintain it in order to emphasise his importance within Somerset society. Wargrave and Downton also, as we saw, served as bases for the royal court. But there were also other manors, some of which would have required residences as points of display to the local gentry, even if they were rarely used by the bishops themselves. A useful example is provided by Witney. Here archaeological excavations and full study of the documentation have shown the presence of a substantial residence. The archaeology revealed a chapel and solar tower, while documentation mentions chambers of sergeants, clerks, knights, esquires, monks and of the almoner.[61] But with the exception of the episcopate of Henry Woodlock, and to a lesser extent of des Roches, it seems to have been an infrequent base for the bishops who, after Edington, rarely seem to have visited. Physically the excavated remains were substantial although not on the scale of the most important residences. We may wonder if Witney should be seen as representative of a few other places outside the diocese which bishops had occasionally visited in the thirteenth century but little thereafter, but where a residence needed to be maintained. West Wycombe, Brightwell, Harwell and Ivinghoe probably fell into this category.[62]

Rebuilding and renewal

The pattern of major residences had already been established by 1200, but it would be modified in the following centuries. Esher was acquired in the thirteenth century, Downton declined and Wargrave grew in importance in the episcopal itineraries, but these were exceptions. This continuity was coupled with a constant pattern of redevelopment: each bishop remodelling particular houses. The bishops might inherit a series of very grand residences, but they also felt the need for change. They might have agreed with Edward VI's description of Bishop's Waltham (once one of the grandest

[51] Roberts, "William of Wykeham's House," 464, 66.

[52] Roberts, "William of Wykeham's House," 473.

[53] D. Len Peach, *The History of Hursley Park* (Winchester: IBM UK Laboratories, 1978) (Medieval references M. Meek), 15.

[54] Roberts, "The Bishop of Winchester's Deer Parks," 83; Edward Roberts, "Medieval Hambledon Manor: chambers for bishops and their stewards," *Proceedings of the Hampshire Field Club and Archaeological Society* 59 (2004): 18.

[55] Edward Roberts, "Overton Court Farm and the Late-Medieval Farmhouses of Demesne Lessees in Hampshire," *Proceedings of the Hampshire Field Club and Archaeological Society* 51 (1995): 91.

[56] Roberts, "Overton Court Farm," 91, 98–104.

[57] For a survey of the Hampshire parks see Roberts, "The Bishop of Winchester's Deer Parks," 67–86, especially 67.

[58] Vivian-Neal and St. George Gray, "Materials for Taunton Castle," 53; Robin L. Storey, *The End of the House of Lancaster* (London: Barrie and Rockliffe, 1966), 91.

[59] Virginia Davis, "Waynflete and the Wars of the Roses," *Southern History* 11 (1989): 10.

[60] HRO: 11M59/B1/232; Courtenay A. Ralegh Radford and A.D. Hallam, "The History of Taunton Castle in the Light of Recent Excavations," *Somersetshire Archaeological and Natural History* 98 (1953): 71–72.

[61] Tim Allen with Jonathan Hiller, *The Excavation of a Medieval Manor House of the Bishops of Winchester at Mount House, Witney, Oxfordshire, 1984–92* (Oxford: Oxford Archaeology, 2002), 196, 206–32.

[62] For West Wycombe see, Roberts. "The Bishop of Winchester's Deer Parks," 67; Roberts, "The Bishop of Winchester's Fishponds," 126.

of the episcopal residence but whose newer buildings were now over a century old), as 'a faire great old house'. As expectations changed, so each episcopate saw the rebuilding and upgrading of some of their residences. It was a process in which they were aided by some of the leading craftsmen of their day.[63] This process of rebuilding can best be seen by examining individual examples, largely among those which continued to be in active use.

By 1200, Wolvesey had already evolved from the two individual elements of the west hall (with the more private accommodation) and the more ceremonial east hall into something like a courtyard plan which remained in place until the palace's destruction in the seventeenth century. In addition to the piecemeal process of repair and minor modifications, there were also major phases of remodelling. At some point in the thirteenth century, the Blois hall was rebuilt, probably by des Roches, with the chambers or gallery to one side being converted into a new aisle for the main hall. This hall was later remodelled by Henry Beaufort in 1441/42 (Figure 5.1). Elsewhere two major changes occurred. Wykeham's major works in 1371–78 cost £565 and included his remodelling of the private accommodation in the tower and west range. Later, in the early fifteenth century his successor, Henry Beaufort rebuilt the chapel.[64]

Southwark was both one of the most important of his residences and a major prestige building for the bishopric, which dominated the view from the Thames. In the early thirteenth century, a massive long range was built, part of which would serve as the undercroft to the hall and great chamber. The hall went through various changes in the succeeding 60 years, and later incorporated the surviving rose window, in *c.*1290–*c.*1330 (Figure 5. 2).[65] It was later further reroofed and refenestrated in *c.*1416.[66] Other major changes included a two storey chamber block for the bishop in 1356/57, a new long chamber that helped to form a household courtyard, and a new kitchen block in the mid fourteenth century. The scale and complexity of this palace at the end of the Middle Ages is aptly shown in Hollar's drawing in *c.*1644–47.[67]

Farnham possessed a major residence in the early thirteenth century. It already possessed the motte or tower with its enclosing wall. This was maintained during the succeeding centuries as in 1290/91, 1346/47, 1349/50, 1352/53 and 1400/01,[68] and there were a series of rooms on the top including a chapel on which £83 was spent in 1338–39, and £283. 10s 2½d in 1352/53 on this and other buildings.[69] Did this reflect the influence of contemporary work on the royal lodgings on the motte at Windsor?[70] In addition and below the motte, there was an aisled hall, lord's chamber, kitchen and a chapel, parts of whose walls still survive. The thirteenth century saw a proliferation of buildings and enlargement, as with the addition of an aisle to the chapel in 1254/55.[71] There was the piecemeal addition of rooms such as in 1338, when a small chamber was built between the lord's chamber and the lord's chapel and the latter was then rebuilt on a larger scale in 1347/48 to become the great chapel. The latter was remodelled and reroofed in 1447/48. [72] Wykeham helped transform the hall, heightening the south wall so that the aisle would become full height. In addition he built a new great chamber in 1386–87, whose roof still survives.[73] Other rooms periodically witnessed minor changes.[74] The final recorded major project was the addition of the new porch tower in 1470–75 at a cost of perhaps £300 (Figure 5.3).[75] Over £100 was spent in years such as 1338/39, 1352/53, 1370/71, 1386–87, 1396, 1400, and 1401.[76]

Esher, as has been seen, was a late acquisition (1245) by the bishopric, but already in major use by the end of the century. We know little of the early buildings, but they were rapidly acquired.[77] The buildings went through various changes, as in 1375/76, when Wykeham spent £127 mainly in enlarging the hall with two extra windows and extending the lord's chamber.[78] But the main transformation was later in the fifteenth century under Waynflete and his successors. Waynflete added a great accommodation tower adjacent to the hall which still survived in the seventeenth century when it was recorded by Aubrey and which has recently been located.[79] Waynflete also built the gatehouse, which survives underneath the details, and additions of William Kent in the 1730s (Figure 5.4).[80] Aubrey in the seventeenth century suggested similarities between the tower and the gatehouse, reinforced by recent excavations, and Aubrey suggests a link between tower and lodging. The gatehouse was completed by 1485, and provides a tree ring dating of 1462–72.[81] The whole programme was probably a

[63] Hare, "Architectural Patronage," 299, 301.

[64] Biddle, *Wolvesey*, 19. The building is not recorded in the pipe rolls, since it was probably accounted for in central accounts that do not survive.

[65] Seeley, *Winchester Palace*, 48–52, 55–59. For the documentation for Southwark see Carlin, "Reconstruction of Winchester House," 33–57.

[66] Seeley, *Winchester Palace*, 81–82.

[67] Seeley, *Winchester Palace*, 75, 70–73, 51, 71.

[68] Robo, *Medieval Farnham*, 144. On Farnham see also Michael W. Thompson, *Farnham Castle Keep, Surrey* (London: HMSO, 1961); Philip D. Brooks, *Farnham Castle: the forgotten years* (Farnham: Farnham and District Museum Society, 1985); Michael W. Thompson, "The Date of 'Fox's Tower', Farnham Castle, Surrey," *Surrey Archaeological Collections* 57 (1960): 85–92.

[69] Robo, *Medieval Farnham*, 150.

[70] Brown, Colvin and Taylor, *HKW* vol. 2, 876.

[71] Robo, *Medieval Farnham*, 133, 137.

[72] HRO: 11M59 B1/185.

[73] HRO: 11M59/B1/138. The timber felling date is 1380: A.K. Moir, 'Dendrochronological analysis of oak timbers from the Bishop's Camera Roof, Farnham Castle Surrey', Tree-ring services: report FACA/27/06.

[74] Robo, *Medieval Farnham*, 140–41.

[75] The recorded cost was about £200, but this missed out at least two years and some items of expenditure. Thompson, "The Date of 'Fox's Tower'," 92.

[76] Hare, "Transformation of a Medieval Episcopal Palace," 31.

[77] See above. HRO: 11M59 B1/28; Steve Thomson and Vaughan Birbeck, "Investigations at Wayneflete's Tower, Esher," *Surrey Archaeological Collections* 95 (2010): 259; D. Stone pers. comm.

[78] HRO: 11M59/B1/128, m29r & v.

[79] Thomson and Birbeck, "Investigations at Wayneflete's Tower, " 262, 267–69.

[80] John Harris, "A William Kent Discovery," *Country Life* 125 (14 May 1959): 1076–78.

[81] Richard Chandler, *The Life of William Waynflete, Bishop of Winchester* (London,1811), 369–70; Anon., "Tree-Ring Date Lists 2006," *Vernacular Architecture* 37 (2006): 121–22.

Figure 5.1: Wolvesey Palace: view of hall from south: the early twelfth century hall, was altered later in the century, transformed in the thirteenth century and reroofed with a new window in 1442/43. Photograph: the author.

product of 1464–67 during which period the building costs became the responsibility of the bishop's cofferer.[82] The hall has completely disappeared above ground, but Aubrey provides evidence of a major rebuilding at the end of the fifteenth century. Although he described it as looking like Westminster hall, the details place it a century later. The escucheons carried by the angels bore the inscription *tibi christe,* probably for *laus tibi christe,* the device of Langton, and the windows showed *sit deo gratia* (probably for *est deo gratia,* that of his successor Fox), suggesting that the rebuilding programme was begun by Langton and completed by his successor Fox, the change from one to the other occurring in 1501.[83] The last changes were made by Thomas Wolsey who both borrowed the house from bishop Fox, and himself subsequently became bishop of Winchester. His new gallery was subsequently removed by Henry VIII and re-erected at Whitehall.[84] In addition, the removal of unused building materials to Hampton Court and Whitehall (Caen stone, bricks, tiles and plaster) suggests that work was either being planned or

Figure 5.2: Southwark Palace: the great hall, remodelled several times, with its additional rose window (*c.*1290–*c.*1330). Photograph: the author.

[82] Edward Roberts has shown, using the pipe books that this was exceptional and suggests convincingly that this major change in the documentation is likely to have resulted from such a major building programme.

[83] John Aubrey, *The Natural History and Antiquities of the County of Surrey*, vol. 3 (London, 1718), 120–21. My thanks to John Crook for help with this.

[84] Brown, Colvin and Taylor, HKW vol. 4 (London: HMSO, 1982), 89–90; Sylvester, Richard S. (ed.), Cavendish's *The Life and Death of Cardinal Wolsey* (London: Early English Text Society, 1959), 123; John S. Brewer (ed.), *Letters and Papers, Foreign and Domestic, Henry VIII, Volume 4, 1524–1530* (3) (London: HMSO, 1875), 6390.

Figure 5.3: Farnham: Waynflete's new residential porch tower (1470–75) abutting the earlier hall. Photograph: the author.

Figure 5.4: Esher gatehouse: Waynflete's new gatehouse (1464–67), as remodelled by Kent in the 1730s from the former inner court. Photograph: the author.

was recently completed.[85] In the reign of Edward VI it was described as 'sumptuously built',[86] There are illustrations of the medieval house in the seventeenth century, in 1606 and by Aubrey.[87]

Bishop's Waltham had been rebuilt by Henry of Blois in the aftermath of the of the civil war of Stephen and Matilda, Subsequently in the thirteenth and early fourteenth century it saw minor rebuilding, a new kitchen and brewhouse in 1252, a new chamber at the entrance to the hall, the rebuilding of the barn in the outer court in 1301/2 to 1305/6, and a new lord's chamber in 1339 and 1340.[88] It was already one of the better used episcopal residences, before its transformation under Wykeham. [89] In order to free up space for the proposed new hall, he built a replacement new bakehouse and brewhouse in 1378–80 on the opposite side of the court. This was followed up by the rebuilding of the hall with an adjacent services and a

[85] Thurley, "Domestic Building Works," 93–94.

[86] Brown, Colvin and Taylor, HKW vol. 4, 90.

[87] These and many other illustrations are included in Penny Rainbow, *A Complete History of the Tower of Esher* (privately printed, 2010). The 1606 drawing is in Floyer's "The Ancient Manor House," 71. See also John Schofield (ed.), *The London Surveys of Ralph Treswell* (London: London Topographical Society, 1987). The Treswell and Aubrey maps are reproduced in Thompson and Birbeck, "Investigations at Wayneflete's Tower, " 262, 264.

[88] HRO: 11M59/B1/23; 91; 92.

[89] The rest of this paragraph is based on, and documented in, Hare, "Bishop's Waltham Palace, Hampshire," 222–54. See also Hare, *Bishops Waltham Palace*.

room above the services in 1379–81 (Figure 5.5). Finally this programme was completed with the construction of a new grandiose kitchen and adjacent services, and a new first floor chamber in 1387–93.[90] Subsequently he rebuilt and remodelled his own private range in 1394–96 (Figure 5.6), with an enlarged and updated great chamber, renewed private accommodation in the adjacent west tower and the links to the hall block. Wykeham spent more and more time here, no doubt enjoying the new building and although his later years showed less activity, these included the construction of a new long chamber and a new gate and chamber in the outer court. Wykeham had spent over £1,500 on these works and thus passed on a transformed palace to his successor, Henry Beaufort. Its role as the pre-eminent country house was further enhanced by Beaufort's building works. He heightened the tower to extend the private accommodation in 1406, and he built a new and much bigger chapel from 1409–27. Finally, in 1438–43 he carried out a major rebuilding programme whose documentation is sadly incomplete, but which cost well over £1000. This programme can be divided into two main sections. He built a large new range of buildings to provide accommodation for guests and household, with addition of a large number of individual heated chambers (Figure 5.7). At the other end of the site the existing buildings were integrated around a covered cloister and some of the rooms were upgraded. The hall, for example, was now provided with glass windows which it had not had before. Beaufort's use of brick, a material fashionable in court circles, as at Herstmonceaux and Tattershall, is its first known use on the bishopric houses,[91] but one that his successor was to use on a much grander scale at Esher and Farnham. Beaufort's successor, Waynflete, needed to do very little, adding a gallery and some panelling. He and his successors refurbished the buildings, in particular refacing the existing timber framed buildings in brick and enclosing the site with a brick wall. This seems to have largely been the work of Langton, three versions of his personal rebus having been found, although this may have been completed by his successor, Bishop Fox.[92]

Highclere already possessed a hall, chapel and chamber but seems to have been much enlarged in the 1240s to make it suitable for the household with the additional chambers of the knights, the clerks and the almoner, wine cellar, larder and salsary. Further expansion occurred between 1265/66 and 1270/71 with a long chamber, a chamber for the steward and for the esquires, as well as that for the bailiff.[93] Edington rebuilt the bakehouse, carried out various alterations to the domestic buildings and invested in some of the demesne buildings, such as in a new barn. But it was his successor, Wykeham, who transformed the place. In 1370/71 he spent £314 on building works here including the rebuilding of the hall, together with a new buttery and pantry and chamber above. However, this seems to have been the end of the main period of activity; in the fifteenth century little was done and the bishops ceased to stay here.[94]

Marwell had been a creation of Bishop Henry of Blois and, as has been seen, contained a church and chantry. Subsequent bishops continued to rebuild it. In the three years 1354–57, bishop Edington spent £237, overlapping with his high-spending at nearby Bishop's Sutton, where he spent almost £400 in four years.[95] Money was spent on a hall porch, new chambers and the service area, a steward's and an almonry chambers, and on the cloisters. The latter lay between church and hall. Henry Beaufort spent on an even more lavish scale. The documentation for his programme of work in 1435–41 is sadly incomplete. In the three surviving documented years between 1434/35 and 1439/40, he spent at least £411. Moreover, the accounts for two years are missing when they would have been sandwiched between the two years of maximum expenditure and it is unlikely that work had simply stopped. In addition we know that the building works continued in 1439/40 when the account is missing,[96] and it was only in 1440/41 that work seems to have reached completion. A total figure of approaching £800 would seem appropriate. Beaufort rebuilt the great hall, lowering and then heightening the walls, replacing the characteristic thirteenth-century exterior, with the windows projecting into the roofline, by a higher levelled aisle, while adding a buttress at one end, and rebuilding its eight windows, adding a major window at the upper end, and reroofing the whole building.[97] Its interior probably now possessed the appearance of the hall at St Cross whose roof was being rebuilt at the same time by the same patron, probably using the same carpenter.[98] The initial phase also involved the inner chamber, a chimney, and a reroofing.[99] Later work seemed to have focussed on the church, with a new porch, leading and paving in the cloisters, glass in two windows beneath the vault, glass from a London glazier for the great window at the west end of the church, and a painter to paint the oriel between the church and the lord's oratory.[100] Further work was carried out by Langton at the end of the

[90] We know little of the kitchen save that its roof was supported on a horizontal wall surface without any gable ends, and that it was sufficiently complex a structure for no less a carpenter than Hugh Herland, the future carpenter of the roof of Westminster hall to spend 133 days on site in 1388 (HRO: 11M59/B2/11/26).

[91] Emery, *Greater Medieval Houses,* vol. 2, 343–55; vol. 3, 308–15.

[92] Hare, "Transformation of a Medieval Episcopal Palace," 245–46.

[93] Phillpotts, "Plague and Reconstruction," 116–17.

[94] Phillpotts, "Plague and Reconstruction," 122–25; 128.

[95] HRO: 11M59/B1/107–09, and 107–110 for Bishop's Sutton.

[96] Coal and iron were recorded as sent to Twyford in the Brokage Book, although some of this might have been for the contemporary St Cross works. Hare, "Miscellaneous Commodities," in *English Inland Trade, 1430–1540: Southampton and its region,* ed. Michael A. Hicks, (Oxford: Oxbow, 2015), 164–65. See also "People, Places, and Commodities 1430–1540," Overland Trade Database, accessed 13 July, 2018, for 1439/40.

[97] HRO: 11M59/B1/179–80.

[98] There has been disagreement about the date of the hall and roof, but the latter has now been dated by dendrochronology to 1437–51, John Hare, "Tree-ring Dating of the Brethren's Hall at St Cross, Winchester," *Hampshire Field Club Newsletter* 56 (Autumn 2011): 17. The roofs for the chambers at Bishops Waltham and St Cross show strong stylistic similarities, and John Lewys was responsible for the work at the former as well as the new roof at Wolvesey.

[99] HRO: 11M59/B1/178 mm20r–20v.

[100] HRO: 11M59/B1/179 mm 21v and 22r.

Figure 5.5: Bishop's Waltham Palace: Wykeham's hall (1378–81) from the east. Photograph: the author.

Figure 5.6: Bishop's Waltham Palace: Great chamber originally built by Henry of Blois, widened, heightened and rebuilt by Wykeham (1394-6). The blocked window of the earlier building contrasts with Wykeham's much grander replacement on the left. Photograph: the author.

fifteenth century. His rebus was included among reused stone from the palace incorporated in Hensting Farm in1659.[101] Moreover, the building works were sufficiently important for them to be extracted and accounted for in a lost household account. Unfortunately few of the Langton accounts survive but this separation was certainly the case in 1495/96.[102] These building works, like his later work at Bishop's Waltham, made heavy use of brick. They were probably finished by 1496/97, when substantial quantities of brick and some tiles were sent from Marwell for the use of St Mary Magdalene hospital (outside Winchester).[103]

The changing character of the episcopal palace

We have seen that several of the residences showed a succession of changes as bishops gradually updated their main houses. The documents, however, tell us more about the presence of building works than about the character of the changes. For this we need to focus more sharply on those where the buildings still exist: which tend to be those that continued as the centre of activity in the fifteenth century.

Wolvesey shows an early and very grand example of the evolution of these residences. A west block and a

[101] Edward Roberts and Maureen Gale, "Henry Mildmay's New Farms 1656–1704," *Proceedings of the Hampshire Field Club and Archaeological Society* 50 (1995): 173–74.

[102] HRO: 11M59/B1/213.

[103] Marwell was a centre of tile production. See John Hare, "The Growth of the Roof-tile Industry in Later Medieval Wessex," *Medieval Archaeology* 35 (1991): 93. Bricks had been used by Beaufort at Bishop's Waltham and on a much larger scale by Waynflete at Esher and Farnham. For the bricks sent to the Magdalene hospital see HRO: 11M59/B1/214.

Figure 5.7: Bishop's Waltham Palace: the farmhouse on the left contains the timber framing of the eastern three chambers of a major lodgings range of the 1440s, while the bakehouse to the right was given an added communal first floor and a connecting gallery. Photograph: the author.

roughly parallel east hall had gradually evolved into a courtyard plan. At Bishop's Waltham, the buildings were grouped around a large roughly rectangular site, but it was only later under Wykeham and Beaufort that they were gradually welded together with the insertion of an inner cloister and a lodgings court. Even the later greenfield creation at Esher seems to have lacked any clear sense of the planned courtyard. Our buildings mark a clear contrast with the planned rectangular courtyards that were becoming common in the fifteenth and sixteenth centuries in lay and ecclesiastical houses like Bodiam, Herstmonceaux, Hatfield, and Knole.[104] Plans also became more complex, as expectations changed. The early printed pipe rolls suggest that at the start of the thirteenth century, most residences were largely restricted to a hall, services and kitchen, and a lord's chamber. Only at Bishop's Sutton was a household room (chamber of clerks) recorded, although others probably existed.[105] But where systematic study of the documentation of an individual house has been made, it suggests that a proliferation of communal chambers soon occurred as at Farnham and Highclere (1240s and 60s), and at Witney where the clerk's chamber existed in 1225/26 and others from 1251/52 onwards.[106] What characterised these house plans more than anything else was a sense of evolution, fitting a more up to date or greatly needed new building into the constraints of the existing plan.

One later but noticeable changes was the shift from these communal rooms to private usage. In the thirteenth century, residences fit for visits of a large household could be distinguished by the presence of communal rooms: chambers for the knights, the esquires, the clerks, the monks. Some such communal rooms survived but by the later fourteenth century expectations were changing. Already under Wykeham, key officials possessed their own room, Nicholas Wykeham at Bishop's Waltham or John de Campeden at Esher, and Farnham. Moreover, it was increasingly expected that individual accommodation would be provided for the household and visitors. A classic example is Beaufort's new lodging range at Bishop's Waltham, which can be reconstructed from the surviving structure and the ground plan. It contained 22 individual chambers, each with its own fireplace and with a communal latrine at one end and a communal room over the bakehouse and brewhouse at the other. Although a timber-framed structure, it bears close similarities to the contemporary stone lodgings which Beaufort built for his almshouse at St Cross. Such proliferation of individual chambers was a common feature of fifteenth-century houses as at Croydon, Hatfield, Knole and Hampton Court, with over 40 examples of two storey lodgings ranges

[104] Emery, *Greater Medieval Houses*, vol.3, 317–19, 343–55, 364–68; Thompson, *Medieval Bishops' Houses, op. cit.*, 146.

[105] *Pipe Roll, 1209*, 42.

[106] Robo, *Medieval Farnham*, 142–43; Phillpotts, "Plague and Reconstruction"; Allen and Hiller, *The Excavation of a Medieval Manor House*, 196.

having been found from the period 1340–1500.[107] The growing demand for accommodation was also reflected in the residential towers built by Beaufort's successor Waynflete at Farnham and at Esher,[108] which paralleled the work of other lords at Buckden and Tattershall.[109]

While the need for particular buildings often remained constant throughout the period, their precise nature varied dramatically over time. The hall, for example remained a feature of any major residence but its character changed. This may still be seen in the ruins of Wolvesey, the headquarters of the diocese in Winchester.[110] The hall remained a key element in the palace plan and with a constant ground plan and foundations from the early twelfth century and the time of Henry of Blois. But it also went through a succession of changes. The hall was already a grand building but de Blois remodelled it on his return from exile in 1158. Later a group of side chambers were incorporated creating a new aisle, thus giving it the fashionable contemporary design of an aisled great hall, with windows breaking into the roof line,[111] as represented for example by that newly built at Winchester Castle, or elsewhere as at the archiepiscopal palace at Canterbury, or Ludgershall.[112] Although the foundations remained the same, the changes at Wolvesey are suggested by the pillar bases for the arcade and the necessary addition of buttresses to support the hall walls. Space may have prevented it having more than one aisle but it would have looked from the outside and from the west, as if it was a full up-to-date thirteenth-century hall. By the later fourteenth or fifteenth centuries, however, such low aisles became disliked, with owners raising the aisle walls to the full height of the building, as at Winchester Castle.[113] This seems to have been done at Wolvesey, Marwell, and Farnham, in all three cases where the reroofing was accompanied by a heightening of the wall. At Wolvesey, a great new window was also added at the north, or high, end.[114] At Esher the hall was lengthened by Wykeham in 1375/76,[115] and was then remodelled and reroofed in the later fifteenth century. At Bishop's Waltham, the hall had always been aisleless since the present structure was built in the aftermath of Blois' return in 1158. Smaller in scale than Wolvesey, it nevertheless reflects its big brother in the blind arcade high upon the wall at the high end. Wykeham enlarged it and emphasised its importance by heightening the walls, and giving it grand new contemporary windows. He also rebuilt the halls at Highclere and East Meon, in both cases building a hall, services and a private room over the services. At both East Meon and Bishop's Waltham this room included a fireplace and was a room of size and importance such as could have served as a private dining room. At Highclere his new hall was a first floor one, as in such contemporary buildings as John of Gaunt's new hall at Kenilworth and Wykeham's own colleges at Oxford and Winchester, but at East Meon he built a ground floor aisleless hall (Figure 5.8). The grandeur of such buildings are reflected in other standing buildings: the great rose window overlooking the hall in the new later thirteenth century hall at Southwark, or, in the absence of the roofs themselves, in the hall roof at St Cross, built at the same time and probably with the same carpenter, John Lewys, as Beaufort's new roofs at Marwell and at Wolvesey.[116] It is important to emphasise both the succession of rebuilding and the building activities of individual bishops at a variety of sites, as with Wykeham at Bishop's Waltham, Farnham, Highclere, East Meon; and Beaufort at Southwark, Marwell and Wolvesey. Earlier, at Taunton the original first floor hall was replaced by a larger ground floor one in the thirteenth century, with over £75 spent on building the hall in 1245/46.[117]

Second only to the hall in its symbolic importance was the lord's great chamber. Its changing nature is aptly shown at Bishop's Waltham where we may compare that of two leading architectural patrons: Henry of Blois at the end of the twelfth century and Wykeham in the late fourteenth, Wykeham rebuilt the chamber on a large and impressive scale. The outer wall was that of the earlier building, still containing a blocked in window but the room was widened by the replacement of the inner wall by one built just outside the earlier wall line. The room was thus widened, heightened both with higher walls and with a shallow pitched roof, and the small earlier window was replaced by a much taller and larger one. From the beginning this was glazed (Figure 5.6). Such changes are seen most clearly here but we can see this chamber being enlarged at Esher, and remodelled by Beaufort at East Meon, It should be emphasised that these changes were concerned with a suite of apartments rather than a single room. At Bishop's Waltham there was the Great chamber but also, probably in the adjacent tower a high chamber, an oratory with a chamber above and the wardrobe, and with an additional storey added by Beaufort on top of the existing tower. At

[107] Patrick A. Faulkner, "Some Medieval Archiepiscopal Palaces," *Archaeological Journal* 127 (1970): 136–38, 140–42; Thompson, *Medieval Bishops' Houses*, 144–47; Thurley, "Domestic Building Works," 87–89; Anthony Emery, "Introductory Reflections after *Greater Medieval Houses of England and Wales,"* in *The Medieval Great House*, ed. Malcolm Airs and Paul S. Barnwell (Donington: Shaun Tyas, 2011), 15.

[108] Thompson, "The Date of 'Fox's Tower'", 85–92; Thompson and Birbeck, "Investigations at Wayneflete's Tower, " 261–62, 65, 67–69.

[109] Emery, *Greater Medieval Houses, vol.* 2, 229–33, 308–15.

[110] Biddle, *Wolvesey*, 32–36.

[111] There is no documentary dating for the building. Martin Biddle raises the possibility of this being the work of John of Pontoise, although opting for des Roches as the most likely. Biddle *Wolvesey,* 15, 35

[112] Brown, Colvin and Taylor, HKW vol. 2, 860, Rady, J, Tatton Brown T and J.A. Bowen, "The archbishop's palace Canterbury," *Journal British Arch. Assoc.*, 144 (1991), 6–10; P. Ellis (ed.), *Ludgershall Castle, Excavations by Peter Addyman 1964–72* (Devizes, Wiltshire Archaeological Society, 2000), 92–94.

[113] Brown, Colvin and Taylor, HKW vol. 2, 860.

[114] Biddle. *Wolvesey,* 19, 36.

[115] HRO 11M59/B1/128.

[116] On John Lewys, see Hare, 241, and Richard Warmington, "Appendix," 250, both in Hare, "Transformation of a Medieval Episcopal Palace"; HRO: 11M59/B1/179 and 180. Derek Keene, *Survey of Medieval Winchester*, vol 1 (Oxford: Oxford University Press, 1985), 283; John Harvey, *English Medieval Architects* (Gloucester: Alan Sutton, 1984), 184. The Saint Cross rebuilding has no documentation, but the hall roof can now be dated to the Beaufort period (1437–51). Hare, "Tree-ring Dating of the Brethren's Hall," 17.

[117] Radford and Hallam, "Taunton Castle," 70.

Figure 5.8: East Meon: Wykeham's new grand hall of 1395–7, in a house rarely visited by the bishops themselves. Photograph: the author.

Bishop's Sutton and Marwell, the bishops spent heavily on their chamber complexes in 1354–58, and at Wolvesey the private accommodation was transformed by Wykeham from 1372/73, while the treasury and exchequer were moved elsewhere.[118] Later, the fashionable galleries were introduced as at Bishop's Waltham and Esher.[119]

The earliest chapels were relatively small buildings, but at Bishop's Waltham and probably Wolvesey, there were two storeyed chapels on the continental pattern. Elsewhere the early chapels were probably modest single storeyed buildings as at Witney.[120] The chapel served the household and the bishop, but larger ceremonial gatherings such as ordination might need to be moved to the parish church, as at Bishop's Waltham. At Farnham, a new much larger chapel was built in 1347–48, which was itself further enlarged and reroofed in 1447–49.[121] In the fifteenth century Beaufort rebuilt the chapels at Waltham and Wolvesey (Figure 5.9). All seem to suggest larger single storey structures. Beaufort also altered and reglazed the important chapel at Marwell.

The accounts also show something of the changing details and expectations. The shift in internal appearance: from the painting of the thirteenth century buildings to the internal timber panelling of the fifteenth, or the growing readiness to fill windows with glass. Thus while Wykeham glazed his new chamber at Bishop's Waltham, his new hall there had to wait for glass until his successor Beaufort.

The bishops of Winchester had been the richest in the country and politically among the most powerful in the land. They spent lavishly on display, on religious foundations and on their residences. The process was continuous, not on every individual house, but on the estate as a whole. The bishops responded to the changing demands and requirements: the increased demand for private accommodation, the smaller number of residences that were required, or changes in fashion, whether in style or in material. Such rebuilding had not ceased before the Reformation. The building materials accumulated by Wolsey at Esher provide a reminder of this. But Esher was the first to be lost to Henry VIII, and in 1551 the new bishop surrendered his estates and houses to the crown in return for a fixed annual payment. Although most of the houses were recovered under Mary, and the bishops continued to possess Southwark, Wolvesey, Bishop's Waltham and Farnham, little rebuilding occurred in the later sixteenth and seventeenth centuries until after the civil war and the decay of the Interregnum.

There were particular peculiarities resulting from the role of these houses as episcopal palaces: the large chapels and the absence of any need for the large extensions required to cater for wives and royal princes.[122] But otherwise these were houses that were in the mainstream of aristocratic residences. We might have expected the bishops of Winchester to spend much more lavishly than their fellow bishops, but comparison with the later archbishops of Canterbury raises an interesting question. The bishops of Winchester created no new residence after Esher in the thirteenth century and there was no wholesale rebuilding of a residence. Instead individual sections were rebuilt in a rather piecemeal fashion. There was no comparison with Archbishop Bourchier's Knole or Archbishop Warham's Otford.[123] Was it because of the distraction of founding and building Oxford Colleges, and if so, why did these bishops take such different paths?

Acknowledgements

This study depends on those who have studied individual houses of the bishopric. I am particularly grateful to

[118] Biddle, *Wolvesey,* 18, 42.
[119] HRO: 11M59/B2/11/101; Thurley, "Domestic Building Works," 93–94.
[120] Allen and Hiller, *The Excavation of a Medieval Manor House*, 27–32.
[121] HRO: 11M59/B1/185; 186.

[122] As seen in the evolving plans at Clarendon and Ludgershall; James and Robinson, *Clarendon Palace*, 25–26, 17–22; Ellis, *Ludgershall,* 14, 247.
[123] Emery, *Greater Medieval Houses,* vol. 3, 364–68, 323; Thurley, "Domestic Building Works," 96–97.

Figure 5.9: Wolvesey Palace: the chapel from NE as rebuilt by Bishop Beaufort. Photograph: the author.

Edward Roberts for much discussion on these houses over the years, and for generously allowing me to use his conclusions on the dating of the Esher buildings under Waynflete. David Stone is working on an edition of the pipe roll documentation for Esher for Surrey Record Society and has very kindly provided me with information on some of the early buildings there. Martin Biddle generously gave me access to the typescripts of the pipe roll documentation for Wolvesey, produced for the Winchester Research Unit. In selecting which additional accounts to look at, I have benefitted from P.D. Brooks and A.C. Graham, *The Bishops Tenants* (typescript Hampshire Record Office [HRO]: 34A/13/1), and from the manorial tabulations of Jan Z. Titow (HRO: 97M97). I have considered the issue of numbers and functions, over a longer period of time in a parallel paper, although inevitably there is some overlap. See John Hare, "Why So Many Houses? The varied functions of the episcopal residences of the see of Winchester, c.1130–c.1680," in *Princes of the Church: bishops and their palaces*, edited by David Rollason, Medieval Archaeology Monograph 39 (Abingdon: Routledge, 2017), 195–215.

Bibliographical update: since writing, the following material on the bishopric of Winchester's houses has appeared:

Hare, John N. "Bishop's Sutton: a forgotten residence of the bishops of Winchester." *Hampshire Field Club and Archaeological Society Newsletter* 64 (2015): 19.

Hare John N. "Bitterne: two medieval buildings." *Hampshire Field Club and Archaeological Society Newsletter* 69 (2018):14–15.

Stone, David, ed. The Accounts of the Manor of Esher in the Winchester Pipe Rolls, 1235-1376 Woking: Surrey Record Society, vol. 46, 2017.

Webster, Chris J. *Taunton Castle*. Taunton: Somerset Archaeological and Natural History Society, 2016.

Bibliography

Unpublished primary sources

Hampshire Record Office (HRO).

Winchester Pipe Rolls

11M59/B1/4. Pont Roches 9 (159272), 1213–14.

11M59/B1/23. Valence 2 (159447), 1251–52.

11M59/B1/28. Valence 8 (159293), 1257–58.

11M59/B1/54. Cons Pontoise 17 (159316), 1297–98.

11M59/B1/91. Trans Orleton 6 (159349), 1338–39.

11M59/B1/92. Trans Orleton 7 (159350), 1339–40.

11M59/B1/107. Cons Edington 10 (159365), 1354–55.

11M59 B1/108. Cons Edington 11 (159366), 1355–56.

11M59/B1/109. Edington 12 (159367), 1356–57.

11M59/B1/110. Cons Edington 13 (159368), 1357–58.

11M59/B1/112. Cons Edington 15 (159370), 1359–60.

11M59/B1/114. Cons Edington 17 (159372), 1361–62.

11M59/B1/123. Cons Wykeham 4 (159380), 1370–71.

11M59/B1/128. Cons Wykeham 9 (159456), 1375–76.

11M59/B1/138. Cons Wykeham 20 (159393), 1386–87.

11M59/B1/178. Trans Beaufort 31 (159433), 1434–35.

11M59/B1/179. Trans Beaufort 32 (159434), 1435–36.

11M59/B1/180. Trans Beaufort 35 (159435), 1438–39.

11M59 B1/185. Cons Waynflete 2 (159439), 1447–48.

11M59/B1/199. (155834), 1446–47.

11M59/B1/213. (155848), 1495–96.

11M59/B1/214. (155849), 1496–97.

11M59/B1/232. (155867), 1521–22.

11M59/B2/11/26. Account roll for Bishops Waltham Manor, 1387–88.

11M59/B2/11/101. Account roll for Bishops Waltham Manor, 1472–73.

Others

34A/13/1. Brooks, P.D. and A.C. Graham. "The Bishops Tenants." Unpublished typescript.

97M97/A33. Titow Research Papers. Wargrave Manor, Berkshire, 1211–1503.

Published primary sources

Aubrey, John. *The Natural History and Antiquities of the County of Surrey*, vol. 3. London, 1718.

Baigent, Francis J., ed. *The Registers of John of Sandale and Rigauld de Asserio, Bishops of Winchester A.D. 1316–1323*. Winchester: Hampshire Record Society, 1897.

Brewer, John S., ed. *Letters and Papers, Foreign and Domestic, Henry VIII*, Volume 4, 1524–1530. London: HMSO, 1875.

Chandler, John, ed. *John Leland's Itinerary*. Stroud: Sutton, 1993.

Deedes, Cecil., ed. *Registrum Johannis de Pontissara Episcopi Wyntoniensis*. Canterbury and York Society, 1924.

Franklin, Michael J., ed. *English Episcopal Acta, VIII: Winchester 1070–1204*. Oxford: Oxford University Press, 1993.

Goodman, Arthur W., ed. *Registrum Henrici Woodlock: Diocesis Wintoniensis A.D. 1305–1316*. Canterbury and York Society, 1940.

Haines, Roy M., ed. *Register of John de Stratford, Bishop of Winchester 1323–1333*, 2 vols. Woking: Surrey Record Society, 2010–11.

Hall, Hubert, ed. *The Pipe Roll for the Bishopric of Winchester, 1208–9*. London: King and Son, 1903.

Hockey, Stanley F., ed. *The Register of William Edington, Bishop of Winchester 1346–1366*, 2 vols. Winchester: Hampshire County Council, 1986, 1987.

Holt, Neville R., ed. *The Pipe Roll of the Bishopric of Winchester, 1210–11.* Manchester: Manchester University Press, 1964.

Kirby, Thomas F., ed. *Wykeham's Register*, 2 vols. Winchester: Hampshire Record Society, 1896, 1899.

Page, Mark, ed. *The Pipe Roll of the Bishopric of Winchester, 1301–2.* Winchester: Hampshire County Council, 1996.

Page, Mark, ed. *The Pipe Roll of the Bishopric of Winchester, 1409–10.* Winchester: Hampshire County Council, 1999.

The National Archives, Anon., *Itinerary of Henry III: 1215–1272*. Unpublished typescript.

The Pipe Roll for the Bishopric of Winchester [hereafter Pipe Roll], 1209, see Hall, H., above.

Pipe Roll 1211, see Holt, N.R. above.

Pipe Roll 1302, see Page, M., above.

Pipe Roll 1410, see Page, M., above.

Secondary sources

Allen, Tim, with Jonathan Hiller. *The Excavation of a Medieval Manor House of the Bishops of Winchester at Mount House, Witney, Oxfordshire, 1984–92*. Oxford: Oxford Archaeology, 2002.

Anon. "Tree-Ring Date Lists 2006." *Vernacular Architecture* 37 (2006): 97–132.

Biddle, Martin, ed. *Winchester in the Early Middle Ages*. Oxford: Clarendon Press, 1976.

Biddle, Martin. *Wolvesey: the Old Bishop's Palace, Winchester*. London: English Heritage, 1986.

Britnell, Richard H. "The Winchester Pipe Rolls and their Historians." In *The Winchester Pipe Rolls and Medieval English Society*, edited by Richard H. Britnell, 1–19. Woodbridge: the Boydell Press, 2003.

Brooks, Philip D. *Farnham Castle: the forgotten years*. Farnham: Farnham and District Museum Society, 1985.

Brown, Reginald Allen, Howard M. Colvin and Arnold J. Taylor. *The History of the Kings Works [HKW]*, vol. 1-2. London: HMSO, 1963.

Carlin, Martha. "The Reconstruction of Winchester House." *London Topographical Record* 25 (1985): 33–57.

Chandler, Richard. *The Life of William Waynflete, Bishop of Winchester*. London,1811.

Colvin, Harold M. ed. *HKW*, vol. 4. London: HMSO, 1982.

Currie, Christopher. "Earthworks in Fisher's Pond and Hassock's Wood." *Newsletter of Hampshire Field Club*, 9 (1988): 15–16.

Davis, Virginia. "Waynflete and the Wars of the Roses." *Southern History* 11 (1989): 1–22.

Davis, Virginia. *William Waynflete, Bishop and Educationalist*. Woodbridge: the Boydell Press, 1993.

Dyer, Christopher. *Standards of Living in the Late Middle Ages*. Cambridge: Cambridge University Press, 1989.

Ellis, P. (ed). *Ludgershall Castle. Excavations by Peter Addyman, 1964–1972*. Devizes: Wiltshire Archaeological Society, 2000.

Emery, Anthony. *Greater Medieval Houses of England and Wales* vol. 2. Cambridge: Cambridge University Press, 2000.

Emery, Anthony. *Greater Medieval Houses of England and Wales* vol. 3. Cambridge: Cambridge University Press, 2006.

Emery, Anthony. "Introductory Reflections after Greater Medieval Houses of England and Wales." In *The Medieval Great House*, edited by Malcolm Airs and Paul S. Barnwell, 1–30. Donington: Shaun Tyas, 2011.

Faulkner, Patrick A. "Some Medieval Archiepiscopal Palaces." *Archaeological Journal* 127 (1970): 130–46.

Floyer, J Kestell. "The Ancient Manor House of the Bishopric of Winchester at Esher." *Proceedings of the Society of Antiquaries* 2nd series, 32 (1919–20): 69–78.

Haines, Roy M. The Church and Politics in Fourteenth-Century England: the career of Adam Orleton c.1275–1345. Cambridge: Cambridge University Press, 1978.

Hare, John N. *Bishops Waltham Palace*. London: English Heritage, 1987.

Hare, John N. "Bishop's Waltham Palace, Hampshire: William of Wykeham, Henry Beaufort and the transformation of a medieval episcopal palace." *Archaeological Journal* 145 (1988): 222–54.

Hare, John N. "Miscellaneous Commodities." In *English Inland Trade, 1430–1540: Southampton and its region*, edited by Michael A. Hicks, 164–65. Oxford: Oxbow, 2015.

Hare, John N. "The Growth of the Roof-tile Industry in Later Medieval Wessex." *Medieval Archaeology* 35 (1991): 86–103.

Hare, John N. "The Architectural Patronage of Two Late Medieval Bishops: Edington, Wykeham and the rebuilding of Winchester Cathedral nave." *Antiquaries Journal* 92 (2012): 273–305.

Hare, John. N. "Tree-ring Dating of the Brethren's Hall at St Cross, Winchester." *Hampshire Field Club Newsletter* 56 (Autumn 2011): 17.

Hare, John N. "Why So Many Houses? The varied functions of the episcopal residences of the see of Winchester, c.1130–c.1680." In *Princes of the Church: bishops and their palaces*, edited by David Rollason, 195–215. Medieval Archaeology Monograph 39. Abingdon: Routledge, 2017.

Harris, John. "A William Kent Discovery." *Country Life* 125 (14 May 1959): 1076–78.

Harvey, John. *English Medieval Architects*. Gloucester: Alan Sutton, 1984.

James, Tom Beaumont. *The Palaces of Medieval England*. London: Seaby, 1990.

James, Tom Beaumont, and Anne M. Robinson. *Clarendon Palace: the history and archaeology of a medieval palace and hunting lodge near Salisbury, Wiltshire*, Reports of the Research Committee of the Society of Antiquaries of London 45. London: Society of Antiquaries and Thames and Hudson, 1988.

Keene, Derek. *Survey of Medieval Winchester*, vol 1. Oxford: Oxford University Press, 1985.

Meekings, Cecil A.F. "The Early Years of Netley Abbey." Reprinted in *Studies in Thirteenth-Century Justice and Administration*, by C.A.F. Meekings, ch xvii, 1–37. London: Bloomsbury Academic, 1981.

Moir, A.K. "Dendrochronological analysis of oak timbers from the Bishop's Camera Roof, Farnham Castle, Surrey." Tree-ring services: report FACA/27/06.

Overland Trade Database, "People, Places, and Commodities 1430–1540." Accessed 13 July, 2018 (the website is currently unavailable).

Page, Mark. *The Medieval Bishops of Winchester: estate, archive and administration*. Winchester: Hampshire County Council, 2002.

Page, William, ed. *The Victoria History of Hampshire and the Isle of Wight*, vol. 3. London, 1908.

Peach, D. Len. *The History of Hursley Park*. Winchester: IBM UK Laboratories, 1978.

Phillpotts, Christopher J. "Plague and Reconstruction: Bishops Edington and Wykeham at Highclere, 1346–1404." In *Fourteenth Century England 1*, edited by Nigel Saul, 115–32. Woodbridge: The Boydell Press, 2000.

Radford, Courtenay. A. R., and Hallam, A.D. "The History of Taunton Castle in the Light of Recent Excavations." *Somersetshire Archaeological and Natural History Society Proceedings*, 98 (1953): 55–96.

Rainbow, Penny. *A Complete History of the Tower of Esher*. Privately printed, 2010.

Roberts, Edward. "The Bishop of Winchester's Fishponds, 1159–1400: their development, function and management." *Proceedings of the Hampshire Field Club and Archaeological Society* 42 (1986): 125–38.

Roberts, Edward. "The Bishop of Winchester's Deer Parks in Hampshire, 1200–1400." *Proceedings of the Hampshire Field Club and Archaeological Society* 44 (1988): 67–86.

Roberts, Edward. "William of Wykeham's House at East Meon, Hants." *Archaeological Journal* 150 (1993): 456–81.

Roberts, Edward. "Overton Court Farm and the Late-Medieval Farmhouses of Demesne Lessees in Hampshire." *Proceedings of the Hampshire Field Club and Archaeological Society* 51 (1995): 89–106.

Roberts, Edward. "Medieval Hambledon Manor: chambers for bishops and their stewards." *Proceedings of the Hampshire Field Club and Archaeological Society* 59 (2004): 180–95.

Roberts, Edward, and Maureen Gale. "Henry Mildmay's New Farms 1656–1704." *Proceedings of the Hampshire Field Club and Archaeological Society* 50 (1995): 169–92.

Robo, Etienne. *Medieval Farnham: everyday life in an episcopal manor*. Farnham: E W Langham, 1939.

Rollason, David, ed. *Princes of the Church: bishops and their palaces*. Medieval Archaeology Monograph 39. Abingdon: Routledge, 2017.

Schofield, John, ed. *The London Surveys of Ralph Treswell*. London: London Topographical Society, 1987.

Seeley, Derek, Christopher Phillpotts and Mark Samuel. *Winchester Palace: excavations at the Southwark residence of the bishops of Winchester*, Museum of London Archaeology (MoLA) Monograph 31. London: MoLA, 2006.

Storey, Robin L. *The End of the House of Lancaster*. London: Barrie and Rockliffe, 1966.

Sylvester, Richard S., ed. *Cavendish's The Life and Death of Cardinal Wolsey*. London: Early English Text Society, 1959.

Thomson, Steve, and Birbeck, Vaughan. "Investigations at Wayneflete's Tower, Esher." *Surrey Archaeological Collections* 95 (2010): 259–70.

Thompson, Michael W. "The Date of 'Fox's Tower', Farnham Castle, Surrey." *Surrey Archaeological Collections* 57 (1960): 85–92.

Thompson, Michael W. *Farnham Castle Keep*. London: HMSO, 1961.

Thompson, Michael W. *Medieval Bishops' Houses in England and Wales*. Aldershot: Ashgate, 1998.

Thurley, Simon. "The Domestic Building Works of Cardinal Wolsey." In *Cardinal Wolsey: church, state and art*, edited by Steven J. Gunn and Peter G. Lindley, 76–102. Cambridge: Cambridge University Press, 1991.

Titow, Jan Z. *English Rural Society*. London: George Allen and Unwin, 1969.

Vincent, Nicholas. "The Politics of Church and State as Reflected in the Winchester Pipe Rolls, 1208–80." In *The Winchester Pipe Rolls and Medieval English Society*, edited by Richard H. Britnell, 157–81. Woodbridge: the Boydell Press, 2003.

Vivian-Neal, Arthur W., and St. George Gray, Harold, "Materials for the History of Taunton Castle." *Somersetshire Archaeological and Natural History Society Proceedings*, 86 (1940): 45–78

Woolgar, Christopher M. *The Great Household in Late Medieval England*. London: Yale University Press, 1999.

6

The Effect of the Black Death of 1348–49 on the Fair of St Giles, Winchester

Paula Arthur

Independent Scholar

Abstract: The pipe rolls of the bishopric of Winchester not only impart in-depth detail about England's wealthiest see in the Middle Ages, but also provide an account of the demographic, economic and social conditions on the estate. This paper examines evidence from the pipe roll of 1348–49 for the impact of the Black Death on the fair of St Giles, one of the four chief fairs in England. The analysis of the pipe roll will focus specifically upon information relating to the Black Death of 1348–49 and assess the immediate impact of the Black Death upon the fair of St Giles. By using other pipe rolls of the bishopric of Winchester both before and after 1348–49 the work also compares and contrasts. Studying such information in conjunction with other years provides a comparative database with which to determine the various stages of decline, if any, after the Black Death of 1348–49 struck Winchester. This paper will search through the information available in the pipe roll as to whether this decline coincided with the arrival of the Black Death, and whether the fair's significant source of income deteriorated due to the visitation of the plague.

Key words: Pipe Roll, Bishopric of Winchester, Fair of St Giles, Winchester, Black Death

This paper examines evidence from the 1348–49 pipe roll of the bishopric of Winchester for the impact of the Black Death on the fair of St Giles in Winchester, one of the four chief fairs in England. The pipe rolls, currently conserved at the Hampshire Record Office in Winchester, impart in-depth details about England's medieval society and economy and are used here to study a key historical event, the onset of the Black Death of 1348 and the effect if any on the fair of St Giles.

The pipe roll itself is written in Latin, the language of most administrative documents in the mid-fourteenth century. Overall the pipe roll for the year 1348–49 is in a reasonable state of preservation, although in many instances a section of the account may be missing or illegible owing to decay. In some cases the deterioration is so bad that the majority of the membrane has disintegrated so as to render the contents almost illegible. In recent years staff at the Hampshire Record Office have carried out extensive and expert repairs, which enable this document to be used with more confidence. The condition and overall appearance of the pipe roll is one of extreme neatness, the letters are written methodically in a small gothic hand in brown ink and the lines of writing are carefully laid out horizontally.

The analysis of the pipe roll focuses specifically upon information relating to the Black Death of 1348–49 and will assess the immediate impact of the disease upon the fair of St Giles. Issues considered include an assessment as to whether the fair attracted the same numbers of people as in years previous to the Black Death, whether the rental income decreased after 1348–49 as well as evaluating receipts, expenditure and wages all in relation to the time of the Black Death. By using other pipe rolls of the bishopric of Winchester the work will compare and contrast different years both before and after 1348–49. Studying such information in conjunction with other years provides a comparative database with which to determine the various stages of decline, if any, after the Black Death of 1348–49 struck Winchester. This paper searches through the information available in the pipe roll as to whether this decline coincided with the arrival of the Black Death, and whether the fair's significant source of income which had been generated in the past to the bishop, deteriorated due to the visitation of the plague.

Black Death

The Black Death was one of the worst natural disasters in history, even today the very name of it conjures up images of fear and despair. In 1347 this great plague arrived in Europe ravaging cities and countryside alike and causing widespread depopulation and death. The Black Death swept into England through France during 1348, crossing the Channel to strike Bristol, London, Plymouth and Southampton.[1] Contemporary chroniclers offered various dates and locations for its first entry into England and it is probable that the bacterium arrived independently in a number of ports and coastal areas over the course of several months before spreading inland. Historians from Seebohm

[1] R. Horrox (trans. and ed) *The Black Death* (Manchester: Manchester University Press, 1994) for contemporary accounts of the arrival of the plague, 62–66.

(1865) to Sloane (2011) have debated evidence of the various aspects of the plague itself to perceived links with the Peasants' Revolt.[2] It is a subject where demographic, economic and social historians can find something to suit their chosen speciality. One thing which remains certain is that the circumstances surrounding the plague are as hotly debated today as they were during the nineteenth century investigations of Seebohm (1865) and Gasquet (1893).[3] Today the plague still retains its position as one of the greatest economic and social factors of the last millennium and retains its importance as one of the foremost topics of medieval history.

Pipe Rolls

The Winchester pipe rolls present a detailed record of the audit process of the bishop's accounts for each financial year which ran from Michaelmas (29 September) to Michaelmas. The pipe rolls of the bishopric of Winchester not only impart in-depth detail about England's wealthiest see in the Middle Ages, but also provide an account of the demographic, economic and social conditions on the estate. The pipe rolls document the years in broken series, from 1208–09 until 1710–11 in the form of one hundred and thirty-seven parchment compilations and would appear to be the best source available for a great estate.[4] They remain the fullest manorial source for demographic, economic and social historians of the Black Death. As records of the wealthiest ecclesiastical landowner north of the Alps, the pipe rolls hold a unique key to unlocking the secrets of the plague which raged through England until the seventeenth century. It is very likely the writer, or writers, of the pipe roll knew people who died of the plague and may very well have seen the plague victims. Even the sheepskins upon which the pipe roll was written were no doubt from flocks on manors where the plague befell. To handle this document is both exciting and evocative of that terrifying era of our island story.

Although the basic form of each manorial account has changed very little over time, the details recorded varied considerably. The pipe rolls record some fifty to sixty manors in a degree of detail unmatched in scope by accounts elsewhere.[5] The documents themselves represent one of the earliest forms of medieval manorial accounting and combine to form a unique set of primary documents and contain much evidence relating to the plague. Using the pipe rolls the historian is able to examine the financial accounts of the Bishop of Winchester's extensive estates, which extended 'far beyond the spiritual boundaries of the see'.[6] From the pipe rolls themselves we can ascertain information about the economic and social circumstances of a 'manorial community in motion', serving to inform us of the relationship between the bishop and his tenants.[7] But the pipe roll is more than a repository of social and economic evidence. The main purpose of the rolls was to record annual accounts, which had been copied from the *compotus* (account) roll of each manor after the accounts had passed through the final stages of auditing. Of the original *compotus* rolls that they duplicate, none survive for the thirteenth century, some survive for the fourteenth century, and a substantial number survive for the fifteenth century.[8] The audit was one of the chief ways in which the bishop controlled the running of his estate. It took place annually after the end of the financial year at Michaelmas, usually at Wolvesey Palace. There, the reeves of each of the bishop's manors and boroughs would present their accounts and hand over whatever money they owed to the bishop's treasurer. The auditors would examine the accounts and frequently queried or disallowed what the reeve claimed, probably on the basis of past accounts or the review which was made halfway through the accounting year. When everything had been settled, the reeve's account and the auditor's additions were then copied onto the pipe roll.

What makes the pipe rolls so valuable is that many of these original accounts, such as the court rolls, are now missing, for some manors there are no rolls, and others are represented in only one or two. None of the surviving manor court rolls are early, which means that the development of jurisdiction on the bishopric estates up to the late fourteenth century can be told only from the pipe rolls. The earliest court roll is for 1331 and relates to the manor of Hambledon.[9] Thus without the pipe rolls a huge vacuum would exist in our knowledge of the accounting system practised by individual manors.

St Giles's Fair

The fair of St Giles in Winchester ranked as one of the foremost and largest fairs in Europe.[10] It was first started by a grant from King William II (c. 1065–1100) to his cousin

[2] F. Seebohm "The Black Death and its Place in English History," *Fortnightly Review*, 2, (1865): part I, 149–60; part II, 268–79; B. Sloane, *The Black Death in London* (Stroud: History Press, 2011).

[3] Seebohm, 'The Black Death and its Place in English History'; F.A. Gasquest, *The Great Pestilence (A.D. 1348–9) now commonly known as the Black Death* (London: Simpkin Marshall, 1893).

[4] The pipe roll of 1348–49 is one of a long series of surviving rent rolls; in all 191 rolls survive from 1208–09 until 1454–55. Thereafter, the accounts continue from 1456–67 until 1710–11.

[5] Notable studies of ecclesiastical estates and their manors include C. Dyer, *Lords and Peasants in a Changing Society. The Estates of the Bishopric of Worcester, 680–1540* (Cambridge: Cambridge University Press, 1980); B.F. Harvey, *Westminster Abbey and its estates in the Middle Ages* (Oxford: Clarendon Press, 1977); I. Kershaw, *Bolton Priory: The Economy of a Northern Monastery, 1286–1325* (London: Oxford University Press, 1973); E. Miller, *The Abbey and Bishopric of Ely: the social and economic history of an ecclesiastical estate from the tenth century to the early fourteenth century* (London: Cambridge University Press, 1951).

[6] M. Page (ed) *The Pipe Roll of the Bishopric of Winchester 1301–02*, Hampshire Record Series, 14 (1996), ix.

[7] A.E. Levett, "The Black Death on the Estates of the See of Winchester," in *Oxford Studies in Social and Legal History*, Vol 5, ed. P. Vinogradoff (Oxford: Clarendon Press, 1916), 144.

[8] T.W. Mayberry, *Estate Records of the Bishops of Winchester in the Hampshire Record Office* (Winchester: Hampshire County Council 1998), 6. The bulk of the rolls are now preserved in the Hampshire Record Office.

[9] Court Rolls 10443 NRA 7893, Winchester College Archives.

[10] J.Z. Titow "The Decline of the Fair of St Giles, Winchester, in the Thirteenth and Fourteenth Centuries," *Nottingham Medieval Studies* xxxi (1987): 58–75. In 1240 the four chief fairs of England were those of Boston, Winchester, St. Ives and Northampton.

Bishop Walkelin of Winchester. Originally it lasted only three days, taking place the day before and after St Giles' Day, (1 September) but over the years the number of days increased. Henry I (1068–1135) extended the fair time to eight days, Stephen (1096–1154) granted the fair a further six days and Henry II (1133–1189) doubled the number of days allowed by his grandfather, King Henry I from eight to sixteen.[11] This period of sixteen days seems to have been regarded as the normal limit during the twelfth and much of the following century.[12] Once one of the foremost fairs in England during the twelfth and thirteenth century, thereafter St Giles fair declined into a local event before finally disappearing at the beginning of the nineteenth century.[13] This paper searches through the information available in the pipe roll as to whether this decline coincided with the arrival of the Black Death, and whether the fair's significant source of income which had been generated in the past to the bishop, deteriorated due to the visitation of the Black Death.

St Giles's fair was a major livestock market, where cattle, cart horses, sumpter horses and palfreys were bought and sold. There seems also to have been an important trade in leather and leather goods, particularly saddles, bridles, boots and gloves. Furs, too were a valuable item of commerce at the fair. Other significant trades included wool, cloth and spices, for which royal, aristocratic, and ecclesiastical households created a vigorous demand.[14] The organisation of the fair began with the period entry, which lasted from the morning of the vigil of the feast of St Giles (29 August) to the nativity of the Virgin Mary (8 September). During this time merchants brought their goods into the fair and paid a toll upon entering the gate, all pleas in the bishop's Pavilion Court were to be begun by summons or attachment. The second period was that designated for trading for the remainder of the sixteen days of the fair which the bishop enjoyed under Henry II's charter of 1155. In this time merchants who wished to bring in goods had to pay a fine to the bishop in addition to a toll, and pleas were to be begun by distraint so as to ensure that all transactions were complete by the time the merchants left. During the third and final period, the bishop's officers went around the fair on foot and ordered the merchants to cease trading and to depart.[15]

As mentioned previously the fair was held every September for a period of sixteen days. During that time all trade in the city was suspended as the Bishop of Winchester and his bailiffs took control of commercial life, moving it lock, stock and barrel to the top of the hill. Semi-permanent streets and shops were erected and levies from tolls and fines were imposed. For the duration of the fair the bishop and his justiciaries were given the keys of the city and collected rent for each booth and taxes on articles sold. Guards were placed on all roads leading to the city and visitors who entered the city for the fair had to pay a toll. Guards were placed at Stockbridge, Romsey, Redbridge, Crab Wood, Hursley, Mansbridge, Otterbourne, Kingbridge, Curbridge, Cheriton and Alresford to levy tolls on merchandise passing over these bridges.[16] While the fair lasted, trade was not permitted to be undertaken outside of the fair within 'a circuit of seven leagues'.[17] The sale of merchandise in any other place other than the fair would end under the penalty of forfeiture of the goods to the bishop.

Before looking in detail at the accounts it is worth describing how the holding of the fair affected, and indeed paralysed, the municipal life of Winchester. On the vigil of St Giles (29 August) the seneschal, with the justice of the bishop's Court of Pavilion, or the treasurer, rode out from Wolvesey Palace and entered the city at Kings Gate where the mayor, bailiff and citizens met them and handed over the city keys and custody as well as those of the South Gate.[18] Here the fair was for the first time proclaimed in the usual form:

> Let no merchant or other for these sixteen days within a circuit of seven leagues round the fair, sell, buy or set out for sale any merchandise in any place other than the fair under penalty of forfeiture of goods to the bishop.[19]

The officers would then ride to the West Gate, where they received the keys, and also the custody of the great weigh beam (tron) of the city which was used for the weighing of wool.[20] Similarly the North Gate and East Gate were placed in the custody of the bishop's officers, who after other proclamations rode out to the bishop's Pavilion of the fair on St. Giles' Hill, where the seneschal and justices held a sitting of the court of the Soke called the 'Cheyne' Court, to summon the bishop's suitors and tenants for service at the fair and Court of Pavilion. Many of the bishop's tenants, were bound to the fair and told to come forward on each Vigil of St Giles, before six in the morning, to offer their service at the Pavilion, and each one was required to

> be prepared with horses and arms as often as may be needful. From among them the Justiciaries shall, at their pleasure, select three or four (or more or fewer, as they may see it will be needful) to serve and tarry in the fair during its continuance, and to carry out the executions and precepts of the said Justiciaries in all places.[21]

[11] G.W. Kitchin (ed) "The Charter of Edward III Concerning St Giles' Fair AD 1349," in *A Consuetudinary of the Fourteenth Century for the Refectory of the House of S. Swithun in Winchester* (London: Elliot Stock, 1886) 43–44.

[12] In 1317 Edward II gave a permanent extension to twenty-four days. The charter of Edward III recognises sixteen days as the normal period, though the actual business of buying and selling within the fair was certainly extended to twenty-four days on several occasions afterwards. Kitchin, "Winchester Chart. of Ed III," 40.

[13] Titow, "The Decline of the Fair of St Giles"; D. Keene, *Survey of Medieval Winchester*, Winchester Studies, vol. 2 (Oxford: Clarendon Press, 1976) 58–75.

[14] Keene, *Survey of Medieval Winchester*, 1117.

[15] Keene, *Survey of Medieval Winchester*, 1113.

[16] Kitchin, Charter Ed III, 52.

[17] Kitchin, Charter Ed III, 46.

[18] Kitchin, Charter Ed III, *passim*. These accounts, though of the fourteenth century, embody practices which were to a large extent carried out in the previous centuries. The Pavilion was the bishop's court house in the fair; it was first recorded *c.*1200.

[19] Kitchin, Charter Ed III, 46.

[20] Kitchin, Charter Ed III, 46. A tron is a type of weighing machine.

[21] Kitchin, Charter Ed III, 49.

A marshal, porter and chamberlain of the Pavilion, three guardians for the three toll-gates, and other officers were appointed, and ultimately the mayor and bailiffs of the city were dismissed and returned to the city, stripped of their position, while the seneschal and justices were at liberty to appoint a new mayor, bailiff and coroner whilst the fair lasted. The seneschal and justices in effect controlled the entire life of the city, for the Pavilion Court not only dealt with actions such as debts between traders at the fair but swept up the whole legal business of Winchester and its suburbs within the seven-league limit, while every function of civic government and the regulation of trade was transferred to the episcopal officials.[22] The Pavilion was the nucleus of the fair. Guards were placed on the roads round Winchester and tolls levied, while in the fair itself at sundown each day the bishop's marshal ordered every stall to be shut until dawn the next day.[23] Only the bishop's officers were allowed to move about the fair and open fires were strictly forbidden.[24] If anyone was to break these rules they would be taken by the officers and brought to the Pavilion where they would be fined. The bishop from the time that the keys and custody of the gates 'have been delivered to him, shall, by his Justiciaries and other Minsters, have custody of the whole City'[25]

Pipe Roll Accounts

The first surviving account of revenue from St Giles's fair to be entered on the bishop's pipe rolls concerns the fair held in September 1287. The early accounts contain little more than grand totals of receipts and expenditure. From 1292 onwards, however, they record the bishop's business at the fair in minute detail so that it is possible to trace not only the overall trends of trade as reflected in the bishop's total income, but also the organisation of the fair and the history of the many shops and properties within it. Looking at the pipe roll from the year 1292, the total receipts received from the fair were originally itemised under separate headings.[26] Generally the format of entry remains fairly consistent throughout the years studied. The accounts begin with the arrears, if any, followed by the tolls received on the South, East and West Gates. It would appear from searching through the pipe rolls that a toll for the North Gate was never collected. The next entry takes the form of rental payments under three separate headings *terragium*, the ground rent or land-tax paid to the bishop for occupying ground at the fair, *boagium*, toll or rent payment for cattle/stock and *seldagium* rent charged on shops or stalls. These items are generally followed by a listing of payments received from various Winchester crafts represented at the fair, as well as the general expenses incurred; for example the wages paid to varying occupations such as the guardians of the road, wages of the crier, costs of the Episcopal household at Wolvesey as well as the cost of maintaining and repairing buildings. All these figures illustrate quite clearly the process of how the fair operated. Studying such information in conjunction with other years provides a comparative database with which to determine the various stages of decline, if any, after the Black Death of 1348–49 struck Winchester.

Collection of tolls

The account of the fair begins with a listing of the tolls paid on the three gates, and this is shown in Table 6.1. Titow states that initially the highest amounts were collected at the South Gate, through which came the traffic from overseas via Portsmouth and Southampton. The lowest amounts were at West Gate where traffic from more local places, such as Newbury, Oxford, Romsey and Salisbury entered the city.[27] The tolls collected at the East Gate, through which most of the London traffic moved via Alton and Alresford, occupied middle position until 1299 where the amount slipped into relative insignificance thereafter.[28]

Titow's findings for the South Gate certainly concur with the figures extracted from the pipe roll of 1301–02. However, after that date the amounts collected at the West Gate are considerably higher than those of the other two gates combined. It would therefore appear that the main body of traders and visitors came from more local places such as Salisbury and Romsey, and this seems to be the case for all the years studied. It is noticeable however that one year more than any other reveals a decrease in the total amount of tolls collected, the first year of the Black Death, 1348–49. The year before, 1347–48, the tolls collected at the South Gate amounted to 17s 10d, by the following year this had decreased to 6s 3½d rising back to 17s 1½d by 1349-50. The tolls collected at the East Gate tell a similar but less dramatic story; the tolls collected during 1347–48 amounted to 4s 4½d decreasing to 3s 8d during the plague year, increasing to 9s 8½d by 1349–50. Finally, the West Gate collected tolls of 36s ½d in 1347–48, decreasing to 15s 6½d during 1348–49, increasing the following year to 39s 2½d.[29] If we combine the tolls received for all three gates, then the impact of the decline in these figures becomes apparent. During the first year of Black Death, the tolls received on the gates had decreased by fifty-six per cent. This is a significant reduction and the only one occurring during the period studied.

[22] Sometimes an actual mayor was appointed by the bishop or the bailiffs replaced by his officers. Whatever the actual measures, the self-government of the city was extinguished for the time. Kitchin, Charter Ed III, 46–47. The craftsmen and traders of Winchester were transferred to the fair in many cases, or forced to cease work.

[23] Kitchin, Charter Ed III, 50.

[24] Kitchin, Charter Ed III, 50.

[25] Kitchin, Charter Ed III, 47.

[26] C.H. Vellacott "Winchester: Fair and Trades," *The Victoria History of the Counties of England A History of Hampshire*, V, ed. W. Page (London, 1912) 36–44.

[27] For a discussion of the road systems in relation to the city gates see M. Biddle ed. *Winchester in the Early Middle Ages: an edition and discussion of the Winton Domesday*, Winchester Studies, 1 (Oxford: Clarendon Press, 1976) 260–63.

[28] Titow "Decline of the Fair of St Giles," 61–62. During 1299 the toll was 34s 4d, but by 1300 it had decreased to 18s 9d and they were never to exceed this sum again.

[29] The Winchester Pipe Rolls, Hampshire Record Office [hereafter HRO] 11M59/B1/100 m26, HRO 11M59/B1/101 m41, HRO 11M59/B1/102 m26.

Table 6.1: Tolls collected for select years 1301–1410

	1301–02			1347–48		1348–49		1349–50		1364–65		1371–72		1409–10[1]
South Gate	£2	19s	6d	17s	10d	6s	3½d	17s	1½d	3s	6½d	3s	6d	0
East Gate		14s		4s	4½d	3s	8d	9s	8½d	4s	7d	6s	4d	0
West Gate		17s	10d	36s	½d	15s	6½d	39s	2½d	36s	2d	25s	3d	0
Total of all Gates	£4	11s	4d	58s	3d	25s	6d[2]	66s	½d	43s	11½d[3]	35s	1d	0

[1] None in this year because deductions of keepers exceeded receipts.
[2] The entry on the pipe roll is stated as 25s 6½d.
[3] This adds up to 44s 3½d but the pipe roll states 43s 11½d.

These figures would seem to suggest that fewer people were travelling to the fair. This could be the result of two main factors, first that there were fewer people alive to travel due to the mortality from plague or secondly it may have been that restrictions were enforced to prevent the movement of people from town to town in an attempt to stop the spread of plague, or people were just too afraid to travel. Although I can find no direct documentary evidence to support the second theory, the pipe roll of 1348–49 does tell us that the tolls collected were 'less this particular year following the great mortality of men'.[30] Here we have a first-hand account telling us purposely that the amounts received from the gates were down this year because of the death of men from the Black Death.

Rents

Another insight into the effect of plague upon the fair can be gained by looking at the various rents paid to the bishop, as shown in Table 6.2. Looking initially at the *terragium*, paid by owners of the shops erected on the site, it becomes evident that the pattern of decrease and increase follows the same form as the tolls received upon the three gates, but what is more noticeable is the longevity of the decrease. For example, in 1347–48 the amount of *terragium* collected amounted to £12 4s 8½d, decreasing to £6 4s 2d for the year of the Black Death. We witness a slight rise to £8 14s 4d for the year directly after the plague, but by 1364–65 this has decreased further to £5 14s 4½d.

By 1362, owing to the second pestilence outbreak, the *terragium* has been recorded as even lower than in the year of the Black Death i.e. £5 17s 3d and one pound of cumin.[31] The account then details a long list of shops left in decay or abandoned for two years or more '2 *terragia* of Ralph Attechurch at the Corner which rendered 4d have stood empty for two years as well as one shop of the Wardens of St John's House which paid a mark for it is in utter decay'.[32] Numerous shops and plots in unnamed parts of the fair are recorded among the defaults of the *terragium* due to the bishop in the second half of the fourteenth and early fifteenth century. The properties of St John's Hospital, the Frary and Kalender and the church of St John in the Soke seem particularly hard hit. References are made regularly to ruinous shops that were in default due to decay or the fact that they had been demolished. A similar story is told for the *seldagium* which proclaimed a figure of £6 10s 10d during 1347–48, however, once again, this decreases to £2 2s 6d for the first year of the plague rising to £5 4s 4d for the year after, decreasing to £2 8s 6d by 1364–65. The last rental figure to look at is that of the *boagium* which had reduced from 10s 8d in 1347–48 to nil the following year, increasing, albeit modestly, to 6d by 1349–50. The entry of a nil return for 1348–49 is highly unusual and would suggest that, for the first time since the fair started, a cattle market was not held that year. One possible reason for this could be the number of cows being paid to the bishop that year as heriots. Heriots were generally paid on the death of the tenant and are found in large numbers in the pipe roll of 1348–49.[33] Payment would usually be in the form of the best live beast or chattel of the deceased tenant, which would then be delivered to the lord. The fact that a cattle market was not held that year provides significant evidence of the scale of the Black Death in Winchester. Looking at the number of cows received as heriots in Table 6.3, one can only imagine the horrors that people of Winchester must have experienced and the effects of the first year of pestilence when, as the contemporary Geoffrey le Baker put it, 'people who one day had been full of happiness, on the next were found dead'.[34]

The *Boagium* separates itself from both the *terragium* and *seldagium* in that by 1364–65 the amount received has rather unusually exceeded the sum collected during 1347–48 i.e. the sum has increased from 10s 8d to 18s 4½d.[35] It would appear that during the first year of the Black Death people may not have had the cattle to bring to the fair or that the majority of people had died and their cattle, instead of being sold at the fair, were given to the bishop as heriots. This certainly links in with the

[30] HRO 11M59/B1/101 m41 '*pro maxima morte hominum*'.
[31] HRO 11M59/B1/115 m38.
[32] HRO 11M59/B1/115 m38.

[33] Paula Arthur, "The Impact of the Black Death on Seventeen Units of Account of the Bishopric of Winchester," Unpublished PhD Thesis University College Winchester/University of Southampton, 2005.
[34] Chronicon Galfridi le Baker de Swynebroke in Horrox, *The Black Death*, 81.
[35] HRO 11M59/B1/100 m26; 11M59/B1/101 m41; 11M59/B1/102 m26.

Table 6.2: Rents paid to the bishop for select years 1301 – 1410.

	1301–02	1347–48	1348–49	1349–50	1364–65	1371–72	1409–10
Terragium	£23 6½d	£12 4s 8½d	£6 4s 2d	£8 14s 4d	£5 14s 4½d[1]	£5 13s 4½d[2]	£1 6s 2½d
Boagium	£1 10d	10s 8d	Nothing	6d	18s 4½d	18s 4d	2s 4d
Seldagium	£10 8s 6d	£6 10s 10d	£2 2s 6d[3]	£5 4s 4d	£2 8s 6d	£1 14s 6d	Nothing declared
Total	£34 9s 10½d	£19 6s 2½d	£8 18s 8d[4]	£13 19s 2d	£9 1s 3d	£8 6s 2½d	£1 8s 6½d

[1] Plus 1lb of cumin.
[2] Plus 1lb of cumin.
[3] This figure does not tally. We are told in the narrative of the accounts that nine windows were rented at 2s 6d which would equal 22s 6d, however the total in the final total of the pipe roll the total is documented as 7s 6d.
[4] The total figure declared in the pipe roll (£8 18s 8d) does not tally with what is actually recorded (£8 6s 8d).

Table 6.3: Number of animal and cash heriots for select years 1301–1410[1]

	1301–02	1347–48	1348–49	1349–50	1364–65	1371–72	1409–10
Horses	0	0	9	1	2	0	0
Plough Horses	2	5	62	1	1	1	2
Cart Horses	2	2	8	0	0	0	0
Mares	2	1	0	0	0	0	0
Colts	0	1	2	0	0	0	0
Bullocks	2	0	23½	0	0	0	0
Oxen	3	7	45	1	1	0	4
Cows	4	1	85½	1	0	3	3
Calves	2	0	11	0	0	0	0
Yearlings	0	1	8	0	0	0	1
Wethers	0	0	10	0	1	0	1
Ewes	0	2	7	0	0	0	0
Pigs	2	0	2	0	0	0	0
Hoggets	0	0	1	0	1	0	0
Total no. of animal Heriots	19	20	274	4	6	4	11
Total Heriots in cash	None	5s + 6@12d	*10@10s + 48@12d	8@12d	None	None	1@4s

[1] Based upon the following units of account spread geographically within the single county of Hampshire – Alresford manor, Alverstoke, Ashmansworth, Beauworth, Cheriton, Crawley, Ecchinswell, Hambledon manor, North Waltham and Woodhay. P.A. Arthur "The Impact of the Black Death on Seventeen Units of Account of The Bishopric of Winchester," Unpublished PhD Thesis (University of Winchester, 2005), 217. Bulls, Hoggs, Lambs, Piglets and Rams have been deleted from this table as no heriots are declared for such beasts.

findings on the number of cattle received by the bishop as heriots. For example, looking through the pipe rolls the number of heriots received in the form of cattle increased considerably during the first year of the Black Death. In 1347–48 just seven oxen were received by the bishop, but by the following year, 1348–49 this had increased to forty-five.[36] The same can be said of cows, during 1347–48 one cow was received as a heriot, but by the following year this had increased to over eighty-five and so the story continues with other animals.[37] By 1364–65 however, only one ox and one cow were received as heriots, the total of all animals received not exceeding six, this may explain the increase in *Boagium* that year and the increase in demand for stock. The year 1371–72 tells a similar story in that 18s 4d was received for the *Boagium*, with only three cows and one plough horse being received in heriots that year.

[36] HRO 11M59/B1/100 m26; 11M59/B1/101 m42.

[37] HRO 11M59/B1/100 m26; 11M59/B1/101 m42.

Once again if we were to take a combined figure of all three-rental incomes we can see that the decrease from 1347–48 to 1348–49 amounts to almost fifty-eight per cent. It would therefore certainly appear that during the first year of the Black Death, fewer shops, stalls and structures were being occupied as well as a smaller supply of stock.

Without doubt the plague played a significant role in the financial deterioration of the fair's once plentiful returns. However the long-term effect was possibly not felt until the second outbreak of 1361/2. Titow supports this theory, for he believed the tremendous mortality of the first plague was in itself cushioned, in so far as its immediate economic effects are concerned, by the presence of very considerable overpopulation on the eve of the outbreak. What strengthens this argument is the fact that in so many manors all holdings vacated through the Black Death were taken up at once without any apparent difficulty.[38]

Titow believed that this suggested a 'countryside teeming with people rather than one starved of them'.[39] This is certainly a plausible argument and corroborates the data found in the pipe rolls studied. However, when the plague struck again in 1361 there was no longer a substantial reservoir of people to cushion its effects and, in spite of the lesser ferocity of its attack, its consequences were more serious and more immediately felt.[40] The basis for this argument hinges upon the figures received for ground-rents (*terragium*) which although dropping significantly in 1349 increased almost immediately with only a few permanent vacancies left unoccupied in the wake of the pestilence. It is difficult to find any figure received after the Black Death that matched the £12 received in 1347–48, but what is certain is that the sums received reduce significantly for each year after 1361, the average amount of ground-rent received between 1361 and 1399 has decreased to £5, whereas the average ground-rent between the years of 1320–1348 was over £13. It is noticeable that after 1361 the rolls dictate a long list of lapsed rents which in the succeeding years grew steadily and progressively longer.[41] This suggests that with the continued recurrence of the Black Death's successive plagues which occurred during 1361, 1369, 1374–79 and 1390–93, the population of Winchester diminished further, this time failing to recover so quickly after the first plague of 1348–49. With less people now available to take up these vacancies it was inevitable that the ground-rents would continue to decrease.

Receipts, pleas and perquisites

Turning to the total receipts received from the fair, Titow maintains that during the period 1189–1250, for which only six annual figures are available, receipts stood well above £100, with the annual average producing a figure of £143 7s 3d.[42] He maintains further that these figures dropped below the £100 line for the first time in 1290; after which they fell below £50 following 1323, decreasing to less than £40 after 1336; dropping permanently below £30 in 1361.[43] However, looking at the evidence contained in the pipe roll this is certainly not the case for the year 1364–65 where receipts are recorded as £48 11s 3d, as noted in Table 6.4. Titow also states that the average amount of total receipts received was below £35 after 1323, no more than £28 after 1336; and less than £21 after 1360. However once again it is difficult to agree with these figures, for example after 1336 the figures for 1347–48 equal £32 16s 5½d and 1349–50 are recorded as £29 14s 5¾d, also for the year 1364–65 the total receipts amounted to £48 11s 3d which is considerably more than the average calculated by Titow. What cannot be ignored is the twenty-seven per cent decrease in receipts which occurred during the first year of plague. This decrease seems fairly short-lived however for, as already mentioned, by 1364–65 receipts are recorded as £48 11s 3d which is significantly more than the amount received during the year before the Black Death.

One item of income which increased directly after the Black Death were the pleas and perquisites of the Pavilion Court.[44] For example, excluding 8s 1d of arrears, the amount received during 1347–48 amounted to 58s 8d, decreasing to 32s 1d in 1348–49. However, the following year this figure has increased substantially to £4 13s 6d, rising to £6 8s 2d in 1361–62 and £7 3s 7d by 1364–65. The pleas and perquisites of the Pavilion Court formed a considerable percentage of total receipts averaging a quarter of the receipts received from 1354 increasing to an average of forty per cent by 1391. In 1373 the payments imposed by the court produced an astonishing seventy per cent of the total receipts received by the bishop.[45] However, the recorded amounts of the court's profits refer to the fines enforced by the court and not necessarily to sums actually collected. Unfortunately, the pipe roll only lists the total sum received and not the circumstances as to the fines imposed, we would need to refer to the court rolls for further details, which are regrettably missing. An example of the type of fine that was imposed can be seen from the Charter of Edward III where the document details a long list of penalties implemented by the justiciaries, for example the justiciaries may taste all casks of wine for sale in the city, and if they find any 'mixed or stale or unwholesome, they shall draw them out of the cellars, knock off their heads, and heavily fine the innkeepers or owners' and so the story continues for cobblers, tailors, bakers, craftsman and many other trades too numerous to list here.[46]

[38] Arthur, 'The Impact of the Black Death, 125.
[39] J.Z. Titow, *English Rural Society 1200–1350* (London: Allen and Unwin, 1969) 71.
[40] Titow "Decline of the Fair of St Giles," 62.
[41] HRO 11M59/B1/117 m46.

[42] Titow "Decline of the Fair of St Giles," 64.
[43] Titow "Decline of the Fair of St Giles," 63.
[44] The Pavilion Court not only dealt with actions as to debts between traders at the fair but swept up the whole legal business of Winchester within the ten-mile limit, C.H. Vellacott *VCH*, 38.
[45] Titow "Decline of the Fair of St Giles," 70; Keene, *Survey of Medieval Winchester* (table 55) 1124–6.
[46] Kitchin, Charter Ed III, 54–55.

Table 6.4: Receipts, pleas and perquisites for select years 1301–1410.

	1301–02	1347–48	1348–49	1349–50	1364–65	1371–72	1409–10
Receipts	£56 7s 2½d	£32 16s 5½d	£23 ¼d	£29 14s 5¾d	£48 11s 3d	£34 3s 9½d	£17 ½d
Pleas & Perquisites of the Pavilion	£2 1s 4d	66s 9d[1]	32s 1d	£4 13s 6d	£7 3s 7d	£6 18s 11d	£13 11s 6d

[1] This figure includes 8s 1d of arrears.

Wages

The pipe rolls provides a great source for extracting information relating to any trends in wages paid and received throughout the periods in question. Despite all this record of change, the wage items of the fair remain more or less the same throughout the period studied as Table 6.5 demonstrates. The wages of the crier are documented as 2s for each of the years studied. Robert Mason took the position of town crier during the period 1348–1350, which would suggest he survived the first year of the Black Death, however after the pipe roll entry of 1349–50 I can find no further trace of Robert Mason.[47]

The amounts received by the keepers of the gates did not alter greatly either. During 1347–48 and 1348–49 each keeper was paid 1½d per day, which amounted to a total of 4s in 1347–48, reducing to 3s in total for the period 1348–49, this decrease in the number of keepers was possibly caused by a decline in the amount of people alive to take on the position of gate keeper after the Black Death.[48] This amount was to continue for the years studied with the exception of the year 1409–10 which recorded nothing 'because the deductions of the keepers exceeded the receipts'. During the period 1348–50 John Bukebrok acted as keeper of the South Gate and Randolph Waltham acted as keeper of the West Gate for two years, but I am unable to trace Randolph Waltham after this date.[49] No other keeper served more than once from the records studied. The guardians/footmen of the road also received a standard amount of remuneration in the form of 2d per day for the period 1301–02 to 1349–50.

After 1364–65, the daily remuneration increased to 3d per day, although the number of guardians had decreased from an average of sixteen to a mere six. Perhaps the increase in the guardian's wages escalated due to the continual onslaught of the Black Death and a shortage of able men to take up the post. Another explanation could be that the bishop had to pay a higher wage to entice the guardians to accept the position. At the 'Passus de Alton', where the road ran near thick woodland infested with outlaws and landless men, the bishop kept strong patrols of men-at-arms mounted and on foot for sixteen days.[50] The occupation of minor sergeant, however received no such increase and remained fixed at 1d per day until 1409–10 where the amount increased substantially to 8d per day. Similarly, payment to the door-keeper of the pavilion continued at the same rate of 4s for all the years studied.[51] Consequently not all occupations were as sensitive to the increase in wages that the fourteenth century has become so synonymous with.

Expenses

Income to the fair was generally declining after the visitation of the Black Death during 1348–49. From the very beginning of the pipe roll we are told the same story as in other units studied; nothing received from the usual providers of income to the bishop, nothing from the officials of ladders and saddlers this year, nothing from the officials of burellers, nor from the official of the garden this year.[52] The London burellers were regular visitors to the fair in the thirteenth century, and between 1292 and 1337 they paid £4 2s a year in seldage to the bishop, but I can find no evidence from the pipe roll that they came to the fair after that date. In 1341 the bishop received 5s rent from the shop at the end of the burellers' seld/booth, which in the following year was demolished.[53] All this must have resulted in a downturn in income. However this was not the case where expenses were concerned for these were far from decreasing in line with income. During the reign of Edward II (1307–1327), gross receipts of the fair rarely exceeded £60 or £61, and the largest sum paid to the treasurer at Wolvesey in any one year was £33 2s ¼d in 1311. By 1346 however we see a different story, the total receipts accomplished the sum of £30 7s 10¼d, while expenses reached £24 13s 9¼d, leaving only between £5 and £6 for the treasurer at Wolvesey.

As can be seen from Table 6.6, the total for expenses remained at a constant £23–£26 between the years 1347–1350, increasingly significantly to £40 17s 2d by 1364–65. By 1371–72 the bishop must have taken stock of the situation as expenses drop to a record low of £6 10s 4d. During 1348–49 the total receipts during the

[47] HRO 11M59/B1/101 m41; 11M59/B1/102 m26.
[48] HRO 11M59/B1/100 m26; 11M59/B1/101 m41.
[49] HRO 11M59/B1/101 m41; 11M59/B1/102 m26.
[50] C.H. Vellacott cites the story of Matthew of Paris stating that robbers of this district were well known. More than a hundred years later the author of *Piers Plowman* (*c*.1360–87) describes the merchant wending his way 'as to Wynchestre fayre' dreading that 'he in derke mete with robbours and reuers, C.H. Vellacott, "Winchester," *VCH*, 39.
[51] Thomas Becket was declared as the door-keeper of the pavilion and seneschal William Clerk the chamberlain of the pavilion during 1349; HRO 11M59/B1/101 m41.
[52] Sellers of coarse woollen cloth known as 'burel' HRO 11M59/B1/101 m41.
[53] Seld was a booth or shop. During the fair long rows of booths or shops or windows were let to individual traders.

Table 6.5: Wages

	1301–02	1347–48	1348–49	1349–50	1364–65	1371–72	1409–10
Wages of the crier	2s	2s	2s[1]	2s[2]	2s	2s	2s
Guardians of the road of Alton	£3 12s[3]	34s 8d	32s	32s	18s	48s	Nothing
Keeper of the East Gate	2s 8d	4s	3s	3s	3s	3s	Nothing
Keeper of the South Gate	2s 8d	4s	3s	3s	3s	3s	Nothing
Keeper of the West Gate	2s 8d	4s	3s	3s	3s	3s	Nothing
Minor sergeants	12s 2d	6s 8d	5s 4d	4s	2s 8d	None declared	2s 8d
Door-keeper of the Pavilion	2s 8d	4s	Document torn	4s	4s	4s	4s
Weigher of the fair	6s 8d	2s		Nothing these years			

[1] Robert Mason.

[2] Robert Mason.

[3] Mounted earn 6d per day, on foot earn 2d per day. Horseman at the pass of Alton were last engaged in 1336.

Table 6.6: Receipts compared with expenses for select years 1301–1410

	1301–02	1347–48	1348–49	1349–50	1364–65	1371–72	1409–10
Expenses of the household	£7 5s 8d	£19 3s 2½d	£15 19s 2d	£20 11¾d	£20 18s 3d	7s 7d	£8 5s 10d
Total of all Expenses	£13 9s 2½d	£24 3s 7½d	£23 ¼d	£26 15s 9¾d	£40 17s 2d	£6 10s 4d	£11 5s 5d
Receipts	£56 7s 2½d	£32 16s 5½d	£23 ¼d	£29 14s 5¾d	£48 11s 3d	£34 3s 9½d	£17 ½d

sixteen days the fair lasted reached £23 ¼d, while the expenses were very heavy in proportion also amounting to £23 ¼d. On this basis, with expenses absorbing receipts, nothing would have been submitted to the treasurer of Wolvesey, John de Nubbelegh. The accounts tell us that during the Black Death £9 3s 2d had to be advanced to the treasurer of Wolvesey in order to meet expenses and balance the account.[54] The fair did not make a profit during 1348–9, unlike the year before the Black Death. The year immediately after the Black Death receipts exceeded expenses by almost £3, which is still a paltry amount in comparison with earlier years.

Conclusion.

It is most probable that the fair of St. Giles had reached its highest point in prosperity under the Angevins. On the first pipe roll of Richard I (1189–1199) the issues of the fair are recorded to have reached the sum of £146 8s 7d peaking to £163 by 1238–39.[55] In the reign of King John (1199–1216) the fair of St Giles stood in almost equal rank with the chief fairs of Boston and St. Ives.[56] The outbreak of the Gascon war in 1294 however appears to be a critical period in the history of the fair as gross receipts soon declined by over one-third and, as expenses had a tendency to keep up, the loss in net issues to the episcopal treasury was even greater in proportion.

By 1346 it is evident that the fair of St. Giles had to a great extent ceased to be of international importance and was gradually sinking to the level of a local Wessex and West Country market. Looking at the tolls collected, it is clear that the increase in local traffic through the West Gate suggested that the majority of traffic entering the fair came from more local places such as Salisbury and Romsey, and that the number of those traders coming from farther afield was beginning to decline. From 1323 the receipts received from the South Gate began to show a steady decline as trade from the overseas market began to diminish. This loss of trade through the South Gate was probably accounted for by troubled relations with Flanders and the Hundred Years War. Tolls at the West Gate on the other hand continued to increase, and from 1330 onwards accounted for the greater part of the business on St Giles's Hill. By 1346 the total receipts during the sixteen days of the fair, only reached the sum of £31 0s 20¾d, while the expenses were very heavy in proportion, amounting to £28 9s 7¾d.[57]

[54] HRO 11M59/B1/101 m42.

[55] Titow, "Decline of the Fair of St Giles," 64.

[56] Cf. Pat. 25 Hen. III, m. 12. Stamford was also in the first rank at least as a cloth fair (cf. Gross, Select Cases on the Law Merchant [Selden Soc.], xxxiii, no. 6).

[57] HRO 11M59/B1/99 m23.

It is clear that the income to the fair, although fluctuating in the period before 1348, declined significantly after the visitation of the Black Death. Income previously received from the tolls had decreased by fifty-six per cent during the first year of the Black Death, and the text of the pipe roll tells us that this was due to the 'great mortality of men'. This is a significant reduction in tolls and the only one occurring during the accounting years studied. Similarly rents received for the *terragium*, *seldagium* and *boagium* declined by more than half following the Black Death. The entry of nil return for the *boagium* during 1348–9 would suggest that, with so many cows being given in death duties, combined with their decrease in value, it was not a time for selling cattle at the fair, especially with the intention of achieving the best possible price. During the first year of the Black Death it is also evident that fewer shops, stalls and structures were being occupied, as well as a much reduced quantity of stock. Only nine *fenestrae* were let to the Cornishmen, for just 2s 6d per window, previously in 1346 the Cornishmen had let twenty eight *fenestrae* and the year before the Black Death thirty *fenestrae* had been let.[58] This number of lets was never to be seen again after the Black Death, with the numbers gradually decreasing each year until 1391 where they returned nil for a number of years thereafter. However, wages paid for those occupations related to the fair remain relatively constant throughout the years studied. This work has demonstrated that the wages of the crier, minor sergeant, door-keeper and the keepers of the gate did not vary greatly during the years studied. The guardians/footman of the road received the standard form of payment until after 1364–65 where their wages increased from 2d per day to 3d per day. Perhaps after the second wave of pestilence the road had become more onerous to travel due to robbers or outlaws. If this was the case then it would not be unreasonable for the bishop to increase the wages earned by the guardians as a form of danger money.

We have seen that the receipts of the fair fell to a record low during the first year of the Black Death. The *terragium*, or ground rents produced only £6 4s 2d and the *boagium* returned nil. In 1353 gross takings were £34 1s 7¾d, and after the deduction of expenses, £9 6s 8½d was paid to the treasurer at Wolvesey and 37s 6d remained in arrears. From the receipts of the fair during the Black Death the expenses of the episcopal household absorbed £15 19s 2d nearly two-thirds of the total of all expenses incurred during the fair. What also cannot be ignored is the twenty-seven per cent decrease in receipts which occurred during the first year of the Black Death. The receipts received during the sixteen days the fair lasted in 1348–49 reached £23 ¼d, whilst expenses were weighted in proportion and amounted to the same. With expenses consuming receipts, £9 3s 2d had to be advanced to the treasurer of Wolvesey in order to meet expenses and balance the account. With this reduction in the fair's income it is possible that by 1371–72 spending was reduced upon the upkeep and maintenance of the fair's shops and stalls, thereby creating a vicious circle of declining revenues. From 1362 onwards references to neglected, derelict, and abandoned structures (shops and stalls) become a main feature of the *terragium* of the accounts. However, by 1364–65 some attempt was made to correct the situation as can be seen from the amount that was spent on the cost of buildings (see Table 6.7). Reading through these entries the majority relate to materials and wages paid for the improvement of shops. By 1362, however, owing to the second pestilence and changing conditions, the improvement, such as it was, had been arrested. In this year the accountant mentions no less than £11 9s 1d as being in arrears from the previous year, and the ground rents were rather lower than in the year of the Black Death, £5 17s 3d and one pound of cumin. 'And no more', explains the accountant. In 1388–89 actual receipts were lower, and are only returned at £21 8s 9½d by including £6 2s 6d arrears. The ground rents had fallen still further to £3 4s 6½d and a pound of cumin – about one eighth of the amount produced a hundred years before. Expenses had been reduced to £11 3s 10d, of which £8 5s 2d was spent at the Wolvesey hospicium for twenty-four days' maintenance. As a result £4 was paid to Sir John de Keton at the treasury, and the rest remained in arrears.

Between 1350 and 1370 a large number of shops on the site of the fair were pulled down. The receipts of the *terragium* indicate *c.* 1330, there were at least forty shops still in use on the fair.[59] The total number of properties let in the fair at this time was probably about ninety. The comparable total of properties in 1292 would have been 750. More shops were pulled down in the years immediately following 1400, and most traders who came to the fair after 1400 probably displayed goods in temporary structures. By 1420 no more than a dozen plots or shops could be let.[60] From this time forth the decline of the fair was steady and irrevocable, and the Black Death had played its part in its gradual deterioration.

In 1420 the combined ground and other rents only produced 14s.[61] Even the old-established shops of the Frary and Kalendars were for the most part abandoned. St John's Hospital income from lettings in the fair fell from a peak of £20 in the second decade of the fourteenth century to virtually nothing in the 1370's. The *Boagium* only reached 5s 4d, besides the agistment fees paid for accommodation in the great meadow belonging to Wolvesey. One item of receipts, however, was rising: the pleas and perquisites of the Pavilion Court which brought in no less than £7 10s 1d. Even with these and 28s of arrears the total receipts came to only £10 5s 7d.[62] As the commercial aspect of the fair was no longer the first consideration, no money was wasted this year in guarding the Alton road, for few merchants passed through the king's forest to St. Giles' Down. On the other hand, in respect of the court officials, 40s was paid to Richard Holte, justiciary of the pavilion,

[58] HRO 11M59/B1/99 m23.

[59] Keene *Survey of Medieval Winchester*, 1122.

[60] Keene *Survey of Medieval Winchester*, 1122.

[61] HRO 11M59/B1/165 m48.

[62] HRO 11M59/B1/165 m48.

Table 6.7: Table of St Giles for select years 1301-1410

	1301–02	1347–48	1348–49	1349–50	1364–65	1371–72	1409–10
Bishop of Winchester	John of Pontoise	William Edington	William Edington	William Edington	William Edington	William Wykeham	Henry Beaufort
South Gate	£2 19s 6d	17s 10d	6s 3½d	17s 1½d	3s 6½d[4]	3s 6d	Nothing[1]
East Gate	14s	4s 4½d	3s 8d	9s 8½d	4s 7d	6s 4d	Nothing
West Gate	17s 10d	36s ½d	15s 6½d	39s 2½d	36s 2d	25s 3d	Nothing
Total of all Gates	£4 11s 4d	58s 3d	25s 6d[2]	66s ½d	43s 11½d[3]	35s 1d	Nil
Receipts	£56 7s 2½d	£32 16s 5½d	£23 ¼d	£29 14s 5¾d	£48 11s 3d	£34 3s 9½d	£17 ½d
Terragium	£23 6½d	£12 4s 8½d	£6 4s 2d	£8 14s 4d	£5 14s 4½d[4]	£5 13s 4½d[5]	£1 6s 2½d
Boagium	£1 10d	10s 8d	Nothing	6d	18s 4½d	18s 4d	2s 4d
Seldagium	£10 8s 6d	£6 10s 10d	£2 2s 6d[6]	£5 4s 4d	£2 8s 6d	£1 14s 6d	Nothing
Total of Terragium, Boagium + Seldagium	£34 9s 10½d	£19 6s 2½d	£8 18s 8d[7]	£13 19s 2d	£9 1s 3d	£8 6s 2½d	£1 8s 6½d
Pleas & Perquisites of the Pavilion	£2 1s 4d	66s 9d[8]	32s 1d	£4 13s 6d	£7 3s 7d	£6 18s 11d	£13 11s 6d
Great beam	£1 8s 5d	Nil	Nil	Nil	Nil	Nil	Nil
Costs of buildings	15s ½d	14s 9d	71s[9]	61s 8d	£15 10s 4d	41s 1d	11d
Expenses of the household	£7 5s 8d	£19 3s 2½d	£15 19s 2d	£20 11¾d	£20 18s 3d	7s 7d	£8 5s 10d
Total of all Expenses	£13 9s 2½d	£24 3s 7½d	£23 ¼d	£26 15s 9¾d	£40 17s 2d	£6 10s 4d	£11 5s 5d

1 Nothing this year because the deductions of the keepers exceeded the receipts.
2 The entry on the pipe roll is stated as 25s 6½d.
3 This adds up to 44s 3½d.
4 plus 1lb of cumin.
5 plus 1lb of cumin.
6 This figure does not tally, we are told that nine windows were rented at 2s 6d which would equal 22s 6d, but the total is documented as 7s 6d.
7 This figure does not tally.
8 Includes 8s 1d arrears.
9 Document torn and illegible.

for his labour, 5s to the chamberlain, John Compton and 4s to the usher. The total expenses reached £8 12s 2d, of which £5 11s was due to the charges of the bishop's house at Wolvesey, and, as 30s was in arrears, only 3s 5d could be paid to the episcopal treasurer.[63] When the bishop ceased to collect tolls at the fair in 1393, his total revenue there was just over a third of the total in 1360, a quarter of that in 1330, a sixth of that in 1300, and a twelfth of what had been received in 1280. It is not surprising, therefore, that the bishop attempted to exploit the judicial rights he enjoyed during the fair as a means to offset the declining income from trade. These attempts are clearly reflected in the receipts of perquisites at the Pavilion Court. By the close of the century it became apparent that the fair had come to exist merely for the profits of the Pavilion Court. In 1488 the ground rent paid was a sorry shilling, no booths were let, and out of the total receipts of £7 9s 11d no less than £7 1s 10d was derived from the perquisites of court.[64] The greatly increased activity of the Pavilion Court on the one hand and the drastic decline in the commercial profitability of the fair on the other, emphasises the point that towards the end of the fourteenth century the primary benefit to the bishop of holding the fair was not the commercial gain, but as Titow argues, the derived political advantage of having the city under his exclusive control for the duration of the fair; however 'as a commercial institution the fair was already moribund'.[65] By the beginning of the reign of Edward III, the fair, which had lost most of the London attendants and a significant part of the overseas trade, was becoming nothing more than a regional fair, the loss of business from London and overseas was an important

63 HRO 11M59/B1/165 m48.

64 HRO 11M59/B1/211 m5.

65 Titow "Decline of the Fair of St Giles," 63.

factor in a decline that was exacerbated by the Black Death and began to be associated with the diminishing status of Winchester as a centre of royal consumption from the end of the reign of Henry III onwards. The decline of trade reflected in the bishop's receipt of tolls and in his overall revenue from the fair continued throughout the fourteenth century. Major economic disruption, such as the outbreak of the Hundred Years' War and the plague of 1349, accelerated this downward trend, the dramatic fall in revenue which was more substantially affected in the long term by the Black Death, was something the bishop had not experienced before as over half of the population died of plague. This and the gradual decay of the fair contributed to the decline of the prosperity of the city. Once the largest fair in Europe, the fair gradually shrank away from the glittering prosperity it had once enjoyed as the jewel under the Angevin rule.

Bibliography

Unpublished primary sources

The National Archives (TNA).

Calendar of the Patent Rolls Preserved in the Public Record Office. Henry III A.D 1216-1272, Patent rolls of the reign of Henry III prepared under the superintendence of the Deputy Keeper of the Records – London: Her Majesty's Stationary Office, 1901–13, 6 vols.

[Selden Soc.], xxxiii, no. 6.

Hampshire Record Office (HRO).

Winchester Pipe Rolls:

11M59/B1/99, cons Edington 2, 1346–47.

11M59/B1/100, cons Edington 3, 1347–48.

11M59/B1/101, cons Edington 4, 1348–49.

11M59/B1/102, cons Edington 5, 1349–50.

11M59/B1/115, cons Edington 18, 1362–63.

11M59/B1/117, cons Edington 20, 1364–65.

11M59/B1/165, trans Beaufort 16, 1419–20.

11M59/B1/211, 1486–87.

Winchester College

Court Rolls 10443 NRA 7893, 1417–1429.

Published primary sources

Page M., ed *The Pipe Roll of the Bishopric of Winchester 1301–2*, Hampshire Record Series, 14 (1996).

Published secondary sources

Biddle M., ed. *Winchester in the Early Middle Ages: an edition and discussion of the Winton Domesday*, Winchester Studies, 1. Oxford: Clarendon Press, 1976.

Dyer, C. *Lords and Peasants in a Changing Society. The Estates of the Bishopric of Worcester, 680–1540.* Cambridge: Cambridge University Press, 1980.

Gasquest, F.A. *The Great Pestilence (A.D. 1348–9) now commonly known as the Black Death.* London: Simpkin Marshall, 1893.

Harvey, B.F. *Westminster Abbey and its estates in the Middle Ages.* Oxford: Clarendon Press, 1977.

Horrox, R., trans. and ed. *The Black Death.* Manchester: Manchester University Press, 1994.

Keene, D. *Survey of Medieval Winchester*, Winchester Studies, 2 vols. Oxford: Clarendon Press, 1976.

Kershaw, I. *Bolton Priory: The Economy of a Northern Monastery, 1286–1325.* London: Oxford University Press, 1973.

Kitchin G.W., ed. *A Consuetudinary of the Fourteenth Century for the Refectory of the House of S. Swithun in Winchester.* London: Elliot Stock, 1886.

Levett A.E. "The Black Death on the Estates of the See of Winchester." In *Oxford Studies in Social and Legal History*, Vol 5, edited by P. Vinogradoff, 7–220. Oxford: Clarendon Press, 1916.

Mayberry, T.W. *Estate Records of the Bishops of Winchester in the Hampshire Record Office.* Winchester: Hampshire County Council, 1998.

Miller, E. *The Abbey and Bishopric of Ely: the social and economic history of an ecclesiastical estate from the tenth century to the early fourteenth century.* London: Cambridge University Press, 1951.

Page, W., ed. *The Victoria History of the Counties of England A History of Hampshire*, vol. V. London, 1912.

Seebohm, F. "The Black Death and its Place in English History." *Fortnightly Review*, 2, (1865): part I, 149–60; part II, 268–79.

Sloane, B. *The Black Death in London.* Stroud: History Press, 2011.

Titow J.Z. "The Decline of the Fair of St Giles, Winchester, in the Thirteenth and Fourteenth Centuries." *Nottingham Medieval Studies* xxxi (1987): 58–75.

Titow, J.Z. *English Rural Society 1200–1350.* London: Allen and Unwin, 1969.

Vellacott C.H. "Winchester: Fair and Trades." In *The Victoria History of the Counties of England A History of Hampshire*, vol. V, edited by, 36–44. London, 1912.

Vinogradoff, P., ed. *Oxford Studies in Social and Legal History*, Vol 5. Oxford: Clarendon Press, 1916.

Unpublished secondary source

Arthur P.A. "The Impact of the Black Death on Seventeen Units of Account of The Bishopric of Winchester." Unpublished PhD Thesis, University College Winchester/University of Southampton, 2005.

7

Catastrophe and Ceramics: A preliminary assessment of the impact of the Black Death of 1348–50 on pottery production in England

Phil Marter

University of Winchester

Abstract: This research focuses on the observation of trends in archaeological data that suggests that the plague of 1348–50 had a significant and visible effect on the medieval pottery industry in England. These trends were identified during the analysis of nationwide pottery production evidence, collected as part of a project for English Heritage and PhD research by the author. The most obvious of these observed phenomena included a general decline in the overall numbers of pottery production centres and a change from seasonal or part-time potting to a more specialised large-scale 'industrial' mode of production. The reasons for these changes are examined against a backdrop of previously highlighted changes in the arts and related medieval craft industries. They are also considered in the light of ongoing debate about the scale and nature of the impact of Black Death in relation to population levels. Finally, it is proposed that because of its particular qualities, that ubiquitous ceramic material culture might provide an ideal measure of societal change in the face of such a catastrophic pandemic event.

Key words: Black Death; plague; pottery production; pottery production centres; English medieval pottery industry; medieval pottery kilns

Introduction

In 2003, I completed an English Heritage-funded project to create a national database of medieval production centres in England,[1] which led shortly afterwards to a more rounded examination of this important medieval craft industry, through what became my doctoral thesis, "Medieval Pottery Production Centres in England, AD 850–1600." This explored the chronological and regional development of pottery production between the mid-ninth and the end of the sixteenth centuries in England.[2] Any work of this nature, spanning such a considerable period and focusing on an entire medieval industry must inevitably consider a variety of chronological, regional and national phenomena. Some of these represented glimpses of local peculiarities, regional traditions and occasionally more wide-ranging change. The study's ambitious scope provided both its 'micro level' weaknesses and its unique 'macro level' vistas of an entire industry.

While the variable quality of collected data and the vagaries of the archaeological record meant it was not always easy to pinpoint specific influences that brought about change within the industry, episodes of artistic and technological development were clearly visible. In addition, observations about the industry's overall fortunes were certainly possible and, because of the overall volume of the data, seem generally reliable in their nature. Around 700 'production centres' were identified during the original research, although it should be emphasised that few have been adequately explored in a systematic, archaeological fashion. This total represents perhaps just 25 per cent of the centres which once existed.[3]

Traditionally, pottery production centres have been identified – or at least classified as such – in a very simplistic way, often through the positive recognition of the kilns used to fire ceramic vessels. These kilns were duly classified and design typologies developed, while other elements of a production centre went unrecognised by archaeologists. Little attention, for example, was given to associated timber structures representing workshops, drying sheds, stores etc., or to clay puddling and extraction pits, or even to the waste heaps of broken pottery lost during firing. Excellent work by McCarthy and Brookes in 1988 attempted for the first time to collate this information from across the nation and to characterise production within the landscape[4]. However, new research for English Heritage was to take this a step further. Data was collected from Historic Environment Records from

[1] Phil Marter, "A National Database of Medieval Pottery Production Centres in England, AD 850–1600," digital database, English Heritage (unpublished, 2003).

[2] Phil Marter, "Medieval Pottery Production Centres in England, AD 850–1600," (unpublished PhD thesis, University of Winchester, 2005). My Directors of Studies were successively, Professor Christopher Gerrard, who initiated the project with me, and after he left for the University of Durham in 2000, Professor Tom James. Assistance at different stages of this extended project came from Professor Andrew Reynolds, the late Professor Mick Aston and Maureen Mellor, President of the Medieval Pottery Research Group. Alex Turner assisted me greatly with GIS aspects of the project.

[3] Marter, "Medieval Pottery Production Centres," 14.

[4] Michael R. McCarthy and Catherine M. Brooks, *Medieval Pottery in Britain, AD 900–1600* (Leicester: Leicester University Press, 1988).

across the country in order to define production centres at specific locales through the consideration of a much wider variety of evidence than previously used. A production centre might then be represented by any single element that could be identified with a degree of certainty to the process of production. In some cases these centres were represented by documentary or place-name evidence, kilns, kiln debris or ceramic wasters. The main purpose of this change in emphasis was to promote understanding of pottery production beyond the traditional 'kiln focus' of the production cycle to include broader manufacturing contexts. In effect this work added both depth and colour to our view of national, regional and in some cases local potting traditions, allowing new appraisals of the industry to be made.

Among the most dramatic of changes visible in the industry's fortunes was an early fourteenth-century hiatus in production. Analysis of the data collected during the original research suggested that there had been a steady increase in numbers of production centres from the ninth to mid-fourteenth centuries as medieval populations rose,[5] and a general decline following the onset of plague (the Black Death in England of 1348–50). In addition, production apparently began to change so that it was no longer a purely seasonal or part-time occupation, but instead an organised manufacturing industry. We also begin to see increased specialisation of production, and attempts to achieve economies of scale as well as production behaviour more familiar in post medieval traditions. So what are the particular mechanics of his change and what evidence do we actually have for it? The answers lie within a growing body of studies of both ceramic and other medieval craft industries that have observed the impact of rising mortality rates in the mid-fourteenth century.[6]

Discussion

It is estimated that the population of England numbered between four and a half and six million by 1348, but following the outbreak of plague it plummeted to between two and a half to three million by 1377.[7] More recently in a brace of major works Ole Benedictow has persuasively argued for a population decline in Europe from 80 to 30 million from 1347–1350, with a mortality rate during the Black Death in England of some 62.5 per cent in rural and urban populations alike.[8] In some areas, for example on the well-documented Bishop of Winchester's estates in southern England, the lethality rate among tenants was in places as high as 75 to 100 per cent.[9] This work on pottery production comes in the wake of a considered revision of the effects of the Black Death on the arts conducted by Phillip Lindley in 1996,[10] which confirmed the significant and sometimes catastrophic effects of the plague on both painting and the plastic arts.

Arts such as painting, and skills such as tomb sculpture were specialist areas in the Middle Ages and involved significant profile, but perhaps comparatively small numbers of people. Pottery, however, was the medieval equivalent of plastic: used by all and relatively durable in the archaeological record. Indeed, the peculiarities of medieval pottery mean that while it shared many links with craft industries such as those of the tile, brick, glass and metal working, it retained crucial differences. In particular, its everyday use in a huge variety of medieval households, its constantly evolving styles and its continual and regular disposal give it unusually varied properties as an indicator of social and economic meaning. As Streeten puts it 'The extent to which pottery can shed light on broader themes of economic history is defined by the contemporary significance of the material'.[11] Its poor showing in early post medieval inventories has in the past led to the inference that pottery was of minor significance in medieval England.[12] However, its relative unimportance to individuals or their households should not be confused with its value in economic terms or its worth in this study as a measure of economic activity. In this respect a thriving economy and healthy population demanded more pots, and this is undoubtedly seen during the thirteenth century prior to the first outbreak of the Black Death.

The increasing number of markets between 1250 and 1350 appears to have provided the ideal commercial opportunities for the sale and distribution of ceramic vessels.[13] These urban markets made it easier for potters

[5] The archaeological and historical sources which yielded this data included Historic Environment Records across the country and data from the Royal Commission on Historic Monuments in Swindon, who provided printouts from their Long Listings and Events Records. The Medieval Pottery Research Group kindly made available the original questionnaires for the Survey of Medieval Pottery Studies in England and an advance copy of the Medieval Pottery Bibliography (an online resource held by the Archaeology Data Service: "Medieval Pottery Research Group Bibliography," accessed 16 July 2018, http://archaeologydataservice.ac.uk/archives/view/mprg_eh_2010/).

[6] See Philip Lindley, "The Black Death and English Art: a debate and some assumptions," in *The Black Death in England*, ed. Mark Ormrod and Philip Lindley (Donington: Shaun Tyas, 2003).

[7] John Hatcher, *Plague, Population and the English Economy 1348–1530* (London: Macmillan, 1977), 68.

[8] Ole J. Benedictow, *The Black Death 1346–1353: the complete history* (Woodbridge: Boydell Press, 2004), 352, 377. Also Ole J. Benedictow, *What Disease was Plague? On the controversy over the microbiological identity of plague epidemics in the past* (Leiden: Brill, 2010), 9 and fn. 14, where the 80 per cent lethality for the plague is set down.

[9] Paula Arthur, "The Impact of the Black Death on Seventeen Units of Account of the Bishopric of Winchester" (unpublished PhD thesis, University College Winchester/University of Southampton, 2005), 228–33; See also Paula Arthur, "The Black Death and Mortality: a reassessment," in *Fourteenth Century England* VI, ed. Chris Given Wilson (Woodbridge: Boydell and Brewer, 2010).

[10] Lindley, "The Black Death and English Art."

[11] Anthony D.F. Streeten, "Craft and Industry: medieval and later potters in south-east England," in *Production and Distribution: a ceramic viewpoint*, ed. Hilary Howard and Elaine L. Morris, British Archaeological Reports (BAR) International Series 120 (Oxford: BAR, 1981), 324.

[12] H.E. Jean Le Patourel, "Pottery as Evidence for Social and Economic Change," in *Medieval Settlement*, ed. Peter H. Sawyer (London: Edward Arnold, 1976), 170; Streeten, "Craft and Industry," 324. These views are not held by Streeten but are identified by him.

[13] Colin Hayfield, *Humberside Medieval Pottery: an illustrated catalogue of Saxon and medieval assemblages from North Lincolnshire and its surrounding region* vol. 1, BAR British Series 140 (Oxford: BAR, 1985), 416.

to sell their wares and enable them to concentrate their time and energy on the production process rather than the marketing of products. Potters were not alone in enjoying the economic growth at this time. Around 1300 the amount of money in circulation reached a higher level than at any other time in the Middle Ages,[14] indicating that trade and exchange were flourishing. Manorial accounts suggest that rural communities also played an important part in this trade boom,[15] and pottery sales would have benefited from the resultant increased commerce, improving the viability of seasonal rural production. Importantly, rural production sites would in some cases also develop some of the key characteristics that would allow them to flourish in the post-plague era. For those centres achieving economies of scale, efficient production and easy access to readily available markets, surviving the plague was undoubtedly more likely.

Certainly, the first half of the fourteenth century witnessed the peak of the medieval pottery industry's achievements. [16] But on comparing total recorded pottery production centres for the fourteenth and fifteenth centuries, we get an idea of the scale of the change that subsequently occurred. The number of production centres in England dropped by 30 per cent to 162 from the fourteenth to the fifteenth century – a significant and noteworthy decline. The data collected from regional Historic Environment Records is not without its problems, however. Pinpointing the precise rapidity of the change brought about by plague is challenging. In most cases, data collected on individual kilns and the majority of production centres enables them to be dated only to a particular century. As a result data for 'fourteenth-century' production contains data from both the early fourteenth-century peak and later fourteenth-century decline of production, with the resulting 'fourteenth-century' data being somewhat homogenised. In this respect, the most immediate effects of the plague are probably disguised. However, some trends are nevertheless visible. So what can we discern? Comparison between production centre numbers and distribution attributed to the fourteenth and fifteenth century reveals some points of note.

While the overall geographical distribution of production centres remains similar between the centuries, several changes occur in the data. Numerically, three regions dominate the fifteenth-century distribution of pottery production centres: those of Yorkshire and Humberside, the South-East Midlands and London and the South-East. The central southern region, the South-East (although remaining numerically significant), the North-West and right across the midlands are the areas that witness the largest decline. The Midlands in particular saw a serious and long-lasting reduction in numbers of individual production centres which continued into the sixteenth century.

Pottery production in the North-East and North-West of England displays many more datable examples of kilns and products in the period before the Black Death and comparatively few following its arrival. In Yorkshire and Humberside the greatest number of productive sites is found in the thirteenth and fourteenth centuries and then numbers decline into the fifteenth. In Derbyshire and Lincolnshire the evidence is less clear but in Nottinghamshire there is a sharp decline between the fourteenth and fifteenth centuries, with a similar pattern in Shropshire, Staffordshire and Worcestershire. In Norfolk the situation is slightly different with a steady decline in sites from the twelfth to the sixteenth century. However, the greatest fall here – almost half – is still between the fourteenth and fifteenth centuries.[17] While Suffolk, Buckinghamshire and Bedfordshire show some growth between the fourteenth and fifteenth centuries, Cambridgeshire and Huntingdonshire decline significantly from six production centres to a single site in that period. In Essex, Sussex and Kent the pattern of decline shows clearly from the thirteenth to the sixteenth century. In West Sussex and Wiltshire the decline was over 50 per cent, while Surrey sites declined by 50 per cent from ten to five, and in Berkshire and Hampshire there is a similar pattern.[18] In the West Country the evidence is not so clear cut. For example, no sites were discovered for Gloucestershire in the fourteenth century while at the same time, Somerset shows a sharp decline.[19]

While zones of pottery production do not conform to county boundaries or modern delineations within which the data was collected, some useful observations can be made by considering regional groupings that may share economic or geographic characteristics. When figures for these areas are consolidated regionally a clear picture emerges: in the North East the number of identified production centres declines from five to two between the fourteenth to the fifteenth centuries; in the North West from 15 to nine; in Yorkshire and Humberside from 35 to 27; in the East Midlands from 26 to 15, and the West Midlands from 22 to 10.[20] East Anglia stays at 14; the South-East Midlands falls from 33 to 29; the South East from 39 to 30; the central Southern region from 31 to 15; and the South West region from 13 to 11.[21] While reduced population was undoubtedly the driving force for these changes it remains likely that regional factors would have determined the exact implications for the industry.

In most cases, production centre survival rates appear to relate largely to local population density, with many of the largest falls in number occurring in areas that saw the most significant growth between 1250 and 1350. It is also noticeable that there is a disproportionately large

[14] Christopher Dyer, "Peasants and Farmers: rural settlements and landscapes in an age of transition," in *The Age of Transition: the archaeology of English culture, 1400–1600*, ed. David Gaimster and Paul Stamper (Oxford: Oxbow, 1997), 62.
[15] Dyer, "Peasants and Farmers," 62.
[16] Marter, "Medieval Pottery Production," 196.

[17] Marter, "Medieval Pottery Production," 106–10; fig. 35, 117.
[18] Marter, "Medieval Pottery Production," 130–36; figs. 47, 48, 50, 53, 138–147.
[19] Marter, "Medieval Pottery Production," figs. 57–58, 152–53.
[20] Marter, "Medieval Pottery Production," figs 60–63, 157–165.
[21] Marter, "Medieval Pottery Production," figs 64–68, 167, 170, 173, 175, 177.

reduction in production in areas of predominantly mixed farming. Lowland areas of England, where arable farming was the norm, see a disproportionately smaller reduction in the occurrence of pottery production centres between the fourteenth and fifteenth centuries. This phenomenon might be explained by Dyer's theory that alternative employment opportunities created by the reduction in labour force, rather than mortality itself, most affected the number of production centres.[22] However, given recent scholarship there may also be other explanations.

Many production centres were located on marginal land, and it was these settlements that usually suffered the most desertion following the onset of plague. Some, like the major site at Lyveden,[23] fell into terminal decline. Lower population brought about changed economic conditions, with less land under cultivation, low and falling rents and increasingly higher wages. The cost of employing labour may have led some production centres to shed part of their workforce, and led others to make their production process as efficient as possible.[24] It is likely that these changes would have created a smaller but more profitable pottery industry for the potting communities that survived the Black Death. Certainly potteries did survive, and in some cases the plague appears to have made little difference to the production of particular wares or certain regional traditions. In Malvern Chase for example, despite the potters of Hanley Castle being recorded as having all died in 1349, no discernible difference in their production output can be seen.[25] While the market for their products was smaller, the potters' rents also reduced, thereby allowing potential profit margins to increase.

Local and national outbreaks of plague continued throughout the fifteenth century, keeping English population levels down. Estimates suggest that they reached a low point of between two and two and a half million around the middle of the century, resulting in widespread agricultural recession.[26]

For those who survived the initial arrival of the plague, the new conditions brought about by depopulation may have allowed changes in their profession, or even their social status. Land holdings per head increased as values and rents fell, with labour becoming scarce enough to increase wages.[27] Many used these opportunities to free themselves from their previous feudal ties or to purchase additional land. The low social status of medieval potters might have ensured that they would be among the first to seize new opportunities and move away from pottery production. Indeed, it has been suggested that 'social improvement' through land purchase, rather than death is the reason for the disappearance of some potting communities in the late fourteenth and fifteenth centuries.[28] However, despite the increased number of written sources available for the fourteenth century, there is little evidence available to identify the fate of individual potters.[29] Even those sources that might shed light on the subject must be treated with caution. For example, research has shown that names that might be associated with the manufacture of pots and the potters' guilds, known at centres such as York, often belonged to metalworkers rather than to earthenware potters.[30]

While the second half of the fourteenth century saw the start of a decline in overall numbers of pottery production centres around the country, it also saw a general expansion in diversity of vessel forms and a corresponding decrease in decoration.[31] Increasingly in the late thirteenth and early fourteenth centuries, urban communities sought to emulate the culinary habits of wealthier members of society by purchasing a wider variety of ceramic vessels whose forms were based on more expensive metal vessels.[32] This led to a broader repertoire of pottery produced at many production centres, perhaps as a result of an increase in individuals' wealth and increased use of metal rather than ceramic cooking vessels.[33] English potters began to innovate in their production to compete with metal workers and with increasing volumes of Continental imports in order to maintain a stake in an increasingly competitive market. Also during the fourteenth century, ceramic drinking vessels began to replace wooden ones, and this trend would ultimately lead to widespread use of stoneware with its superior properties for holding liquids.

This increase in vessel diversity is linked in part with the development of kiln technology. Returning briefly to the ninth and twelfth centuries, kiln types were most commonly either 'clamp kiln' (bonfire kilns) or single-flued types, reflecting much earlier potting traditions. The twelfth and thirteenth centuries not only saw a rise in the number of production centres but also an increase in double and 'multi-flued' kilns that formed part of what Barton described as a 'minor industrial revolution'.[34] Given that the primary function of the kiln flue is to regulate and control firing conditions within the kiln it seems most likely that at least part of this 'revolution' with

[22] Christopher Dyer, "The Social and Economic Changes of the Later Middle Ages and the Pottery of the Period," *Medieval Ceramics* 6 (1982): 38.
[23] Glen Foard, "The Medieval Pottery Industry of Rockingham Forest, Northamptonshire," *Medieval Ceramics* 15 (1991): 16.
[24] Hayfield, "Humberside Medieval Pottery," 403.
[25] Alan G. Vince, "The Medieval and Post-Medieval Ceramic Industry of the Malvern Region: the study of a ware and its distribution," in *Pottery and Early Commerce: characterisation and trade in Roman and later ceramics*, ed. D.P.S. Peacock (London: Academic Press, 1977), 285.
[26] Hatcher, *Plague, Population*, 39.
[27] Dyer, "Social and Economic Changes," 32.
[28] Dyer, "Social and Economic Changes," 38.
[29] McCarthy and Brooks, *Medieval Pottery in Britain*, 77. See also Dyer, "Social and Economic Changes," 37.
[30] H.E. Jean Le Patourel, "Documentary Evidence and the Medieval Pottery Industry," *Medieval Archaeology* 12 (1968): 102.
[31] Sarah Jennings, *Medieval Pottery in the Yorkshire Museum* (York: The Yorkshire Museum, 1992), 27. See also Beverly Nenk, "Highly Decorated Pottery in Medieval England," in *Pottery in the Making*, ed. Ian Freestone and David R.M. Gaimster (London: British Museum Press, 1997), 97.
[32] Nenk, "Highly Decorated Pottery," 97.
[33] Jennings, *Medieval Pottery*, 27.
[34] K.J. Barton, *Pottery in England, from 3500BC–AD1730* (London: David and Charles, 1975), 36.

its multiple flues, was aimed at improving kiln efficiency and production quality, and at achieving higher firing temperatures. In addition, the number of flues a kiln had appears to be linked directly to the type of fuel being used to fire it, as Le Patourel had claimed back in 1968.[35] Hence multi-flued kilns were most prevalent in areas where coal became the fuel of choice during the industries' twelfth, thirteenth and early fourteenth-century rise, and double-flued kilns continued to be favoured in the south, where wood remained the most viable fuel source.[36] We reach a point – at the height of Barton's mini industrial revolution – where the early fourteenth century presents the Medieval pottery industry in its largest and most varied guise, with the entire range of kiln types on display.

In the second half of the fourteenth century we see a decline in the number of single and double-flued kilns, while numbers of multi-flued kilns seem to have been little affected. In fact, in the West Midlands, multi-flued kilns appear to have replaced double-flued technology. Interestingly, in contrast to this increased kiln sophistication in some regions, numbers of clamp kilns appear to increase in the second half of the fourteenth century, perhaps representing local production solutions to a reduction in traded wares.[37]

A continued reduction in the overall numbers of kilns took place in the fifteenth century.[38] Clamp, single, double and multi-flued kilns all continued in use with single- and double-flued kilns being preferred in the South of England and multi-flued kilns in the North, a pattern repeated in the sixteenth century. Multi-flued kilns occurred in largest numbers in the West Midlands, where the total reaches a peak in the late fifteenth century before they disappear in the early sixteenth century.[39]

In summary, the data for kiln type and design are patchy and may be inconclusive. However, what is apparent is that clamp kilns in general decline significantly between the fourteenth and fifteenth centuries, while multi flued kilns make a significant appearance in the fifteenth century.[40] This change characterises a broad trend towards increasing scale of production, and very much reflects an industry in transition.

Context and Conclusions

The Black Death remains a contentious topic of study, particularly, for example, regarding the nature of the disease, and of course no research is ever complete. However, after a long period in which estimates of Black Death mortality were firmly anchored at about 30 per cent – as seen for example in Philip Ziegler's 1969 account – estimates have steadily risen, through Rosemary Horrox's 47 per cent (1994) to Benedictow's 62.5 per cent in 2010, with some regional studies such as that by Paula Arthur (2005, 2010) suggesting higher mortality hot-spots.[41] Evidence for the small number of attested places where populations were extinguished (always a troublesome topic because, when all are dead, who is left to report total mortality?) has increased, for example by George Watts's revelation of the reported deaths of all tenants at Quob, on the Abbot of Titchfield's lands in southern Hampshire.[42]

If the data on pottery production set down here may be relied on to present a picture of changes in the production of a fundamental commodity for all of society, then such a steep reduction may quite reasonably be argued to have been caused by the onset of the Black Death and successive plagues. It is important to emphasise that any commentary on the fate of the pottery industry must be tempered with an understanding of its relationship with other trades and crafts. Many of the production techniques used by potters probably developed in conjunction with those found in metal working or the manufacture of glass, plaster and cement. Indeed, ethnographic study suggests it would not have been unusual to find all four of these industries located in close proximity.[43] The fuel sources and markets on which pottery production relied would also have stimulated the development of related industries such as charcoal production and iron smelting.

In Berkshire, a kiln at Ashampstead was located in common woodland exploited largely by the charcoal burning industry,[44] and in the Rockingham and Whittlewood Forests of Nottinghamshire, charcoal burning, iron and pottery production evidently existed side by side.[45] Many of the inhabitants of forest settlements may well have been involved in the production processes for all three of these industries. Other craftsmen such as tile makers would have exerted at least some influence over the medieval potter, perhaps in the form of shared skills, distribution networks or labour force. Sometimes, for example, potters fired a few tiles in their pottery kilns, as at West Cowick, Humberside,[46] and sometimes they worked alongside the tilers. In some cases, as at Lacock, Nottingham and Rye,[47] pottery kilns and tile kilns existed side-by-side at a production centre. At Lacock, two pottery kilns were found on the same spot

[35] Le Patourel, "Documentary Evidence," 118.

[36] Marter, "Medieval Pottery Production," 225–40, figs. 84–99. A series of diagrams is presented showing regional kiln distributions, by type and date. Dates are defined by 50 year blocks. It should be noted that in many cases original source data was not complete enough to allow a kiln type to be defined, suggesting this distribution to be an indication of reality only.

[37] Marter, "Medieval Pottery Production," 235, fig. 94.

[38] Marter, "Medieval Pottery Production," 236–37, figs 95 and 96.

[39] Marter, "Medieval Pottery Production," 243–44.

[40] Marter, "Medieval Pottery Production," 248.

[41] See Benedictow, *What Disease was Plague;* Philip Ziegler, *The Black Death* (London: Collins, 1969); Rosemary Horrox (ed.), *The Black Death* (Manchester: Manchester University Press, 1994); Arthur, "The Impact of the Black Death," "The Black Death and Mortality."

[42] D.G. Watts, "The Black Death in Dorset and Hampshire," *The Hatcher Review* 5, no. 46 (1998): 21–28.

[43] Owen S. Rye, *Pottery Technology: principles and reconstruction* (Washington D.C.: Taraxacum, 1981), 1, 9.

[44] Lorraine Mepham and Michael J. Heaton, "A Medieval Pottery Kiln at Ashampstead, Berkshire," *Medieval Ceramics* 19 (1995): 31.

[45] Foard, "The Medieval Pottery Industry," 13.

[46] H.E. Jean Le Patourel, "Pots and Potters," *Medieval Ceramics* 10 (1986): 8.

[47] Le Patourel, "Pots and Potters," 8–10.

as two tile kilns and were constructed using the same techniques, suggesting a degree of co-operation between potters and tilers.[48] While potters usually worked for a socially varied clientele, tilers in contrast usually received commissions from the king, religious houses or wealthy magnates. These clients demanded the latest designs from tilers, whose production designs may have led potters to experiment with new motifs on their pottery.[49]

Designs used by iron workers also appear to have influenced pottery made at Grimston, Lincoln, Toynton, Coventry and Leicester.[50] At Nash Hill, Lacock, dragon decoration on one of the thirteenth-century jugs from the site has very close affinities with images appearing in contemporary manuscripts,[51] reflecting the possibility of artistic links that may have existed between sections of the potting community and other craft industries. Further afield, practical cross-trade innovation was taking place. The development of high quality lead-glazed pottery in the Huy-type pottery industry of the middle Meuse valley appears to have occurred through the close relationship developed between the potters and local town-based metalworkers. Here, it has been suggested, a glaze probably developed through waste recycling by experienced potters who employed lead-protoxide, a well-known by-product of cupellation,[52] to decorate their newly developed oxidised ware.[53]

Potters could also be engaged in supplying products to other trades. Pots could be supplied wholesale to merchants for the storage and transport of foodstuffs. During major building projects potters might be engaged in the production of floortiles, rooftiles or, more commonly, ridge tiles alongside their normal pottery vessels. In some places refractory clays, such as those used at Stamford or for Surrey Whiteware production, could be used to make vessels that could withstand very high temperatures. Crucibles were made from this clay and supplied to metalworkers.[54] These inter-linked elements of industry, craft and art provide a challenging backdrop to any commentary purporting to observe the impact of catastrophic change. In particular, anecdotal evidence tempts us to assign meaning where it might not belong, or to make generalisations based purely on inference. This should not, however, preclude us from attempting to propose possibilities alongside the appropriate caveats. There is value in this endeavour. Important works by others have contributed significantly to our understanding of the impact of the Black on Medieval life and these provide encouragement that the fate of craft industries can be accessed via studies of material culture.

In revisiting debates about the effects of the Black Death on culture Lindley rightly observes that the 'central problem with Millard Meiss's work' (1952, on the profound consequences of the effects of the plague on art, artists and patrons in Florence and Siena after the Black Death) was that the author assumed 'a direct connection between art and society'. Any such simplistic relationship must be questionable. However, the effects on art – with the deaths of major practitioners such as the Lorinzettis in Siena, and the increased conservatism in art of new patrons after the Black Death in both cities, must be and may be attributed to the effects of plague both through mortality and through alterations in mentality.[55]

In his re-evaluation of changes in the arts and architecture in England around the middle of the fourteenth century, Lindley was able to show breaks in traditions and/or production in a range of specialities. The deaths of three royal masons, the Ramseys, of whom William had designed the Chapter House of Old St Paul's died, also William Joy who designed the presbytery at Wells and William la Bole, head mason at Westminster Abbey, along with the master mason at York Minster and the Black Prince's master mason. In metalwork all eight of the wardens of the Cutlers Company in London died, and half the council of the Goldsmiths. Such high proportions of mortality among select groups, Lindley avers, would have had a disproportionate effect on the arts. John Maddison's unique study of the transition in Lichfield diocese from Decorated to Perpendicular architecture directly attributes the change to the Black Death. The abrupt cessation of work on the lavish Decorated Chapter House at Ely may well result from a similar cause. Further evidence is adduced from losses among tomb-brass engravers and tomb-sculptors such as those who produced the Hastings tomb and effigy at Abergavenny, Gwent, the last of its type, and from the cessation of work by the Fitzwarin Psalter Group of manuscript producers and embellishers: a 'serious hiatus in English manuscript illumination'. While poorer and more remote churches experienced a 'decline in quality' of work there; some royal works such as the glazing of St Stephen's chapel, Westminster, proceeded – but only because of national impressment of glaziers from across the land. Great glazing schemes are not found in provincial England between Kettlebarn's Great West Window at York in 1339 and Thomas of Oxford's scheme at Winchester College, Hampshire, in the 1390s. Other detailed and cogent cases are presented by Lindley.[56]

There is plenty of evidence that wages rose after the Black Death since government attempts, such as first the Ordinance and then the Statute of Labourers' limitation

[48] Michael R. McCarthy *et al.*, "The Medieval Kilns on Nash Hill, Lacock, Wiltshire," *Wiltshire Archaeological and Natural History Magazine* [WANHM] 69 (1974): 97–145.
[49] Le Patourel, "Pots and Potters," 7.
[50] Le Patourel, "Pots and Potters," 10.
[51] C.K. Pankhurst, "A Dragon from Nash Hill, Lacock," in "The Medieval Kilns on Nash Hill, Lacock, Wiltshire," ed. Michael R. McCarthy *et al*, *WANHM* 69 (1974): 154–60.
[52] A high-temperature refining process for metals such as silver and gold, in which base metals are separated by being absorbed into the walls of a cupel.
[53] Wolfram Giertz, "Middle Meuse Valley Ceramics of Huy-type: a preliminary analysis," *Medieval Ceramics* 20 (1996): 33–64.
[54] John Schofield and Alan G. Vince, *Medieval Towns* (London: Leicester University Press, 1994) 108.
[55] Lindley, "The Black Death and English Art," 146.
[56] Lindley, "The Black Death and English Art," 136–40.

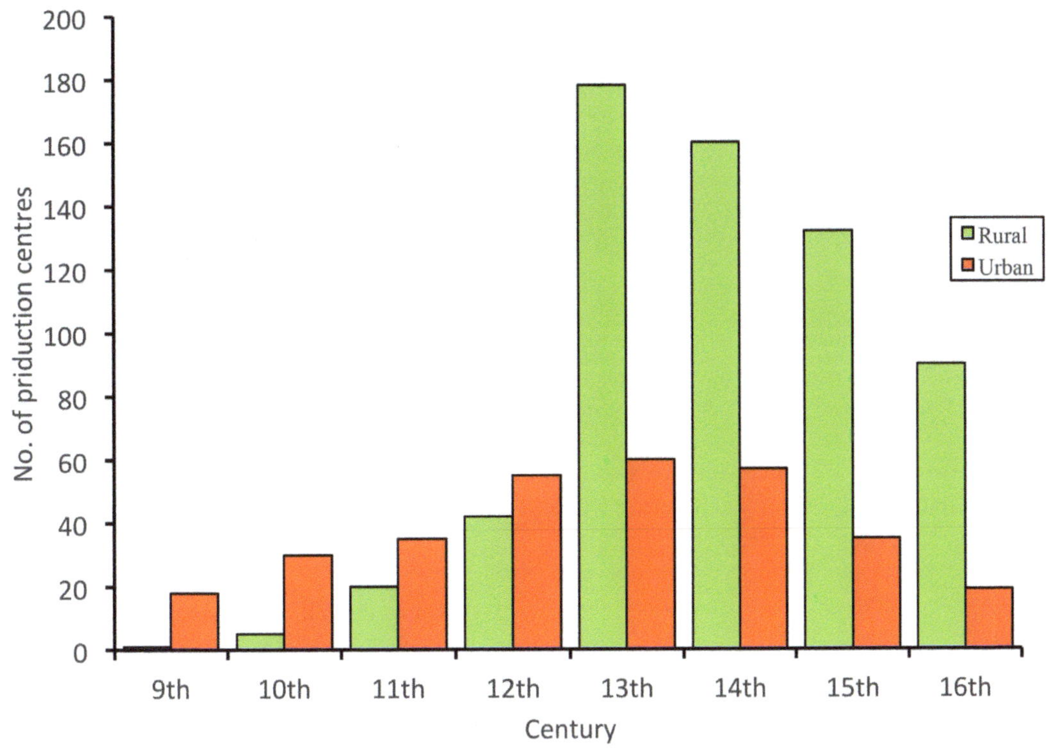

Figure 7.1: Urban and rural production centres by century (Marter, "Medieval Pottery Production," 252).

of wages in 1351, attempted to turn the clock back. The Sumptuary law of 1363 was a further attempt to control not only clothing but also diet among the lower ranks of society. Chaucer's 'Canterbury Tales' of 1387 were surely, in the wake of the Great Revolt of 1381, an attempt by the court poet to reassure the elite and to send pilgrims back down the pilgrim route to Canterbury up which peasants had marched to behead Archbishop Sudbury in London, six years earlier. It is no surprise that Chaucer organised his pilgrims by rank and degree.

Lindley raises various legitimate questions about other potential causes for the breaks in production, changes in style, and loss of practitioners from the late fourteenth century in the arts. So what of the potters and pottery production? If population decline was on the scale of some 60 per cent immediately following the plague, potters are bound to have suffered. One aspect of recent work is that it proposes matching mortality in both rural and urban societies. Potters are not usually, like so many artisans, known to us by name. However, what is observable in the surviving record is what is currently estimated to be a 30 per cent decline in pottery production sites from the fourteenth to the fifteenth centuries, as outlined above. This matches earlier, and similarly tentative proposals for mortality in society at large; a 30 per cent rate which has doubled in recent years.

While other causes and complexities may apply to explain the decline in numbers of pottery production centres from the fourteenth to the fifteenth centuries (e.g. Dyer's suggestion of increased opportunity for alternative work and lifestyles for potters), for the moment it is reasonable to suggest that the pottery industry, as with other aspects of the arts, may have been severely affected by the Black Death. For the pottery industry these changes primarily manifest themselves in reduced numbers of production sites (detailed earlier in this work) and changes in types of kilns and production locations – from urban to rural (see Figure 13.1). The complex and multi-facetted industry of pre-plague society appears therefore to have been transformed by the altered economic conditions brought about by the onset of the Black Death.

By the fifteenth century there were fewer but larger production centres. The industry was more dynamic and robust than at any time since the Roman period, with greater efficiency and potential profit margins available to potters. This dynamism is reflected in larger potting tenements than in previous periods and in some of the largest production centres of the medieval period.[57] Evidence from across the country suggests that potting was usually no longer a purely seasonal or part-time occupation, but an organised manufacturing industry.[58] How far conclusions can be drawn about the broader meaning of a fall in production centre numbers given this transformation remains to be seen. However, research has already begun to suggest that in some urban centres such as Southampton plague impacted on the local economy to the point where its effects can be seen in the archaeological record.[59] Until

[57] Dyer, "Social and Economic Changes," 38. See also Marter, *A National Database*.

[58] Marter, "Medieval Pottery Production," 257.

[59] Duncan H. Brown, "The Social Significance of Medieval Pottery," in *Not so Much a Pot, More a Way of Life*, ed. Christopher G. Cumberpatch and Paul W. Blinkhorn (Oxford: Oxbow, 1997), 95–112.

levels of pottery consumption and of production volume can be viewed on a national scale and data compared pre- and post-plague, the truth may remain elusive. Yet whilst we might not see artistic changes in pottery production as observed in other craft industries we do appear to see the impact of changed economic circumstances brought about by the Black Death. These changes are manifest in technology, scale of production and the relationship between potters and their markets.

It is also worth reminding ourselves that, as with any complex and dynamic entity, the medieval pottery industry cannot be properly understood purely by analysing statistical data or observing distribution patterns hundreds of years after the event. However, the value of such a broad overview of a national data set is that it does afford us a first glimpse into the potential scale of the effects on one aspect of ordinary medieval society; the ubiquitous qualities of the humble ceramic vessel perhaps providing a unique opportunity to witness the terrible impact of the Black Death on a national scale. An everyday item used by the everyday person might just be the perfect barometer of population health during this turbulent period. While there must certainly be caveats placed on our assumptions about pottery and the plague, it is hoped that this initial foray into the debate might stimulate further discussion.

Bibliography

Published secondary sources

Arthur, Paula. "The Black Death and Mortality: a reassessment." In *Fourteenth Century England VI*, edited by Chris Given Wilson, 49–72. Woodbridge: Boydell and Brewer, 2010.

Barton, K.J. *Pottery in England, from 3500BC–AD1730.* London: David and Charles, 1975.

Benedictow, Ole J. *The Black Death 1346–1353: the complete history.* Woodbridge: Boydell Press, 2004.

Benedictow, Ole J. *What Disease was Plague? On the controversy over the microbiological identity of plague epidemics in the past.* Leiden: Brill, 2010.

Brown, Duncan H. "The Social Significance of Medieval Pottery." In *Not so Much a Pot, More a Way of Life*, edited by Christopher G. Cumberpatch and Paul W. Blinkhorn, 95–112. Oxford: Oxbow, 1997.

Dyer, Christopher. "The Social and Economic Changes of the Later Middle Ages and the Pottery of the Period." *Medieval Ceramics* 6 (1982): 33–42.

Dyer, Christopher. "Peasants and Farmers: rural settlements and landscapes in an age of transition." In *The Age of Transition: the archaeology of English culture, 1400–1600*, edited by David Gaimster and Paul Stamper, 61–76. Oxford: Oxbow, 1997.

Foard, Glen. "The Medieval Pottery Industry of Rockingham Forest, Northamptonshire." *Medieval Ceramics* 15 (1991): 13–20.

Giertz, Wolfram. "Middle Meuse Valley Ceramics of Huy-type: a preliminary analysis." *Medieval Ceramics* 20 (1996): 33–64.

Hatcher, John. *Plague, Population and the English Economy 1348–1530.* London: Macmillan, 1977.

Hayfield, Colin. *Humberside Medieval Pottery: an illustrated catalogue of Saxon and medieval assemblages from North Lincolnshire and its surrounding region* vol. 1, BAR British Series 140. Oxford: BAR, 1985.

Horrox, Rosemary ed. *The Black Death.* Manchester: Manchester University Press, 1994.

Jennings, Sarah. *Medieval Pottery in the Yorkshire Museum.* York: The Yorkshire Museum, 1992.

Le Patourel, H.E. Jean. "Documentary Evidence and the Medieval Pottery Industry." *Medieval Archaeology* 12 (1968): 101–26.

Le Patourel, H.E. Jean. "Pottery as Evidence for Social and Economic Change." In *Medieval Settlement*, edited by Peter H. Sawyer, 169–79. London: Edward Arnold, 1976.

Le Patourel, H.E. Jean. "Pots and Potters." *Medieval Ceramics* 10 (1986): 3–16.

Lindley, Philip. "The Black Death and English Art: a debate and some assumptions." In *The Black Death in England*, edited by Mark Ormrod and Philip Lindley, 124–46. Donington: Shaun Tyas, 2003.

McCarthy, Michael R., *et al.* "The Medieval Kilns on Nash Hill, Lacock, Wiltshire." *Wiltshire Archaeological and Natural History Magazine* 69 (1974): 97–160.

McCarthy Michael R., and Catherine M. Brooks. *Medieval Pottery in Britain, AD 900–1600.* Leicester: Leicester University Press, 1988.

Medieval Pottery Research Group. "Medieval Pottery Research Group Bibliography." Accessed 16 July, 2018. http://archaeologydataservice.ac.uk/archives/view/mprg_eh_2010/.

Mepham, Lorraine, and Michael J. Heaton. "A Medieval Pottery Kiln at Ashampstead, Berkshire." *Medieval Ceramics* 19 (1995): 29–43.

Nenk, Beverly. "Highly Decorated Pottery in Medieval England." In *Pottery in the Making*, edited by Ian Freestone and David R.M. Gaimster, 92–97. London: British Museum Press, 1997.

Pankhurst, C.K. "A Dragon from Nash Hill, Lacock." In "The Medieval Kilns on Nash Hill, Lacock, Wiltshire," edited by Mike R. McCarthy *et al. WANHM* 69 (1974): 154–60.

Rye, Owen S. *Pottery Technology: principles and reconstruction.* Washington D.C.: Taraxacum, 1981.

Schofield, John, and Alan. G. Vince. *Medieval Towns.* London: Leicester University Press, 1994.

Streeten, Anthony D.F. "Craft and Industry: medieval and later potters in south-east England." In *Production and*

Distribution: a ceramic viewpoint, edited by Hilary Howard and Elaine L. Morris, 323–46. Oxford: British Archaeological Reports, 1981.

Vince, Alan G. "The Medieval and Post-Medieval Ceramic Industry of the Malvern Region: the study of a ware and its distribution." In *Pottery and Early Commerce: characterisation and trade in Roman and later ceramics*, edited by D.P.S. Peacock, 257–305. London: Academic Press, 1977.

Watts, D.G. "The Black Death in Dorset and Hampshire." *The Hatcher Review* 5, no. 46 (1998): 21–28.

Ziegler, Philip, *The Black Death.* London: Collins, 1969.

Unpublished secondary sources

Arthur, Paula. "The Impact of the Black Death on Seventeen Units of Account of the Bishopric of Winchester." Unpublished PhD Thesis, University College Winchester/University of Southampton, 2005.

Marter, Phil. "A National Database of Medieval Pottery Production Centres in England, AD 850–1600." Digital database, English Heritage. Unpublished, 2003.

Marter, Phil. "Medieval Pottery Production Centres in England, AD 850–1600." Unpublished PhD thesis, University of Winchester/University of Southampton, 2005.

8

Balancing Military Ambitions with Civilian Interests: The English Occupation of Normandy, 1417 to 1450

Anne Curry

University of Southampton

Abstract: It is one thing to conquer an area and quite another to win over the hearts and minds of its inhabitants, especially when occupation is sustained by the continuing presence of soldiers. This essay explores this problem with regard to the English conquest and occupation of Normandy in the first half of the fifteenth century. It highlights changes over time as well as space, exploring the views of both occupier and occupied. The English needed to ensure the military effectiveness of their soldiers whilst also preventing excesses in their behaviour towards the native population. Control and conciliation were both needed but there was often a narrow line between them.

Key words: England; Normandy; military occupation; military discipline

Relations between soldiers and civilians have been brought into stark relief by recent military engagements of the British army in Afghanistan and Iraq. Two main lessons emerge relevant to this present discussion. First, that in the context of occupation/peace keeping/or however one wishes to define these kinds of invasions, politics plays a major role, 'interfering', if we can put it that way, with military concerns. It is not just a straight fight between armies of opposing sides, where we can more easily weigh up strengths and weakness and explain victory and defeat, but a complex, and often problematic, mix of strategic and political determinants in which there are several players with diverse responses—the local population, which is itself unlikely to be homogeneous; the new and old regimes, their rulers and their officials; and the soldiers themselves.

The second lesson from the present is that soldiers are precisely that. They are trained to fight. Arguably it is easy for an army to take territory by advancing from one place to the next, especially if the enemy is not strong enough to retaliate. The real challenge comes later, namely in occupying the conquered area and interacting with the civilian population. I have heard from military experts that at the invasion of Iraq relatively little thought had gone into training soldiers for the aftermath of invasion, and that it was not always easy for those who had been fired up for action to 'come down' from that frame of mind, or to identify with the role of peacekeeper. There have been moves to remedy this since but the continuing existence of an army in conquered territory raises another important question. Is their presence to be read as a continuation of war or as a means of establishing and preserving a peace? The victor's claim is that the enemy has been defeated. In this scenario the civilian population expects peace, and victors have to be seen to provide it.

It is easy to dismiss past contexts as less complex than those of today. Yet while weapons may have been less destructive and communications less instant, the same basic issues prevailed. From my researches on the conquest and occupation of Normandy by the English in the first half of the fifteenth century I would certainly say that the two lessons mentioned above apply as much in that context as in modern warfare. Battles such as Agincourt were fought between professional armies, although their outcomes indirectly affected others. By contrast, the conquest and occupation of territory directly involved and impacted upon civilians, thereby raising important dilemmas for would-be conquerors and occupiers as well as for the people they conquered and over whom they imposed a military occupation.

Yet the concept of occupation would be lost on the English of this period. King Henry V invaded to recover possession of what he considered was his by right as a claimant to the crown of France.[1] Subsequent documents speak of 'notre duché', 'notre peuple', 'notre ville de Rouen' etc. After 1422 Henry VI ruled France as king by virtue of the treaty of Troyes, the terms of which had been agreed by a legitimate French ruler, Charles VI, and ratified by nobles, clergy and people. In no way, then, did the English political position include any notion of occupation of Normandy or anywhere else in France. Indeed Henry's line was that he had come to liberate the Normans from French tyranny.

But what of the Normans themselves? From our modern liberal perspective it is hard to imagine their not seeing the English presence as an occupation. After all, it began with military invasion and with siege warfare involving, at least on some occasions, bombardment, starvation, personal and communal cost. It was sustained by an English military

[1] For a full discussion of this period see Christopher Allmand, *Lancastrian Normandy: the history of a medieval occupation 1415–1450* (Oxford: Clarendon Press, 1983). See also Anne Curry, "Lancastrian Normandy: the jewel in the crown," in *England and Normandy in the Middle Ages*, ed. Anne Curry and David Bates (London: Hambledon Press, 1994), 235–52.

presence throughout, with around 45 garrisons. These were reinforced at moments of perceived crisis, and with many expeditionary and field armies passing through. Virtually all of the captains of garrisons, and all of the senior officials (the *baillis* who were in charge of the administrative divisions known as *bailliages*) were Englishmen.[2] Indeed the first *bailli* to be appointed by Henry in Normandy was Sir John Popham jnr, who was given charge of the *bailliage* of Caen on 24 December 1417, shortly after the composition of Falaise which had given Henry effective control of this area of the duchy.[3] The Popham family had held the manor of that name, midway between Winchester and Basingstoke since at least the twelfth century. Sir John senior (d. 1418) was constable of Southampton Castle at the time of Henry V's expeditions of 1415 and 1417 which sailed from the port. His son (d. 1463) served with his cousin Stephen in the retinue of Edward, duke of York in the Agincourt campaign. In March 1417 he had crossed to reinforce Harfleur but then joined the main expedition for the conquest of Normandy in August 1417. In addition to the *bailliage* of Caen, he was also appointed captain of Bayeux in January 1421. He served in France almost continuously to 1430, and in the mid-1430s carried out a number of key roles between England and France in both military and diplomatic activity.[4] A high proportion of the soldiers present in the duchy were English. Between 1415 and 1450 at least 50 Hampshire men took out letters of protection as they prepared to cross for service in France, but this figure by no means includes all soldiers of Hampshire origins: only the wealthier men with landed interests needed to take out protections from any actions in their absence.[5] Normans who refused to accept English rule were deprived of their lands which were then given to Englishmen.[6] Sir John Popham, for instance, was granted houses in Caen and Bayeux as well as the lordships of Torigni-sur-Vire and Planquery.[7]

On the face of it, therefore, we have a government which claimed legitimacy but which was only sustained by a military presence. Yet the situation is more complex.[8] After the initial period of military emergency, such as with expulsion of women and children from Harfleur after its capture, effort was made to preserve local institutions and to confirm existing privileges and lands at least of those – and they were the majority of Normans – who acquiesced to the rule of the English kings. Local opinion was taken into account – arguably more so than under previous French rule – through the regular calling of the Estates. Indeed, the introduction of stricter controls on the behaviour of soldiers was often prompted by complaints against them voiced at such assemblies.[9] The local inhabitants continued to play a role in their own defence. Some joined the garrisons and fought alongside English soldiers. There was intermarriage, sexual as well as commercial intercourse, friendship, business partnership, money lending, and many other relationships between occupier and occupied.[10]

We could conclude that that without military aid from the Valois kings the Normans could not offer meaningful resistance and therefore for the most part did not try to do so. Given the size of the population (600,000) the proportion of Normans committing acts against the occupier was small. In other words, they simply learned to live with their English rulers, so much so that in the heartlands of Normandy by the early 1430s there was little need for a large military presence to be maintained at all.[11]

Older French historical works tend to suggest that in their heart of hearts the Normans harboured enmities and a desire to be liberated.[12] This was certainly the impression that they gave when they were liberated in 1449–50, offering a warm welcome to Charles VII. But had they given as equally warm a welcome to Henry VI, to Bedford, to Henry V? Was their response no more and no less than pragmatic? If so, this would suggest that there was a standard civilian response to soldiers. In sociological terms this is simply the response of the powerless unarmed to the powerful armed. It confirms, if there was any need for confirmation, that soldiers were a distinct professional group characterised not only by their legitimate ownership of weapons but also their skill in using them. In this respect, then, Lancastrian Normandy is perhaps not so different from German-occupied Normandy between 1940 and 1944, where acts of opposition were as disproportionately small.

Should we talk of 'a rule of fear'? The efforts of the English rulers of Normandy would suggest that this was not the intention. Politics come into the equation again. The English could hardly claim to be legitimate rulers if

[2] Anne Curry, "The *Baillis* of Lancastrian Normandy: English men wearing French hats," in *The Plantagenet Empire*, Harlaxton Medieval Studies 26, ed. Peter Crooks, David Green and W. Mark Ormrod (Donington: Shaun Tyas, 2016), 359–70.

[3] *Rotuli Normanniae in turri Londoniensis asservati Johanne et Henrico Quinto Angliae regibus*, ed. Thomas D. Hardy (London, 1835), 231–32.

[4] Anne Curry, "Popham, Sir John (c. 1395–1463)," *Oxford Dictionary of National Biography*, 2008 (https://doi.org/10.1093/ref:odnb/22542).

[5] Adrian Bell, Anne Curry, Andy King and David Simpkin, *The Soldier in Later Medieval England* (Oxford: Oxford University Press, 2013), table 6.3.

[6] Christopher Allmand, "The Lancastrian Land Settlement in Normandy 1417–50," *Economic History Review* 21, 3 (1968): 461–79.

[7] *Annual Report of the Deputy Keeper of the Public Records* 41 (1880), 686; 42 (1881), 367; Archives Nationales de France JJ 174/291.

[8] For a case study see Anne Curry, "Bourgeois et soldats dans la ville de Mantes pendant l'occupation anglaise de 1419 à 1449," in *Guerre, Pouvoir et Noblesse au Moyen Âge:* Mélanges en l'honneur de Philippe Contamine, ed. Jacques Paviot and Jacques Verger (Paris: Presses de l'Université de Paris-Sorbonne, 2000), 175–84.

[9] For an example of 1423 see Pierre Adolphe Chéruel, *Histoire de Rouen sous la domination anglaise* (Rouen, 1840), 85–91.

[10] Anne Curry, "Sex and the Soldier in Lancastrian Normandy, 1415–50," *Reading Medieval Studies* 14 (1988): 17–45; "Isolated or Integrated? The English soldier in Lancastrian Normandy," in *Courts and Regions of Medieval Europe*, ed. Sarah Rees Jones, Richard Marks and Alistair Minnis (Woodbridge: York Medieval Press, 2000), 191–210.

[11] Joseph Stevenson, ed., *Letters and Papers Illustrative of the Wars of the English in France during the Reign of Henry VI*, Rolls Series 186 part 2 (London, 1864), 540–46; Anne Curry, "English Armies in the Fifteenth Century," in *Arms, Armies and Fortifications in the Hundred Years War*, ed. Anne Curry and Michael Hughes (Woodbridge: The Boydell Press, 1994), 49–60.

[12] Roger Jouet, *La résistance à l'occupation anglaise en Basse-Normandie (1418–1450)*, Cahier des Annales de Normandie 5 (Caen, 1969): 15–19.

they did not take the interests of the local population to heart. They may also have realised that a happy population was much more likely to be a peaceful one, and therefore themselves adopted a pragmatic view of how soldiers should interact with civilians. Such a situation would be boosted by the need to rely upon local supplies of food, horses, and armaments, as well as labour for construction of fortifications.

But does the relationship work in reverse? Does a civilian population behave as it is treated? Is violence met with violence, compromise with compromise, peaceful treatment with peaceful response? It would be meaningful to probe these questions comparatively across time. This would reveal the continuities of politico-military activity as well as the disjunctures, especially in cross-cultural conflicts. It is significant that in fifteenth-century Normandy both occupiers and occupied were Christians. Once the papal schism that began in 1378 came to an end in 1417, both accepted the authority of the same pope. They were both bound by the same moral and ethical belief systems and also by a general principle of non-resistance to authority. Furthermore, there were also strong linguistic ties. The English nobility and gentry – men who occupied the positions of military commanders, captains and *baillis* – all read and spoke the 'French of England'. Indeed, this gave the English an advantage in their invasions of France during the Hundred Years War.[13] Some Englishmen who came to Normandy as soldiers or settlers married local women and integrated into the population and some even chose French allegiance at the Reconquest by Charles VII (1449–50) in order to keep the lands they had gained through their Norman wives.[14]

In addition, the English and Normans had very similar systems of government and social structures, and wholly comparable legal codes and procedures. The legacy of the Anglo-Norman duchy reinforced this despite the loss of the duchy to Philip Augustus in 1204. It is important to remember that there had been French royal garrisons in Normandy before the invasion of the English in 1415. The French crown had fully exploited its rights to require service, such as the *arrière-ban*, *corvée* and *guet et garde*, from the native population, and taxation systems of the *aides*, *fouage*, *gabelle* and *quatrièmes* were well established. The English simply took all of these over.

Both English and Normans had a similar understanding of social hierarchy and an acceptance of properly constituted governmental authority. Their shared concept of the legitimate leaders of society is exemplified in the Household Book of Richard, earl of Warwick when captain of Rouen.[15] Here we see frequent formal dinners held in the castle of Rouen where the bourgeois of Rouen and their wives sat side by side with the leading English military commanders and their womenfolk. The inhabitants of the Norman capital had welcomed the young Henry VI during his visit to France in 1430–32. He had stayed in Rouen throughout the trial of Joan of Arc, both residing in the same castle. His visit had seen the foundation of the University of Caen as a Norman rival to the University of Paris. On the whole the Normans had accepted English rule. This was partly because the English promoted Norman identity, but also because the English ruled by virtue of the treaty of Troyes which the French crown had accepted. Whilst there might be an alternative power base south of the Loire up to 1429, and more widely after that date, there was no alternative power base within Normandy itself. The Norman nobles who remained after the initial invasion of the English, or who returned in the peaceful conditions after the treaty of Troyes and subsequently the English victory at the battle of Verneuil in August 1424 – which removed for a while any Dauphinist military threat within the duchy – proved loyal to the English. Those who had chosen exile saw their influence decline as the English occupation continued. The clergy were on the whole compliant towards English rule. Only at first was there any sense of emergency military rule. As the years passed, the English ruled through existing institutions and often through existing personnel in local government, law and the Church.

It would be very instructive to compare occupations of this kind with those involving peoples with different social, cultural and religious mores. Such differences go a long way towards explaining the difficulties faced, for example, by the crusader states, and by Western powers in today's conflicts. It may be, too, that different kinds of cultures have different perceptions of the purpose of soldiers. Are they protectors of the civilian population, or enforcers of the will of the conqueror, or both? As Philippe Contamine shows, the notion of the soldier as protector of the civilian population was a strong one.[16] Both the French and English had similar disciplinary codes stemming from a common Christian tradition which tried to limit violence against non-combatants, especially clergy, women and peasants.

Another factor to throw into the debate must be timescale. The longer an occupier had been able to establish his presence in an area then the greater the level of social and economic peace, and the higher the rate of acquiescence. English actions against the civilian population diminished as time went on. However, a geographical dimension needs to be added in. The attitude of the occupied was influenced by their proximity to military action and to the presence

[13] Denise Angers, "La guerre et la pluralisme linguistique: aspects de la Guerre de Cent Ans," *Annales de Normandie* 43 (1993): 125–39; Anne Curry, Adrian Bell, Adam Chapman, Andy King and David Simpkin, "Languages in the Military Profession in Later Medieval England," in *The Anglo-Norman Language and its Contexts*, ed. Richard Ingham (Woodbridge: The Boydell Press, 2010), 74–93.

[14] Anne Curry, "Soldiers' Wives in the Hundred Years War," in *Soldiers, Nobles and Gentlemen: Essays in honour of Maurice Keen*, ed. Peter Coss and Christopher Tyerman (Woodbridge: The Boydell Press, 2009), 201.

[15] Warwickshire County Record Office CR/1618/W, 19/5, folio 18v, 30r, 127v. Four bourgeois of Rouen accompanied the countess of Warwick to Paris for the coronation of Henry VI in December 1431 (f. 135r).

[16] Philippe Contamine, "The Soldier in Late Medieval Urban Society," *French History* 8 (1994): 1–13. See also Craig Taylor, *Chivalry and the Ideals of Knighthood in France during the Hundred Years War* (Cambridge: Cambridge University Press, 2013), chapters 5 and 6.

of Valois-held territory and soldiers. For instance, when there were false reports that the English had been defeated at the battle of Verneuil in 1424, anti-English actions by civilians briefly increased until the truth of the matter was known.[17] In 1433, the English considered that 12 soldiers were enough to defend Bayeux 'because the enemy who supported the Dauphin were a very long way away from the city'.[18] We must distinguish between the heartlands of Normandy and the frontiers. Some places, such as Avranches close to the never-conquered Mont St Michel, always saw a large military presence as did the Norman capital, Rouen. The exact geographical dimensions varied across time. The *pays de Caux* was peaceful and well away from action in the 1420s and early 1430s, but a war zone in the late 1430s after French recovery of Harfleur and many other places. Harfleur was recovered in 1440, and thereafter housed a garrison of 200, twice as many as before its loss. Dieppe remained in Valois hands, with its population supporting 400 French soldiers rather than the 60 English soldiers of the 1420s and early 1430s.[19] The recovery by the French of Louviers and Évreux in 1440–1441 led to great insecurities in that area, exacerbated by repeated English efforts to recover the lost places.

We can also see different phases of the occupation, although these are blurred at the edges. In the initial conquest of 1415 the English gave priority to military considerations. This is seen most obviously in the expulsion of many of the inhabitants of Harfleur and the introduction of English settlers in order to ensure the security of the town as an English military base.[20] In the second invasion of 1417 the English imposed their will on the first major conquest, Caen, by a public burning of its records and donation of houses in the town to soldiers and administrators but as the conquest continued existing rights and privileges of the Normans were confirmed. The military success of the English, and the lack of French royal support, had the effect of persuading the Normans to accept English rule. In turn the English authorities ordered soldiers not to damage any Norman who was 'bulleté', that is, who had formally submitted. Henry V had always emphasised the need for his soldiers to behave responsibly. Requirements for them to take due regard of the rights of civilians increased as garrisons were established in the main centres of population.[21] As a corollary, the establishment of good relations made Normandy secure and permitted the English to expand their area of conquest towards Paris. The premature death of Henry V in 1422 triggered an increase in resistance and Franco-Scottish invasion into Normandy but the English victory at Verneuil in August 1424 reinforced the state of submission. Indeed in military terms this enabled a major reduction in the size of garrisons within Normandy, thereby releasing troops for the invasion of Maine. The English could afford to give priority to civilian interests, as is revealed in a further wave of formal restrictions on the behaviour of soldiers and garrison captains.[22] But the reversals of 1429–30 renewed English suspicions towards the local population. For instance, the recruitment of Normans and French into the garrisons, which had increased in the years of peace, was now limited.[23] However, there was still considerable emphasis on ensuring that soldiers behaved well towards civilians, and this no doubt helped the English to maintain their rule and for the war to be fought largely outside Normandy.

The winter of 1435–6 was the real turning point since war came into the duchy and stimulated resistance once again, especially in the *pays de Caux*.[24] Even though all of the disciplinary ordinances remained in place, English troops were increasingly seen as oppressors. This was no doubt because of the need, for the first time since 1420, to carry out so many military actions within Normandy itself, which put pressure on food supplies and necessitated high taxation levels at a time of general economic decline.[25] It is not surprising that we can detect relief on the part of the Normans when a state of truce was negotiated with Charles VII in May 1444. Interestingly too, the English commanders were aware of the problem of how soldiers might behave when they had no fighting to do. Captains were ordered not to allow their men to spend more than one day 'sur les champs' for fear that they might harass or oppress the local population.[26] Subsequently there were efforts made to force soldiers who were now surplus to requirements to return to England.[27] At the end of the day, however, the diminution of the English presence in the duchy enabled Charles VII to recover the duchy easily. The events of 1449–50 replicate those of 1417–19 and reveal once more that civilians were wholly pragmatic in their response to a large scale military invasion.[28]

---

[17] Pierre Le Cacheux, ed., *Actes de la Chancellerie d'Henri VI concernant la Normandie sous la domination anglaise (1422–35)* 2 (Rouen and Paris: Société de l'Histoire de Normandie, 1907–08), items CCCXXXVI; CCCLV.

[18] "Adversarii ex part Dophini multum remoti a dicta civitate," *Letters and Papers*, vol. 2 part 2, 541.

[19] Anne Curry, "The Impact of War and Occupation on Urban Life in Normandy, 1417–1450," *French History* 1 (1987): 169.

[20] Anne Curry, "Henry V's Harfleur. A Study in Military Administration, 1415–1422," in *The Hundred Years War (Part III). Further considerations*, ed. L.J. Andrew Villalon and Donald J. Kagay (Leiden and Boston: Brill, 2013), 259–84.

[21] Anne Curry, "Disciplinary Ordinances for English Garrisons in Normandy in the Reign of Henry V," in *The Fifteenth Century XIV: Essays Presented to Michael Hicks*, ed. Linda Clark (Woodbridge: The Boydell Press, 2015), 1–12.

[22] Benedicta Rowe, "Discipline in the Norman Garrisons under Bedford, 1422–35," *English Historical Review* 46 (1931): 194–208.

[23] Anne Curry, "Foreign Soldiers in English Pay. Identity and unity in the armies of the English Crown 1415–1450," in *Routiers et mercenaires pendant la guerre de Cent Ans. Hommage à Jonathan Sumption*, ed. Guilhem Pépin, Françoise Lainé and Frédéric Boutoulle (Bordeaux: Ausonius Editions, 2016), 311.

[24] Denise Angers, "La résistance à l'occupant anglais en Haute–Normandie," *Annales de Normandie* 36 (1986): 37–55; 91–104.

[25] Guy Bois, *The Crisis of Feudalism. Economy and society in eastern Normandy c.1300–1550*, Past and Present Publications (Cambridge: Cambridge University Press, 1984).

[26] Paris, Bibliothèque Nationale pièces originales 2623 Salvain 47.

[27] Anne Curry, "Les 'gens vivans sur le pais' pendant l'occupation de Normandie, 1417–1450," in *La guerre, la violence et les gens au Moyen Age. 1: Guerre et violence*, ed. Philippe Contamine and Olivier Guyotjeannin (Paris: CTHS, 1996), 209–21.

[28] Anne Curry, "Towns at War. Relations between the towns of Normandy and their English rulers 1417–1450," in *Towns and Townspeople in the Fifteenth Century*, ed. John Thomson (Gloucester: Alan Sutton, 1988), 149–60.

A study of Normandy under English rule suggests that it was never possible to prevent clashes between soldiers and civilians. The frequent reissuing of disciplinary ordinances and the launching of enquiries shows that the behaviour of soldiers was not always as the English rulers might have hoped. Furthermore, it was only possible to control soldiers who were in receipt of pay. Those who fell outside this system – the unemployed soldiers who chose to, or had little option but to, live off the land – were a constant cause of civilian complaint. Equally crucial was the personality of the captain. Today much attention is given to the choice of suitable commanders and their training. There are some parallels to this in English Normandy. An excellent closing example can be found in the disciplinary ordinances which were published at the Estates of Normandy at Caen in December 1423, which defined the qualities expected in a captain.

> Avons ordonné et ordonnons que pour la garde et seureté des chasteaulx et forteresses de notre dit duchié soient ordonnées et commises notables et souffisans persones de bonne fame et renommée, lesquelles seront tenues et astrainctes de bien et deuement gouverner les gens de leur retenue, de les tenir ensemble, et de les garder et deffendre de pillier, robber ne faire grief, dommaige ou molestation a noz bons et loyaulx subgiez.[29]

In order to protect the interests of civilians, the behaviour of soldiers towards them had to be regulated. This was all the more necessary in this period when there had to be continuing reliance on the local population not only for taxation and food supplies but also in the payment of watch and maintenance of fortifications. The civilian input to the occupation of Normandy was crucial, yet the English could never be fully sure they could trust the local population. Therefore they had always to ensure the military effectiveness of their soldiers. The tensions inherent in a military occupation were never resolved. Perhaps they never can be.

Acknowledgements

This discussion began as a contribution to a lecture series at the University of Lille on the history of military occupations, which was published in Revue du Nord 402 (2013), 967–76.

Bibliography

Primary Sources

British Library (BL).

BL, Birch MS 4101 f.65

The National Archives (TNA).

Annual Report of the Deputy Keeper of the Public Records 41 (1880).

Annual Report of the Deputy Keeper of the Public Records 42 (1881).

Warwickshire Record Office (WRO).

CR/1618/W, 19/5, folio 18v, 30r, 127v. Four bourgeois of Rouen accompanied the countess of Warwick to Paris for the coronation of Henry VI in December 1431.

Bibliothèque Nationale, Paris.

Pièces originales 2623 Salvain 47.

Others

Actes de la Chancellerie d'Henri VI concernant la Normandie sous la domination anglaise (1422–35), edited by Pierre Le Cacheux, two vols (Rouen and Paris: Société de l'Histoire de Normandie, 1907–08).

Letters and Papers Illustrative of the Wars of the English in France during the reign of Henry VI, edited by Joseph Stevenson, three volumes in two parts (London: Rolls Series, 1861).

Rotuli Normanniae in turri Londoniensis asservati Johanne et Henrico Quinto Angliae regibus, ed. T.D. Hardy (London, 1835).

Secondary sources

Allmand, Christopher. *Lancastrian Normandy: The history of a medieval occupation 1415–1450.* Oxford: Clarendon Press, 1983.

Allmand, Christopher. "The Lancastrian Land Settlement in Normandy 1417–50." *Economic History Review* 21, 3 (1968): 461–79.

Angers, Denise. "La résistance à l'occupant anglais en Haute-Normandie." *Annales de Normandie* 36 (1986): 37–55.

Angers, Denise. "La guerre et la pluralisme linguistique: aspects de la Guerre de Cent Ans." *Annales de Normandie* 43 (1993): 125–39.

Bell, Adrian, Anne Curry, Andy King, and David Simpkin. *The Soldier in Later Medieval England.* Oxford: Oxford University Press, 2013.

Bois, Guy. *The Crisis of Feudalism. Economy and Society in Eastern Normandy c.1300–1550*, Past and Present Publications. Cambridge: Cambridge University Press, 1984.

Chéruel, Pierre Adolphe. *Histoire de Rouen sous la domination anglaise*, two volumes in one part. Rouen, 1840.

Clark, Linda, ed. *The Fifteenth Century XIV: Essays Presented to Michael Hicks*. Woodbridge: The Boydell Press, 2015.

[29] British Library, Birch MS 4101 f.65; Rowe, "Discipline in the Norman Garrisons," 202. (We have ordered and now order that for the guard and safekeeping of the castles and fortresses of our duchy of Normandy should be appointed and commissioned notable and sufficient persons of good name and reputation who should be required and expected to govern the men in their retinue well and in due manner, to hold them together, and keep them and forbid them from pillaging, robbing or committing any kind of grief, damage or molestation against our good and loyal subjects.)

Contamine, Philippe. "The Soldier in Late Medieval Urban Society." *French History* 8 (1994): 1–13.

Coss, Peter and Christopher Tyerman, eds. *Soldiers, Nobles and Gentlemen: Essays in honour of Maurice Keen*. Woodbridge: The Boydell Press, 2009.

Curry, Anne. "The Impact of War and Occupation on Urban Life in Normandy, 1417–1450." *French History* 1 (1987): 157–81.

Curry, Anne. "Sex and the Soldier in Lancastrian Normandy, 1415–50." *Reading Medieval Studies* 14 (1988): 17–45.

Curry, Anne. "Towns at War. Relations between the towns of Normandy and their English rulers 1417–1450." In *Towns and Townspeople in the Fifteenth Century*, edited by John Thomson, 148–72. Gloucester: Alan Sutton, 1988.

Curry, Anne. "Lancastrian Normandy: the jewel in the crown." In *England and Normandy in the Middle Ages*, edited by Anne Curry and David Bates, 235–52. London: Hambledon Press, 1994.

Curry, Anne. "English Armies in the Fifteenth Century." In *Arms, Armies and Fortifications in the Hundred Years War*, edited by Anne Curry and Michael Hughes, 39–68. Woodbridge: The Boydell Press, 1994.

Curry, Anne. "Les 'gens vivans sur le pais' pendant l'occupation de Normandie, 1417–1450." In *La guerre, la violence et les gens au Moyen Age. 1: Guerre et violence*, edited by Philippe Contamine and Olivier Guyotjeannin, 209–21. Paris: CTHS, 1996.

Curry, Anne. "Bourgeois et soldats dans la ville de Mantes pendant l'occupation anglaise de 1419 à 1449." In *Guerre, Pouvoir et Noblesse au Moyen Âge: Mélanges en l'honneur de Philippe Contamine*, edited by Jacques Paviot and Jacques Verger, 175–84. Paris: Presses de l'Université de Paris-Sorbonne, 2000.

Curry, Anne. "Isolated or Integrated? The English soldier in Lancastrian Normandy." In *Courts and Regions of Medieval Europe*, edited by Sarah Rees Jones, Richard Marks and Alistair Minnis, 191–210. Woodbridge: York Medieval Press, 2000.

Curry, Anne. "Popham, Sir John (c. 1395–1463)." *Oxford Dictionary of National Biography*, 2008. https://doi.org/10.1093/ref:odnb/22542.

Curry, Anne. "Soldiers' Wives in the Hundred Years War." In *Soldiers, Nobles and Gentlemen: Essays in honour of Maurice Keen*, edited by Peter Coss and Christopher Tyerman, 198–214. Woodbridge: The Boydell Press, 2009.

Curry, Anne. "Henry V's Harfleur. A Study in Military Administration, 1415–1422." In *The Hundred Years War (Part III). Further considerations*, edited by L.J. Andrew Villalon and Donald J. Kagay, 259–84. Leiden and Boston: Brill, 2013.

Curry, Anne. "Disciplinary Ordinances for English Garrisons in Normandy in the Reign of Henry V." In *The Fifteenth Century XIV: Essays Presented to Michael Hicks*, edited by Linda Clark, 1–12. Woodbridge: The Boydell Press, 2015.

Curry, Anne. "Foreign Soldiers in English Pay. Identity and unity in the armies of the English Crown 1415–1450." In *Routiers et mercenaires pendant la guerre de Cent Ans. Hommage à Jonathan Sumption*, ed. Guilhem Pépin, Françoise Lainé and Frédéric Boutoulle, 303–16. Bordeaux: Ausonius Editions, 2016.

Curry, Anne and David Bates, eds. *England and Normandy in the Middle Ages*. London: Hambledon Press, 1994.

Curry, Anne, Bell, Adrian, Chapman, Adam, King, Andy and Simpkin, David. "Languages in the Military Profession in Later Medieval England." In *The Anglo-Norman Language and its Contexts*, edited by Richard Ingham, 74–93. Woodbridge: The Boydell Press, 2010.

Curry, Anne and Michael Hughes, eds. *La guerre, la violence et les gens au Moyen Age. 1: Guerre et violence*. Paris: CTHS, 1996.

Curry, Anne and Michael Hughes, eds. *Arms, Armies and Fortifications in the Hundred Years War*. Woodbridge: The Boydell Press, 1994.

Ingham, Richard, ed. *The Anglo-Norman Language and its Contexts*. Woodbridge: The Boydell Press, 2010.

Jouet, Roger. *La résistance à l'occupation anglaise en Basse-Normandie (1418–1450)*, Cahier des Annales de Normandie 5 (Caen, 1969): 15–19.

Paviot, Jacques and Jacques Verger, eds. *Guerre, Pouvoir et Noblesse au Moyen Âge: Mélanges en l'honneur de Philippe Contamine*. Paris: Presses de l'Université de Paris-Sorbonne, 2000.

Pépin, Guilhem and Françoise Lainé and Frédéric Boutoulle, eds. *Routiers et mercenaires pendant la guerre de Cent Ans. Hommage à Jonathan Sumption.* Bordeaux: Ausonius Editions, 2016.

Rees Jones, Sarah and Richard Marks and Alistair Minnis, eds. *Courts and Regions of Medieval Europe*. Woodbridge: York Medieval Press, 2000.

Rowe, Benedicta. "Discipline in the Norman Garrisons under Bedford, 1422–35." *English Historical Review* 46 (1931): 194–208.

Taylor, Craig. *Chivalry and the Ideals of Knighthood in France during the Hundred Years War.* Cambridge: Cambridge University Press, 2013.

Thomson, John, ed. *Towns and Townspeople in the Fifteenth Century*. Gloucester: Alan Sutton, 1988.

Villalon, L.J. Andrew and Donald J. Kagay, eds. *The Hundred Years War (Part III). Further considerations.* Leiden and Boston: Brill, 2013.

9

The Late-Medieval Inns of Hampshire: Their Architecture and Plan-Form

Edward Roberts

Independent Scholar

Abstract: This essay on the standing remains of Hampshire's medieval inns leads to a fundamental questioning of Pantin's analysis and classification of the plan-form and functions of medieval inns. It starts from an examination of The Angel Inn at Andover where, remarkably, not only does a substantial amount of the mid-fifteenth-century frame survive but also the original building contract and detailed accounts are still kept in the archives of Winchester College. The recent discovery of the remarkable lodging range of the former George Inn at Alton, tree-ring dated to 1501, adds to our understanding of an important component of a medieval inn because it is clear that these were lodgings for less important guests who had to share unheated rooms intended for multiple occupancy and shared garderobes. Documentary evidence shows beyond doubt that these two buildings were designed as inns but some large medieval houses were converted to inns at an early date. How can we distinguish between purpose-built and converted inns and how can we distinguish between inn-like structures that were and were not inns without surviving documentary evidence? To try to answer these questions the surviving buildings, including The White Horse at Romsey, The George Inn at Odiham and The Swan Inn and Falcon Inn at Kingsclere, are considered. Pantin's attempt to divide medieval inns into either a 'courtyard' or a 'gatehouse' type fails to fit the surviving evidence and, in fact, most purpose-built medieval inns appear to have both features. In dealing with these fundamental questions of typology and definition, further questions naturally arise. How were inns used and by what manner of person and why does no inn building survive in Hampshire (or elsewhere in England) from before the mid-fourteenth century?

Key words: Inn; alehouse; tavern; lodging; courtyard; gatehouse; gallery; market

Introduction

It is scarcely an exaggeration to say that the scholarly study of the English medieval inn was largely initiated by W A Pantin. His intimate knowledge of both the documentary sources of English medieval history and of medieval vernacular architecture made him supremely well-qualified to write the seminal essay 'Medieval Inns' published in 1961.[1] Serious students of English medieval inns now build on the foundations laid by Pantin. Some have focussed on economic and social history, notably Alan Everitt who dealt mainly with a slightly later period, and John Hare.[2] Others have written on the standing remains of medieval inns in terms of their architecture and plan-form although this approach has been much less fully developed, partly because some historians still undervalue the potential contribution of architectural history, and in particular vernacular architecture, to their discipline.[3] A few general works on English medieval history and archaeology have referred briefly to Pantin's typology of the plan-forms of inns and there have also been detailed studies of the architecture of individual inns, such as The George Inn, Norton St. Philip and The New Inn, Oxford.[4] Regional studies of vernacular architecture occasionally touch on medieval inns in a given county, for example Hertfordshire and Hampshire,[5] but no regional study entirely devoted to the architecture and plan-form of medieval inns is known to the present author. This essay attempts to fill this gap.

[1] William Abel Pantin, "Medieval Inns," in *Studies in Building History*, ed. Edward Martyn Jope (London: Odhams Press, 1961), 166–91.

[2] Alan Everitt, "The English Urban Inn, 1560–1760," in *Perspectives on English Urban History*, ed. A. Everitt (London: Macmillan, 1973), 91–137; John Hare, "Inns, Innkeepers and the Society of Later Medieval England," *Journal of Medieval History* 39 (2013): 477–97; John Hare "Winchester College and the Angel Inn, Andover: a fifteenth-century landlord and its investments," *Proceedings of the Hampshire Field Club and Archaeological Society* 60 (2005): 187–97.

[3] Christopher Dyer, "History and Vernacular Architecture," *Vernacular Architecture* 28 (1997): 1–8.

[4] E.H.D. Williams, J. and J. Penoyre and B.C.H. Hale, "The George Inn, Norton St. Philip, Somerset," *Archaeological Journal* 144 (1987): 317–27; Julian Munby et al., "Zacharias's: a fourteenth-century Oxford new inn and the origins of the medieval urban inn," *Oxoniensia* 57 (1992): 249–309.

[5] John T. Smith, *English Houses 1200–1800: the Hertfordshire evidence* (London: HMSO, 1992), 150–54; 170–74; Edward Roberts, *Hampshire Houses 1250–1700: their dating and development* (Winchester: Hampshire County Council, 2003), 179–83; 193–94.

Late-medieval alehouses, taverns and inns

In July 1577 Queen Elizabeth's Privy Council required a certificate to be made of the true and just number of all the innholders (innkeepers), taverners and alehouse keepers within the county of Southampton – now Hampshire.[6] This implies, of course, that the Council and those who compiled the certificate thought they had a fairly clear idea how inns could be distinguished from alehouses and taverns. Indeed, the certificate was drawn up in three discrete columns precisely for this reason. In practice, these distinctions may not have been watertight and they certainly became more blurred during the seventeenth century. Today the terms inn, tavern and alehouse can be applied almost indiscriminately to a public house,[7] and this loosening of meaning can be a trap for historians. For example, in a chapter specifically devoted to medieval buildings in Hampshire, the fourteenth-century Blue Boar in Winchester has been rather confusingly called an inn. It was indeed a post-medieval public house – and in that loose sense a post-medieval inn – but there is no physical or documentary evidence to show that it was ever a *medieval* inn; that is, a medieval building supplying lodgings and drink to travellers which was distinct from an alehouse or tavern.[8] In order, as far as possible, to avoid this potential confusion, the year 1600 has been chosen as an approximate end-date for this essay and for the close of a rather protracted late Middle Ages.

So what were the distinctions that were apparent to Elizabeth's Council? In the later Middle Ages, alehouses were considerably more numerous establishments in Hampshire than inns. The certificate of 1577 recorded 324 alehouse-keepers but only 67 innkeepers in the county and in 1410 there were only nine inns in Winchester but 27 alehouses.[9] In the period between 1400 and 1600 alehouses in Hampshire, and probably elsewhere, served the poorer classes, who drank ale and not wine. It is thus not surprising that keeping an alehouse in sixteenth-century Winchester implied social inferiority and was usually a secondary occupation, perhaps carried on in the ale-seller's home.[10] It is hard to know what an alehouse might have looked like, although it was probably relatively humble and perhaps not unlike some of the smaller late-medieval houses that still survive in Hampshire.[11]

Taverns, on the other hand, formed a select minority of drinking establishments where wine was drunk and, unlike ale, wine was a luxury commodity. In 1577, 324 alehouse keepers were recorded in Hampshire but only 14 taverners.[12] Taverns catered for the more prosperous members of urban society, and taverners were among the wealthier property owners of late-medieval Winchester.[13] Winchester's taverns invariably had cellars and a remarkable survival takes us beyond the documentary records to see a fourteenth-century tavern substantially unaltered.[14] At Number 42 High Street, Winchester there is a stone-lined cellar and, above it, a building composed of three timber-framed chambers stacked one above the other on three floors.[15] This building has been tree-ring dated to 1316–52 and in 1380 was called The Paradise Tavern with shops and chambers built above: '*le Taverne de Paradys simul cum shopis et cameris superedificatis*'.[16]

The medieval Latin word for an inn, *hospitium*, could mean the great household of a lay or ecclesiastical magnate or the house in which the household was accommodated; in effect, a private inn. Pantin's conclusion that it was not until the fourteenth century that, in England, the word *hospitium* was applied to a public inn has remained unchallenged.[17] Thereafter the word 'inn' was generally understood to apply to both the private houses of the rich and public establishments, although in late-medieval Winchester from the mid-fourteenth century onwards the word *hospitium* seems only to have been applied to public inns.[18] It is likely that public inns were developed in the later Middle Ages because an expansion of trade and travel called for a network of establishments offering superior accommodation to travellers, and especially to the gentry and great landowners as they progressively concentrated on upgrading a few major residences and leased or sold their minor properties.[19] A telling example of this process is the behaviour of the Stonors, a landed family who bought a London house in the 1340s but later sold it and stayed at public inns instead.[20] As Pantin pointed out with regard to public inns, while people of inferior rank who stayed at them would eat together in the hall, 'persons of superior rank had their meals and drinks served in a variety of private rooms'.[21] Thus inns provided a home from home for the upper ranks of society so that the President of Magdalen College, Oxford was content to stay annually at the College's Bell Inn, Andover with his retinue of clerks,

[6] TNA: SP12/117/74.
[7] Derek Keene, *Survey of Medieval Winchester*, 2 vols (Oxford: Oxford University Press, 1985), 168–69; 277.
[8] Anthony Quiney, *The Traditional Buildings of England* (London: Thames and Hudson, 1990), 92; Keene, *Survey of Medieval Winchester*, 1067; Elizabeth Lewis *et al.* (eds) *Medieval Hall Houses of the Winchester Area* (Winchester: Winchester City Museums, 1988), 66–69.
[9] TNA SP12/117/74; Keene, *Survey of Medieval Winchester*, 276.
[10] Keene, *Survey of Medieval Winchester*, 165–68; 267.
[11] Roberts, *Hampshire Houses, passim.*
[12] TNA SP12/117/74.
[13] John Schofield and Alan Vince, *Medieval Towns* (London: Leicester University Press, 1994), 75; Keene, *Survey of Medieval Winchester*, 275–76.
[14] Keene, *Survey of Medieval Winchester*, 274.
[15] Tom Beaumont James and Edward Roberts, "Winchester and Late Medieval Development: from palace to pentice," *Medieval Archaeology* 44 (2000): 190, 198.
[16] Keene, *Survey of Medieval Winchester*, 567; James and Roberts, "Winchester and Late Medieval Development," 190; Roberts, *Hampshire Houses*, 250.
[17] Pantin, "Medieval Inns," 166.
[18] Keene, *Survey of Medieval Winchester*, 167.
[19] Christopher Dyer, *Standards of Living in the Later Middle Ages* (Cambridge: Cambridge University Press, 1989), 99–101; Hare, "Inns, Innkeepers," 447–49.
[20] Caroline M. Barron, "London 1300–1400," in *The Cambridge Urban History of Britain: vol. 1, 600–1540*, ed. David M. Palliser (Cambridge: Cambridge University Press, 2000), 440.
[21] Pantin, "Medieval Inns," 187.

servants and horses.[22] Similarly, Sir John Paston in the mid-fifteenth century stayed so frequently at The George near St. Paul's Cathedral in London that he could refer to 'my chamber' there, and 'Walops chamber' at The White Hart Inn, Alresford in 1571 was probably the regular room of a member of the Wallop family who were then wealthy and powerful gentry in Hampshire.[23]

Site, survival and builders.

A few of Hampshire's medieval inns were built in villages; for example, The Pelican Inn at Hursley. But even this stood on a trade route beside the road from Winchester to Romsey and the west of England.[24] Generally, however, the evidence of both standing remains and documentary sources shows that inns were predominantly situated in town centres. The Dolphin Inn stood in Southampton's English Street (now the High Street) and the medieval inns of Winchester all stood in the central area of the High Street.[25] Unfortunately, there are no upstanding remains of medieval inns in Southampton and The Red Lion public house in the High Street, sometimes called 'an historic inn', is in fact a typical fourteenth-century 'burgess house'.[26] Similarly, The George Inn in Winchester High Street, built by Mark le Fayre probably in 1412, survived, albeit in a post-medieval form, until the 1950s when it was replaced by the present Barclays Bank.[27]

Turning to the smaller towns, Basingstoke, Andover and Alton in the north of the county enjoyed an increased prosperity in the fifteenth century that would have encouraged inn-building.[28] Of the three inns recorded at Basingstoke in 1543, the George and the Swan have not survived and in 1965 the Angel, which stood on the south side of London Street (formerly the Market Place) was swept away during radical post-war redevelopment.[29] Fortunately, prior to demolition, a superb wall painting was photographed on the entire wall of an upper room. This painting, of possibly late sixteenth-century date, suggested the superior quality of a late-medieval inn.[30]

In some other small towns, the destruction has been a little less depressingly complete. Andover retains a substantial element of the Angel Inn, which was built in 1445–53 and is the finest and most complete medieval inn in the county.[31] Its status is attested by a magnificent fireplace drawn in the 1970s by Richard Warmington before it was removed and lost.[32] The Bell Inn, on which work began in 1534 and which also occupied a large and important site in the High Street, was demolished in 1969–70.[33]

At Alton, three medieval inns survive in some form in key commercial locations along the High Street and its extension, Crown Hill. The most significant survival is the lodging range of the former George Inn, built in 1501.[34] At Crown Hill, the Crown Inn (formerly Hyde Abbey's Pelican Inn) the fine, moulded ceiling beams of a ground-floor room suggest a building date *c.* 1500 when wealthy guests expected to experience the kind of high-status accommodation that they enjoyed at home. It was acquired by the Crown at the Dissolution in 1539 and by *c.* 1570 reference is made to the Crown formerly called the Pelican.[35] Finally the Swan Inn, on the south side of the High Street and near to the former George Inn, was recorded as early as 1498. However, it is now a mainly eighteenth- and nineteenth-century building.[36] Similarly, the former George Inn, Alresford was built in the early fifteenth century but rebuilt after the great fire in 1689 (Figure 9.1). It still occupies a wide street frontage with a gatehouse fronting Broad Street, the former market street of the town.[37] In Broad Street, too, was the Hart Inn of which no trace remains.[38] Another Hart Inn (now called The White Hart) was first recorded in 1501 and still stands beside the former market place and at the cross roads in the centre of Overton. It has a fine early-seventeenth century hall range.[39]

In Romsey Market Place, the Swan Inn was called an inn (*hospicium*) as early as 1477.[40] It was an impressive building with framing suggestive of a building date of

[22] Magdalen College Archives Oxford (MCAO): LE/12.

[23] Caroline M. Barron, "The Lords of the Manor," in *The Making of Britain: The Middle Ages*, ed. Lesley M. Smith (London: Macmillan, 1985), 110; Isabel Sanderson, *Dwellings in Alresford*, vol. 1 (privately published, 1973), 47; HRO: 1571P/21.

[24] HRO: 83A02/5.

[25] Colin Platt, *Medieval Southampton* (London: Routledge and Kegan Paul, 1973), 242; Edward Roberts and Karen Parker, eds, *Southampton Probate Inventories 1447–1575*, Southampton Records Series, vols 34 and 35 (Southampton: Southampton University Press, 1991, 1992), xvi; Keene, *Survey of Medieval Winchester*, 168.

[26] Platt, *Medieval Southampton*, 101.

[27] Keene, *Survey of Medieval Winchester*, 167, 481–82; Nikolaus Pevsner and David Lloyd, *The Buildings of England: Hampshire and The Isle of Wight* (Harmondsworth: Penguin, 1967), 715.

[28] John Hare, "Regional Prosperity in Fifteenth-Century England: some evidence from Wessex," in *Revolution and Consumption in Late-Medieval England*, ed. Michael A. Hicks (Woodbridge: Boydell and Brewer, 2001), 112–15.

[29] Francis J. Baigent and James E. Millard, *A History of the Ancient Town and Manor of Basingstoke*, 2 vols (London: C.J. Jacob, 1889), 561–65; Barbara Applin pers. comm.

[30] Elizabeth Lewis and Ross Turle, "Early Domestic Wall Paintings in Hampshire," *Proceedings of the Hampshire Field Club and Archaeological Society* 61 (2006), 201; 210.

[31] Edward Roberts, "A Fifteenth-Century Inn at Andover," *Proceedings of the Hampshire Field Club and Archaeological Society* 51 (1992), 153–70; Hare, "Winchester College and the Angel Inn, Andover," 187–97.

[32] Richard Warmington, "A Medieval Fireplace from Andover," *Hampshire Field Club and Archaeological Society Newsletter* 2, no.3 (1972), 11–12; Linda Hall, "Fixtures and Fittings," in *Hampshire Houses 1250–1700: their dating and development*, ed. Edward Roberts (Winchester: Hampshire County Council, 2003), 89.

[33] Richard Warmington, "Rebuilding of 'Le Belle' Inn, Andover, 1534," *Post Medieval Archaeology* 10 (1976), 131–41.

[34] Jane Hurst and Edward Roberts, "The George Inn, Alton," *Alton Papers* 4 (2000): 3–20; Edward Roberts, "A Sixteenth-Century Lodging Range at Alton, Hampshire," *Vernacular Architecture* 31 (2000): 81–83; Roberts, *Hampshire Houses*, 181–82.

[35] Jane Hurst, *Alton's Inns* (privately published, 2004), 40–47.

[36] V.F. Smith, "The Swan at Alton," *Hampshire Field Club Local History Newsletter* 1 (1980), 25–26; Hurst and Roberts, "The George Inn, Alton," 7–15.

[37] Louis F. Salzman, *Building in England down to 1540* (Oxford: Clarendon Press, 1952), 493–95; Andrew J. Robertson, *A History of Alresford*, revised edn (Alresford: Laurence Oxley, 1969), 25.

[38] Sanderson, *Dwellings in Alresford*, 47.

[39] HRO: 83A02/8; Stan Waight "The Hampshire lands of Corpus Christi College, Oxford and their management 1500–1650," *Proceedings* of the *Hampshire Field Club and Archaeological Society* 51 (1996), 174–75.

[40] Sheila Himsworth, *Winchester College Muniments*, vol. 2 (Chichester: Phillimore, 1984), 803–04.

Figure 9.1: The former George Inn, Broad Street, Alresford. It was built for Winchester College in the early-fifteenth century and rebuilt after a fire on 1689. Although no longer an inn, the building occupies a generous street frontage of c. 20 metres width facing the medieval market place. The central gatehouse still leads to a generous courtyard. Photograph: the author.

*c.*1600 which survived until a mid-twentieth century fire and radical rebuilding. Although the present structure resembles the outline of the former inn, there is now 'not an ancient beam in the place'.[41] Also in the Market Place at Romsey is the White Horse, which comprises a front range through which a gatehouse leads to a narrow courtyard with galleried lodgings on one side, all with framing typical of *c.*1500.

The George Inn, Odiham is a large complex with a hall range dated 1486/7 and a cross-wing of 1474, both of which face the High Street close to where the town's market house formerly stood.[42] Its original quality is attested by evidence of close-studded exterior walls, finely-moulded beams and a door-head in the hall with a crisply-carved floral pattern. Two inns in Kingsclere, the Swan Inn and the Falcon, are early conversions from private houses. The Swan comprises a large hall and cross-wing built in 1449 and, although first recorded in the Winchester College Muniments in 1452, it was not called an inn until 1533. Similarly, the Falcon, a large courtyard complex built in 1445–77 and 1482, was described in 1521 as 'a tenement late of John Kent between the vicarage and the highway' and was not recorded as an inn until 1626.[43]

Of the ancient monastic institutions which owned a considerable part of the best land in late-medieval Hampshire, only Hyde Abbey's Pelican Inn (now the Crown) at Alton remains.[44] The bishop of Winchester, an even greater landowner in the late Middle Ages, owned no inns at all in the county. It was the colleges founded between the late fourteenth and early sixteenth centuries that were the most active in building or acquiring inns. Magdalen College, Oxford was building the Bell in Andover in 1534. Corpus Christi College, Oxford acquired the Hart in Overton and the Pelican in Hursley soon after the College's foundation in 1517.[45] Winchester College built the Angel Inn at Andover and the George Inn at Alresford in the early fifteenth century and had built or acquired the Swan Inn in Romsey by 1477.[46] The College also converted private houses to inns, such as the Swan and the Falcon inns in Kingsclere and owned several other inns, such as the Swan at Stockbridge, of whose medieval fabric there is apparently no trace.[47] The archives of laymen who built or acquired inns have survived less frequently but it is recorded that Thomas Butler, earl of Ormonde, had the George built at Alton in 1501 and Robert Cresswell, a member of a prosperous Odiham family, owned the Swan in Alton in 1554.[48] As we have already seen, Mark le Fayre, a wealthy citizen of Winchester, built the George Inn there in the early fifteenth century.[49]

Purpose-built late-medieval inns in Hampshire.

What can we know about the physical appearance, the architecture and the plan-form of the late-medieval inns of Hampshire? In rare and very valuable cases there are both standing structures and relevant documentary sources. Two outstanding examples are the Angel in Andover and the George at Alton. The construction of the Angel between 1445 and 1455 and its subsequent development are recorded in extraordinary detail in Winchester College's magnificent archives.[50] Moreover, at the Angel a substantial and uncommonly revealing proportion of the original timber frame survives on a large plot, some 90 by 50 feet (Figure 9.2). This roughly square area gave sufficient room for an ample courtyard on one side of which, facing the town's High Street, is the framing of a gatehouse, a splendid two-bay hall with scissor-braced hall truss and flanking cross-wings on two floors for important guests.[51] It is probable the high-status rooms in these cross-wings were heated by magnificent fireplaces, one of which survived until recently.[52] On another side of the courtyard there still remains a gallery that led to a range of smaller and unheated rooms on the first floor. The rooms beneath were formerly stables but have now been converted to a public bar with all traces of their original

[41] Phoebe Merrick, pers. comm.

[42] Sheila Millard and Edward Roberts, "Odiham Fairs, Markets and Market Buildings," *Hampshire Field Club Local History Newsletter* 43 (2005), 19–21.

[43] Roberts, *Hampshire Houses*, 235; Edward Roberts, Daniel Miles and Martin Bridge, "Hampshire Dendrochronology Project," *Vernacular Architecture* 38 (2007): 127; Himsworth, *Winchester College Muniments* vol. 2, 579; 582–83.

[44] Roberts, *Hampshire Houses*, 201; Hurst, *Alton's Inns*, 40–47.

[45] Warmington, "Rebuilding of 'Le Belle' Inn, Andover, 1534," 131–41; HRO: 83A02/5.

[46] Salzman, *Building in England down to 1540*, 493–95; Himsworth, *Winchester College Muniments* vol. 2; 554–55.

[47] Himsworth, *Winchester College Muniments* vol. 2, 582–83; 803; 909.

[48] Hurst and Roberts, "The George Inn, Alton," 3–20; Roberts, "A Sixteenth-Century Lodging Range at Alton," 81; Smith, "The Swan at Alton," 25–26.

[49] Keene, *Survey of Medieval Winchester*, 151; 481–82.

[50] Roberts, "A Fifteenth-Century Inn at Andover," 153–70; Hare "Winchester College and the Angel Inn, Andover," 187–97.

[51] Roberts, "A Fifteenth-Century Inn at Andover," 153–70.

[52] Warmington, "A Medieval Fireplace from Andover"; Hall, "Fixtures and Fittings," 89.

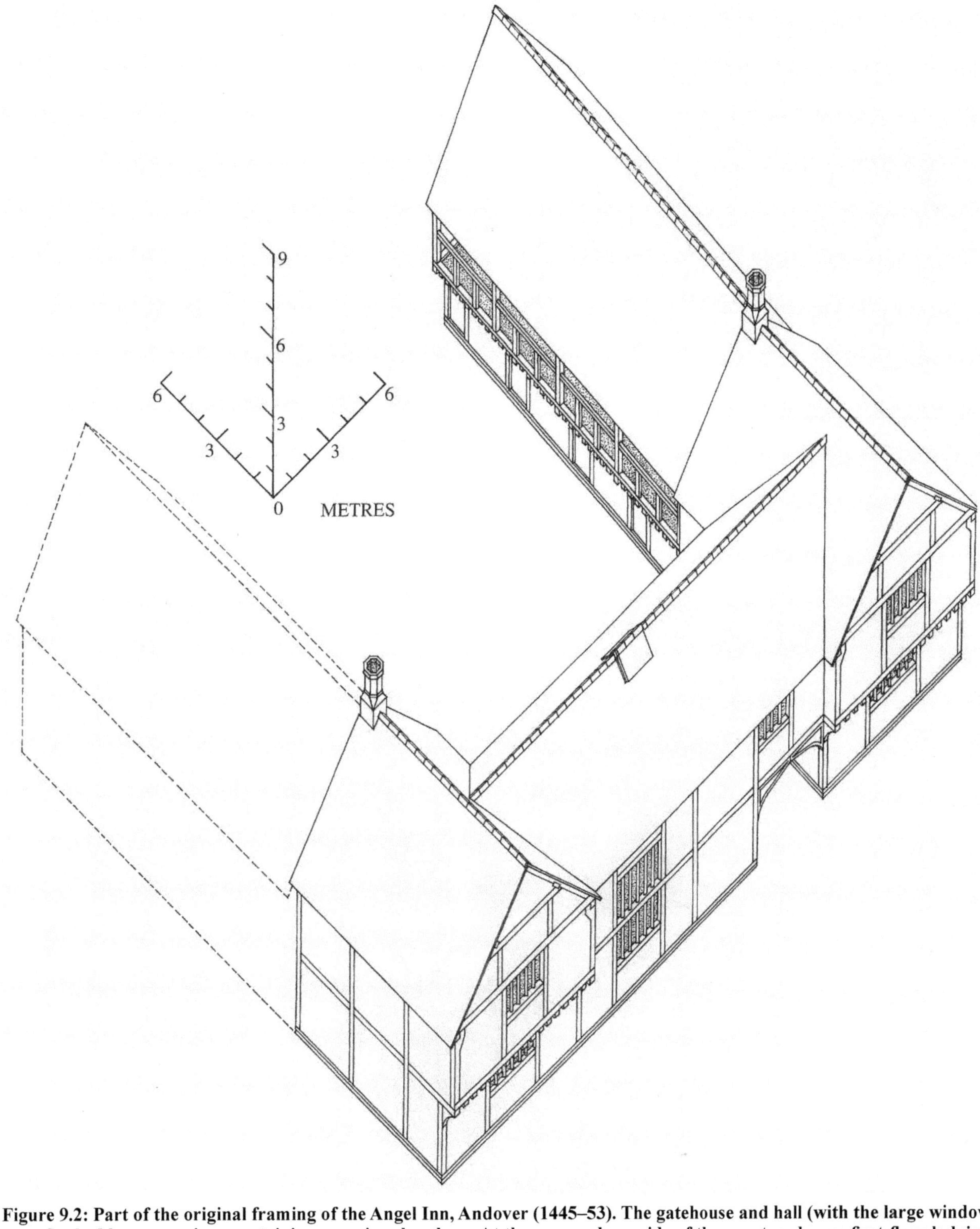

Figure 9.2: Part of the original framing of the Angel Inn, Andover (1445–53). The gatehouse and hall (with the large window) were flanked by cross-wings containing superior chambers. At the rear and one side of the courtyard were first-floor lodgings accessed from a gallery. Drawing: Jonathan Snowdon.

function removed.[53] Documentary sources also show that the early sixteenth century Bell Inn in Andover was a purpose-built inn and had, until demolition in 1969–70, a hall facing the High Street there with two flanking cross-wings and originally a large courtyard with service rooms and stables behind in a manner that echoes the plan of the Angel.[54]

As with the Angel, there is not only documentary evidence to show that the former George in Alton was a purpose-

[53] Roberts, "A Fifteenth-Century Inn at Andover," 153–70.

[54] Warmington, "Rebuilding of 'Le Belle' Inn, Andover, 1534," 132.

built medieval inn (in this case tree-ring dated to 1501), but also significant physical remains of that date.[55] The range that faced the High Street has been at least partly replaced with shops but along one side of a courtyard is an important unheated lodging range (Figure 9.3). The information from an early nineteenth-century annotated drawing and from a substantial timber frame allows a reconstruction of this range to be made with considerable confidence. It originally contained five or six first-floor chambers (of which four survive largely intact). Two of these chambers shared access to the gallery and to a single garderobe; the other two had independent access both from the gallery and to separate garderobes.[56] Although only the door-frames to these garderobes survive, their placement above the river leaves no doubt as to their purpose (Figure 9.4). They may indeed be unique features for Pantin writes that, although in larger, private houses in the fifteenth and sixteenth centuries guests were sometimes provided with a lodging that comprised a chamber with a garderobe, 'there seems to be no trace of this practice in the inns, either in extant remains or in the inventories'.[57]

Diagnostic features of medieval inns

The richness of both the documentary and the physical evidence for the Angel in Andover and the George in Alton is unfortunately very rare. More frequently, and still of some value, we have documentary records that shed light on the physical appearance of inns which have now disappeared without trace or have been completely rebuilt in post-medieval form. For example, a building contract dated 1418 survives for the George Inn, Alresford together with copious references to its development during succeeding centuries but, as we have seen, the building was completely rebuilt after a disastrous fire in 1689.[58] Often the reverse is the case: a medieval inn-like structure survives but without documentary evidence to show that it was a purpose-built inn. So could there be *physical features* of such structures which demonstrate that they really were purpose-built late-medieval inns? At this point it is necessary to distinguish between inns like the Angel in Andover that were planned and built as inns from the start and inns such as the George in Salisbury, which were merchant's courtyard houses but which were converted to inns in the late-medieval period by the addition of extra lodgings.[59] It may be said that the George was in part purpose-built. If diagnostic features of entirely, or partly, purpose-built late-medieval inns could be established, the number of such buildings for research would be significantly increased.

Pantin was well aware of the problem. He wrote, 'There is at the outset a certain amount of difficulty in finding surviving medieval buildings, which we can be certain were built or used as inns during the medieval period: for not every medieval building now used as an inn was necessarily so from the beginning'. To illustrate this point he quoted John Stow, the Elizabethan historian, who wrote the following of a tavern that Pantin argues was also an inn: it was 'sometime the Jewes Synagogue, since a house of Fryers, then a Noble mans house, after that a Marchauntes house... and now a Wine Taverne'.[60] Derek Keene seemed almost to despair of distinguishing between late-medieval houses and inns without documentation when he wrote, 'Most inns in later medieval Winchester were probably structurally indistinguishable from the larger private houses, which could readily be adapted for the purpose by building additional ranges of chambers and stabling'.[61] On the other hand, the need to expand accommodation for guests and horses may point to a crucial way of distinguishing between private and public inns, as we shall see.

If it is true that in fourteenth-century England public inns developed from private inns, it is not surprising that significant physical similarities remained between the two. Wealthy travellers would expect to be accommodated in inns that offered them the facilities they were familiar with in their own homes. These would include a gatehouse through which they could ride and which could be securely closed, and a courtyard around which were disposed lodgings for their servants, stables for their horses and suitably furnished rooms for their own comfort. However, Pantin has suggested that there were at least two main diagnostic features of late-medieval public inns that set them apart from private houses: galleries and a multiplicity of rooms.

Taking galleries first, Pantin wrote:

> The essential purpose of the inn gallery was to give independent access to a series of rooms. In private houses, passage rooms were tolerated till a very late date, down to the eighteenth and nineteenth centuries; but in inns there was a much earlier demand for privacy from a multitude of separate travellers, especially merchants, who would want a room where they could lock up their valuables.[62]

The point about the acceptability of passage rooms in private houses is generally true, although in royal or episcopal palaces, where household guests might be both numerous and strangers to each other, galleries were sometimes desirable. For example, at Bishop's Waltham palace there remain six self-contained lodgings each with its own door accessed from a first-floor gallery.[63] Thus

[55] Hurst and Roberts, "The George Inn, Alton," 3–20.

[56] Roberts, *Hampshire Houses*, 181–82.

[57] Pantin, "Medieval Inns," 187.

[58] Salzman, *Buildings in England down to 1540*, 493–95; Himsworth, *Winchester College Muniments* vol. 2, 21–23; Robertson, *A History of Alresford*, 25.

[59] Royal Commission on the Historical Monuments of England, *Ancient and Historical Monuments of the City* of *Salisbury*, vol. 1 (London: HMSO, 1980), xlvi.

[60] Pantin "Medieval Inns," 166.

[61] Keene, *Survey of Medieval Winchester*, 167–69.

[62] Pantin, "Medieval Inns," 168.

[63] Richard Warmington, "Beaufort's Range of Lodgings" in John Hare, "Bishop's Waltham Palace, Hampshire," *Archaeological Journal* 145 (1988): 222–54.

Figure 9.3: An impression of the courtyard of the former George Inn, Alton in the early-16th century. The gatehouse range fronting the High Street has been remodelled but the lodging range is largely intact, although the gallery and stairs shown in a 19th-century sketch have been removed. Drawing: Bill Fergie.

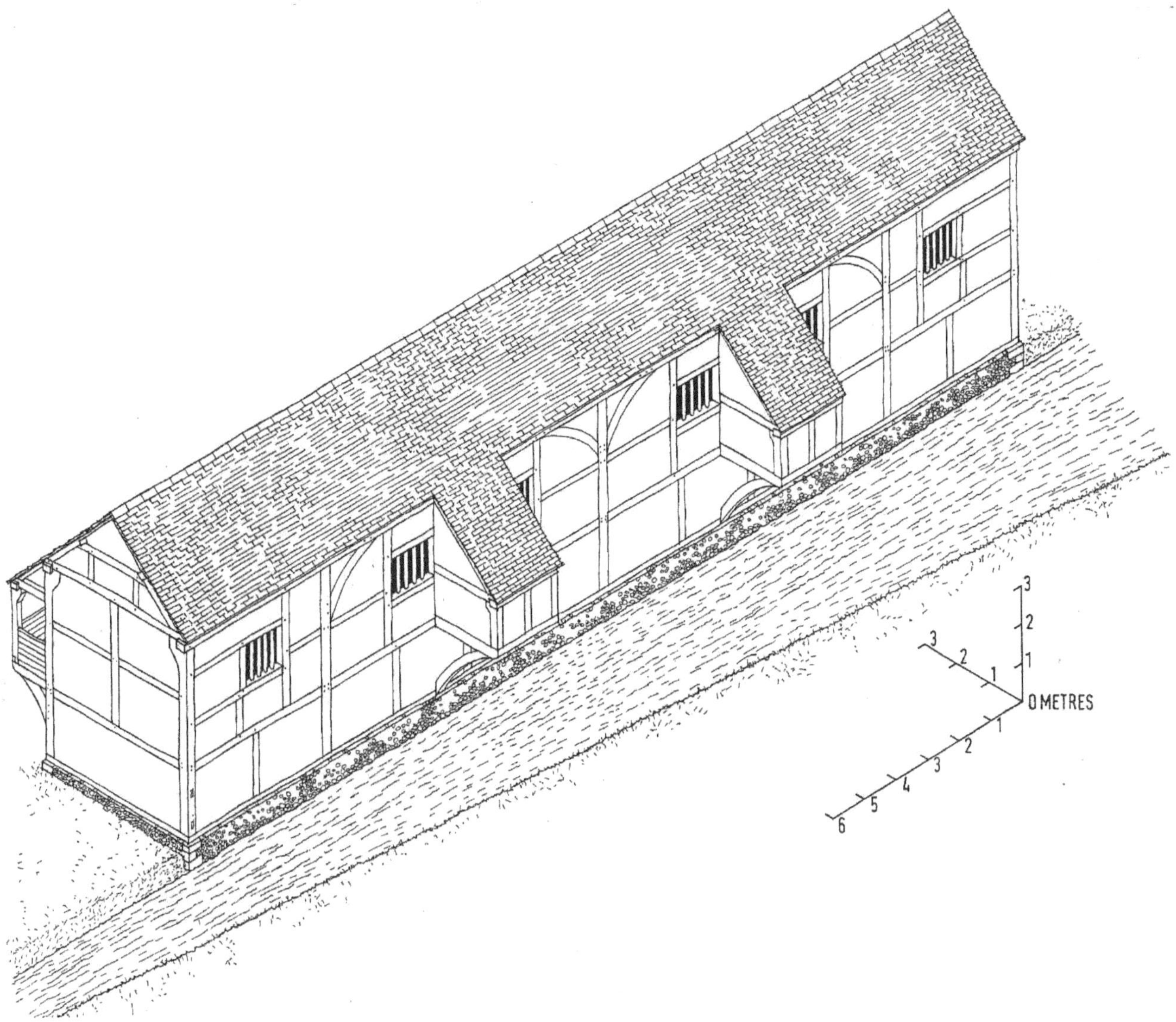

Figure 9.4: The surviving lodging range at the former George Inn, Alton as viewed from the River Wey. The garderobes that jetty over the river have been removed but are evidenced by framing for doors. Drawing: Jonathan Snowdon.

J.T. Smith's claim that medieval inns in Hertfordshire have 'one architectural feature by which they can be infallibly be recognised, the first-floor galleries needed to provide access to any considerable number of rooms' needs qualification.[64] It may be that all medieval inns had galleries giving access to self-contained rooms, but they were not the only buildings with this feature.

The weaker claim that most late-medieval buildings with galleries and access to self-contained rooms were inns can perhaps be demonstrated by a thorough survey of late-medieval probate inventories. As a tentative first step towards such a survey, it may be noted that the inventory of William Braxtone, the elder, yeoman and innholder of the Chequer inn in Winchester High Street, dated March 1573, lists 13 bedchambers, two of which were the 'mydle' and 'farther gallerye chamber'.[65] However, in attempting to distinguish inns from private houses it should be noted that some of the latter also had galleries of a kind that might be called 'open-hall galleries'. Such galleries were not uncommon features of town houses built at a right angle to the street in which a gallery crossing a central open hall provided a convenient link between two flanking first-floor chambers. Such galleries may still be found at the Red Lion, High Street, Southampton, Number 58 French Street, Southampton, and at Numbers 33–34 High Street, Winchester.[66] In a study of Southampton probate inventories made between 1447 and 1575, six of the larger houses had galleries. Only one of these was recorded as an inn. This was Edward Willmott's Dolphin Inn, which had both a gallery and 'a gallery without', the latter implying a gallery in the open air around a courtyard.[67] In the other five inventories there are no references to inns or innkeepers. They do, however, contain references to houses with galleries but not 'galleries without' and it is feasible, although it is impossible to be certain, that these houses had 'open-hall galleries'.

The existence of multiple rooms is the second principal defining characteristic of medieval inns suggested by Pantin. He writes that the familiar combination of the principal parts of the private inn – the kitchen, hall and chamber – will presumably play an important part in the plan of a public inn, 'but with certain necessary modifications: instead of the single solar or chief chamber, there will be a multiplication of chambers with, if possible, independent access'.[68] Of course, not all inns were large and not all buildings with multiple rooms were inns but could private houses and public inns, both with many rooms, be distinguished from each other? Again, the documentary evidence of probate inventories can be illuminating. To return to Edward Willmott, innkeeper of the Dolphin Inn, Southampton; in 1570 most of his 18 bedchambers appear to have been intended for guests. Some were given names to enable easy recognition by strangers, such as 'the draggine' and 'the Lyon'; others probably indicated the names of frequent quests, such as 'Younges chamber' and 'Harrys chamber'. It is likely that 'the Kendalmens chamber' was frequented by clothiers from Kendal in Cumberland coming to sell their cloth in Southampton. Only one room name indicated a member of the family or household; 'Mrs Willmottes chamber'.[69] In contrast to this innkeeper's inventory, the probate inventory of Thomas Mill of Southampton, gentleman, made in 1566, named 23 rooms of which only eight were chambers with beds and only one of these was called 'the gesten chamber'. Others indicated rooms of family members or household servants, such as 'the Cheldrens Chamber' and 'the Maidens chamber'.[70]

Two uncertain examples of purpose-built inns

The Angel, Andover was undoubtedly an entirely purpose-built medieval inn. In contrast, the Falcon in Kingsclere was built in the fifteenth century as one or more private dwellings but is first recorded as an inn in the seventeenth century. The Falcon, although built around a courtyard, has no gallery or multiplicity of rooms with separate access. In fact it appears to be a loose agglomeration of buildings rather than a planned inn. There are, however, two fine late-medieval buildings in Hampshire which were certainly used as public inns before the year 1600. These are the White Horse, Romsey and the George, Odiham. Unfortunately, there is no documentary evidence to show that they were entirely or partly purpose-built as inns and the evidence of their standing remains needs to be discussed.

The White Horse Inn, Romsey was called an inn by 1572 when John Uvedale, a member of important local gentry family, lay dying there in a room containing a box of his deeds and conveyances, and again in1610 when Lucilla Dixon was the innholder and there was a hall, a great chamber and four 'gallery chambers'.[71] It still has a hall with a large chamber above and a gatehouse leading from Romsey's Market Place to a narrow courtyard. Beside the courtyard a single range, now with three storeys but originally with two, has a gallery, or part of a gallery, with at least three doorways of 'Tudor' form leading to separate rooms (Figure 9.5). Uvedale's box of deeds and conveyances at the White Horse show the need for gentlemen to have private lockable rooms when they stayed at public inns; a point emphasised by the eleven locks with their keys held in 1477 by Thomas Kokys, lessee of the Swan Inn, also in Romsey Market Place.[72] The gallery giving access to probably lockable rooms strongly suggests that the White Horse was at least in part a purpose-built inn and while its hall and gatehouse

[64] Smith, *English Houses 1200–1800*, 150.
[65] HRO: 1573B/16/2; Karen Parker, pers. comm.
[66] Platt, *Medieval Southampton*, 101; Roberts, *Hampshire Houses*, 183–86.
[67] Roberts and Parker, *Southampton Probate Inventories*, 1991, xvi; Roberts and Parker, *Southampton Probate Inventories*, 1992, 280–9
[68] Pantin, "Medieval Inns," 168.
[69] Roberts and Parker, *Southampton Probate Inventories*, 1992, 280–89.
[70] Roberts and Parker, *Southampton Probate Inventories*, 1992, 244–45.
[71] HRO: 1572B/106; HRO: 1610B21/22.
[72] Himsworth, *Winchester College Muniments* vol. 2, ii, 803–04.

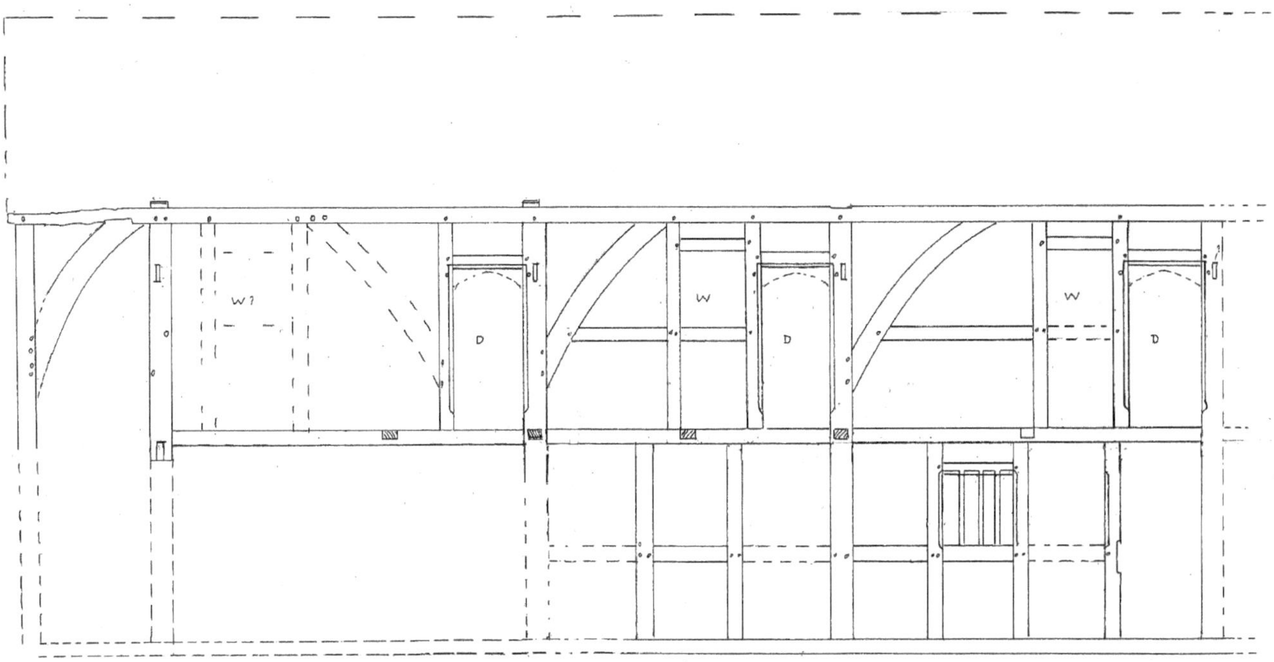

Figure 9.5: A section through the ground floor and first-floor gallery of the lodging range at The White Horse, Romsey. On the first floor, there are at present only three doorways whose jambs have pegs for 'Tudor' door-heads, although there may originally have been at least one more. 'D' signifies a door and 'W' a probable window. Drawing: the author.

range could be elements of either a private or a public inn, the fact that they are typologically of a similar date to the gallery range suggests that they may have been part of the same building campaign.

The George Inn at Odiham is a fine building facing the town's High Street (Figure 9.6). The property is first recorded in 1544 but it is not until 1584 that we have a reference to the George 'now called an inn', implying perhaps that it had recently been converted from the house of a wealthy townsman.[73] It is built on a fairly narrow plot that would only admit a rear lodging range on one side, as at the White Horse, Romsey. Two timber-framed ranges to the rear of the parlour and beside a courtyard (now a garden) appear to date to the late fifteenth century, although their much-altered interiors bear no indication of a gallery or multiple rooms. The hall range and cross-wing, tree-ring dated to 1486/7 and 1474 respectively, flank an entrance approximately 6 ft 9 in wide (1.81m) that could perhaps be called a gatehouse (Figure 9.7). This entrance is situated at the socially 'low' end of the hall and could function as a cross passage, which would be an arrangement typical of a private medieval house except that it is uncommonly wide for a private dwelling.[74] Moreover, there does not appear to be evidence for an original door from this passage (or gatehouse) to a service room, which again was a standard feature of a private dwelling. Instead, there are two doors from the courtyard giving access to two suites of rooms in the cross-wing: one is a suite of three rooms on two floors and the other a suite of two ground-floor rooms one of which had two windows, one looking towards the street and another to a carriageway at the side. Could this perhaps have been suitable for an innkeeper on the look-out and ready to receive guests? The hall, too, is not typical of a medieval private house. As well as having a door to an aligned room that may be called the parlour, it had a doorway with an elaborately carved door-head that now leads to a post-medieval passage with stairs.[75] Could this echo an original inn pentice or stairs to a gallery? Unfortunately, while some of the evidence is suggestive of a purpose-built inn – at least in part – it is too ambivalent for firm conclusions to be drawn.

Pantin's typology of medieval inns

The part of Pantin's article 'Medieval Inns' that has been most quoted by later historians but which is also the most problematic is his typology of inn plan-forms. He introduces his typology with the words 'I think we can distinguish two sorts of medieval inn plan'; these are

> (A) what may be called *the Courtyard type*, where the main buildings lie back from the street, ranged around a courtyard' and '(B) what may be called *the Block or Gatehouse type*, where the main part of the inn constitutes a solid block or range directly on the street, containing the principal rooms, and incorporating a gateway or passageway as a prominent feature.[76]

Pantin immediately cautions against an exaggeration of the contrast between the two types, a distinction that was only a working hypothesis for examining and classifying

[73] Roberts, *Hampshire Houses*, 240; HRO: 47M81/PZ22; HRO: 79M79/E/T44.

[74] Edward Roberts, "The George Inn," *The Odiham Journal* 20 (spring 1994); Roberts, *Hampshire Houses*, 153–54, 240.

[75] Hall, "Fixtures and Fittings," 64.

[76] Pantin "Medieval Inns," 167–68.

Figure 9.6: An impression of the George Inn, Odiham in the late-15th century as viewed from the High Street. The hall range with a gateway or gatehouse (1486/87) is to the left and a cross-wing (1474) to the right. Drawing: Bill Fergie.

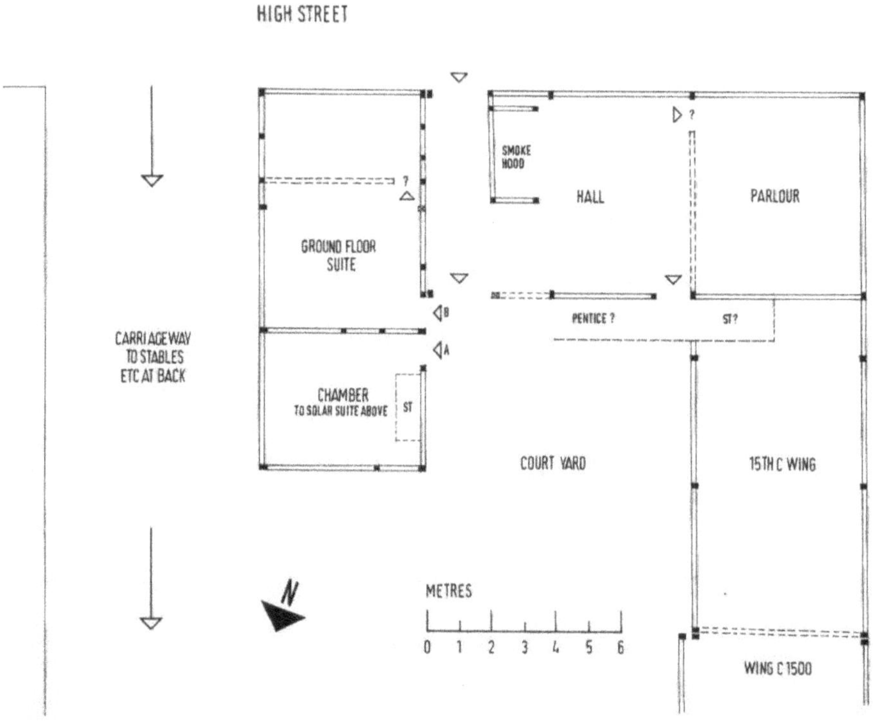

Figure 9.7: A plan of the hall range (right) and cross-wing (left) at the George Inn, Odiham. Note that (1) access to both suites of rooms in the cross-wing is from the courtyard and not from the gatehouse (or cross-passage and (2) there is a door that leads from the side of the hall to a modern staircase which may replace an original pentice and gallery. Both of these features would be unusual in a late-medieval house. Drawing: Jonathan Snowdon.

examples. Some historians have echoed Pantin's caution: for example, J.T. Smith, who wrote on Hertfordshire inns.[77] Others have been bolder. Margaret Wood wrote without qualification 'Medieval inns fall into two classes, the courtyard and the gatehouse plan' and Schofield and Stell simply refer to 'two common plan-forms, courtyard or gatehouse'.[78]

Pantin offers a detailed discussion of six inns of the courtyard type and eight of the blockhouse type but, as his discussion develops, his typology seems to unravel. The Angel Inn at Andover is his first example of a courtyard type and he admits that it 'is perhaps not quite an orthodox example of what I have called the "Courtyard" type'.[79] Indeed the main rooms of the Angel do not 'lie back from the street' as the typology would require but instead the hall, gatehouse and principal chambers face Andover High Street. The same was true of the Bell, Andover. All eight of Pantin's examples of inns of supposedly blockhouse type had courtyards but their courtyards were small because the inns occupied a restricted site.[80] It is not clear how small a courtyard was required to be before an inn ceased to count as a courtyard type, and attempts to apply Pantin's typology to inns in Hampshire cause similar uncertainty. The White Horse Inn at Romsey, for example, has not only a gatehouse but also a narrow courtyard with only room for a single range of lodgings on one side of it. It is not at all clear to which of Pantin's inn types it should be ascribed.

To a large extent Pantin laid the foundations for the serious study of the late-medieval English inn. This essay is an attempt to test and develop his conclusions by focussing upon the inns of a single county but it would be interesting to see whether studies of other counties would match those of Hampshire. Would, for example, the social status of builders, the urban or rural situation of inns and the problems of interpreting Pantin's typology of inns be similar? Pantin's discussion of inn typology is, however, more nuanced than has been suggested by some later historians who have quoted him without due qualification. He also wrote in sufficient detail and with enough clarity to allow critical amendment. He was after all, exploring a new field and suggesting hypotheses for future research. His achievement was a significant and lasting one.

Addendum

Since writing this paper, there have been two important additions to the list of pre-1600 inns in Hampshire. The White Hart (tree-ring dated to 1419-51) and The Raven (tree-ring dated to 1572-3) are both situated at Hook which, before 1600, was a sparsely populated area beside the main London Road to Basingstoke, Salisbury and on to Exeter. Unlike most inns discussed in this paper, they depended on transit trade rather than their position in a commercial centre.[81]

Acknowledgements

John Hare generously gave advice throughout the preparation of this paper. I also offer warm thanks for their help to Michael Bullen, Robin Darwall-Smith, Bill Fergie, Linda Hall, Jane Hurst, Phoebe Merrick, Martin Morris, Karen Parker and Jonathan Snowdon. It is very sad to record that Barbara Applin, Sheila Millard and Stan Waight, whose help was deeply appreciated, have died since this essay was completed.

Bibliography

Unpublished primary sources

Hampshire Record Office (HRO).

47M81/PZ22, schedule of the deeds of the George Inn, Odiham.

79M79/E/T44, lease of property in Odiham, 1584.

1572B/106, will of John Uvedale of Romsey, gentleman.

1573B/16/2, inventory of William Braxtone of Winchester, innkeeper, 1573.

1571P/21, will and inventory of Joan Oakley of New Alresford, widow, 1571.

1633A64/1 and 2, will and inventory of Richard Pope innholder of the Angel Inn, Andover.

83A02/5, "The Pelican Farm, formerly the inn of The Pelican in the parish of Hursley, Hampshire, 1516–1858," note by Waight, S. 1994.

83A02/8, "The estates of Corpus Christi College, Oxford in Overton, Quidhampton and Polhampton, Hampshire," note by Waight, S. 1996.

Magdalen College Archives Oxford (MCAO) Leases.

LE/12, lease of The Bell Inn, Andover, 1635.

The National Archives (TNA).

SP12/117/74, Certificate of innholders, taverners and alehouse keepers in Hampshire, 1577.

[77] Pantin "Medieval Inns," 168; Smith *English Houses 1200–1800*, 246.

[78] Margaret Wood, *The English Mediaeval House* (London: Phoenix House, 1965), 193; John Schofield and Geoffrey Stell, "The Built Environment 1300-1540," in *The Cambridge Urban History of Britain: vol. 1, 600–1540*, ed. David M. Palliser (Cambridge: Cambridge University Press, 2000), 388–89; see also John M. Steane, *The Archaeology of Medieval England and Wales* (Beckenham: Croom Helm, 1985), 115.

[79] Pantin "Medieval Inns," 169.

[80] Warmington, "Rebuilding of 'Le Belle' Inn, Andover, 1534," 132; Pantin "Medieval Inns," 179.

[81] W. Fergie, J. Hare, and E. Roberts, "Two Historic Inns in Hook. Part I: The White Hart," *Hampshire Field Club and Archaeological Society Newsletter* 70, (2018): 1–3; W. Fergie, J. Hare, and E. Roberts, "Two Historic Inns in Hook. Part II: The Raven," *Hampshire Field Club and Archaeological Society Newsletter* 71, (2019): 26–27.

Published primary sources

Himsworth, Sheila. *Winchester College Muniments* vol. 2. Chichester: Phillimore, 1984.

Roberts, Edward, and Karen Parker, eds. *Southampton Probate Inventories 1447–1575, I*, Southampton Records Series, 34. Southampton: Southampton University Press, 1991.

Roberts, Edward, and Karen Parker, eds. *Southampton Probate Inventories 1447–1575, II*, Southampton Records Series, 35. Southampton: Southampton University Press, 1992.

Secondary sources

Baigent, J. Francis and James E. Millard. *A History of the Ancient Town and Manor of Basingstoke*, 2 vols. London: C.J. Jacob, 1889.

Barron, Caroline M. "The Lords of the Manor." In *The Making of Britain: The Middle Ages*, edited by Lesley M. Smith, 101–18. London: Macmillan, 1985.

Barron, Caroline M., "London 1300–1400." In *The Cambridge Urban History of Britain: vol. 1, 600–1540*, edited by David M. Palliser, 395–440. Cambridge: Cambridge University Press, 2000.

Dyer, Christopher. *Standards of Living in the Later Middle Ages*. Cambridge: Cambridge University Press, 1989.

Dyer, Christopher. "History and Vernacular Architecture." *Vernacular Architecture* 28 (1997): 1–8.

Everitt, Alan. "The English Urban Inn, 1560–1760." In *Perspectives on English Urban History*, edited by A. Everitt, 91–137. London: Macmillan, 1973.

Fergie, W., John Hare and Edward Roberts. "Two Historic Inns in Hook. Part II: The Raven." *Hampshire Field Club and Archaeological Society Newsletter* 71, (2019): 26–27.

Fergie, W., John Hare and Edward Roberts. "Two Historic Inns in Hook. Part I: The White Hart." *Hampshire Field Club and Archaeological Society Newsletter* 70, (2018): 1–3.

Hall, Linda. "Fixtures and Fittings." In *Hampshire Houses 1250–1700: their dating and development*, edited by Edward Roberts, 63–115. Winchester: Hampshire County Council, 2003.

Hare, John. "Bishop's Waltham Palace, Hampshire." *Archaeological Journal* 145 (1988): 201–54.

Hare, John. "Regional Prosperity in Fifteenth-Century England: some evidence from Wessex." In *Revolution and Consumption in Late-Medieval England*, edited by Michael A. Hicks, 112–15. Woodbridge: Boydell and Brewer, 2001.

Hare, John. "Winchester College and the Angel Inn, Andover: a fifteenth-century landlord and its investments." *Proceedings of the Hampshire Field Club and Archaeological Society* 60 (2005): 187–97.

Hare, John. "Inns, Innkeepers and the Society of Later Medieval England." *Journal of Medieval History* 39 (2013): 477–97.

Hurst, Jane. *Alton's Inns*. Privately published, 2004.

Hurst, Jane, and Edward Roberts. "The George Inn, Alton." *Alton Papers* 4 (2000): 3–20.

Keene, Derek. *Survey of Medieval Winchester*, 2 vols. Oxford: Oxford University Press, 1985.

James, Tom Beaumont and Edward Roberts. "Winchester and Late Medieval Development: from palace to pentice." *Medieval Archaeology* 44 (2000): 181–200.

Lewis, Elizabeth, Edward Roberts and Kenneth Roberts, eds. *Medieval Hall Houses of the Winchester Area.* Winchester: Winchester City Museums, 1988.

Lewis, Elizabeth, and Ross Turle. "Early Domestic Wall Paintings in Hampshire." *Proceedings of the Hampshire Field Club and Archaeological Society* 61 (2006): 200–07.

Millard, Sheila and Edward Roberts. "Odiham Fairs, Markets and Market Buildings." *Hampshire Field Club Local History Newsletter* 43 (2005): 19–21.

Munby Julian, with J. Ashdown, B. Durham, D. Haddon-Reece, M. Henig and C. Jeuckens. "Zacharias's: a fourteenth-century Oxford new inn and the origins of the medieval urban inn." *Oxoniensia* 57 (1992): 249–309.

Pantin, William Abel. "Medieval Inns." In *Studies in Building History*, edited by Edward Martyn Jope, 166–91. London: Odhams Press, 1961.

Pevsner Nikolaus and Lloyd, David. *The Buildings of England: Hampshire and The Isle of Wight.* Harmondsworth: Penguin, 1967.

Platt, Colin. *Medieval Southampton.* London: Routledge and Kegan Paul, 1973.

Quiney, Anthony, *The Traditional Buildings of England.* London: Thames and Hudson, 1990.

Roberts, Edward. "A Fifteenth-Century Inn at Andover." *Proceedings of the Hampshire Field Club and Archaeological Society* 51 (1992): 153–70.

Roberts, Edward. "The George Inn." *The Odiham Journal* 20 (spring 1994): 20–23.

Roberts, Edward. "A Sixteenth-Century Lodging Range at Alton, Hampshire." *Vernacular Architecture* 31 (2000): 81–83.

Roberts, Edward. *Hampshire Houses 1250–1700: their dating and development.* Winchester: Hampshire County Council, 2003.

Roberts, Edward, Daniel Miles and Martin Bridge. "Hampshire Dendrochronology Project." *Vernacular Architecture* 38 (2007): 125–28.

Robertson, Andrew J. A *History of Alresford*, revised edn. Alresford: Laurence Oxley, 1969.

Royal Commission on the Historical Monuments of England. *Ancient and Historical Monuments of the City of Salisbury*, vol. 1. London: HMSO, 1980.

Salzman, Louis F. *Building in England down to 1540*. Oxford: Clarendon Press, 1952.

Sanderson, Isabel. *Dwellings in Alresford*, vol. 1. Privately published, 1973.

Schofield, John, and Geoffrey Stell. "The Built Environment 1300–1540." In *The Cambridge Urban History of Britain: vol. 1, 600–1540*, edited by David M. Palliser, 371–394. Cambridge: Cambridge University Press, 2000.

Schofield, John, and Vince, Alan. *Medieval Towns*. London: Leicester University Press, 1994.

Smith, John T. *English Houses 1200–1800: the Hertfordshire evidence*. London: HMSO, 1992.

Smith, V.F. "The Swan at Alton," *Hampshire Field Club Local History Newsletter 1* (1980): 25–26.

Steane, John M. *The Archaeology of Medieval England and Wales*. Beckenham: Croom Helm, 1985.

Waight, Stan. "The Hampshire lands of Corpus Christi College, Oxford and their management 1500–1650." *Proceedings of the Hampshire Field Club and Archaeological Society* 51 (1996): 167–85.

Warmington, Richard. "A Medieval Fireplace from Andover." *Hampshire Field Club and Archaeological Society Newsletter 2*, no.3 (1972): 11–12.

Warmington, Richard. "Rebuilding of 'Le Belle' Inn, Andover, 1534." *Post Medieval Archaeology* 10 (1976), 131–41.

Warmington, Richard. "Beaufort's Range of Lodgings." In John Hare, "Bishop's Waltham Palace, Hampshire." *Archaeological Journal* 145 (1988): 201–54.

Williams, E.H.D., J. and J. Penoyre and B.C.H. Hale. "The George Inn, Norton St. Philip, Somerset," *Archaeological Journal* 144 (1987): 317–27.

Wood, M. *The English Mediaeval House*. London: Phoenix House, 1965.

10

The People Project: the residents of Southampton 1485–1603

Cheryl Butler

Independent Scholar

Abstract: This essay focuses on a big data project which maps the lives of over 18,000 people resident in Southampton between 1485–1603, and calls extensively on the wealth of documentary material that survives in the Southampton Archives. Having such a large dataset over a hundred year period enables trends to be mapped but also the minute detail of individual lives to be recorded and analysed. It is particularly useful for engaging with the lives of ordinary people such as craftsmen, migrants, women as well as burgesses and the urban elite. The essay also illustrates that the growing number of such studies, enabled by new technology, can more easily facilitate cross referencing of data to the mutual benefit of individual research studies.

Key words: The People Project; Tudor Southampton; crafts; genealogy; databases; local archives; urban experience; migrants; women

Professor Tom James is a champion of the academic study of local history and, in particular, the archives and documents of Southampton. One of the most useful books he produced for the Southampton Records Series, for which he was a long-time general editor, was *Southampton Sources.*[1] This volume is comprised of a list of sources for the history of Southampton from the Domesday survey to 1900. It provides a chronological list of sources for Southampton people in the middle ages and succeeding centuries.[2] In producing this volume Professor James hoped the descriptive nature of the list would encourage those interested in the history of Southampton to make use of sources scattered through different archives to gain a rounded picture of town history[3] and to suggest ways in which Southampton studies might be developed in the future. James's volume was produced a century after J.S. Davies's seminal *A History of Southampton* which was, in turn, inspired by John Speed's earlier history.[4] Both quoted heavily from original Southampton documents; documents which, when published, were largely uncatalogued and written at a time without the assistance of modern technology. In the century that followed Davies, the Historical Manuscripts Commission, the Southampton Record Society and the Southampton Records Series made many of the original documents more readily available for wider study.

Professor James encouraged many of his students to consider using the un-transcribed documents still in the archives as the subject of doctoral research, introducing them to a rich vein of original source material and providing opportunities for new volumes for the Southampton Records Series. He also converted many into champions of local history in general and the study of Southampton's unique resources in particular. One such resulting study is The People Project, which aimed to follow James's lead in raising the profile of the history and heritage of Southampton and, in particular, its wealth of original documents. By using new technology, the aim was to produce an open-source, searchable database which would encapsulate all surviving references to people living in Southampton between 1485 and 1603. As *Southampton Sources* shows, the Tudor period had a range of surviving original source material, but a manageable number of documents for the original two-year research period. The documents were also in English, an advantage when the project would need to engage with volunteer researchers in order to comb as many documents as possible in a relatively short time.

The project was fortunate to gain support from the Heritage Lottery Fund but it was still a massive undertaking for a non-university led large scale research programme. In the end, a modest £6,000 budget was used to develop a website and database and a core of twenty amateur historians led by some of Professor James's former doctoral students recorded entries onto a database which can be searched over a number of categories: craft, date, name, nationality, parish, year, and gender. Those volunteers not used to reading original documents turned first to the printed volumes of the Record Society and the Records Series. The project was also fortunate that several researchers of Southampton, including Professor James, donated their research notes including summaries of all the surviving Southampton wills. Earlier researchers like Barry Chinchen had also, for the sheer joy of the exercise,

[1] T. B. James, *Southampton Sources 1086–1900* Southampton Records Series [hereafter SRS] 26 (1983).

[2] James, *Southampton Sources* xiii.

[3] James, *Southampton Sources* xiii.

[4] J.S. Davies, *A History of Southampton* (London and Southampton: Gilbert and Co. and Hamilton Adams and Co., 1883); E.R. Aubrey (ed.), *The History and Antiquity of Southampton, with some conjectures concerning the Roman Clausentium: written about the year 1770* Southampton Record Society [hereafter SRSoc] 8 (1909).

transcribed all the surviving Southampton Stewards books and the only surviving parish register for St Michaels, which saved hours of work. Southampton's material records are, however, such a rich source that there are many documents still awaiting their editor. The project has reviewed many of these un-transcribed documents such as the muster rolls, stall and art lists and large volumes such as the 'Book of Instruments' all worthy of detailed study in their own right. The volunteers also undertook to study palaeography meeting on a monthly basis to transcribe many of the loose leaf single documents and dockets which had not previously been scrutinised at all. The original project target was for a database of 5,000 individuals but this was far exceeded, and it was decided to continue the work past the original two year study, so that now well over 18,000 individuals are entered into the database. Research has continued with about 20 percent of the surviving Southampton documents still to be addressed.[5]

One of the outputs expected from the People Project was to link with other historians, genealogists, academics, researchers and writers to provide research data from the Southampton records for their particular area of study. In addition the People Project also made links with other longitudinal studies to supply additional source material linked to those studies. The Overland Trade project has developed a database around Southampton's unique set of surviving Brokage books.[6] As the editor of the accompanying book to the project, Professor Michael Hicks, has observed, the brokers who compiled the records sometimes failed to state the occupation and domicile of the traders and carters and the books do not record the whole business of any carter. The Overland Trade project covers the period from 1430 to 1540, so there is a significant overlap of years with The People Project. The People Project can answer some of the questions as to domicile and additional business of some of the carters, in turn the Overland Trade project has provided information for the database on the goods carters carried, the distances travelled and the merchants for whom they worked.

An example of how the two databases can work together is the biography of Thomas Blake. Blake worked as a carter for some twenty-five years and when not working for merchants like William James carrying iron to Winchester, he worked regularly on corporate projects. His main cargoes were clay and gravel which he delivered to a range of building projects including improvements to houses, the Bargate prison and work on the West Quay. In 1513–14 he carried ten thousand bricks down to West Hall, the town property where Brankini de Marini the Genoese merchant lived, to build a wall. Blake lived in the parish of All Saints and rented parcels of land around the Ronceval and the Marlands, so it is possible that he was not only carrying the gravel and clay but also supplying it from his land.[7] Occasionally, he carried higher quality cargo like wine that was being sent to the Bishop of Winchester, or he was sent further afield to bring timber into the town from the forest. Not all the stewards' books for the period 1508–1533 survive but for most that do Blake appears as a preferred carter for corporate projects. The pay that Blake received seems to depend on the type of cargo and the distance travelled. For loads of clay and gravel he would receive 3d or 4d. If he was making a number of journeys he could earn 12d a day. When he took food and necessaries to the law day place on the common for the Court Leet, he received 12d. For his journey to the Bishop of Winchester his wage was 3s 4d. He could expect if he was loading a large cargo such as timber that he would have a couple of men to help him load and they would also be paid by the town. The lay subsidy of 1524 assessed Blake's goods at £16.[8] By combining the data recorded by both projects it can been seen that the carters' carriage work covers both long journeys for merchants and short trips within the town boundaries. There are 297 carters on The People Project database, some are not involved in overland trade and some are operating in years when there are no brokage books, so we can begin to develop a more rounded picture of their working life.

The England's Immigrants project[9] has less of a crossover, as this project has a focus from the mid fourteenth century up to the 1530s however the juxtaposition of the two studies has highlighted some particular traits in Southampton's alien settlers. The England's Immigrants database records all the aliens living in England and their payment of alien subsidy taxes. The entries generally record the place of birth of the subject and what subsidy collections they contributed to. For the period 1470–1550 there are 37 entries for Southampton with a significant proportion being merchants from Italy.[10] One of the most significant of the 37 is the Florentine merchant Christopher Ambrose. His entry records him paying alien subsidies from 1463 and his denization in 1472, however his entry on The People Project database is much more significant. Ambrose begins to appear in the Southampton records from 1462 when he arrived to take up a position as clerk with the Florentine factor in the town, Angelo de Aldobrans, who was living in the prime location of West Hall on Bugle Street. By 1466, Ambrose was the only Florentine tenant in the town. After he became a denizen he took an English apprentice, James Harrison, and began his climb up the offices of the town becoming town steward. He went on to become bailiff, then sheriff at a very difficult time in the town's history, when the mayor, Watkin William, was on the run having

[5] See www.tudorrevels.co.uk/records.php to search the database.

[6] See www.overlandtrade.org.

[7] B. Chinchen, Stewards Books 1511–31 unpublished transcriptions, Cope Collection, Hartley Library, University of Southampton.

[8] Full citations can be found on the Tudor Revels database by entering the name of the person, viewing all information on their timeline and the references to the archive material used. A full bibliography is also contained on the database. This is an on-going research project and data is continually being updated.

[9] See www.englandsimmigrants.com.

[10] If the timescale on the England's Immigrants database is put back to 1450, the numbers rise to 185 primarily because of the presence of entries from Genoese and Florentine merchants.

become involved in the Buckingham Rebellion against Richard III.[11] Ambrose survived the turmoil to become mayor himself in 1486–87, as the Tudors took control of the country, and he served again in 1497–98. Ambrose used his mayoral income to improve the port, repairing walls and quays, paving the area around God's House and having the public toilet cleaned at the Withdraught House. He had a wife living in Southampton who paid a craft fine in 1483–84 and at least two sons, John and Robert, with Robert being made burgess in 1508–09 by which time his father was either dead or returned to Florence. Ambrose's significant property portfolio included six tenements, three cellars, the wool house warehouse, a barn, lofts and a market place. Ambrose's example shows that it was possible for an alien merchant, not only to have a successful trading career in Southampton, but also to become integrated enough for it to cause no comment that held the position of mayor on two occasions.[12] His wealth and contribution to the town economy was probably of more significance than his nationality.

There were at least 97 Italians who lived in the town as long term residents between 1485 and 1603, and a number are also to be found in the England's Immigrants project but The People Project also picks up more transitory residents such as the galleymen of the galleys *Faliez, Captain* and *Hampton* whose skills were recognised and they were put into service in 1492–93. Fourteen men laboured for between five and 45 days at 6d a day on repairs to the cranes and haulage systems required to take cargoes on and off the visiting trading vessels. The People Project can also help to fill in gaps, such as the entry for Vanflotyng on the England's Immigrants database. He is known to be male and living in St Michael and St John's ward in 1524 but the deterioration of the documents makes it impossible to read his first name. He can be identified from The People Project as the same person as Nicolas Flotter working on repairs to the town fortifications in 1512–13.

There are over two and a half thousand aliens who appear in the The People Project database. Italians, Dutch, German, Portuguese and Spanish are significant minorities and there are even three Hungarians, as in 1590 John Battane, Matthias Perrus and Michael Vornet are recorded as being in the port with letters allowing them to collect money to help repay the ransoms that had been paid to release them from Turkish captivity.[13] The largest groups of immigrants are French speakers from France and the Low Countries who came to England in waves following on from persecution and rebellion in their places of origin. This is particularly prevalent in the last quarter of the sixteenth century when there were constant complaints from locals about the number of incomers and under-tenants that were over-pressing the town and heightening the risk of fire, and sickness.[14] It seems these claims were not over-exaggerated. When town officials were sent around to record the numbers of lodgers in buildings around the town, in 1575, Arthur Pitt who was leasing the building now known as Tudor House was found to have under-tenants living there, a Frenchman, his wife, two servants, and 17 other men, women and children. In addition, there were two severe outbreaks of plague in 1583 and 1603 which both decimated the immigrant enclave but also would have given evidence to locals that their fears were not unfounded.[15]

In total there are currently 2,394 French speaking immigrants on The People Project database who make their home in Southampton in the sixteenth century. Unlike previous immigrant waves that came to Southampton, the French speaking Protestants of the sixteenth century came in much greater numbers over a concentrated period and came for religious reasons and as refugees rather than the earlier economic migrants from Italy and the Low Countries. Although, in fact, they did contribute to the town's economy, the numbers who came, their separation from the wider community and the fact that many ignored several of the town's ordinances around trade did not endear them to the local population.[16] However the longitudinal nature of The People Project shows that by the end of the Tudor period the two communities were starting to inter-marry and families like the Delamottes were renting the West Hall for their weaving and dying business, whilst others were taking on official positions in town governance.

Throughout the late fifteenth and sixteenth centuries there was a steady flow of Dutch, German and Flemish immigrants who coalesced around certain industries: brewing, glazing and gunnery. Some are easily identified as immigrants, such as Roland Johnson, also known as Rowle Beerbrewer and Rowle le Fleming, and with his brother Rutt and the Adrians were the town's official brewers in the 1480s and 1490s.[17] There were no English brewers on the official list. Interestingly, none of these men appear on the alien hosting data, although there is an Adrian Johnson who is by trade a cooper. There are other Southampton residents who are obviously foreign, but without the firm evidence of identification in the records, for example the Breme family. Peter Breme senior was living in Southampton from at least 1552 and at the muster of 1555–56 was listed as an able-bodied gunner, and owner of two handguns. A year later he became one of the town's official gunners earning an annual wage of 53s 4d which included nearly three yards of red kersey and two and a

[11] R. C. Anderson (ed.), *The Assize of Bread Book 1477–1517*, SRSoc 23 (1923), 2n.

[12] For an overview of Ambrose's career see A.A. Ruddock, *Italian Merchants and Shipping in Southampton 1270–1600*, SRS 1 (1951), 83, 102, 123, 131, 183, 185, 203, 214, 216.

[13] E.R. Aubrey and G.H. Hamilton (eds), *Books of Examination and Depositions 1570–94*, SRSoc 16 (1914), 76.

[14] See A. Spicer, *The French-Speaking Reformed Community and their Church in Southampton 1567–c.1620*, SRS 39 (1997).

[15] H.M. Godfray (ed.), *Registre de l'Eglise Wallonne de Southampton 1567–1779* Huguenot Society of London (London 1889).

[16] F.J.C. Hearnshaw and D.M. Hearnshaw, *Court Leet Records 1578–1602* SRSoc (1906), 180, 217, 228, 235, 262, 301.

[17] C.B. Butler (ed.), *The Book of Fines: The Annual Accounts of the Mayors of Southampton Vol I 1488–1540*, SRS 41 (2007), xvii n37, 55.

half of white cotton for his livery. His occupation was as a glazier, and in 1563–64 he worked on what was the largest civic project of the period, the construction of the town's new alms house. There he glazed three windows using 26ft of glass at a cost of 9d a foot. He was versatile, being able to play the drum and flute, which he did to entertain Elizabeth I when she visited the town in 1568–69.[18] His sons Peter and Thomas and daughter Catherine survived him in 1572, and the boys followed in his footsteps as glaziers, gunners and fife and drum players. Most interestingly Peter the younger acted as a translator in 1593 for a case which involved Flemish witnesses in an action resulting from privateering bought before the Southampton Admiralty Court, which suggests the family were originally from Flanders.[19] In references to early gunners in the town the Dutchmen Deryk and Balfer Lynne were given financial inducements to remain in the town to serve as gunners, which suggests a pragmatism in regard to immigrants who could provide knowledge and experience not available from the local population.[20] The year they were employed as official gunners was 1512, at the time of Henry VIII's first French War.

What is perhaps surprising is the lack of named Spaniards in the town. Up to eleven Spanish ships arrived in 1487, and there was an increase in trade after the Treaty of Medina del Campo and the formation of the Andalusian Company in 1530, which was governed with the advice from merchants of London plus two from Bristol and two from Southampton.[21] In the early Tudor period the Spanish often travelled in combined fleets with the Italians which perhaps masked the numbers of Spanish in the town as they probably used the Italian factors to facilitate the landing of cargoes. In addition, the Spanish economy was buoyant and there were not the incentives to become economic migrants. The Portuguese, however, make much more of a showing, particularly through their involvement in the woad trade. Between 1552 and the 1570s, a number of merchants such as John Alfonso, Salis Constayia, Manuel Diaz, Jaspar Gonsalin, Ferdinand Jakes, Francis Lessons and Angelo Mannella were all granted licences to trade woad. Jacob Honne was living in the town for at least four years and Angelo Mannella rented West Hall whilst in Southampton between 1559 and 1564. Other Portuguese merchants traded in sugar and alum.[22] Dominic Green suggested in his research about the Portuguese in England that these merchants were using the money they made to support Don Antonio, the Portuguese pretender to the throne, during the period that country was governed by Philip II of Spain.[23] What is certainly true is that Don Antonio was in Southampton in the lead up to the abortive counter-armada and was made an honorary burgess of the town.[24] The small Portuguese enclave were expelled in 1589 with the mayor assisting the process paying a Frenchman 6s to carry away the Portuguese.[25]

Turning to the indigenous population and the usefulness of The People Project database as a resource for historians and researchers, Louise Fairbrother has used the resource for her PhD thesis. This examines how the town government of Southampton organised its industry and trade in the sixteenth century, with specific focus on the way in which it controlled the three groups involved: burgesses, freemen and strangers.[26] The database has been extremely useful in helping to identify those people whose names appear in primary sources and to determine the occupations of these people as these details are not always noted in the specific documents used to record these groups. The strength of the database is that it draws on a large variety of sources.

Familiarity with the richness of the source material in Southampton on occasion makes it easy to take for granted the breadth and scope of the content. Professor Robert Tittler, who has written extensively on late medieval and early-modern English towns, has in recent years, been making a study of regional art and paintings of which there are many notable survivors. He illustrated in a talk at the University of Southampton in 2011, called Portraiture and Memory, the significance of this art as the face of a town, and that its subjects linked to a town's mythology and memory, but that it was mostly created by unknown hands. The People Project was able to identify a number of regional painters at work in Southampton, which currently stands at twelve, including Deaf Robert who painted the Bargate with Tudor roses to welcome Princess Catherine of Aragon in 1501.[27] Others include Henry Mason, Harry Matthew and William Painter who made the town arms at Stoneham in 1528–29 and Richard Dashwell who was provided with parchment, felt and canvas in 1569–71 and was the possible maker of the early map of Southampton now held at the Hartley Library.[28] The painters worked on many civic projects including painting the lions that stood outside the town gates, decorating buildings and churches inside and out, and produced the surviving paintings of the towns legendary founders Bevis and Ascupart which were for many centuries fixed to the outside of the Bargate. The painter we know most about is Jan Luchtyng who flourished between 1546 and 1564. As his name suggests he was from the Low Countries, his wife was called Edith and his surviving children were Ellen, Neme, Jane and John. He must have feared for his life in 1553 when he made his will but did not die until 1564 when his will

[18] C. B. Butler (ed.), *The Book of Fines: The Annual Accounts of the Mayors of Southampton Vol II 1540–1571,* SRS 43 (2009), 55–6, 77, 79.
[19] Aubrey and Hamilton (eds), *Books of Examination and Depositions,* 125.
[20] H.W. Gidden (ed.), *The Book of Remembrance of Southampton Vol III,* SRSoc 30 (1930), 84–5; Chinchen Steward's Book 1513–14, 41.
[21] G. Connell-Smith, *The Forerunners of Drake* (London and New York: Longmans, Green and Co., 1954), xviii, 44, 65.
[22] Butler (ed.) *Book of Fines Vol II*, 2, 37, 41–2, 46.
[23] D. Green, *The Double Life of Doctor Lopez*, (London: Century, 2003).
[24] Southampton Record Office [hereafter SRO] SC3/1/1 Burgess Admissions.
[25] C.B. Butler (ed.), *The Book of Fines: The annual Accounts of the Mayors of Southampton Vol III 1572–1594,* SRS 44 (2010), 161.
[26] L. Fairbrother, "Burgesses, Freemen and Strangers: The Organisation of Industry and Trade in Southampton, 1547 to 1603," PhD thesis, University of Southampton, 2018.
[27] Chichen, Stewards Book 1550–51, 44.
[28] Butler (ed.) *Book of Fines II*, 97 and *III*, 80.

and probate inventory listed the goods in his shop, which included many artists' materials.[29] His money included ducets and guilders. It is likely that he perished in the plague outbreak of 1563–64 as his wife, Edith, was then charged with painting the crosses on the doors of infected people in that same year, in her husband's stead.[30] Luchtyng was featured in the National Portrait Gallery exhibition, Elizabeth I and Her People in 2014.[31]

The growing interest in genealogy sets a challenge for amateur genealogists in understanding the wide range of source material prior to parish records and census data, where potential nuggets might be found, and it can even be a challenge for seasoned historians. American historian Stephen Moore, in his study of Henry Carpenter and John Parker, knew they were connected to the Plymouth mayor and privateer William Carpenter and that the family had connections with Southampton, but in his own words had hit 'a brick wall'.[32] John Parker and his family are on The People Project database and Henry Carpenter was a privateer operating in the town, turning up in the Admiralty court having seized a Portuguese ship. He served on the *Elizabeth* the ship the town provided to the campaign led by Essex and Raleigh which sacked Cadiz.[33] He later went on to serve as Sheriff of Southampton in 1611. The Staveley family researchers had undertaken a major study and already found the Southampton Staveleys of the sixteenth century, but had not found one Geoffery Staveley who was murdered by William Brown in 1489–90. All Brown's goods were sold off as part of his sentence, one of the income perks the mayor enjoyed.[34] Researchers of the Elzies, Dymoks, Demes and Cottons have all exchanged information with the project which has enhanced both areas of research. Genealogists who had tracked Almaric du Laeke to Southampton had found the trail cold until introduced to Emery Lakes, petty customer and licensed wine seller. Emery had arrived in Southampton in 1539 from his native Clifton in Nottingham, which information he supplied to the Bishop's Consistory Court whilst giving evidence in a defamation case in 1589.[35] In this case he witnessed Mary Elzie accuse Mary Waterton of cuckolding her husband Richard, the town clerk. According to those who knew her, Mary Waterton was 'incontinent of her body'.

There are challenges to a study like The People Project, especially in regard to the type of records that survive. The survival of just one of the parish registers for the period, that of St Michael and St John, is both exciting in the detail it supplies on women of the town and the number of pregnancies and infant mortality endured, as well as the effects of epidemics which produced so many widows.[36] It is also frustrating to know how much detail is forever lost for the parishes of Holy Rood, St Lawrence and the most populous, All Saints. There was an assumption that most People Project records created would be those for men, and probably for those men at the top of Southampton society, however, even though the balance is in the favour of men there are over 4,400 women on the database. There is also a mix of the community, and although we know most about the burgesses we can also trace those on the margins, the poor, common women and those with disability. Women become much more visible in the documents as widows but even so we can see them operating as sole traders in a wide range of occupations: barbers, bakers, butchers, carters, cooks, goldsmith, healers, hucksters, inn-keepers, mercers, merchants, midwives, nurses, painters, prostitutes, purse-makers, rope-makers, silk-women, servants, shepsters, smiths, tipplers and wool packers. Of course in some trades we just have an occasional woman mentioned but there are reasonable numbers working as bakers, hucksters, and merchants and there are some trades in which women are dominant such as silk-women and wool packers.[37] Many single women can be found as servants often in the household of relatives, but a number are also without that protection and particularly young women working in alehouses and inns could find themselves the prey of their masters and their customers.[38]

There were women who 'pushed' themselves into the records, often because they were the subject of controversy. The following example is a detailed picture of one family living in Southampton in the sixteenth century. The family matriarch, Mary Janverin, had a long life being born around 1539 and dying in the reign of James I. The Janverins were at the heart of many of the turbulent events that affected not only Southampton but England in the sixteenth century.

Edward Marcant was the proprietor of a substantial inn next door to St Lawrence church called The Star. He was an incomer to the town arriving in Southampton from Jersey at the start of the Tudor period in 1490, aged ten. Marcant was often involved in controversy, having been accused of being a knave by a Jersey mariner and was reported as selling beer in unlawful and unsealed measures as well as being reported for harbouring Portuguese traders giving them inside information on the price of cloth. He was married to a woman called Anne, of whom little is known. They had at least two children but their son died young, leaving their daughter Mary as their heir. Marcant died in 1552, at which time his daughter had been married to his

[29] E. Roberts and K. Parker (eds), *The Southampton Probate Inventories 1447–1575, Vol I (1447–1566)* and *Vol II (1566–1575)* SRS 34–35 (1992), 201–23.
[30] Butler (ed.) *Book of Fines Vol II*, 2, 35.
[31] T. Cooper, *Elizabeth I & Her People* (London: The National Portrait Gallery, 2014), 127.
[32] Pers. Comm.
[33] SRO SC5/2 crew list of the *Elizabeth*.
[34] Butler (ed.) *Book of Fines Vol I*, 7–8.
[35] Hampshire Record Office [hereafter HRO] Consistory Court Deposition Book, 21M65/C3/9, 463–8.
[36] St Michael Parish Register 1552–1878, SRO PR7/1.
[37] For a full picture of women in Tudor Southampton see C. Butler, "Hiding in documents: The lives women in a patriarchal society – sixteenth century Southampton," *The Local Historian*, 48.2 (2018): 90–103.
[38] C. Butler, "'Incontinent of her body': women, society and morality in Tudor Southampton," *The Local Historian*, 47.2 (2017): 96–110.

former apprentice Stephen Abarrow, probably aged only 14. Through Mary, Stephen inherited The Star inn and was also made burgess in place of his late father-in-law due to his marriage. The marriage however was short-lived, Stephen died in 1557, probably of plague, and left Mary still in her teens and the mother of two toddlers. For nine years Mary remained a widow bringing up her sons alone but in 1566 she took a second husband, another incomer from Jersey. Peter Janverin was born in 1528 and had moved to Southampton in 1559–60. He was soon in trouble with the town authorities for selling wine without licence and was even dis-burgessed in 1563 for colouring goods. Peter was restored to his burgesship in 1566 around the time of his marriage to Mary and that marriage was probably one of the reasons he was let back into the franchise. He was a widower himself with three young sons, the youngest only a baby born in the same year as his marriage to Mary, so it likely his first wife died in childbirth. Like his predecessor, Peter also took on the tenancy of the Star Inn. Peter's behaviour did not improve with his marriage and he fell out with neighbours and was attacked by local landowner and merchant James Betts. He was regularly fined for keeping hides in his loft, for not scouring his ditches, receiving stolen wax, having false weights and measures and allowing foreign meal men to sell their wares in his inn. Peter was also a merchant, heavily involved in trade, underwriting a number of business ventures for large sums of money for merchants from Jersey, Newbury, Reading, Salisbury, Trowbridge and Bristol, the latter involving a business deal with John Gitto who had to repay him £212. He also took shares in voyages to Bordeaux and was part-owner, with Denis Rowse, of a ship of 80 tons, *The Jonas*, which Hugh Rider took on a fishing expedition to Newfoundland. Peter can also be found defending his servant Elizabeth Allen in a case of defamation in 1573 when John Mill accused Elizabeth of trying to entice his servant John Collbrook into marriage. Collbrook's parents also weighed in objecting to the marriage, Janverin supervised the courtship and Elizabeth and John did marry. It may have been that he was protecting his own interests if, for example, Elizabeth had found herself unmarried and pregnant her master, Peter Janverin, would have been financially responsible for her and her child.

Peter was a member of the French Church which he had joined in 1567, and sometimes had preachers staying at his house. This was the church of the French speaking Protestants that had fled to the town from the Low Countries and France, and the church was of Calvinist leanings. His wife, on the other hand, was accused of being a recusant.[39] Peter was asked to look after the son of Lawrence Williams on the death of his father and to make sure to find John a good master, and see he went to school. Peter also of course was step-father to William and Thomas Abarrow and they appeared as his servants at musters, and Thomas became a member of the French Church in 1576. Peter's own three sons attended the King Edward VI School and Lawrence went onto Winchester College and Oxford, although he never matriculated.[40]

Peter took on official roles in town governance, being a collector of the poor rate and following the same trajectory as Edward Marcant, becoming Sheriff in 1581–82, but he never became mayor. This may have been because of the activities of his wife Mary. As well as the five children they had from previous marriages, William and Thomas Abarrow and Nicholas, Edward and Lawrence Janverin, Peter and Mary had at least three children themselves, John, Walter and Mary. During the early years of their marriage there is not much evidence of Mary in the records, as she probably was having to focus on looking after the children. Mary was still helping run the inn because in 1576 she was left 20s for her kindness by one of her guests, Michael Heroult, when he died whilst staying at the Star. In the 1580s and 1590s when Peter might have hoped for the highest office Mary was in trouble with the town governors on more than one occasion. In 1584, she was summoned to the Audit House for insulting a woollen draper, ten years later she was in trouble for calling the mayor, John Hopton, a bankrupt, pokey knave, amongst other things. In the same year, she boxed the ears of the wife of another mayor, John Gregory, for sitting in Mary's pew in St Lawrence. She also called Mrs Gregory a 'kitchen coff' for not letting Mary's daughter, another Mary, sit with her. This altercation may also have been an outcome of the religious persuasion of the Janverin women. Peter Janverin, when quizzed at the Audit House, told the mayor that his wife would not come to the Audit House as she did not consider herself an Audit House bawd. He was not called on to defend his wife further as he died in 1596.

Mary's altercation with the Gregory family was not the first. Back in 1573, she had given evidence in a case involving Gregory's daughter, Marie Dingley. Dingley had fallen out with Margery Singleton over a dress sold to her by Dingley, which had developed a hole in the material. Mary Janverin's role in the resulting argument came when she apparently witnessed Singleton accuse Dingley of witchcraft after the views of the town shearmen had been canvassed about the damaged dress. They were of the opinion that the hole was un-mendable with the conclusion that it must have been caused by witchcraft. The protagonists all found themselves in the bishop's court giving evidence. The case must have been resolved as all the women involved continue to appear in the records and do not seem to have been damaged by the investigation.[41]

As to the fates of their various children, William Abarrow, after serving his step-father went on to become a town porter and beadle. Thomas Abarrow also served his step-father and became a merchant working with other members of the French Church, like Matthew Sohier and Arnold

[39] Hearnshaw and Hearnshaw, *Court Leet*, 359.

[40] See C. F. Russell, *A History of King Edward VI School Southampton* (Cambridge: Privately Published, 1940), 47–9 for a summary of the Janverin family.

[41] HRO 21M65/C3/5 1573, 215–17.

le Clerque, providing the victuals for *The Dove* in 1579. He also followed the family trait of using false measures, which was reported in the court leet in 1584–85.[42] Edward Janverin also became a merchant working with a range of merchants in New Sarum and can be found sub-letting one of his properties to six French immigrants in 1585. Lawrence disappears from the records once he went away to College and Nicholas became a shoe maker and died in 1612. The children Mary and Peter had together were altogether more colourful than their other siblings. John married a woman called Winifred Austen and had three children, but also had an illegitimate child, Leonard, who his parents arranged to be bought up by William Brown in 1595. He was a tippler and a clothier having received one of the £25 loans Thomas White had bequeathed to the town for the support of poor young men to help them set up their trade, although it was noted that John was not a poor man. He was later in trouble for selling cloth in his house rather than in the Linen Hall. Walter Janverin also had a child, Rose, and he chose the career of a mariner. He was involved in a number of privateering adventures, although others accused him and his compatriots of actually acting as pirates. In 1602, he was one of the crew on the *Margaret and John* with Edmund Boneham and Thomas Tomkins which privateered two Venetian Ships, the *Jesus* and the *Balbiana*. The Venetian ambassador complained to King James who issued a proclamation against piracy specifically naming Janverin, Boneham and Tomkins.[43] In 1603, Walter was arrested and the trial for piracy was held in Southampton. Seven sailors were condemned to death in December, including Walter. Six were executed but Walter was spared at the request of the Venetian secretary as the son of honest parents who were willing to pay compensation of £150. He was in trouble again in 1610 when the mayor sent the constable to apprehend him, but the constable found his 'dore was shut and that he was not within'. An order was made for his arrest.[44]

Peter and Mary's daughter Mary married a man called Gerrard Swift. Her parents' inn was searched in 1589 looking for Gerrard who was thought to be hiding there fleeing from a charge of theft. Francis Walsingham wrote to the mayor of Southampton about the alleged robbery and said that Swift had used forged documents to obtain a goods of a ship of Pierre Halle of Dieppe. Walsingham also threatened that if Swift was not found his father-in-law would answer for it. Swift was eventually arrested in 1590 and charged with forging the Lord Admiral's seal and other warrants and it was ordered that whilst he was in the Marshalsea prison he was not to be allowed to have paper or to write to anyone but the council. Swift escaped in 1593 but was recaptured and sent to the galleys at Chatham. The next year he escaped again but was promised a safe conduct by the Lord Admiral if he turned himself in. When he did so however he was imprisoned in the Gatehouse at Westminster. In 1597, when he escaped for a third time and was found in Southampton, it was ordered that on his return to London his legs were to be bound under his horse and his arms pinioned. He was sent to Newgate and again forbidden pen and ink. In 1598, he claimed to have been wrongly accused of forging a petition for a Newgate prisoner, and that prisoner later said he had been tortured to implicate Swift. The man was afterwards executed for coining. Cecil ordered Swift's house to be searched for forged signatures. Swift complained that the Lord Admiral had personal spite against him and that the Lord Admiral had been bound by order of the council to provide for Swift's wife and his brother but had not done so and instead had tried to seduce Mary Swift. Swift was hung in 1598. His brother Jasper was known to be a Catholic and there is a suspicion that Swift had been forging documents to enable Catholics to leave the country.[45]

After the death of her husband Mary Swift was reported in Court Leet in 1602 for not attending church for over twelve months, suggesting that Mary along with her mother were recusants. Her brother Walter and cousin Walter Earle each provided £40 surety and Mary herself provided another 100 marks. It was noted that at the time she was living in her mother's house. Mary senior was ordered to present herself at the Audit House but she sent a message to say she was sick in bed and could not come. Mary Janverin made her will in 1608 making her daughter her residual heir. The last time we see Mary in the records is that same year when the burgess wife Alice James called her a 'common whore'. Mary retorted that she was never known to be but of 'good and honest conversation'.[46]

Previously to the work of The People Project odd snippets about the Janverin family appear in various commentaries in some Record Series volumes but it was not until all those pieces of information were pulled together along with data from un-transcribed sources that a more in-depth picture of a merchant family of Southampton could be drawn. They are in many ways a typical family of the period, well off, running a substantial inn but still, like most people in the town being involved in merchant activity whilst breaking rules around weights and measures which affected the daily life and staple foods of ordinary people. Like many others Peter and Mary married more than once due to the early deaths of their spouses. The family spread across the religious divide that was becoming more prominent in the country at the time, with several of the men in the family being prominent in the Calvinist Protestant church whilst the women appear to be of Catholic persuasion. They are involved in one of the earliest recorded incidents of witchcraft in the records, at a time just prior to large scale witchcraft trials of the reign of James I. The family were involved in privateering but at a period when, with peace

[42] Butler (ed.), *Book of Fines III*,.98; SRO SC/13/2/2–10 Muster Books 1577, 1583, 1583–4; SRO SC2/6/5 Books of Instruments, 71, 131, 163.
[43] R. C. Anderson (ed.), *The Book of Examinations 1601–2* SRSoc 26 (1926), xxi–v, 7, 24, 56.
[44] Russell, *History of King Edward VI School*, 48–9.
[45] Anderson *Examination 1601–2*, xxv–xxvii.
[46] HRO 1608A/057; J. W. Horrocks (ed.), *The Assembly Books of Southampton Vol II 1609–10* SRSoc 21 (1920), 63; Hearnshaw and Hearnshaw *Court Leet*, 359.

with Spain imminent and when privateering was no longer sanctioned by government, they had like others turned to piracy. They were incomers to the town, but they prospered and managed to navigate difficult waters and some of the challenging issues of the period. Despite their various infringements, family members served as Sheriffs of Southampton, the second most senior post in the corporate hierarchy. In a patriarchal society Mary Janverin is found operating an inn, defying the corporation, defending her children and living a full life dying in her bed in around her 70th year.

One of Professor James's earliest pieces of research, when he was working on his PhD was to investigate the geographical origins of the burgesses of Southampton, illustrating the pull the town had in attracting men from across the country to settle there. Like Professor Colin Platt who wrote biographies of the merchant families of medieval Southampton, he was and is interested in the lives of ordinary people in urban environments and the academic study of history that is local but also has wider importance in giving a more nuanced and richer picture of life in towns, towns which were becoming a vital force in national and international affairs in the sixteenth century. The People Project also illustrates the range of different records that are available to use as sources, as the single document studies that Hicks and Fairbrother have undertaken have shown, there is additional data available to enhance those studies in unexpected source material. As Professor James illustrated in his *Southampton Sources* volume but also in his *The Urban Experience* source book, produced in 1983 when interest in urban history was at its height, there is a rich variety of material in the archives of towns from across the country. The People Project aims to add the history of individuals to the spectrum of urban experience championed by Professor James.

Bibliography

SRS – Southampton Records Series.

SRSoc – Southampton Record Society.

Unpublished primary sources

Hampshire Record Office (HRO).

21M65/C3/5: Consistory Court Deposition Book, 1573.

21M65/C3/9: Consistory Court Deposition Book, 19 Jan 1582/3–16 May 1590.

1608A/057: Will of Mary Janverin.

Southampton Archives (SRO).

SC3/1/1: Burgess Admissions, 1496–1704.

SC5/2: Crew list of the *Elizabeth.*

SC6/1/1–37: Court Leet Records, 1549–1570.

SC/13/2/2–10: Muster Books 1577, 1583, 1583–84.

SC2/6/5: Books of Instruments, 1576–86.

PR7/1: St Michael Parish Register 1152–1878.

University of Southampton.

Chinchen, B., Southampton Stewards Books 1511–51 unpublished transcriptions, Cope Collection, Hartley Library.

Published primary sources

Anderson, R. C., ed. *The Assize of Bread Book 1477–1517*, SRSoc 23 (1923).

Anderson, R. C., ed. *The Book of Examinations 1601–2*, SRSoc 26 (1926).

Aubrey, E.R. and G.H. Hamilton, eds. *Books of Examination and Depositions 1570–1594*, SRSoc 16 (1914).

Aubrey, E.R., ed., *The history and antiquity of Southampton, with some conjectures concerning the Roman Clausentum: written about the year 1770*, SRSoc 8 (1909).

Butler, C.B., ed. *The Book of Fines: The Annual Accounts of the Mayors of Southampton Volume I 1488–150*, SRS 41 (2007).

Butler, C.B., ed. *The Book of Fines: The Annual Accounts of the Mayors of Southampton Volume II 1540–1571*, SRS 43 (2009).

Butler, C. B., ed. *The Book of Fines: The Annual Accounts of the Mayors of Southampton Volume III 1572–1594*, SRS 44 (2010).

Gidden, H.W., ed. *The Book of Remembrance of Southampton Vol III*, SRSoc 30 (1930).

Godfray, H.M. *Registre de l'Eglise Wallonne de Southampton 1567–1779* Huguenot Society of London (1889).

Hearnshaw F.J.C. and D.M. Hearnshaw. *Court Leet Records 1578–1602*, SRSoc 1–2 (1906).

Horrocks, J.W., ed. *The Assembly Book of Southampton Vol II 1609–10*, SRSoc 21 (1920).

James, T.B., *Southampton Sources 1086–1900*, SRS 26 (1983).

Richardson, R. C. and T.B. James, eds. *The Urban Experience a Sourcebook, English, Scottish and Welsh Towns, 1450–1700.* Manchester: Manchester University Press, 1983.

Roberts, E. and K. Parker, eds. *The Southampton Probate Inventories 1447–1575, Volume 1 (1447–1566)*, SRS 34 (1992).

Roberts, E. and K. Parker, eds. *The Southampton Probate Inventories 1447–1575 Volume 2 (1566–1575)*, SRS 35 (1992).

Ruddock, A.A. *Italian Merchants and Shipping in Southampton 1270–1600*, SRS 1 (1951).

Spicer, A. *The French-Speaking Reformed Community and their Church in Southampton 1567–c.1620*, SRS 39 (1997).

Published secondary sources

Butler, C. "Hiding in documents: The lives women in a patriarchal society – sixteenth century Southampton." *The Local Historian*, 48.2 (2018): 90–103.

Butler, C. "'Incontinent of her body': women, society and morality in Tudor Southampton." *The Local Historian*, 47.2 (2017): 96–110.

Connell-Smith, G., *The Forerunners of Drake*. London and New York, Longmans, Green and Co.,1954.

Cooper, T., *Elizabeth I and Her People.* London: National Portrait Gallery, 2014.

Davies, J.S., *A History of Southampton. Partly from the MS. of Dr. Speed, in the Southampton Archives.* London and Southampton: Gilbert and Co. and Hamilton Adams and Co., 1883.

Green, D., *The Double Life of Doctor Lopez.* London: Century, 2003.

Platt, C. *Medieval Southampton: The port and trading community, A.D. 1000–1600.* London and Boston: Routledge Kegan Paul 1973.

Russell, C.F., *A History of King Edward VI School Southampton.* Cambridge: Privately Published, 1940.

Websites

Tudor Revels: www.tudorrevels.co.uk/records.php

England's Immigrants: www.englandsimmigrants.com

Overland Trade Project: www.overlandtrade.org

Unpublished Secondary source

Fairbrother, L. "Burgesses, Freemen and Strangers: The Organisation of Industry and Trade in Southampton, 1547 to 1603." Unpublished PhD thesis, University of Southampton, 2018.

11

Gender, space and status in the sixteenth-century English Deer Park: with reference to the Framlingham Park Game Roll (1515-19) and George Penruddock's Ranger's Book (1572-75)

Amanda Richardson

University of Chichester

Abstract: It has been argued that the gendered spatial divisions identified inside medieval buildings, based on public/private, extended into the landscape so that parks, like gardens, were notionally 'female space'. The premise is given impetus by Mary Thomas Crane's assertion that 'real privacy... was, until well into the seventeenth century... attainable only outdoors'. Most recently, Christopher Ward has extended the thesis regarding the sixteenth century, noting the juxtaposition of fallow deer with the female body in contemporary art, and positing that their controlled nature made parks suitable loci for female recreation. But does the theory stand up to documentary scrutiny? This paper will discuss who hunted where, as recorded in game rolls for two high-status, long established deer parks – Framlingham Great Park (Suffolk) and Clarendon Park (Wiltshire). Although the gendering of space in sixteenth-century parks may have gained impetus through the increasing variety of internal divisions, the results no doubt echo late-medieval practice.

Key words: Clarendon; gender; space; landscape; deer parks; medieval hunting; Framlingham; royalty; nobility; masculinity, animal history

Introduction

This paper could not have been written without Tom James, whose name will always be synonymous with Clarendon. Together with Chris Gerrard, he guided me from an early interest in the medieval palace and its famous tiled pavements, discussed in this volume by Mary South, towards a fascination with the landscapes of the Middle Ages, particularly forests and deer parks. Since I first wrote on the subject some fifteen years ago, studies of medieval and early modern deer and deer parks, and the fallow deer within them, have emerged from a narrow medieval and regional focus to encompass a wider temporal and geographical range.[1] Yet the parks of the sixteenth century, sitting awkwardly between their medieval predecessors and the designed country house landscapes of the 1700s,[2] rarely receive singular attention despite the resurgence of royal interest in parks under the early Tudors, and Henry VIII and Elizabeth I's well-known enthusiasm for hunting.[3] Indeed, in *Deer and People* (2015), a publication resulting from the AHRC-funded, multi-period fallow deer project, just two of 24 chapters address the early modern period in any meaningful detail.[4] The lacuna is perplexing since more country houses were constructed between 1570 and 1620 than in any other 50-year period,[5] most alongside newly-made parkland.

This paper attempts to leap the traditional medieval/early modern divide by expanding on the main themes that have arisen to date regarding sixteenth-century deer parks – namely gender and space, the meanings behind royal

[1] Fallow was the deer species invariably maintained in medieval and early modern deer parks, although keeping imparked red deer became fashionable in the seventeenth century. Recent works include Christopher S. Ward, "Cultural Depictions of the European Fallow Deer (*Dama Dama*) 6000 BCE to 1600 CE," PhD Thesis, University of Nottingham, 2017; Amanda Richardson, "Pale Reflections? Deer parks in contemporary writings from the sixteenth to the later nineteenth century," in *A Fresh Approach: essays presented to Colin Platt in celebration of his eightieth birthday*, ed. Claire Donovan (Bristol: Trouser Press, 2014); Richard Almond, "Femmes Fatale: iconography and the courtly huntress in the later Middle Ages and Renaissance," in *Deer and People*, ed. Karis Baker et al. (Oxford: Windgather, 2015); Marilyn L. Sandidge, "Hunting or Gardening: parks and royal rural space," in *Rural Space in the Middle Ages and Early Modern Age: the spatial turn in premodern studies*, ed. Albrecht Classen (Berlin: Walter de Gruyter, 2012).

[2] The depredations of the seventeenth century during and after the civil wars caused such a fracture that it is difficult to measure continuities and contrasts in this period.

[3] Simon Thurley, *The Royal Palaces of Tudor England: architecture and court life 1460–1547* (London: Yale University Press, 1993), 68; Amanda Richardson, "'Riding like Alexander, Hunting like Diana': gendered aspects of the medieval hunt and its landscape settings," *Gender and History* 24, no.2 (2012); Richard Almond, *Daughters of Artemis: the huntress in the Middle Ages and Renaissance* (Woodbridge: D.S. Brewer, 2009).

[4] Almond's "Femmes Fatale," and Mandy de Belin, "English Icons: the deer and the horse," in *Deer and People*, ed. Karis Baker et al. (Oxford: Windgather, 2015).

[5] Susan Lasdun, *The English Park: royal, public and private* (New York: Vendome Press, 1992), 27.

hunting, and the increased subdivision of outdoor areas. It will do this with reference to the Framlingham Park Game Roll (1515–19) and George Penruddock's Ranger's Book (1572–75),[6] paying particular attention to the gender and status of those who hunted following claims that the benign, enclosed and relatively private terrain of parks led to their association with women.[7] That is, women's symbolic spatial segregation, based on notions of public and private, identified by Roberta Gilchrist, Oliver Creighton and others inside medieval and early modern buildings extended out into the landscape through the enclosure of certain areas.[8] This premise has so far been explored chiefly in regard to late-medieval parks – and then at a rather basic level.[9] It is given impetus by the work of Mary Thomas Crane who states, regarding the 1500s and 1600s, that 'real privacy... was, until well into the seventeenth century... readily attainable only outdoors'.[10] Most recently, Christopher Ward has extended the thesis in relation to the sixteenth century. He notes the juxtaposition of butchered fallow deer with the female body in contemporary art, positing that the controlled circumstances of deer parks made them suitable loci not only for the performance of femininity, but also of rites of passage for adolescents of both sexes.[11]

In the later sixteenth century this gendering of space may have gained impetus – or was driven by – the increasing use of internal divisions in parks, such as paddocks and deer courses, which created yet more exclusive areas. Where possible, therefore, the location of kills at Clarendon and Framlingham will be taken into account, as well as the protagonists' gender, although other themes may emerge regarding the impact on the landscape of the social and cultural shifts of the mid-sixteenth century.[12] At the very least, the documents provide snapshots into the operation of hunting towards the start and end of the 1500s, demonstrating the ways in which a park enabled its owner or guardian to host visitors to the required standard.[13]

The Parks

Framlingham Great Park (Suffolk) may have existed from the early twelfth century although the first documentary reference dates to 1270.[14] The castle passed to the Howards in 1483 and by the time of the Game Roll it was in the hands of Thomas Howard second Duke of Norfolk, who died there in 1524 after an illustrious career in royal service.[15] The Game Roll outlines numbers of deer dispatched by hunters and park staff, or which died of disease, over a five-year period from 1515–19. It was compiled by the duke's parker Richard Chambyr, and has been lauded by Richard Cummins for its vivid depiction of 'the scale of hunting in a large park of fallow deer in... the early Tudor period and of its carefully supervised nature'.[16] In the 1570s the Great Park contained around 500–650 acres (200–260 ha) and held 400 fallow deer, a doubtless depleted figure following the fall of the third duke in 1546, after which the castle passed in and out of royal hands and the park became neglected. By its disparkment in 1580 the herd had apparently risen to 1,600 animals. This number is perhaps indicative of the total in the early sixteenth century, since Chambyr lists up to 200 deer gifted annually to Norfolk's neighbours, servants and tenants.[17]

George Penruddock's Ranger's Book similarly sets out annual tallies of deer slaughtered or killed by disease, this time over four years in the royal park of Clarendon (Wiltshire). At around 4500 acres (1821 ha) this park dwarfed Framlingham and is widely accepted as the largest purpose-made deer park to have existed in medieval Europe. It may also have been constructed in the early twelfth century, although a park is first recorded in 1223.[18] Unlike Framlingham Great Park at the time of the Game Roll, by the 1570s it was no longer associated with a major residence, the royal palace at its centre having been abandoned around 1500. Nevertheless, Clarendon Park reputedly still held *c.*7,000 fallow deer in the early seventeenth century, and remained Crown property until 1660.[19]

During the 1570s Clarendon Park's wardenship was vested in Henry Herbert of Wilton House, second earl of Pembroke (1534–1601), who appointed as his deputy Sir George Penruddock (d.1581), sometime sheriff and

[6] John Cummins, *The Hound and the Hawk: the art of medieval hunting* (London: Phoenix Press, 2001), Appendix 2 (hereafter Appendix 2); Wiltshire and Swindon Archives, Papers of the Penruddocke Family of Compton Chamberlayne, Wiltshire and Swindon Archives [WSA] 549/8, ff.7–23d.

[7] Ward, "Cultural Depictions," 216; Naomi Sykes, "Animal Bones and Animal Parks," in *The Medieval Park: new perspectives*, ed. Robert Liddiard (Macclesfield: Windgather, 2007), 55; Richardson, "'Riding like Alexander," 216–63; Naomi Sykes, "Animals: the bones of medieval society," in *Reflections: 50 years of medieval archaeology, 1957–2007*, ed. Roberta Gilchrist and Andrew Reynolds (Leeds: Maney, 2009), 358; Stephen A. Mileson, *Parks in Medieval England* (Oxford: Oxford University Press, 2009), 41.

[8] See Roberta Gilchrist, *Gender and Archaeology: contesting the past* (London: Routledge, 1999), 109–45; Oliver H. Creighton, "Castle Studies and the European Medieval Landscape: traditions, trends and future research directions," *Landscape History* 30 (2009).

[9] For example, Richardson, "Riding like Alexander," 260–63.

[10] Mary T. Crane, "Illicit Privacy and Outdoor Spaces in Early Modern England," *Journal for Early Modern Cultural Studies* 9, no. 1 (2009): 5.

[11] Ward, "Cultural Depictions," 224–46; 254–58.

[12] It should be noted that the version of the Framlingham Park Game Roll used here is the annotated document, originally published in Evelyn P. Shirley's *Some Account of English Deer Parks* (London: John Murray, 1867), so that the data taken from it are not definitive.

[13] Ward, "Cultural Depictions," 158.

[14] Magnus Alexander, *Framlingham Castle, Suffolk: the landscape context – desk-top assessment*, Research Department Report Series no. 106 (Cambridge: English Heritage 2007), 26.

[15] David M. Head, "Howard, Thomas, second duke of Norfolk (1443–1524)," *Oxford Dictionary of National Biography*, accessed 11 April 2017, http://www.oxforddnb.com/view/article/13939; Alexander, *Framlingham Castle*, 21.

[16] Cummins, *The Hound and the Hawk*, 62–63.

[17] Alexander, *Framlingham Castle*, 44; Roger B. Manning, *Hunters and Poachers: a cultural history of unlawful hunting in England 1485–1640* (Oxford: Clarendon Press, 1993), 10.

[18] *Rotuli Litterarum Clausarum I, 1204–1224* (London: Record Commission, 1833), 541.

[19] John Britton (ed.), *The Natural History of Wiltshire by John Aubrey FRS: written between 1656 and 1691* (London: Wiltshire Topographical Society, 1847), 59; Tom Beaumont James and Christopher M. Gerrard, *Clarendon: landscape of kings* (Macclesfield: Windgather, 2007), 104.

MP for Wiltshire. Penruddock, a keen huntsman, was installed at Ivychurch House, Alderbury, adjacent to the park and set in the grounds of the ruined Augustinian priory of Ivychurch.[20] He enjoyed overall charge of the park and its six keepers until his death in 1581, no doubt a fitting reward for his services to the earl, for whose father he had been standard bearer at the siege of St Quentin (1557).[21] His Ranger's Book demonstrates that in the late sixteenth century Clarendon Park remained an important recreational space for notable local gentry families, and it played a significant part in the resurgence of the immediate area from *c.*1551, when Pembroke leased the manor of Ivychurch, characterised by a 'great rebuilding' in the area around the time the Ranger's Book was compiled.[22]

Licit and Illicit Hunting: gendered, spatial and temporal boundaries

The prevalence of poaching among the Elizabethan gentry and nobility seems to have coincided with a perceived need to preserve the martial spirit at a time when formal hunting was thought to have become more feminised.[23] Theoretically, anyone owning greyhounds could course deer lawfully if they owned land worth £2 per annum (although not at night or by entering a park uninvited, in which circumstances groups of three or more constituted a riot).[24] Liminal and illicit forms of coursing therefore co-existed alongside more formal versions in and around early-modern parks. Yet poaching is not mentioned at all at Clarendon in the 1570s, perhaps indicating that the park was very tightly policed by its staff: Robert Bright the forester of Shergallgate; Richard Boothe the park's ranger; John Townsend, forester of Whitmarsh; Robert Donnington the launderer, and Greene, Batter, Jockey and Roger, the park's quarter keepers, all of whose individual contributions to deer management and dispatch are listed by George Penruddock. Misfortunes did, however, occur, including a poignant episode on 13 May 1573, when Robert Penruddock's servant 'killed one of Bright's tame deer'.[25]

An illuminating snapshot of how these early-modern park keepers (and no doubt George Penruddock himself) might have lived, alongside their various animals, can be found in the memoirs of Anthony Ashley Cooper, first Earl of Shaftesbury (1621–83). Describing what he saw as a vanishing world, Shaftesbury portrayed his godfather Henry Hastings (1562–1650), a keeper of the New Forest, as 'the copy of our nobility in ancient days in hunting'. Henry, who 'rode to the death of a stag as well as any' until his final years, occupied a house 'perfectly of the old fashion, in the midst of a large park well stocked with deer'. It was:

> not so neatly kept as to shame him… the great hall strewed with marrow bones, full of hawks' perches, hounds, spaniels, and terriers, the upper sides of the hall hung with the fox-skins of this and the last year's skinning… [and] guns and... huntsmen's poles in abundance… On a great hearth [in the parlour]… lay some terriers and the choicest hounds and spaniels... two of the great chairs [with]... litters of young cats in them which were not to be disturbed… The windows… served for places to lay his arrows, crossbows... and other such like accoutrements; the corners of the room full of the best chose hunting and hawking poles… hawks' hoods, bells, and such like… His table cost him not much, though it was very good to eat at, his sports supplying all but beef and mutton.[26]

The close bond between early modern hunters and their dogs is further demonstrated by the section on healing canine infirmities in the *Boke of Hunting* (1576), which recommended, among other cures, restorative baths and wine-based medicines administered through table napkins.[27]

Not surprisingly then, dogs appear frequently in both documents, often highlighting the differing nature of the two parks and perhaps also the shift to formalised coursing in the intervening period. Mentions in the Framlingham roll indicate a reasonably fluid boundary – and thus rather less 'control' than Cummins has suggested.[28] In summer 1515 'a dog came in and killed a [doe]', while two others belonging to a Mr Dallyng of Laxfield (*c.*7 miles north of Framlingham) brought down another doe and a fawn.[29] The following year, while chasing a sower with their dogs three men gained entry to the park, killing a doe and two fawns; on a separate occasion while Chambyr led the duke's deer home they were forestalled by Walter Warrener whose bitch chased a doe into the park and killed it, and in 1519 a fawn was savaged to death by a 'mastife beche and a spanyell'. A few entries indicate the possible consequences for such misconduct. In 1516 John Pulsham 'cam rydyng be the wey and fownd a [doe] without [the

[20] Richard F. Atkinson, *The Manors and Hundred of Alderbury: lords, lands and livery* (Alderbury: R.F. Atkinson, 1995), 71; James and Gerrard, *Clarendon*, 49.

[21] Stanley T. Bindoff, "Penruddock, Sir George (d.1581), of Ivy Church and Compton Chamberlayne, Wilts., Broxbourne, Herts. and Clerkenwell, Mdx," Member Biographies, The History of Parliament, accessed 22 May 2018, http://www.historyofparliamentonline.org/volume/1558-1603/member/penruddock-sir-george-1581.

[22] For example, John Stockman, keeper of the king's rabbits at Clarendon, another member of Pembroke's household, built Barford House at nearby Downton in 1569, and Sir Thomas Gorges constructed Longford Castle near Alderbury *c.*1576. See Amanda Richardson, *The Forest, Park and Palace Of Clarendon, c.1200–c.1650: reconstructing an actual, conceptual and documented Wiltshire landscape*, British Archaeological Reports British Series 387 (Oxford: BAR Publishing, 2005), 109.

[23] Manning, *Hunters and Poachers*, 14; Ward, "Cultural Depictions," 216.

[24] Roger B. Manning, "Unlawful Hunting in England, 1500–1640," *Forest and Conservation History* 38, no. 1 (1994): 17.

[25] WSA 549/8, f.12d.

[26] William D. Christie, *A Life of Anthony Ashley Cooper, First Earl of Shaftesbury, 1621–1683*, vol 1 (London: Macmillan, 1871), Appendix, xiv–xvii.

[27] *Turbervile's Booke of Hunting 1576* (New York: Clarendon Press, 1908), 221–36. Until the 1940s the text was attributed to George Turbervile, but it is now believed to have been compiled by George Gascoigne.

[28] Cummins, *The Hound and the Hawk*, 62–63.

[29] Cummins, Appendix 2, 262.

park] and hys doge kylled hym and he hyng his dog', and in 1519 at fawning time the dog of a shoemaker from Dennington managed to gain entry, despatching two does. Chambyr records that the cobbler declined the dog's return, upon which it was 'hynge... upon a tre'. A happier fate awaited one of two coursing dogs that killed a sorrel (a three-year old fallow buck) in the park, at which Chambyr approached the owner and master and dog were duly reunited.[30] Such brutal penalties survived well into the eighteenth century, by the end of which they were recognised to be less than effective deterrents – a conclusion borne out at sixteenth-century Framlingham.[31]

The dogs most frequently recorded in the Penruddock document are the earl of Pembroke's hounds, testifying to Clarendon Park's recurrent use by its guardians, including Penruddock and various hunting companions, which may have made it difficult for poachers to operate. Pembroke's dogs are often mentioned alongside deer which made 'sewtes' for them; probably a reference to training for coursing (hunting by sight with greyhounds) since 'suit' derives from pursuit.[32] A doe and a fawn were killed in this way on 25 November 1573 followed by another doe and fawn on 6 December.[33] Furthermore, in August 1575 Richard Booth, the park's ranger, calculated that since the previous Michaelmas 96 winter deer (i.e. does and fawns) had been killed there either by warrant or 'for sewtes for howndes'.[34] Since does and fawns appear invariably to have been the 'suits', it is possible that these dogs were being trained in the sport of coursing, saving bucks for the main event in the due season. Indeed Richard Blome, in *The Gentleman's Recreation* (1686), 'first collected from antient and modern authors', recommended coursing greyhounds at least thrice weekly throughout the year.[35]

In his 1576 *Booke of Hunting*, adapted from Jacques du Fouilloux's *La Venerie* (1573) and contemporaneous with the Penruddock document, Gascoigne noted that whereas deer coursing was unfashionable in France, 'we in England do make great account of such pastime' – a discrepancy resulting from the sheer number of parks in England and the lack of more challenging game such as wild boar and wolves.[36] Accordingly he set out the rules, revealing an intricate sport which we might otherwise imagine to have been rather haphazard. The dogs were divided into 'teasers', released singly or in pairs to isolate a suitable deer from the herd; 'sidelayes', which were then let slip at its flanks, and finally 'backsets', which ran at the deer face on so that 'they may the more amaze him [and]... with the help of the... teasers and sidelayes... pull him downe'. All this was bet on and due to the strength of red deer stags, which 'wil beare sometimes foure or five [brace] of Greyhoundes', the rules concerning fallow bucks were more stringent. Thus, a hound that 'pinched' a red deer won the wager but 'in coursing of a Fallow deare, your Greyhounde must pinche and holde'. This indicates a high level of training, and indeed Gascoigne adds that young dogs should never be let slip 'without the companie of some old [fleshed] dog: for every dog wil not byte a Deare at the firste course'.[37] Evidence for such training exists – in the form of the 'suits' – in the 1570s at Clarendon, testifying to the rising popularity of coursing with greyhounds in parks by the later sixteenth century.[38] Certainly nothing similar appears in the earlier Framlingham roll, in which the dogs mentioned invariably belonged to poachers.

Notwithstanding the apparent lack of poaching at Clarendon in Penruddock's time, the park was clearly vulnerable following the reduction of royal interest from the later fifteenth century. A gang from a range of social strata including husbandmen, labourers, tilers and yeomen is recorded as entering it in 1488.[39] Unusually, female involvement is evident during the reign of Henry VIII when Margaret York of the adjacent village of Laverstock actively encouraged her servants to poach and resist the keepers, even inviting along the local gentry, who would not lack 'meat, drink, lodging nor good cheer' if they hunted in Clarendon Park, in which, she claimed, her land had unlawfully been enclosed.[40] Generally though, poaching was an almost entirely male affair, raising issues of the performance of masculinity in such unlawful but often glorified acts, and also of parks as notionally female spaces, at once symbolically 'safe' and capable of violation.[41]

The appeal of poaching is outlined by Gascoigne, who declared that hunting nocturnally with dogs required a great deal more skill than coursing by day. However, since he had vowed 'to be friend to [all] Parkes, Forrests, and Chaces' he would not 'expresse the experience which hath bene dearer unto me'.[42] Indeed the decline of the martial imperative in hunting in the 1500s and the evolution of more 'feminised' forms of hunting in the unthreatening space of parks may have popularised masculine risk-taking.[43] As Ward puts it, poaching by night provided an 'opportunity for the "macho" poacher to penetrate

[30] Cummins, Appendix 2, 263-5.

[31] Peter B. Munsche, *Gentlemen and Poachers: The English Game Laws 1671–1831* (Cambridge: Cambridge University Press, 1981), 82.

[32] It is just possible that the 'suits' were protective jackets for Pembroke's hunting dogs (see John B. Friedman, "Coats, Collars, and Capes: royal fashions for animals in the early modern period," *Medieval Clothing and Textiles* 12 [2016]). However, the context makes this unlikely, and deer skins used in this way would have been a by-product rather than recorded as the cause of the animals' deaths.

[33] WSA 549/8, ff 19d.

[34] WSA 549/8, f.23d.

[35] Richard Blome, *The Gentleman's Recreation* (London: Freeman Collins, 1686), frontmatter; 49.

[36] *Turbervile's Booke*, 246; Matthew M. Stokes, "Blood Sports: violence and the performance of masculinity in early modern drama," PhD Thesis, University of Boston, 2015, https://open.bu.edu/handle/2144/14047, 155, 162.

[37] *Turbervile's Booke*, 246–47.

[38] See Stokes, "Blood Sports," 158.

[39] TNA: PRO DL 39/2/20, m.15.

[40] TNA: PRO STAC 2/11/31; Manning, *Hunters and Poachers*, 177.

[41] Richardson, "Riding like Alexander," 266; Ward, "Cultural Depictions," 179, 209.

[42] *Turbervile's Booke*, 250.

[43] Stokes, "Blood Sports," 157–71.

the terrain where young women would in daytime freely move'.[44] These poachers were frequently young men, for whom the activity represented a rite of passage into manhood and/ or genteel status,[45] and they were often found on the peripheries of parks whether by night or by day. In one instance at Framlingham in 1518, John Crispe and John Chyrie 'broute a [sorell] in to the parke and kyllyd hyme ther' after coursing with their dogs in 'Holfereth', clearly outside the pale.[46] This is noteworthy because apart from the locations to which Framlingham's deer were sent, Holfereth is one of the only place names mentioned in the entire document. However, other references to dogs chasing deer *into* the park make it clear that the original – or ostensible – activities invariably took place immediately outside. It would seem that 1516 was an especially bad year. Walter Warrener 'browt [?a doe] in to the parke and kyllyd here', and John Foxe and 'yonge Thomas Hyllys', described as 'lads' and accompanied by a William Tendyclone, chased a Sower inside the pale after coursing hare, killing a doe 'with fawne, and another fawne'. In the same year John Pulsham the elder took advantage of a deer which had leapt outside the pale, where he was conveniently waiting.[47]

Two clergymen poachers are mentioned at Framlingham, and in contrast both were found *inside* the park rather than on its peripheries. On Holy Rood eve (13 September) in 1515 Richard Chambyr caught John Bowse, parish priest of Tannyngton, red-handed (or almost) 'with his bow bent [pointing at the herd] and an arrow in it'. Then in September 1517 the parson of Kettleburgh was apprehended by night in the park on the Thursday after Michaelmas Day. Perhaps the priests felt more at home in an arguably 'feminised' space, or were using the park's boundaries to hide their decidedly unclerical activities, hunting being forbidden to them under Canon Law.[48] What can be said with certainty is that both were apprehended during buck season, the maleness of the prey perhaps affirming the skills expected of manhood.[49] Unfortunately it is impossible to compare 1570s Clarendon because references to the clergy are naturally fewer on the other side of the Reformation. None at all are mentioned as poaching, although their medieval predecessors at Ivychurch priory had indulged frequently, often in groups.[50]

Documentary evidence for solitary poachers is generally scant in the early modern period. Instead, like their cherished hounds they usually roamed in packs, their forays often planned immediately beforehand in taverns or inns.[51] Such may have been the case when the Salisbury clothier Thomas Ray met Barnaby Legate, a carpenter, at a farmhouse near Clarendon in June 1606. Legate persuaded Ray and two others to accompany him into the park after dusk but Ray claimed he resisted entering it for fear of offending the earl of Pembroke, instead minding the horses until his companions returned 45 minutes later with a dead buck.[52] One gang member was servant to Giles Estcourte, sometime JP for Wiltshire and clerk of Salisbury's statute merchant, named in the Penruddock document as receiving venison from the park, with which he – and his household – were no doubt familiar.[53] Opportunism could also be a spur to action, as when the sixteenth-century gentleman John Quennell visited Hampshire to attend a baptism. After the celebratory supper he and his companions went to Odiham Park and caused their greyhounds to leap the pale, resulting in the slaughter of five deer.[54] That they happened to have a pack of dogs with them, however, suggests a level of premeditation.

The legitimate sport of coursing became much more formalised and demarcated in the sixteenth-century landscape. At the new royal park at More (Hertfordshire) in 1535 an area was enclosed in which all trees were felled, affording 'a great plain laund for the king's course', described by Roger Manning as akin to a bear-pit. Timber structures built on masonry piers gave shelter for the deer, and two standings were erected to provide views over the proceedings. The manner in which such areas operated is evident at Oatlands (Surrey), where deer held in a pen and released upon command were slaughtered 'with darts and spears' by the ageing Henry VIII from the royal standing.[55] Indeed Henry, whose infirmities from the mid-1530s precluded his riding to hounds, seems to have made coursing along delineated tracks fashionable. The purpose of a standing, in conjunction with a deer course, was to allow spectators – who would have betted on the outcome – to observe deer being pursued along the course, the hound nearest the deer when it passed a given point being the winner.[56] What is noteworthy is the nomenclature; the word 'standing' derived from the 'stand' (the position taken up by archers in medieval bow and stable hunts), while the fence replaced the beaters. Thus, the already status-affirming medieval hunt was made doubly concrete for early modern observers, as was the performance of status and gender in the landscape.

At Clarendon a fenced deer course about one and a half miles (2.4 km) long and eighty yards (*c.* 70m) wide is shown on a map of *c.* 1640, with a standing half-way along.[57] It has been suggested that the course and standing were constructed under Henry VIII. No written evidence exists for it in that period but it was certainly there by the early

[44] Ward, "Cultural Depictions," 217.
[45] Manning, *Hunters and Poachers*, 171, 183.
[46] Cummins, Appendix 2, 265.
[47] Cummins, Appendix 2, 264, 263.
[48] Manning, *Hunters and Poachers*, 177.
[49] Ward, "Cultural Depictions," 244.
[50] See Richardson, *The Forest, Park and Palace*, 121–26.
[51] Katharine W. Swett, "'The Account between Us': honour, reciprocity and companionship in male friendship in the later seventeenth century," *Albion* 31, no. 1 (1999): 16; Manning, "Unlawful Hunting," 20.
[52] Manning, *Hunters and Poachers*, 187.
[53] Anon ('M.N.'), "Estcourt, Giles (d.1587), of Salisbury, Wilts." Member Biographies, The History of Parliament, accessed 22 July 2018. http://www.historyofparliamentonline.org/volume/1558-1603/member/estcourt-giles-1587.
[54] Manning, *Hunters and Poachers*, 19.
[55] Manning, *Hunters and Poachers*, 199; 24.
[56] James and Gerrard, *Clarendon*, 110.
[57] John Fletcher, *Gardens of Earthly Delight: the history of deer parks* (Oxford: Windgather, 2011), 110.

seventeenth century. In 1630–33, 500 oaks were felled for 'making the Paddock Course',[58] which probably followed the route of a predecessor mentioned in 1603 when *c*.£46 was accounted for repairs, including to the 'Great Rails' and 'parrocks'.[59] These were probably the deer course/ paddock course itself and the enclosures (parrocks) into which deer were corralled ahead of their pursuit along it. A comparable course was constructed in the 1630s at Lodge Park in Gloucestershire, described in 1634 as accompanied by 'hansome contriv'd Pens... where the Deere are kept, and turn'd out for the Course'.[60]

Gascoigne commented that in such pailed or railed courses 'it is easie to see whiche way the cource is to be made: since the Deare...cannot [swerve]'. Coursing, therefore, provided recreation 'without unmeasurable toyle and payne' contrasting with par force hunting, in which 'the pastyme be great, yet... the toyle and payne is also exceedyng great'.[61] This relative ease may lie behind women's association with paddocks, little parks and other more enclosed areas. Their connection in contemporary thought with parks generally is evident in John Coke's comment in 1550 that '[In England] it is a fine thing to see what a great number of parks there are, wonderfully full of venison... so that when the ladies... divert themselves, they draw their bows and kill these animals, which is a very exquisite pleasure'.[62] From a French perspective this was not good sport, since 'killing a beast in a park is not hunting... It is not to be wondered at that the English ladies kill them with a bow, for the poor beasts go where they want them to'.[63] Thomas Elyot (d.1546) concurred, opining that killing deer in parks with bows or greyhounds 'containeth no commendable solace and exercise'. Elyot associated coursing with greyhounds with studious men or those otherwise lacking in martial courage – and with gentlewomen 'which fear neither sun nor wind for impairing their beauty... Peradventure they shall be thereat less idle than... at home in their chambers'.[64] Thus in contrast to the masculine practice of poaching, often on the peripheries of parks, the parks themselves and their internal enclosures (such as Clarendon's parrocks) may have provided, or were meant to appear to provide, 'safe' terrain for women to take their recreation. It is informative, therefore, to consider the gender of hunting participants in the two parks, and if possible to identify precisely where in them women hunted. This is problematic for Framlingham since the Game Roll rarely identifies locations, although neither it nor the Penruddock document gives the impression of a landscape dominated by female hunters.

For Framlingham in 1515–19 six women are mentioned: Lady Vere (Elizabeth Trussell, second wife of John de Vere, fifteenth earl of Oxford), the Prioress of Campsey (Elizabeth Everard), 'Thomas Cook's daughter', Lady Bowser (Katherine Bourchier, wife of John, second Baron Berners), [65] Mistress Margaret Hassett, and Mary Tudor, younger sister of Henry VIII, known in the roll as 'the French queen'. In contrast, a full 82 male names appear.[66] Most of the women (and indeed the vast majority of the men) received gifts of venison, with Mary the only lady recorded as having hunted in person, killing four bucks in summer 1516 and possibly two fawns (a third fawn is recorded by Chambyr as having been 'sent for' by her).[67] However, that Katherine Howard, Lady Berkeley (d.1596), great granddaughter of the second duke, devoted herself to hunting and was considered exceptionally proficient with the longbow, suggests that Howard women commonly spent many hours in the field.[68] John Smyth (d.1640), who knew Katherine in old age and claimed she showed him her 'bowes, arrowes, glove, bracer, [and] scarfe', remembered her wistfully recalling her hunting years.[69]

In George Penruddock's Ranger's Book, 97 men's and 12 women's names appear for 1572–75 including Elizabeth I, receiving deer by warrant and for her visit to the park in 1574, although she is not recorded as having taken part in the action.[70] Most of those named received gifts, with only 19 men listed as killing deer themselves, of which five were the park's keepers, and (again) just one woman definitely hunted. This was George Penruddock's wife Anne, who killed two bucks in the parrocks on one occasion in September 1573 – not much of a tally since Penruddock alone finished off eight bucks in the parrocks over three occasions in 1572–73, on one of which he was accompanied by the earl of Pembroke. But Lady Penruddock also hunted at Whitmarsh, inside the park and relatively close to her home at Ivychurch. Not once is she recorded as hunting in the more open space of the launds or the more liminal area of the Out Woods, unlike her husband.

It has been noted that deer in extremely large parks such as Clarendon could be more wild than tame, and that hunting in such spaces was akin to a hunt in open landscapes or woodland.[71] The park's less obviously enclosed spaces

[58] PRO E 178/4728.

[59] TNA: PRO E 101/542/21, *ff*.1–3; TNA: PRO E 101/140/14, m.4. Oliver Rackham interprets the 'parockes' made in 1542–4 at Fairmead Park, Epping Forest, as enclosures into which deer were corralled for this purpose. See Rackham, "Lodges and Standings." In *Epping Forest through the Eyes of the Naturalist*, ed. Mark W. Hanson, (Romford: Essex Field Club, 1992), 15.

[60] Katie Fretwell, "Lodge Park, Gloucestershire: a rare surviving deer course and Bridgeman layout," *Garden History* 23, no. 2 (1995): 136.

[61] *Turbervile's Booke*, 247.

[62] Quotes from Stokes, "Blood Sports," 159; 169–70.

[63] Quoted in Emma Griffin, *Blood Sport: hunting in Britain since 1066* (London: Yale University Press, 2007), 64.

[64] Stanford E. Lehmberg (ed.), *Sir Thomas Elyot: the book named the governor, 1531* (London: Dent, 1962), 68.

[65] "Houses of Austin nuns: Priory of Campsey," in *A History of the County of Suffolk*, vol. 2, ed. William Page (London, 1975), 112–15; James P. Carley, "Bourchier, John, second Baron Berners (*c*.1467–1533)," *Oxford Dictionary of National Biography*, accessed 5 July 2017, http://www.oxforddnb.com/view/article/2990.

[66] Unfortunately Shirley did not transcribe the recipients or slayers of a further 537 deer he took care to list. However, given the male-to female ratio in the printed version, the vast majority are likely to have been men.

[67] 'The queen came again and killed four bucks', p.261.

[68] Manning, *Hunters and Poachers*, 13.

[69] John Maclean (ed.), *The Berkeley manuscripts: the lives of the Berkeleys, lords of the honour, castle and manor of Berkeley... from 1066 to 1618, by John Smyth (1567–1640)* (Gloucester: J. Bellows, 1883–85), 285.

[70] See below.

[71] Griffin, *Blood Sport*, 65.

may therefore have appealed to men, especially those with a martial background like George Penruddock. Of 12 named kill sites in the Ranger's Book associated with Penruddock, Lord Pembroke or a few named local gentlemen, the Out Woods, on the park's southern boundary, appear a full six times. The Launds appear twice (if one counts Bright's Lodge at Shergallgate on the site of the present Ranger's Lodge, adjacent to them), the wooded Goodales coppice once, and the parrocks three times. In these locations 26 deer were killed, all male except for a single doe, presumably caught in the crossfire since she appears to have met her end alongside a prickett, but it is noteworthy that the vast majority (21 animals) were mature bucks. The data reflect the timing of the visits, which occurred in buck season, but may also represent a choice of more challenging terrain by the male nobility and gentry, and of what they perceived to be worthy prey. As Matthew Stokes puts it, in the sixteenth century 'the rising popularity of coursing... and shooting at animals from blinds in enclosed parks had threatened to remove most of [hunting's] physical hardship and danger'.[72]

Deeper analysis of the men and women listed highlights differences in the ways these two parks were used. Of the 82 men named in the Framlingham document 12 were clergy, 18 were knights (listed as 'sir') and four were members of the secular nobility – Thomas Howard second Duke of Norfolk (1443–1524), his third son Lord Edmund Howard (1478–1539), Lord Christopher Willoughby (c.1482–1540), younger brother of the 11th Baron Willoughby de Eresby, and Lord Curzon (1491–1550). The Duke of Norfolk himself appears only four times, receiving or giving deer by warrant, while in contrast the Earl of Pembroke is mentioned 30 times in the Penruddock document, often hunting himself, and a further nine entries record deer being dispatched by his hounds. The discrepancy may be accounted for by the ages of the Duke and Earl; Norfolk was around 72 years of age and Pembroke 38 when the respective documents were begun.

Of the 97 men named in the Penruddock document, 10 were titled 'my lord', seven as 'sir' and seven were clergy. The remaining 73 appear as 'Mr' or without a title. In contrast with Framlingham, then, a marginally wider social mix benefited from Clarendon Park in the 1570s. In addition, many more men's names are recorded more than once, suggesting a landscape thrown open to a favoured circle of local gentry after the palace had gone out of use. Aside from Pembroke, George Penruddock and the keepers, however, no huntsman appears more than once although the presence of hunting parties – the keepers Bright and Batter 'made their frind(es) ij corse[s]',[73] and 'Mr Thistelltwhaite and other gentillmen' killed a sorrel and a pricket in the Out Woods[74] – indicates that the park was a locus for the affirmation and construction of male group identities at various social levels.

[72] Stokes, "Blood Sports," 158.
[73] WSA 549/8, f.13d.
[74] WSA 549/8, f.16.

In the end, though, evidence in the two documents to back up the spatial theories relating to women to parks is tentative at best. Anne Penruddock died in 1573, the same year she is recorded as hunting, and in any case the documents' chronological parameters mean that they can only provide a snapshot. Nevertheless, it is possible to discern Lady Penruddock's networks of patronage from her gifts of venison. In 1573, Robert Bright killed a buck 'by my ladies gifte' to William Herbert which was sent to a Mistress Estcourte; Edward Green, the forester of Shergallgate, sent bucks on her behalf to Thomas Marshall, Miles Matthew and a Mr Earthe, and the keeper George Batter sent others to Mr Tucker, John Penruddock and a Mr Proctor. There were also gifts to London. Such benefactions show that Clarendon Park was still managed much as in medieval times; its venison a means of securing local and wider patronage, sustaining largesse and demonstrating social status.

The Authority to Govern, the Power to Hunt – Royal Women at Framlingham and Clarendon

The women named in the Framlingham Game roll were from a narrower social range than the men, with four of the six mentioned from the seigneurial strata, as were eight of the 12 listed in the Penruddock document – a comparable tally. Alongside the heavy use of Clarendon Park by Lord Pembroke, and despite that park's arguably wider accessibility in the 1570s, parks clearly remained exclusive spaces in which status, as well as gender was played out. This performance was perhaps even more defined by the multiplicity of internal divisions, in which the constructedness of the social order was made doubly clear against the background of the status-affirming hunt.[75]

Mary Tudor's 1516 visit to Framlingham occurred in the year of her return from France with her second husband, Charles Brandon, Duke of Suffolk. Brandon's family is pointedly absent from the Framlingham Game Rolls, having only twice received a buck from the park in a ten-year period, which may represent a rift stretching back to the Wars of the Roses when Suffolk and Norfolk took opposite sides.[76] Two years earlier, Mary's first meeting with her previous husband Louis XII (d.1515) near Abbeville had involved Louis 'unexpectedly' discovering his bride's party while hunting, accompanied by a party of 200 (whose surprise was probably dimmed by the couple's ostentatious matching outfits of crimson velvet and cloth of gold).[77] Although the setting for such staged nuptial meetings was fluid, the hunt was a relatively frequent

[75] Amy L. Tigner, *Literature and the Renaissance Garden from Elizabeth I to Charles II: England's paradise* (London: Routledge, 2012), 16.
[76] Diarmaid MacCulloch, *Suffolk and the Tudors: politics and religion in an English county 1500–1600* (Oxford: Oxford University Press, 1986), 57.
[77] Retha M. Warnicke, "Henry VIII's Greeting of Anne of Cleves and Early Modern Court Protocol," *Albion* 28 (1996): 583; Erin A. Sadlack, *The French Queen's Letters: Mary Tudor Brandon and the politics of marriage in sixteenth-century Europe* (Basingstoke: Palgrave Macmillan, 2011), 69. James IV of Scotland had first met his new bride in a similar faux-hunting scenario in 1503 (Warnicke, "Henry VIII's Greeting," 584).

feature in them. In sixteenth-century literature it was often a metaphor for courtship, marriage and seduction, all of which gained further impetus in the idealised space of a park, which by the early modern period functioned also as symbolic of long and successful lineage.[78] Not all of Mary and Louis's meeting was romantic hyperbole, however, since Mary was an accomplished huntswoman. A chronicler at Abbeville had enthused – highlighting the link between hunting and good rule – that 'she loves the hunt and shoots an arrow in the English fashion so well that it is a marvel… this will be a lady of boldness… she is not afraid of anything, and here rules wisely her people as one could wish'.[79] Indeed, although much good work has been done on medieval women and hunting, the links between gender, authority and hunting in the sixteenth century remain underexplored.

The hunting skills of Elizabeth I, whose visit to Clarendon Park in 1574 is recorded in the Penruddock document, were viewed similarly. Until recent analysis of the Ranger's Book,[80] the only known detail came from an account of 1578, which first describes her reception by the earl of Pembroke on Friday 3 September at Wilton House, on return from her progress to Bristol. Although the queen is unlikely to have entered Clarendon Park in the same fashion, the account gives context for her visit and hints at the pomp which no doubt took place there. Mirroring the format of royal entries, Pembroke ranged scores of liveried horsemen on a hill five miles from Wilton, 'one from another about seaven foot, and about fifteene foot from the highway… and another ranke of the Earl's Gentlemen's servants… about a stone's cast behind their masters stood on horsebacke in like order'.[81] Elizabeth's procession entered the gate of Wilton House to a volley of gunfire, before proceeding through the outer court, 'beset on bothe sides… with the Earles men as thicke as could be standing one by another'. The following day she chose ('appoynted') to hunt in Clarendon Park, although one suspects the choice had already been made for her since the Earl:

> Had prepared a very faire and pleasant banquett [house] for her to dyne in; but that day happened soe great raine, that although it was fenced with… [tapestries], yet it could not defend the wett, by meanes whereof the Queen dyned within the Lodge, and the Lords dyned in the Banquett-house; and after dinner the rayne ceased for a while, during which tyme many deare coursed with greyhounds were overturned; soe, as the tyme served, great pleasure was shewed.[82]

The 'lodge' was probably that originally built by Edward III, originally called 'the lodge on the laund',[83] which stood opposite the palace site on the launds, close to a system of paddocks shown on the parliamentary map of *c.*1650 and close to the deer course first recorded in 1603.

Thanks to the transcription of the Penruddock document, we now know that a full 340 bucks were killed during Elizabeth's visit,[84] in what the above account suggests was a relatively short period of time. It is unclear how many of these beasts were merely butchered to celebrate the occasion,[85] but the coursing would have been a magnificent spectacle, underscored by the banqueting house's enveloping tapestries. The proceedings must have been comparable to the 1541 deer drive at Hatfield Chase, Yorkshire, presided over by Henry VIII, in which over 200 deer were brought down in one day.[86] Although thwarted by the weather, Pembroke probably aimed for the type of entertainment provided for Elizabeth at Cowdray House (Sussex) in 1591, for which 'delicate bowers' were constructed,[87] and when:

> Her Highness took a horse with all her train and rode into the park where was a… bower prepared, under which were her Highness's musicians… a crossbow by a nymph with a sweet song delivered into her hands to shoot at the deer (about some thirty in number) put into a paddock; of which number she killed three or four and the Countess of Kildare one.[88]

That same evening, Elizabeth ascended Cowdray's 'banqueting tower' to watch greyhounds coursing and killing 16 bucks below.[89]

From *c.*1560 the aristocratic garden (and by inference the park) was increasingly idealised 'both as a physical space and a mental construct', allowing it to cement 'political and personal aspirations and to map... the nation'.[90] Hunting in such spaces both created and broadcast social relationships between the monarch and the aristocracy, and the visitors who accompanied them.[91] Elizabeth's journeys have recently been re-evaluated as social spectacles in which the exchange of power and influence with her highest subjects was enacted,[92] and Clarendon

[78] Warnicke, "Henry VIII's Greeting," 567; Ward, "Cultural Depictions," 187, 193.

[79] Sadlack, *The French Queen's Letters*, 72.

[80] See Richardson, *The Forest, Park and Palace*, and James and Gerrard, *Clarendon*.

[81] John Nichols, *The Progresses and Public Processions of Queen Elizabeth*… vol. 1 (London: Society of Antiquaries, 1823), 409.

[82] Nichols, *The Progresses and Public Processions of Queen Elizabeth*… vol. 1, 409..

[83] See Richardson, *The Forest, Park and Palace*, 74–82. 'Launds', from which the word lawn derives, were the open, grassy areas in parks where deer were kept.

[84] WSA 549/8, f.23.

[85] James and Gerrard, *Clarendon*, 110.

[86] Griffin, *Blood Sport*, 70.

[87] Caroline Adams, "Queen and Country: the significance of Elizabeth I's progress in Surrey, Sussex and Hampshire in 1591," PhD thesis, University of Chichester, 2012, 155.

[88] Cited in Keith Thomas, *Man and the Natural World: changing attitudes in England 1500–1800* (London: Allen Lane, 1983), 147.

[89] Manning, *Hunters and Poachers*, 201.

[90] Tigner, *Literature and the Renaissance Garden*, 5.

[91] David Rollason, *The Power of Place: rulers and their palaces, landscapes, cities, and holy places* (Woodstock: Princeton University Press, 2016), 151.

[92] Felicity Heal, "Giving and Receiving on Royal Progress," in *The Progresses, Pageants, and Entertainments of Queen Elizabeth I*, ed. Jayne E. Archer et al. (Oxford: Oxford University Press, 2007), 47.

Park was thus a backdrop against which the second earl of Pembroke enacted his ambition. Indeed, he enjoyed royal favour for most of his life and James I's grant of Clarendon Forest and Park to his son William, the third earl, conferred the most complete control ever to a subject over a royal hunting reserve.[93] At the same time Elizabeth's queenly authority and right to rule were simultaneously reinforced, especially given Clarendon's ancient association with the Crown. For her, hunting was more than a pleasurable pastime; it was a performance to be viewed through the lens of the monarch's unique political and social position.[94] Moreover in a Renaissance world of resurgent classical learning contemporaries perhaps understood the allusions to the Emperor Domitian's legendary slaughter of hundreds of wild animals at a time in his park. Thus the queen, aged 40 at the time of her visit, confirmed her right to govern, 'because [she still] had the power to hunt', just as her father Henry VIII had done despite illness and obesity in his later years.[95]

The early modern royal hunt was also a metaphor for military power, the deer acting as surrogates for the monarch's enemies;[96] an allegory perhaps doubly resonant in view of Elizabeth's sex, which prevented her from personally leading military manoeuvres. Moreover, the queen's own love of the hunt may have strengthened further the links between women and parkland hunting. Her image as virginal huntress was a key element in her symbolic armoury; her pride in her chastity precluding her riding to hounds on a standard hunting-saddle (or at least preventing her being depicted doing so) – an activity believed to loosen the 'man's seat' in women.[97] It is therefore no surprise that like other sixteenth-century ladies, Elizabeth instead chose to course deer or shoot at them in enclosures.

That the ideological power stemming from hunting communicated fitness to rule is apparent in George Gascoigne's claim, published in 1575, a year after the queen's visit to Clarendon, that Brutus, legendary founder of British civilisation (and supposed ancestor of the Tudors), first introduced hunting to Britain.[98] According to Sir Thomas Cockayne in 1591, the sport was later regulated by King Arthur's knight Sir Tristram, who invented 'the terms in hunting, hawking and measures of blowing'.[99] Such allusions to lineage, chivalry and the advancement of civilisation intertwined with the place of hunting, and parks, as significant elements in late sixteenth-century English national identity.[100] Two years after Elizabeth's visit to Clarendon, William Lambarde published his *Perambulation of Kent* (1576), listing the county's 52 parks ahead of its markets and fairs, thus underscoring their centrality to the lives of his gentry readership,[101] and the sheer number of parks in England was proudly relayed by countless others. Among these was the antiquarian John Stowe, who declared with pride in his *Annales of England* (1580, revd 1592) that there were 'more parks in England than in all Europe besides'.[102] Thus the hunt, its quarry, and the landscapes in which it was performed symbolised a glorious royal past and a noble present, bestowing a mythical character on the English polity,[103] and indeed the realm. Little wonder that the 'hard landscaping' of parks in the later sixteenth century was harnessed to emphasise such notions.

Conclusions: Constructed Spaces, Idealised Places

There is little solid evidence in either the Framlingham Park Game Roll or George Penruddock's Ranger's Book to corroborate the spatial theories regarding women and parks recently put forward – which is not to say they are invalid. As this paper has shown, women, parks and the forms of hunting that took place within them were firmly linked in the sixteenth-century mindset. Most notably, although women are largely invisible at both Framlingham and Clarendon, it transpires that men often occupied the peripheries, either by choice of terrain or by virtue of their status and/or the unlawful nature of their hunting. What is clear is that while much good work has been done on *medieval* women and hunting, wider links between gender, authority, hunting and landscape in the sixteenth century remain fully to be explored. Undoubtedly over the sixteenth century the landscapes in which hunting was performed acquired heightened levels of theatricality,[104] evident in the marking out of areas within parks such as Clarendon with its deer course, standing and systems of paddocks, in which we did find one woman, Anne Penruddock, hunting.

Matthew Johnson has linked the proliferation of lists in early-modern documents to enclosure in the landscape, seeing in each an attempt to rationalise and order the world,[105] and in the late-sixteenth century parks, like gardens, became more carefully contrived and subdivided.[106] This conceptual shift through the 1500s is echoed in the very structure of the Framlingham and Penruddock documents. The first merely lists people alongside the deer they killed or were warranted, although unlike Penruddock, Richard Chambyr dated his accounts not only by regnal year, but also by year since his appointment as keeper.[107]

[93] Manning, *Hunters and Poachers*, 30.
[94] Stokes, "Blood Sports," 171–72.
[95] Rollason, *The Power of Place*, 156.
[96] Manning, *Hunters and Poachers*, 196.
[97] Ward, "Cultural Depictions," 199.
[98] George Gascoigne, *The Noble Art of Venerie or Hunting* (London: Thomas Purfoot, 1611), 3.
[99] Quoted in Dan Beaver, "The Great Deer Massacre: animals, honor, and communication in Early Modern England," *Journal of British Studies* 38, no. 2 (1999): 189.
[100] Richardson, "Pale Reflections," 176.
[101] Cited in Susan Pittman, "Elizabethan and Jacobean Deer Parks in Kent," *Archaeologia Cantiana* 132 (2012): 53, 55.
[102] Quoted in Shirley, *Some Account of English Deer Parks*, 28. For other examples see Richardson, "Pale Reflections."
[103] Beaver, "The Great Deer Massacre," 190.
[104] Linda L. Peck, *Court Patronage and Corruption in Early Stuart England* (London: Routledge, 2003), 19; Heal, "Giving and Receiving," 48.
[105] Matthew H. Johnson, *An Archaeology of Capitalism* (Oxford: Blackwell, 1996), 78, 206.
[106] Griffin, *Blood Sport*, 70.
[107] MacCulloch, *Suffolk and the Tudors*, 56.

Penruddock's document, arranged primarily according to the hunting calendar, gives either the name of the underkeeper as a guide to location or refers more explicitly to deer 'recoverid in greenes walk', 'killed in the parrocks' or 'died in the Lawnde' and so on.[108] In contrast, the only locations noted in the Framlingham document are outside the park, for example the occasional town to where the venison was sent. As such, poaching inverted not only the normative assumptions and techniques of hunting,[109] but also its conventional locations, which were increasingly marked out clearly inside parks for all to see.

The emphasis on order apparent in George Penruddock's Ranger's Book was echoed in late sixteenth-century elite landscapes, at a time when texts on gardening and husbandry had begun to express scientific interest in the natural world, promoting the relationship between man and nature as a reflection of the Divine plan.[110] Orderliness and harmony were therefore emphasised, the new repertoire of park architecture helping to avoid what, in Gervase Markham's words, might otherwise be 'a Chaos of confusednesse'.[111] Structures like the paddocks at Clarendon and Cowdray along with deer courses, bowers, standings and banqueting houses, also amplified novel divisions of social space. Likewise they obfuscated the division between 'outside' and 'inside', 'bowers' being found in both early modern houses and gardens, in which settings they often offered greater privacy.[112] Indeed it has been argued that garden buildings served similar functions to the upper chambers of medieval gatehouses, whose large windows afforded pleasant views over parks and whose interior decoration, frequently including tapestries, suggests their purpose as venues for pleasurable activities.[113] The arras hangings of Elizabeth I's banqueting house at Clarendon replicated such arrangements, underscoring an increasingly blurred division between indoor and outdoor space.

Parks were thus the backdrop against which Tudor and Stuart landowners began to explore and develop the 'dialogue between architecture and landscape' that would dominate subsequent centuries,[114] culminating in the eighteenth-century country house landscapes that would obscure the significance of post-medieval deer parks both physically and in terms of modern scholarly endeavour. In fact an argument can – and should – be made that the deer park reached its height of significance in the 1570s, when country-house building was reaching a zenith,[115] when George Gascoigne was writing on genteel hunting, and when William Lambarde was emphasising the importance of parks to his county gentry readership. Not coincidentally this was also when George Penruddock compiled his Ranger's Book, which, in its level of description and detail, deserves a great deal more attention.

Acknowledgements

I would like to thank several people for their comments and ideas. My gratitude goes to Nicola Clark, Eloise Kane, Naomi Sykes and Richard Thomas for a lively Twitter discussion regarding the 'suits' for hounds. Thanks also to Mark Allen for reading drafts, and to Ken Taylor for putting up with yet more conversations about deer. My greatest thanks, however, go to Tom James for supervising my PhD, occasioning the discovery of the Penruddock document, and to Chris Gerrard for inspiring my interest in medieval (and post-medieval) landscapes.

Bibliography

Unpublished primary sources

The National Archives (TNA).

DL 39/2/20. File of Wiltshire forest eyre... 21 August, 3 Hen VII... Clarendon forest.

STAC 2/11/31. Court of Star Chamber: Proceedings, Henry VIII. Plaintiff: Edward Cressett, ranger of Clarendon Park... Defendant: Margaret Yorke: compassing to destroy the King's game... and causing her servants to assault the keepers.

Wiltshire and Swindon Archives (WSA).

549/8. Papers of the Penruddocke Family of Compton Chamberlayne (1570–75), ff.7–23d.

Published primary sources

Blome, Richard. *The Gentleman's Recreation.* London: Freeman Collins, 1686.

Britton, John, ed. *The Natural History of Wiltshire by John Aubrey FRS, Written Between 1656 and 1691.* London: Wiltshire Topographical Society, 1847.

Gascoigne, George. *The Noble Art of Venerie or Hunting.* London: Thomas Purfoot, 1611.

Lambarde, William. *A Perambulation of Kent... written in the yeere 1570, first published in the year 1576...* London: Baldwin, Cradock and Joy, 1826.

Lehmberg, Stanford E., ed. *Sir Thomas Elyot: the book named the governor, 1531.* London: Dent, 1962.

Rotuli Litterarum Clausarum I, 1204–1224. London: Record Commission, 1833.

Maclean, John, ed. *The Berkeley Manuscripts: the lives of the Berkeleys, lords of the honour, castle and manor of Berkeley... from 1066 to 1618, by John Smyth (1567–1640).* Gloucester: J. Bellows, 1883–85.

[108] WSA 549/8, f.13; f.15.

[109] Beaver, "The Great Deer Massacre," 197.

[110] Paula Henderson, *The Tudor House and Garden* (London: Yale University Press, 2005), 31, 146.

[111] Gervase Markham, *The English Husbandman* (London 1613–15, new edn 1635), ch. II, quoted in Henderson, *The Tudor House and Garden*, 31.

[112] Crane, "Illicit Privacy," 8.

[113] Henderson, *The Tudor House and Garden*, 70, 69.

[114] Felicity Heal, "Food Gifts, the Household and the Politics of Exchange in Early Modern England," *Past and Present* 199, no.1 (2008): 44.

[115] Susan Lasdun, *The English Park: royal, public and private* (New York: Vendome Press, 1992), 27.

Markham, Gervase. *The English Husbandman*. London 1613–15, new edn 1635.

Nichols, John. *The Progresses and Public Processions of Queen Elizabeth...* vol. 1. London: Society of Antiquaries, 1823.

The Framlingham Park Game Roll. Appendix 2. In Cummins, John, *The Hound and the Hawk: the art of medieval hunting*. London: Phoenix Press, 2001.

Turbervile's Booke of Hunting 1576. New York: Clarendon Press, 1908.

Published secondary sources

Alexander, Magnus. *Framlingham Castle, Suffolk: the landscape context – desk-top assessment*. Research Department Report Series no. 106. Cambridge: English Heritage 2007.

Almond, Richard. *Daughters of Artemis: the huntress in the Middle Ages and Renaissance*. Woodbridge: D.S. Brewer, 2009.

Almond, Richard. "Femmes Fatale: iconography and the courtly huntress in the later Middle Ages and Renaissance." In *Deer and People*, edited by Karis Baker *et al.*, 257–68. Oxford: Windgather, 2015.

Anon ('M.N'.). "Estcourt, Giles (d.1587), of Salisbury, Wilts." Member Biographies, The History of Parliament. Accessed 22 July 2018. http://www.historyofparliamentonline.org/volume/1558-1603/member/estcourt-giles-1587.

Atkinson, Richard F. *The Manors and Hundred of Alderbury: lords, lands and livery*. Alderbury: R.F. Atkinson, 1995.

Beaumont James, Tom, and Christopher M. Gerrard. *Clarendon: landscape of kings*. Macclesfield: Windgather, 2007.

Beaver, Dan. "The Great Deer Massacre: animals, honor, and communication in early modern England." *Journal of British Studies* 38, no. 2 (1999):187–216.

Bindoff, Stanley T. "Penruddock, Sir George (d.1581), of Ivy Church and Compton Chamberlayne, Wilts., Broxbourne, Herts. and Clerkenwell, Mdx." Member Biographies, The History of Parliament. Accessed 22 May 2018. http://www.historyofparliamentonline.org/volume/1558-1603/member/penruddock-sir-george-1581.

Carley, James P. "Bourchier, John, second Baron Berners (*c.*1467–1533)." *Oxford Dictionary of National Biography*. Accessed 5 July 2017. http://www.oxforddnb.com/view/article/2990.

Christie, William D. *A Life of Anthony Ashley Cooper, first Earl of Shaftesbury, 1621–1683*, vol. 1. London: Macmillan, 1871.

Crane, Mary T. "Illicit Privacy and Outdoor Spaces in Early Modern England." *Journal for Early Modern Cultural Studies* 9, no. 1 (2009): 4–22.

Creighton, Oliver .H. "Castle Studies and the European Medieval Landscape: traditions, trends and future research directions." *Landscape History* 30 (2009): 5–20.

Cummins, John. *The Hound and the Hawk: the art of medieval hunting*. London: Phoenix Press, 2001.

de Belin, Mandy. "English Icons: the deer and the horse." In *Deer and People*, edited by Karis Baker *et al.*, 248–56. Oxford: Windgather, 2015.

Fletcher, John. *Gardens of Earthly Delight: the history of deer parks*. Oxford: Windgather, 2011.

Fretwell, Katie. "Lodge Park, Gloucestershire: a rare surviving deer course and Bridgeman layout." *Garden History* 23, no. 2 (1995): 133–44.

Friedman, John B. "Coats, Collars, and Capes: royal fashions for animals in the early modern period." *Medieval Clothing and Textiles* 12 (2016): 61–94.

Gilchrist, Roberta. *Gender and Archaeology: contesting the past*. London: Routledge, 1999.

Griffin, Emma. *Blood Sport: hunting in Britain since 1066*. London: Yale University Press, 2007.

Head, David M. "Howard, Thomas, second duke of Norfolk (1443–1524)." *Oxford Dictionary of National Biography*. Accessed 11 April 2017. http://www.oxforddnb.com/view/article/13939.

Heal, Felicity. "Food Gifts, the Household and the Politics of Exchange in Early Modern England." *Past and Present* 199, no.1 (2008): 41–70.

Heal, Felicity. "Giving and Receiving on Royal Progress." In *The Progresses, Pageants, and Entertainments of Queen Elizabeth I*, edited by Jayne E. Archer *et al.*, 46–61. Oxford: Oxford University Press, 2007.

Henderson, Paula. *The Tudor House and Garden*. London: Yale University Press, 2005.

Houston, Robert A. *Bride Ales and Penny Weddings: recreations, reciprocity, and regions in Britain from the sixteenth to the nineteenth century*. Oxford: Oxford University Press, 2014.

Johnson, Matthew H. *An Archaeology of Capitalism*. Oxford: Blackwell, 1996.

Lasdun, Susan. *The English Park: royal, public and private*. New York: Vendome Press, 1992.

MacCulloch, Diarmaid. *Suffolk and the Tudors: politics and religion in an English county 1500–1600*. Oxford: Oxford University Press, 1986.

Manning, Roger B. *Hunters and Poachers: a cultural history of unlawful hunting in England 1485–1640*. Oxford: Clarendon Press, 1993.

Manning, Roger B. "Unlawful Hunting in England, 1500–1640." *Forest and Conservation History* 38, no. 1 (1994): 16–23.

Mileson, Stephen A., *Parks in Medieval England.* Oxford: Oxford University Press, 2009.

Munsche, Peter B. *Gentlemen and Poachers: The English Game Laws 1671–1831.* Cambridge: Cambridge University Press, 1981.

Page, William, ed. "Houses of Austin nuns: Priory of Campsey." In *Victoria County History: a history of the county of Suffolk*, vol. 2, edited by William Page, 112–15. London, 1975.

Peck, Linda L. *Court Patronage and Corruption in Early Stuart England.* London: Routledge, 2003.

Pittman, Susan. "Elizabethan and Jacobean Deer Parks in Kent." *Archaeologia Cantiana* 132 (2012): 53–81.

Rackham, Oliver. "Lodges and Standings." In *Epping Forest through the Eyes of the Naturalist*, edited by Mark W. Hanson, 8–17. Romford: Essex Field Club, 1992.

Richardson, Amanda. *The Forest, Park and Palace Of Clarendon, c.1200–c.1650: reconstructing an actual, conceptual and documented Wiltshire landscape*, British Archaeological Reports British Series 387. Oxford: BAR Publishing, 2005.

Richardson, Amanda. "'Riding like Alexander, Hunting like Diana': gendered aspects of the medieval hunt and its landscape settings." *Gender and History* 24, no.2 (2012): 253–70.

Richardson, Amanda. "Pale Reflections? Deer parks in contemporary writings from the sixteenth to the later nineteenth century." In *A Fresh Approach: essays presented to Colin Platt in celebration of his eightieth birthday*, edited by Claire Donovan, 169–80. Bristol: Trouser Press, 2014.

Rollason, David. *The Power of Place: rulers and their palaces, landscapes, cities, and holy places*. Woodstock: Princeton University Press, 2016.

Sadlack, Erin A. *The French Queen's Letters: Mary Tudor Brandon and the politics of marriage in sixteenth-century Europe*. Basingstoke: Palgrave Macmillan, 2011.

Sandidge, Marilyn L. "Hunting or Gardening: parks and royal rural space." In *Rural Space in the Middle Ages and Early Modern Age: the spatial turn in premodern studies*, edited by Albrecht Classen, 389–406. Berlin: Walter de Gruyter, 2012.

Shirley, Evelyn P. *Some Account of English Deer Parks*. London: John Murray, 1867.

Swett, Katharine W. "'The Account between Us': honour, reciprocity and companionship in male friendship in the later seventeenth century." *Albion* 31, no. 1 (1999): 1–30.

Sykes, Naomi, "Animal Bones and Animal Parks." In *The Medieval Park: new perspectives*, edited by Robert Liddiard, 49–62. Macclesfield: Windgather, 2007.

Sykes, Naomi. "Animals: the bones of medieval society." In *Reflections: 50 years of medieval archaeology, 1957–2007*, edited by Roberta Gilchrist and Andrew Reynolds, 347–62. Leeds: Maney, 2009.

Thomas, Keith. *Man and the Natural World: changing attitudes in England 1500–1800*. London: Allen Lane, 1983.

Thurley, Simon. *The Royal Palaces of Tudor England: architecture and court life 1460–1547*. London: Yale University Press, 1993.

Tigner, Amy L. *Literature and the Renaissance Garden from Elizabeth I to Charles II: England's Paradise*. London: Routledge, 2012.

Warnicke, Retha M. "Henry VIII's Greeting of Anne of Cleves and Early Modern Court Protocol." *Albion* 28 (1996): 565–85.

Unpublished secondary sources

Adams, Caroline. "Queen and Country: the significance of Elizabeth I's progress in Surrey, Sussex and Hampshire in 1591." PhD thesis, University of Chichester, 2012.

Stokes, Matthew M. "Blood Sports: violence and the performance of masculinity in early modern drama." PhD Thesis, University of Boston, 2015. https://open.bu.edu/handle/2144/14047

Ward, Christopher S. "Cultural Depictions of the European Fallow Deer (*Dama Dama*) 6000 BCE to 1600 CE." PhD Thesis, University of Nottingham, 2017.

12

'Disorders in Religion': The Misbehaving Laity of Elizabethan Winchester

Susan K. Parkinson

Independent Scholar

Abstract: Some may argue that the Reformation concluded in 1559 with Elizabeth's Settlement of Religion, however this was not true of Winchester. This paper provides some insight into how the Settlement was received in this city and focusses on the survival of Catholicism. Local and national sources have been consulted, including evidence provided by the city governors, visitations, the Consistory Court and local courts, bishops' registers, churchwardens' accounts, wills and probate inventories, and the national government. They reveal that Protestantism was not welcomed in Elizabethan Winchester, and the bishops despaired at the conservatism and obstinacy in the cathedral, the college, the gaol, and the city government. Recusants and seminary priests repeatedly troubled the authorities. The defiance of the city remained a problem until the last decade of Elizabeth's reign, when the sources suggest Winchester was conforming more readily and becoming more receptive to Protestantism.

Key words: Winchester, Catholics, Recusancy, Horne, laity, non-communicating

Introduction

In August 1561, Robert Horne,[1] the newly consecrated bishop of the diocese of Winchester, wrote to William Cecil, the Queen's Principal Secretary, to complain about 'disorders in religion'. He found that both 'the common sort' and 'the better sort' of people in the diocese were not conforming to the Elizabethan Settlement of Religion.[2] In 1559, Elizabeth I had established the Church of England by a moderate set of reforms designed to embrace people from across the religious spectrum. Recognition of her role as Supreme Governor of that Church, use of her new Prayer Book and attendance at church services, was less than that demanded by Edward VI, but it proved too great a request for the people of the city of Winchester. The religious changes were received coolly by the laity in Winchester where, within days of the Act of Uniformity being passed by Parliament, the Spanish Ambassador noted to Philip II that 'in the neighbourhood of Winchester they have refused to receive the church service book… and the clergy of the diocese had assembled to discuss what they should do. No mass was being said, whereat the congregations were very much disturbed'.[3] Horne thus faced an uphill battle as he endeavoured to 'reduce th[e] Inhabitaunts of the Citie of Winchester to good uniformytie in Religion' as they did not 'well like and allowe' the new doctrine. He was to find them to be 'veray stubborne'[4] in their persistence in their 'disorders in religion'. It is to these 'disorders in religion' displayed by the laity of the city of Winchester that this paper will now turn.

This paper considers the most pressing 'disorders in religion' that perturbed Horne and his successors. These were: recusancy and non-communicating, Catholic services, and finally the laxity and sympathy of important lay persons: churchwardens, keepers of the gaol and the city governors.

Recusancy and Non-Communicating

The 1559 Act of Uniformity had ordered that anyone not attending church, should be fined 12d. for each absence by the churchwardens.[5] Early in Elizabeth's reign, it became apparent to the government that many people in Winchester were not attending their parish church or taking Communion. The government consistently attempted to address the problem of Winchester's recusancy throughout Elizabeth's reign. Their despair can be traced in the official correspondence of the State Papers, whilst their

[1] Robert Horne (1519?–1580), graduate of St John's College with BA, MA, BD and DD (1536–49). He was a zealous advocate of the reformed doctrines, and being a man of learning and a powerful preacher, he soon obtained ecclesiastical preferment as vicar of Matching in Essex (1546), rector of All Hallows in London (1550), chaplain to Edward VI (1550), dean of Durham (1551), and prebendary of Bugthorpe in York Minster (1552). Under Mary I, Horne was deprived of his deanery, his goods were confiscated and he became an exile. He was restored to the deanery in 1559. On White's deprivation at Winchester, Horne was consecrated as Bishop in February 1561. Ralph Houlbrooke, "Horne, Robert (1513x15–1579), bishop of Winchester." *Oxford Dictionary of National Biography*. https://doi.org/10.1093/ref:odnb/13792

[2] The National Archives [hereafter TNA] SP12/19/36.

[3] Spanish Calendar No.39, 78, cf. John E. Paul, "Hampshire Recusants in the time of Elizabeth I, with special reference to Winchester," *Proceedings of the Hampshire Field Club and Archaeological Society*, XXI, pt.2, (1959), 63.

[4] TNA SP12/21/7. [Jan. 1562, Horne to Cecil]

[5] Gerald Bray, (ed.), *Documents of the English Reformation*, Library of Ecclesiastical History, (Cambridge: James Clarke, 2004), 332.

lack of success can be witnessed in the official figures for recusancy and non-communicating.

The Act of 1581 'to retain the Queen's Majesty's subjects in their due obedience', made recusancy an indictable offence. A fine of twenty pounds per month of absence, replaced the 12d. fine for each absence. This fine was beyond the means of most recusants; imprisonment was the statutory penalty for failure to pay the fine. In 1586 this was changed to forfeiture to the crown of two-thirds of the recusant's lands, and all his goods and chattels. This did not affect those who did not own land and had few possessions, but some people were dispossessed, and became debtors to the crown. Yet throughout the 1580s, recusancy continued to be a major problem in Winchester. In October 1580, the Privy Council told the newly appointed bishop, John Watson,[6] that they had been informed that, many 'in the towne of Winchester...were fallen away in Relligion'.[7]

In December 1582 the English counties certified their number of recusants to the government. Hampshire was the third most recusant county, reporting 132 recusants, somewhat behind Lancashire with 428, and Yorkshire 327, but nevertheless the most recusant southern county, with double the recusant total of neighbouring Surrey.[8]

The recusants 'obstinately absent themselves' from Communion, and encourage others to do the same, leading by their own example. Of those guilty of this 'soden backeslyding' in religion, many have affirmed to the bishop that 'their consyences would not serve them to come to church'. 'Others have bouldy affirmed that yt is necessarye to have masse, and they hope to heare yt, and th[a]t they had rather heare beare baytinges then the devyne service'.[9]

In the Recusant Rolls of 1581–92, Winchester appears an important centre of Catholicism and recusancy, with over one fifth of Hampshire recusants living in Winchester.[10] The same is true of the Exchequer Pipe Rolls, where prominent Winchester recusants, such as Anthony Uvedall, Richard Warneford, Anthony Norton and Henry Norton, are recorded almost every year from 1591 to 1602.[11] Between November 1601 and November 1602, twenty-five Winchester recusants faced the Exchequer.[12] A variety of people had been reported from Winchester – these included both male and female, married, single or widowed, and both gentry and the occupations of yeoman, husbandman, labourer, tailor and net-maker were represented. The offenders came from the parishes of St Bartholomew, St Mary Kalendar, and St Michael. Many wives were presented with their husbands. The evidence from the Exchequer suggests that many in Winchester were obstinate recusants, but we should remember that only those with money or land tended to be penalised by the Exchequer fines – it is thus necessary to consider the recusants subjected to the Winchester Consistory Court in order to gauge a fuller picture of Catholic dissent.

The surviving Consistory Court Books are incomplete for Elizabeth's reign, with gaps occurring in 1571, 1580, 1584–85, 1592, and 1597–98, and so all figures quoted below perhaps would be higher if all records had survived. We must also remember that the actual figures for recusancy and non-communicating are likely to be far greater than the actual number reported to both the Exchequer and Consistory Court.

During Elizabeth's reign, the surviving Consistory Court records name 131 recusants, 89 non-communicants, and 23 people cited for both offences either in the same case, or at a separate time to the Consistory Court. Of this total of 243 religious deviants, eight were repeating offenders for recusancy, and three for non-communicating. Most Winchester parishes seem to have reported to the Court, with St Thomas, St Maurice, St Mary Kalendar, St Bartholomew, and St Michael in the Soke, and St Clements all reporting over twenty deviants each.

Some citations were for not attending church on a specific occasion, or not taking communion on a religious occasion, usually Easter. Other cases, however, involved lengthy periods of recusancy or non-communicating. Thomas Ynges, William Cowdry, and Lawrence Smith, from St Thomas's in Winchester, were cited at Court in 1599, 'for not receiving the Co[mmun]ion these vij yeres'.[13]

Some people refused to conform, even after appearing at the Consistory Court. Thomas Brabon and his wife, of St Mary Kalendar in Winchester, had appeared at the Court, cited for recusancy in December 1576.[14] Yet nine years on, in 1585, Thomas Brabon's name appeared in 'A Catalogue of Papistes refusing to come to Church'.[15]

---

[6] John Watson (1520–1584), educated at Oxford, BA (1539), MA (1544), MD (1575). He became known as a reformer under Edward VI, and in 1551 he became second prebend in Winchester Cathedral. He managed to retain his prebend during Mary's reign, and added the rectories of Kelshall (Herts) and Winchfield (Hants) to it in 1554. He became chancellor of St Paul's Cathedral in 1558, and after Elizabeth's accession he was made archdeacon of Surrey in 1559, rector of South Warnborough (Hants) in 1568, and master of the hospital of St Cross, Winchester, around the same time. He was appointed dean of Winchester in 1570, and succeeded Horne as Bishop of Winchester in 1580. Jane Reedy Ladley, "Watson, John (c. 1520–1584), bishop of Winchester." *Oxford Dictionary of National Biography* https://doi.org/10.1093/ref:odnb/28844

[7] John Roche Dasent (ed.), *Acts of the Privy Council of England* (London: Stationery Office, 1890–3), 244.

[8] TNA SP12/156/42.

[9] BL Cotton Titus B III fos.73, 81.

[10] T.J. McCann, and Hugh Bowler (eds), *Recusants in the Exchequer Pipe Rolls, 1581–1592*, Catholic Record Society Record Series 71 (1986); Hugh Bowler (ed.), *Recusant Rolls no 2, 1593–1594. An abstract in English with an explanatory introduction by Dom Hugh Bowler*, Catholic Record Society Record Series 57 (1965); Hugh Bowler (ed.), *Recusant Rolls no 3, 1594–1595 and recusant roll no. 4, 1595–1596. An abstract in English*, Catholic Record Society Record Series 61 (1970).

[11] TNA E377/4–9.

[12] TNA E377/11.

[13] Hampshire Record Office [hereafter HRO] 21M65 C1/27 f.3.

[14] HRO 21M65 C1/19 f.100v.

[15] TNA SP12/183/15.

At the Winchester Consistory Court sessions, some recusants were eager to voice their religious objections at being forced to attend church. In the summer of 1583, Humphrey Rofe of St Maurice's parish insisted that 'the latten service is necessary'.[16] In October 1598, John Clemence and Ralph George from St Maurice[17] and William Hall, a Winchester gentleman, were summoned to the Court for their recusancy.[18] The following month, Richard Smith,[19] Anthony Norton gentleman, Stephen Henslowe gentleman, Thomas Goter, Mary White, Thomas Grove alias Canterton, Mary Goter and Jacob Lake, all from St Clement's parish, were cited to the Consistory Court. All these recusants were charged with long-term or frequent recusancy – all responded by saying that their consciences would not permit their attendance at church. Almost all were excommunicated for their obstinacy.

There are frequent references in the State Papers to the problem of recusant wives and widows in Winchester, and the statistics of the Consistory Court seem to confirm that the female population caused the authorities greater distress than their male counterparts. In November 1580, Bishop Watson wrote to Walsingham that the husbands of recusant wives were demanding to know why they were being punished for their wives' recusancy, when they themselves attended divine service. The husbands were bound over to ensure their wives compliance. Watson also notes that 'there are allso diverse widdowes w[i]thin ye diocesse w[hi]ch are very backward and abstaine from coming to Churche'.[20] The 1603 survey counted 149 recusant men, and 249 recusant women in the Winchester diocese, so it seems the female population were still giving the authorities more cause for concern than their male counterparts, even at the end of Elizabeth's reign.[21] In May 1590, the Privy Council had estimated Hampshire recusants to exceed three hundred – this non-conformity thus seems to have continued unabated.[22] As late as March 1596, the bishop of Winchester informed the government that 'the country abounds with recusants' and Jesuits.[23]

Beyond Elizabeth's reign, concern about the level of recusancy in Winchester continued. The survey of recusants, non-communicants and communicants in each parish in 1603, the first year of James I's reign, provides some useful figures on Catholics in Winchester. The Winchester parishes returned a total of 66 recusants and 26 non-communicants. The total number of communicants for Winchester was 1,755; adding both types of religious deviant to this total, gives us a possible communicative adult population in the Winchester parishes of 1,847. Of the 1,847 people who could have taken communion and attended church, 66 persons, or 3.6 per cent, were recusant, and 26 persons, or 1.4 per cent, were non-communicant.[24] In 1607 Bishop Bilson of Winchester expressed concern in his visitation about the continuing existence of 'recusants' and 'notorious papists'.[25]

Catholic Services

The Winchester recusants were supported in their 'disorders in religion' by the provision of secret Catholic services, provided by the seminary priests.

As early as June 1574, the Privy Council expressed their concern about 'certein secrett assemblies and uses of massinge' in Hampshire, and the bishop and JPs were instructed to search all suspected places.[26] Around 1578, the government listed seventy ports, creeks and landing places in the county, which could be used.[27]

Some Winchester residents offered the priests their homes and consequently protection from the authorities. Private masses and Catholic services were being held behind some closed doors in Winchester homes. In 1576 'a great store of vestments, books and other massing tools to serve lewd purposes' were found in Alexander Dering's house in the Soke of Winchester.[28] Dering was a committed recusant, cited in the Consistory Court in 1570.[29] He had been deputy registrar to Bishop Gardiner.[30]

Jane Knight, widow of St Michael's in Winchester, made her will in June 1580. Her preamble read 'I give my sowle to Allmighty God my redeemer desiring him of his bitt[e]r passion and tender mercy to accept and receive this my simple bequest into his holy handes', and she left money to the cathedral and to St Michael's church. She then made a very interesting bequest of 'certeine Church orname[n]tes w[hi]ch in truste I deliv[er]ed to Mr William Hoorde', and then left 'diverse specialities and writinges to be delivered to Mr Wright for safekeeping'.[31] Jane Knight was a recusant and non-communicant, cited twice in the Consistory Court for these offences in 1568 and 1570, and named as 'Mistress Knight widow' in Horne's list of Winchester recusants in 1577.[32] William Hoorde was entrusted with the task of protecting the Catholic service equipment, as he was a key Winchester recusant, a gentleman from St Mary Kalendar, and 'a v[ery] backward & obstinat p[er]son in matters of Religion', who was to be imprisoned in the House of Correction in November 1580 and was named in the Inquisition of April 1583.[33] In 1585, his name appeared in 'A Catalogue of Papistes refusing to come to Church'.[34]

16 HRO 21M65 C1/22 fos. 138, 141v., 143, 146.
17 HRO 21M65 C1/26 fos.12, 32.
18 HRO 21M65 C1/26 f.22.
19 HRO 21M65 C1/26 f.32.
20 TNA SP12/144/36.
21 BL Harleian 280 (now 157).
22 TNA PC2/17 fos.649–50.
23 TNA SP12/256/1021.
24 BL Harleian 595 f.213v.
25 HRO 21M65 A1/29 f.25.
26 *APC 1574*, pp.257–58.
27 TNA SP15/25/129.
28 TNA SP12/108/40.
29 HRO 21M65 C1/14 fos.202, 205, 270.
30 Adrienne Rosen, "Economic and social aspects of the history of Winchester, 1520–1670," DPhil thesis, University of Oxford, 1975, 89.
31 HRO 1584B/47.
32 HRO 21M65 C1/12 f.5v., C1/14 f.202, PRO SP12/117/10.
33 TNA SP12/144/31, SP12/160/26.
34 TNA SP12/183/15.

In November 1580, the Privy Council suspected William Hoorde of dispersing the Jesuit Challenge. He refused to say where he received it, and we are left wondering if Jane Knight may have aided his acquisition.[35] Suddenly one becomes aware of a Catholic network operating within the city. Sadly, Jane Knight's will does not list any witnesses, and the identity of Mr Wright, whom she left the written material to, is uncertain. There is no Mr Wright cited in the surviving Consistory Court records, nor is a Mr Wright recorded in any of the lists of Winchester recusants. It is possible that Jane was referring to John Wright, rector of St Maurice's church from 1577, and so hinting at his non-conformity.

The influence of the Jesuit priests in Winchester is very evident from the alarm they caused in official circles. In November 1580, Bishop Watson, Sir Henry Radcliffe and others wrote to the Privy Council to inform them that they had apprehended, Elizabeth Saunders, sister of Dr Saunders. They found lewd and forbidden books in her possession and a protestation or challenge of the Jesuits. On her examination they found 'grete obstinacie in p[er] servereance of her profession'. She was committed to the House of Correction in Winchester.[36]

In November 1583, Dr. Bennett of St Cross, Winchester, wrote to Cecil regarding the backwardness in religion in the county, but particularly in the city of Winchester. One reason for the people's non-compliance, he found to be the delayed execution of the two traitors who had 'a marvelouse perverse and most obstinate resolution against the regime[n]t and sov[er]ainte of her Ma[jes]tie in ecc[lesiastica]l causes'. The long delay of their execution had caused great harm, with 'both religion towards god, and obedience toward her Ma[jes]tie' decaying and decreasing daily amongest the people of Winchester. This was owing to the people's 'favour and liking of them', and 'great numbres [were] caried awaie with them into stubborn recusancie'.[37] It is likely that Dr. Bennett was referring to John Body and John Slade, two schoolmasters, who had been supporting the seminary priests. They had been convicted of treason for denying the royal supremacy, and were executed in the autumn of 1583, Slade in Winchester, and Body in Andover.[38]

A search for the 'findinge of Jesuits Priestes' in suspected houses in Winchester was organised on 10 December 1583 at the request of the bishop, who had heard that an assembly was due to meet to hear mass in Winchester. Jenkins and the bishop's servants checked the house of Richard Warnforde, a prominent Winchester recusant, who was most suspected by Jenkins, but found nothing except suggestions that they should try Lady West's house. Lady West, wife of Sir Owen West, lived in St Peter's Street, which was particularly associated with Catholicism from the 1570s onwards.[39] In December 1578 masses had reportedly been held at Lady West's home, and those present included Mr Brig and Mr Bryant, both described as priests and recusants; widow Burt of Long Parish and her two daughters; Jacques that served Lady Peys; and Byrd.[40] Lady West harboured the priest, John Ballard, who later instigated the Babington plot against Elizabeth I.[41] In the search of December 1583 'divers newe and olde papisticall bookes printed and written' were found. In a secret place underground, they uncovered an iron cheste, which contained 'all mann[er] of massing Apparrell', including a chalice; a box of singing cakes; velvet altar cloths; an ivory pax set in wood; two Agnus Dei (both broken but one stuck together so the inscriptions could be read); two double papers imprinted with stars; twenty-four bugles on a string; a paper of myrre; three round glasses like beadstones, which appeared to be another hallowed item; and 'divers newe masse bookes, Manuells and Cathechismes'. The searchers learnt from the confession of Fraunces, the servant of Lady West, that the iron chest had been in the Ladies' Chamber until that morning, when the house learnt that there was to be a search in the city, at which time it was removed to the underground hiding-place for concealment. Elsewhere in the house, about forty old mass and Latin service books were found, and in the Ladies' Chamber, the search party found a 'Superaltare'. The named items were all seized, with some being retained by the searchers, the others being sent to Sir Francis Walsingham for his perusal. The servant was imprisoned and Lady West remained at her house. The bishop with John White, the mayor, and many aldermen, signed the letter to Walsingham which asked for his direction in this matter.[42]

In February 1585, John Gardiner (alias Owen), Roger Brierton and Walter Treveven were apprehended in Winchester by Stephen Cheston and Thomas Bedham, after they had escaped from London upon the detection of Dr. Parry's conspiracy. They were examined by Richard Bird the mayor, and JPs in Winchester on suspicion of papistry. John Owen confessed 'and saieth that he is A Catholique and A seminarie prieste', and had dined at the Warnefords' house in Winchester. He refused to say where or with whom, he had been harboured during the period 13 to 28 February when he was known to have been in the city. Roger Brierton also admitted to being a firm Catholic recusant, but like Owen, refused to confess his harbourers in Winchester. Walter Treveven also admitted recusancy, but gave no details of his Winchester harbourers.[43] In

[35] TNA SP12/144/31.
[36] TNA SP12/144/31, *APC 1580*, 270.
[37] BL Lansdowne 39/183 (original reference 46).
[38] TNA SP12/151/15. John Body, layman and schoolmaster, had entered Winchester College in 1562, and was a fellow of New College 1568–76.
[39] Barbara Carpenter Turner, *A History of Winchester* (Chichester: Phillimore, 1992), 90.
[40] TNA SP12/127/42. Byrd is likely to be James Bird, son of the mayor, Anthony Bird, who was executed for his non-conformity in 1593.
[41] E.S. Washington, "Hampshire and the Catholic Revival of the 1580s." In John Webb, Nigel Yates and Sarah Peacock (eds) *Hampshire Studies presented to Dorothy Dymond on the occasion of her ninetieth birthday* (Portsmouth: Portsmouth City Council, 1981), 62; *Calendar of State Papers Domestic 1581–90*, no.14, 135.
[42] TNA SP12/164/14.
[43] TNA SP12/177/3 I.

March 1585, the bishop found Owen and the two other men had three times refused to be examined on oath, and so sent them onto London, for further examination, as he felt they had more to reveal. It was known that 'persons ignorantly waiward or maliciously discontent' in Winchester had offered the seminary priest and the two Catholics 'harbour and intertaynment'.[44]

Roger Dickenson was found in Winchester around 1585, assisting Thomas Stanney. Dickenson laboured in Winchester for several years, 'a man of great virtue' who had attended Catholics imprisoned in Winchester gaol, providing for all necessities, temporal and spiritual.[45] He was sheltered and aided by Ralph Miller, a poor, illiterate Catholic, the father of ten children, whose home was nearby at Slackstead, but who spent most of his time in Winchester gaol. Miller was perceived by the Council to be 'a verie daungerous and il affected member in thoes partes', and was imprisoned in Bridewell, after revealing the names of English recusants in France, including Lady Paulet's eighteen-year old son.[46] Dickenson's work lay among the poor and the prisoners of Winchester. He had already been committed for his religion and examined by the government as early as January 1584, and had been named by Thomas Dodwell and Lord Hunsdon as 'now apprehended and in prison' in February 1584. It appears his former name was Lasey, and he had been accommodated by Lady West and possibly also by the Beckinsawes in Winchester.[47] Seemingly he escaped, or was released, as he was arrested at Winchester in January 1591[48] and was sent to London with Miller. He was imprisoned in the Clink and interviewed by the Privy Council before returning to Winchester for his trial. In July 1591 Dickenson and Miller were executed together at Winchester.[49] At the same time as these men were sentenced, several young women were condemned to death for having confessed to priests, and heard masses. The public pronouncement of death was postponed until the next day. When the ladies heard sentence pronounced against the priest and layman but not against themselves, they asked not to be separated from their father and brother for they were guilty of the same offences. The judges ordered that they be returned to prison. This was a measure of the following the seminary priests were able to attract amongst the lower classes as well as with the gentry.[50]

A list of Catholic prisoners in the Winchester gaol was recorded in February 1591. Twelve of these had been found with the seminary priest – Richard Jonson.[51]

[44] TNA SP12/277/3.
[45] J. H. Pollen, (ed.), *Unpublished Documents Relating to the English Martyrs Vol. 1 1584–1603*, Catholic Record Society Record Series 5 (1908) 203 – letter of 1 October 1592.
[46] TNA SP12/173/64.
[47] TNA SP12/168/33–34.
[48] TNA SP12/167/59, *APC 1590–1*, 234–35.
[49] Godfrey Anstruther, *The Seminary Priests: A Dictionary of the Secular Clergy of England and Wales 1558–1603* (Ware: St. Edmund's College, 1968), 103.
[50] Pollen, *Unpublished Documents*, 203 – letter of 1st October 1591.
[51] HRO 44M69/G3/112.

Benjamin Beard, grandson of Mrs. Ticheborne of Winchester, and a former Winchester scholar, had been acting as an informant to the government, advising them of the activities and location of Jesuit priests. In March 1594 he suggested to Lord Keeper Pickering that if he was freed from his current imprisonment before Easter, he 'can do the like service at Winchester'.[52] In writing to Morgan Jones at Gray's Inn, in the same month, Benjamin Beard explained that he could go to Winchester Castle, where his uncle, Gilbert Tichborne 'and divers other friends and kindred remain for their consciences', and he would gain much information from them. He also explained that Mrs. Ticheborne had harboured two priests, Fenell and Richards, continually in her house, and whenever a search was made, the priests fled for three or four days. Benjamin Beard also alleged that Jerome Heath of Winchester was not a recusant, nor suspected for his religion, but 'in time of disturbance', he harboured such priests.[53] Also in the opening months of 1594, writing to Mr Jones, a former fellow scholar at Winchester, and now also a prisoner, Benjamin Beard told him that John Ticheborne, the son of Mrs. Ticheborne, was a seminary priest.[54] In March 1597 Nicholas Tichborne, under examination by Attorney General Coke and Solicitor General Fleming, denied the suggestion that Roger Ticheborne had ever heard any sermons by a seminary priest in his house, or in his mother's house. The examination continued into who had attended mass in Mrs. Ticheborne's house, and William Ringwood, Francis Ticheborne, and Thomas Ticheborne were named.[55]

The Laxity of Key Laity

The various Elizabethan bishops of Winchester had cause to complain to the Privy Council about certain groups of the laity who were not assisting in their quest to deal with the 'disorders in religion'. These were: the churchwardens, the keepers of the gaol and the city's governors.

From the churchwardens' accounts and the records of the Consistory Court, it is possible to see the reluctance of the churchwardens to conform to the prescribed religious changes.

In the 1559 Injunctions, Elizabeth ordered that each church should possess the largest volume of the bible, written in English, within three months of the visitation.[56] Yet it was not until between 1566 and 1569, that St John's church in Winchester sold the bible it had been using during Mary's reign, and purchased a new one.[57] The churchwardens were cited at the Consistory Court for failing to provide a copy of the Great Bible in October 1570, but it would seem that this had already been done very recently.[58]

[52] TNA SP12/248/10, SP12/248/88.
[53] TNA SP12/248/30.
[54] TNA SP12/248/88.
[55] TNA SP12/262/67.
[56] TNA SP12/262/67, 336–37.
[57] HRO 88M81W/PW1 fos.27v., 29.
[58] HRO 21M65 C1/14 f.169.

In 1570, the church of Colebrook lacked a Great Bible and in 1588, St Michael's churchwardens were also reported to the Consistory Court for lacking a bible.[59] Many Winchester churchwardens were presented to the Court for lacking the Paraphrases; with St Maurice's and St Cross's in 1562 and 1566; St Bartholomew's in 1562 and 1570; St Mary's in 1570; whilst in November 1570, the judge ordered that the churchwardens of St Cross should pay 22d. for their continuing lack of the Paraphrases.[60] Of course, failure to purchase books does not necessarily indicate refusal to conform: the parish may simply have been too poor to comply, but unfortunately the churchwardens' accounts have not survived for these parishes.

In 1566–69 St John's churchwardens in Winchester, reported they had exchanged the chalice for a communion cup at a cost of 11s. 6d.[61] In 1595–96, the accounts list a silver chalice, and do not mention a communion cup, so we are left wondering if the church really had conformed.[62] Unfortunately the 1590 inventory does not resolve this, as neither the chalice nor communion cup were listed.[63] Only as late as 1570–73 did the church finally sell its cross for £4 13s. 4d., again hinting at its reluctance to accept the permanence of the Elizabethan Church.[64] St Peter Chesil did not sell its chalice until 1565 or 1566, whilst the churchwardens of Kingsgate were reported to the Consistory Court in November 1570, for not having a communion cup.[65] Also in November 1570, the churchwardens of St Lawrence's were reported to the Court, for not taking Communion that year, and for having superstitious vestments in the church. They were ordered to destroy the vestments, and in December 1570, they certified that they had sold the offending articles to Lancelot Johnson.[66] On 10 December 1572 the churchwardens of St Thomas's were ordered by the Court to surrender the Mass Book and two grails, previously discovered by the visitation officials, to the Court. Nothing more is mentioned about this case in the following Court book, so it is likely that these churchwardens did comply.[67] Yet at the end of the century, churchwardens from St Thomas's were reported to the Consistory Court for their lack of 'a sufficient bible & a surples', so it is likely that this church conformed only as far as it was forced to.[68]

From the inventory of St John's church in Winchester in January 1597, it would appear that some Catholic servicing equipment had survived. The inventory lists two altar cloths of blanched damask embroidered and one of them with a fringe of silk, and an old altar cloth of embroidered silk.[69]

[59] HRO 21M65 C1/14 f.310v., C1/24 f.3.
[60] HRO 21M65 C1/8 fos.37v., 38v., C1/10 fos.18, 46, C1/14 fos.169, 308v. and 312v.
[61] HRO 88M81W/PW1 f.28.
[62] HRO 88M81W/PW1, f.55.
[63] HRO 88M81W/PW1, f.59.
[64] HRO 88M81W/PW1, f.31v.
[65] HRO 3M82W/PW1, f.4, C1/14 f.310v.
[66] HRO 21M65 C1/14 f.310v., f.314v.
[67] HRO 21M65 C1/15 f.125v.
[68] HRO 21M65 C1/27 f.5.
[69] HRO 88M81W/PW2, f.3v. They were also present in the inventory of 1590 HRO 88M81W/PW1 f.59.

The churchwardens of four Winchester parishes were also involved in the organisation of a forbidden Catholic celebration. On 30 June 1569, the churchwardens of St Bartholomew, St Maurice, St John's in the Soke and St Mary Kalendar, were all presented to the Consistory Court for holding bonfires in their parishes, and the following month, the judge warned them to conform. No other names are mentioned, other than for the parish of St Bartholomew, who implicated Edith Sidford, Anna Collock, John Ustman, Alice Eve, Thomas Ludloe and John Hering.[70] The celebrations of Midsummer Day and the Feast of St John the Baptist by bonfires was seen by many, including the Consistory Court, as a popish practice. St John Day's was still the midsummer holiday under the Elizabethan Church, but the use of bonfires, whilst common under Henry VII, was already less frequent under Henry VIII.[71] No further Winchester bonfires were recorded in the extant Court Books, so it seems the parishes did comply, and the midsummer of 1569 was the last to be celebrated with a bonfire.

In May 1584, Bishop Cooper[72] explained to Cecil that the churchwardens had already presented over four hundred recusants, but that this was probably far from the total owing to 'the slackenes of the Churchwardens'. He felt that Hampshire was in need of 'extraordinarie authoritie'.[73] From the visitation records and Consistory Court cases, it is possible to see the laxity of the Winchester churchwardens, in both attending the visitations and presenting their bills.

St. Peter Colebrook's churchwardens missed the two visitations held by the bishop in 1591 and 1592. The churchwardens from St Thomas' failed to attend three visitations, those of 1572, 1580, and 1591. St Lawrence's failed to send churchwardens on four occasions in 1589, 1590, 1591 and 1592. The poorest attenders, however, were from St Swithun upon Kingsgate and St Mary Kalendar whose churchwardens each missed seven visitations.[74]

In October and November 1575, the churchwardens of St Swithun's were warned four times by the Court to exhibit their bill.[75] Also in October 1575, the churchwardens of St Lawrence's had to exhibit their bill at the Court, and in October 1577, the churchwardens of St Michael's in

[70] HRO 21M65 C1/12 fos. 124v., 125, 126, C1/13 fos. 39v., 40, 42v., 43
[71] David Cressy, *Bonfires and Bells: National Memory and the Protestant Calendar in Elizabethan and Stuart England* (London: Weidenfeld and Nicolson, 1989), 25–26, 81, and David Cressy, *Travesties and Transgressions in Tudor and Stuart England* (Oxford: Oxford University Press, 2000), 165.
[72] Thomas Cooper (1517?–1594). He was educated at Magdalen College school, and took a degree in physic, finding himself unable to take orders during the reign of Mary I, owing to his Protestant views. After Mary's death, he became a zealous preacher. He became dean of Christchurch in 1567, dean of Gloucester in 1569, and Bishop of Lincoln in 1570–71. In 1584, on the death of Watson, he became Bishop of Winchester. Margaret Bowker, "Cooper, Thomas (*c.*1517–1594), theologian and bishop of Winchester." *Oxford Dictionary of National Biography*, https://doi.org/10.1093/ref:odnb/6229
[73] BL Lansdowne 42/41 (99).
[74] Susan K. Parkinson, "The Religion of the People in Winchester and Southampton *c.*1558–c.1603," PhD thesis University of Southampton, 2003, Figure 9 of Appendices, 203.
[75] HRO 21M65 C1/18 fos. 18, 20v., 25, 31.

the Soke were warned by the judge to exhibit their bill.[76] On 28 March 1579, the churchwardens of St Swithun, St Thomas, St Bartholomew and St Clement were presented at the Court for not presenting their bills at visitation.[77] In 1582, the churchwardens of St Peter Colebrook were cited at the Court for not presenting their bill at visitation.[78]

Even if a churchwarden did name a person as a recusant, and they were found guilty of their 'disorder in religion' by the Consistory Court, they could relax happy in the knowledge that it was easier to attend mass inside the Winchester gaol than in their own homes. On many occasions the bishops had cause to express concern over the lax imprisonment of the city's gaol keepers. Hints to the religious persuasions of the keepers of the gaol can be found by close-reading of their wills, together with a search of the Consistory court records.

In 1583, Edmund Yateman of St Clement's parish in Winchester, and keeper of city's gaol, left a will containing an ambiguous religious preamble and one religious bequest. However, it is Yateman's list of witnesses to his will, which attracts our attention. The names of key Hampshire recusants appear there – Gilbert Wells and Richard Warneford.[79] Yateman's wife had been cited as a recusant in the Consistory Court of 1581.[80]

David Ringstead, the under-keeper of Winchester gaol, was imprisoned in June 1586, on suspicion of carrying priests from place to place for the past three or four years. The bishop sent him to the Clink for imprisonment.[81] Both Ringstead and his wife, from St Maurice in Winchester, had also been presented to the Consistory Court for recusancy in July 1583 and were excommunicated by the judge after Ringstead told the Court 'he had bynn a papist these iij yeres well knowen'.[82] They were both listed as recusants in the Inquisition of April 1583.[83]

'Disorders in religion' certainly did persist in the gaol. In January 1583, Sir Richard Norton, William Wright and Thomas Fleming searched Winchester gaol. In the chambers of Richard Warneford and Mr Howrd, they found a huge amount of Catholic material, which included five massing ornaments, a set of beads, two wax candles, a super altar, a vestment, a mass book and various devotional and controversial works of theology. In John Slade and John Body's chamber, the searchers found Catholic writings on purgatory and the mass, and in Traverse's chamber, there were more written works on the Schism and the Catholic faith. In Mercy Deane's chamber, the searchers found 'A Greate Masse Booke in Latyn'.[84]

By 1599 the gaol could still not be regarded as a secure prison. Edward Kenyon, a seminary priest, was committed to the gaol in September of that year to the care of the keeper, William Uvedale and an underkeeper, Thomas Garnet. Bishop Bilson wrote ordering the keeper to keep a close eye on Kenyon and to treat him as a traitor who had confessed to being a seminary priest, and was therefore guilty of high treason. The seminary priest was allowed freedom to roam around the prison and grounds, and to receive visitors, despite the bishop's orders that he be strictly confined. Not surprisingly he escaped before his trial.[85]

Bishop Horne also had cause to complain about the aldermanic elite of the city of Winchester were not innocent of such 'disorders in religion' either, and did not actively use their power and influence to encourage others to conform. Again, it is the close-reading of their wills, cross-referenced with the cases of the Consistory Court, that allow us to see that Horne was not wrong in his concern.

Bishop Horne did not feel many Winchester city governors could be trusted as 'all that bear authority there, except for one or two', were 'addict to the old superstition'.[86] He saw Winchester as setting an example of religious disobedience within his jurisdiction and cited Robert Hodson the mayor, Bethel the elder and Bethel the younger, William Lawrence,[87] White, Pottenger and Coreham, as men sympathetic to Catholicism.[88]

It is likely that the White mentioned by Horne was Giles White who had served the town as Chamberlain from 1558 to 1560. White had held minor legal office under Bishop Gardiner.[89] Despite being a known Catholic, in 1565 White was elected as mayor. The preamble to his will made in October 1571 was Protestant, trusting to be saved by the merits of the death of Jesus Christ, but his testament does not entirely convince us that White was fully converted. His will includes an unusual extra phrase – 'God grannt of his mercie that I may die in the trewe feith'. We wonder what White felt was the true faith. One of his executors was Roger Hoorde, perhaps a relation to William Hoorde, the recusant gentleman of Winchester.[90]

Despite Horne's obvious displeasure, William Lawrence went on to become mayor of the city in 1574–75, escheator of Hampshire and Wiltshire in 1569, and deputy Clerk of the Peace in 1575. He also continued to serve as bailiff

[76] HRO 21M65 C1/18 f.18.
[77] HRO 21M65 C1/20 f.112.
[78] HRO 21M65 C1/22 f.2.
[79] TNA PROB11/65/ 23 ROWE.
[80] HRO 21M65 C1/21 fos. 167, 169.
[81] TNA SP12/190/26, SP12/190/42.
[82] HRO 21M65 C1/22 f.138.
[83] TNA SP12/160/26.
[84] TNA SP12/158/16 (listed 9 in the Calendar).

[85] TNA SP12/273/23 vii, cf. Godfrey Anstruther, *The Seminary Priests*, 196–97.
[86] Mary Bateson, (ed.), "A Collection of Original Letters from the Bishops to the Privy Council 1564, with returns of the Justices of the Peace and others within their respective dioceses classified according to their religious convictions," *Camden Miscellany, Vol. IX*, Camden Society New Series LIII (London: Royal Historical Society, 1895), 54.
[87] William Laurence had been mayor of Winchester under both Edward and Mary's reigns, in 1548–49, 1553–55.
[88] Ibid., 56.
[89] Rosen, "Economic and social aspects of the history of Winchester," 89.
[90] HRO 1574B/182.

of the Bishop's liberty from 1557 to his death in 1580.[91] Like Giles White, Lawrence had been a legal official for Gardiner and had testified for him in 1550.[92]

John Pottenger's career in the city administration was also not inhibited by earning the displeasure of Horne, as he continued to be chamberlain of Winchester from 1563–65, and was re-appointed from 1577–1585. He was presented for recusancy in 1572, and three recusants were found at his house after his death.[93]

Stephen Bethell's will of 1577 indicates that he was perhaps not fully committed to the Elizabethan Church as it included a non-committal preamble.[94] Roger Coreham was a noted recusant from Hyde.[95]

The proceedings of the Winchester borough mote record that Robert Hodson was not allowed in an election, owing to his excommunication.[96] Despite living until 1572–73, Hodson does not appear to have held any further senior posts in the city government. His will, made in July 1572, suggests his conversion to Protestantism, as he trusted 'to be numbred amonge his electe', although his inventory showed his ownership of a dozen silver spoons of the apostles.[97] Furthermore, his widow's inventory of 1581 included the dozen apostles' spoons.[98] Their son, William, became mayor of Winchester twice in Elizabeth's reign, so either the family had converted to Protestantism, or else others in the city's government were not biased against Catholic families sharing the reins of power.

In March 1564, the proceedings of the Winchester borough mote note that Robert Hodson, mayor, and Richard Bird, bailiff, were to appear before the Privy Council.[99] Robert Hodson, Richard Bird, Richard Burton and John Mynnell, also of Winchester, were to appear before the Council to be investigated on religious matters.[100] The Chamberlain's Account Roll of Winchester in 1564 recorded a payment of £6 to Robert Hodson and £4 to Richard Bird, to cover their travelling expenses to London. It would appear therefore, that the city government at least sympathised with the religious views of its mayor and bailiff.[101] On 24 November 1564, Hodson, Bird and Mynnall were discharged from the Marshalsea, after bonds of £100 had been taken from each of them.[102] Again, Catholicism did not dissuade others from electing Richard Bird as MP for Winchester in 1571.[103]

There are other references in the Consistory Court cases that may be of relevance here. In 1576, the wife of John White was cited for recusancy at the Consistory Court.[104] She may have been the wife of John White, mayor of Winchester in 1583–84, and 1593–94.

In 1582, a Richard Burd, of St Mary Kalendar in Winchester, was presented to the Consistory Court, for not taking Communion on Easter Sunday, and calling the parson a knave.[105] This may have been the same Richard Bird who was mayor of the city in 1571–72 and 1577–78. Likewise there was a Richard Cooke, presented to the Court for non-communicating at the last Easter Communion, along with his wife, in 1586. They were also alleged to have been receiving 'divers suspicious persons' at their house.[106] It is possible that this was the same Richard Cooke who was mayor of Winchester twice in 1579–80 and 1591–92.

In the Inquisition of April 1583, James Bird of St Lawrence's in Winchester, son of Anthony Bird, the mayor, was listed as a recusant.[107] The surviving Consistory Court records do not detail any case involving James Bird, however he appears to have been executed for his persistent recusancy in Winchester in March 1593.[108] In 1578, a member of the 'Byrd' family is noted to have attended masses at Lady West's house in Winchester.[109]

Conclusion

This paper has attempted to describe the 'disorders in religion' that Horne first noted in 1561, and that were to plague the government and the ecclesiastical authorities throughout the reign of Elizabeth I. This paper has focused on the 'disorders' of the laity; however for the city of Winchester this is only half the story of Catholic survival – for a fuller picture it is necessary to look at the roles played by the parish clergy, and the staff of Winchester Cathedral and Winchester College. The bishops of Winchester were to find little active support from these quarters in their quest to eradicate the old religion in the city. The Elizabethan Settlement of Religion had settled nothing for the Catholics of Winchester and they persisted in their 'disorders in religion' for the remainder of the sixteenth century.

[91] P.W. Hasler, (ed.) *House of Commons: 1558–1603*, The History of Parliament Trust, Vol. 2 (London: Stationery Office, 1981), Hasler, *The History of Parliament*, 442, Tom Atkinson, *Elizabethan Winchester* (London: Faber and Faber, 1963), 220–21. William Laurence had also been M.P. for Winchester in 1553, 1554, 1555, 1558, 1559 and 1563.

[92] Rosen, "Economic and social aspects of the history of Winchester," 89.

[93] Rosen, "Economic and social aspects of the history of Winchester," 89.

[94] HRO 1577/B005.

[95] Carpenter Turner, *A History of Winchester*, 89. She spells his surname as Corham.

[96] HRO WB2/1 f.46.

[97] HRO 1573B/072.

[98] HRO 1581B/063.

[99] HRO WB2/1 f.64v.

[100] TNA PC2/9 f.114.

[101] HRO W/E1/93 (the last entry on the reverse of the roll).

[102] TNA PC2/9 f.125.

[103] Hasler, *House of Commons*, p.173.

[104] HRO C1/19 f.81v.

[105] HRO C1/22 f.80v.

[106] HRO C1/23 f.3.

[107] TNA SP12/160/26.

[108] Bishop Challoner, *Memoirs of Missionary Priests, and other Catholics of both Sexes that have suffered death in England on religious accounts from the year 1577 to 1684*, Volume 1 (Manchester: Mark Wardle, 1803), 158

[109] TNA SP12/127/42 – possibly from December 1578. The Christian name is unclear, but the last two letters appear to be "es", making it more likely that this is James Bird, than Richard.

Acknowledgements

The author would like to acknowledge the University of Southampton, where she received a scholarship to study for her doctoral thesis, noted in the bibliography. Chapter two of that thesis forms the basis for this paper.

Bibliography

Unpublished Primary sources

British Library (BL).

Cotton Titus B III.

Harleian 280 (now 157).

Harleian 595.

Lansdowne 39/183 (original reference 46).

Lansdowne 42/41 (99).

The National Archives (TNA).

E377/4–9: Recusant Rolls (Pipe Office Series), Nov 1594–Nov 1600.

E377/11: Recusant Rolls (Pipe Office Series), Nov 1601–Nov 1602.

PROB11/65/23 ROWE: Sentence of Rose Holford or Holdford of London, Jan 1583.

SP12: State Papers Domestic, Elizabeth I

SP15: State Papers Domestic, Edward VI–James I: Addenda

Hampshire Record Office (HRO).

3M82W/PW1: St Peter Chesil, Churchwardens' account book, 1566–1642

21M65 A1/29: Bishop's Registers: Register of Thomas Bilson.

21M65 C1/8: Office Act Book, 1562–63.

21M65 C1/10: Office Act Book, 1566.

21M65 C1/12: Office Act Book, 1568–69.

21M65 C1/13: Office Act Book, 1569–70.

21M65 C1/14: Office Act Book, 1570.

21M65 C1/15: Office Act Book, 1572–73.

21M65 C1/18: Office Act Book, 1575–76.

21M65 C1/19: Office Act Book, 1576–77.

21M65 C1/20: Office Act Book, 1578–79.

21M65 C1/21: Office Act Book, 1581–82.

21M65 C1/22: Office Act Book, 1582–83.

21M65 C1/23: Office Act Book, 1586–87.

21M65 C1/26: Office Act Book, 1598–1603.

21M65 C1/27: Office Act Book, 1599–1600.

44M69/G3/112: Manuscript calendar of prisoners in the County Gaol, 12 February 1591.

88M81W/PW1: Winchester St John's Parish Churchwarden's account book, 1549–1596, 1605.

88M81W/PW2: Winchester St John's Parish Churchwarden's account book, 1596–1824.

1573B/072: Will and inventory of Robert Hodson of Winchester, 1573.

1574B/182: Will and inventory of Giles White of St Lawrence, Winchester, 1574.

1577B/005: Will and inventory of Stephen Bethell of Winchester, 1577.

1581B/063: Will and inventory of Frideswide Hodson of St Mary Kalendar, Winchester, 1581.

1584B/47: Will of Jane Knight of St Michael, Winchester, 1584.

W/E1/93: Winchester Chamberlains' account roll 5–6 Elizabeth, 1563–64.

WB2/1: Winchester Corporation Proceedings in Borough Mote, 1552–1575.

Published Primary Sources

Bateson, Mary, ed. "A Collection of Original Letters from the Bishops to the Privy Council 1564, with returns of the Justices of the Peace and others within their respective dioceses classified according to their religious convictions." In *Camden Miscellany, Vol. IX*, Camden Society New Series LIII, London: Royal Historical Society, 1895.

Bowler, Hugh, ed. *Recusant Rolls no 2, 1593–1594. An abstract in English with an explanatory introduction by Dom Hugh Bowler*, Catholic Record Society Record Series 57 (1965).

Bowler, Hugh, ed. *Recusant Rolls no 3, 1594–1595 and recusant roll no. 4, 1595–1596. An abstract in English*, Catholic Record Society Record Series 61 (1970).

Bray, Gerald, ed. *Documents of the English Reformation*, Library of Ecclesiastical History, Cambridge: James Clarke, 2004.

Challoner, Bishop. *Memoirs of Missionary Priests, and other Catholics of both Sexes that have suffered death in England on religious accounts from the year 1577 to 1684*, Volume 1. Manchester: Mark Wardle, 1803.

Calendar of State Papers Domestic: Elizabeth, 1581–90, "Queen Elizabeth – Volume 164: December 1583," ed. Robert Lemon (London, 1865), 134–143. *British History Online* http://www.british-history.ac.uk/cal-state-papers/domestic/edw-eliz/1581-90/pp134-143.

Dasent, John Roche, ed. *Acts of the Privy Council of England*, London: Stationery Office, 1890–93.

McCann, T.J. and Dom Hugh Bowler, eds. *Recusants in the Exchequer Pipe Rolls, 1581–1592*, Catholic Record Society Record Series 71 (1986).

Pollen, J. H., ed. *Unpublished Documents Relating to the English Martyrs. Vol. 1 1584–1603*, Catholic Record Society Record Series 5 (1908).

Published secondary sources

Anstruther, Godfrey. *The Seminary Priests: A Dictionary of the Secular Clergy of England and Wales 1558–1603.* Ware: St. Edmund's College, 1968.

Atkinson, Tom. *Elizabethan Winchester.* London: Faber and Faber, 1963.

Bowker, Margaret. "Cooper, Thomas (c. 1517–1594), theologian and bishop of Winchester." *Oxford Dictionary of National Biography*. 23 Sep 2004. Accessed 24 Feb. 2020 https://doi.org/10.1093/ref:odnb/6229

Carpenter Turner, Barbara. *A History of Winchester.* Chichester: Phillimore, 1992.

Cressy, David. *Bonfires and Bells: National Memory and the Protestant Calendar in Elizabethan and Stuart England.* London: Weidenfeld and Nicolson, 1989.

Cressy, David. *Travesties and Transgressions in Tudor and Stuart England.* Oxford: Oxford University Press, 2000.

Hasler, P.W. ed. *House of Commons: 1558–1603*, The History of Parliament Trust, 3 vols. London: Stationery Office, 1981.

Houlbrooke, Ralph. "Horne, Robert (1513x15–1579), bishop of Winchester." *Oxford Dictionary of National Biography*. 3 Sep. 2004; Accessed 24 Feb. 2020

https://doi.org/10.1093/ref:odnb/13792

Ladley, Jane Reedy. "Watson, John (c. 1520–1584), bishop of Winchester." *Oxford Dictionary of National Biography.* 23 Sep. 2004; Accessed 24 Feb. 2020.

https://doi.org/10.1093/ref:odnb/28844

Paul, John E., "Hampshire Recusants in the time of Elizabeth I, with special reference to Winchester." *Proceedings of the Hampshire Field Club and Archaeological Society*, XXI, pt.2 (1959): 61–82.

Washington, E.S. "Hampshire and the Catholic Revival of the 1580s." In *Hampshire Studies presented to Dorothy Dymond on the occasion of her ninetieth birthday.* 51–72, Portsmouth: Portsmouth City Council, 1981.

Webb, John; Yates, Nigel; and Peacock, Sarah (eds) *Hampshire Studies presented to Dorothy Dymond on the occasion of her ninetieth birthday.* Portsmouth: Portsmouth City Council, 1981.

Unpublished secondary sources

Parkinson, Susan K. "The Religion of the People in Winchester and Southampton c.1558–c.1603." PhD thesis, University of Southampton, 2003.

Rosen, A. "Economic and social aspects of the history of Winchester, 1520–1670." DPhil thesis, University of Oxford, 1975.

13

Two College Gardens: Recent investigations in Wadham and Merton Colleges, Oxford

John Steane

Independent Scholar

Abstract: Tom James's interest in parks (particularly Clarendon Park) is only matched by his fascination with his ancestors, one of whom was the Bodleian Library's earliest librarian. This contribution is therefore apposite being on two gardens of Oxford Colleges, Wadham and Merton. The garden at Wadham is discussed using 17th-century sources and a recent resistivity survey. The Fellows' Garden at Merton College goes back to the Middle Ages but this paper centres on the recent felling of a lime avenue and a resistivity survey undertaken at the same time.

Key words: John Wilkins; walls; planning; mount; paths; arbours; resistivity surveys; medieval garden; lime avenue

Introduction

In a volume dedicated to Tom James and consisting largely of papers connected with the areas of his historical and archaeological activities, namely, Hampshire, Wiltshire and the ancient kingdom of Wessex, it might be thought anomalous to include one devoted to the garden history of two Oxford colleges. But, in truth there are connexions between Tom, Wessex, and the oldest English university. A literary link that springs to mind is in Thomas Hardy's *Jude the Obscure*, an account of the struggles, ultimately unsuccessful, of a Wessex-based and aspiring stone mason to enter the University of Oxford, or Christminster as Hardy calls it. A personal connexion is that Tom James, an avid reader in the Bodleian Library, had a distinguished ancestor of the same name, namely Bodley's first librarian Thomas James (1572/3–1629) whose portrait is displayed in the library and whose life is given due prominence in the *Dictionary of National Biography*. His contribution to the early library included a first catalogue of its riches, and a negotiation with the Stationers Hall which obtained for the library copies of all books published in England. Tom has also himself been deeply involved in researching and writing up the gardens and park of Clarendon.[1]

Part one: Wadham College

Initial interest in the garden of Wadham College was sparked by an exhibition in the Bodleian Library which took place between 1 February and 2 May 1998 entitled 'The Garden, the Ark, the Tower and the Temple'.[2] This exhibition was not primarily concerned with topographical considerations. Instead it was centred on the ideas of Oxford-based intelligentsia who gathered in the 1630s and 1640s around Samuel Hartlib. For them the Old Testament stories of the Garden of Eden 'symbolised the ideal state when the earth has been spontaneously fertile, labour was easy and fulfilling and human life had been grounded in a complete knowledge of words and things'.[3] Among this group of influential scientists was John Wilkins, warden of Wadham College from 1648–59. Wilkins was interested in gardens and it seems highly likely that he was involved in the creation of the complex of gardens which appear in the background of David Loggan's bird's eye view of the college published in the 1675 edition of *Oxonia Illustrata*. Wilkins was chaplain to Lord Saye and Sele in the 1630s and may well have been inspired by the layout of the gardens at Broughton Castle, shown in Cambridge University's aerial photograph (Figure 13.1).

A detailed and admirable account of the gardens had already appeared in the college history.[4] A trawl through the college archives produced a number of previously unpublished references supplementing this study, and concurrently the college agreed (through the kind offices of the late Professor Richard Sharpe) to fund a resistivity survey of the gardens. This aimed to locate the buildings of the Augustinian Friary which preceded the college on the site and to see whether the gardens in Loggan's bird's eye view ever existed in reality. Other areas tested included the back quad between the seventeenth-century college buildings and Holywell Street and the Warden's Garden. A minute examination of the walls (with the help of the geologist Philip Powell) followed. A visit was paid with Scott Mandelbrote to Broughton Castle where Lord

[1] Tom Beaumont James and Christopher M. Gerrard, *Clarendon: Landscape of Kings* (Macclesfield: Windgather, 2007).

[2] Bodleian Library, University of Oxford, *Bodleian Library Record* 16, no. 3 (April 1998): 204–06.

[3] *Bodleian Library Record* 16, no. 3 (April 1998): 204–06.

[4] David J. Mabberley, "The Gardens," in *Wadham College Oxford*, ed. Clifford S.L. Davies and Jane Garnett (Oxford: Wadham College, 1994).

Figure 13.1: Broughton Castle, Oxfordshire. A moated house and gardens. These appear as three square features on the island to the west of the house. The two northernmost appear to have a central feature. Taken in April 1949. Reproduced with permission of the Cambridge University Collection of Aerial Photography Copyright reserved.

Saye and Sele showed us his gardens, some of which may have been known to Wilkins when he was chaplain to the household in the 1630s. The rest of this part of the paper attempts to bring together the results of this study. It can be summarised under six headings: site, walls, paths, mount, pleached avenues and furnishings.

Site

The site now occupied by Wadham College lies north of the medieval walled city. It had been in the hands of an Augustinian Friary since the thirteenth century. At the Dissolution the Friary does not seem to have been very prosperous; its buildings were ruinous and according to Dr John London, the king's commissioner, it only had six or seven acres of land.[5] The site was then leased to various tenants, sold on to various buyers and ended up in the hands of the City of Oxford in 1588–89. Dorothy Wadham bought it for £600 in March 1609.[6] It consisted of an approximate rectangle of about 5½ acres, bounded south by Holywell Street and west by the street now known as Parks Road to just short of Wadham Cottages.[7] To the east it was bounded by a bank, later part of the

[5] William Page (ed.), *The Victoria History of the County of Oxford* [hereafter *VCH Oxon*], vol. 2 (London: Archibald Constable, 1907), 147.
[6] Nancy Briggs, "The Foundation of Wadham College Oxford," *Oxoniensia* 21 (1956): 66.
[7] Herbert E. Salter and Mary D. Lobel (eds), *VCH Oxon*, vol. 3 (London: Oxford University Press, 1954), 279.

Civil War fortifications.[8] It was enclosed to the north by an east-wall which still bounds the Fellows' Garden. Within this area the college was built and, as was said at the time, 'the ground wheare the Colledg shall be, buylt, contayneth between 4 and 5 acres and ys the most absolutest place that Oxford canne yelde & hath a very strong wall about yt of viii foote highe which will save 300 li'.[9] The Warden and Fellows to begin with leased the northern two acres but resumed their possession of this land in 1645 and 1650 and laid out the gardens which are the main subject of this paper. The ground to the north apparently belonged to Merton College in 1704 and was 'in occupation of William Haynes gardener or his under tenants'. The college obtained a lease of this land and extended the Warden's Garden. A further area was bought from Merton College in *c.*1835 making the additions up to 3¼ acres.[10] The college sold a substantial strip along South Parks Road to the Trustees of Rhodes House in 1925.

Walls

With Philip Powell, geologist, formerly at Oxford University Museum, we walked round the walls in January 2002. We also studied the plans of the college garden in Agas's map of Oxford in 1578 (Figure 13.2),[11] Loggan's map of 1675 (Figure 13.3) and Jackson's of 1893. The site of the Augustinian Friary is likely to have been walled and a number of these walls appear to have survived the Friary's dissolution and demolition. There are three large rectangular blocks of land shown on the Agas plan which confirm the 1893 plan. The two to the south are drawn with continuous lines which we think indicate walls. That to the north is shown by a connection which may indicate a hedge. The extent of walling to the south of the site is less clear but it seems that the Friary property butted up against Holywell Street on the south (belonging to Merton College) and the junction of Parks Road with Broad Street (modern street names) at the south west corner. It is likely that the west end of Holywell Street including the site of the King's Arms public house was already built up in the late Middle Ages. When physically examined it would seem that the wall along the western edge of Wadham College's property had been built in three phases. The lowest part up to two metres in places is of Corallian limestone rubble similar to that used in the early eleventh century St Michael's Church tower and Oxford Castle, the lower part of Merton College library (*c.*1280s) and the city wall (in 1230). There are no architectural features which can indicate a more precise dating. This wall was repaired and heightened using large blocks of Headington freestone together with a few blocks of Taynton stone,[12] and very rarely a few limestone lumps reddened by fire. Some of this material seems to have been freshly quarried but much is evidently second-hand. We suggest that some of these repairs and heightening took place in the early seventeenth century and were associated with the college's foundation. The wall very clearly figures in Loggan's 1675 bird's eye view of the city (Figure 13.3). The last two to three feet of the upper part of the wall with a projecting band of stone, capped by a tapering coping course could have been added in the last century or so. It is similar in style to the upper part of the wall bounding Trinity College gardens and Parks Road only a stone's throw away. It would serve to reduce traffic noise in the Warden's Garden. The cross wall which runs east-west and bounds the Warden's Garden on the north and continues to enclose the Fellows' Garden on the north may also be medieval in date. It shows a similar construction to the west wall (Figures 13.5 and 13.6), that is the lower one metre is of Corallian limestone rubble and the upper one metre 40 or so has much good Headington freestone but lacks the final capping and projecting band. Loggan's 1675 bird's eye view of Oxford certainly shows a high and continuous wall at this point.

The north-south wall separating the present Warden's Garden from that of the Fellows', can be dated with assurance. The land to the north of the college buildings acquired by the foundress was let for a period of 30 years and the college had only a narrow strip of land running close under its wall. John Burrows was the first tenant. He was a gardener from Holywell and paid £8 annually, a substantial sum. He covenanted to have the ground at the end of his term 'well and sufficiently furnished with apple trees, pear trees and other fruit trees of 20 years' growth...fit for any orchard',[13] In the event the lease was terminated for Warden Estcott (d. 1644) resumed for his use the western part of the land,[14] and in 1650 the rest of the land to the north of the college was taken in from market gardens and used for laying out the elaborate Fellows' Garden. The wall between the two gardens must date from the period 1644–50. It appears pictorially for the first time on the Loggan bird's eye view and plan in *Oxonia Illustrata*, 1675. Structurally it is inferior to those already described, being made of limestone rubble without the small Corallian blocks seen in the walls enclosing the garden. It has big blocks of Headington stone with very wide mortar joints and appears to be of a single phase. It is of neater construction on the side facing the 'important' side.

When acquiring a site for an institution outside the protective walls of a medieval town such as Oxford it made good sense to surround it with walls. Bishop William of Waynflete surrounded the property which housed Magdalen College with such a strong wall.[15] There was also a symbolic reference to the first garden

[8] Anthony Kemp "The Fortifications of Oxford during the Civil War," *Oxoniensia* 42 (1977): 246; R.T. Lattey *et al.*, "A Contemporary Map of the Defences of Oxford," *Oxoniensia* 1 (1936): 171.

[9] Briggs, "Foundation," 69.

[10] Lawrence Stone, *Catalogue of Muniments of Wadham College* (London: Historical MSS Commission, National Register of Archives, 1962).

[11] BL Gough Maps Oxfordshire 4.

[12] W.J. Arkell, *The Geology of Oxford* (Oxford: Oxford University Press, 1947).

[13] Stone, *Catalogue of Muniments*, 78, 182.

[14] Stone, *Catalogue of Muniments*, 78, 768.

[15] John M. Steane, "The Grounds of Magdalen College 1480–1880," *Oxoniensia* 63 (1998): 92.

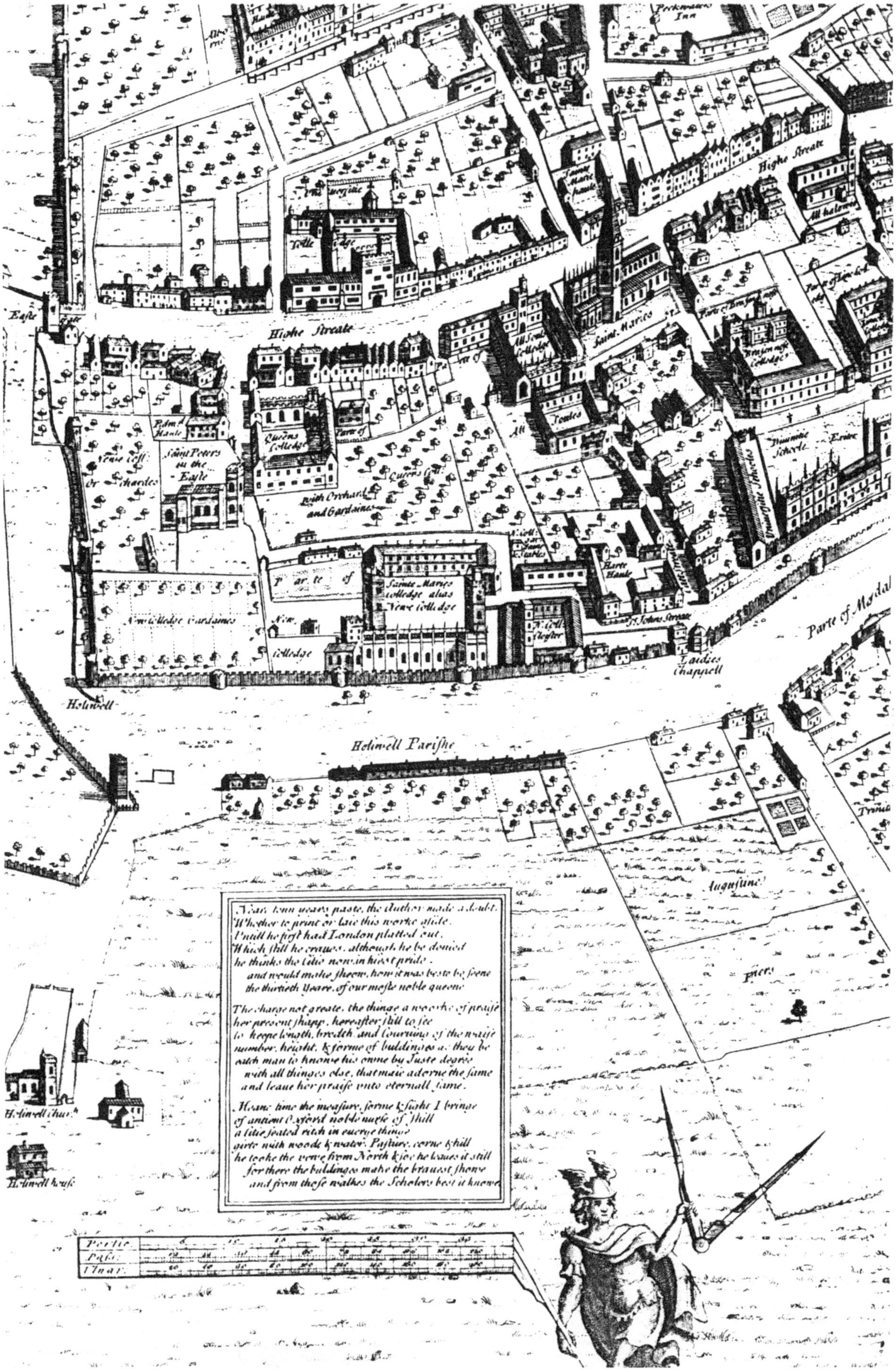

Figure 13.2: Agas's map of Oxford, 1578. The site of the future Wadham College is seen as three rectilinear spaces to the bottom right. Courtesy of Bodleian Library.

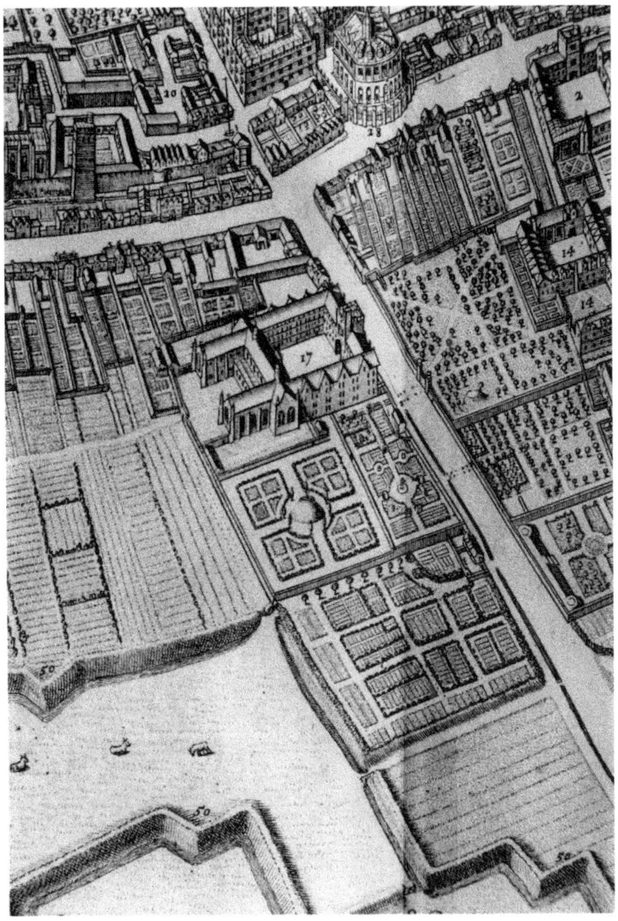

Figure 13.3: David Loggan's bird's eye view of Wadham College 1675 showing the eastern boundary, part of the Civil War fortifications, the Fellows' and Warden's gardens and ? market gardens beyond. Source: *Oxonia Illustrata* 1675.

Figure 13.4: David Loggan's engraving of Wadham College and its gardens from his *Oxonia Illustrata* of 1675. The plum pudding shaped mount is clearly visible with paths leading up to it from four directions. Source: *Oxonia Illustrata* 1675.

mentioned in the Old Testament, the Garden of Eden. Horticultural writers such as William Lawson and John Evelyn recommended walling in the garden. Lawson in his *Country House-wife's Garden* (1617) stated that both garden and orchards 'require a strong and shrouding fence'.[16] Evelyn in his *Elysium Britannicum*, gives detailed instructions, including the making of 'a good strong and substantial wall of two foote in thickness, and thirteen foote in height, either of brick, stone or such materials as may neither decay, nor leave any uneven & ragged surfaces, receptacles for snails and other noxious insects…'.[17] Such a wall not only provided security, it could also be used to train up fruit trees and other plants. Practically every college garden in Loggan's engravings of Oxford and Cambridge is depicted with trees trained up espalier fashion on the sides of the wall.

Planning

Turning to the planning of the Fellows' Garden as shown in Loggan's engraving and confirmed by the resistivity survey (Figures 13.4 and 13.7), we find that it is basically a square subdivided into four smaller squares, each bounded by a path on all four sides. Four of these paths meet in the middle where there was a plum-pudding-shaped mount topped with a statue. Each of the smaller squares was split up in two with four small beds, rectangular in shape except where their corners adjoin the circular mount; here they follow the shape of the circular feature. Again, writers in the early and mid-seventeenth century agree about the superiority of square plans. Bacon in his essay on gardens, recommended that 'it is best to be square, en-compassed on all the four sides by a stately arched hedge'.[18] Parkinson in his *Paradisi in Sole* (1629) confirms that 'the four square is the most usually accepted with all, and doth best agree to any mans dwelling being... behinde the house all the backe windows thereof opening into it'.[19]

It is possible that in its original form Wadham's garden was more complex in plan and that the version seen in the Loggan engraving is a simplified or diluted layout. Intricate knot designs were labour intensive. Bacon scorned them

[16] William Lawson, *The Country House-wife's Garden* (1617. London: Breslich and Foss, 1983), 21.
[17] John E. Ingram (ed.), *Elysium Britannicum: or The Royal Gardens*, by John Evelyn (Philadelphia: University of Pennsylvania Press, 2001), 95.
[18] Oliphant Smeaton (ed.) *Francis Bacon's Essays* (London: Dent, 1935), 139.
[19] John Parkinson, *Paradisi in Sole: paradisus terrestus* (1629. London: Methuen, 1904), 3.

Figure 13.5: Wall bounding west side of Wadham College gardens. Note three different builds, flaggy limestone at base, large blocks in middle then coping. Photograph: the author.

Figure 13.6: The eastern boundary of Wadham College garden. Ramp forming part of Civil War fortifications. Philip Powell in mid distance. Photograph: the author.

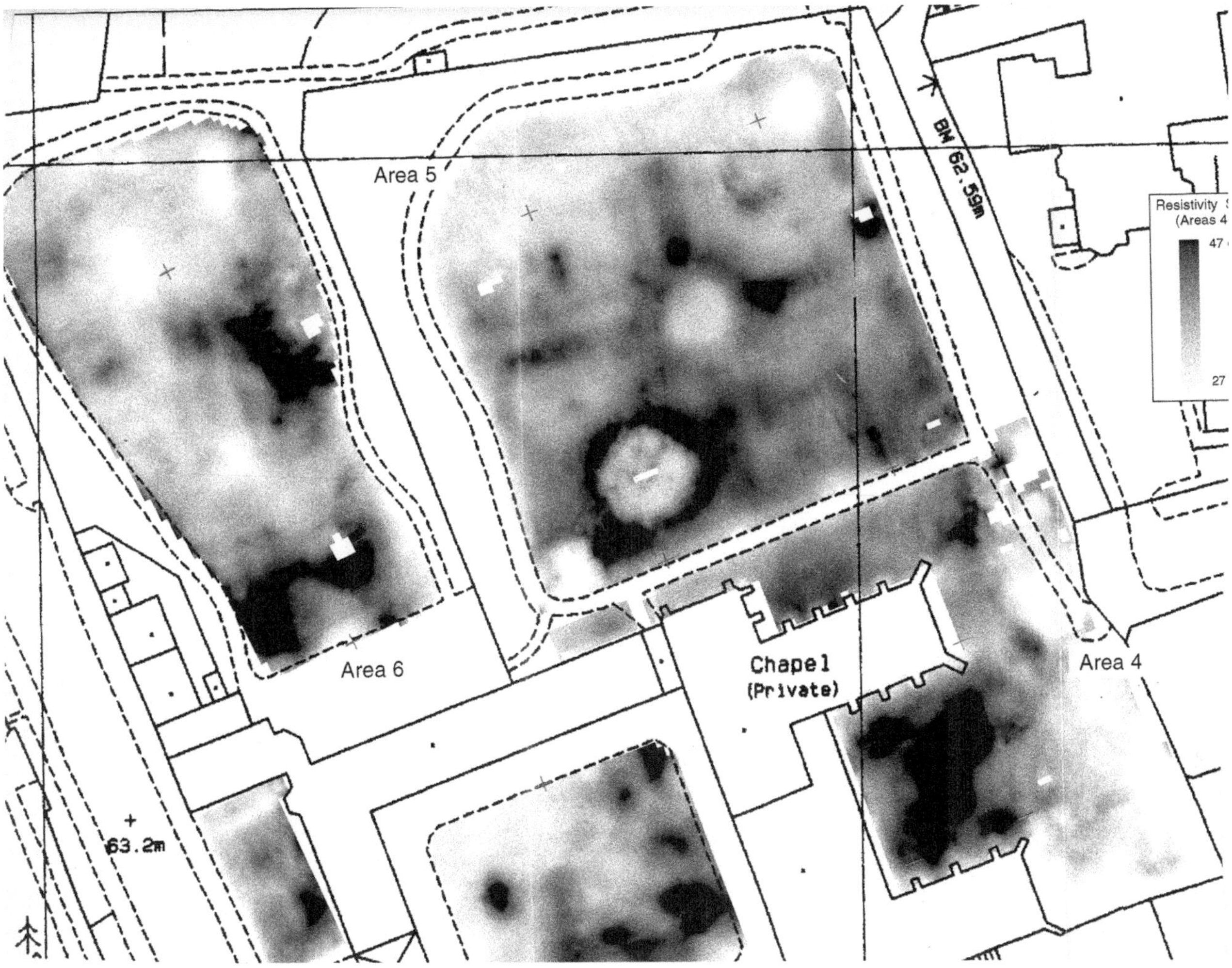

Figure 13.7: Resistivity survey of Fellows' Garden at Wadham College. Note central feature where the mount stood. The circular anomaly bottom right is a large beech tree. Bartlett-Clark Consultancy.

'as for making of knots or figures with divers coloured earths... they be but toys; you may see as good sights many times in tarts'.[20] Also, practical gardeners recognised that plants grow quickly into bushes and do not take kindly to the sort of regulation imposed by Renaissance pattern books. It does seem from Loggan that the Wadham garden by 1675 was split into four quadrants each of four beds, apparently lined with box or some lower growing, easily snippable substitute.

The resistivity survey first proved that the Loggan layout had been realised in the ground. The central area of low readings may result from compression of the ground beneath the former mound. Traces of at least three of the four main paths can be seen extending from the central feature to the north, east and west. Other anomalies could possibly relate to the ornamental features containing obelisks which are shown at the centre of each group of parterres in the 1732 engraving by W. Williams. The low reading in the south west quadrant is to be explained by the presence of a large beech tree.

Before the obelisks were raised, probably an 18th-century feature, focal points in the layout were provided by topiary in the form of closely clipped conical trees. Evelyn claims that he was the first to bring the yew into fashion as 'a succedaneum to cypress, whether in hedges, or pyramids, cones, speres, bowls or what other shapes'.[21] The Wadham trees may well have been yew.

The Mount

The central feature to which all four paths led is the plum pudding-shaped mound with a statue on top. Mounts have a long pedigree. The Normans threw up mottes which were capped by timber or stone towers. Such is the great motte of Oxford Castle. Monasteries constructed mounts as calvaries in their gardens. There was one in Padua's Botanical Garden, the earliest such garden in Europe, started in 1545. Olivier de Serres considered that they were a good place to grow native and exotic herbs, 'in short the private physic garden be grown on artificial hills, thus saving time and space and giving a variety of aspect

[20] Smeaton *Francis Bacon's Essays*, 139.

[21] Quoted in Reginald T. Blomfield, *The Formal Garden in England* (London: Macmillan, 1892), 159.

to suit the different kinds of herbs'. A second and more important function was that it provided a prospect from which the garden could be viewed as a whole. There are mounts at two sides of the moated garden at Lyveden New Bield, Northamptonshire.[22] From its height the contrast between the ordered pattern within the enclosing walls of the garden and the disorderly landscape without might be noted. If there were complicated designs of knot gardens they could be appreciated from above. John Evelyn went further. He thought the raising of mounts enabled men 'to heighten and exalt our contemplations'. He lists the biblical references to mounts especially the Mount of Olives, 'our Blessed Saviour affected the mountains more than all the place of the earth'. Incidentally on a more earthly plane he considered they were appropriate places to pile the earth dug out from fish ponds.

Wadham's mount had three distinctive features, the staircase which went up in two flights, the railing at the top and the figure of Atlas holding a globe (Figure 13.4). Evelyn recommends statuary in a garden:

> As a garden without water hath no life, as deprived of its radicall humor so without sculpture it has no action; for by this it is that we reppresent the figures of those (greate) Heros & Genious's that have so well deserv'd of Gardens & so much celebrated by the Antients.[23]

He thought that heroes and demi-gods (such as Atlas) should be represented as 'a degree bigger & represented a dubble proportion to the life'.[24] On a marginal note he states that:

> some of them may be made to speake or sing by passing a long pipe of lead through their bolt's to the mouth, the other extreame conveyed underground to some seacret place where the lead orifice being made somewhat open like a tunnel one may speake or sing a whisper to the affright & amusement of the ignorant.[25]

It is likely that he wrote this passage with Wadham's statue in mind. In his diary,[26] speaking of his visit to Oxford and Warden Wilkins he stated 'he had also contrived a hollow statue, which gave a voice and uttered words by a long concealed pipe that went to its mouth, whilst one speaks through it at a good distance'.

Warden Wilkins had other equally entertaining but more serious and scientific gadgets operating in his garden. He showed Evelyn 'the transparent apiaries, which he had built like castles and palaces, and so ordered them one upon another, as to take the honey without destroying the bees' .[27] Such a curiosity came into the possession of the early Ashmolean Museum. One is described in the 1685 catalogue as 'a beehive with glass windows through which one can see the bees making their honey'.[28] Robert Plot had no doubt that Warden Wilkins, or rather Wilkins the Bishop of Chester which he had now become, had first invented 'the new sort of Boxes, or Colony Hives for bees'.[29]

Water Features

Although they are not discernible in Loggan's 1675 view of the college garden, we are told that there were water features. Plot mentions an Engine contrived by Wilkins when he was Warden 'though long since taken hence, whereby, of but few Galons of Water forced through a narrow Fissure, he could raise a Mist at a due Distance between the Sun and the mist might see an exquisite Rainbow in all its proper Colours'.[30]

Paths and Avenues

It is clear from the layout that the garden was meant as a place wherein the Warden and Fellows could walk at all times. It was criss-crossed with paths whose gravel composition provided a well-drained walking surface. Evelyn justified the creation of such paths 'since it is by them alone that the severall parts and distinctions of a Garden are as well formed as by hedges, wales (walls), palisads and other enclosures whatsoever, not to mention the most agreable use they afford us for health, pleasure (&) buisinesse & conversation'.[31] He thinks there should be:

> an (ample) Walke leading quite about the whole Imparkment, or out Wales, besides those which are to be set out, passing to the particular *enclosures, Labyrinths, Groves, mounts* etc. every of which, even to the smalest *Alle & bed Path* should have a universal intercommunication, there being nothing more odious & prepostrous than to necessitate a returning by the same steppes.[32]

He thinks such paths should be '30 or 35 foote in breadth; if they (much) exceede not 1200 foote in length', and proportionately less wide to fit smaller lengths. He gives detailed instructions about their making. 'Let the Labourers dig, clense and accurately pick & make levell the ground, empting carring away the mould'. Upon this he suggests is laid 'a bed of lime, chalke (rubbish), old bricks, pottshards,

[22] John M. Steane, "The Development of Tudor and Stuart Garden Design in Northamptonshire," *Northamptonshire Past and Present* 5, no.5 (1977): 16–17; Bruce Bailey, Nikolaus Pevsner and Bridget Cherry, *The Buildings of England: Northamptonshire* (new edn, London: Yale University Press, 2013), 404–08.
[23] Ingram, *Elysium*, 204.
[24] Ingram, *Elysium*, 205.
[25] Ingram, *Elysium*, 206.
[26] Austin Dobson (ed.), *The Diary of John Evelyn* (1906. Repr London: Routledge, 1996), 29.
[27] Esmond S. de Beer (ed.), John Evelyn, *Diary* (Oxford: Oxford University Press, 1959), 13 July 1654, 341.
[28] Arthur MacGregor *et al.*, *Manuscript Catalogues of the Early Museum Collections 1683–1886* part 1, BAR International Series 907 (Oxford: BAR Publishing with the Ashmolean Museum, 2000), 15.
[29] Robert Plot, *Natural History of Oxfordshire* (1676. 2nd edn, Oxford: Leon Lichfield, 1705), 268.
[30] Plot, *Natural History*, 240.
[31] Ingram, *Elysium*, 126.
[32] Ingram, *Elysium*, 126.

flints, rough gravell, (broken glasse) or whatsoever hard & impenetrable rubbish you can procure... which will be of greate effect to resist the weede and abate the Worme, being well beaten and rammed (downe)'. On this the gravel is cast, first coarse and then ever finer layers.[33] It all sounds very much as if a Roman road was being made. The paths are 16 inches in thickness. Assuming that something along these lines was carried out in the construction of the paths at Wadham, it is not surprising that they showed up as distinct features in the resistivity survey. They must largely still survive within the first metre and under the turf of the Fellows' Garden. Evelyn completes his description by recommending making the paths cambered 'to carry off the raine & water which falls from heaven' and then to roller it, plentifully washing the roller, to harden the walk.[34] The considerable works required to make such walks are echoed in the sixteenth- and seventeenth-century accounts at Magdalen College where the water walks were laid out bordering the college meadows.[35]

Arbours

Another feature that seventeenth-century garden makers were keen to provide were arbours and tunnels made of clipped, trained and leafy foliage. Loggan's engraving of the Wadham garden shows in the south western corner what may be an avenue running parallel to the north side of the main quadrangle, below the Warden's lodging. Evelyn recommends 'for cover's walkes so make the Allee seeme broader to the Eye than the open and free; and therefore should they be design'd narrower in proportion to the length, which likewise will much facilitate the Archment above'. He was of the view that lime made a good tree for avenues, 'the most proper and beautiful for walks, as producing an upright body, smooth and even bark, ample leaf, sweet blossom, the delight of bees and a goodly shade at the distance of eighteen or twenty five feet...it is also very patient of pruning'.[36] In order to prune and to clip it was essential to have 'ladders of severall sizes for length and strength one made with a stage to plash, bind and doe high-worke upon'. Such close walks were to be 12 foot high.[37] For evidence of this at Merton College, see the second part of this paper.

The extension to the Warden's Garden was made in the late eighteenth century. A wall was built to enclose the gardens attached to the cottages (occupied today by the gardener and under-gardener) facing onto Parks Road. The doorway leading into the college garden from the cottages has a two-centred arch and moulded jamb stones (Figure 13.8). It has two stones of Taynton type in the head, clearly not made for its present position or function and is apparently second-hand material from a medieval building. It is suggested that it was derived from stone of

Figure 13.8: 'Gothic' arch, possibly built of remains from Augustinian Friary. Photograph: the author.

the Augustinian Friary, the predecessor on the college site. If so it is the sole remaining architectural fragment apart from the enclosure wall and apart from the remains of the Friary described by John Blair.[38]

Part 2: Merton College Garden

The college founded by Bishop Walter de Merton in 1264 moved to Oxford in 1274. It occupied a long narrow site in the south east of the walled city where there had been a series of tenements with houses facing onto Merton Street and stretching south down to the city wall, and during the Middle Ages it extended its property to the east taking in a number of houses and gardens. These latter became the Fellows' Garden. This part of the paper aims to contribute to our knowledge about this garden and its development over 500 years and in particular to publish a resistivity survey carried out in 1996.

What is known already

Two detailed articles have been written by Mr T. Braun about the history of the garden up to 1720 and after

[33] Ingram, *Elysium*, 128–29.
[34] Alexander Hunter (ed.), John Evelyn's *Sylva, or a Discourse of Forest Trees* (York: A. Ward for J. Dodsley, 1776), 130.
[35] Steane, "The Grounds of Magdalen," 1998.
[36] Hunter, Evelyn's *Sylva*, 201.
[37] Ingram, *Elysium*, 88, 143.

[38] See W. John Blair, "A Monastic Fragment at Wadham College, Oxford," *Oxoniensia* 41 (1976).

Figure 13.9: Bartlett-Clark consultancy in action. Wadham College Archaeogeophysical Survey, 1999. Photograph: the author.

Figure 13.10: Extract from David Loggan's bird's eye view of Merton College, 1675. The Warden's Garden with summerhouse at top (south) with rails and knot garden and pleached arbour below. Source: *Oxonia Illustrata* 1675.

1720.[39] The college in 1993 commissioned a report on the historical evolution of the garden.[40] It drew heavily on Braun's research and was illustrated by a series of maps and plans including those of Agas (1578); Hollar (1643); Loggan (1675, see Figure 13.10); Williams (1724); Faden (1789); Hoggar (1850) and the Ordnance Survey of 1878, 1900, 1921, 1947 and 1970. These studies have established the main lines of the evolution of the garden and a succinct account appeared in Alan Bott's 1993 *Short History*.[41]

The Merton Limes

The college undertook a major reshaping of the urban landscape of Oxford by authorising the felling of an avenue of limes in the Fellows' Garden in the summer of 1996 (Figures 13.11, 13.12). These trees had been there since the eighteenth century and were the sole surviving element of formal garden layouts otherwise vanished over the years. Merton College's garden was on the Register of Parks and Gardens of special historic interest compiled by English Heritage under the National Heritage Act of 1983.[42] The trees concerned were situated in the central (City and University) conservation areas, and were subject to the six weeks notification of intended works to the city council. Eventually the City Council, the college and English Heritage agreed that the trees be removed but a condition was imposed that an archaeological watching brief should accompany the operation. I was approached by Dr Sarah Bendall of the College Garden Committee to organise this. My proposals included a resistivity survey of the whole garden as well as a record of the felling procedure and subsequent analysis of the timber. These the college generously agreed to fund. Ian Gourlay of the University Forestry Institute, Department of Plant Sciences was present at the felling and undertook the analysis. Our observations confirm in some respects what was known but also added new material of some significance.

The Resistivity Survey

This technique records the electrical resistance of the soil which is itself regulated by the moisture content of the ground. Since stone and brick features (such as walls and paths) have lower moisture content than earth-filled features

[39] T. Braun, "The Fellows' Garden until 1720," *Postmaster* (1985); "The Garden from 1720," *Postmaster* (1986).

[40] Cobham Resource Consultants, *Merton College Gardens: a report* (Abingdon, 1993).

[41] Alan Bott, *Merton College: a short history of the buildings* (Oxford: Merton College, 1993), 42–47.

[42] Historic England, Register of Parks and Gardens of Special Historical Interest in England, part 34, Oxfordshire (London, no date).

Figure 13.11: Lime avenue before felling of trees. Photograph: Vernon Brooke.

Figure 13.12: Lime tree showing burrs where it has been pollarded and possibly pleached. Above, the two trunks merge. Photograph: Vernon Brooke.

they will produce readings of higher resistance. Similarly tree holes, bedding trenches, post holes and ditches will all show up in suitable conditions in a mapping of high and low resistance. This produces a pattern of buried features that exist within a metre of the present surface without the necessity of putting in a spade or disturbing the turf. Such a survey was carried out with success at Magdalen College and published in *Oxoniensia*.[43]

The interpretation of the results

The survey located a number of features from earlier garden layouts (Figure 13.13) and indeed from the earlier use of the land before the college acquired it. Salter (1936) reckoned that 'the most potent sign of the depopulation of Oxford is given by the garden of Merton College. Owing to the pestilence of 1349 there were not enough inhabitants to fill the houses of Oxford... the back streets were deserted and Merton was able to buy for a trifle the site of twelve deserted houses'.[44] Prior to 1313 when a series of seven academic halls existed in the land now occupied by the Fellows' Garden, the area comprised a series of eight burgage plots running from Merton Street down to the City wall.[45] These included Nun (Hall), St Alban's Hall, Hart Hall, St Stephen Hall, Elm (Helen) Hall, St Lawrence

[43] See Steane, "The Grounds of Magdalen College." Also Northamptonshire Archaeology, "Resistivity Survey at Merton College, August 1996" (Northampton, 1996).

[44] Herbert E. Salter, *Medieval Oxford* (Oxford: Oxford Historical Society, 1936), 88.

[45] Jeremy I. Catto (ed.), *The History of the University of Oxford: vol. I, the early Oxford schools* (Oxford: Clarendon Press, 1984), map 3.

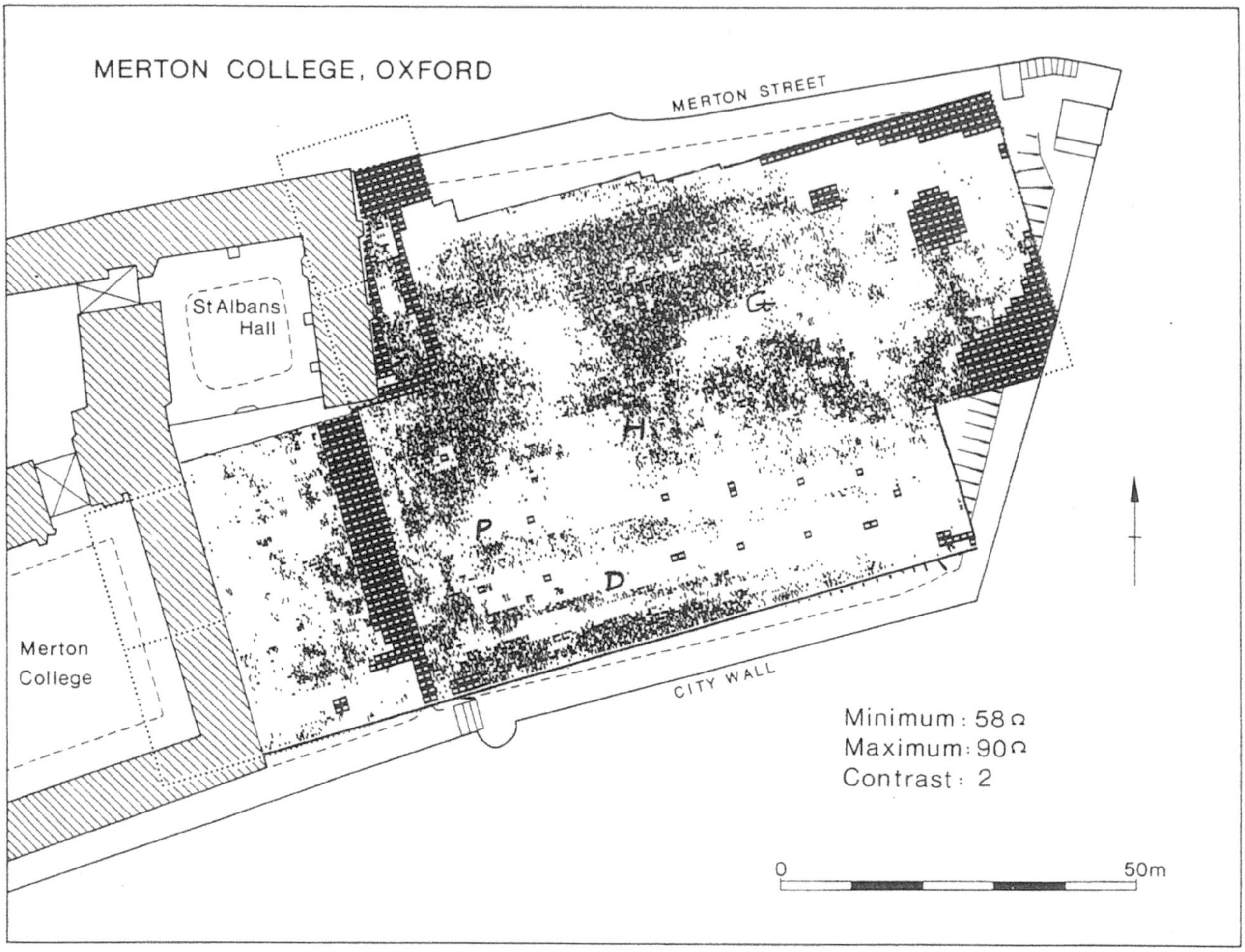

Figure 13.13: Resistivity survey. Courtesy of Northamptonshire County Council.

Hall and Runcival Hall. HB Salter in his survey of Oxford, has reconstructed the history of these tenements.[46] Robert Peberdy (pers. comm.) reckons that the original medieval tenement plots were three perches (49½ ft) wide along the street front. He has calculated that at the east side of Merton's Front Quad there were two plots which were occupied in the Middle Ages by Nun Hall and St Alban's Hall; the present Merton Fellows' Garden as far eastward as the sharp turn in Merton Street occupies seven original tenement plots. There are three features, numbered K to L in the Northampton report,[47] which may denote the ditches running north-south dividing these plots. They point towards an east-west feature which is approximately parallel with the city wall and may represent the boundary of the previous intra-mural road. K and L are spaced about 20 m apart, K and P are about five metres apart.

By 1465 the earlier arrangement of plots together with the buildings upon them had been amalgamated (and presumably the buildings removed) to form Merton College's present garden.[48] The College put the north wall bounding the Fellows' Garden into good repair when Henry Milton and a mason called Blake were employed in making a wall for the Great Garden in 1500. This garden, however, may have been within the site of Fellows' Quad, as suggested by Martin and Highfield.[49] What is certain is that the north wall of the garden bounding Merton Street is of a number of different phases possibly indicating the gradual increase of the college's holding in this area.

The next piece of evidence for the development of the garden is Agas's map of 1578 showing trees planted in most of the garden and a division between an area of land adjacent to the city wall and the Warden's Garden. There are a series of disconnected high resistance features running north-south of St Alban's Quad which may indicate related walls of the sixteenth century Warden's Garden. Virtually the same layout as shown by Agas appears in Hollar's map of 1643, but by the time of Loggan's survey of 1675 the main part of the Fellows' Garden had been formalised with subdivision into four plots, each hedged.[50] The garden was transformed into roughly the same plan as that at Wadham College (Figure 13.14). There are two areas of high density (marked G and M in the Northampton report) which may

[46] Salter, *Medieval Oxford,* 198–200; 247–48.
[47] Northamptonshire Archaeology, "Resistivity Survey."
[48] Braun, "The Garden from 1720," 45.
[49] Geoffrey H. Martin and John R.L. Highfield, *A History of Merton College, Oxford* (Oxford: Oxford University Press, 1997), 36.
[50] Braun, "The Garden from 1720," 40, 48.

Figure 13.14: Features possibly related to Loggan's survey of 1675. The south terrace is in place showing steps leading up to it from an avenue of trees. There is another building in Loggan's map at the junction of the Fellows' and Warden's gardens. Courtesy of Northamptonshire County Council.

relate to the Loggan layout. Loggan also recorded the east terrace showing steps leading up to it from an avenue of trees. His bird's eye view also shows the Warden's summer house (Figure 13.10). This Anthony Wood objected to. He described how:

> The Wardens garden must be altered, new Trees planted, Arbours made, Rootes of choice flowers bought etc. All which the unnecessary yet the poor college must pay for them; and all this to please a woman. Not content with these matters, there must be a new Summer-House built at the south end of the Warden's Garden, wherein her Ladyship and her Gossips may take their pleasure, and any Eves Dropper of the family may harken what any of the Fellows should accidentally talk of in the passage to their owne Garden.[51]

It lasted until about 1800 and appears in the series of drawings made by J.B. Malchair.[52]

Faden's map of 1789 shows the Warden's Garden to be divided into a series of flower beds (Figure 13.15), while the Fellows' Garden was covered with rows of trees. For a fellow such as John Warnford 'it delighted in vertuous studies as he did and would walk several times with him in shady recesses and retired walks to each others' comfort'.[53] It seems that the lime avenue which is the principal subject of this paper was already in existence, and indeed was the successor of an earlier avenue in the same position that appears on the Loggan map (Figure 13.14). The southern terrace has also appeared adjoining the city wall, with the steps at the south western end but the bastion shown at the south eastern corner of Loggan's map has gone. We have evidence for two further features of the eighteenth-century layout, both of which appear in Malchair's drawings. Evidently there was a winding path between two masses of trees, presumably a serpentine feature beloved of eighteenth-century gardeners such as William Kent at Rousham. Seemingly there was the erection of the Fellows' Summer House in 1709.[54]

Hoggar's map, dated 1850 (Figure 13.16), showed the present (until 1996) lime avenue apparently straddling a path leading on to the eastern terrace. The rest of the garden at this time was laid out with clumps of trees or shrubs connected by the sinuous path. The path seems to show up clearly in the resistivity survey but it may of course be an earlier feature. Resistivity does not distinguish between periods; it simply records the multi-period mesh of activity. Hoggar showed the Warden's Garden to contain a central flower bed. This does not show on the resistivity survey.

The Ordnance Survey plan of 1875 indicates that by this period the Fellows' Garden was almost completely covered by trees. These have been largely removed in the present century apart from a group of sycamores and a mulberry tree. The felling of the limes has almost completed the process.

The felling of the limes

The limes were cut down between 2 and 12 September 1996. One was left *in situ*. Following felling, ten complete stem cross-sections were cut and stored for closer detailed analysis. The rest of the commentary relies heavily on information provided by Ian Gourlay. The method used was as follows: Two radii were cut from each disk. Two slices (one above the other) were cut from each radius. After drying for three months all samples were polished and subsequently examined under a low-power microscope in order to define growth rings. A thin application of Vaseline was used in order to enhance cell colour change. The highest ring count was recorded for each sample.

The mean maximum total ring count across the nine trees sampled was 220: the maximum was 232. This means that the planting period was within a few years of 1776. Notable periods of fast or slow growth were observed in the majority of samples as follows: Wide rings showing fast growth years 1–20 (1776–96). Again growth rings 70–90 (1846–66) were noticeably wider. Narrow growth ring years 96–112 (1871–88) and very narrow rings, years 140 to the felling (1919–96). All the trees had been reduced in height according to the college gardener 35 years ago.

There were interesting indications of former management practices. At a height of approximately six to eight feet there were large areas of swollen burrs (c/f Figure 13.12), such growth indicating pruning or major disturbance to the trees' growth at this point. Above this for approximately seven to eight feet in some trees there was a longitudinal depression indicative of two stems joining together. In other trees one could still see daylight through the tree at this point between two separate stems. At approximately 15 feet the twin stems were noticed as coalescing as one stem and here was a further area of swelling of burrs and sucker growth. The speed of growth, age and height of the trees at the points where twin stems diverge and then merge again suggests the following. At an age of 5–15 years selecting and training of the twin stems began. At this stage it may be suggested that the trees may have been encouraged by pruning and training to form a tunnel or arch-like effect. It may be that the young branches were pleached (entwined and trained) possibly initially to a frame, resulting in a regular form of hedge requiring frequent trimming. This explanation accounts for a number of square sectioned (i.e. hand forged) nails driven into the stems 120 years ago.

The phenomenon of the two stems being brought together to form a single stem is probably to be explained by a change of garden design. Instead of pleached hedges it now became fashionable to have an avenue, and the trees were permitted to resume their upward growth unimpeded.

[51] Nicolas R. Kiessling, *The Life of Anthony Wood in His Own Words* (Oxford: Bodleian Library, 2009), 85.
[52] Corpus Christi College (CCC) MS 443, 1.19 and VI, 7 and 9.
[53] Kiessling, *The Life of Anthony Wood*, 43.
[54] Martin and Highfield, *A History of Merton College*, 236 and plate 22.

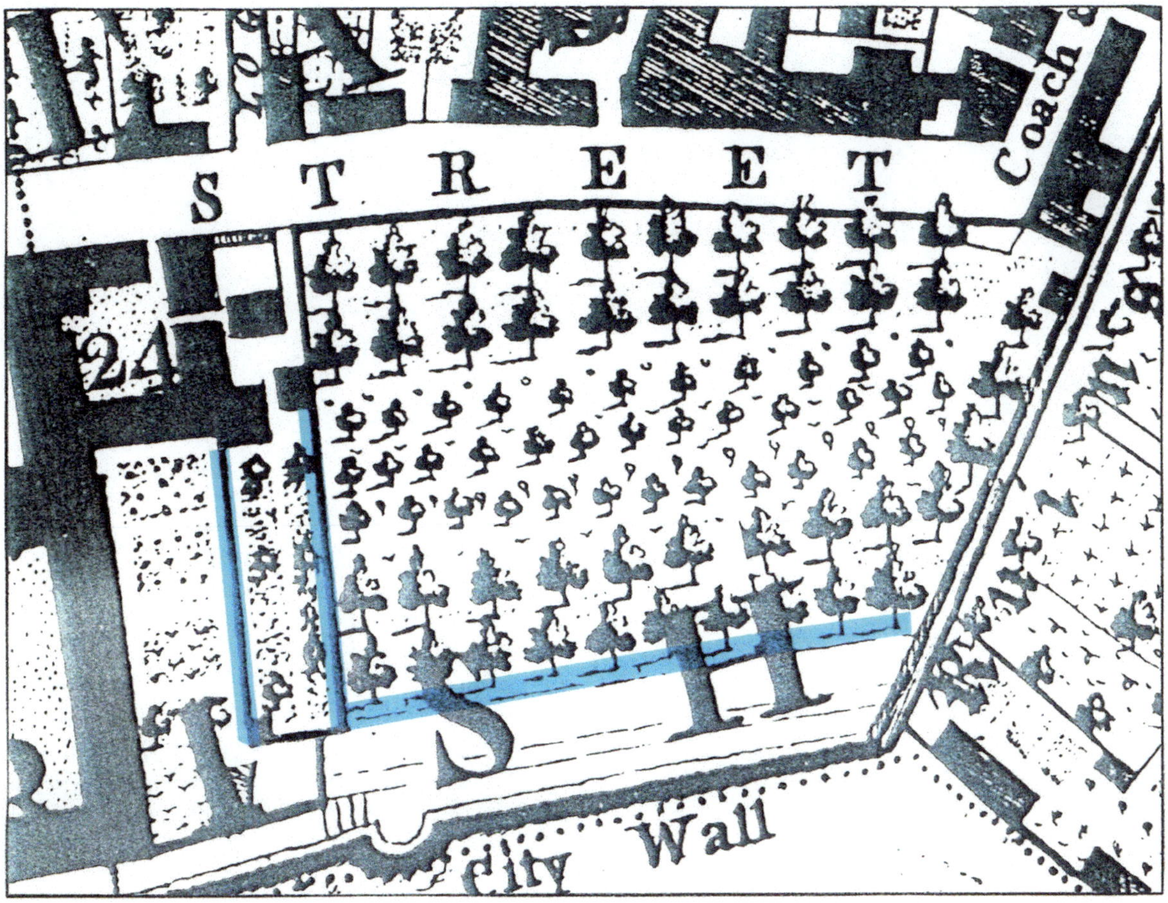

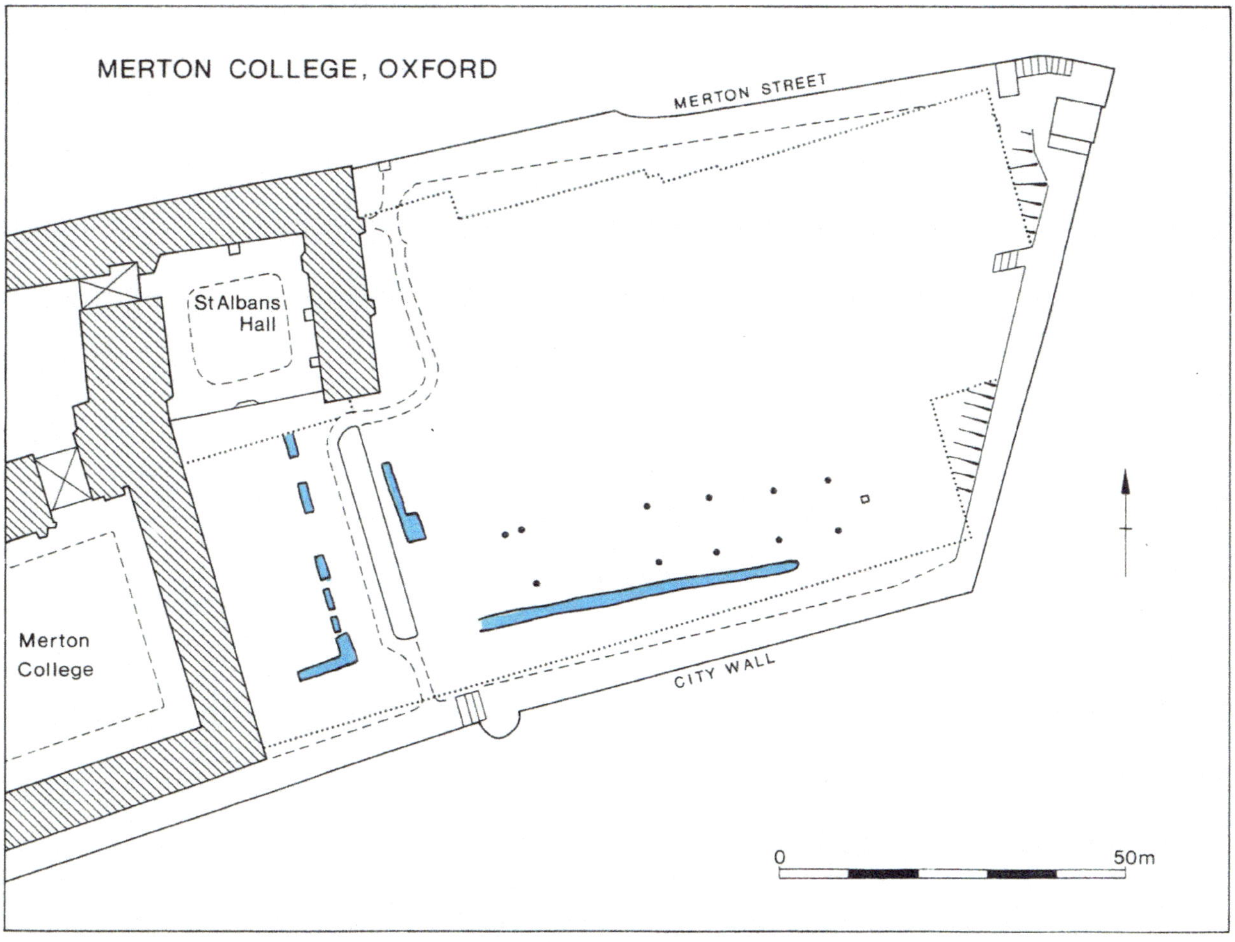

Figure 13.15: Features possibly relating to Faden's map of 1789. The Warden's Garden was covered by rows of trees. The lime avenue is apparently there at this date. Courtesy of Northamptonshire County Council.

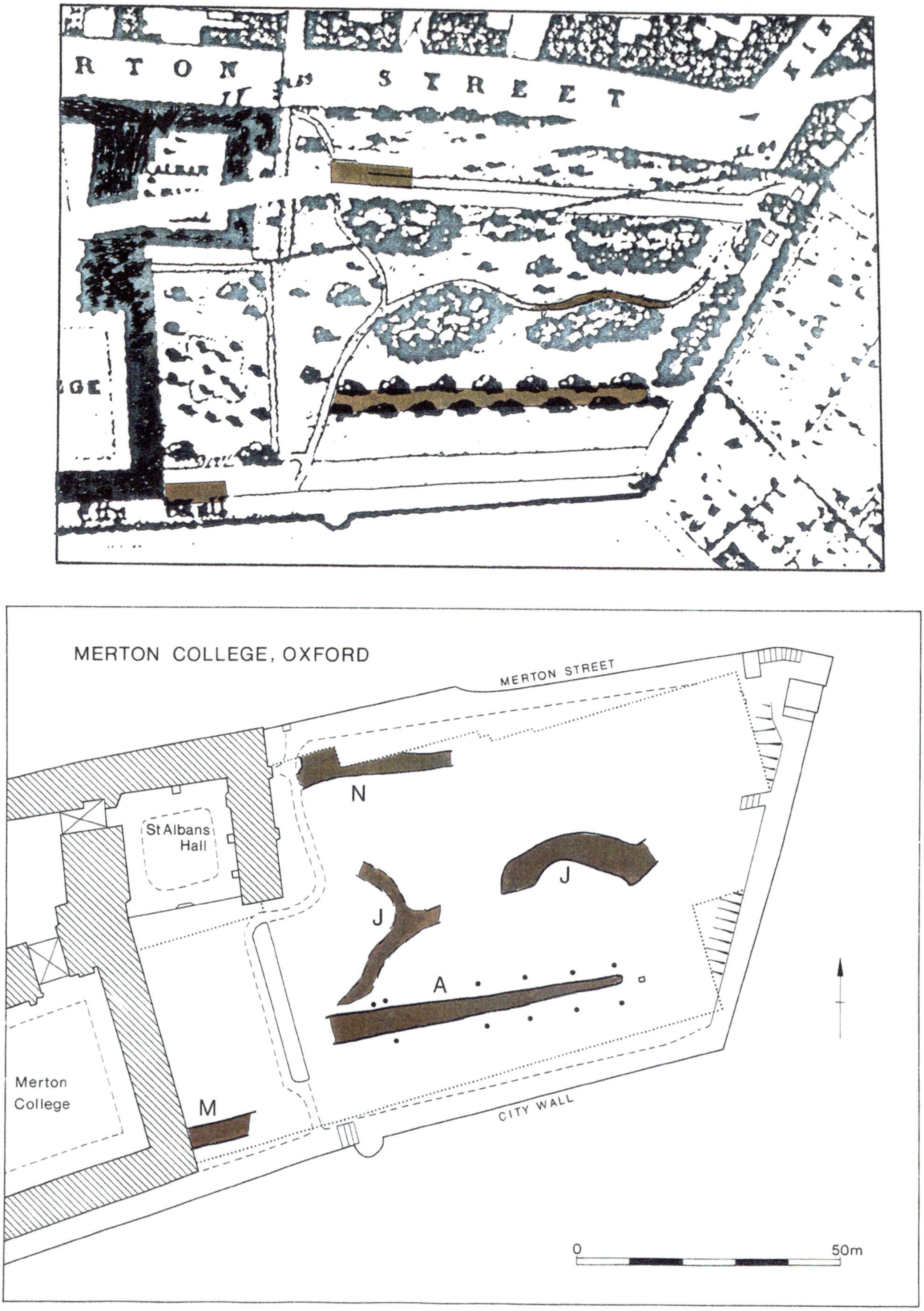

Figure 13.16: Hoggar's map, dated 1850, shows the present lime avenue flanking a path leading to the eastern terrace. The rest of the garden is laid out at this time with clumps of trees connected by a sinuous path. Hoggar showed the Warden's Garden containing a central flower bed but there is no evidence of this from the resistivity survey. Courtesy of Northamptonshire County Council.

The question of whether it was necessary or wise to fell the limes arises. One tree had fallen in the summer of 1992 and 'the remains of that tree and of three others… identified as being immediately hazardous were felled on the grounds of public safety in 1993'.[55]. Of the incomplete avenue one tree, not felled, remains. Ian Gourlay reported on the condition of the others, stating that 'despite some decay higher in the trees especially around the wounds caused by the tops having been reduced in the past, and other broken branches, there appeared to be little major decay or decline. The butt sections, after felling, showed little decay at ground level, only one out of the nine was hollow'. The college, however, was advised that the lime trees were a potential hazard and that more would have to be felled in the near future on safety grounds, and it felt that it had to act on this advice. Despite a vigorous campaign by Tom Braun to replace the limes with a like avenue, a more random scheme is now in place. Oxford has thus lost an ancient piece of formal tree planting. However, one can see an excellent example of a (nineteenth-century) pleached lime avenue, such as Merton College had, at Arley Hall, Cheshire.

Acknowledgements

For part one on Wadham College I should like to thank Scott Mandelbrote; the late Professor Richard Sharpe; Philip Powell; Lord Saye and Sele, and the Warden and Fellows. For part two, Merton College, my gratitude goes to the following: John Ashdown and Edith Gollnast for information on planning history; Dr Pigott for expertise on limes; Brian Dix for advice on garden archaeology; the late Dr Roger Highfield for commenting on an earlier text; Dr Sarah Bendall for advice; Vernon Brooke for photographs; Ian Gourlay for expertise in recording the limes, and the Warden and Fellows of Merton College for interest and support.

Bibliography

Unpublished primary sources

Corpus Christi College (CCC).

MS 443. Sketchbooks of J.B. Malchair [*c.*1730–1812].

Bodleian Library (BL).

Gough Maps Oxfordshire 4. Ralph Agas's bird's eye view of Oxford (1578).

Published primary sources

de Beer, Esmond S., ed. John Evelyn, *Diary*. Oxford: Oxford University Press, 1959.

Hunter, Alexander, ed. John Evelyn's *Sylva, or a Discourse of Forest Trees*. York: A. Ward for J. Dodsley, 1776.

Ingram, John E., ed. *Elysium Britannicum: or The Royal Gardens*, by John Evelyn. Philadelphia: University of Pennsylvania Press, 2001.

Kiessling, Nicolas R. *The Life of Anthony Wood in His Own Words*. Oxford: Bodleian Library, 2009.

Lawson, William. *The Country House-wife's Garden* (1617). London: Breslich and Foss, 1983.

Loggan, David. *Oxonia Illustrata*. Oxford: Sheldonian Theatre, 1675.

MacGregor, Arthur, *et al. Manuscript Catalogues of the Early Museum Collections 1683–1886* part 1, BAR International Series 907. Oxford: BAR Publishing with the Ashmolean Museum, 2000.

Parkinson, John. *Paradisi in Sole: paradisus terrestus* (1629). London: Methuen, 1904.

Plot, Robert. *Natural History of Oxfordshire* (1676). 2nd edn, Oxford: Leon Lichfield, 1705.

Smeaton, Oliphant, ed. *Francis Bacon's Essays*. London: Dent, 1935.

Stone, Lawrence. *Catalogue of Muniments of Wadham College*. London: Historical MSS Commission, National Register of Archives, 1962.

Secondary sources

Arkell, W.J. *The Geology of Oxford*. Oxford: Oxford University Press, 1947.

Bailey, Bruce, Nikolaus Pevsner, and Bridget Cherry. *The Buildings of England: Northamptonshire*. New edn, London: Yale University Press, 2013.

Beaumont James, Tom, and Christopher M. Gerrard. *Clarendon: Landscape of Kings*. Macclesfield: Windgather, 2007.

Blair, W. John. "A Monastic Fragment at Wadham College, Oxford." *Oxoniensia* 41 (1976): 161–67.

Blomfield, Reginald T. *The Formal Garden in England*. London: Macmillan, 1892.

Bodleian Library, University of Oxford. *Bodleian Library Record* 16, no. 3 (April 1998).

Bott, Alan. *Merton College: a short history of the buildings*. Oxford: Merton College, 1993.

Braun, T. "The Fellows' Garden until 1720." *Postmaster* (1985): 45–50.

Braun, T. "The Garden from 1720." *Postmaster* (1986): 7–13.

Briggs, Nancy. "The Foundation of Wadham College Oxford." *Oxoniensia* 21 (1956): 61–81.

Catto, Jeremy I., ed. *The History of the University of Oxford: vol. I, the early Oxford schools*. Oxford: Clarendon Press, 1984.

[55] Dr S. Bendall, pers. comm.

Cobham Resource Consultants. *Merton College Gardens: a report*. Abingdon, 1993.

Dobson, Austin, ed. *The Diary of John Evelyn* (1906). Repr London: Routledge, 1996.

Historic England, *Register of Parks and Gardens of Special Historical Interest in England*, part 34, Oxfordshire. London, no date.

Jackson Thomas G. *Wadham College, Oxford.* Oxford: Clarendon Press, 1893.

Kemp, Anthony. "The Fortifications of Oxford during the Civil War." *Oxoniensia* 42 (1977): 237–41.

Lattey, R.T., *et al*. "A Contemporary Map of the Defences of Oxford." *Oxoniensia* 1 (1936): 161–73

Mabberley, David J. "The Gardens." In *Wadham College Oxford*, edited by Clifford S.L. Davies and Jane Garnett, 100–22. Oxford: Wadham College, 1994.

Martin, Geoffrey H., and John R.L. Highfield. *A History of Merton College, Oxford.* Oxford: Oxford University Press, 1997.

Northamptonshire Archaeology. "Resistivity Survey at Merton College, August 1996." Northampton, 1996.

Page, William, ed. *The Victoria History of the County of Oxford*, vol. 2. London: Archibald Constable, 1907.

Pigott, D. "The Clones of Common Limes (Tilia X Vulgaris Hayne) planted in England during the Seventeenth and Eighteenth Centuries." *The New Phytologist* 121 (1992): 487–93.

Salter, Herbert E. *Medieval Oxford.* Oxford: Oxford Historical Society, 1936.

Salter, Herbert E., and Mary D. Lobel, eds. *VCH Oxon*, vol. 3. London: Oxford University Press, 1954.

Steane, John M. "The Development of Tudor and Stuart Garden Design in Northamptonshire." *Northamptonshire Past and Present* 5, no.5 (1977): 1–23.

Steane, John M. "The Grounds of Magdalen College 1480–1880." *Oxoniensia* 63 (1998): 91–104.

14

Brief Lives? Artefacts, memory and the afterlife of medieval monuments

Christopher M. Gerrard

Durham University

Abstract: A single post-medieval artefact, found during excavations at Clarendon Palace in the 1930s, provides a detailed case study in biographical approaches to archaeological objects. Historical, social and political contexts combine to reveal a complex story which suggest that evidence for later activity on medieval sites might be worthy of further consideration and should not be so easily dismissed as the litter of later generations. In this case, a late-seventeenth century coronation medallion may have had personal significance for Henry Hyde, the second Earl of Clarendon.

Key words: Post-medieval archaeology; special deposits; biographies of artefacts; Clarendon Palace; medallion; the Hyde family

Introduction

The recovery of post-medieval and early modern objects from later medieval sites has attracted little attention from the archaeologist. Theirs is a predictable story, or so it would seem, an uninteresting scatter of debris quickly dismissed as the litter of stone robbers, iconoclasts and antiquaries. And questioning this assumption proves by no means straightforward. Even a cursory survey reveals that many sites occupied in later Middle Ages continued in use in some shape or form; only a rare few were entirely abandoned. Of those that were, just a small proportion have been investigated and their excavators have not always been kind even to these. When the medieval monuments of Church and State came to be 'cleared' in the first half of the twentieth century, later layers were removed with little thought. Trenches were run around the edges of buildings, 'chasing' the walls and leaving the deposits in the centre to be shovelled away.[1] The aim was to reveal the layout of the principal buildings on the site and explain it all in a guidebook; later finds were only selectively retained,[2] and the end result is that we know little about them. Even today, when our knowledge of post-medieval artefacts is so much better developed, the costs of post-excavation often mean that more attention is paid to artefacts from the main phases of occupation on the site. All too often, the unintended consequence is that we know less than we should about later activities on medieval sites, clandestine or otherwise; our understanding of their full 'life cycle' is curtailed.

[1] For example, Peter Fergusson and Stuart Harrison, *Rievaulx Abbey: community, architecture and memory* (London: Yale University Press, 1999).

[2] For example, at Dunstanburgh Castle, Northumberland. See Robert C. Bosanquet, "Excavations at Dunstanburgh Castle in 1931," *Archaeologia Aeliana* 13, 4th series (1936): 279–92.

This paper challenges the notion that the afterlife of medieval monuments in Britain is a simple tale of decay, thieving, careless tourists and recycling. It offers a richer set of explanations inspired by the notion that there is a significant relationship to be unravelled between objects and people, even for such a well-documented period of our human past.[3] Here I draw particularly upon recent discussions of archaeological 'memory',[4] material mnemonics,[5] 'special deposits',[6] and biographies of artefacts,[7] in order to emphasise that what happens to objects can sometimes tell us about people and their attachments to particular places. I will take one artefact as my main case study and, in the spirit of this volume, my choice is an object first published by Tom James and Annie Robinson in 1988 in their account of the history and archaeology of Clarendon Palace in Wiltshire.[8] As we shall see, this is a rare example of a post-medieval artefact from a medieval site that links person, historical event, place and property, and one that raises broader issues about the way in which material culture was deployed.

[3] Elizabeth DeMarrais, "The Materialization of Culture," in *Rethinking Materiality: the engagement of mind with the material world,* ed. Elizabeth DeMarrais, Chris Gosden and Colin Renfrew (Oxford: Oxbow Books, 2004), 11–22.

[4] For example, Ruth M. Van Dyke and Susan E. Alcock (eds), *Archaeologies of Memory* (Oxford: Blackwell, 2003).

[5] Katina T. Lillios and Vasileios Tsamis (eds), *Material Mnemonics: everyday memory in prehistoric Europe* (Oxford: Oxbow Books, 2010).

[6] Richard Bradley, *The Passage of Arms: an archaeological analysis of prehistoric hoard and votive deposits* (Oxford: Oxbow Books, 1998).

[7] Chris Gosden and Yvonne Marshall, "The Cultural Biography of Objects," *World Archaeology* 31 (1999): 169–78; Roberta Gilchrist, *Medieval Life: archaeology and the life course* (Woodbridge: Boydell, 2012).

[8] Tom Beaumont James and Anne M. Robinson, *Clarendon Palace: the history and archaeology of a medieval palace and hunting lodge near Salisbury, Wiltshire,* Reports of the Research Committee of the Society of Antiquaries of London 45 (London: Society of Antiquaries and Thames and Hudson, 1988).

Discovery

Among the finds recovered during the 1930s excavations at Clarendon Palace is a late-seventeenth century artefact that has always struck me as curious: a medallion or medal of William and Mary, very likely struck in honour of their coronation on 11 April 1689.[9] The medal is made of pewter and, at about 4cm across, somewhat larger than a coin; it is also pierced near its rim, so it was suspended at some point in its life (Figure 14.1). Its precise findspot is not known and this is hardly a surprise given that the workforce on the site in the 1930s comprised inexperienced students and labourers brought together by the Universities Council for Unemployed Camps.[10] This workforce undoubtedly brought some useful skills to bear but there is little doubt that the impression of serenity and order conveyed by the 1930s site photographs is not the full story. Even with his willing band of more experienced helpers, it cannot have been easy for the 25 year old supervisor John Charlton to control the excavation. As a result, we know almost nothing of the precise circumstances of this particular find, although sketchy museum records suggest that it was recovered immediately north of the Antioch Chamber, and from its date we can deduce that it must have been deposited long after the palace had fallen into disuse in the last quarter of the fifteenth century.

The object

Coronations in the seventeenth century were, in some respects, not so very different from the grand royal occasions of today. The coronation of William and Mary in 1689 was a moment of public celebration, even though there was some uneasiness about the succession. Across the country there were speeches, parades and feasting. The diarist Narcissus Luttrell noted 'great splendour and joy' at 'several places' including Scotland where 'the evening concluded with the ringing of bells, bonefires, &c'.[11] In London, by far the largest city in Europe at this time, the streets were cleaned and freshly gravelled for processions, pageants, poetry and bonfires. Bells rang, conduits ran with wine, and, at the end of the day, there were fireworks.[12] Luttrell noted:

> The 11th [April], the coronation of their majesties king William and queen Mary was performed at Westminster... there was a great appearance and crowd of people. The ceremony at the Abby being over, they returned to Westminster Hall, where was a splendid dinner to entertain the nobility and persons of quality: the house of commons dined also in an adjacent place to the Hall at their majesties charge, and had each of them a medal in gold given them, of about 50s. value.[13]

The coronation was an opportunity to press home a political message, an image of the new monarchy, and it was in this context that the William and Mary coronation medals were minted – as a badge to symbolise a cause and to legitimatise the Glorious Revolution. By this date medals were by no means a novelty; they had already circulated in England for many years. The first medal minted for an English coronation was for Edward VI in 1547 and there had been others since then to exploit public interest in Elizabethan feats such as Drake's circumnavigation of the globe and the defeat of the Spanish Armada. More recently, the English Civil War had transformed medals into visible emblems of personal political loyalties; there was even a medal struck for the first Earl of Clarendon by engraver Thomas Simon.[14]

At previous coronations, a limited number of medals were distributed during the ceremony itself, apparently being tossed out to assembled spectators.[15] On this occasion, both Luttrell and the diarist John Evelyn reported that all who attended the coronation feast received 'a Medaile of Gold' and this included members of the House of Commons who were present in Westminster Hall for the 'greate feast'. Evelyn, slightly more conservative in his monetary estimate, calculated his medal's value at 'five and fourty shill'.[16] Either way, they were valuable and exclusive objects; fewer than 1500 were minted from a design commissioned by the Crown from the reputable medallist John Roettiers. However, our Clarendon find was not among them – nor is it a copy of Roettiers' approved design in a more affordable base metal. It is in fact one of several alternative versions struck for the event, most of which carry the busts of the royal couple on one side and some kind of insignia on the reverse.[17] The propaganda messages on these unofficial versions could be distinctly unsubtle: one depicts an old oak tree torn up by the roots lying next to a young orange tree, complete with the legend *Meliorem lapsa locavit* ('His place is filled by a better'). It took little imagination to see that James II, a Catholic, was represented by the oak while his eldest daughter's husband (and his own nephew) William of Orange was 'the better' and a Protestant. Like the Elizabethan medals that had gone before, their purpose was to reinforce the 'stamp' of the royal title.

---

[9] James and Robinson, *Clarendon Palace*, 199–200.

[10] John Field, "Able Bodies: work camps and the training of the unemployed in Britain before 1939," unpublished paper delivered at The Significance of the Historical Perspective in Adult Education Research, University of Cambridge, Institute of Continuing Education, 2009; John Field, "Student Volunteering in Britain between the Wars: summer camps and the unemployed," unpublished paper delivered at the Institute for Volunteering Research, Conference on Students, Volunteering and Social Action: 1880–1990, Toynbee Hall, London, 25 November 2010.

[11] Narcissus Luttrell, *A Brief Historical Relation of State Affairs from September 1678, to April 1714*, 6 vols (Farnborough: Gregg International Publishers, 1857 [republ 1969]), vol. 1, 522.

[12] Carolyn A. Edie, "The Public Face of Royal Ritual: sermons, medals, and civic ceremony in later Stuart coronations," *Huntington Library Quarterly* 53, no.4 (1990): 311–36.

[13] Luttrell, *A Brief Historical Relation of State Affairs*, 520–21.

[14] Mark Jones, *The Art of the Medal* (London: British Museum Publications, 1979), 67–72.

[15] Edie, "The Public Face of Royal Ritual," 323.

[16] Esmond S. de Beer (ed.), *The Diary of John Evelyn, vol. 4 Kalendarium, 1673–1689* (Oxford: Clarendon Press, 1955), 633.

[17] William Till, *Descriptive Particulars of English Coronation Medals: from the inauguration of King Edward the Sixth to our present sovereign the Queen Victoria* (London: Longman, Orme, Brown, Green and Longmans, 1846).

Figure 14.1: The coronation medal of William and Mary found at Clarendon Palace in the 1930s and now in Salisbury Museum. Note the piercing close to the rim. Copyright: David Cousins and The Salisbury Museum.

An analysis of the artefact therefore provides us with our first set of clues. The Clarendon medal appears to be of the more affordable kind available to private buyers. Quite possibly its purchaser would have first learnt of it through an advertisement in a London newspaper where novelties such as medals and portrait prints were announced. This was a recent phenomenon; retail advertisements had appeared for the first time in 1668 and, in this new market, the twice weekly *London Gazette* had an almost unchallenged monopoly. Among the medical services, descriptions of army deserters, missing children and thieving servants,[18] there were also adverts for medals which could be viewed and acquired at the establishments of goldsmiths, booksellers and cutlers. The demand for these purchases perhaps came from Protestants with libraries and 'closets' or smaller studies where they could privately advertise their allegiances.[19] In this case, only a small number may have been produced; only one other example of this particular design is known, recovered by a metal detectorist from a field near Cookham, north of Maidenhead.[20]

The people: Clarendon, the Hydes and Queen Mary II

To explain how this medallion came to be buried at Clarendon Palace there are some significant pointers in Queen Mary's background (Figure 14.2). Mary was one of eight children born to Lady Anne Hyde, the first of James II's two wives, and a grand-daughter to Frances Aylesbury and Edward Hyde, first Earl of Clarendon (1609–74), who came to own the Clarendon estate after the Civil War.[21] Mary would have been 12 years of age when Edward died in Rouen in 1674.[22] This timeline shows that, by the time of Mary's coronation in 1689, the title and ownership of Clarendon Park had long since passed to Edward's eldest son Henry Hyde (1638–1709). Henry was Mary's uncle, and both he and his brother Lawrence were brothers-in-law to the exiled King James and had been highly favoured under the previous monarch. Henry was appointed Lord Privy Seal (Feb–Sept 1685) under James, Lord Lieutenant of Ireland (Sept 1685–Feb 1687) and a Privy Councillor (1680–89) (Figure 14.3), while his influential brother Lawrence, the Earl of Rochester, became First Lord of the Treasury (1679–84), Lord President (1684–85) and Lord Treasurer (1685–86) (Figure 14.4).[23]

There is, however, absolutely nothing to suggest that either the first or the second Earl actually lived on the Clarendon estate. During the seventeenth century there was no suitable grand residence to be found there, only a number of lodges occupied by tenants, keepers and foresters to which we might add 'severall small beggarly cottages' which may have been pulled down.[24] The grandest of all the houses in Clarendon Park in Edward and Henry's day was probably that in the possession of George Cooper MP at or near the site of Palmer's Lodge, not far from

[18] Claire H.L. George, "Marketing Medals in Early Modern Britain," *The Medal* 42 (2003): 23–26.
[19] Antony Griffiths, "Advertisements for Medals in the *London Gazette*," *The Medal* 15 (1989): 4–6.
[20] Portable Antiquities Scheme (PAS) SUR–925737.

[21] Tom Beaumont James and Christopher M. Gerrard, *Clarendon: landscape of kings* (Macclesfield: Windgather Press, 2007), 104–06.
[22] For background see Eveline Cruickshanks, *The Glorious Revolution* (London: Macmillan, 2000); Tim Harris, *Revolution: the great crisis of the British monarchy 1685–1720* (London: Allen Lane, 2006).
[23] Anon., *An Essay Towards the Life of Lawrence, Earl of Rochester* (London: John Morphew, 1711), 171; Harris, *Revolution*, 105–06.
[24] Thomas H. Lister (ed.), *Life and Administration of Edward, First Earl of Clarendon: letters and papers*, vol. 3 (London: Longman, Orme, Brown, Green, and Longmans, 1837), 326–57.

Figure 14.2: Queen Mary II in a portrait by Jan van der Vaart. Mary II (1662-1694) was the eldest child of James II and his first wife Anne Hyde. She married William of Orange in 1677 and their coronation took place in Westminster Abbey on 11 April 1689. Copyright: Wikimedia Commons / Public Domain.

the present mansion.[25] James Ayres (see chapter sixteen) describes a possible hunting lodge encased within that building. Edward Hyde, the first earl, mostly lodged in London, and after 1664 and until his exile in 1667 he was at his lavish new home at Clarendon House in Piccadilly. When he was in the country at all, Edward spent his time at his estate near Oxford at Cornbury which he had purchased in 1661. The alterations and additions made at Cornbury House by architect Hugh May are usually ascribed to the first earl, but the work also seems to have continued in his absence and after his death in 1674,[26] so presumably Henry, the second earl, was involved too. In spite of his investment, however, Henry seems to have had little time for Cornbury, preferring to be closer to Parliament and the royal court in London. Even after James II dismissed him from office in 1687 and his ties to the capital were loosened, he spent just a few weeks there each year, his visit in March 1687 being one such occasion.[27] At the time of Mary's coronation, Henry was distracted at his wife's Tudor home at Swallowfield Park outside Reading in Berkshire; between June 1688 and the summer of 1689, and with the help of the architect William Talman he was pulling out old glass and wainscoting, demolishing and rebuilding walls to create an H-shaped layout of which very little survives today.[28] While Cornbury lay empty, it was therefore Swallowfield that occupied Henry's time and his ever more limited funds; matters were made worse by the need to raise funds for his eldest son's marriage settlement. As his financial position became steadily gloomier, so by 1694 Henry was selling off his father's pictures and the library at Cornbury and in around 1697 he sold the entire Oxfordshire estate to his brother, the earl of Rochester, who soon after tried to tempt the Duke of Shrewsbury into a tenancy in February 1699.[29] The sale of Cornbury, however, failed to stop Henry's financial slide and, according to one biographer, he engaged in reckless speculations such as digging for coal in Windsor Forest.[30] Two years before his death in 1709, mounting debt finally obliged him to sell off the Clarendon estate that bore his title. As was said at the time, by this point in his life 'he almost wanted bread to eat'.[31]

It can be established from this abbreviated biography that Mary had an association with the Clarendon estate through her uncle Henry for the five years that remained of her life after her coronation; the Queen died unexpectedly of smallpox in late December 1694 at the age of 32. But there may have been other family links to Clarendon too. Writing in his *Monumenta Britannica* (compiled in 1688–89), the Wiltshire-born antiquary John Aubrey relates the discovery of 'severall Roman coynes: and some English coines... and two old Andirons six foot high' at Clarendon Park.[32] These finds, Aubrey tells us, are 'in the countrey w[it]h mr Hyde my Lord's Agent'. The phrasing is perplexing here because, on the face of it, the 'mr Hyde' being referred to cannot be the second Earl, Henry Hyde; Aubrey must be referring to another member of the family. We cannot identify this individual with certainty but among the candidates is William Hyde, whose will survives for 1691 and who died 'at Clarendon'.[33] There were also other Hydes not very far away; Alexander Hyde (1598–1667), Bishop of Salisbury from 1665 to 1667, was first cousin to Edward, the first Earl of Clarendon,[34] and of his 11 brothers, the

[25] Beaumont James and Gerrard, *Clarendon: landscape of kings,* 101.

[26] English Heritage, British Listed Buildings, "Cornbury House, Cornbury and Wychwood." Accessed 6 July 2018. http://www.britishlistedbuildings.co.uk/en-252455-cornbury-house-cornbury-and-wychwood.

[27] Samuel W. Singer (ed.), *The Correspondence of Henry Hyde, Earl of Clarendon, and his Brother Lawrence Hyde, Earl of Rochester: with the diary of Lord Clarendon from 1687 to 1690...* (Milton Keynes: Lightning Source, 2012), 167.

[28] Singer, *The Correspondence of Henry Hyde,* 279; 285; English Heritage, British Listed Buildings, "Swallowfield Park and Adjoining Stable Block, Swallowfield." Accessed 6 July 2018. https://www.britishlistedbuildings.co.uk/101313056-swallowfield-park-and-adjoining-stable-block-swallowfield#.W0IB6be0Xcs.

[29] Singer, *The Correspondence of Henry Hyde*, 344–47.

[30] Sidney Lee, "Hyde, Henry (1638–1709)," *Dictionary of National Biography* (London: Smith, Elder and Co, 1891).

[31] Robert Beddard (ed.), *A Kingdom without a King: the journal of the provisional government in the Revolution of 1688* (Oxford: Phaidon, 1988), 201.

[32] John Fowles and Rodney Legg (eds), *Monumenta Britannica: or, a miscellany of British antiquities* (Sherborne: Dorset Publishing Company, 1980), 971.

[33] The National Archives (TNA) PROB 11/405/282. Will of William Hyde of Clarendon Park, Wiltshire, 1691.

[34] Stephen Wright, "Hyde, Alexander (1596x8–1667)," *Oxford Dictionary of National Biography* (2004), accessed 29 January, 2013, http://www.oxforddnb.com/view/article/14324.

Figure 14.3: Henry Hyde, 2nd Earl of Clarendon with his wife, Theodosia. Here in an oil painting by Peter Lely. Henry was the eldest son of Edward Hyde, the 1st Earl of Clarendon, and his second wife, Frances Aylesbury. Henry succeeded to the earldom on his father's death in 1674. Copyright: Wikimedia Commons / Public Domain.

barrister and politician Robert (1595/6–1665) might also make a plausible 'mr hyde'.[35] Whatever the case, it would appear that there were Hydes living at Clarendon at the time of the coronation in 1689. Once more, Henry Hyde himself seems to have been a regular visitor. The will of one Clarendon Park resident, Christopher Ewer, who died in 1680, reveals a long string of debts including 15 shillings to the Earl of Clarendon's coachman and groom, and fully £80 to Henry Hyde himself.[36] Quite how Ewer could ever have managed to build up such a large debt is a mystery; he goes unmentioned in Henry Hyde's diaries for 1687–90,[37] but there was very likely a family connection. We can deduce this from the will of William Hyde, who wished 'to bee decently buried at West Grimstead neare my uncle and aunt Ewer'. William's executrix was his cousin Mary Ewer 'of Clarendon Parke' who went on to receive the residue of his goods, moneys and chattels after his funeral and legacies had been paid off.[38]

This biographical detail provides a second useful set of clues. We can show that one of the faces on the medal is that of Queen Mary, who was a niece of the second Earl of Clarendon, Henry Hyde. At the time of her accession, Henry owned Clarendon Park where the royal palace lies and where the medal in question was discovered. Although Henry did not himself live at Clarendon, preferring to spend his time in London, at his Oxfordshire estate or at his wife's family home, it seems very likely that he did visit and that he allowed at least some of the lodges in the Park to be occupied by members of his extended family. William Hyde, in particular, may have acted on Henry's behalf in administering his Wiltshire property, a role that would have been of acute interest to Henry given his increasingly precarious financial position.

[35] Wilfrid Prest, "*Hyde, Sir Robert* (1595/6–1665)," *Oxford Dictionary of National Biography* (2004), accessed 29 January, 2013, http://www.oxforddnb.com/view/article/14334.

[36] Wiltshire and Swindon History Centre (WSHC), P4/1680/4(i). Account, Inventory, Will of Christopher Ewer, 1680.

[37] Singer, *The Correspondence of Henry Hyde.*

[38] TNA PROB 11/405/282, 1691.

Figure 14.4: Lawrence Hyde, Earl of Rochester (1642–1711), painted c.1685–87 by William Wissing. Thomas Macaulay (1889, 125) described him as a 'rancorous party man.. he drank deep and when he was in a rage – and he very often was in a rage – he swore like a porter'. Copyright: Wikimedia Commons / Public Domain.

The place: the afterlife of a medieval palace

To deepen this inquiry further, it is important to establish what was going on at the end of the seventeenth century at the medieval palace site; evidence that can be pieced together from archaeological and antiquarian records as well as from documentary sources. A good place to begin is with William Stukeley's sketch of 1723 (Figure 14.5). On that day in August, Stukeley took up position at the south-western corner of the palace site and, from that vantage point, he drew the remains of the gatehouse at the west end of the site, the walls of the north-west range along the edge of the scarp and the distinctive crag of the east gable of the Great Hall which still stands today. By 1723 it seems clear that none of the buildings there were roofed or otherwise in use.

One intriguing piece of documentary evidence allows us to creep a little closer to what was happening at the palace site a generation or so earlier. The inventory of 1680 of 'all the goods and chattels' of Christopher Ewer sets out his possessions in the various rooms of a house at an unstated location somewhere in Clarendon Park.[39] Mention is made of a 'dungeon chamber', a Bird room, a Room within the stable and, significantly, the 'Parliament hall'; no specifics are given as to what goods were stored there but this cannot be other than the palace site. Until recently there has been some cause to doubt the case for later activity on the site because the assemblage reported upon by James and Robinson contains so few post-medieval objects.[40] True, there are a handful of fragments of sixteenth–seventeenth century vessel glass and a mid-sixteenth century jetton but very little else bar a seventeenth-century wheel lock pistol.[41] Even if there are records (but no surviving finds) of stonewares and clay pipes excavated from the gatehouse,[42] these were barely sufficient to prove occupation; in 1988 none of the Clarendon pottery at all could be satisfactorily dated after 1250. Today, however, that picture is quite changed. Re-excavation of the spoil heaps and fieldwalking across the palace site have produced further post-medieval finds and plentiful pottery (Figure 14.6);[43] sufficient to suggest that the finds collection reported upon in 1988 had been carefully pre-selected by the 1930s excavators so as to exclude later material. Happily, the archaeological evidence now seems to be in tune with the documentary sources and, taken together, these strongly suggest that Christopher Ewer's house lay immediately south-east of the palace. The most satisfactory conclusion is that Ewer lived at the cottage at 'King's Mannour', as it was recorded on the 1650 estate map, and that he made some use of standing structures immediately to the north such as the old gatehouse. The cottage, as it stands today, can be dated to the second half of the eighteenth century with various later extensions and re-facings,[44] so its earliest structural phases date to perhaps 70 years after Ewer's death; there must be an earlier building on the same site.

This third set of clues indicates that parts of the ruined medieval palace were still being put to occasional use towards the end of the seventeenth century. Judging by the evidence from Stukeley's drawing of 1723 and the lack of post-medieval masonry and reconstruction evident on the site today, there were no new buildings erected there – rather it was the open spaces created by the palace layout that were used for outside storage for a house at 'King Mannour', now beneath King Manor Cottage. Artefacts recovered from the old spoil heaps would strongly support this suggestion. Furthermore, in 1680 'King Mannour' was occupied by a member of the Ewer family, possibly a family relation of the Henry Hyde who owned Clarendon Park.

The national narrative

The identification in Christopher Ewer's inventory of a 'Parliament Hall' and 'dungeons' is an important reminder of the role of Clarendon 'the place' in national historical narratives of the seventeenth century. Among the earlier antiquarians, John Leland had noted the park and the priory

[39] WSHC P4/1680/4(ii). Account, Inventory, Will of Christopher Ewer, 1680.

[40] James and Robinson, 169–265.

[41] Robert J. Charleston, "Vessel Glass," in *Clarendon Palace*, ed. James and Robinson, 194–96; Alison R. Goodall, David A. Hinton, and Tom Beaumont. James, "Copper-alloy Objects," in *Clarendon Palace*, ed. James and Robinson, 207.

[42] James and Robinson, *Clarendon Palace*, 81.

[43] Alejandra Gutiérrez, *Clarendon Park: medieval and later pottery*, unpublished typescript report (2004).

[44] RCHME, *King Manor Cottage, Clarendon Park, Wiltshire* (1979), Architectural Records Section, Buildings Index file 50317.

Figure 14.5: William Stukeley's sketch of August 1723 of the ruins at Clarendon Palace. Copyright: Wikimedia Commons / Public Domain.

at Ivy Church in *c.*1542,[45] but William Camden's *Britannia*, first published in 1586 in Latin and then expanded and translated into English in 1610, probably under Camden's own direction, made some important additions. Not only does Camden mention Clarendon's 'very large and goodly parke' and its 'house of the Kings', he also tells us that 'heere in the yeere 1164 was made a certain recognition and record of customes of the Kings of England before Clergie, Judges and Barons of the Realme which were called The Constitutions of Clarendin. Of which so many as the Pope approved have been set downe in the Tomes of the Councels, the rest omitted, albeit Thomas Becket, the Archbishop of Canterburie and the rest of the Bishops approved them all'. While there may be some doubt that Camden actually visited Clarendon, he was certainly aware of the historic events that had once taken place there. And when Thomas Fuller came to provide his own account for his *Church History Of Britain*, he too felt able to offer a lengthy account of the parliament in 1164, of Thomas Becket first consenting to the new laws and later 'recanting on his own act'.[46]

By the middle of the seventeenth century then, historical events of the Middle Ages were already linked with Clarendon 'the place' and this perhaps explains why there had already been antiquarian diggings on the site before John Aubrey compiled his *Monumenta Britannica* in 1688/89. In spite of the vogue of classicism current at the time, this awareness of Clarendon then proliferated in antiquarian and historical narratives during the last two decades of the seventeenth century. Royalists like John Nalson and Robert Brady, and Whig critic James Tyrrell in his three-volume *General History of England* all follow a familiar script and tell of 'the famous Council at Clarendon' and the 'Bishops, Abbots, Priors, and chief Men of the Kingdom' who were present.[47] The stout opposition of Thomas Becket to the Constitutions of Clarendon features large. And when Edmund Gibson came to update Camden's work in 1695,[48] he was able to add still further detail. In the 1701 edition of *Britannia*, Clarendon was noted as 'famous for two Parliaments held there, the one in the Reign of Henry II [that is, in 1164], and the other of Edward II [that is, in 1317], and since for giving the Title of Earl to Edward Hyde... he was succeeded by his Eldest Son Henry, now Living'.[49] By the time William Stukeley

[45] Lucy Toulmin Smith (ed.), *The Itinerary of John Leland in or About the Years 1535–43*, vol. 1 (London: George Bell, 1907–10), 268–69.

[46] Thomas Fuller, *The Church History of Britain* (London: John Williams, 1655), 312–13.

[47] John Nalson, *Impartial Collection of the Great Affairs of State...* (London: S Mearne et al., 1682), 505; Robert Brady, *A Complete History of England: from the first entrance of the Romans... unto the end of the reign of King Henry III*, vol. 3 (London: Thomas Necomb, 1685); James Tyrrell, *The General History of England*, part 2 (London: W. Rogers et al., 1696–1704), 8.

[48] Edmund Gibson (ed.), *Camden's Britannia, newly Translated into English: with large additions and improvements* (London: E. Gibson, 1695), 94; 108.

[49] William Camden, *Britannia Abridg'd with Improvements, and Continuations, to this Present Time...* (London: Joseph Wild, 1701), 165.

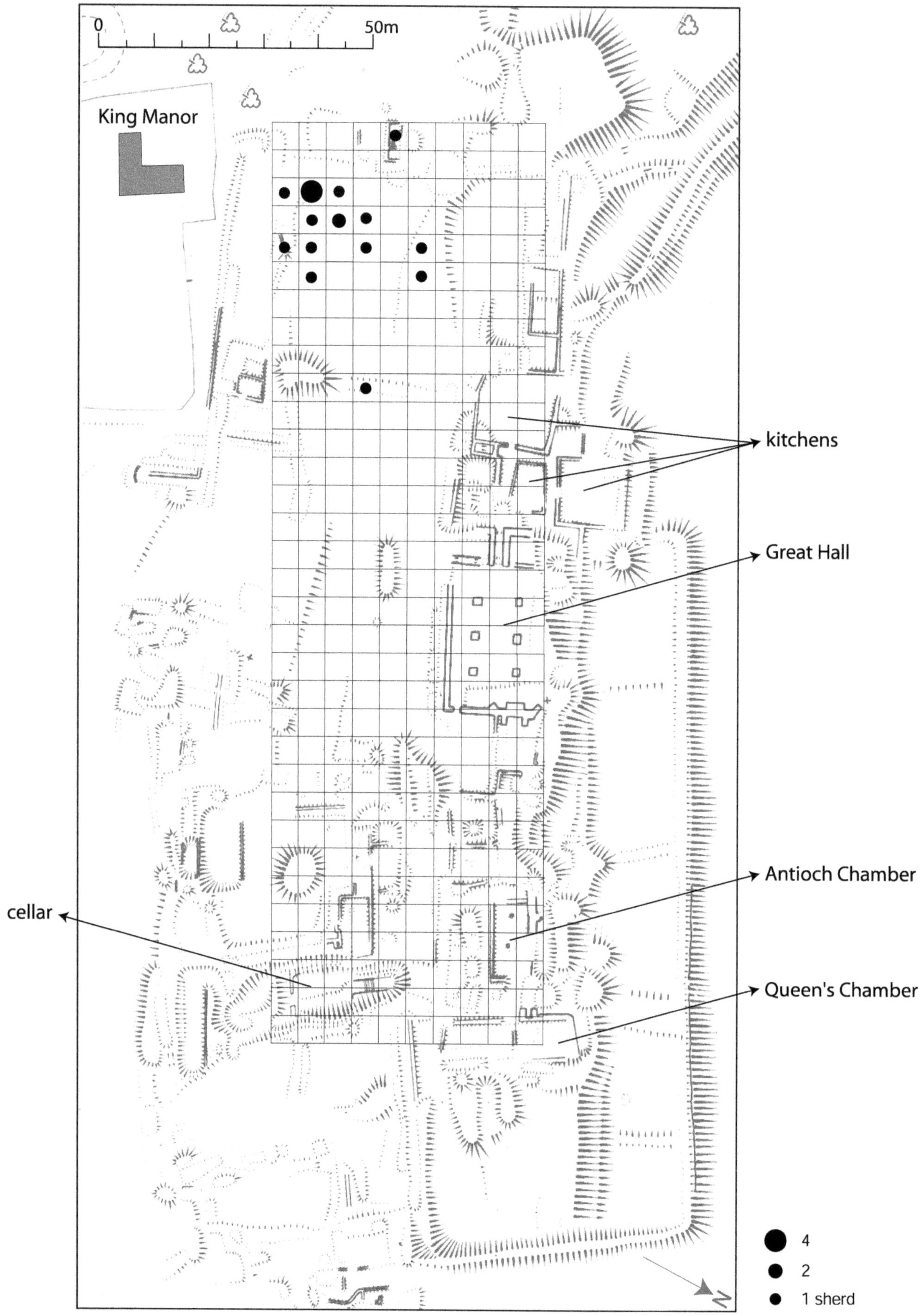

Figure 14.6: Distribution of post-medieval pottery at Clarendon Palace recovered from a 5m grid by fieldwalkers in 1994, here superimposed over a plan of the site created by the RCHM(E) and labelled with some of the principal buildings. Crown copyright. Historic England archive.

visited in August 1723 with his friends Lord Thomas and Lady Betty Herbert, he would have known the place and its historical associations well enough – even if he mistakenly ascribed the buildings of the palace to King John.

For the purposes of this essay, the important point to stress is that by the end of the seventeenth century Clarendon, its palace and the Constitutions were long established features of the national historical narrative. By now the site was firmly associated with the names of Henry II and Thomas Becket and it therefore spoke to debates about Church and State as well as to the antiquity of English institutions, its laws and legal history. We have seen how this narrative had become more generous in its detail during the course of the century, and especially so during its last two decades – at precisely the moment when the medal is likely to have been deposited at the palace. By this time there were no less than 368 titles about English history in circulation; and these were not books that idled on the shelves, they were bought and sold, borrowed, catalogued, perused and took centre stage among intellectual and social activities of the day.[50]

The act: culprits and motives

Taking these different sets of clues into account, the first, and least satisfactory, explanation for the medal being left or buried at the site is that it was accidently lost there. This seems wholly implausible; the medal is large and weighty, it seems unlikely to have slipped from the neck unnoticed and the coincidence of its loss at a known former royal palace on Hyde property stretches credulity too far.

A second explanation is that Queen Mary herself was responsible. This seems unlikely given what we now know of the financial value of the artefact, its likely provenance and its means of acquisition. Once more, there are no records of any royal visits to Clarendon at this time. This should not surprise us given that Mary's uncle Henry Hyde, the second Earl of Clarendon, was among those loyal to James II who would not swear allegiance to this new regime. Both Henry and his brother Lawrence held Anglican beliefs that made them wary of James' Catholic leanings and eventually resulted in their resignation from office in December 1686/January 1687. At the same time they were also staunchly royalist and, rather than favouring a breach in the succession, both men sought the conditional restoration of James following his flight.[51] In addition, Rochester and Clarendon stood to gain handsomely from James' survival and would have confidently expected to return to office.[52]

But the fate of the two brothers under the new regime was to be very different; while Rochester worked his way back into favour with William and Mary and subsequently became Lord Lieutenant of Ireland (1700–02), Henry was imprisoned in the Tower for seven weeks in 1690 and for a further six months in 1691 after he became involved in Jacobite intrigues.[53] As a 'nonjuror', Henry still considered himself to be bound to the lawful monarch – James II – and would not transfer his allegiance. The fact that the king had left the country in no way absolved him from this; Henry took the view that James II ruled with an authority from God that could not be broken. Allegiance for Henry Hyde was not dependent merely upon possession of the throne and he believed those who took their oath to William to be 'naive and misguided, at worst cynical and pragmatic'.[54] On this basis, it seems very unlikely indeed that Mary, William's queen, would ever have been welcome at Henry's Wiltshire home.

A second possible culprit is Lawrence Hyde, the Earl of Rochester. He was a political survivor, loved by James II but also with 'a large share in the esteem of both [William and Mary], particularly of the Queen, to whom he had the honour to be Maternal Unkle'. The occasion for his 'placing' of the medal might have come in 1694 when Queen Mary passed away. Lawrence is known to have put up a statue to Queen Mary 'in the middle of his most delicious Garden at Petersham'.[55] Alternatively, another opportunity might have presented itself when the estate was finally sold off by Henry Hyde in 1707 – for while Lawrence was able to save Cornbury he was not able to do likewise with Clarendon and 1707 symbolised the end of the Hyde connection with the Park, when the link between title and estate established by the first earl was finally broken. For Lawrence the motive might have been commemorative appropriation or nostalgia. However, while Lawrence had access to Clarendon, there is nothing to suggest that he was ever there. We cannot place him 'at the scene'.

A third possible culprit is Henry Hyde himself. Like his brother, Henry had opportunity but he is also known to have been at Clarendon, quite possibly at 'King Mannour' with his indebted relation Christopher Ewer who lived immediately adjacent to the palace site. Henry was also the most directly affected personally by the succession of William and Mary; unlike his brother he had not compromised his principles and, as a result, he suffered imprisonment and found himself in ever more extreme financial circumstances. It might be said also that the conflicts of duty and friendship felt by Henry echoed those of Thomas Becket at the Constitutions of Clarendon. Thomas Becket opposed Henry II, just as Henry Hyde did

[50] Daniel R. Woolf, *Reading History in Early Modern England* (Cambridge: Cambridge University Press, 2000), 113–23; 236–44.

[51] Harris, *Revolution*, 210; 319.

[52] Beddard, *A Kingdom without a King*, 36.

[53] Harris 2006, *Revolution*, 362; William A. Speck, "Hyde, Henry (1638–1709)," *Oxford Dictionary of National Biography* (2004), accessed 29 Jan 2013, http://www.oxforddnb.com/view/article/14329; William A. Speck, "Hyde, Lawrence, first earl of Rochester (bap. 1642, d.1711)," *Oxford Dictionary of National Biography* (2004), accessed 29 Jan 2013, http://www.oxforddnb.com/view/article/14332.

[54] David M. Jones, *Conscience and Allegiance in Seventeenth Century England: the political significance of oaths and engagements* (New York: University of Rochester Press, 1999), 216–22.

[55] Anon., *An Essay Towards the Life of Lawrence, Earl of Rochester*, 18, 23.

James II; both were to suffer for their convictions. But even if we cannot accept this direct association, the medal might have caused Henry to reflect upon his link with the royal house, his fate and his loss of place in society. For Henry, this would have been a mnemonic object deliberately hidden at an emotionally charged place, a mundane object perhaps but one with deep personal significance. To these generalities we can also add two specific personal interests; not only did Henry have an interest and knowledge of medieval history as author of *History and Antiquities of the Cathedral Church at Winchester*, he had also amassed a fine collection of medals.[56]

Discussion

The use of coins and medals as 'special deposits' is not unknown in other contexts. In 1489 coins and a medal engraved for the occasion were tossed into the foundations of a new palace construction in Florence[57] and when the foundation stone for the new St Peter's in Rome came to be laid by Julius II in 1506, he descended a ladder to reach the foundations and deposited an earthenware pot there containing 12 medals with inscriptions referring to the ceremony.[58] The placing of coins was said to invoke God's protection and seems to have been prevalent in eastern Europe in the seventeenth century, especially during the construction of religious houses. Known examples include Bila Hora (near Prague) in 1628, Valtice (Czech Republic) in 1631, Chartreuse in Vvaldice in 1632, the Capuchin monasteries near Sušice in Bohemia (modern Czech Republic) in 1651 and at Nisa in Silesa in 1659 .[59] Other kinds of 'foundation deposit' are also documented elsewhere across Europe,[60] indeed one is argued by James Ayres (see chapter sixteen) at the hunting lodge on the site of Clarendon House in the seventeenth century, and while I do not wish to argue here that the Clarendon medal is a foundation deposit, it is interesting that the medal should have been considered an appropriate vehicle for commemoration; presumably this is because medals like coins are portable and carried unambiguous associations that enabled people to connect with buildings and sites. In this context the medal could invoke memory and stimulate recollection; the medal is concealed – taken out of circulation and 'sacrificed'. According to this interpretation I see the Clarendon medal as a 'closing', 'termination', or 'leave-taking' deposit in which the intention would have been to decharge the meaning of the place through the 'killing' of an object.[61] The burial of the medal I interpret as a fleeting act by an individual whose motives we can only now dimly reconstruct but may be tied to the ending of the relationship between person and place.

Whether or not this interpretation is acceptable to the reader, the Clarendon case study does raise questions about the occurrence of post-medieval objects at the sites of later medieval monuments. While there has been some consideration of the adaption and conversion of medieval architecture in a post-medieval world, mostly for monasteries but also, more recently, for castles,[62] a detailed survey of the artefactual evidence is long overdue. Post-medieval finds at medieval sites are usually attributed to continued occupation. Thus, for example, the North Gatehouse at Launceston Castle (Cornwall) continued as the residence of the constable and, although no buildings were left standing in the bailey by the mid-seventeenth century, it later became the site of the county gaol; hence the deposition of post-medieval artefacts.[63] In other cases, objects are said to have been left behind by visitors and picnickers,[64] or else represent the debris generated during demolition and robbing. At the Cistercian abbey at Hulton (Staffs), for example, archaeological evidence suggests that medieval structural materials and artefacts of value were gathered up from various buildings and brought into the nave for disposal and recycling. Lead from the roof, window frames and even smaller items such as crucifix pilgrim badge were cast into ingots in bowl hearths that had been cut into the floor of the church, and then sold on. Broken tools, among them a bone knife handle and a chisel blade, may have belonged to agents dismantling the church.[65] Most evocatively, faunal remains of shrews, voles, mice and frogs from the church suggest an assemblage derived from owl pellets, probably from a barn owl that

[56] Henry Hyde and Samuel Gale, *The History and Antiquities of the Cathedral Church of Winchester: containing all the inscriptions upon the tombs and monuments…* (London: Printed for E. Curll, 1715); Lee, "Hyde, Henry (1638–1709)," *Dictionary of National Biography*.

[57] Ann Crabb, *The Strozzi of Florence: widowhood and family solidarity in the Renaissance* (Ann Arbor: University of Michigan Press, 2000).

[58] Ferdinand Gregorovius, *History of the City of Rome in the Middle Ages 1506–1534* (New York: Italica Press, 2000).

[59] Tomas Kleisner, "An Unknown Medal for the Foundation of Sušice Monastery, 1651," *Sbornik Narodniho muzea v Praze, A-Historia* 61 (2007): 87–93.

[60] For example, Ralph Merrifield, *The Archaeology of Ritual and Magic* (London: Batsford, 1987); Brian Hoggard, "The Archaeology of Counter-Witchcraft and Popular Magic," in *Beyond the Witch Trials: witchcraft and magic in Enlightenment Europe*, ed. Owen Davies and Willem de Blécourt (Manchester: Manchester University Press, 2004), 167–86; Sonja Hukantaival, "Hare's Feet under a Hearth: discussing 'ritual' deposits in buildings," in *Hortus Novus: fresh approaches to medieval archaeology in Finland*, ed. Visa Immonen, Mia Lempiäinen and Ulrika Rosendahl (Turku: Society for Medieval Archaeology in Finland, 2007), 66–75; Vesa-Pekka Herva, "Buildings as Persons: Relationality and the life of buildings in a northern periphery of early modern Sweden," *Antiquity* 84 (2010): 440–52.

[61] For similar ideas see Travis W. Stanton, M. Kathryn Brown and Jonathan B. Pagliaro, "Garbage of the Gods? Squatters, refuse disposal, and termination rituals among the Ancient Maya," *Latin American Antiquity* 19, 3 (2008): 227–47.

[62] Richard K. Morris, "Monastic Architecture: destruction and reconstruction," in *The Archaeology of Reformation 1480–1580*, ed. David Gaimster and Roberta Gilchrist (Leeds: Maney, 2003), 235–51. For castles e.g. Sarah Speight, "Castles as Past Culture 2: adaptation and identity in the post-life of castles," *The Castle Studies Group Journal* 21 (2007–08): 268–75; Sarah Speight, "Castles as Past Culture: living with castles in the post-medieval world," *Château Gaillard* 23 (2008): 247–56.

[63] Andrew Saunders, *Excavations at Launceston Castle, Cornwall*, Society for Medieval Archaeology monograph 24 (Leeds: Maney, 2006).

[64] For example, Ewan Campbell and Alan Lane, "Excavations at Longbury Bank, Dyfed, and Early Medieval Settlement in South Wales," *Medieval Archaeology* 37 (1993): 25.

[65] Noel Boothroyd, "Introduction: finds," in *Excavations at Hulton Abbey, Staffordshire 1987–1994*, ed. William D. Klemperer and Noel Boothroyd, Society for Medieval Archaeology monograph 21 (Leeds: Maney, 2004), 150.

nested there once parts of the roof had been removed.[66]

Not only does Hulton illustrate the kind of archaeological detail now sadly lost to us for Clarendon Palace and for many other sites, it also causes us to reflect on the general principles that might govern the discard of objects on archaeological sites. Among the most important of these to consider are economy of effort, the value of the refuse and its potential impediment to other activities.[67] If the Clarendon medal is judged to have little economic value and in no way can be considered a physical hindrance, we might expect the maximum economy of effort during its disposal. In other words, it should have been found together with most of the other low value domestic debris at the west end of the palace site, but it was not, it was found some distance away on a part of the site that does not seem to have been adapted for use or renovated in the late seventeenth century. This suggests to me that we should look beyond simple refuse disposal to explain its deposition.

Conclusions

This paper has sought to broaden the scope of discussion about post-medieval objects and to emphasise the active role of material culture in the seventeenth century. I argued at the outset that there can be a strong bond between objects and people, and that material culture can be an affirmation of social and cultural identity, and I believe the Clarendon medal to be an example of that. In this case the life course of the object and whoever buried it were entwined not simply through possession but also through their social, cultural and biographical associations. To unravel these associations I have considered different historical, social, political and archaeological contexts and made use of a biographical approach in which I envisage an object that has been given meaning and contemporary value.

But this paper has been as much about place as about object. Once the royal house at Clarendon had ceased to be maintained in the last quarter of the fifteenth century its roofs collapsed, materials from the site were robbed and antiquarians began to root among the spoil to recover finds. There was some minor refurbishment of spaces to act as service and farm buildings but, as far as one can tell, the site of the royal palace never slipped from the memory; it was never 'lost'. The site remained available, visually and sensually, to later visitors and it served to anchor the past in the post-medieval present. Clarendon might be described as a historically 'layered' landscape and therefore a fruitful context for a statement about memory and its re-working through the burial of the coronation medal on the site. And damaged though the archaeology at Clarendon Palace may be, there is surely sufficient here to suggest that in future we should pay closer attention to later activities on our medieval sites.

Acknowledgements

I am grateful to Robin Skeates and Richard Hingley for discussions during the preparation of this paper and for corrections made by Alejandra Gutiérrez. I am especially grateful to Peter Saunders, Curator Emeritus at The Salisbury Museum for organising the photographs of the Clarendon medallion and to David Cousins who was the photographer.

Bibliography

Unpublished primary sources

The National Archives, PROB 11/405/116. Will of William Hyde of Clarendon Park, Wiltshire, 1691.

Wiltshire and Swindon History Centre, P4/1680/4. Account, Inventory, Will of Christopher Ewer, 1680.

Published primary sources

Anon. *An Essay Towards the Life of Lawrence, Earl of Rochester*. London: John Morphew, 1711.

Brady, Robert. *A Complete History of England: from the first entrance of the Romans... unto the end of the reign of King Henry III*, vol. 3. London: Thomas Necomb, 1685.

Camden, William. *Britannia Abridg'd with Improvements, and Continuations, to this Present Time...* London: Joseph Wild, 1701.

de Beer, Esmond S., ed. *The Diary of John Evelyn, vol. 4 Kalendarium, 1673–1689*. Oxford: Clarendon Press, 1955.

Gibson, Edmund, ed. *Camden's Britannia, newly Translated into English: with large additions and improvements*. London: E. Gibson, 1695.

Hyde, Henry, and Samuel Gale. *The History and Antiquities of the Cathedral Church of Winchester: containing all the inscriptions upon the tombs and monuments...* London: Printed for E. Curll, 1715.

Lister, Thomas H., ed. *Life and Administration of Edward, First Earl of Clarendon: letters and papers*, vol. 3. London: Longman, Orme, Brown, Green, and Longmans, 1837.

Nalson, John. *Impartial Collection of the Great Affairs of State...* London: S Mearne *et al.*, 1682.

Singer, Samuel W., ed. *The Correspondence of Henry Hyde, Earl of Clarendon, and his Brother Lawrence Hyde, Earl of Rochester: with the diary of Lord Clarendon from 1687 to 1690...* Milton Keynes: Lightning Source, 2012.

[66] Umberto Albarella, "Small Bones from Samples," in *Excavations at Hulton Abbey*, ed. William D. Klemperer and Noel Boothroyd, 145–46.

[67] For example, Margaret E. Beck, "Midden Ceramic Assemblage Formation: a case study from Kalinga, Philippines," *American Antiquity* 71 (2006): 27–52; Douglas C. Wilson, William L. Rathje and Wilson W. Hughes "Household Discards and Modern Refuse: a principle of household resource use and waste," in *The Ethnoarchaeology of Refuse Disposal*, ed. Edward Staski and Livingston D. Sutro, Anthropological Research Papers 42 (Tempe: Arizona State University, 1991), 41–51.

Toulmin Smith, Lucy, ed. *The Itinerary of John Leland in or About the Years 1535–43*, vol. 1. London: George Bell, 1907–10.

Tyrrell, James. *The General History of England,* part 2. London: W. Rogers et al., 1696–1704.

Published secondary sources

Albarella, Umberto. "Small Bones from Samples." In *Excavations at Hulton Abbey, Staffordshire 1987–1994*, edited by William D. Klemperer and Noel Boothroyd, Society for Medieval Archaeology monograph 21, 145–46. Leeds: Maney, 2004.

Beaumont James, Tom, and Christopher M. Gerrard. *Clarendon: landscape of Kings*. Macclesfield: Windgather Press, 2007.

Beck, Margaret E. "Midden Ceramic Assemblage Formation: a case study from Kalinga, Philippines." *American Antiquity* 71 (2006): 27–52.

Beddard, Robert, ed. *A Kingdom without a King: the journal of the provisional government in the Revolution of 1688.* Oxford: Phaidon, 1988.

Boothroyd, Noel. "Introduction: finds." In *Excavations at Hulton Abbey, Staffordshire 1987–1994*, edited by William D. Klemperer and Noel Boothroyd, Society for Medieval Archaeology monograph 21, 149–51. Leeds: Maney, 2004.

Bosanquet, Robert C. "Excavations at Dunstanburgh Castle in 1931." *Archaeologia Aeliana* 13, 4th series (1936): 279–92.

Bradley, Richard. *The Passage of Arms: an archaeological analysis of prehistoric hoard and votive deposits.* Oxford: Oxbow Books, 1998.

Campbell, Ewan, and Alan Lane. "Excavations at Longbury Bank, Dyfed, and Early Medieval Settlement in South Wales." *Medieval Archaeology* 37 (1993): 15–77.

Charleston, Robert J. "Vessel Glass." In *Clarendon Palace: the history and archaeology of a medieval palace and hunting lodge near Salisbury, Wiltshire*, edited by Tom Beaumont James and Anne M. Robinson, 193–99. London: Society of Antiquaries and Thames and Hudson, 1988.

Crabb, Ann. *The Strozzi of Florence: widowhood and family solidarity in the Renaissance.* Ann Arbor: University of Michigan Press, 2000.

Cruickshanks, Eveline. *The Glorious Revolution.* London: Macmillan, 2000.

DeMarrais, Elizabeth. "The Materialization of Culture." In *Rethinking Materiality: the engagement of mind with the material world,* edited by Elizabeth DeMarrais, Chris Gosden and Colin Renfrew, 11–22. Oxford: Oxbow Books, 2004.

Edie, Carolyn A. "The Public Face of Royal Ritual: sermons, medals, and civic ceremony in later Stuart coronations." *Huntington Library Quarterly* 53, no.4 (1990): 311–36.

English Heritage. British Listed Buildings, "Cornbury House, Cornbury and Wychwood." Accessed 6 July 2018. http://www.britishlistedbuildings.co.uk/en-252455-cornbury-house-cornbury-and-wychwood.

English Heritage. British Listed Buildings, "Swallowfield Park and Adjoining Stable Block, Swallowfield." Accessed 6 July 2018. https://www.britishlistedbuildings.co.uk/101313056-swallowfield-park-and-adjoining-stable-block-swallowfield#.W0IB6be0Xcs.

Fergusson, Peter, and Stuart Harrison. *Rievaulx Abbey: community, architecture and memory.* London: Yale University Press, 1999.

Fowles, John, and Rodney Legg, eds. *Monumenta Britannica: or, a miscellany of British antiquities.* Sherborne: Dorset Publishing Company, 1980.

Fuller, Thomas. *The Church History of Britain.* London: John Williams, 1655.

George, Claire H.L. "Marketing Medals in Early Modern Britain." *The Medal* 42 (2003): 23–26.

Gilchrist, Roberta. *Medieval Life: archaeology and the life course.* Woodbridge: Boydell, 2012.

Goodall, Alison R., David A. Hinton, and Tom Beaumont James. "Copper-alloy Objects." In *Clarendon Palace: the History and Archaeology of a Medieval Palace and Hunting Lodge near Salisbury, Wiltshire*, Reports of the Research Committee of the Society of Antiquaries of London 45, 193–99. London: Society of Antiquaries and Thames and Hudson, 1988.

Gosden, Chris, and Yvonne Marshall. "The Cultural Biography of Objects." *World Archaeology* 31 (1999): 169–78

Gregorovius, Ferdinand. *History of the City of Rome in the Middle Ages 1506–1534.* New York: Italica Press, 2000.

Griffiths, Antony. "Advertisements for Medals in the *London Gazette*." *The Medal* 15 (1989): 4–6.

Harris, Tim. *Revolution: the great crisis of the British monarchy 1685–1720.* London: Allen Lane, 2006.

Herva, Vesa-Pekka. "Buildings as Persons: relationality and the life of buildings in a northern periphery of early modern Sweden." *Antiquity* 84 (2010): 440–52.

Hoggard, Brian. "The Archaeology of Counter-Witchcraft and Popular Magic." In *Beyond the Witch Trials: witchcraft and magic in Enlightenment Europe*, edited by Owen Davies and Willem de Blécourt, 167–86. Manchester: Manchester University Press, 2004.

Hukantaiva, Sonja. "Hare's Feet under a Hearth: discussing 'ritual' deposits in buildings." In *Hortus Novus: fresh approaches to medieval archaeology in Finland*, edited by Visa Immonen, Mia Lempiäinen and Ulrika Rosendahl, 66–75. Turku: Society for Medieval Archaeology in Finland, 2007.

James, Tom Beaumont, and Anne M. Robinson. *Clarendon Palace: the history and archaeology of a medieval palace and hunting lodge near Salisbury, Wiltshire*. Reports of the Research Committee of the Society of Antiquaries of London 45. London: Society of Antiquaries and Thames and Hudson, 1988.

Jones, Mark. *The Art of the Medal*. London: British Museum Publications, 1979.

Jones, David M. *Conscience and Allegiance in Seventeenth Century England: the political significance of oaths and engagements*. New York: University of Rochester Press, 1999.

Kleisner, Tomas. "An Unknown Medal for the Foundation of Sušice Monastery, 1651." *Sbornik Narodniho muzea v Praze, A-Historia* 61 (2007): 87–93.

Lee, Sidney. "Hyde, Henry (1638–1709)." *Dictionary of National Biography*. London: Smith, Elder and Co, 1891.

Lillios, Katina T, and Vasileios Tsamis, eds. *Material Mnemonics: everyday memory in prehistoric Europe*. Oxford: Oxbow Books, 2010.

Luttrell, Narcissus. *A Brief Historical Relation of State Affairs from September 1678, to April 1714*, 6 vols. Farnborough: Gregg International Publishers, 1857 [republ 1969]. vol. 1.

Merrifield, Ralph. *The Archaeology of Ritual and Magic*. London: Batsford, 1987.

Morris, Richard K. "Monastic Architecture: destruction and reconstruction." In *The Archaeology of Reformation 1480–1580*, edited by David Gaimster and Roberta Gilchrist, 235–51. Leeds: Maney, 2003.

Prest, Wilfrid. "Hyde, Sir Robert (1595/6–1665)." *Oxford Dictionary of National Biography*. Accessed 6 July, 2020. http://www.oxforddnb.com/view/article/14334.

RCHME. *King Manor Cottage, Clarendon Park, Wiltshire* (1979), Architectural Records Section, Buildings Index file 50317.

Saunders, Andrew. *Excavations at Launceston Castle, Cornwall*, Society for Medieval Archaeology. Leeds: Maney, 2006.

Speck, William A. "Hyde, Henry (1638–1709)." *Oxford Dictionary of National Biography* (2004). Accessed 6 July, 2020. http://www.oxforddnb.com/view/article/14329.

Speck, William A. "Hyde, Lawrence, first earl of Rochester (bap. 1642, d.1711)," *Oxford Dictionary of National Biography* (2004). Accessed 6 July, 2020. http://www.oxforddnb.com/view/article/14332.

Speight, Sarah. "Castles as Past Culture 2: adaptation and identity in the post-life of castles." *The Castle Studies Group Journal* 21 (2007–08): 268–75.

Speight, Sarah. "Castles as Past Culture: living with castles in the post-medieval world." *Château Gaillard* 23 (2008): 247–56.

Stanton, Travis W., M. Kathryn Brown and Jonathan B Pagliaro. "Garbage of the Gods? Squatters, refuse disposal, and termination rituals among the Ancient Maya." *Latin American Antiquity* 19, 3 (2008): 227–47.

Till, William. *Descriptive Particulars of English Coronation Medals: from the inauguration of King Edward the Sixth to our present sovereign the Queen Victoria*. London: Longman, Orme, Brown, Green and Longmans, 1846.

Van Dyke, Ruth M., and Susan E. Alcock, eds. *Archaeologies of Memory*. Oxford: Blackwell, 2003.

Wilson, Douglas C., William L. Rathje, and Wilson W. Hughes. "Household Discards and Modern Refuse: a principle of household resource use and waste." In *The Ethnoarchaeology of Refuse Disposal*, edited by Edward Staski and Livingston D. Sutro, Anthropological Research Papers 42, 41–51. Tempe: Arizona State University, 1991.

Woolf, Daniel R. *Reading History in Early Modern England*. Cambridge: Cambridge University Press, 2000.

Wright, Stephen. "Hyde, Alexander (1596x8–1667)." *Oxford Dictionary of National Biography* (2004). Accessed 6 July, 2020. http://www.oxforddnb.com/view/article/14324.

Unpublished secondary sources

Field, John. "Student Volunteering in Britain between the Wars: summer camps and the unemployed." Unpublished paper delivered at the Institute for Volunteering Research, Conference on Students, Volunteering and Social Action: 1880–1990, Toynbee Hall, London, 25 November 2010.

Field, John. "Able Bodies: work camps and the training of the unemployed in Britain before 1939." Unpublished paper delivered at The Significance of the Historical Perspective in Adult Education Research, University of Cambridge, Institute of Continuing Education, 2009.

Gutiérrez, Alejandra. *Clarendon Park: medieval and later pottery*. Unpublished typescript report 2004.

15

Clarendon House, Wiltshire: Its evolutionary details

James Ayres

University of Bath: School of Architecture

Abstract: The medieval palace and its associated deer park have been very extensively re-excavated and re-evaluated by Professor Tom Beaumont James and his colleagues over the last several decades. In contrast, the rather sad decline of Clarendon House was to result in its derelict condition. Fortunately, its new owners were determined to rescue the house as a family home. To this end they invited Prof. James to produce an historical Report and he asked the author to join him in this venture. The following account gives a brief overview of the house so as to provide a context for an examination of various details which helped in the dating of the three principal phases in the history of this building.

Key words: Architecture; building; carpentry; cast iron; joinery; stone carving; timber

Clarendon lies at the hub of twelfth-century English history, the centre around which events turned. It was there, in 1164 that Henry II began his lethal dispute with Thomas à Becket and, in the same year, the Constitutions of Clarendon were promulgated. Just two years later the Assize of Clarendon brought English criminal law under the overarching control of the crown.[1] Of recent years the re-excavation and re-evaluation of Clarendon Palace and its parkland has been undertaken by Professor James of the University of Winchester and his colleagues and their achievement is reflected in their publications on this Scheduled Ancient Monument and its setting.[2] Consequently when the entire estate was sold in 2006 its new owners turned to Tom James for an historical analysis of Clarendon House, as distinct from the Palace. In 2007 I was invited to assist with this research. It should be added that the house was, at this stage, in a ruinous condition. Consequently, and despite its underlying grandeur, our working conditions were sometimes squalid. It therefore says much for Tom's good humour that the whole enterprise was so thoroughly enjoyable.[3] Furthermore the current owners of the house and its estate are to be applauded for rescuing this important building – without their resources and imagination the final collapse of Clarendon House would have been inevitable.

The following account aims to show how the details in the surviving building explain the evolution of Clarendon House from the late seventeenth to the early nineteenth centuries. In doing so it has been necessary to touch on the wider context in which this building history took place. Following the Restoration of the monarchy in 1660 Clarendon Park was alienated from royal ownership. The estate was briefly held by George Monck (1608–70) the first Duke of Albemarle but then, in 1665, it passed to Edward Hyde (1609–74) who took his title as first Earl of Clarendon from this newly acquired estate. By 1667 the Earl was out of favour and spent the remainder of his life in voluntary exile on the Continent. It was there that he wrote his *History of the Rebellion and Civil Wars in England* (1702–04). So successful was this posthumous publication that the Clarendon Building (built 1712–13) in Oxford was named in his honour by the University Press.

The seventeenth-century lodge

The Hydes' principal country seat was Cornbury Park, Oxfordshire.[4] Consequently their Wiltshire estate was probably seen as little more than the basis for their title and a source of income – besides it was good hunting country. Also by this time Clarendon Palace, after decades of conflict and royal exile, was all but uninhabitable. A print showing William Stukeley and others visiting the Palace in August 1723 shows it as a complete ruin.[5] For these reasons some sort of habitable *pied à terre* within the estate was presumably thought to be necessary. Indeed, within the core of the surviving and later Clarendon House, the fragments of a much smaller late seventeenth century brick building with stone dressings was revealed.

These fragments were buried within the fabric of the south side of the north-west rooms of the later house

[1] Dan Jones, *The Plantagenets: the kings who made England* (London: Harper Press, 2012), 69; 71; 96.

[2] For example, Tom Beaumont James and Anne M. Robinson, *Clarendon Palace: the history and archaeology of a medieval palace and hunting lodge near Salisbury, Wiltshire*, Reports of the Research Committee of the Society of Antiquaries of London 45 (London: Society of Antiquaries and Thames and Hudson, 1988).

[3] Tom Beaumont James and James Ayres, "Clarendon House," unpublished reports 2007–09.

[4] John M. Steane and James Ayres, "Cornbury Estate, Oxfordshire: Kingstanding Farm and Walcot Barn," unpublished report (2004).

[5] Tom Beaumont James, *Clarendon: landscape, palace, mansion* (Salisbury: Salisbury and South Wiltshire Museum, 2010).

(Figure 15.1). Some of this evidence was located in the space above the barrel vaults of the cellar and below the boards of the ground floor. Here a fine water table was discovered, its handsome off-set being marked within the English bond brickwork by a masoned stone torus. In addition a pocket in the brickwork close to the foundation was found to contain animal bones most notably parts of a horse. Remains immured in this way are almost certainly a builder's offering.[6] From an architectural point of view the most significant detail to be recovered was found on the first floor immediately above the surviving segment of water table. Here the rusticated brickwork of the corner was treated as a lesene pilaster on the north face and as long and short quoins to the west, with a masoned stone cornice returning on both elevations (Figure 15.2). On this floor one half of a north facing window was recorded with a finely worked flat arch in rubbed brick. Elsewhere, a further detail that raised important questions was an area of brickwork set at an angle of forty five degrees to the structure as a whole. This is located just outside the south east corner of the present main staircase well (Figure 15.1). This feature lines up with the footings of a north-south wall found in the east-west passage running the length of the basement.

Taken as a whole these fragments of evidence could suggest a relatively long low two storey building of three bays and just one room deep with a bay window at its eastern end. Although this suggests a fairly small structure its detailing is certainly patrician. Furthermore, the small vernacular building with a cupola (smoke louvre?) shown in a watercolour of 1791 located a few yards to the north-west of the house, could well have been a detached kitchen – a facility that would have relieved pressure on space in the lodge.

In some respects this lodge may have resembled some of the long low brick buildings with stone dressings in Salisbury's cathedral close,[7] which date to 1717. The dimensions of the bricks (9 x 4¼ x 2½ ins. / 22.8 x 10.8 x 6.3 cm) in the lodge are consistent with a date of between 1666 and 1695.[8] Thermoluminescence commissioned by Tom James and carried out by Professor Ian Bailiff (University of Durham) gave a date range of *c.*1666–95. This conforms well to the first earl's departure from England (1667) and his death in 1674 when the estate passed to his son Henry (1638–1709), the second earl.

In these circumstances it is likely that Henry Hyde constructed a hunting lodge on the estate in the late 1680s; a suitable destination and purpose for his occasional visits from Oxfordshire. In this respect it may be significant that Clarendon House in Piccadilly (built 1664–67), designed by Sir Roger Pratt, was demolished in 1683. The hunting lodge at Clarendon Park may have resembled the overall form, but not the materials, of the Duke of Beaufort's 'Swangrove' on the Badminton estate, a late seventeenth-century Bath stone pavilion reworked by William Killigrew of Bath in *c.*1703.[9] Swangrove with its

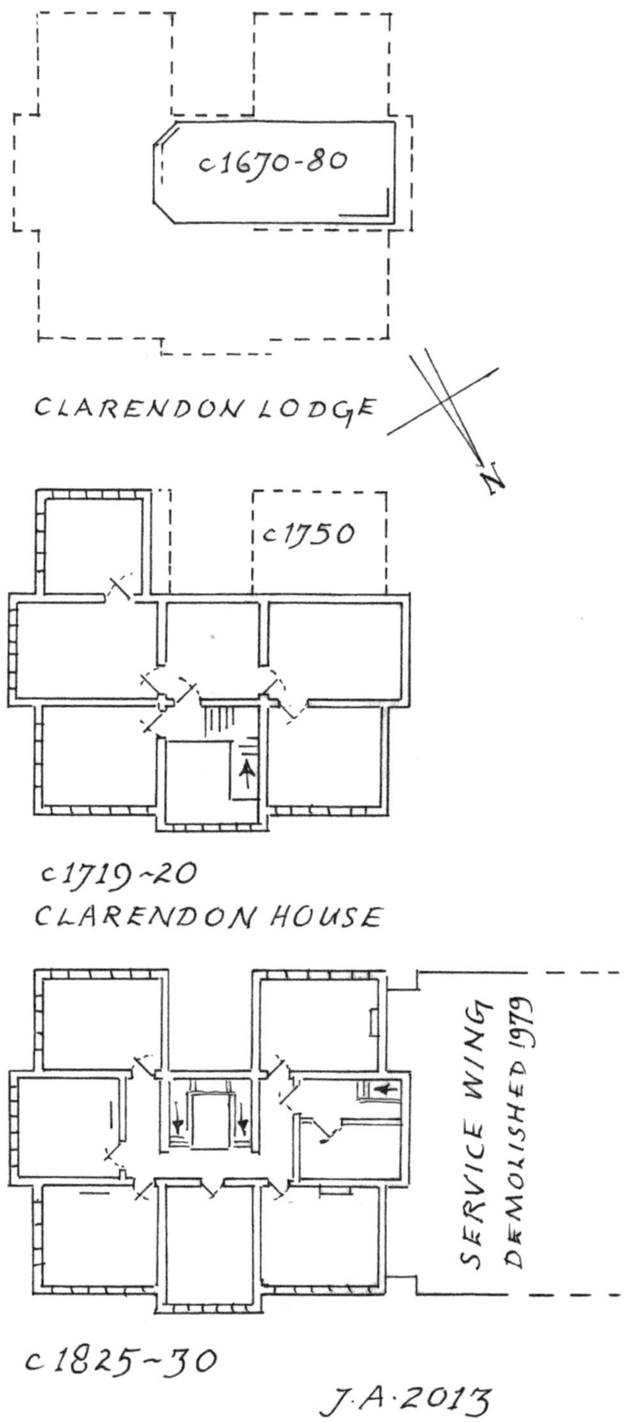

Figure 15.1: Plans showing the possible evolution of Clarendon from a late seventeenth-century Lodge to an early eighteenth-century House with amendments and additions of 1825–30. Drawing: the author.

[6] James Ayres, *Domestic Interiors: the British tradition 1500–1850* (New Haven and London: Yale University Press, 2003), 4.

[7] Nos. 56A and 56B The Close. See Royal Commission on Historical Monuments of England (RCHME), *Salisbury: the houses of the Close* (London: HMSO, 1993), 177.

[8] Nathaniel Lloyd, *A History of English Brickwork* (1925) (reprint, Woodbridge: Antique Collector's Club, 1983), 98–99.

[9] Min Hogg, "Swangrove," *The World of Interiors*, March 2003.

Figure 15.2: Two sides of the north corner of the late seventeenth-century Clarendon Loge, built by the Hydes. On the east front (right) the rusticated quoins are long and short whereas those on the south elevation (left) are treated as a pilaster or lesene. These differing features are united by the return of the masoned cornice which is surmounted by a pulvinated base for the upper zone. Drawing: the author.

very small flanking pavilions linked by a pair of curtain walls to the main lodge is, in its planning, Palladianism in miniature – a characteristic it shares with Ebberston Lodge (1718) in Yorkshire by Colen Campbell.[10]

The eighteenth-century house

In 1695 Sir Benjamin Bathurst purchased Cirencester Park for his eldest son Allen, later the first earl Bathurst. Sir Benjamin's second son Peter was presented with Clarendon Park in 1707.[11] The Bathursts were known for what the plantsman Stephen Switzer (1682–1745) was to term 'extensive or forest gardening' – more sylviculture than horticulture.[12] This sense of priorities was well summarised by Alexander Pope in his line 'Who plants like Bathurst or who builds like Boyle [Burlington]'.[13] For this reason a few years appear to have elapsed before a fully realised house would envelop the small hunting lodge – a necessary development to establish a fully-fledged country seat. Nevertheless, the pristine condition of some of the rodel on the brickwork of the earlier lodge demonstrates that only a few years elapsed before these fragments were enveloped by the later house.[14]

On its northern and eastern frontages Clarendon House has a distinct yet subdued Baroque character. As a late manifestation of this idiom it is consistent with the date 1719 recently found scratched in plaster in the basement (Figure 15.3). These two elevations, the entrance and park frontages, are faced with Tisbury or Chilmark stone from the quarries just to the west of Salisbury, some 15 miles distant from Clarendon. The entrance front survives very much as illustrated in a watercolour of 1791 except that the land has risen (or been raised) somewhat. This has had the effect of obscuring the plinth and its mullioned windows to the basement so that the overall height and status of the house has been marginally diminished.

[10] Dana Arnold (ed.), *The Georgian Villa* (Stroud: Sutton, 1996), 81.

[11] Christopher Hussey, "Cirencester House, Gloucestershire," *Country Life* 107 (16 June 1950); Tom Beaumont James and Christopher M. Gerrard, *Clarendon: Landscape of kings* (Macclesfield: Windgather, 2007), 108.

[12] Christopher Hussey, *English Gardens and Landscape 1700–1750* (London: Country Life, 1967), chapter 11.

[13] Hussey, *English Gardens,* 79.

[14] See Timothy Easton, "The Painting of Historic Brick," *Weald and Downland Open Air Museum Magazine* (spring 2001): 26–29.

Figure 15.3: Sgraffito inscription in plaster by the builders who worked on Clarendon House in 1719. This was found in a plaster wall in one of the vaulted brick cellars. Drawing: the author.

The importance of the north front is indicated by the slightly projecting central bay surmounted by a segmental pediment. This divides the facade into three bays, each three windows wide. Centred on this composition is a rusticated stone door-case which, as the principal entrance, is given further emphasis by its Doric entablature. This is fully enriched with mutules under the cornice and trigliphs and guttae in the frieze.[15] The keystone to the semicircular door-head breaks into this scholarly classicism in a Baroque or Mannerist fashion.

On both the northern and eastern ranges the windows are encompassed by flat architraves supported, on the ground floor by simple consoles and on the first floor by projecting flat aprons. Unlike the north frontage the eastern elevation is surmounted by a triangular pediment and is seven rather than nine bays wide. The projecting middle bay, three windows wide, is anchored by a strong central emphasis from the apex of the pediment with its recessed lunette in its tympanum, to the architrave of the first floor window down to the door with its surmounting pediment and supporting consoles.

The building work at Clarendon seems to have been amended and then suspended in about 1720. Perhaps this may be associated with the South Sea Bubble which burst in the autumn of that year and resulted in a stock market collapse. This may explain why the remaining elevations were to be constructed of brick from the brickfield within the estate, a short distance to the north east of the house. Limited funds appear to have caused a hesitant approach to the building work at the south east corner of the site. The confident brick barrel vaults in the cellars of the northern range give way in the south east corner to cheaper 'naked flooring' of timber although the summer beams are of substantial scantlings. Archaeological investigation in the ground floor of the adjacent room to the west revealed the lower part of the west wall of a south wing giving the house an 'L' plan (Figure 15.1). This wing was built of brick with stone dressings and as such may have been considered as secondary – a possible service wing. Nevertheless when serious building work resumed this wing was enlarged and a further south wing was added to the west. These last amendments were probably built before the middle of the century.

Much of the splendour of Clarendon House is dependent upon its size and setting. For its realisation much was well within the competence of an artisan building craftsman in consultation with his client. Certainly, Earl Bathurst fulfilled the role as the patron for his recreation of Cirencester Park and it is possible his younger brother followed this approach. In its details Clarendon does betray a number of possible influences. For example, in Oxford Hawksmoor's Clarendon Building (built 1712–13) has similarly flat architraves on its external elevations.[16] Perhaps it was Hawksmoor's carpenter at Greenwich, John James (1673–1746) who played some part in the design of this Wiltshire house. James certainly worked in the district and in neighbouring counties. Indeed towards the end of his life he was an architectural adviser to the Dean and Chapter of Salisbury Cathedral. Perhaps the most persuasive justification for this attribution is a series of small engravings in James's translation (1707) of Pozzo's book on perspective.[17] Here the vignettes that decorate the letter A on a number of pages include a house with its central bay surmounted by a segmental pediment (Figure 15.4). Here the resemblance to the north front of Clarendon, and the west elevation of Cirencester Park, is striking.

From such architectural speculations let us now turn to the masonry. In the Salisbury district Chilmark and Tisbury stone from the quarries some ten miles west of the Cathedral city have a long history. Because of its softness it was often reinforced with bands or chequerwork of flint and was used in this way for the Bishop's Palace. A similar chalk-like material known as clunch in East Anglia was

[15] Batty Langley and Thomas Langley, *The Builder's Jewel: or, the youth's instructor, and workman's rembrancer* (London, 1768), 20–21, plate 12 (1741).

[16] Geoffrey Tyack, *Oxford: an architectural history* (Oxford: Oxford University Press, 1998), 150–51.

[17] Andrea Pozzo, *Rules and Examples of Perspective proper for Painters and Architects*... John James's translation, 1707 (Rome, 1693).

Figure 15.4: The house shown in this initial letter A resembles the north front of Clarendon and one of the elevations of Cirencester Park, Gloucestershire – each belonging to a member of the Bathurst family. This vignette appears on several pages in John James's translation (1707) of Pozzo's *Rules and Examples of Perspective* (1693). James, a carpenter by profession and an architect by trade may have taken some role in the design of Clarendon House. Drawing: the author.

reinforced in much the same way by adjacent areas of flint.[18] At Clarendon the masons were evidently confident in their use of Chilmark because it was noted that boasters were used to give the ashlar a decorative treatment known as corduroy work or batting. Surprisingly much of this surface decoration remains after some three hundred years. Perhaps the most remarkable example of the use of this ostensibly frail material is the Palladian Bridge at Wilton (1737) which has survived despite its proximity to water.

Many of the domestic buildings in the Close at Salisbury were faced with ashlar of Chilmark in the first decades of the eighteenth century. These include Arundels (refaced *c.* 1720), Malmesbury House (refaced 1705), Mompesson House (1701) and Myles Place (brick with Chilmark dressings, 1718).[19] Of these Myles Place has a reasonably secure date which corresponds closely to the work on Clarendon. The extensive use of Chilmark stone in the Salisbury area at this time suggests the presence of a tradition for this tractable yet difficult material among local masons and carvers. Most impressive of all was the decorative carving that was used to enrich many of these buildings, not least the lascivious fruit that embellish the consoles on the east front at Clarendon (Figure 15.5). Other examples include the cartouches on Mompesson House and on Myles Place. The latter carries the coat of arms of Eyre impaling Hyde (for Francis Eyre who married Anne Hyde, the daughter of Bishop Alexander Hyde – Figure 15.6). In creating these details the carvers were compelled to adopt very special methods in working the cloying nature of Chilmark. This may well have included the use of woodcarving tools which would be consistent with the undercutting and 'backing-off' that characterises much of this work.

The individuals responsible for these carvings have yet to be identified. One possible candidate is the mason Richard Macy of Salisbury who on 13 March 1715/16 took on Henry S. Rogers as an apprentice for a premium of £13.[20] A generation later, as the decoration that enriched Baroque architecture was displaced by an austere Palladianism, carvers were probably compelled to find alternative applications for their skills. For example the father and son Joseph and Josiah Lane of Tisbury established a reputation as builders of grottos working at Stourhead (*c.* 1750) and also Bowood. Even as late as 1792 the younger Lane built a grotto at Wardour Old Castle.[21] A close contemporary of Joseph Lane was the mason John Moore, also of Tisbury who, in 1755 took three apprentices for a full seven years. According to London trade regulation this was a maximum number of trainees for a single master but it suggests that there was ample work.[22]

Amendments to the house *c.* 1825–1830s

As it stands today the faintly Baroque external elevations of Clarendon House leave the visitor totally unprepared for its interiors. The experience is comparable to a visit to Kingston Lacy in Dorset where the 1660s external elevations make a curious prelude to Sir Charles Barry's interiors of 1835–39. At Clarendon it was John Peniston (1779–1848) who was appointed to build a stable block, re-order the inside of the house and add a service wing (demolished 1979), which practically doubled its size.

The house and its estate were inherited, in 1824, by Frederick H. Hervey-Bathurst (1810–1900) following the death of his father in that year. As a minor his inheritance was managed by his great uncle Sir William Fremantle (1766–1850). To modernise and rework the early eighteenth-century house Fremantle appointed Peniston, a local architect based in Salisbury. Peniston's family and forebears were bricklayers, and they may even have worked as such on Clarendon House. In this respect his background was comparable to that of the architect Sir John Soane (1753–1837). Indeed, the latter changed the spelling of his name from Soan to Soane, a convenient way of distancing himself from his trade-based relatives. In much the same way Peniston went to some lengths to stress his professional status and regularly emphasised his address at No. 28 in the Cathedral Close. His lease on

18 Alec Clifton-Taylor and A.S. Ireson, *English Stone Building* (London: Gollancz, 1983), 110.

19 RCHME, *Salisbury: the houses of the Close.*

20 Christabel Dale (ed.), *Wiltshire Apprentices and their Masters 1700–1760* (Devizes: Wiltshire Archaeological and Natural History Society, 1961), xiv.

21 Ingrid Roscoe, *Biographical Dictionary of Sculptors in Britain 1660–1851* (New Haven and London: Yale University Press, 2009).

22 Dale, *Wiltshire Apprentices*, xiv.

Figure 15.5: Console (two views) which supports the pediment over the east door. For comparison see Figure 15.6. Note the corduroy work on Chilmark ashlar. Drawing: the author.

that house was granted to him by the Chapter in 1807 on the understanding that he would repair it. By 1819 he had entirely rebuilt this dwelling; so Sir William Fremantle can have been under no illusions as to the radical approach that his chosen architect took to 'repairs'.[23] Nevertheless Peniston was a highly successful architect with clients throughout Wessex and beyond. Moreover his practice was to be continued by his son John Michael (1807–58) and his grandson Henry (1832–1911) – three generations, all of whom had a hand in the work at Clarendon.[24]

The Penistons' activities are remarkably well documented in the archive of their correspondence in the Wiltshire and Swindon History Centre at Chippenham (previously the Wiltshire Record Office, Trowbridge). Of particular relevance here are the letters that relate to Clarendon – some 80 in all. The abridged version of this archive, edited by Michael Cowan,[25] provides what is, in effect, a useful index – but the original documents remain essential reading. The letters are catalogued by number and date sequence, and for Hervey-Bathurst's house the first item (257) is dated 24 May 1825 when Fremantle's agent Webb was asked to report on Clarendon House. Fremantle would continue to act on his guardian's behalf at Clarendon until at least 18 December 1830 by which time Hervey-Bathurst had achieved, or was approaching, the age of majority.

By 4 March 1828 the architect submitted his outline scheme for extensive repairs and alterations which, he estimated, would cost £3,883 with an additional £1,000 or £2,000 for a stable block. On 5 May the plans had reached a stage when Peniston was in a position to discuss the proposals with Sir William. Although the architect was indisposed with gout he was able to send his 21 year old son John to London for this meeting. In this same letter Peniston confirms that whilst he 'will be pleased to direct the work [he] has for some years declined the building himself'. This proved to be a recurring theme with the ex-bricklayer attempting to assert his professional status. In this he was not entirely successful for he was to comment later that he 'unexpectedly' found himself functioning at Clarendon as a 'general contractor' in addition to his role

[23] RCHME, *Salisbury: the houses of the Close*, 137.
[24] Pamela M. Slocombe (ed.), *Architects and Building Craftsmen with Work in Wiltshire*, Part 2 (Trowbridge: Wiltshire Record Office, 2006).
[25] Michael Cowan, (ed.), *The Letters of John Peniston, a Salisbury Architect, Catholic and Yeomanry Officer, 1823–1830*, Wiltshire Records Series 50 (Trowbridge: Wiltshire Record Society, 1996).

Figure 15.6: Pediment of *c.*1719 over the door of number 69 Walton Canonry, The Close, Salisbury Cathedral. The cartouche carries the arms of Eyre impaling Hyde. The stonework of the domestic buildings in the Close as at nearby Clarendon House appear to be products of a Salisbury centred school of masons and carvers working in Chilmark stone. Photograph: the author.

as architect. The presence of his cousin, the builder James Peniston, at nearby Winchester Street, Salisbury, seems to have complicated the architect's position.

At an early stage in the project Peniston gives some consideration to those items that were to be sourced at some distance from Wiltshire. For example, he notes (16 June 1828) that the pair of scagliola columns that were to mark the divide between the entrance hall and the new staircase were likely to cost about £30 each unless second hand ones could be found. In that same letter reference is made to his sketch for a proposed conservatory. By 28 June he writes to Messrs Jones and Clark, Metallic Hot House Manufacturers of Birmingham for a design and price for such a structure. This was to be built between the two south wings of the house (but was, much later, displaced by a ballroom). In this aspect of the work Peniston, his client and, more particularly, Messrs Jones and Clark the designers and suppliers, were in the vanguard of technology and taste. Paxton's great Conservatory at Chatsworth was not built until 1836 although Lewis Vulliamy's hot house at Syston New Hall, demolished *c.*1935,[26] was built in 1822 and Peniston's letters show that he was in touch with Vulliamy. He was also in correspondence with Edward Blore (1787–1879) who used the same Birmingham manufacturers for a conservatory at Norman Court, Hampshire (28 June 1828). On 5 July Peniston writes to Jones and Clark seeking clarification of their estimate of £430, asking if it included a furnace.

By 1 October 1828, with detailed designs and costings in place, the architect was in a position to revise upwards his estimate of 4 March to £8,000 but it is not clear if this included the stable block which he was also to build. So radical was this scheme for the house that the goods and chattels that it housed were likely to get in the way of building work. The architect's letter of 24 October 1828 states that Sir William's agent Webb had visited Clarendon House 'and arranged for inventories of the furniture and library'. By 7 November the rooms in which these articles were stored were identified and a Clarendon tenant (Mr Parry) agreed 'to take the pictures and glasses [mirrors?]'. On 26 November it was decided that the 'Furniture will be stored in the staddle barn' although the books remained 'a problem'. In this same letter Peniston reports that with the work on the garden wall being complete he was able to 'discharge' one hundred employees – a note

[26] John Cornforth, *English Interiors 1790–1848: the quest for comfort* (London: Barrie and Jenkins, 1978), fig. 88.

that is indicative of the number of men engaged on this undertaking.

Some faltering communication between Peniston and the Hot House Manufacturers compelled him to write (23 April 1829) stating that 'unless I hear from you quickly and satisfactorally I must regretfully apply elsewhere'. This evidently had the desired effect for by 23 August the components for the conservatory had arrived at Southampton. It seems that this shipment included mortice locks for the doors and very probably, the sash pulleys by W. Bullock of Birmingham. This midlands manufacturer supplied ironmongery of this type for John Nash's work on Buckingham Palace in 1825–30.[27] It is very probable that the cast iron balusters (Figure 15.7) for the main staircase were supplied by Messrs Jones and Clark, the designers and manufacturers of the conservatory. All these supplies were sourced in the midlands, the cradle of the industrial revolution, and then transported by boat to Southampton and thence to Clarendon by means of wagons.

Figure 15.7: Details of the main staircase of *c.*1828 – the balusters are cast iron. Drawing: the author.

In some ways the most visible contribution that Peniston made to the early- eighteenth century house was also the most superficial. This concerned its high quality rubbed brick south and west elevations. The finish of such details as the flat arches over windows and doors show that this brickwork was intended to be visible. However, these elevations were, in tone, colour and material, at variance with the stone elevations to their north and east. The new regime was determined to unify the building by rendering the brick with stucco. In addition 'the offices', presumably Peniston's service wing and the stable block, were to have 'Roman cement' applied to the brickwork but 'only to colour the walls' (5 August 1828). In the late eighteenth century the diluted use of stucco as a form of distemper was used as a mural treatment on the brick built stable block at Crichel House, Dorset which may have been designed by James Wyatt (1746–1813).[28] Fragments of this surface treatment survive on the stable blocks at both Clarendon and Crichel.[29] It seems that Peniston purchased his stucco from Messrs Grieve, Grellier and Morgan, Roman Cement Manufacturers of Belvedere Road, Waterloo Bridge Road, London. This company certainly supplied him with 'three casks of coarse plaster' for Spetisbury House, Dorset (25 May 1830).

With the exception of the cellars, which were largely left untouched, Peniston's work on the interiors was radical in the extreme. For example, the original principal staircase was probably located in the north entrance hall. The architect maintained this generous space exclusively as the entrance vestibule but he moved the staircase to the south. Certainly, the present staircase-well has been cut through a floor since its joist pockets were identified in the flank walls. Indeed, so uncompromising were his amendments that on 2 June 1828 he was compelled to admit that 'many of the walls have been weakened by serious alterations'. This probably explains an additional skin of brickwork, identified at some points, where it served as a means of buttressing the structure. Not that these issues were to prevent Peniston from proceeding with his schemes. By 11 and 13 March 1829 he reports that 'The space is cleared for the intended staircase'. This flight rises and divides to afford an almost ceremonial means of access to the upper rooms – mostly bedrooms. This feature is comparable to the stairs at Onslow Hall, Shropshire, designed by Edward Haycock in *c.*1820, and Birch Hall, Essex, by Thomas Hopper *c.*1844. All had cast iron balusters like the stair at Clarendon but sadly Birch Hall and Onslow Hall were both demolished in 1955.[30]

The addition of the service wing to the west, coupled with other alterations, resulted in 'a want of light in the Corridors'. Accordingly a proposal was made 'to gain it [daylight] by inserting openings in the Walls next to the Staircase' (9 December 1828). The following year (23 March 1829) reference is made to 'semicircular openings'.

[27] Charles Brooking, pers. comm.

[28] John Cornforth, "The Building of Crichel." *Design and Practice in British Architecture: Studies in architectural history presented to Howard Colvin,* Architectural History 27 (1984): 268–69.

[29] John M. Steane and James Ayres, "Crichel House, Dorset," unpublished report, September/ October 2003.

[30] Roy Strong, Marcus Binney and John Harris, *The Destruction of the Country House, 1875–1975* (London: Thames and Hudson, 1974), figs. 306, 308.

As realised this treatment is very similar to the stair well to Wyatt's Claverton Manor, near Bath, built *c.*1820.[31] This resemblance may not be entirely coincidental. Sir Jeffry Wyatt (Wyattville 1776–1840) was appointed by George IV to make considerable alterations to Windsor Castle. At Windsor it is very likely that Wyatt met Sir William Fremantle who was then the Treasurer to the royal household and, by 1827, Deputy Ranger of Windsor Great Park – the Ranger being the monarch.

The early eighteenth-century house was a compact box with most rooms illuminated by external windows. The addition of the service wing increased the need to obtain 'borrowed light', especially in the western zones in the house. In the late nineteenth century the roof, and the ceilings below it, were fitted with sky-lights and, at the first floor level, glazed grills, manufactured by Hayward Brothers of London, were inserted in some floors. In addition to the supply of ready-made components the correspondence is peppered with references to the sourcing of building materials. On 26 October 1828 the architect writes to the timber merchant Charles Baker of Southampton for 'a considerable number of deals', in the sense of scantlings,[32] as the 'Works at Clarendon will require many loads of Memel timber' and also 'well seasoned Christiana deals, red and white'. Memel timber came from the Baltic but Christiana, today's Oslo, being in close proximity to the North Sea, was a port that remained largely free of ice so that timber was generally available from Norway throughout the year. Curiously, few if any of the doors in the house were made of mahogany although they were hung on the finest quality ormolu rising-butt hinges.

With regard to carpentry Peniston 'found the timbers of the old roof even worse than expected' (7 February 1829) and it was to be entirely rebuilt in soft-wood. On 26 November 1828 the sawyers were 'busy in cutting out Timbers for the new roof'. There may then have been some delay with the slaters' work for, on 9 December, Peniston complains that 'nothing can be done towards the Plastering 'til the roof is on'. By June 'the Joiners [were] proceeding simultaneously with the Plasterers'. As with all building undertakings the sequencing of the work was of fundamental importance. On 26 Nov 1828 the joiners were preparing 'New Sash Frames, Doors etc', and by 7 April 1829 they were fixing their work. This would have been the point at which the windows of the 1719 house, with their wide ovolo glazing bars, were replaced by sashes with narrow astragals.

Perhaps among the most significant features in the Peniston interiors are the decorative plaster ceilings that adorn most of the ground floor rooms – those in the first floor chambers have good but simple cornices. To what extent Peniston was involved in the design of these ceilings is not known. However, for his work at Thornhill House, Dorset (9 March 1829), he supplied a 'pattern for the coffers of the ceiling'. As for the execution of the decorative plasterwork at Clarendon it has not proved possible to identify a master craftsman. The most likely man was Porter who is known to have worked in the house and who, for another job, was sent drawings by Peniston for a modillioned plaster cornice.[33] By 1830 Porter is known to have settled in Salisbury. Another possible plasterer is Wallis of Southampton (7 October 1824) but a third candidate for this work, a man named Padden, may be excluded as Peniston considered him incompetent (1 October 1830).

Although all these ceilings were worked to a similar idiom, evidently by the same hand, they differ in their details. In general they share a Greek Revival character appropriate to the tastes of their time although in some cases an almost Turkish accent gives them a somewhat Byronic flourish. Most of these ceilings have now been restored to their former glory with the exception of the formal dining room (N.W. corner of the ground floor). Sadly, in the recent restoration, the joists that sustained this plasterwork from above were found to be in such poor condition that RSJs were inserted and a secondary ceiling suspended below them. This inevitably led to some destruction of this decorative plasterwork and has eclipsed the surviving fragments. When complete this ceiling was conceived as a celebration of nature's bounty and its provision of grain and grape – a theme appropriate to the function of the room it graced (Figures 15.8 and 15.9).

As Peniston's interventions in the house drew to a conclusion the need to provide chimneypieces became apparent. Few of these now survive in the house. On the first floor a modest marble example with *paterae* at the corners survives in a bedroom.[34] For the principal rooms on the ground floor more substantial and sculpturally more significant chimneypieces were required (although none survived in-situ in 2007–09). An undated letter (Cowan no. 926) refers to 'several marble chimneypieces for re-erection at Clarendon House' which had been 'laid out for examination at Mr Brown's store in Exeter Street'. This is a reference to F. Brown of Salisbury (fl. 1829–40) whose father had been appointed master mason to the Cathedral in 1804.[35] A letter of 16 October 1829 alludes to the arrival of a consignment of plaster from London but 'not the chimneypieces', which indicates a source for the latter in the capital. Of the many sculptors capable of doing such work in London at this time we know that Edward Gaffin supplied Peniston with chimneypieces (11 March 1829).[36] Thomas and Edward Gaffin established a marble carving business that flourished for just over a century from *c.*1800. Various addresses are given for this establishment

[31] James Ayres, "Claverton and its Manors," *America in Britain* 39 (2001): 10–13.

[32] James Ayres, *Building the Georgian City* (New Haven and London: Yale University Press, 1998), fig. 81.

[33] Cowan, *The Letters of John Peniston*, 1238, 1613.

[34] For a comparable example dated 1828, see Ayres, *Domestic Interiors*, fig. 292.

[35] Roscoe, *Biographical Dictionary of Sculptors*.

[36] Gaffin, not Griffin as transcribed by Cowan, *The Letters of John Peniston*, 985.

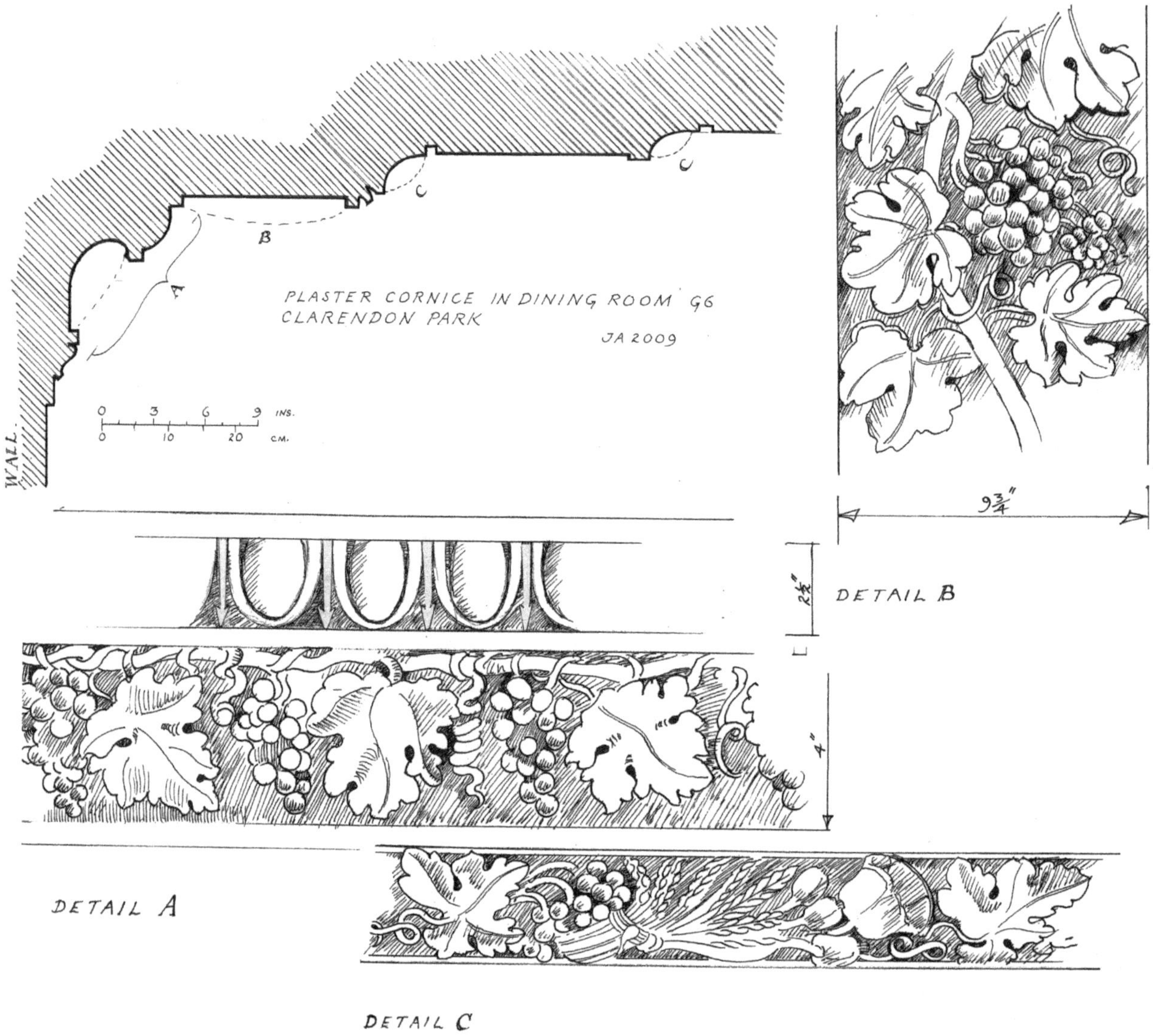

Figure 15.8: Details of the decorative plaster ceiling of *c.*1829 in the formal dining room at Clarendon House. Drawing: the author.

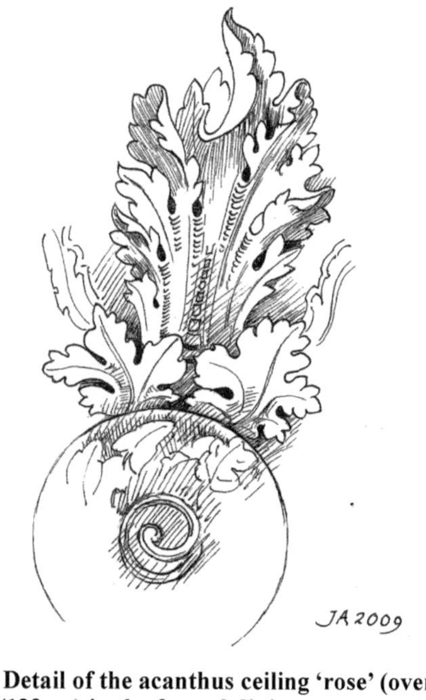

Figure 15.9: Detail of the acanthus ceiling 'rose' (overall diameter 4ft/122cm) in the formal dining room on the ground floor in the north-west corner of Clarendon House. Drawing: the author.

including 63 Regent Street, London. From 1827 Peniston was writing to the Gaffins at Kensington Place, Millbank, Westminster. One rather fine marble mantelpiece, possibly by the Gaffins, was in store in the staddle barn in 2007–2009.

By 2 March 1830 the architect reports, with some satisfaction if exaggeration, that 'another fortnight will complete our work on the house, except the entrance hall' with its marble floor. Two months later (30 April) the painters were finishing the third coat but they would allow the summer to pass before applying the fourth and final coat. As three coats of paint were generally considered adequate this final coat, after months of drying, demonstrates the very high standards of workmanship that were sought and achieved at Clarendon.

Bibliography

Published secondary sources

Arnold, Dana, ed. *The Georgian Villa*. Stroud: Sutton, 1996.

Ayres, James. *Building the Georgian City*. New Haven and London: Yale University Press, 1998.

Ayres, James. "Claverton and its Manors." *America in Britain* 39 (2001): 10–13.

Ayres, James. *Domestic Interiors: the British tradition 1500–1850*. New Haven and London: Yale University Press, 2003.

Beaumont James, Tom, and Christopher M. Gerrard. *Clarendon: Landscape of kings*. Macclesfield: Windgather, 2007.

Clifton-Taylor, Alec, and A.S. Ireson, *English Stone Building*. London: Gollancz, 1983.

Cornforth, John. *English Interiors 1790–1848: the quest for comfort*. London: Barrie and Jenkins, 1978.

Cornforth, John. "The Building of Crichel." *Design and Practice in British Architecture: Studies in architectural history presented to Howard Colvin*, Architectural History 27 (1984): 268–69.

Cowan, Michael, ed. *The Letters of John Peniston, a Salisbury Architect, Catholic and Yeomanry Officer, 1823–1830*, Wiltshire Records Series 50. Trowbridge: Wiltshire Record Society, 1996.

Dale, Christabel, ed. *Wiltshire Apprentices and their Masters 1700–1760*. Devizes: Wiltshire Archaeological and Natural History Society, 1961.

Easton, Timothy. "The Painting of Historic Brick." *Weald and Downland Open Air Museum Magazine* (spring 2001): 26–29.

Hogg, Min. "Swangrove." *The World of Interiors*, March 2003.

Hussey, Christopher. *English Gardens and Landscape 1700–1750*. London: Country Life, 1967.

Hussey, Christopher. "Cirencester House, Gloucestershire." *Country Life* 107 (16 June 1950).

James, Tom Beaumont. *Clarendon: landscape, palace, mansion*. Salisbury: Salisbury and South Wiltshire Museum, 2010.

James, Tom Beaumont, and Anne M. Robinson. *Clarendon Palace: the history and archaeology of a medieval palace and hunting lodge near Salisbury, Wiltshire*, Reports of the Research Committee of the Society of Antiquaries of London 45. London: Society of Antiquaries and Thames and Hudson, 1988.

Jones, Dan. *The Plantagenets: the kings who made England*. London: Harper Press, 2012.

Langley, Batty, and Thomas Langley. *The Builder's Jewel: or, the youth's instructor, and workman's rembrancer*. London, 1768.

Lloyd, Nathaniel. *A History of English Brickwork* (1925). Reprint, Woodbridge: Antique Collector's Club, 1983.

Pozzo, Andrea. *Rules and Examples of Perspective Proper for Painters and Architects,* John James's translation (1707). Rome, 1693.

Roscoe, Ingrid. *Biographical Dictionary of Sculptors in Britain 1660–1851*. New Haven and London: Yale University Press, 2009.

Royal Commission on Historical Monuments of England. *Salisbury: the houses of the Close*. London: HMSO, 1993.

Slocombe, Pamela M., ed. *Architects and Building Craftsmen with Work in Wiltshire*, Part 2. Trowbridge: Wiltshire Record Office, 2006.

Strong, Roy, Marcus Binney and John Harris. *The Destruction of the Country House, 1875–1975*. London: Thames and Hudson, 1974.

Tyack, Geoffrey. *Oxford: an Architectural History*. Oxford: Oxford University Press, 1998.

Unpublished secondary sources

James, Tom Beaumont, and James Ayres. "Clarendon House." Unpublished reports 2007–09.

Steane, John M., and James Ayres. "Crichel House, Dorset." Unpublished report, September/ October 2003.

Steane, John M., and James Ayres. "Cornbury Estate, Oxfordshire: Kingstanding Farm and Walcot Barn." Unpublished report 2004.

16

God's House Chapel, the French Church, and Remembering Southampton's 'Huguenot' Past

Andrew Spicer

Oxford Brookes University

Abstract: The commemoration of the bicentenary of the Revocation of the Edict of Nantes in October 1885 focused attention on the Huguenot diaspora and the communities they established in southern England. At Southampton, exiles from the southern Netherlands had formed a community in 1567 and services continued to be held in St Julien's chapel at God's House Hospital. Academic and popular publications recounted the foundation and early history of the community, with particular reference to the French church's register. By 1885, the congregation used a French translation of the Anglican prayer book rather than the Reformed liturgy of the Huguenots. Services were attended by Channel Islanders and French-speaking people passing through the port rather than Huguenot descendants. Pastors focused on the religious needs of French-speaking residents as well as Southampton's seamen. Even the French congregation's use of God's House chapel was questioned during the nineteenth century and when the building was restored, it was primarily to serve the residents of God's House Hospital. While traces of Southampton's 'Huguenot' history survived, the French church did not memorialise its past.

Key words: French church: God's House Hospital; Huguenot; immigration; memory; mission to seamen; Queen's College Oxford; Southampton

In July 1889, the Huguenot Society of London held its summer conference in Southampton and Winchester.[1] The prospect of visiting Southampton appealed because 'in addition to the French church, there are other churches of interest... old town records and other important documents to be inspected'. The conference opened in the municipal buildings with 'a cordial welcome of characteristic Hampshire heartiness' from the mayor, who expressed his pleasure in seeing in Southampton 'so many representatives of the Huguenots who had formerly sought and found a refuge there, and who had done so much to promote the trade and general prosperity of the town'. The visitors inspected 'various ancient documents, maces and other objects of interest'. After luncheon, they made their way to St Julien's chapel where they heard a paper on the history of God's House hospital delivered by the Rev. J. Aston Whitlock, vicar of Holy Rood and steward of God's House. Whitlock's lecture discussed the hospital's foundation in the twelfth century and the history of the French Reformed community which had worshipped in its chapel since 1567. Under the guidance of Mr Shore, 'a gentleman possessing great local knowledge and an experienced archaeologist', the conference 'visited the most important monuments and relics of the past in Southampton – not only those connected with the Huguenots but with more ancient times, in which the city abounds'.[2] These sites included God's House tower, 'the legendary Canute's House', French Street, 'the No. 4 vault in Simnel Street', St Michael's church '(in which are a very remarkable font and several old church books, one... bearing on the cover the name of Guillaume, a former churchwarden)' and 'the peculiar arcaded portion of the ancient town wall commonly supposed to be the remains of King John's waterside palace'. After dinner and toasts at the South-Western Hotel, the Society heard a paper by W.J.C. Moens on 'The Walloon Settlement and French Church at Southampton'. The following day, the conference continued with a visit to Winchester with its cathedral and the hospital of St Cross but as the President later noted there was little there especially connected with the Huguenots, apart from 'the inscribed tablet to the memory of the liberated galley-slave, Jean Serres, who suffered for his religion'.[3]

The Society's visit reflected the increasing interest in the Huguenot diaspora and their settlements during the late nineteenth century.[4] In Southampton, the French

[1] This paragraph is based on "Summer Conference at Southampton and Winchester, July 19, 20 1889," *Proceedings of the Huguenot Society* [hereafter *PHS*] 3 (1888–91): xlvii–li.

[2] Henry Austen Layard, "Address to the Sixth Annual General Meeting of the Huguenot Society of London," *PHS* 3 (1888–91): lxxx. On Thomas William Shore, see H.C.G. Matthew and Brian Harrison (eds), *Oxford Dictionary of National Biography*, 60 vols, Oxford, 2004 [hereafter *ODNB*], L, 424–25.

[3] Layard, "Address," lxxx–lxxxi; "Summer Conference," lii–liii.

[4] See Andrew Spicer, "1885: French Protestantism and Huguenot identity in Victorian Britain," in *Histoire, mémoire et identités en mutation. Les huguenots en France et en diaspora (XVIe–XXIe siècles)*, ed. Philip Benedict, Hugues Daussy and Pierre-Olivier Léchot (Geneva: Droz, 2014).

Reformed community had been closely associated with the medieval chapel of St Julien at God's House hospital, where they had worshipped for more than three and a half centuries. Yet during the society's visit to the chapel, the pastor Auguste Bellet spoke of his regret of 'there not being a larger attendance at the services at St Julian's. He trusted, however, that the interest excited by the visit of the Huguenot Society would do much to induce those in Southampton and the neighbourhood who had Huguenot blood in their veins, to attend the church and help in the work carried on in connection with it'.[5] Although the minister had only been appointed in March 1889, Moens – vice-president of the Huguenot Society – expressed the hope that 'the importance and well-doing of this well-established French church, so important in Southampton, where so many French and Channel Islanders are to be found, may long continue under his watchful and diligent care'.[6]

Bellet's comments reflected the apparent paradox of growing interest in the Huguenots' heritage at a time when the survival of the French-speaking congregations was threatened.[7] In Southampton, the congregation's right to worship in St Julien's chapel had been challenged earlier in the century. Furthermore, God's House hospital had been redeveloped in the late 1850s with new buildings for the brethren and sisters; the demolition and replacement of the medieval chapel was even contemplated. Had this proposal gone ahead, it would have eradicated all structural traces of the Huguenot presence in Southampton. This essay will focus on the association between the French church and God's House chapel amidst the growing nineteenth-century interest in the history of the Huguenot diaspora and their settlements.

I The French Church and God's House Chapel

The French church had been established in 1567 by refugees escaping religious persecution in the southern Netherlands, as the Spanish government attempted to restore order following the hedge-preaching, iconoclasm and rebellion of the *Wonderjaar*.[8] These exiles had appealed to the mayor and corporation of Southampton for permission to settle in the port because they could not 'endure and abide our consciences to be burdened and in especiall to beare the intolerable clogge of the Spanish Inquisicon'. They had left the southern Netherlands 'without regard for the loss of our goodes or native Co[u] ntrey to seeke out an other place of habitacon where it may be lawfull for us to live quietly and Christian like'.[9] From the outset, Channel Islanders trading or passing through Southampton had gathered with these religious exiles and their descendants to worship in their own language. The community grew further with the arrival of Huguenot refugees escaping religious persecution and the associated socio-economic dislocation caused by the religious wars in France, particularly in the wake of the St Bartholomew's Day massacres in 1572. With assimilation and integration into the host community as well as the more favourable religious climate on the continent, the French church was on the verge of collapse by the mid-seventeenth century. However, its fortunes were revived by a new influx of Huguenot refugees fleeing increasing religious persecution in France under Louis XIV, which culminated in the Revocation of the Edict of Nantes in 1685. These exiles and their descendants, together with the Channel Islanders, ensured the survival of the French church.

In 1853, the church closed following the death of the minister Frederick Vincent, but a subsequent appeal or 'memorial' called for a new appointment and the resumption of services. The Charity Commissioners noted the following year that they had 'received differing opinions as to the necessity or the benefit of continuing such services with reference to the failure of the objects for which they were established'. In spite of these reservations, an order in Chancery was obtained to restructure the church's government, leading to the appointment of a board of trustees responsible for its charitable funds. Services resumed in October 1856, with Hubert Napoléon Dupont as the new minister of the French church.[10] The Charity Commission had also questioned in 1854 'the constitution and Proprietorship of the Chapel... particularly the fact or degree of its [French church's] connexion with the Hospital of God's House'.[11] Their rights to the chapel had been the source of a dispute with the steward of God's House, William Wilson, several decades earlier.

The initial settlers had been assigned the chapel in 1567 by Robert Horne, Bishop of Winchester, who had written to William Cecil explaining that:

> they can not lyve without great disordres amonge themselves and sectes dangerous to the naturall subjectes, onles by your good meanes also they may have lycence to gather together into some one churche and so to lyve undre some godly discipline ... and there is for that purpose a churche that well be spared and fytt for them withoute the molestation of any [of] the parishes of Hampton.[12]

[5] "Summer Conference," xlix.

[6] W.J.C. Moens, "The Walloon Settlement and the French Church at Southampton," *PHS* 3 (1888–91): 75; Edwin Welch (ed.), *The Minute Book of the French Church at Southampton, 1702–1939*, Southampton Records Series [hereafter SRS] 23 (1979) [hereafter *Minute Book*], 134–35.

[7] Spicer, "1885: French Protestantism," 391–422; A. Spicer, "'A Survival of a Distant Past': J.A. Martin and the Victorian revival of the French church at Canterbury," *Southern History* 34 (2012): 100–38.

[8] Andrew Spicer, *The French-speaking Reformed Community and their Church in Southampton, 1567–c.1620*, Huguenot Society New Series 3 / SRS 39 (1997), 2–21.

[9] British Library, London, Cottonian MSS, Vespasian FIX, f. 230. For an examination of the negotiations, see Spicer, *French-speaking Reformed Community*, 22–34.

[10] Southampton City Archives, Southampton [hereafter SCA], D/FC3/10/1–5, D/FC5 (Acc.7134) Livre du Clerc (unpaginated), D/S1/5/18; *Minute Book*, 9, 100–02, 104.

[11] SCA, D/S 1/5/18. See also *Hampshire Advertiser*, 18 August 1855.

[12] The National Archives, Kew [hereafter TNA], SP12/43/16.

Horne was referring to the medieval hospital of God's House, founded in the 1190s but in the possession of Queen's College, Oxford since the fourteenth century.[13] There is no indication that the college was formally consulted or even granted the refugees permission to use God's House chapel, but they did pay for it to be reglazed at this time.[14] The first French Reformed service was held in October 1567, when the Guernsey minister Nicholas Baudouin preached to the new community in the presence of the mayor and corporation as well as the bishop of Winchester.[15] Although the exact arrangements are unclear, the refugees appear to have shared the chapel with those living at the hospital; the God's House accounts show that money continued to be spent on bread and wine for communion for the brethren.[16] This ad hoc arrangement continued into the nineteenth century, when Dr Wilson attempted to establish the respective rights of the college and the congregation to the chapel.

The failure to determine these rights and a dispute over the chapel's keys led in February 1829 to Queen's College giving the French congregation notice to quit by the following Lady Day.[17] A report on the state of the French church noted that:

> What is particularly remarkable is that it is by mere sufferance that the French Service is performed there: the *Chapel, Hospital*, and the *whole Building* belong to... *Queen's College, Oxford.* Dr Wilson, Vicar of Holy Rood, in which Parish this Foundation lays, lives on the premises and performs English Service every Wednesday in the... French Chapel, which he claims as his right from the college, altho' (he told me) he will not oppose the continuation of the French Service on the Sunday.[18]

An elder of the French church, Mr Le Fevre, claimed that according to the '*Patent from Queen Elizabeth* in 1567 the Chapel was appointed for the *Walloon Protestants* who fled from the Persecution of the Duke of Alva and took refuge in Southampton'.[19] There had been unsuccessful attempts by the minister to locate letters patent for the establishment of the community in 1825 and 1827.[20] Although letters patent were granted for some settlements, this was not the case for all the Elizabethan foreign communities.[21] Legal advice was sought as to whether 'after the length of time which the elders have had possession can they be ejected without any other process, or further notice'.[22]

The resulting legal opinion outlined the history of the congregation's use of the chapel, showing that 'from time out of mind' they had repaired the building, for example with a levy on the 'heads of families' to finance a new roof in 1702. However, a donation of £21 towards the cost of repairs in July 1788 'keeps up a connection between the College and the chapel'. It was noted that 'the College aim only to retain their membership', but questioned whether 'after 263 years of quiet possession, can the College by any & what legal or equitable means get the congregation out'. It concluded that as the elders were not recognised as a body in law but 'in their individual character only', their possession of the chapel only stretched back to the election of the most senior elder in 1786. Furthermore 'the title of the elders is mere possession only. They possess no grant or Document from the College or the Crown. What documents they did possess, are lost'.[23] The dispute led to the cessation of services, until the college offered a lease to the congregation. Although minded to accept the offer, the elders first sought a further legal opinion as to whether this would be justified, as it would be an admission of the college's rights to the building and the abandonment of their own claims.[24] The matter was ultimately resolved with the congregation's agreement to pay the college 6s 8d per annum for the use of the building.[25]

II God's House Hospital and Chapel

During the late 1850s, Queen's College was criticised in the local press for its management and trusteeship of God's House hospital. In April 1856, the *Southampton Examiner* thundered 'You rich ecclesiastics of Oxford, are you not ashamed of the neglected, dilapidated, and deserted state of the God's House Establishment in Winkle-Street?' It was claimed that 'the Provost and Fellows of Queen's College, pounce on the lion's share [of the income from 'the property committed to their trust'], and that their Steward, resident at Southampton, reserves but a very small share for the four aged men and four aged women, now resident in this neglected and dilapidated Almshouse establishment'.[26] Parallels were drawn between God's House and the more notorious accusations of corruption levelled against the earl of Guilford at the hospital of St Cross near Winchester.[27] Guilford had been appointed to the mastership by his father Brownlow North, Bishop of Winchester. In the God's House case, it was claimed that the bishop, North's successor Charles Sumner, had failed to act because the steward William Wilson was his brother-in-

[13] See John M. Kaye (ed.), *The Cartulary of God's House, Southampton*, 2 vols, SRS 19–20 (1976) [hereafter *Cartulary of God's House*], I, xxv–li.

[14] The Queen's College Archives, Oxford [hereafter QCA], GHA Box 4 (7); Spicer, *French-speaking Reformed Community*, 100–01.

[15] Johannes H. Hessels, *Epistulae et tractatus cum Reformationis tum ecclesiae Londino-Batavae historiam illustrantes*, 3 vols (London, 1889–97), III, 2555–56; Spicer, *French-speaking Reformed Community*, 34, 102.

[16] QCA, GHA Boxes 4, 5.

[17] SCA, D/FC3/8/6, 11a.

[18] *Minute Book*, 183–84. The notice to quit was accompanied by 'a verbal message "that if the Right of the College was admitted, the performance of Divine Worship would not be interfered with'. SCA, D/FC3/8/11a.

[19] *Minute Book*, 184.

[20] SCA, D/FC3/8/1–4.

[21] Spicer, *French-speaking Reformed Community*, 22.

[22] SCA, D/FC3/8/8a.

[23] SCA, D/FC3/8/11a.

[24] SCA, D/FC3/8/13b.

[25] SCA, D/FC1; *Minute Book*, 184n.

[26] SCA, TCBox 58/3 "The Almshouse Establishment of God's House." From the 'Southampton Examiner', April 1856.

[27] Peter Hopewell, *Saint Cross: England's oldest almshouse* (Chichester: Phillimore, 1995), 106–12.

law.[28] In 1858, the town corporation decided to investigate the accusations levelled against the college's management of the almshouses. This prompted a heated exchange of letters, in which the college challenged the authority of the corporation to undertake such an enquiry. Furthermore, the college had a couple of months earlier accepted the recommendation made by the charity commissioners in their 1855 report. They increased the allowances for the residents, and were already in discussions about rebuilding the hospital. Protracted 'technical difficulties' concerning their new statutes prevented them from acting sooner but 'any statement that the College has diverted to its own use one farthing belonging to the brethren and sisters is utterly false and calumnious'.[29]

At the forefront of the vitriolic press campaign was an un-beneficed cleric and eccentric, Herbert Smith, who took a keen interest in social welfare, particularly for the elderly, and charitable foundations such as almshouses. A frequent writer to the newspapers regarding the God's House hospital, he also published tracts on the issue largely drawing on his correspondence with the charity commissioners, the bishop of Winchester and others, as well as letters in local newspapers.[30] His obituary stated that 'Almost unaided, he was the means of greatly benefiting the inmates of God's House Almshouses'.[31] Smith himself claimed that he had spared Queen's College, the Southampton corporation and the God's House estate 'the annoying and ruinous intervention and expense of the law' through his campaign 'to correct the abuses of this ancient Catholic Religious House of Charity – a Home for the Aged Poor Saints, or respectable Aged Poor'. Through his actions, he argued, 'the allowance to the eight aged almsmen and women has been increased from two to five shillings per week, and the hospital has been rebuilt'.[32]

Even after the construction of the new buildings, which opened in July 1860, Smith continued to press the Charity Commissioners to make the college fulfil what he regarded as their obligation for 'the constant residence of a clergyman within the hospital establishment, to minister to the spiritual necessities of the aged inmates, and to perform Divine Service in the English language twice every Lord's day in the Chapel of the Hospital'. Wilson had, with the college's permission, demolished the decayed steward's lodging so there was nowhere for a resident clergyman to live within the hospital.[33] Furthermore, Smith did not mention the French church's use of the chapel, probably considering their spiritual needs as secondary to the intentions of the founders of 'the ancient Catholic establishment'.

This criticism ignored the significant work undertaken by Wilson and his refurbishment of the chapel, which was in 'a very dilapidated condition'.[34] Even allowing for artistic licence and a romantic view of the building, its decayed and fairly ramshackle appearance and the poor condition of the stonework can be seen in the engraving from 1817 (Figure 16.1). In January 1829, Wilson wrote to P. Le Fevre concerning 'the interior of the Chapel of God's House [which] wants considerable reparations, the floor in many parts is altogether decayed, and the seats are some of them broken down'. He went on to ask 'whether you propose to undertake this reparation yourself or… are willing to cooperate with the Wednesday evening congregation in making suitable accommodation for the performance of divine worship'.[35] The French congregation provided £35 towards the costs of these repairs, which Wilson estimated at £130. Further funds were raised from the townspeople; the bishop donated £10 and the Dock Company, £50. Wilson expressed the hope that if more money was raised then 'part of the Chapel, which is now misappropriated to a store might be formed into a gallery, at an addition[al] expence of 30£. Thus the building would be completely a consecrated Place & there would also be a considerable increase of sittings'.[36]

In November 1839 a letter to the bursar of Queen's College reported that during Wilson's repairs to the chapel they 'uncovered the beautiful pillars and restored the ornaments at the chapiter [capitals?]'.[37] It seems that the work also exposed the gravestones of past members of the French congregation.[38] Attempting to restore the ceiling plaster revealed the poor condition of the roof, which needed to be replaced.[39] The work undertaken was extensive with the final cost being £210 8s 10d, including the new gallery, seating, pulpit and desk.[40]

In spite of this extensive refurbishment, R. Critchlow was asked in September 1861, after completion of the residential blocks, to provide a report on the state of the chapel and an estimate for repairing the building. His report was extremely critical and Critchlow observed that 'in this case to restore will be to rebuild or nearly so':

> I will begin with the roof. The part once their chancel is as far as the design goes in its original state but from the care that has been taken in getting it together and its

[28] SCA, TCBox 58/3 "The Almshouse Establishment of God's House"; *ODNB*, LIX, 661; Hopewell, *Saint Cross*, 106–12.

[29] QCA, 4G181; SCA, TC Box58/3; *Hampshire Advertiser*, 15 January 1859. In 1889, the corporation again questioned the income the college derived from the God's House estate, considering it to be 'the result of the energy and enterprise of the people of Southampton'. SCA, TC Box 58/3; *Hampshire Advertiser*, 23 March 1889, 3 April 1889.

[30] SCA, TCBox 58/3 *Extracts from documents on God's House Hospital are brought forward in this Paper for the Town Council of Southampton, and the public generally, to aid and to prepare the way for a searching enquiry, that the Hospital may be restored to its ancient efficient state.*

[31] *Hampshire Telegraph*, 7/6/1876. See also R. Preston, '"The eccentric and reverend Mr Smith": the Reverend Herbert Smith, 1800–1876', *Journal of the Southampton Local History Forum* (Summer 2007): 9–22.

[32] *Hampshire Chronicle*, 12 January 1861, 3 August 1867.

[33] *Cartulary of God's House*, I, lxxxvi–lxxxvii; QCA, 4G181.

[34] SCA, D/S1/5/6.

[35] SRO, D/FC3/2/5iii.

[36] SCA, D/S1/5/6.

[37] QCA, 4G173.

[38] SCA, D/S4/43/6.

[39] QCA, 4G174, 176

[40] SCA, D/S1/5/6.

Figure 16.1: An engraving of God's House Chapel and Winkle Street, Southampton, 1817. Local Studies and Maritime Collection, Southampton City Council.

> bold and massive proportions I am of [the] opinion that the timbers were exposed to the eye and not ceiled [sic] to as is now the case. The new roof is entirely modern and the timbers of the chancel roof are far from being sound so that a new roof would be necessary for the whole building.
>
> The North and South walls are out of perpendicular but not enough as to be any detriment to the general stability of the building the external part of them is at present composed of Composinall [sic] stones and oyster shells. The stone dressings of the windows have been taken away and their place supplied by Compo and bricks so that the whole of the present outer surface of the wall would have to be cut away and stone dressings and proper walling stone substituted. The inner portion of the walls on the north side and east end have been battened to keep out the damp which of course it has not done as it arises from the soil coming up the wall about 2 feet so that it will be necessary to clear away the soil. The battening must be taken away, the plaster hacked off the walls and the internal walls must be replastered. The pillar and arch dividing the chancel from the nave are in good preservative and of beautiful design and will only require scraping. The floor though not very old is rotten in some places and will soon be so all over owing to damp and a deficient ventilation to the floor timbers so that the floor would have to be taken up the soil dug out to a depth of 15 inches and air bricks introduced below the floor level, the materials sound and fit to be used again. There is an encaustic tile floor under the boarded floor of the altar but it is not in very good preservation. There is a gallery across the west end of the nave which I propose to take away. The west doorway I propose to close up and to open the south doorway from the quadrangle. The tower need not in my opinion be done anything to. The interior arrangement of pews, pulpit &c are estimated for the same as for the proposed new Chapel. All the windows need to be reglazed.[41]

This critical report not only identified extensive work that Critchlow considered was needed but also intended to reverse some of the changes made a couple of decades earlier. The tone of the report may also have been influenced by his alternative proposal to erect a new place of worship.

The architect provided the college with plans and elevations for a new chapel; these sketches were not 'a finished study but merely to give an idea of what might be done for the sum named' (Figures 16.2–16.5). The new building would have been erected in the space between the accommodation for the hospital's male and female residents.

> The new chapel would be built of Swanage stone with Combe Down stone dressing to the door and windows and Cosham Down stone to the Chancel arch. The inner surface of the walls would be of brick of various colours in bands. The floor where are no seats of black and red tiles. The seats ofen [sic] deal stained and varnished with stall of plain character for the brothers and sisters. The roof would be open as shown by the section covered with boards, felt and plain dark coloured tiles. The chapel would seat about 30 worshippers besides the brothers and sisters; an unnecessary number you will say perhaps but any thing smaller would not look well... I am told that the congregation attending the present chapel does not average more than ten in number.[42]

It is clear that Critchlow intended this chapel to be used principally by the hospital brethren and sisters, but for aesthetic reasons it would be slightly larger than was strictly necessary. It would be built in the Gothic style with a rose window above the altar at the east end and an early English-style window formed of five lancets over the west door; its use of brickwork was intended to complement the neighbouring almshouses. The design shows that there was no intention to salvage any of the existing chapel's fabric and incorporate it in the new design.[43] Furthermore, even with the envisaged extra capacity, this chapel would have been inadequate for accommodating the French congregation.

Critchlow estimated that the restoration of the existing chapel would cost £580, although if the roof was left it would be £400. A completely new chapel would only amount to £600. Initially the college may have contemplated

[41] QCA, 4G180.
[42] QCA, 4G180.
[43] QCA, 4G179; *Cartulary of God's House*, I, lxxix.

Figure 16.2: Architect's drawing of the side elevation of the proposed new chapel, God's House Hospital, Southampton, 1861. The Queen's College, Oxford, 4 G 179. Published with permission of the Provost and Fellows to The Queen's College, Oxford.

Figure 16.3: Architect's drawing of the west front of the proposed new chapel, God's House Hospital, Southampton, 1861. The Queen's College, Oxford, 4 G 179. Published with permission of the Provost and Fellows to The Queen's College, Oxford.

building afresh, as they had further plans drawn up.[44] In the end, the decision was taken to refurbish the existing building although the replacement of the east window with three lights probably owed something to Critchlow's new design. The north door which gave access onto the street was also blocked during the restoration, perhaps

Figure 16.4: Architect's drawing of a cross section of the proposed new chapel, showing the interior of the east end, God's House Hospital, Southampton, 1861. The Queen's College, Oxford, 4 G 179. Published with permission of the Provost and Fellows to The Queen's College, Oxford.

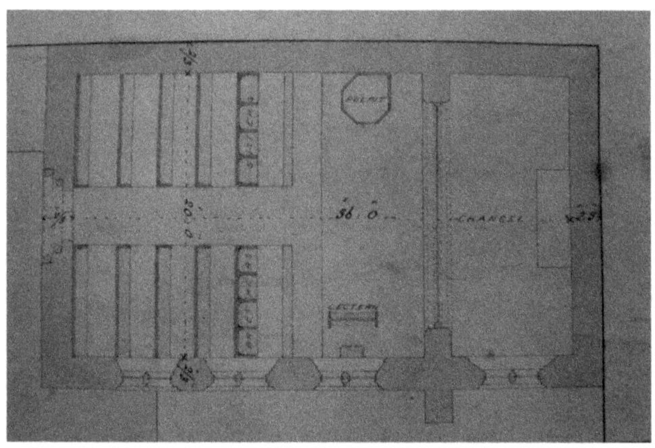

Figure 16.5: Architect's drawing of the interior plan of the proposed new chapel, God's House Hospital, Southampton, 1861.The Queen's College, Oxford, 4 G 179. Published with permission of the Provost and Fellows to The Queen's College, Oxford.

to connect the chapel more directly with the residents of God's House rather than considering the convenience of its other users. One further significant change was made to the adjoining tower over the entrance to the quadrangle, which was refaced and the original pitched roof replaced with a flat one (Figure 16.6).[45]

Contemporaries were critical of the work carried out on the chapel. The *Journal of the Society of Architects*

[44] QCA, 4G180; *Cartulary of God's House*, I, lxxix n.

[45] QCA, 4G180; *Cartulary of God's House*, I, lxxvii.

Figure 16.6: View of God's House, chapel and tower, Winkle Street, Southampton. Photograph: the author.

commented that 'the church is worth a visit, although suffering from over restoration' but did note the 'fine transitional arch between the nave and chancel'.[46] The 'Roving Correspondent' of *The Building News* was even more scathing:

> Little of the old chapel is now to be seen. Before the restoration a blocked up Norman entrance and an obtusely pointed double window existed on the street side; now alas! these have disappeared, to the writer's astonishment. Why not have made the old doorway available? A tower gateway adjoins the chapel. The restored side, to the street, consists of a few single slightly pointed windows with shafted jambs in the Norman Transitional style. The east gable has triplet, also obtusely pointed. Broad, flat, buttress-like masses of smooth ashlar work occur at the angles and side of the chapel, projecting only six inches, for what reason does not appear, except, perhaps for the sake of conforming to the style literally. Mr. Critchlow, the architect, seems to have carried out the restoration in a characteristic spirit, though the fine coursed jointing spoils the walling.[47]

A later article in the *Hampshire Advertiser* pointed out what had been lost during the course of the restoration:

> The ancient building has been cased on the exterior with stone, and at the east three lights have taken the place of a window, which was beautiful for its tracery, as may be seen from some of the cusps and foliations lying about the court. On some of the stones may yet be seen the 'marks' of the masons, who were members of a guild, and each had his distinct symbol to put on his own work when finished, and the artisan could thus be traced by the initiated. The ivy-grown tower is a charming piece of late perpendicular.[48]

A plan of the interior of the chapel before its refurbishment shows that there was a gallery across one bay at the west end (Figure 16.7). The seating on the ground floor extended virtually to the altar enclosure, on the edge of which was the pulpit.[49] The focus on the east end conformed to Anglican liturgical practices and presumably accorded with the religious needs of the hospital's residents as well as the French church. In the early eighteenth century, this congregation had abandoned the Reformed liturgy for a form of worship broadly conforming to the Church of England and the use of the Book of Common Prayer translated into French.[50] The *Hampshire Advertiser* account continued by describing the interior:

> Turning into the chapel from the court the chancel arch at once strikes the eye. It is of great beauty. The western entrance under the gate-tower is through a deeply-recessed doorway. On the south side of the chancel are two niches, one of which may have been used as a piscina, and the other as a credence-table. There are two portable fonts here, one of marble, having an indistinct name and the date 1731 scratched on it. In the chancel are stalls, four on each side, for the brethren and sisters. The chancel and nave can accommodate about a 100 people.[51]

This restored interior, nonetheless, retained some medieval features such as the chancel arch, holy water stoup and piscina (Figure 16.8). The internal arrangement, seen in a photograph published in 1894 (Figure 16.9), may have been influenced by Critchlow's design for the new chapel. A distinct chancel has been created with the seating confined to the nave, apart from the stalls closer to the altar, presumably for the brothers and sisters of the hospital. The flooring of the nave is also red and black encaustic tiles.

When the chapel reopened in 1864, there was a dispute between the college and the French church over the provision of seating. The college decided not to re-pew the interior, apart from providing for the hospital residents, but permitted the French Protestants to provide seats, which 'must not be fixed but moveable'. The French church argued that their charitable status meant that their funds could not be directed towards providing replacement seating. The matter was ultimately resolved when the college provided compensation of £30.[52]

The surviving furnishings date mainly from the late nineteenth century and were donated by members of the French congregation. In April 1889, the minister Louis Napoléon Seichan wrote to the college stating that he had been unable to find the £50 necessary for the reredos and other church ornaments. Providentially the shipbroker and

[46] "The Archaeological Excursions," *Journal of the Society of Architects*, September 1899, 267.

[47] Reprinted in *Hampshire Advertiser*, 30 September 1865.

[48] *Hampshire Advertiser*, 3 July 1886.

[49] QCA, 4G179.

[50] See Andrew Spicer, "Conformity, Nonconformity and Occasional Conformity: The Church of England and the French Church in Southampton, *c.*1662–1723', forthcoming.

[51] *Hampshire Advertiser*, 3 July 1886.

[52] *Minute Book*, 113–15.

Figure 16.7: Architect's drawing of the interior plan of God's House chapel, Southampton, 1861.The Queen's College, Oxford, 4 G 179. Published with permission of the Provost and Fellows to The Queen's College, Oxford.

Figure 16.8: Interior view towards the east end of God's House chapel, Southampton. Photograph: the author.

long standing member of the congregation J.W. Deal had offered to provide the reredos and his mother donated 'a magnificent cross in brass' to the church.[53] The reredos must have been provided shortly afterwards as it can be seen in a late nineteenth-century photograph of the interior (Figure 16.9). It was inscribed with the Commandments and the Lord's Prayer but was removed from the chapel in 1935.[54] The photograph also shows the substantial panelled communion table, also donated by Deal. The decorative arcading across the front has the emblems of the four evangelists beneath each trefoil arch and the

[53] QCA, S206.

[54] *Minute Book*, 153. See also *Southern Daily Echo*, 16 February 1935.

Figure 16.9: Interior view of the east end of God's House chapel, Southampton, in the late nineteenth-century, from J. Aston Whitlock, *A Brief and Popular History of the Hospital of God's House Southampton* (Southampton, 1894).

Agnus Dei in the centre (Figure 16.10).[55] Among the other furnishings are the 'oak lectern (given by Capt. G. Allix)' and the 'folding oak chair for the pastor's use (given by Mr de Carteret)', which still remain in the chapel, the latter with a brass plaque recording the donation in 1887 (Figures 16.11 and 16.12).[56] The congregation had raised the £25 needed for a harmonium in 1857, which after further fundraising was replaced with an organ in 1890 (Figure 16.13).[57]

III Historians and Southampton's Huguenots

From the mid-nineteenth century, there was growing popular and academic interest in the history of the foreign congregations established in England during the sixteenth and seventeenth centuries. In 1846, John Southerden Burn published *The History of the French, Walloon, Dutch and other Foreign Protestant Refugees settled in England*; the first major study of the foreign churches. The work drew heavily on the registers of baptisms, marriages and deaths from these communities as well as other anecdotes from their archives. With the introduction of civil registration of births, deaths and marriages in 1837, Burn had been appointed as secretary to a royal commission charged with collecting non-parochial registers, which were then deposited in the Public Record Office.[58] Unlike other communities, the Southampton register, handed over in December 1837, commenced shortly after the church's establishment.[59] Furthermore after listing those present at the first administration of the Lord's Supper in December 1567, the register recorded the admission of subsequent church members. In the same volume, details

[55] SCA, D/FC3/18.

[56] SCA, D/FC3/18.

[57] SCA, Livre du Clerc; *Minute Book*, 135; *Hampshire Advertiser*, 8 March 1890.

[58] John Southerden Burn, *The History of the French, Walloon, Dutch and other Foreign Protestant Refugees* (London: Longman, 1846), vi; *ODNB*, VIII, 878–79.

[59] *Minute Book*, 100.

Figure 16.10: Late nineteenth-century altar table and cross, God's House chapel, Southampton. Photograph: the author.

Figure 16.11: Oak lectern donated by Capt. G. Allix, God's House chapel, Southampton. Photograph and copyright: the author.

Figure 16.12: Oak chair donated by Mr de Carteret, God's House chapel, Southampton. Photograph: the author.

Figure 16.13: Interior view towards the west end of God's House chapel, Southampton. Photograph: the author.

of baptisms, marriages and deaths were kept from the church's foundation onwards. The register also included anecdotal details and early disciplinary decisions about individuals barred from the Lord's Supper. There was also a list of fasts held as the community prayed for their co-religionists in France and the Netherlands, or about matters that affected them more directly such as outbreaks of plague.[60] Burn's coverage of the Southampton community

[60] TNA, RG 4/4600; Andrew Spicer, "The Consistory Records of Reformed Congregations and the Exile Churches," *PHS* 28 (2003–07), 650–51.

runs to 10 pages, beginning with two pages discussing its foundation based on documents in the British Library but the remainder of his text is transcriptions and extracts from the register.[61] This account of the congregation's history appears to have formed part of the evidence presented to the Charity Commissioners during their investigation of the French church's charities.[62] Samuel Smiles similarly made extensive use of the register in *The Huguenots. Their Settlements, Churches and Industries in England and Ireland*, which was first published in 1867 but went through a number of editions. His approach was more analytical than Burn, using the entries to provide a more detailed examination of the origins of these immigrants and the history of their community.[63] Substantial extracts from these works appeared in local newspapers shortly after their publication.[64]

Earlier histories of Southampton had tended to be more cursory in their accounts of the French church. In the late eighteenth century, John Speed's manuscript history of the town erroneously dated the community's foundation to an unsuccessful scheme to settle some French Protestants and introduce 'silk weaving manufacture' in 1668. Nonetheless, he claimed that they worshipped at God's House chapel 'by the leave of Queen's College and the Licence of the Bp. of Winchester'.[65] Sir Henry Englefield's *A Walk through Southampton* (1805), even in its 'considerably augmented' second edition merely noted that God's House chapel was 'very ancient, but has been so defaced by repair, that few traces of its original form are visible'. It made no reference to the French congregation.[66] John Duthy's *Sketches of Hampshire* (1839) focused principally on the foundation and medieval history of God's House but did go on to mention that the chapel was 'allotted to the Protestants from the Netherlands in the reign of queen Elizabeth' and that 'the congregation of French Protestants that now use the chapel, was established in the year 1567'. He also published as an appendix the appeal to the mayor and corporation that could be found in the British Library.[67]

The most thorough examination of the French church, in the broader context of the port's history, appeared in J. Silvester Davies's *A History of Southampton* (1883). Like Burn and Smiles, he made extensive use of the register, but the publication by 1872 of the *Calendar of State Papers Domestic* meant that new material was presented on the negotiations for the establishment of the community. Davies's coverage also went further than earlier accounts by going beyond the register to examine its history in the seventeenth and eighteenth centuries. He discussed the threat to the existence of the French church posed by Archbishop Laud in 1635, the impact of the Revocation of the Edict of Nantes in 1685, conformity with the Church of England in 1711–12 and the schisms within the congregation in the 1720s. He relied on the church's minute book for the later history of the community. Davies' contextualisation of the French community within the religious and economic life of Southampton remained the definitive study for more than a century.[68]

Alongside Davies's *History of Southampton*, two articles published in the *Proceedings of the Huguenot Society of London* also contributed to establishing the chapel's history. These were based on the papers delivered by the steward of God's House, J. Aston Whitlock, and W.J.C. Moens at the Huguenot conference in 1889. Whitlock mainly focused on God's House chapel, its establishment and subsequent history including its use by the French church.[69] The real historian of the French church according to Moens was Humphrey Marett Godfray who had been recently been appointed as Greffier to the Royal Court of Jersey and had completed a transcript of the Southampton register, the typescript of which was displayed at the Huguenot conference. Godfray's legal work had prevented his attendance 'and, in fact, doing anything in the way of a Paper, as he has not yet completed the search necessary in order to find the details which are still wanting in what has been written on the subject by the late Mr. J.S. Burn, Mr. Smiles, and the Rev. Silvester Davies, to whom all owe so much for the history of Southampton'. For his paper, Moens relied upon these authors as well as 'adding somewhat from sources to which they had not access'.[70]

Under the auspices of the Huguenot Society of London, Godfray's transcription of the church's register was published at Lymington in 1890: *Registre des baptesmes, mariages & mortz, et jeusnes: de l'eglise wallonne et des isles de Jersey, Guernesey, Serq, Origny....*[71] It was the fourth volume for a Society dedicated to 'Huguenot Genealogy and Heraldry, and Huguenot Church and other registers'. In 1885, Moens had addressed the Society about the importance of identifying and publishing records relating to the Huguenot diaspora and took an active role in the process.[72] The Society established a Register Committee; the first volumes were published at Lymington, 'where the work will have the advantage of being from time to time supervised if needful by a member

[61] Burn, *History of the French, Walloon, Dutch ... Refugees*, 80–89.
[62] *Hampshire Advertiser*, 18 August 1855.
[63] Samuel Smiles, *The Huguenots: their settlements, churches, and industries in England and Ireland* (London: Harper and Brothers, 1867), 134–40, 347–48, 471–81.
[64] *Hampshire Advertiser*, 28 March 1846, 8 January 1870.
[65] John Speed, *The History and Antiquity of Southampton*, ed. E.R. Aubrey, Southampton Records Society 8 (1909), 110–12.
[66] Henry Englefield, *A Walk through Southampton* (Southampton: Baker and Fletcher, 1805), 49.
[67] John Duthy, *Sketches of Hampshire: embracing the architectural antiquities, topography &c of country adjacent to the River Itchen ...* (Winchester, 1839), 455–56, 471–73.
[68] John Silvester Davies, *A History of Southampton: partly from the MS. of Dr. Speed, in the Southampton Archives* (Southampton: Gilbert and Company, 1883), 403–22.
[69] J. Aston Whitlock, "Domus Dei or the Hospital of St Julian, Southampton," *PHS* 3 (1888–91): 42–52.
[70] Moens, "The Walloon Settlement," 53–76.
[71] Humphrey Marret Godfray (ed.), *Registre des baptesmes, mariages & mortz, et jeusnes : de l'eglise wallonne et des isles de Jersey, Guernesey, Serq, Origny, &c.: etablie a Southampton par patente du roy Edouard six et de la reine Elizabeth*, Publications of the Huguenot Society 4 (1890).
[72] W.J.C. Moens, "French and Walloon Church Registers in England," *PHS* 1 (1885–86): 17–56.

of the Register Committee, Mr Moens, who resides near the town'.[73] In reviewing the work, *The Athenæum* applauded the Huguenot Society in its endeavours but considered that 'the chief interest of the Southampton register' was in the list of fasts held by the community, which 'enable us to see contemporary events from the standpoint of the refugees in our midst'.[74]

In 1894, Rev. J. Aston Whitlock published *A Brief and Popular History of the Hospital of God's House Southampton*; a relatively short work, it mainly concentrated on the medieval history of the foundation although it described the reconstruction of the mid-nineteenth century. However, the later history of God's House is mainly given through the 11 pages describing the French church and its use of the chapel. Although based on archival research and published histories – 'some of them have not always rewarded our labours' – the book, particularly for the French church, goes over well-established ground.[75] *The Athenæum* commented:

> It is not quite fair to call this book a history. Brief it certainly is – there are but sixty-four pages printed in large type; as to its being popular there is room for differences of opinion; we should rather call it scrappy and disconnected. The author however deals fairly with his readers. He tells them in the preface that lest he should weary the eyes of his readers he has used 'as few foot-notes and inverted commas as possible'. This is all very well in a romance but in a history, unless it be a mere school compendium, references are an absolute necessity for every one who reads for any higher purpose than amusement.[76]

In spite of being somewhat derivative, the publication of William Wyndham Portal's *Some Account of the Settlement of Refugees [L'Eglise Wallonne] at Southampton and also of the Chapel of St Julian* ... in 1902 was received more positively. Portal was President of the Hampshire Field Club and had given a paper on this subject to the society in God's House chapel. It was reported that 'Mr Portal's family being of Huguenot origin gave additional interest to his remarks'.[77] His family had fled persecution at Castres in Languedoc and sought refuge in England. In the early eighteenth century, they were involved in establishing the paper manufacture first at South Stoneham on the outskirts of Southampton and then later at Laverstoke Mill near Whitchurch, Hampshire. Although there is no reference to the family in the register, other papermakers at South Stoneham do appear, so it is probable that Portal's ancestors were members of the French congregation. Besides discussing God's House Chapel, Portal's book also used Godfray's *Registre* to recount the French church's history. The final section was on 'The Papermaking Industry as practised by the Southampton Refugees'. He identified papermakers in the local records as well as providing an account of his family's contribution but in a spirit akin to Smiles's work, demonstrating the economic significance of the Huguenot diaspora.[78] After praising 'this delightful quarto', *The Athenæum* concluded:

> The skill, industry and probity of this famous Huguenot race have resulted in its establishment as one of the most influential families in Hampshire. The interest of this volume is much enhanced by the fact that so many details are furnished by one of Huguenot descent.[79]

IV Views of God's House Chapel

Although there were a number of engravings and etchings of God's House tower, the chapel does not seem to have attracted the same degree of attention from Victorian artists and novelists as the French church in Canterbury.[80] There are some early nineteenth-century views of Winkle Street and God's House, which depict the exterior of the chapel before its restoration (Figure 16.1). A similar lithograph of the view down the street towards the town quay appears to have been the inspiration for the illustration used in Burn's *History of the French, Walloon, Dutch and other Foreign Protestant Refugees settled in England* (Figure 16.14).[81] The building attracted the attention of two pioneers of photography: the local man Thomas Hibberd James whose image shows the stark appearance of the restored building (Figure 16.15), and Catharine Weed Ward (née Barnes) who captured the interior in *c.*1896 (Figure 16.16).[82]

The novelist William Harrison Ainsworth set an important scene there in *Cardinal Pole, or the Days of Philip and Mary: an historical romance* (1863). He described Philip's arrival at Southampton before his wedding to Queen Mary at Winchester in 1554. In the novel, the king came ashore incognito where he came across 'a beautiful little chapel' dedicated to 'St Julian', the patron of travellers, and 'ancient even at the period of our history':

> Vespers were being celebrated within the sacred pile as Philip and his conductor passed it; perceiving which, the Prince determined to go in and perform his devotions. Accordingly they entered the little edifice.
>
> Dimly lighted by the tapers burning at the altar, its massive round pillars, semicircular arches, small

[73] "Report of the Council to the Third Annual General Meeting, Wednesday, June 8, 1887," *PHS* 2 (1887–88): xxxv, xxxvi.
[74] *The Athenæum*, No. 3327, 1 August 1891.
[75] J. Aston Whitlock, *A Brief and Popular History of the Hospital of God's House Southampton* (Southampton: Henry March Gilbert, 1894).
[76] *The Athenæum*, No. 3478, 23 June 1894.
[77] "Hampshire Field Club and Archaeological Society. Annual Report… April 8th 1902," *Proceedings of the Hampshire Field Club* 4 (1899–1905): 2; *Portsmouth Evening News*, 14 October 1902.
[78] William Wyndham Portal, *Some Account of the Settlement of Refugees, l'Église wallonne, at Southampton: also notes on the papermaking industry, as practised by the Southampton refugees* (Winchester, 1902).
[79] *The Athenæum*, No. 3959, 12 September 1903.
[80] See Andrew Spicer, "Victorian Vignettes of the French Church at Canterbury," *PHS* 29 (2012): 716–18.
[81] Burn, *History of the French, Walloon, Dutch ... Refugees*, 80.
[82] Adrian B. Rance, *A Victorian Photographer in Southampton: Thomas Hibberd James* (Southampton: Paul Cave, 1980), 56–57.

Figure 16.14: Lithograph of God's House chapel and Winkle Street from J.S. Burn, *History of the French, Walloon, Dutch and other Foreign Protestant Refugees settled in England* (London, 1846).

Figure 16.15: Photograph of God's House chapel and Winkle Street, Southampton, in the late nineteenth century by Thomas Hibberd James. Local Studies and Maritime Collection, Southampton City Council.

> windows, and deeply-recessed doorway, could only be imperfectly seen. Within the chancel, the arch of which was of great beauty, three black marble flags told where the traitorous nobles were laid. Here also, side by side, were recumbent statues of the founders of the fane, sculptured in alabaster.
>
> Except the officiating priest and his assistants, there were only two female devotees in the chapel, both of whom were kneeling before the altar. Philip took a place near them. For some minutes he was so absorbed in his devotions that he did not notice the person beside him, further than remarking that she was young; but as he raised his eyes, he caught sight of a face that at once riveted his attention. Never had he beheld features so exquisitely beautiful, or so sweet in expression. No nun could have a holier or purer look.[83]

This fictional account seems to be the basis for the occasional references to the Spanish king attending mass at God's House in 1554, in histories of the hospital.[84]

V God's House Chapel and Southampton's Huguenot Past

In spite of the interest in the history of the French church, God's House chapel did not become a monument to Southampton's 'Huguenot' past. This is in marked contrast to the situation in Canterbury, where the indefatigable minister Joseph Auguste Martin emphasised the symbolic importance of the French church as a 'precious relic of a truly remarkable period of faith', 'a Religious Monument, but at the same time … a solemn protest against the baneful spirit of Roman Catholicism … a living witness to future generations of the intolerant and persecuting measures

Figure 16.16: Catherine Weed Ward (1851–1913), Interior of the Walloon Church, Southampton. George Eastman House, Rochester, NY. Ref: 4817–12. Courtesy of George Eastman House, International Museum of Photography and Film.

[83] William Harrison Ainsworth, *Cardinal Pole, or the Days of Philip and Mary: an historical romance*, 3 vols (London: Chapman and Hall, 1863), vol. 1, 117–18.
[84] Whitlock, "Domus Dei," 46; Whitlock, *Brief and Popular History*, 41.

of Rome'.[85] The reasons for this difference are probably two-fold, relating to the surviving associations with the 'Huguenot past' as well as the use made of God's House chapel during the later nineteenth century.

Although the Huguenot Society visited God's House chapel in 1889, the subsequent report was silent about the place where a French-speaking congregation had worshipped for more than three centuries or any features of the building. Past alterations and the restoration of the chapel in the early 1860s meant that there were few tangible traces of the Huguenot presence at God's House, such as the biblical verses in French seen by visitors to Canterbury cathedral's crypt.[86] It is not known how the chapel was configured by the original settlers or the seventeenth-century immigrants, but these arrangements were probably swept away after the congregation adopted a variant of the Anglican liturgy. So by the later nineteenth century, there was generally nothing in the chapel that could be regarded as specifically 'Huguenot'.

The one notable exception is the handful of gravestones to members of the congregation. While some of these dated back to the late seventeenth century, such as the French inscription marking the grave of the two-year-old daughter of the minister Anthoine Cougot, who died in 1693, others commemorated later ministers of the church such as Isaac John Barnouin (d.1797) and Hubert Napoléon Dupont (d.1875). Nineteenth-century accounts noted that beneath the altar there were also memorials to other prominent members of the congregation: Colonel Lewis de Belleau (d.1739); Mary, daughter of Nicolas Pescod and wife of Adam de Cardonnel (d.1708); and Peter de Vaux (d.1742).[87] These were relatively simple commemorations that lacked 'heroic' epitaphs like that of Jean Serres of Montauban viewed during the Huguenot Society's visit to Winchester cathedral.[88] There was quite rightly a degree of scepticism about the label next to a damaged memorial brass depicting a Catholic priest, which claimed it commemorated the first Reformed minister Walerand Thévelin (Figure 16.17).[89]

These relatively humble memorials were also overshadowed by a monument that had been erected in the chapel in the mid-eighteenth century by John,

Figure 16.17: Brass memorial plaque depicting a medieval priest wearing ecclesiastical vestments, God's House chapel, Southampton. Photograph: the author.

Earl Delawarr, which commemorated the burial of the conspirators executed for plotting against Henry V.[90] The inscription reads:

> Richard, Earl of Cambridge,
> Lord Scrope of Masham,
> Sir Tho. Gray of Northumberland,
> Conspired to murder King
> Henry Vth, in this town, as he
> was preparing to sail with his
> army against Charles the Sixth,
> King of France, for which
> conspiracy they were executed
> and buried near this place,
> in the year
> MCCCCXV

In fact, only the earl of Cambridge was interred, with his decapitated head, within the chapel.[91] During the Huguenot Society's visit, the local historian Mr Shore 'mentioned that the architect who was engaged in restoring the church some twenty-five years ago… told him that in the chancel had been found the skeleton of a very tall man,

[85] Joseph A. Martin, *Christian Firmness of the Huguenots and a Sketch of the History of the French Refugee Church of Canterbury* (Canterbury: S.W. Partridge, 1881), 144–46. See also Spicer, '"A Survival of a Distant Past"'.

[86] Spicer, '"A Survival of a Distant Past"', 131; *The Times*, 25 February 1882; Rowland E. Prothero, *The Life and Correspondence of Arthur Penrhyn Stanley*, 2 vols (London: John Murray, 1893), vol. 1, 428; Richard J. King, *A Handbook for Travellers in Kent and Sussex* (London: John Murray, 1858), 177; Richard J. King, *Handbook to the Cathedrals of England: Southern division* (London, 1861), 385.

[87] SCA, D/S4/43/6; Davies, *History of Southampton*, 459n; *Hampshire Advertiser*, 3 July 1886.

[88] *Hampshire Advertiser*, 27 July 1889; Henry Austen Layard, "Address to the Fifth Annual General Meeting of the Huguenot Society of London," *PHS* 3 (1888–91): xxvi–xxvii; "Summer Conference," lii–liv; Layard, "Address," lxxxi.

[89] Davies, *History of Southampton*, 459; *Hampshire Advertiser*, 3 July 1886.

[90] Davies, *History of Southampton*, 459; *Hampshire Advertiser*, 3 July 1886.

[91] Thomas B. Pugh, *Henry V and the Southampton Plot of 1415*, SRS 30 (1988), 122–23, 135n.

decapitated, which led him to the belief that the Earl of Cambridge was buried there'.[92] The connection with the Southampton Plot provided another or rival point of interest for visitors to the chapel, which was mentioned in guides for visitors and popular histories of the town, alongside the French services that commenced more than a century later.[93]

VI The French Church and Southampton's Huguenot Past

Besides the competing historical associations in God's House chapel, there was a degree of ambivalence in how the nineteenth-century French congregation viewed their past. In October 1885, there was a resurgence of popular interest in the Huguenot diaspora, culminating in services and events to mark the bicentenary of the Revocation of the Edict of Nantes in London and Canterbury.[94] Services had resumed at Southampton in August 1885 with the appointment of a new minister, Louis Napoléon Seichan, but there is no record of the bicentenary, two months later, being remembered in the town.[95] However, attention was drawn to the congregation in some newspapers and periodicals. The *Guernsey Magazine* reported that after his first service in Southampton, Seichan was met 'with greetings of welcome by several of the congregation, some of whom were direct family descendants of an ancestry who worshipped in that place over two centuries ago, and others of real Huguenot noted family names'.[96] Similar sentiments had been expressed two years earlier in an article on 'Huguenot Anglicans' in *The Foreign Church Chronicle and Review*. Together with the Savoy church in London, 'to very many English families of Huguenot descent', the church of '"St Julien" Southampton, stand as monuments to the memory of those forefathers of ours who suffered for the sake of the Reformation, and to all hearty Christians they cannot but be more or less interesting mementoes of the past'.[97]

It was this Huguenot past that Joseph Martin commemorated at Canterbury, with services marking the bicentenary of the Revocation as well as what he mistakenly regarded as the foundation of the church at Canterbury in July 1550 and 'the Festival of the Reformation' in late October or early November. According to Martin, the latter event was 'in memory of the greatest event for good, which in the dispensations of God, had ever been brought about since the first publication of the Gospel'.[98] These developed into celebrations of the Protestant faith at which prominent local clergy preached sermons and were attended by the corporation.

The situation in Southampton was rather different, where the congregation did not hold similar commemorations, although the mayor and corporation were occasionally invited to attend services. In August 1894, the pastor Auguste Bellet wrote to the mayor and corporation, 'pointing out that there was a special mission at that church, and asked the Mayor, in the name of the old Huguenots, so hospitably received by Southampton 300 years ago, to attend divine service at St Julien's Church on Sunday the 23rd September or the following Sunday'.[99] The corporation robed at the Audit House before making their way to the French church.

> The greater portion of the service was conducted in French, although the hymns and canticles were sung to well-known Anglican music … the pastor addressed the congregation for a few minutes in English before the sermon, and expressed the deep pleasure that it gave him to see the Mayor and Corporation in attendance … Their attendance that day showed that in spite of the difference in the languages of the nations there was nothing between them and Christ. He was heartily pleased to welcome them there that day, his mind reverting to the times when the English in Southampton gave their people refuge from the fierce religious persecutions of their countrymen in France. A collection was taken in aid of French mission work.[100]

While the minister acknowledged the French church's past, it was the present missionary work which had prompted the invitation of the corporation to the service.

The seeming indifference to the church's past was probably a reflection of the congregation's membership by the mid-nineteenth century and the role that St Julien's had come to fulfil. An appeal was made in 1853 for the reopening of the church and the appointment of a new minister. Notes made against the names of the petitioners show that a number of them were either relative newcomers to the port, or were Channel Islanders, rather than the descendants of Huguenot families.[101] The appeal reflected their origins and practical concerns:

> That the closing of their place of Worship is fraught with inconvenience & disappointment, not only to the memorialists, but to the many individual families, & travellers passing this way to and from France, and the Channel Islands; and that, as this was the only Church in Southampton having French service, the fact of its closing is regarded with deep regret by all who are

[92] "Summer Conference," 1. See also Thomas W. Shore, *A History of Hampshire including the Isle of Wight* (London: Elliot Stock, 1892), 236.
[93] [Philip Brannon], *The Stranger's Guide and Pleasure Visitor's Companion to Southampton* (Southampton, s.d.), 57; *Hampshire Advertiser*, 3 July 1886.
[94] Spicer, "1885: French Protestantism," 391–92, 399, 418.
[95] SCA, D/FC3/15; *Minute Book*, 130.
[96] *The Guernsey Magazine. A Monthly Illustrated Journal*, October 1885.
[97] P. Ahier, "Sympathy with Huguenot Anglicans," *The Foreign Church Chronicle and Review for the year 1883*, 94.
[98] Martin, *Christian Firmness*, 98; Spicer, '"A Survival of a Distant Past"', 120–22.
[99] *Hampshire Advertiser*, 11 August 1894, 8 September 1894, 19 September 1894.
[100] *Hampshire Advertiser*, 26 September 1894.
[101] SCA, D/FC3/10/1, D/FC5 (Acc.7134). In 1876, the French church was described as 'frequented chiefly by Jersey people connected with shipping', *Hampshire Advertiser*, 29 April 1876.

> interested in maintaining the important position which Southampton has attained.[102]

Similar sentiments were expressed again in 1875 when another request was made to appoint a new minister.[103] This broader interest was also indicated by notices in the newspapers which highlighted the possible appeal of the church for local people or visiting gentry 'who keep French servants' or the opportunity provided by the 'interesting Huguenot Church' for the 'numerous people who have been trained in French go to worship in that graceful language exclusively used by the St. Julien's congregation. No better way of keeping what we learnt than to practise it'.[104] While some townspeople, and Channel Islanders such as the clerk Samuel James Carrel, were longstanding members of the congregation, there was also a more transient element which did not have the same established links.[105] The church appears to have been well-attended; the Charity Commissioners were informed that there were some 40 to 50 persons ready to attend and when it did reopen in 1856 congregations varied between 120 and 146. Some 200 attended the service following the restoration in 1864.[106]

This broad membership was important for the continued survival of the congregation; in spite of the success of the Huguenot Society's visit, the publicity did not encourage descendants of the earlier settlers to attend services. Even the Society's vice-president, Moens, apparently showed no interest in the church, in spite of his relative proximity at Boldre and close interest in the New Forest and Hampshire affairs in general.[107] One important and notable exception was Sir William Wyndham Portal. During the Huguenot Society's visit in 1889, Portal had been described by the dean of Winchester as 'a most worthy and earnest Huguenot, who even at this present day, represented one of the many important industries which the refugees introduced into this country'.[108] He served as President of the Huguenot Society from 1908 to 1911 but also took a close interest in the history of Hampshire. According to his testimonial in *The Times*:

> Truly he was a remarkable man. To his undoubted business capacity he added a zeal for his county of which I know no parallel. In addition to the many public offices which he held, all of which he filled with peculiar distinction and success, he found time to care for the natural and archaeological beauty of his county, bringing to that task a trained knowledge of both archaeology and architecture. That the beauty of Hampshire, both in its buildings and scenery, remains so little spoilt is in the first degree due to the unceasing vigilance of Sir William Portal. Our great cathedral was in his constant care. In him the cathedral has lost its greatest friend. The famous old hospital of St Cross was preserved and beautified by his wisdom and great generosity.[109]

The French church should also be added to these achievements. He had published an account of the congregation in 1902, became a trustee of the church in 1912 and was an important benefactor. In 1915, Portal presented a solid silver chalice and paten to the church for its services. Before presenting these liturgical items, he observed: 'It is not often that some of us have the opportunity of entering this little church – the smallest I suppose in Southampton – and where divine worship has been conducted ever since its erection in the twelfth century'.[110] After briefly recounting the history of the congregation, he concluded:

> It was in that same reign of Queen Anne that my ancestor, a Huguenot refugee from France and the first of our name to settle in Hampshire, was associated with the important paper-making industry at South Stoneham, and was an attendant at this church. And so it is that I offer this gift to the Church of the "Strangers" for the use of the congregation. 'May every blessing continue to attend both those who minister and those who worship here'.[111]

Portal later published two short works that reflected on his family's history and economic contribution to the county: *The Story of Portals Ltd of Laverstoke. A Brief Account of 200 years Successful Making of Good Papers* (London, 1925); *Abraham Portal – born 1726, died 1809 – and his Descendants* (Winchester, 1925).

Portal therefore provided an important link between the French church and its Huguenot history. However, there were few tangible traces of that past within God's House chapel. This was a building which had other significant associations with Southampton's past more than a century and a half before the arrival of the Walloon refugees in 1567. Although the congregation in the later nineteenth century acknowledged their antecedents, it had evolved from its original foundation to one that also served the cultural and religious needs of the more transient population of Southampton. As a result there was not the same drive to commemorate and celebrate anniversaries such as the bicentenary of the Revocation or the beginnings of the Reformation.

[102] SCA, D/FC5 (Acc.7134).
[103] SCA, D/FC5 (Acc.7134).
[104] *Hampshire Advertiser*, 25 December 1841, 17 January 1891.
[105] Carrel, a hairdresser in Southampton, was appointed clerk in October 1856 and resigned in 1871 to return to his birthplace on Jersey. SCA, D/FC5 (Acc.7134); *Minute Book*, 103, 117.
[106] SCA, D/FC5 (Acc.7134); Andrew Spicer, "The 'Livre du Clerc' of the French Church in Southampton," *The Huguenot Society Journal* 30 (2014): 196; *Hampshire Advertiser*, 18 August 1855.
[107] *ODNB*, XXXVIII, 491. A donation to the organ fund was made by Sir Henry Peek, another vice-president of the Society, *Hampshire Advertiser*, 8 March 1890.
[108] *Hampshire Advertiser*, 27 July 1889.
[109] *The Times*, 1 October 1931.
[110] *Minute Book*, 148; *Winchester Diocesan Chronicle*, February 1916, 29; Charles Poyntz Stewart, "Address to the Thirty-Second Annual General Meeting of the Huguenot Society of London," *PHS* 11 (1915–17): 175–76.
[111] *Winchester Diocesan Chronicle*, February 1916, 29.

VII Worship at God's House Chapel

In 1886, the *Hampshire Advertiser*'s account of St Julien's in its series 'Churches in and around Southampton' observed: 'St Julian's affords an instance of the Catholicity of the Church of England, being used for services in the French language, a service in the mother tongue on Tuesday evenings, and for the "Missions to Seamen" services every Sunday evening'.[112] Although God's House chapel remained synonymous with the French congregation, it never had exclusive use of the building. While the actual arrangements are unclear, they had shared the chapel with the hospital's brethren and sisters from its establishment in 1567. During the nineteenth century, God's House chapel also came to be associated with other services besides those conducted for French-speaking worshippers.

From the 1820s, William Wilson held services within the chapel on Wednesday evenings and these continued under his successor, Whitlock, on Tuesdays. Although some pews had been provided by Wilson, the furnishings by the end of the century had largely been donated by members of the French congregation. As the French congregation had adopted the Anglican liturgy in the early eighteenth century, apart from language there was perhaps little difference between their services and those held by the vicar of Holy Rood. This was markedly different from the situation in Canterbury, which had initially used a French translation of the Book of Common Prayer but their pastor Martin had introduced a new and distinctive liturgy for the congregation. In contrast to the altar and altar rails erected in God's House chapel, the new furnishings at Canterbury included a communion table around which the participants sat to receive the Lord's Supper in the Reformed manner.[113]

Certainly some members of the Southampton congregation were concerned to maintain the liturgical practices of the French church, particularly with the spread of ritualism. Tractarianism had initially made little headway in this primarily evangelical town and Wilson had preached on several occasions against ritualism. However, by the 1870s it had become established in several parish churches, particularly St Lawrence's and St Michael's.[114] Some alarm was expressed by Thomas Mollet, clerk of the French church, in 1875 following the death of Hubert Dupont. He noted that 'many changes have been made in nearly all the parishes of the town. The new form of Anglicanism that is to say "Ritualist" having penetrated from nearly all sides that we ask ourselves what will be the future history of our church and congregation'. He expressed the hope that the congregation would retain their liberty and that a 'Ritualist' would not be instituted. Following the appointment of Alphonse Dupont in 1877, Mollet wrote to the minister concerning the 'usages of the church' including wearing a black robe for preaching the sermon.[115]

The photographs of the church interior indicate that the congregation had moved in that direction by the 1890s (Figures 16.9 and 16.16). By this time, ritual practices such as the use of candles and vestments had been adopted by other churches in Southampton, although not Holy Rood.[116] The impetus for these changes at God's House presumably came from the ministers; Louis Seichan wrote about the provision of an altar and reredos in 1889. In the same year, following his appointment Auguste Bellet investigated the 'usages and customs' of the French church and challenged Mollet's right to conduct services. There was a long-running dispute between the minister and the clerk, during which Mollet disrupted services, perhaps because of differences over how they were conducted.[117] The photograph taken by Catharine Weed Ward shows a high altar with candles and vestments, two of the hallmarks of the ritualist movement (Figure 16.16). These liturgical arrangements and furnishings were presumably also acceptable to the parishioners of Holy Rood who gathered there for their weekly services. Whereas the furnishings at Canterbury underscored the congregation's Reformed traditions, at God's House the decision to embrace the more ceremonial traditions of the Church of England meant that it was little different from some of the town's parish churches.

VIII Mission to Seamen

During the course of the nineteenth century, God's House chapel came to be associated with the Mission to Seamen as well as the spiritual welfare of the navvies employed in the construction of the docks from the late 1830s.[118] The chapel's position close to the Town Quay and new docks meant that it was ideally suited for this emerging mission. As early as 1824, Queen's College had received a request from one Heath for the use of the chapel to preach to sailors, to which they agreed so long as there was no objection from the French elders.[119] To improve access to the chapel, Wilson ordered an entrance to be opened on to Winkle Street; it was the key to this door which caused the dispute between the steward and elders in the late 1820s.[120]

In the following decade, Wilson took steps to develop this mission to the port's workers. By November 1839, he had received a grant of £100 from the Pastoral Aid Society to

[112] *Hampshire Advertiser*, 3 July 1886.
[113] Spicer, '"A Survival of a Distant Past"', 120, 137–38.
[114] Alfred Temple Patterson, *A History of Southampton, 1700–1914*, 3 vols, SRS 11, 14, 18 (1966, 1971, 1975), vol. 2, 69–70, vol. 3, 34; Nigel Yates, *Anglican Ritualism in Victorian Britain, 1830–1910* (Oxford: Oxford University Press, 1999), 396; J. Carne Waram (ed.), *Tourist's Church Guide 1876* (London: G.J. Palmer, 1876), 76–77: W. Nigel Yates, "'Bells and Smells': London, Brighton and South Coast Religion Reconsidered," *Southern History* 5 (1983): 135–36.
[115] SCA, D/FC5 (Acc.7134). See Yates, *Anglican Ritualism*, 56
[116] Comparison can be made over candles on the altar (whether lighted during services) and the use of vestments between the mid-1870s and mid-1890s: Carne Waram, *Tourist's Church Guide 1876*, 76–77; [English Church Union] (ed.), *Tourist's Church Guide 1894 and 1895* (London, 1894), 280–81. St Julien's church is not recorded in either issue.
[117] QCA, S206; SCA, D/FC 5 (Acc. 7134); Spicer, "Livre du Clerc," 198; *Minute Book*, 138–41.
[118] Temple Patterson, *History of Southampton*, vol. 2, 12.
[119] SCA, D/FC3/8/11a.
[120] SCA, D/FC3/8/11a.

employ a cleric 'for the especial benefit of the labourers and to officiate to them on the afternoon and evening of Sundays. The Dissenters have agreed not to step… between me and them if I can carry out that plan, otherwise they have talked of opening their own room for assembling'.[121] Wilson's initiative was the result of a campaign led by Major Frederick Hill to improve the religious provision for dock workers, whose spiritual life had been neglected and many of whom 'live[d] without God'. As the *Hampshire Advertiser* later reported: 'the spiritual, moral and physical condition of our men-of-war's men, merchant seamen, fishermen, and bargemen led to the foundation of the noble enterprise, and it was determined to bring religious ministrations near to them, afloat and at home; and to provide greater facilities for united worship as well as to meet their social needs'. Wilson presumed that the college would have no objection to God's House chapel being used for these services; he intended that the chapel 'would be exclusively devoted to the use of the Dockmen during 2 services on every Sabbath without interfering with the morning service of the French congregation'. Wilson had refurbished the chapel to prepare it for this mission to seamen.[122]

When these services began in 1840 between 20 and 30 men attended, who 'seemed to use their prayer books as if they were accustomed to divine service'.[123] Numbers increased in the following weeks. Responding to criticism in local newspapers, Hill stated that there had never been less than 17 worshippers but their numbers were steadily increasing with 39 and 48 present at recent services, 'exclusive of women and children'. Furthermore he noted that after the last service 14 men had remained behind: 'some to request [that] they might be supplied with bibles and testaments, others to have their children put to our Sunday or weekly schools'.[124] A report later in the year claimed that the response of 'the offer of Christian friendship to the dockmen is felt and welcomed by them', to the extent that the chapel was barely large enough to accommodate them at the last service.[125] Seamen filled the chapel at times of tragedy, such as in 1840 when Wilson preached following the 'drowning of six of their companions'.[126]

In the mid-1870s it was decided to combine the ministry of the French church with that of chaplain to the port's seamen. The post would be financed by both the French church and the Missions to Seamen Society. Services in English would be held for the mariners, and it was hoped that French sailors and pilots in the town would be encouraged to attend the church.[127] In 1878, Alphonse Dupont reported that in just under six months since his appointment, he had made 400 visits to the ships in port, 150 visits to sailors on shore and held 100 services especially for sailors.[128] This combined post only lasted until 1883, when Dupont's chaplaincy was terminated, precipitating a crisis in the financing of the French church's ministry.[129] Although services continued to be held at God's House, the following year the new chaplain gave a negative view of the arrangements: 'The only provision for the sailors was in the St Julien's Church in Winkle Street, an out of the way place not easily found by seamen, and there they were only permitted to be on sufferance after the Sunday evening services'.[130] The situation changed dramatically with the establishment of a seaman's mission on the Town Quay, which opened on to Winkle Street resulting in a significant increase in church attendance.[131]

The Mission for Seamen illustrates how the use of God's House chapel developed over the course of the nineteenth century. Although the relationship with the French church can only be gleaned from fragmentary references, increasingly large congregations of seamen gathered there on Sunday evenings. While the French church's association with God's House remained, the missions represented an important evolution in the role of the medieval chapel during the nineteenth century.

IX Conclusion

On 19 June 1864, some 200 people gathered in the newly restored chapel at God's House where they heard sermons preached in the morning and afternoon by Abraham Le Sueur, the rector of Grouville, Jersey. He then assisted the minister of the French church in the administration of communion. Recording this occasion in the 'livre du clerc', Thomas Mollet concluded: 'This church was consecrated 1567, rebuilt 1864'.[132] While the congregation and its ministers acknowledged the church's foundation and history on this and other occasions, it was not something they dwelled upon or commemorated with special anniversary services. This was a congregation which served the needs of the French-speaking community of nineteenth-century Southampton and those passing through the town, rather than the descendants of the Huguenot refugees from earlier centuries.

The increasing interest in the history of the Huguenots, especially around the bicentenary of the Revocation of the Edict of Nantes in 1885, had little impact on the Southampton congregation. Unlike the French church in Canterbury, there were few tangible reminders in God's House chapel of the congregation's past, apart from some gravestones, particularly after its controversial restoration. The furnishings installed in the later nineteenth century meant that the chapel's appearance differed little from

[121] QCA, 4G173(2); Temple Patterson, *History of Southampton*, vol. 2, 12.
[122] QCA, 4G173(2); SCA, D/S 1/5/6; *Hampshire Advertiser*, 7 May 1840, 17 October 1840, 3 July1886.
[123] *Hampshire Advertiser*, 2 May 1840.
[124] *Hampshire Advertiser*, 5 September 1840.
[125] *Hampshire Advertiser*, 10 October 1840.
[126] *Hampshire Advertiser*, 6 June 1840.
[127] SRO, "Livre du Clerc"; *Minute Book*, 121, 124–25; *Hampshire Advertiser*, 29 April 1876, 18 September 1878.
[128] *Hampshire Advertiser*, 18 September 1878.
[129] *Minute Book*, 128–30.
[130] *Hampshire Advertiser*, 15 November 1884.
[131] *Hampshire Advertiser*, 4 November 1885.
[132] SCA, D/FC5 (Acc. 7134).

some parish churches in Southampton. Perhaps for these reasons, histories of the Southampton congregation tended to focus more on the wealth of material presented in its register rather than their place of worship. With the notable exception of Sir William Portal, this earlier history rather than the contemporary congregation attracted the attention of and support of the Huguenot Society and others interested in the foreign congregations in general.

Although the French church had never had exclusive use of God's House chapel, during the nineteenth century they increasingly shared it with other congregations. Services in French continued to be held on Sunday mornings and afternoons, but the chapel was also used during the week by the parishioners of Holy Rood and increasingly by the Seamen's Mission on Sunday evenings. In spite of this, God's House chapel remained synonymous with the French congregation with all its historic associations. While acknowledging this past, the church and its ministers were more concerned to meet the religious needs of the French-speaking residents and visitors to Southampton rather than memorialise its past.

Select Bibliography

PHS – *Proceedings of the Huguenot Society.*

SRS – Southampton Records Series.

SRSoc – Southampton Record Society.

Archives

The Queen's College, Oxford

Southampton City Archives, Southampton

Published primary sources

Godfray, Humphrey Marret (ed.). *Registre des baptesmes, mariages & mortz, et jeusnes : de l'eglise wallonne et des isles de Jersey, Guernesey, Serq, Origny, &c.: etablie a Southampton par patente du roy Edouard six et de la reine Elizabeth*, Publications of the Huguenot Society 4 (1890).

Hessels, Johannes H. *Epistulae et tractatus cum Reformationis tum ecclesiae Londino-Batavae historiam illustrantes*, 3 vols. London, 1889–97.

Kaye, John M., ed. *The Cartulary of God's House, Southampton*, 2 vols. SRS 19–20 (1976).

Speed, John. *The History and Antiquity of Southampton*, edited by E.R. Aubrey. SRSoc. 8 (1909).

Welch, Edwin, ed. *The Minute Book of the French Church at Southampton, 1702–1939*. SRS 23 (1979)

Secondary Sources

Ainsworth, William Harrison. *Cardinal Pole, or the Days of Philip and Mary: an historical romance*, 3 vols. London: Chapman and Hall, 1863.

[Brannon, Philip]. *The Stranger's Guide and Pleasure Visitor's Companion to Southampton.* Southampton, s.d.

Burn, J. Southerden, *The History of the French, Walloon, Dutch and other Foreign Protestant Refugees*. London: Longman, 1846.

Davies, Silvester J. *A History of Southampton: partly from the MS. of Dr. Speed, in the Southampton Archives*. Southampton: Gilbert and Company, 1883.

Duthy, John. *Sketches of Hampshire: embracing the architectural antiquities, topography &c of country adjacent to the River Itchen*...Winchester, 1839.

Englefield, Henry. *A Walk through Southampton.* Southampton: Baker and Fletcher, 1805.

[English Church Union], ed. *Tourist's Church Guide 1894 and 1895*. London: English Church Union, 1894.

Hopewell, Peter. *Saint Cross: England's oldest almshouse*. Chichester: Phillimore, 1995.

King, Richard J. *A Handbook for Travellers in Kent and Sussex*. London: John Murray, 1858.

King, Richard J. *Handbook to the Cathedrals of England: Southern division*. London: John Murray, 1861.

Layard, Henry A. "Address to the Fifth Annual General Meeting of the Huguenot Society of London." *PHS* 3 (1888–91): xxvi–xxvii.

Layard, Henry A. "Address to the Sixth Annual General Meeting of the Huguenot Society of London." *PHS* 3 (1888–91): lxxix–ciii.

Martin, Joseph A. *Christian Firmness of the Huguenots and a Sketch of the History of the French Refugee Church of Canterbury.* Canterbury: S.W. Partridge, 1881.

Moens, W.J.C. "French and Walloon Church Registers in England." *PHS* 1 (1885–86): 17–56.

Moens, W.J.C. "The Walloon Settlement and the French Church at Southampton." *PHS* 3 (1888–91): 53–76.

Patterson, Alfred Temple. *A History of Southampton, 1700–1914*, 3 vols. SRS 11, 14, 18, 1966, 1971, 1975.

Portal, William Wyndham. *Some Account of the Settlement of Refugees, l'Église wallonne, at Southampton: also notes on the papermaking industry, as practised by the Southampton refugees*. Winchester, 1902.

Poyntz Stewart, Charles. "Address to the Thirty-Second Annual General Meeting of the Huguenot Society of London." *PHS* 11 (1915–17): 175–76.

Prothero, Rowland E. *The Life and Correspondence of Arthur Penrhyn Stanley*, 2 vols. London: John Murray, 1893.

Pugh, Thomas B. *Henry V and the Southampton Plot of 1415.* SRS 30 (1988).

Rance, Adrian B. *A Victorian Photographer in Southampton: Thomas Hibberd James*. Southampton: Paul Cave, 1980.

Shore, Thomas W. *A History of Hampshire including the Isle of Wight*. London: Elliot Stock, 1892.

Smiles, Samuel. *The Huguenots: their settlements, churches, and industries in England and Ireland.* London: Harper and Brothers, 1867.

Spicer, Andrew. *The French-speaking Reformed Community and their Church in Southampton, 1567–c.1620*, Huguenot Society New Series 3 / SRS 39 (1997).

Spicer, Andrew. "The Consistory Records of Reformed Congregations and the Exile Churches." *PHS* 28 (2003–07): 640–63.

Spicer, Andrew. "'A Survival of a Distant Past': J.A. Martin and the Victorian revival of the French church at Canterbury." *Southern History* 34 (2012): 100–38.

Spicer, Andrew. "Victorian Vignettes of the French Church at Canterbury." *PHS* 29 (2012): 716–18.

Spicer, Andrew. "1885: French Protestantism and Huguenot identity in Victorian Britain." In *Histoire, mémoire et identités en mutation. Les huguenots en France et en diaspora (XVIe–XXIe siècles)*, edited by Philip Benedict, Hugues Daussy and Pierre-Olivier Léchot, 391–422. Geneva: Droz, 2014.

Spicer, Andrew. "The 'Livre du Clerc' of the French Church in Southampton." *The Huguenot Society Journal* 30 (2014): 193–99.

Spicer, Andrew. "Conformity, Nonconformity and Occasional Conformity: the Church of England and the French church in Southampton, c.1662–1723." Forthcoming.

Waram, J. Carne, ed. *Tourist's Church Guide 1876.* London: G.J. Palmer, 1876.

Whitlock, J. Aston. "Domus Dei or the Hospital of St Julian, Southampton." *PHS* 3 (1888–91): 42–52.

Whitlock, J. Aston. *A Brief and Popular History of the Hospital of God's House Southampton.* Southampton: Henry March Gilbert, 1894.

Yates, Nigel. *Anglican Ritualism in Victorian Britain, 1830–1910*. Oxford: Oxford University Press, 1999.

Yates, W. Nigel. "'Bells and Smells': London, Brighton and south coast religion reconsidered." *Southern History* 5 (1983): 122–53.

17

The Administration and Organisation of the Census in Nineteenth Century Winchester

Mark Allen

University of Winchester

Abstract: The nineteenth century censuses have become central not just to demographic surveys of the period, but also to family and local historians. Yet these documents are, as Peter Tillott pointed out in 1972, littered with idiosyncrasies and inaccuracies. We do not have the original householders returns between 1841 and 1901 and are entirely dependent upon the reading and understanding of temporarily employed enumerators, many of whom were described by contemporaries at the General Register Office as unfit for the purpose. This paper considers how well enumerators carried out their instructions, and studies them as a body of men (they were all male). It is possible to see the extent to which the elite of Winchester were involved and also how the same families undertook the role of enumerators from one census to the next. The way individual enumerators interpreted their instructions also allow us insight into the differing understandings of what their role was and longitudinal analysis of the CEBs shows how well the enumerators did their job, and the extent to which this changed over time.

Key words: Census Enumerators' Books; corrections; enumerators; Registrars; Winchester

In 2006, Tom James and I published an edition of the 1871 census for Winchester, which included an introductory essay analysing the structure and content of the Census Enumerators' Books [hereafter CEBs]. Tom, with the eye of a medievalist, looked at how the books were put together, identifying examples of different handwriting in each, focusing on the enumerators and exploring how the CEBs themselves were used to put together the published census report. This paper expands upon Tom's examination of the enumeration process, extending the analysis to cover each census from 1841 to 1901, using around 6,000 colour images of the CEBs that are not normally available for public inspection, and which were not available to us in 2006. The essay is in four sections. First, the role and function of enumerators is considered. The physical state of Winchester's CEBs are then assessed before an analysis of local officers and the material contained in the CEBs is undertaken.

The question of how well enumerators carried out their task caused problems for contemporaries. They were meant to display a number of characteristics:

> He must be a person of intelligence and activity; he must read and write well, and have some knowledge of arithmetic; he must not be infirm or of such weak health as may render him unable to undergo the requisite exertion; he should not be younger than 18 years of age or older than 65; he must be temperate, orderly and respectable, and be such a person as is likely to conduct himself with strict propriety, and to deserve the goodwill of the inhabitants of his district. It will also be desirable that he should be well acquainted with the district in which he will be required to act; and it will be an additional recommendation if his occupations have been in any degree of a similar kind.[1]

The 1841 *Census Report* was generally positive, noting that 'careful inspection of the Schedules … has enabled us to announce that [the enumerators'] duties were carefully and intelligently discharged'.[2] In 1861 it was reported that 'no difficulty was experienced in procuring the services of a highly respectable body of enumerators, including clergymen and many other professional men who undertook the work from public motives'.[3] By 1871 the mainly positive view of enumerators was maintained, in that 'no one…will consider that they were overpaid' and that they 'have done their country good service; they have all sent in their books in time…and there is every reason to believe that the books which have yet to be examined will be found, as on previous occasions, creditable to them as a body, and in many instances deserving of the highest praise'.[4]

[1] The National Archives [hereafter TNA] RG27/1, 26–27. Also reproduced in M. Drake, "The census, 1801–1891," in *Nineteenth-Century Society. Essays in the use of quantitative methods for the study of social* data, ed. E.A. Wrigley (Cambridge: Cambridge University Press, 1972), 25.

[2] *Parliamentary Papers*, 1843 XXVII.1 [C.587], 1841 Enumeration Abstract, 1–2 of preface.

[3] *Parliamentary Papers*, 1863 LIII [C.3221], 1861 Census General Report, 1.

[4] *Parliamentary Papers*, 1871 LIX.659 [C.381], 1871 Census Preliminary Report, ii.

The tone of comments regarding the enumeration process changed in 1881. The 1841 census had been conducted under the first Registrar General, Thomas Lister,[5] and those from 1851–71 had been overseen by his successor George Graham and the Superintendent of Statistics at the General Register Office, William Farr, who wrote most of the early census reports. The retirement of these two men before the 1881 enumeration and their replacement with Sir Brydges Henniker and the strident Dr William Ogle, may have something to do with how the enumerators were now viewed.[6] The *Preliminary Report* highlighted how it was 'increasingly difficult to take the whole census in a single day', presumably because the increase in population was not met by an increase in the number of enumerators.[7] The *General Report* noted that:

> enumerators received but scanty remuneration for services which were by no means light or simple; and it is out of the question to expect that an army of men, each... expected to do the work of a fairly adequate clerk while he is paid at a far lower rate, can be raised for a temporary purpose, and that no difficulty shall occur with any of them. It is satisfactory, however, to be able to state that, disregarding a few exceptional cases, the enumerators performed their part, within the limits of their capacity... as well as could reasonably be expected. There were often, it is true, omissions and inaccuracies which had to be set right afterwards... but such omissions and inaccuracies are the unavoidable incidents of every census, and we have no reason to believe that they were more frequent on the present than on preceding occasions.[8]

This rather backhanded comment about the limits of enumerators' capacity was then demonstrated by disclosing that enumeration books 'were found to be most deficient, and to show the most serious amount of inaccuracy ... [in] the matter of boundaries. ... the enumerators and the local registrars in a vast number of cases failed altogether to unravel their intricacy'.

By 1891 there had been wider debate about the census as a whole, with a Treasury Committee appointed in 1890 to look into the taking of the census, which revealed William Ogle's thoughts on the shortcomings of the enumeration process in more detail.[9] During evidence to the committee he stated that enumerators were 'on the whole, rather a poor lot', and, after describing what they should be capable of, he stated that he 'doubted whether there are 40,000 men of that character to be got for a temporary job'.[10] He also stated:

> there are good... and bad enumerators, and indifferent enumerators; but their mere handwriting and the general aspect of their work shows that many of them are very illiterate men; the kind... who spelt butcher 'bousher'; they are often that kind of man.[11]

So, what had caused this change in attitude towards census enumerators? Had their jobs got more difficult, were they less capable than previously, and do the surviving CEBs demonstrate that, at least in the case of Winchester, they were 'rather a poor lot'? Or did Winchester's enumerators do a better job than some?

It is impossible to evaluate how 'accurate' the enumerators were, as the researcher would need to compare the CEBs with the original householders' schedules, which have been destroyed.[12] Many householders also did not know the information requested of them. This is particularly the case relating to ages and birthplaces, but it can be applied to other information like family relationships. The censuses are replete with examples of people who apparently aged considerably more (or less) than the ten years between enumerations, and Michael Anderson discovered that around 14 per cent of a sample of 475 people identified in both the 1851 and 1861 censuses had different birthplaces. Although some differences were insignificant, 'in half of these cases migrants became non-migrants and *vice versa*'.[13]

The nature of occupational information was a further problem. Unlike age or birthplace which, theoretically, had a single precise answer, a householder's occupation was subjective. He or she may have followed more than one trade, as was the case with William Dyer, an

[5] Lister was the chief of three Census Commissioners, but he died in 1842 before publication of the report, so that report just bears the signatures of the other two commissioners. *Parliamentary Papers*, 1904 CVIII.1 [C.2174], 1901 Census General Report, 8.

[6] The changing role of the General Register Office, which undertook the census, is analysed by Edward Higgs, "The state and statistics in Victorian and Edwardian Britain. Promotion of the public sphere or boundary maintenance," in *Statistics and the public sphere, Numbers and the people in modern Britain c.1800–2000* eds Tom Crook and Glen O'Hara (London: Routledge, 2011), 67–83.

[7] *Parliamentary Papers*, 1881 CXVI.1 [C.2955], 1881 Census Preliminary Report, ii.

[8] *Parliamentary Papers*, 1883 LXXX.583 [C.3797], 1881 Census General Report, 3.

[9] For a discussion of some of the aims, and the eventual results of 'the battle for control of the census', see Simon Szreter, *Fertility, class and gender in Britain, 1860–1940* (Cambridge: Cambridge University Press, 1996), 114–120. A slightly different take on this is given by Edward Higgs, *Life, Death and Statistics. Civil Registration, census and the work of the General Register Office, 1836–1952* (Hatfield: Local Population Studies, 2004), 124–27.

[10] *Parliamentary Papers*, 1890, LVIII.13 [C.6071], Treasury Committee connected with the taking of the census, Minutes of Evidence, paras. 33, 34.

[11] *Parliamentary Papers*, 1890, LVIII.13 [C.6071], Treasury Committee connected with the taking of the census, Minutes of Evidence, para. 2409.

[12] Edward Higgs, *Making Sense of the Census Revisited. Census Records for England and Wales 1801–1901. A Handbook for Historical Researchers* (London: The Institute of Historical Research/The National Archives of the UK, 2005), 24. He contends that household schedules were probably destroyed by the Census Office after they had been used to check the CEBs.

[13] M. Anderson, "The Study of Family Structure," in *Nineteenth-Century Society. Essays in the use of quantitative methods for the study of social* data, ed. E.A. Wrigley (Cambridge: Cambridge University Press, 1972),75. For ages see Higgs, *Making Sense Revisited*, 83–87. A general survey on accuracy is P. Tillott, "Sources of inaccuracy in the 1851 and 1861 censuses," in *Nineteenth-Century Society. Essays in the use of quantitative methods for the study of social* data, ed. E.A. Wrigley (Cambridge: Cambridge University Press, 1972), 82–133.

enumerator in St Thomas parish in 1841. He listed his occupation as a woolstapler – and 'late woolstapler' in 1851 – but his residence in the cemetery lodge and a subsequent comparison of his signature in burial registers for West Hill Cemetery shows he was also the cemetery's sexton from 1840 until his death in 1852.[14] The same is true of Charles Mayo, listed as a surgeon in each census from 1841 to 1861, but he was also registrar of births, and deaths, signing off every enumeration book for Winchester. This is left unmentioned in his census entries. His successor, William Etheridge, took the opposite view, highlighting his status as registrar in 1871 but neglecting altogether to mention that he was also a solicitor's clerk. Winchester's third Registrar, Frank Spire, took yet another approach, stating both his roles in 1901 – solicitor's clerk and registrar of births and deaths.[15]

It is true also that copying material from householders' schedules to CEBs introduced inaccuracies. In 1890, giving evidence to the Treasury Committee into the Census, Dr Ogle stated that 'there was an additional chance of error introduced by copying' and Frank Tupper, a registrar in Clerkenwell declared that 'there would be a great risk' that copying mistakes made by enumerators could never be detected and that removing CEBs from the process would eliminate one element of doubt.[16] In 1911, it was noted that the reasons CEBs were no longer used included the fact that 'it ... led, despite the checking provided for in the regulations, to many copyists' errors, some... purely accidental... and others due to mistaken emendations from misinterpretation of the replies'.[17] But considering the use to which the CEBs were originally put – to provide national-level statistics – miscopying even several thousand entries in a population of around 40 million was statistically insignificant. However, when local researchers use the census to address distinctive social and economic features of places with small populations, such inaccuracies are amplified.

To suggest that errors were introduced by enumerators also assumes that householders produced perfect answers in the first place. This is clearly not the case, as Ogle stated, 'I really attribute the inadequacy of the returns to the stupidity of the men who filled them up, not the enumerator' and that householders had 'no notion of accuracy'.[18] It is clear that many householders' answers were imperfect, illustrated by the case of one family. A diligent enumerator, Charles White, told the Treasury Committee of how he eventually obtained correct information from a partially paralysed man in his district in 1881.[19] This man initially described himself as a cooper, but upon further inquiry turned out to be a shoeblack. White's 1881 enumeration book contains one such entry: a Henry March.[20] He was aged 34, from Bristol in Gloucestershire and his wife, Louisa, was born in Devon but did not know where. In 1891, when White was again the enumerator, they had each aged 11 years. Henry's birthplace, although still Bristol, was described as in Somerset, while his wife appears to have remembered that she was born in Exeter.[21] By 1901, Henry was a widower in the Mile End Old Town workhouse, so a different person enumerated him. He was thus able to get away with claiming to be a cooper, while his birthplace had returned to Gloucestershire.[22] White described him in 1881 as a partially paralysed imbecile. Ten years later he was described merely as paralysed and in 1901 no mention was made of any disability.

Clearly there were inaccuracies in the above information, but they were more likely caused by Henry March than the enumerator and were relatively unimportant as far as statistical summaries go. Occupational terms were subjective. People sometimes gave different descriptions in official questionnaires like the census than they might in a trade directory when they were seeking trade. It was also questioned whether a parent might wish to describe their child as an idiot or imbecile, as the census required. In the Henry March case, his wife's county of birth remains the same even if the exact birthplace is not always clear; ages were often approximated and Bristol straddled Gloucestershire and Somerset's county boundary, so it is patently one of many such cases. The information on March's disability is the most inconsistent, and this was the one element of the census that Ogle considered of little use. So, the census's 'accuracy' is impossible to ascertain, although it is possible to get some understanding of who the enumerators were and whether they were likely to be diligent. It is also possible to use the internal evidence of their CEBs to discover whether they were up to the task.

The physical state of the Winchester enumeration books

The original CEBs are not normally available for public scrutiny but The National Archives made those for Winchester available for this research. Higgs has detailed their format but their physical state today is worth noting.[23] The abstraction process led to more changes to the 1841 books than would be seen with later ones. There is also one

[14] For Dyer's signature as enumerator see TNA HO/107/409/9 fo.50v. His occupation is shown in both TNA HO107/410/5 fo.3v and TNA HO 107/1674 fo. 347. The West Hill Cemetery burial register shows his identical signature, see Hampshire Record Office [hereafter HRO] W/J3/1, 18. Dyer's employment start and end dates are shown in the Directors' Book of Proceedings for West Hill Cemetery, meetings of 31 July 1840, and 14 October 1852. HRO W/J3/16, 14.

[15] For Mayo, see TNA HO 107/409/9 fo. 8; TNA HO 107/1674 fo.34v; TNA RG9/691 fo. 74v. For Etheridge, TNA RG10/1211 fo. 5v; TNA RG11/1232 fo. 94 v. Spire's entry is found at TNA RG13/1081 fo. 159.

[16] *Parliamentary Papers*, 1890, LVIII.13 [C.6071], Treasury Committee connected with the taking of the census, Minutes of Evidence, 43, paras. 1022–23; 101, para. 2463.

[17] *Parliamentary Papers*, 1917 XXXV.483 [C.8491], 1911 General report, 10.

[18] *Parliamentary Papers*, 1890, LVIII.13 [C.6071], Treasury Committee connected with the taking of the census, Minutes of Evidence, 105, para. 2540.

[19] *Parliamentary Papers*, 1890, LVIII.13 [C.6071], Treasury Committee connected with the taking of the census, Minutes of Evidence, 82, para. 1850.

[20] TNA RG11/481 fo. 76.

[21] TNA RG12/307 fo. 113.

[22] TNA RG13/338 fo.104.

[23] Higgs, *Making Sense Revisited*, Appendices 2 and 3, 169–188.

missing CEB in 1841, for the parish of Winnall, the only such loss for Winchester across the period, meaning the identity of this district's enumerator is unknown.[24] The books themselves are portrait booklets with blue covers, each containing a label – red for institutional books, black for others – with the number of the enumeration district; many also have the enumerator's name on the cover. The first page contains a description of the district, in an anonymous hand, but it is the same one for each district. Also, on this page are notes indicating the initials or names of the clerks in London who abstracted information for the final census report, and the date on which each was completed.

The unique characteristic of the 1841 Winchester CEBs, compared to those later in the century, is how they were rearranged. If a district contained more than one area to be considered in the published report, it was physically detached from that book and rebound, making a second book but without a distinctive blue cover. When the area to be detached was found halfway down a page in the original book, part of that page was copied, presumably in London (the handwriting differs) and crossed out in the original. For example, in St Maurice parish the extra-parochial area of Bishop Morley College was originally included in the middle of the district (pages 18 and 19 of 31) but it has been crossed out on both pages and repeated separately.[25] Sometimes this process got very messy. In St Swithun parish (District 14) the Cathedral Close was excised, meaning that the bottom four lines of page three were crossed out; the facing page as it exists today (originally from a different book, as its page number is 28, but crossed out) was left blank, pages four to six are missing entirely, and page seven (originally page 29 but crossed out) has a blank first six lines with the rest of the page completed in a different hand in ink, as opposed to the rest of the St Swithun book, completed in pencil. The 'missing' pages then turn up as a separate enumeration book with the reverse changes. Here, page one (actually a page 26 crossed out) was blank; page two *only* contained the bottom four entries, in the same pen-hand, with pages four to six written in the same pencil hand of the main St Swithun book, while page seven is crossed out except for the first six entries. In extreme cases, as can be seen in St Faith parish, where the main book has been butchered to produce three distinct districts, this can end up looking unduly chaotic.[26] This process would have been extremely time-consuming, and was thankfully abandoned after 1841.

Uniquely, in 1841 enumerators were provided with pencils to complete their CEBs. In Winchester, eleven districts were entered in pencil, whilst all twelve institutional books and a further six ordinary CEBs were completed in ink.[27] Pencil does make later interventions from both local officers and London clerks more obvious, so this is an advantage when studying the originals from these books.

Later CEBs are all landscape documents and those for 1851 are on blue paper, meaning that later interventions stand out; no others were printed on coloured paper. Pencils were not generally used by enumerators after 1841, and all CEBs thereafter were completed in black ink, with the exception of that for Chilcomb in 1851, where the enumerator used blue ink. None has been left bound in its original form. CEBs were generally grouped together in sets that together made up Winchester sub-district.[28] In the case of Winchester, only the books for 1851 and 1881 remain bound together today, and the 1861 books are held together with treasury tags, the hole for which passes through the printed part of the page, so no information is lost. The CEB pages for 1871, 1891 and 1901 have been left loose but are tied together in bundles. This reorganisation or binding of the books seems to have been done during the abstraction process, as each set of books, excepting 1881, has a covering page detailing the initials or names of people abstracting different pieces of information for all the CEBs held together in that book, together with the date that this was done. In 1891 and 1901 the front covers are printed tables with spaces for abstractors to sign and date their work. In 1871 and earlier, the original cover was blank but abstractors filled in the same information on the page. In 1881 CEBs, at least for Winchester, these covers either never existed or have been lost, and each group of CEBs has a plain brown cover. Summary totals of males, females and total population in each group of bound-together CEBs were provided inside the front cover on some books.

Excepting Winnall parish in 1841, each CEB for Winchester survives. There are three apparent smaller-

[24] TNA HO107/404/20. According to the census report it contained details of 27 inhabited houses, a population of 49 men and 64 women (113 people in total).

[25] The re-written page is at TNA HO107/409/1 fo.1 and the crossed-out originals may be found at TNA HO107/409/6 fo 38, 38v. Bishop Morley College is located on the northern boundary of the cathedral close and is for widows of clergymen. The St Swithun/Cathedral Close example is to be found at TNA HO107/410/12 fo4v-5v and TNA HO107/410/13.

[26] See TNA HO107/410/5, particularly pages 7–19 in the original book. The two additional districts extracted from this can be found at TNA HO107/409/3 and TNA HO107/410/4.

[27] The following districts were completed in pencil: St Bartholomew Hyde, Weeke, St John, the first of the two districts for St Maurice, the first of the two St Thomas districts, St Lawrence/Cathedral Yard, the Vill of Milland, St Swithun/Cathedral Close, St Faith and Chilcomb. The following were completed in ink: The second districts for St Maurice and St Thomas, respectively, St Mary Kalendar, St Peter Chesil, St Peter Colebrook and St Michael. It is unknown how Winnall's CEB was completed.

[28] By way of example, the CEBs for 1851 (TNA HO107/1674) were bound together as follows. Sub-district 3a contains Weeke, St Thomas (2 districts), the Barracks (two districts), St Bartholomew Hyde and St Mary Kalendar with St Lawrence and the Cathedral Yard. Sub-district 3b contains St Maurice (two districts, one with Bishop Morley College), St Peter Colebrook and Wolvesey Palace, St Swithun with Winchester College and the Cathedral Close, St Michael and the Vill of Milland, St Faith and St Cross Hospital, the County Gaol, St Peter Chesil, St John and Winnall. In 1861 and thereafter there were at least three bound groups of CEBs rather than two. Chilcomb was in the Twyford sub-district in 1851 (TNA HO107/1675), which is not bound. Chilcomb was in the Twyford sub-district (no. 4) until the 1891 census, when it was transferred to Winchester although the parish was at least partly in the municipal borough for the whole period.

scale losses in later CEBs, which require further explanation. Modern researchers working from microform or genealogical websites would believe the six preliminary pages and pages 1–4 of District one in 1861, containing entries covering most of Winchester's Cathedral Close, are missing. This seems to have been an error during reproduction as the pages do survive, along with a seventh page of abstracted information on a slip of paper.[29] The two preliminary pages containing the abstract of page totals and the dated signatures of enumerator, registrar and superintendent registrar for St Bartholomew Hyde parish in 1861 do not survive, however, and the same is true for all of the preliminary pages for St Peter Chesil parish in 1881[30]. On both occasions these are the first districts in a bound volume. They appear to have been lost relatively soon after being worked on by clerks in London as the folio numbers stamped on the books when they were bound together both follow their logical sequence without these pages being present. We know the 1861 enumerator of St Bartholomew Hyde was John Castell, however, as he signed the district's description, on a page which does survive.

One advantage of examining the CEBs in colour is the ability to distinguish between interventions made by a variety of people other than the enumerator. This sometimes meant the registrar, who had access to the original householders' schedules, correcting miscopied information, as with the entries for Amelia Evans and Annie Alder in 1871.[31] Evans's entry has the occupation 'General Servant' added in different handwriting to the enumerator in red pen, and the birthplace for Alder is changed from Ringwood to nearby Alderholt. This must have come from someone with access to the original schedules.

Other interventions were made by clerks in London to aid abstraction of information. In 1841 these were limited to a few vertical marks next to some occupations and ticks next to birthplaces not in Hampshire. Occasionally, some occupations were crossed out in red, usually for those under the age of 16 listed as servants or pupils, but ages were generally left untouched. In 1851, such interventions mainly occurred in six areas: every head of household was noted with a vertical line in black crayon or pencil by a clerk; entries for the widowed also had a vertical line added in red whilst married couples were noted by a slash in red; ages were marked in a similar manner (although sometimes in black); every birthplace listed as anywhere other than Winchester; and any disabilities disclosed had a slash in red through them once abstracted. Clerks also added notes to occupations to aid the abstraction process. These fall into three categories and are best described by example. On page two of the St Cross Hospital entries, William Lambert, a Brother of St Cross Hospital, gave his occupation as Brother of St Cross and ex-Excise Officer.[32] Excise Officer was highlighted by red brackets placed around this portion of his occupation, indicating that it was this which would be abstracted in preference to his rank at the hospital. His grandson, a 'Toolman' – changed to Toolmaker in red crayon – had '10 11' added to show the particular occupational class his profession was to be coded with, and two further Brothers of St Cross who gave no other occupations had the word 'Alms' added to their occupations to give an idea of where they would be abstracted. Other clarifications like 'Serv', 'Dom' or 'No occ' appear frequently in the CEBs. Sometimes the red additions obscure the original text on black and white images, but they are frequently easier to see in colour.

In later censuses interventions developed. Ages were either crossed through or ticked in each CEB, usually in a different colour for each sex, although the exact colour used varied between censuses, and sometimes between CEBs in the same census. At different times ages were ticked in grey and blue (1861) grey and red (1871), red and blue (1881) blue (1891) and black and red (1901). Red pencil slashes in different directions for married and widowed people were added to CEBs in 1861, and in 1871 all marital statuses were marked off in grey pencil and in blue pencil in 1881. By 1901 this column was left completely untouched by clerks.

Birthplaces were marked off in a similar fashion at each census, although from 1861 it was the non-Hampshire born that were highlighted, usually in black pencil (1861, 1881) or blue (1871, 1891), as opposed to the non-Winchester natives of 1851. By 1901 ticks in black ink were used on such birthplaces, and throughout, disabilities were struck through in various colours.

The treatment of occupations in CEBs is noteworthy. In 1861 there were only 91 interventions in total in the occupation column, 50 of them in just three districts. Almost all interventions noted people with no occupations or highlighted the classification of a given occupation, with only two additions, presumably by the registrar. Similarly, interventions are relatively rare in the occupation column in 1871, but there are more in 1881, usually in blue pencil clarifying which occupational groups a given trade should be placed in. By 1891 significant additions began to be made by clerks in an attempt to classify given occupational terms, and in 1901 a single CEB contains around one and a half times the number of interventions for the whole of 1861. Indeed, almost every occupation given either received a red annotation to aid classification, a red circle to highlight the term classified, or a thick blue pencil slash to indicate it was dealt with.

Local Districts and Officers

From 1841, each registration sub-district for births and

[29] TNA RG9/691 fo. 1–6v.

[30] For 1861 see TNA RG9/692 fo. 1–3, and for 1881 see TNA RG11/1233 fo. 1.

[31] TNA RG10/1210 fo. 16v. See "Introduction," in *The 1871 Census for Winchester*, eds Mark Allen and Tom James (Winchester: Wessex Historical Databases, 2006), 2.

[32] TNA HO107/1674 fo. 334.

deaths was divided into enumeration districts, its registrar organising household schedules to be distributed in the week before the census. Each enumeration district was then overseen by a temporary enumerator employed to collect household schedules, help householders complete them if they were unable to do so, and then copy the material into a CEB. The CEBs and schedules were then checked against each other by registrars, signed off by superintendent registrars (who only viewed the CEBs) and sent up to the census office in London where abstraction of information was completed over a period of two to three years, the resulting statistics published by Parliament. It has recently been suggested that up to a quarter of responses by householders had to be amended by enumerators, indicating that their job was important, although the same text goes on to say that we do not know how much information was improved nor how many errors were introduced by this process.[33] Once their job was complete, enumerators were paid and returned to their everyday lives. The process remained virtually identical at each subsequent census up to and including 1901.[34] The exact boundaries of enumeration districts were tweaked by registrars at each census, meaning that the number of districts at successive Winchester censuses was rarely the same. Nevertheless, many enumerators served at successive censuses, sometimes in the same district.[35] Enumerators were retained in 1911, their duties amended with householders' schedules used for abstraction purposes. So, we are left with the CEBs. They are neither the end-product nor the original census returns, but working documents produced with no expectation that they would be examined by researchers, and their survival has been rather fortunate.

The hierarchy of census administration started at the Registrar General. Winchester registration district, controlled by a superintendent registrar, was based on the New Winchester and Hursley poor law unions and consisted of five sub-districts, reduced to four in 1901. One of these sub-districts, also named Winchester, comprised the city parishes and was controlled by a registrar. Winchester had three superintendent registrars in the nineteenth century, and all lived in the city. The *Hampshire Advertiser* noted that the role was jointly held with that of clerk to the Board of Guardians of the New Winchester Union, giving this person a wide network of suitable enumerators.[36] John Ventham served from the creation of the role until his death in 1856. He was an actuary, clerk to the poor law guardians of Winchester, a pavement commissioner an alderman, and mayor of Winchester in 1854/5. He was replaced by Edward Williams Faithfull, a solicitor and another alderman (as was his father, as well as mayor) in the city. Upon his death in 1879, his son Frank Faithfull – another solicitor – became the next superintendent registrar.[37]

Likewise, there were only three registrars for the Winchester sub-district in the period. Charles Mayo fulfilled this role up to August 1869;[38] he was the son of a clergyman, surgeon to the Royal Hampshire County Hospital for 60 years and, like John Ventham, had been mayor, although he achieved this on three occasions (1839/40, 1844/5 and 1851/2).[39] Mayo died, aged 88, in 1876. William Etheridge, who had been a clerk in the solicitor's firm of both Edward and Frank Faithfull, undertook this role between 1869 and his death in 1891.[40] Frank Spire, another solicitor's clerk, became Winchester registrar in March 1901, a month before the census.[41] Local newspapers are silent on the recruitment of enumerators, and as with Frank Tupper, the registrar in Clerkenwell who gave evidence to the Treasury in 1890 stated, most of Winchester's enumerators appear to have been friends and acquaintances of these men.[42] All three registrars had extensive contacts with other men through their roles in the poor law, as registrars and Winchester's corporation. Further investigation will doubtless expose many of these informal links to enumerators.

Registrars were also required to act as enumerators if the nominated enumerator could not undertake the role. This appears to have happened once in Winchester, with Frank Spire being the enumerator of the district of the combined parishes of St Lawrence, St Swithun and the Vill of Milland in 1901. As Spire had been the registrar for less than a month, he may have already been assigned this role under his predecessor, but it is also possible that he replaced at the last minute someone unable to undertake the work.

William Harwood noted in 1995 that 'enumerators constituted the main interface between the population and the census data. On their diligence, intelligence and literacy depended in large measure the quality of the

[33] Gunnar Thorvaldsen, *Censuses and census takers. A global history* (London: Routledge, 2018), 290.

[34] Most census reports detail the enumeration process. See also Higgs, *Making Sense Revisited*, 14–19 and D. Mills and K. Schürer, eds, *Local Communities in the Victorian Census Enumerators' Books* (Oxford: Leopard's Head Press, 1996), 16–26. From 1851, enumerators replaced registrars in distributing household schedules before census night. From 1911, CEBs were no longer used and household schedules and an Enumerators' Summary Book were completed.

[35] M. Drake and D.R. Mills, "A Note on Census Enumerators," *Local Population Studies Society Newsletter*, 29 (2001): 6, notes one example in Minster Lovell in Oxfordshire and Wildsmith has found one person who enumerated five successive censuses, two farmers who did so four times, and a bootmaker and carpenter who did so three times. J. Wildsmith, "The 1871 Census Enumerators in the Subdistrict of Witney," *Local Population Studies Society Newsletter*, 17 (1995): 3–5.

[36] *Hampshire Advertiser*, 22 February 1879, 6 col. 6.

[37] *Hampshire Chronicle*, 25 January 1879 and 15 February 1879.

[38] Etheridge was appointed in 21 August 1869. *Hampshire Chronicle*, 28 August 1869, 5, col. 1.

[39] *Hampshire Advertiser*, 28 May 1879, 3, col. 4.

[40] See Etheridge's obituary in *Hampshire Chronicle*, 23 February 1901, 5.

[41] *Hampshire Chronicle*, 16 March 1901. This also relates how Spire got the post over George Read, an overseer on Colebrook Street. Read was an enumerator for Chilcomb in 1891.

[42] *Parliamentary Papers*, 1890, LVIII.13 [C.6071], Treasury Committee connected with the taking of the census, Minutes of Evidence, para 909.

data we can now access'.[43] Although each enumerator was identified by name at least once in each CEB, we know surprisingly little about them; even their total number at each census is unclear. Both the 1841 and 1851 censuses contain three different counts that might equate to enumerators. The *Census Report* for 1841 only mentioned a figure of 'not less than 35,000' enumerators, although there were 30,689 ordinary enumeration books and 1,761 institutional ones (a total of 32,450) issued, and the expenses for the 1851 census noted that 32,353 enumerators were paid in 1841.[44] In 1851, 30,610 districts in England and Wales, approximately 40,000, enumerators and 38,000 enumeration books (both including Scotland) are noted at different times.[45] Ten years later, 30,329 enumeration districts and *c.*31,000 CEBs were noted in *General Report*, but the expenses gave a more precise number of 31,144, enumerators.[46] In 1871, their number was clearly stated, and at this time the total number of institutional enumerators was distinguished from those employed to work on 'ordinary' CEBs. Even so, the totals differ between published expenses, and the preliminary and final *Census Report*.[47] The expenses of the census do not appear to distinguish the number of payments to enumerators after 1871, and thereafter only in 1881 was all information given explicitly in the published *Report*.[48] The 1891 *Report* stated only the number of districts, adding that an enumerator was appointed for each, so the number of districts and enumerators were presumably the same, but the work of Drake and Mills indicates that some enumerators worked on two districts and, in just a few cases, three districts.[49] The 1901 census gave a figure in the *Preliminary Report* only.[50] Table 17.1 summarises numbers of local officers involved in census taking between 1841 and 1901, as far as can be ascertained.

Just as their numbers nationally are difficult to determine, relatively little work has analysed enumerators. Analyses relying on the census tend not to focus on them, transcriptions rarely do more than name them and written work on enumerators tends to focus on their identification.[51] Two exceptions to this are Arkell's work on 89 enumerators in Cornwall in 1851 and that of volunteers published by Drake and Mills, which focused on 449 enumerators up to 1891 in rural areas or small market towns across the country and in different years.[52] Arkell's work concentrated on just one year, and the Drake and Mills sample was balanced between the years. There were 144 enumerators from 1881, with no other sampled year containing more than 90 enumerators, and only 35 and 34 from 1841, and 1891 respectively. This current work looks at a single sub-district, but addresses each census year up to 1901.

Adding together the number of enumeration districts in Winchester at each census gives a total of 141, of which 118 were ordinary (i.e. non-institutional) districts and 23 were institutional. In 1841, Thomas Lister expected enumerators to cover ordinary households, and the principal officer of an institution to be treated as the enumerator for each establishment, with the responsibility for signing off that work.[53] From 1851, only institutions above a certain size were given institutional books, smaller ones being treated as part of the ordinary district and covered by the enumerator working on the surrounding households. Uniquely, the 1841 census saw 12 institutional returns completed and

[43] W. Harwood, *Chaps and Maps. St Ives and the Census* (Stockton on Tees: Ella Publications, 1995), 9.

[44] The figure of *c.*35,000 could be taken to mean 'local officers' which included registrars and superintendent registrars, and by this count there were just over 35,000 in total. See *1841 Census Report*, 1 and 38. The number of enumeration books was noted in "A History of the 1841 Census," TNA RG27/1, 42 and 77. The expenses, taken from the 1851 account, noted that 'the payments to local officers for the year 1841 were made from the poor rate, and the amounts stated here have been obtained from returns furnished by the clerks to the several Boards of Guardians'. See *Parliamentary Papers*, 1854 XXXIX.333 [442], Return of expenses for census of Great Britain, 1841 and 1851, 1.

[45] See *Parliamentary Papers*, 1851 XLIII.73 [1399] Census of Great Britain, 1851 Census Report: Tables of Population and houses, iii; *Parliamentary Papers*, 1852–53 LXXXV.1 [1631], 1851 Census Report: Population Tables, I, xi and xviii; *Parliamentary* Papers, 1854 XXXIX.333 [442], Return of expenses for census of Great Britain, 1841 and 1851, 1.

[46] *Parliamentary Papers*, 1863 LIII [C.3221], 1861 Census General Report, 2 and 3; *Parliamentary Papers* 1863, XXIX.249 [544], Return of expenses of Census of England and Wales in 1861, 1.

[47] The General Report stated 32,543 enumerators were employed as well as its appendix noting that there were 31,916 enumeration districts and 627 institutions (totalling the same as the number of enumerators). The Preliminary Report, however, had previously given the figure as 32,606 and the expenses for the census differed from the Preliminary Report by a single person, at 32,605. As the General Report was published later it may well be that this reflected the number of individuals who undertook the role, rather than the number payments made, which was quoted in the other two sources. *Parliamentary Papers*, 1871 LIX.659 [C.381], 1871 Census Preliminary Report i.; *Parliamentary Papers*, 1873 LXXI [C.872–I], 1871 Census General Report, x and 169; *Parliamentary Papers*, 1875 XLII.155 [377], Expenses incurred in taking census in 1871, 2.

[48] *Parliamentary* Papers, 1883 LXXX.583 [C.3797], 1881 Census General Report, 3.

[49] Drake and Mills, "A note on Census Enumerators," 3.

[50] *Parliamentary Papers*, 1893–94 CVI.629, [C.7222], 1891 Census General Report, 1–2. The number of sub-districts at the time of the census, differed from the number at the time of the report (2,110), as noted on page 2 of that report; *Parliamentary Papers*, 1901 XC.1, 1901 Census Preliminary report, v, x. The number of sub-districts was stated in the final General Report for 1901, 14.

[51] D. Butler, *Durham City: The 1851 Census* (Durham: Durham Historical Enterprises, 1992), 5, names the enumerators at the head of each district but gives no other details. N. Goose, *Population Economy and family structure in Hertfordshire in 1851. Volume 1: The Berkhamstead region* (Hatfield: University of Hertfordshire Press, 1996) and *Volume 2: St Albans and its region* Hatfield: University of Hertfordshire Press, 2000) do not include enumerators' names in the transcription. The same is also true of the CD-ROM produced by Southampton Special Collections Library, *Southampton 1871 Census* (Southampton: Southampton City Council, 2004). Other works on enumerators include M. Drake, "A note on the enumerators," *Local Population Studies Society Newsletter*, 14 (1994): 12–15; B. Woollings, "An Orsett Census Enumerator," *Local Population* Studies, 56 (1996): 54–9; Wildsmith, "Witney," 3–5; W. Harwood, *Callington and the Census* (Stockton on Tees: Ellar Publications, 1998), 8–13; W. Harwood, *Chaps and Maps*, 9–13. See also Mills and Schürer, *Local Communities*, 22–23.

[52] T. Arkell, "Identifying Census Enumerators. Cornwall in 1851," *Local Population Studies*, 53 (1994): 70–75, reprinted in Mills and Schürer *Local Communities*, 36–41; Drake and Mills, "A Note on Census Enumerators," 3–9. Kidderminster, Droitwich and Worcester were the only places examined that were larger than small market towns. They were included for 1881 only, and, overall, more enumerators from 1881 (144) were analysed compared to other years. The next highest total was 86, in 1851.

[53] TNA RG27/1, 7.

Table 17.1: Number of local officers at the taking of each census, 1841–1901

	1841	1851	1861	1871	1881	1891	1901
Enumerators	32,353	30,610	31,144	32,543	34,711	35,507	38,200
Registrars	2,184	2,190	2,191	2,196	2,175	2,122	2,064
Superintendents	622	624	631	627	630	633	635
Total	35,159	33,424	33,966	35,366	37,516	38,262	40,899

noted in the published report for Winchester, but only four were completed in institutional books, and most were very small. Cheyney Court Prison, for example, only contained three people. Thereafter, Winchester had four institutions which sometimes qualified for an institutional book: the barracks, the county hospital, the county gaol and the workhouse. All four were completed in institutional CEBs in 1841, 1891 and 1901, with just the gaol and barracks treated in that fashion in 1851, 1871 and 1881. In 1861, all except the hospital completed institutional CEBs.

The 18 institutional books were completed by 13 different heads of the institutions over time. They were compelled to enumerate, and it is clear that many, especially in the barracks, simply delegated this duty to others and signed off the completed book, as the CEBs contain various different hands. Sometimes names and ages were completed in one hand, and additional details like birthplaces were completed in another. Whilst it is probable that some principal officers, like the Master of the workhouse, did complete the CEB, due to his access to the admission registers containing nominal information, for others it is less likely.[54] The barracks in 1841, for example, was signed off by Lieut. Col. Charles Wellesley, but it is unlikely that the Duke of Wellington's younger son completed the details for each soldier in the barracks personally. The same is undoubtedly true for Colonels Arthur Wombwell and William Moberley, who signed off the barracks CEBs in 1881 and 1901, respectively, but were not in the barracks on census night.[55] In 1871 it is clear from the several different hands that more than one person completed the CEBs of the barracks, yet a rather lowly soldier, 22 year old Harry Croxford, signed the CEBs as the 'Sergeant for Enumerator'. The governor of the gaol and the chief surgeon of the hospital signed off the CEBs for these places at each enumeration.[56]

The number of non-institutional districts varied. In 1851 and 1891 the city had only 15 enumeration districts: in 1841, 1861 and 1871 there were 17 districts; 18 in 1901, and 19 in 1881. The basis of each district was the civil parish, but the detail of census organisation in the city is more complex. The majority of enumeration districts equated directly to parishes.[57] Some sparsely populated parishes were paired together in a single enumeration district, those most commonly found together being St Lawrence and St Swithun.[58] Although small parishes geographically, each with small populations and in the city centre, they were not adjacent. Other larger parishes, like St Faith, were split into two or three districts. Both St Thomas and St Maurice, located in the city centre, were variously divided into two districts (1841, 1851, 1891, and 1901) or three (1861–1881). Other parishes were originally single districts (for example Weeke and St Bartholomew, Hyde) but later, as their suburban population increased they were split into two districts. Still other districts like Chilcomb were only partly within the city's boundary and were combined with other places outside its limits to form enumeration districts of sufficient size.[59] In such cases the whole district is analysed here, as this is what the enumerator was asked to work on. By the time of the 1901 census some of these parishes, like Weeke and St Faith, had been divided into 'Within' and 'Without' parishes, not just for census purposes. In addition to these issues a number of extra parochial areas in the city were enumerated alongside parishes they were geographically surrounded by or adjacent to. [60] The proliferation of such areas, alongside the infancy of the civil registration system, accounted for the relative complexity of the 1841 census results compared to those of later ones. The 1891 CEBs for Winchester also show considerable additions in red ink, clearly some years later, which indicates where individual properties that were outside the municipal boundary in 1891 had been added to the city by a boundary change in 1900. By 1911 many of these complications had been resolved by the formation of a single parish for the city of

[54] It was Joseph Steel in 1841, John Haysman in 1891 and Charles Deller in 1901.

[55] Wombwell was in Southgate St and Moberley in Clifton Road.

[56] The gaol's governor at successive censuses was William Barber, Henry Barber (in 1851 and 1861), Charles West Hill (until 1891) and Frank Lodge, in 1901. The hospital was signed off by Arthur Paul in 1841, Thomas Langdon in 1861, Harry Tuppen in 1891 and Drummond Ferguson in 1901.

[57] Examples include St Peter Colebrook, St Peter Chesil, St Michael and St Mary Kalendar (except 1841, where St Mary Kalendar was paired with the smaller parish of St Lawrence).

[58] St Swithun and St Lawrence were paired at each census between 1861 and 1881, with a small extra parochial area known as the Vill of Milland included in the district as well in 1891 and 1901. In both 1841 and 1851 St Swithun was paired with the Cathedral Close, and St Lawrence was paired with the Cathedral Yard in 1841 and the much more populous parish of St Mary Kalendar in 1851.

[59] In the case of Chilcomb there was always a part of the parish which was outside the city, but the enumeration district also included the village of Morested and a small place known as 'no man's land'.

[60] Examples include the Cathedral Close, as well as a number of alms houses or organisations providing help for the needy. For example, Bishop Morley College, Christ's Hospital, St Cross Hospital and St John's Hospital.

Winchester.

Looking at non-institutional districts, all Winchester enumerators were men.[61] The name of each was recorded in the preliminary information, and this survives in all but three cases.[62] A comparison of names, signatures and handwriting in each CEB indicates 118 districts being enumerated by 89 individuals, of whom 61 (68 per cent) only acted as enumerator for one census. Most enumerators have been identified. Sometimes this was straightforward, as in the case of Robert Hayles in 1851, who signed the front page of his CEB and put his age, occupation and address underneath. It was assumed that the enumerator lived in the sub-district, a process followed by Wildsmith, meaning that large numbers of enumerators were identified as they were the only adult of that name in the area.[63]

Some 12 enumerators cannot yet be positively identified. Two relate to districts where their names do not survive, and four districts were enumerated by William and Harry Gaiger. There is more than one person of each of those names who would have been able to enumerate, and identification has not been assumed. William Gaiger, for example, enumerated in 1851 and 1871 because his signature is the same. Yet there were three William Gaigers in the city at both censuses. One can be excluded as he was aged only nine in 1851. The others were, respectively, a 29 year old cellarman and a schoolteacher aged 40 in 1851. The schoolteacher is most likely, especially as his 1877 obituary noted his long association with St Thomas parish (where this man was an enumerator), that he had been an assistant overseer and that his son, William Charles Gaiger, was also an enumerator.[64] He also had a brother, named Henry, but whilst it is tempting to identify both men – and some of the others so far unidentified – by such circumstantial evidence, further investigation of other documentary evidence is necessary. The remaining men, though, provide a good idea of what a Winchester enumerator would be expected to be like.

A considerable body of men (24) enumerated in the city more than once, demonstrating satisfaction with their performance.[65] The most frequent enumerator was Charles Johnson, who enumerated St Peter Colebrook parish in 1871, then St Mary Kalendar parish in 1881, 1891 and 1901. Three other men enumerated on three occasions: James Masters (St John parish in 1841, 1851 and 1861); Samuel Ventham (one of the St Maurice districts in 1851, 1861 and 1871) and Harry Humby Bailey (the district containing St Michael and the Vill of Milland in 1881, plus part of St Thomas in 1891 and 1901). Bailey and Johnson each only enumerated a district they lived in once (both in 1891), but Masters and Ventham always enumerated the parish they lived in, although on one occasion Ventham was actually enumerating a different part of the parish he inhabited. Overall, enumerators were to be found living in their district of enumeration 60 per cent of the time, but a clear pattern emerges over time. While Charles Mayo was registrar, enumerators worked in the districts they lived in for 79 per cent, 73 per cent and 60 per cent of the time, at successive censuses. Under William Etheridge this figure fell to 24 per cent, six per cent and 40 per cent of the time. However, at Frank Spire's appointment as registrar in 1901, nobody lived in the district they enumerated, perhaps indicating difficulties finding enumerators across the city. When widening this out to examine just the parish of enumeration rather than the specific district within the parish, the figures are higher. However, there is still a general decline from almost 86 per cent of enumerators living in the parish they enumerated in 1841 to only 22 per cent doing so in 1901. The 1881 census saw particular difficulties in this regard, with only 16.7 per cent of enumerators living in the parish they enumerated.

As shown in Figure 17.1, Winchester's youngest enumerator was 16 years old, and the oldest two were James Burnage, who, aged 72 enumerated Weeke parish in 1901, and Charles Coles aged 70, who enumerated the small district of St Lawrence and St Swithun in 1871. The mean age of enumerators was 40.82 years, or 41.08 years excluding those who completed institutional CEBs. This is around two years younger than the mean age of Drake and Mills's sample but it remains 'solidly middle aged'.[66]

Unlike Drake and Mills, there is no discernible peak in the frequency of ages ending 0 or 5, excepting the six enumerators aged 40, indicating that rounding up of ages was less pronounced and that Winchester enumerators were probably more aware of their precise age than those elsewhere. Overall, 28 per cent of enumerators were in their thirties, with just under 30 per cent in their forties. It is, though, notable that just under a quarter of enumerators were over 50 years old at each census.

According to the available evidence, there were usually between three and five enumerators at each census with previous experience of the role in Winchester. It is not a surprise, therefore, that these people had a higher average age, and that a larger number of new enumerators were younger. The mean average age was 38, but this was especially low for new enumerators in the first three

[61] Whilst there are no obvious signs that women were directly involved in enumerating Winchester's Victorian population there have been occasions elsewhere. See S. Lumas, "Women Enumerators," *Local Population Studies Society Newsletter*, 14 (1994): 3–5. It is possible that some of the unidentified handwriting, where more than one person completed a CEB, could have belonged to women.

[62] In 1841 the Winnall CEB has not survived; there is no signature in the barracks in 1851; St Peter Chesil's preliminary pages have not survived in 1881. Even in this last case, a comparison of the handwriting indicates it's at least possible that the 1881 enumerator was William Masters, the same man who enumerated the district in 1871 who is still resident in the parish at the later enumeration.

[63] Wildsmith, "Witney," 3.

[64] *Hampshire Advertiser*, 22 December 1877, 6.

[65] A further four institutional districts were enumerated by the same man more than once. One, the county gaol, was enumerated by Charles West Hill three times, between 1871 and 1891. The younger Wellington signed off two barracks districts, but both were in 1841.

[66] Drake and Mills, "A note on Census Enumerators," 4.

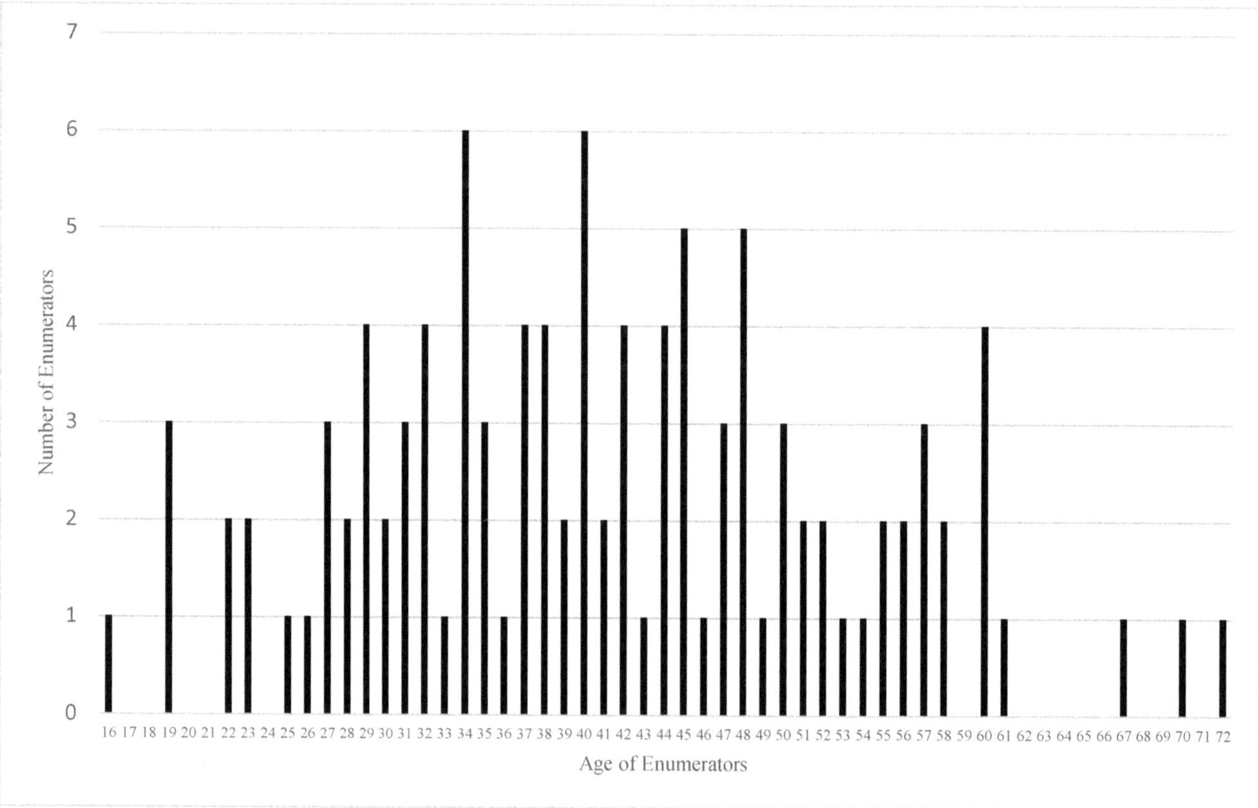

Figure 17.1: Age of Winchester Enumerators, 1841–1901

censuses (excluding 1841, where all enumerators were new), whose average ages were 34.8, 35.7 and 33 years, respectively. The two exceptional censuses regarding enumerators were 1881 – when only three enumerators from previous years were used (and so there was a higher average age) – and 1901, when there was an even split (nine each) between new and experienced Winchester enumerators.

The other notable feature of Winchester enumerators across districts and across time is the extent to which family involvement is traceable. Samuel Ventham's family is a case in point. The Venthams were a respected family of umbrella makers in Winchester, of which no fewer than five can be traced as enumerators at various points in nineteenth-century Winchester. As already noted, Samuel enumerated three times. His brother, Edward, enumerated the neighbouring district to Samuel's in St Maurice parish in 1851 (actually the one where Samuel lived) and part of St Faith parish in 1861. Samuel's son, Samuel Robert Ventham also enumerated in St Maurice parish in 1871, next to his father, and Edward's son Henry A.W. Ventham was an enumerator in St Faith parish in 1881. Finally, Edward's other son, Edward Selwyn Ventham, is clearly shown by name as the enumerator for St Peter Colebrook parish in 1861.[67]

This last example, however, throws up a conundrum, possibly revealing Winchester's youngest enumerator, at 16 years of age. Edward Selwyn Ventham was not enumerated in Winchester, or anywhere else by name, in 1861, despite being listed as an enumerator in the city. He is difficult to trace. In 1851, he is found as a son of Edward Ventham, aged six and born in Winchester.[68] This would have made him 16 in 1861 – theoretically too young to enumerate. When he died in 1864, aged only 19, he was specifically noted as the 'eldest son of Mr E Ventham' in the local newspaper, and this detail is noted in the consecrated (i.e. Anglican) burial register for West Hill cemetery.[69] There is, though, no civil birth or baptismal record for Edward Selwyn in or around 1845, either in Winchester or anywhere else in the UK. The closest is an Edward Selwyn Ventham, baptised in St John's church in Winchester on 28 June 1838, some seven years earlier. This would make him 23 years of age when he enumerated, but in 1841 there is a burial (in non-Anglican ground) in the West Hill cemetery for a child of this name, aged three years and ten months, indicating a birth of May 1837, about a month before civil registration began.[70] So, while it is perfectly possible that Edward Selwyn Ventham was aged 16 in 1861, there must be some doubt to his precise age.

67 TNA RG9/693 fos 1 and 3v.

68 TNA HO107/1674 fo.414.

69 *Hampshire Chronicle*, 9 April 1864, 4 and 5, and 16 April, 4. Burial Register: HRO W/J3/2, 202, no. 4267.

70 Ancestry.com. *England, Select Births and Christenings, 1538–1975* [database on-line]. Provo, UT, USA: Ancestry.com Operations, Inc., 2014. Burial: HRO W/J3/6, 1.

A sixth Ventham, John, the first superintendent registrar, is possibly also related, but a direct family line has not yet been traced. Yet William Etheridge, Winchester's second registrar, was definitely related to two other enumerators. His brother, George, enumerated St Bartholomew Hyde parish in 1901, and another William Etheridge, the uncle of both men, enumerated Winnall parish in 1851 and 1861. Other families involved in enumerating Winchester's census include the father and son both named John Castell, who worked on St Bartholomew Hyde parish. The father completed the book in 1841 and 1851, as did the son in 1861 – a month after his father's death – and 1881. James Masters, enumerated St John parish between 1841 and 1861 and his nephew, William Masters, enumerated the neighbouring parish of St Peter Chesil in 1861 and 1871. The son of the four-time enumerator Charles Johnson, Alfred, enumerated in 1891 and 1901, and, indeed, the handwriting of the father's book in 1901 looks suspiciously like his son's ten years earlier, so it is possible that the work between father and son was shared. Finally, the Gaiger family was also heavily involved in enumeration. William Charles Gaiger enumerated part of St Thomas parish in 1861 and 1871, and his father, William, although not absolutely identified as enumerator, is the most likely candidate of the William Gaigers to have enumerated other parts of St Thomas in 1851 and 1871. In addition, one of the Henry Gaigers most likely to have been the enumerator in St Mary Kalendar in 1851 and 1861 was the brother of William.

According to Drake and Mills, 'occupation provides a clue to the effectiveness of the enumerator', but they go on to say that they are 'notoriously difficult to handle'.[71] While bearing this in mind, it is still useful to get an idea of what occupations Winchester enumerators followed. Table 17.2 indicates the occupations most frequently returned by Winchester's enumerators.

These eight occupational groups account for almost two thirds of enumerators' occupations in Winchester. While those working as collectors or relieving officers provide a network where the registrar could easily find potential enumerators, and clerks, accountants and solicitors are also among a social group who were expected to be both capable and diligent. However, the group of tradesmen needs further explanation. It was diverse, containing a blacksmith, cooper, cordwainer, three tailors, an umbrella maker and a woolstapler, among others. These occupations clearly describe part of what these people did, but many of them hide other networks and roles. For example, the Sexton William Dyer who kept the records of the cemetery company, is the woolstapler, and the gardener, John Castell, actually spent many years as a relieving officer in Winchester – an occupation he chose not to list in 1851.[72]

Corrections and Errors in Winchester CEBs

The overall job that enumerators did in Winchester can be addressed by examining the differences in housing and population totals between the preliminary and final census statistics, which is shown in Table 17.3. To produce the preliminary report, registrars were asked to summarise the totals given in the CEBs after they had corrected them, and these were then forwarded to London to produce the preliminary statistics before abstraction took place. For Winchester, there is only published information on the municipal borough from 1861 onwards.

Table 17.2: Occupations followed by Census Enumerators, 1841–1901, as indicated in CEBs.

Occupation	Number
Rate Collector, Overseer or Relieving Officer	16
Various Tradesmen	15
Clerks in Civil Service	12
Accountant or their clerks	11
Solicitor or solicitor's clerk	10
Other Clerks	7
Publican or Brewer	7
Building Trades	5

Table 17.3: Preliminary and Final Population of Winchester Municipal Borough, 1861–1911.

		Houses	People
1861	Prelim	2385	14784
	Final	2392	14776
	Difference	-7	8
1871	Prelim	2718	14705
	Final	2720	16366
	Difference	-2	-1661
1881	Prelim	2996	17469
	Final	2990	17780
	Difference	6	-311
1891	Prelim	3307	19073
	Final	3305	19073
	Difference	2	0
1901	Prelim	4015	20919
	Final	4017	20929
	Difference	-2	-10
1911	Prelim		23380
	Final	4577	23378
	Difference		2

[71] Drake and Mills, "A Note on Census Enumerators," 7.
[72] *Hampshire Chronicle*, 23 March 1861, 5, col. 3.

The major differences were the 1871 and 1881 populations; respectively 1,661 and 311 fewer in the preliminary reports compared to the final total. The preliminary pages of the 1871 CEBs do not show how that total came to be so different, and it seems likely that there was an error in the figures sent to London by the registrar. The initial count of 14,705 was certainly a mistake, being a slight reduction in the population from 1861 when the number of houses in the city increased by over 300. The difference of 311 in the 1881 population is also not obvious from the corrections made to the CEBs during abstraction. It seems most likely that this was due to an error by the registrar in adding the total in Winchester barracks. It was covered by two enumeration books, with 312 people in one of them, and it seems likely that the registrar only included one book for the barracks in his total. Beyond this, the greatest difference lay in seven houses too few and eight individuals too many being counted in the preliminary report of 1861. So, the enumerators in Winchester seem to have done a fair job. For the 1841 and 1851 censuses, comparisons only exist between the initial and final reports at the level of the registration district. Similar results can be gleaned here, with just three inhabited houses missing from the preliminary observations in 1841, and one in 1851, from over 4,000 dwellings. In 1841 the population totals match precisely, although the number of males and females are different by eight between the two reports (too many females and too few males in the preliminary observations). The differences for 1851 are more marked between males and females, where overall the population differs by just three individuals, but 111 individuals in the preliminary report were listed as female – corrected to males by the time of the final report.

Ultimately, though, the CEBs give the best indication of how successfully the enumerators' carried out their tasks. This analysis of the text will be divided into three parts. At the start of each book (except in 1841 where they appeared at the end) were some summary pages, completed by the enumerator or registrar, giving overall totals for the number of schedules, houses and people in the district. A second part, which appeared in every census, was what became known as the abstract of totals for each page, listing the same information about houses and people, but for each page. Then, the detail of the CEBs themselves forms the third part of this analysis. As the 1841 books were of a different format, these are dealt with first.

Enumerators were asked, up to and including 1881, how many people were either temporarily present or absent from the district, and also (in 1841 and 1851) whether they slept in barges, tents, caravans or other temporary accommodation. In 1841, only two enumerators completed this, with one person noted as inhabiting a barn in Weeke, while one enumerator wrote that upon enquiry nobody was temporarily present or absent. Ten years later only three enumerators entered this information, with 40 people temporarily present and 11 absent in St Maurice parish, 17 temporarily present and five absent in St Peter Colebrook, and three temporarily absent in St Peter Chesil. In 1861, 12 districts completed this return and only five left it completely blank, with 87 people in total known to be temporarily absent and 47 temporarily present. In 1871 only, information was required also on the number of schedules the enumerators completed for householders unable to do so themselves. This has previously been analysed, but six enumerators did not bother to complete this information at all.[73] The 1881 census saw only five districts note this information, with only 37 people temporarily present (23 in one district – St Faith, by Henry Ventham) and nine individuals temporarily absent. Overall, therefore, this summary information was only occasionally completed.

The 1881 summary page allowed for either the registrar or a clerk in London to add other information relating to smaller institutions not completing their own institutional CEBs. So, for example, some almshouses, female refuges, schools and lodging houses were listed at this point. It was not comprehensive, however, as the Diocesan Training College (now the University of Winchester) was clearly enumerated but is missing from the list of places of note.[74]

The last two censuses with CEBs removed information on those temporarily absent or present, in favour of more information on the number of houses and people in each civil parish wholly or partly making up the district, to be completed by the enumerator. The same information for a variety of subdivisions above the level of the civil parish was to be completed by the registrar. In 1891 only two enumerators – Samuel Russell in St Faith and Edwin Snook in St Peter Colebrook and Winnall – got all the totals in their districts correct. Three others made only a single small error: Philip Yates in St Thomas added up the number of men in the district erroneously, Edwin Tubb added his schedules up wrongly in St Maurice and George Stillman counted 138 properties with fewer than five rooms rather than the correct total of 137. The registrar only got all his totals correct in five out of 15 non-institutional districts. In 1901, four enumerators' summaries and five registrar's summaries were correct, plus all the institutional ones and a further five enumerators' summaries only had errors in one section of the summary.

The abstract of information on a page-by-page basis was the only summary information found in the CEBs for every year. In 1841, 15 books were entirely correct with no crossings out, although many were institutions with very small populations. Indeed, institutional books contain the most error-free abstraction of totals at subsequent censuses. The abstract of totals for the County Gaol was perfect at every census, as were those for the hospital and barracks in 1861, the workhouse in 1891 and the barracks, hospital and workhouse in 1901.

For non-institutional books abstracts of totals were less likely to be completed without crossings out – often the

[73] Allen and James, "Introduction," 19–20.
[74] TNA RG11/1231 fo. 38.

result of corrections made during the abstraction process where male ages had been spotted in the female column in CEBs, or vice versa. In 1851, a clerk named Charles Badcock checked and signed many Winchester CEBs, noting the number of what he termed 'errors' found, with the result that every non-institutional book had some crossings out, something which also occurred in 1891. In 1861, Edward Ventham in St Faith was the only enumerator to complete his abstract of totals without an error; in 1881 abstracts of totals pages were completed in an exemplary fashion in four books, rising to five in 1901.

The vast majority of CEBs only had a few crossings out in the abstract of totals, as was the case in 13 districts in 1851. But the exceptions showed poor understanding or carelessness. On four occasions in 1851 the abstract of totals pages looked rather messy due to multiple crossings out. The book, signed by Robert Hayles, contained 15 errors, the part of St Thomas parish enumerated by John Norris had 18, Samuel Ventham's district had 29 and William Heward's district contained summary errors on every page, largely down to him erroneously entering the total population in the column for the number of inhabited houses. He appears to have corrected these errors himself, but another 34 mistakes corrected later in red ink leave this summary page looking rather untidy. Whilst Norris enumerated again in 1861, and Ventham in both 1861 and 1871, neither Hayles nor Heward did so.

There are a number of examples of enumerators not understanding what was required in this part of the CEB. This was something Dobraszczyk found as early as 1801 in London with an overseer, John Puckle, who did not quite follow the prescribed form.[75] In 1861, George Phillips's book for St Maurice parish saw him keep a running total of the number of schedules per page, rather than for the number of schedules on each page. So, instead of page 29, the last in the book, showing the four schedules copied into the CEB on that page, it originally showed 188, the number of schedules the whole book contained.

By 1881, the book completed by Henry Ventham saw this page entirely re-written with a new, error-free abstract of totals pasted over the top of what must have been something containing errors. Indeed, this book had a larger number of changes than average made by both the enumerator and other hands. For example, the prison governor and his family were erroneously included, before being crossed out in red ink by a different hand, despite the fact that they were also enumerated in the gaol.[76]

In 1891, for the first time, it is possible to see errors going uncorrected despite being spotted. Two examples where an age had been entered into the wrong column which should have resulted in a correction to the number of males and females at the bottom of the page or in the summary tables for Weeke parish, and a similar change that was recorded on the page in St Maurice parish, but went uncorrected in the abstract of totals.[77] In 1901, perhaps the most error-strewn was George Berry's abstract of totals. Every one of the total number of schedules on the first 26 pages was crossed out because Berry had mistakenly entered the totals for inhabited houses in that column.[78] Errors in this part of the CEBs, though, are largely mistranscriptions, rather than mathematical errors, as postulated by Drake and Mills.[79]

The third section of analysis here relates to the main part of the CEBs. The 1841 CEBs are perhaps best dealt with separately due to excessive crossings out caused by sections being physically excised from one book and added to another, with an entirely different hand re-writing partially completed pages. This was presumably done in London, as all abstraction occurred there. Interventions in a different hand in 1841 were largely confined to occupations like 'wife', 'pauper' or 'gent' being crossed out, usually with a red pen. In St Bartholomew Hyde, entries were completed in pencil in the main, with the addresses added in ink.[80] Only very rarely did changes occur to the substantive text in the CEB. An example of this was in St Maurice parish, where two occupations of 'Hatter' and one 'Butcher' are in ink, overlaying pencil text underneath.[81] It is uncertain whether this was merely an attempt to make an unclear occupation more visible, or to make a correction. The only clear evidence of a change made was for St John's Hospital, where Sussannah Andrews's entry gave her age as 59, later changed, in a different hand, to 60.[82] While it was possible that this was done to round the age up to 60, the evidence suggests this was not normal practice. Indeed, on the same page Sarah Smith's entry remained as 59, so it is possible that Andrews's age was changed by someone with access to the original householder's schedule.

Aside from additions made to occupations in order to aid classification, the largest number of interventions across all the Winchester CEBs is seen in the age column, usually where women's ages were inserted in the male column, or *vice versa* (Table 17.4).

Although there remained a large number of corrections to be made to ages, in the later censuses the enumerators themselves spotted and corrected many of their errors, with far fewer remaining to be picked up by registrars and London-based clerks. So, by 1881 only 39 per cent of ages that were corrected in some way were changed by anyone other than the enumerator, falling to 24 per cent in 1891 and 19 per cent by 1901. This was despite it being clear by 1881 that more than one person checked the ages, with

[75] Paul Dobraszczyk, "'Give in your account': Using and Abusing Victorian Census Forms," *Journal of Victorian Culture*, 14.1 (2009): 6–11.

[76] TNA RG11/1231 fo.40.

[77] TNA RG12/936 fo. 65v and RG12/937 fos. 88v. and 64. Entries for William Warren and Charles Griffin.

[78] TNA RG13/1081 fo. 4

[79] Drake and Mills, "A note on the Census Enumerators," 4–5.

[80] TNA HO 107/410/1 and 2.

[81] TNA HO 107/409/6, 12 and 40.

[82] TNA HO 107/409/8, fo.3

Table 17.4: Age corrections in Winchester CEBs, 1841–1901

Year	By Different Hand	Corrected by enumerator	Total
1841	29	6	35
1851	96	50	146
1861	43	50	93
1881	86	134	220
1891	68	210	278
1901	39	205	244

some corrections in red and others in either blue or black, even on the same page.

The other age-related correction that became less common was the number of unknown ages appearing in CEBs. In 1851, ages originally given as unknown were changed to specific ages on 22 occasions. In all but five instances, these were ages ending in '0' or '5' so were probably approximations. Such approximations continued, as in 1891 where William Kelly, an Irish general labourer whose stated age was originally 'between 60 & 70' became a 65 year old.[83] By 1901 there are only a handful of examples, with unknown ages far more likely to be akin to the case of two steamroller labourers listed as 'about 20' and 'about 30'. Neither their Christian name, marital status nor birthplace was known either, so that the men themselves were probably no longer around to give this information when the enumerator called.[84] Only occasionally can factual errors be spotted, as with one example where an entire page of boys in the Industrial School appeared in the female column, and one occasion where the age of an apparently 115 year old child, living with her parents, was corrected in a different hand to 15.[85]

There was a clear change in policy over how to deal with other information after 1881. Before this time, changes were occasionally made to occupations or birthplaces which could only have come from consultation with household schedules, but amendments to these two pieces of information or, indeed, marital statuses, was rare. Birthplace changes, for example, usually related to London-born people stating Middlesex or Surrey as their county of birth when the place was in the other county. These changes would be found on no more than around a dozen occasions at each enumeration before 1891. From 1891, corrections to the county of birth in another hand become far more frequent, as do tweaks made to occupations. Counties of birth were being checked far more carefully. St Bartholomew Hyde parish, which was covered in two districts, saw 21 interventions, all relating to counties of birth distant from Hampshire or other countries/continents, like Turkey, Australia or West Africa. In 1901, the new question from 1891 about the nature of employment was tweaked, so people had to state whether they were employers, workers or working on their own account. Large numbers of people did not complete this particular column, so a substantial number of interventions are of the type 'W' or 'O', or even 'Own' to signify classifications as to the person's occupational status. The two districts that made up St Thomas parish, for example, saw around 72 such interventions, and this was fairly typical.

Despite these issues, the enumerators in Winchester were clearly carrying out their duties with care and when errors were made, they were often contrite. In Chilcomb in 1901, an extra slip of blue paper was glued to one of the CEB pages and a family's details attached accompanied by a note from the enumerator stating, 'This part of No.5 Schedule was, by mistake, entered under the wrong headings, for which the enumerator is very sorry'.[86]

Handwriting was always legible, even though three enumerators in particular had scruffy scripts. Both the 1861 CEB for Frederick Holdaway and Walter Lovelock's short book in Weeke parish in 1881, although perfectly legible, contained many minor ink blots and crossings out on several pages. In 1891, William Futcher, in St Maurice, habitually left a blank line between households, but possibly also entered the details column-by-column, since on the third page of his book birthplaces slipped one line out of alignment, and the abstractor was forced add an extra mark to each birthplace to make clear which entry each stated birthplace belonged to. Futcher, a school attendance officer aged only 28, had possibly the most difficult handwriting to decipher in the whole set of books for Winchester and it is perhaps fortunate that ten years later he appears not to have been in Winchester.

There were also enumerators who misunderstood elements of their role, especially relating to the question of schedule numbers, what they were and when to assign new ones to a group of people. William Etheridge in Winnall neglected to list any schedule numbers in his book for Winnall in 1851, and ten years later he had problems understanding the numbering of schedules again, especially relating to lodgers in houses, so only the first five pages contain uncorrected schedule numbers. The 1861 CEB of James Masters in St John also saw him make some errors in the numbering of his schedules. Neither Frank Small, in St Peter Chesil in 1891, nor George Berry in St John ten years later understood that uninhabited houses should not receive schedule numbers. Eight pages of Small's 28-page book and seven of Berry's had to be corrected.[87] The 1881 book by Sydney Tuthill also displayed difficulty with schedule numbering.[88] He was particularly prone to counting the first line of each page as a new household,

[83] TNA RG12/938 fo. 26v.
[84] TNA RG13/1082 fo. 50.
[85] TNA RG12/937 fo.13; RG13/1083 fo. 56. Entry for Alice Rogers.
[86] TNA RG13/1083 fo. 66v. and 67.
[87] TNA RG13/1081 fos. 8–11.
[88] TNA RG11/1231 fos. 62–69v., 134–155v., especially fo. 135.

even if it was a continuation of a family group from the previous page, doing this on 17 occasions in his book. Wilson Lomer, in St John parish, attempted to avoid this by starting each page with a new household, but the unfortunate consequence was that while some pages had one or two blank lines at their end, he crammed two or even three extra entries, on five occasions, at the end of other pages.[89]

Enumerators were also allowed assistants to help them and there is some evidence of this, to varying degrees, in Winchester. In 1861, Henry Gaiger's district of St Mary Kalendar contains one household, that of the county magistrate, Robert Rawlins, written in the hand of William Gaiger, who enumerated part of St Thomas parish, strengthening the case for these two men being the Gaiger brothers, as opposed to others of that name mentioned earlier. It is likely that these Gaigers were brothers, and they clearly did some work together.[90] Edward Williams's 1881 district in Weeke contains two entries at the end in a different hand; ironically one of these entries belongs to the household of Sydney Tuthill, another enumerator.[91] The first page of Charles Tanner's book in the same year was also in entirely different handwriting to the rest of the book.[92] In the barracks, the entries for the Hampshire Militia in 1881 are in a different hand to the rest of the book, and the birthplaces of these individuals were largely limited to Hampshire or England, with very few specific places of birth given. James Burnage also had help in his district in 1901, with pages 1–13, 17–35 and 43 onwards in one hand, but the intervening pages in a different one.[93]

Some enumerators simply missed or repeated material. In 1901, an enumerator clearly felt he had forgotten to complete Ada Ayling's entry, adding it between two lines, not noticing he had already enumerated her further up the page. This was deleted by another hand in red ink.[94] In 1891, Alfred Johnson in St Michael seems to have neglected to total the number of houses with fewer than five rooms on many pages, although he did enumerate them individually. As a result, 12 page totals either had to be added or corrected in blue crayon, compared with only three pages correctly totalled by Johnson himself. Samuel Ventham, in 1861, did not give himself any occupation in his own district, and the term 'Rent and Rate Collector' was added in a clearly very different hand. Other enumerators were a little old fashioned, several using the archaic spelling of the word 'laborer', and one, in 1861, spelling tailor as 'taylor' throughout. Still others made rather comical errors: one house on Eastgate Street in 1861 has an unnamed head as 'lying dead', while in 1881 in what was either a joke or a momentary lack of concentration, an Italian travelling musician named 'Mark Antony' was corrected in red ink to 'Mary' in John Rodwell Carling's district of St Maurice parish.[95]

These issues do not impede our understanding of the books, however. Indeed, sometimes through the prejudices of individual enumerators we get an insight into the society in which they lived. Edward Ventham, in 1851, obviously affected by a sense of moral outrage, felt it necessary to annotate his CEB. On three occasions, he targeted unmarried female residents of beer shops. Two were in Lower Brook Street, and the other in Union Street, all working-class parts of the city. In James Gilman's beer shop lodged Jane Holdaway, Fanny Weeks, Ellen Bond and Susan Tucker. Their response when asked their occupation was transcribed as 'What a queer question to ask – and if one does, [one] is not likely to obtain the truth'. Ventham added that these women were 'On the Town' and, in case any doubt remained regarding their virtue, he added at the foot of the page that 'Two soldiers came after twelve o'clock and left before five in the morning and are believed to have returned to the Barracks in time to be enumerated with those that slept there. Names and Regt. U.K.'.[96] Similarly, in William Luckett's beer house Miriam Butterly, Betsey Stead and Martha Merritt, all servants, were listed as 'Soldiers [sic] waiting maid', Ventham adding that 'this reply was given to enumerator on enquiring for 'occupation'. This house is frequented by soldiers'.[97] Finally, in Catherine Paul's beer house, Mary Ann Cook's given occupation, 'Household Servt', was queried by Ventham, presumably because she was unmarried with a one year old child. Rosanna Goodall, listed as a household servant, had the same query mark next to her occupation and, above this, Ventham added that she was also 'On the Town'.[98] All these beer shops were unnamed in the census, but all three individuals running them had problems with the courts, either through violence or renewing licenses. Gilman was landlord of The Lamb, Luckett the Three Hearts – described as 'a beer-house of very low repute' – and Paul, the Woolpack.[99] These comments in 1851 are the only times prostitution is mentioned in Winchester's censuses, save for inhabitants of the gaol or workhouse.[100]

Finally, in 1891, Samuel Russell in St Faith provided extra information to those reading his book. At least two people were described as 'out of employ', and people with no formal disability listed are noted to have 'spinal disease', 'one leg' and 'paralysed'. Three entries missing the household heads have additions noting 'Head of H away' and 'Head Retd at St Cross Hospital', and 'Dr White [the coroner] away'.[101]

[89] TNA RG11/1233 fos. 47–70v.
[90] TNA RG9/692 fo.30v and RG9/691 fo. 67–88v.
[91] TNA RG11/1231 fos. 104v and 105.
[92] TNA RG11/1232 fo. 60.
[93] TNA RG13/1082 fos. 133–155v.
[94] TNA RG13/1082 fo. 57.
[95] TNA RG9/693 fo. 82v.
[96] TNA HO 107/1674 fo. 210.
[97] TNA HO 107/1674 fo. 225 v. One of the unmarried women, aged 22, had a four year old daughter.
[98] TNA HO 107/1674 fo. 223.
[99] *Hampshire Chronicle*, 13 October 1849, 4 col. 3.; 28 August 1852, 4, col 3; 13 October 1860, 4 col. 5.
[100] There are a few examples elsewhere. See Roger Hutchinson, *The butcher, the baker, the candlestick maker. The story of Britain through its census, since 1801* (London: Little, Brown, 2017), 111–114.
[101] TNA RG12/936 fos. 4v., 5, 5v, 8, 9v, 15, 16v, 19.

Conclusion

How well did Winchester's enumerators perform their tasks, and are there changes over time? Well, one thing is certain. The increase in population was far greater than the proportional increase in enumerators, both nationally and in Winchester. Nationally, on average, each enumerator dealt with 452 people in 1841, and 852 in 1901. This can also be seen in Winchester, where the non-military population grew from 9,889 in 1841 to 20,413 in 1901.[102] There were always between 15 and 19 non-institutional enumerators in Winchester, meaning that, on average, each enumerator dealt with a population of 549 in 1841. This went up at every enumeration, until in 1901 there were, on average, 1,021 people in each Winchester enumeration district. Yet the time allocated to complete the enumeration locally remained the same as it had been in 1841. Enumerators were instructed to have their completed CEBs and other material sent up to the local registrar within a week of receiving them, registrars got a fortnight to check them and superintendent registrars were expected to have sent the CEBs to London about a month after enumeration.[103] It is hardly surprising, therefore, that as time went on enumerators grumbled about having to do the copying. There was increased dissatisfaction with this element of their work, although this was not something noted in Winchester.

The evidence from the CEBs shows that Winchester's enumerators were generally diligent people who performed their roles well. All but four of them fell within the prescribed age range, most were men who wrote well and whilst many summary tables had issues, few of the problems appear to have centred on mathematical incompetence. While confusion could sometimes remain, the same was true with householders and their schedules, especially relating to questions on occupation, even at the end of the century.[104] They followed occupations that engendered respect, and appear to have had the goodwill of Winchester's inhabitants as instances of people not providing the required information were rare. Even then, enumerators were resourceful enough to provide information required. Whilst evidence exists for them becoming more pressured in the last two censuses of the century, this does not invalidate what they provided. As Tom and I concluded in 2006, 'all in all … the census is as detailed a snapshot of Winchester as we are likely to find. The efforts of the 'amateur' enumerators … who created the CEBs so quickly from the schedules is a magnificent testament to nineteenth-century organisational skill'.[105]

[102] Allen and James, "Introduction," 8. Winchester's military population in the barracks would skew the figures somewhat, with there being 1,485 people out of a total population of 14,776 in 1861, for example, which is just over 10 per cent of the entire population.

[103] In 1851 when an extra day was provided for enumerators to copy material, and in 1911 the time was reduced to five days, in part because the Summary Books took less time to complete than CEBs had. These deadlines are shown in the instructions for local officers at each census (RG27/1 for 1841, RG27/3 for 1861, etc.). The instructions for 1851 do not survive separately, but are reproduced in the *1851 General Report*.

[104] Dobraszczyk, "Using and Abusing," 16–17.

[105] Allen and James, "Introduction," 56.

Acknowledgements

I wish to express thanks to The National Archives, and especially David Priest, for allowing access to the original CEBs and giving permission to digitally photograph each page relating to Winchester. Thanks are also due to Professor Kevin Schürer for providing a specific article and his thoughts on enumerators. None of this could have been done without Tom James who, as supervisor, colleague and friend has been helped in more ways that I can remember over many years.

Bibliography

Published primary sources

The National Archives (TNA).

HO107/403/16 and 404/15: 1841 census, Chilcomb parish.

HO107/404/7–8: 1841 census, Weeke parish and New Winchester Union Workhouse.

HO107/409 and 410: 1841 census for City of Winchester.

HO107/1674: 1851 census, Winchester sub-district.

HO107/1675 fo. 1–16v.: 1851 census, Chilcomb and Morestead parishes.

RG9/961–963: 1861 census, Winchester sub-district.

RG9/964 fo. 90–101v.: 1861 census, Chilcomb and Morestead parishes.

RG10/1209–1212: 1871 census, Winchester sub-district.

RG10/1213 fo. 94–106: 1871 census, Chilcomb and Morestead parishes.

RG11/1231–1233: 1881 census, Winchester sub-district.

RG11/1234 fo. 98–110: 1881 census, Chilcomb and Morestead parishes.

RG12/936–938: 1891 census, Winchester sub-district.

RG13/1081–1083: 1901 census, Winchester sub-district.

RG13/1084 fo. 1–22: 1901 census, parishes of Abbots Barton, Chilcomb without, Sparsholt, Lainston and Weeke without.

RG27/1: 'A History of the 1841 Census'.

RG27/3: Forms and instructions issued for taking the 1861 Census

RG27/4: Forms and instructions issued for taking the 1871 Census

RG27/5: Forms and instructions issued for taking the 1881 Census

RG27/6: Forms and instructions issued for taking the 1891 Census

Hampshire Record Office (HRO).

Hampshire Advertiser, 1877–1879.

Hampshire Chronicle, 1849–1901

W/J3/1: West Hill Cemetery Company consecrated burials register, 1840–1854.

W/J3/2: West Hill Cemetery Company consecrated burials register, 1854–1870.

W/J3/6: West Hill Cemetery Company unconsecrated burials register, 1841–1907.

W/J3/16: West Hill Cemetery Directors' Book of Proceedings, 1840–1919.

Published Primary Sources:

British Parliamentary Papers (BPP).

Abstract of the answers and returns made pursuant to Act 3 and 4 Vict. c.99 and 4 Vict. c. 7. Enumeration Abstract. Part 1, England and Wales and Islands in the British Seas, BPP, 1843, 1.

Census of Great Britain, 1851: Tables of Population and houses in the divisions, registration counties, and districts of England and Wales; in the counties, cities, and burghs of Scotland; and in the islands in the British seas, BPP, 1851, XLII.

Population Tables Part I. Numbers of the inhabitants in the years 1801, 1811, 1821, 1831, 1841 & 1851. Vol 1. Report; objects of the census and machinery employed; results and observations; appendix of tabular results and summary tables of England and Wales. BPP, 1852–3, LXXXV.

1861 Census of England and Wales. Vol. III, General report; with appendix of tables, BPP, 1863, LIII.

Census of England and Wales, 1871, preliminary report, and tables of population and houses enumerated in England and Wales, and in islands in British seas on 3 April 1871, BPP, 1871, LIX.

Census of England and Wales 1871. General report, (Vol. IV), BPP, 1873, LXXI, pt. II.

Preliminary report and tables of population and houses for England and Wales, and in islands in the British seas on 4 April 1881, BPP, 1881, CXVI.

Census of England and Wales 1881, Vol. IV, General report and tables, BPP, 1883, LXXX.

1891 Census of England and Wales. Vol. IV, General report, with summary, tables and appendices. BPP 1893–4, CVI.

1901 Census of England and Wales. Preliminary report and tables of population and houses enumerated in England and Wales and in islands in the British seas on 31 March 1901, BPP, 1901, XC.

Census of England and Wales (63 Vict. c.4), 1901 General report (with Appendices), BPP, 1904, CVIII.

Census of England and Wales. 1911. (10 Edward VII and 1 George V, ch. 27.) General report with appendices, BPP, 1917.

Comparative statement of the expenses of the census of Great Britain in 1841 and 1851, number of persons enumerated, heads of Information comprised in enquiry, and cost per 1,000 of the population, BPP, 1854, XXXIX, 1.

Return of expenses of Census of England and Wales in 1861, number of persons enumerated, heads of information comprised in enquiry, and cost per 1,000 of the Population; with comparisons of former charges in 1841 and 1851, BPP, 1863, XXIX, 1863.

Expenses incurred in taking census in 1871 for England and Wales, Scotland and for Ireland: with comparisons of former charges in 1841, 1851, and 1861, BPP, 1875, XLII, 2.

Report of the committee appointed by the Treasury to enquire into certain questions connected with the taking of the census with evidence and appendices, and the Treasury minute appointing the committee, BPP, 1890, LVIII.

Electronic Primary Sources

Ancestry.com. *England, Select Births and Christenings, 1538–1975* [database on-line]. Provo, UT, USA: Ancestry.com Operations, Inc., 2014.

Southampton 1871 Census CD-ROM (Southampton: Southampton City Council, 2004).

Secondary Sources

Allen, Mark and Tom James, eds. *The 1871 Census for Winchester.* Winchester: Wessex Historical Databases, 2006.

Anderson, Michael. "The Study of Family Structure." In *Nineteenth-Century Society. Essays in the use of quantitative methods for the study of social* data, edited by E.A. Wrigley, 47–81. Cambridge: Cambridge University Press, 1972.

Arkell, T. "Identifying Census Enumerators. Cornwall in 1851." *Local Population Studies*, 53 (1994): 70–75.

Butler, D. *Durham City: The 1851 Census.* Durham: Durham Historical Enterprises, 1992.

Dobraszczyk, Paul. "'Give in your account': Using and Abusing Victorian Census Forms." *Journal of Victorian Culture*, 14.1 (2009): 1–25.

Drake, Michael and Dennis Mills. "A Note on Census Enumerator." *Local Population Studies Society Newsletter*, 29 (2001): 3–9.

Drake, Michael. "A note on the enumerators." *Local Population Studies Society Newsletter*, 14 (1994): 12–15.

Drake, Michael. "The census, 1801–1891." In *Nineteenth-Century Society. Essays in the use of quantitative methods for the study of social* data, edited by E.A. Wrigley, 7–46. Cambridge: Cambridge University Press, 1972.

Goose, Nigel. *Population Economy and family structure in Hertfordshire in 1851. Volume 1: The Berkhamstead region.* Hatfield: University of Hertfordshire Press, 1996.

Goose, Nigel. *Population Economy and family structure in Hertfordshire in 1851. Volume 2: St Albans and its region.* Hatfield: University of Hertfordshire Press, 2000.

Harwood, William. *Callington and the Census.* Stockton on Tees: Ellar Publications, 1998.

Harwood, William. *Chaps and Maps. St Ives and the Census.* Stockton on Tees: Ella Publications, 1995.

Higgs, Edward. "The state and statistics in Victorian and Edwardian Britain. Promotion of the public sphere or boundary maintenance." In *Statistics and the public sphere, Numbers and the people in modern Britain c.1800–2000* edited by Tom Crook and Glen O'Hara, 67–83. London: Routledge, 2011.

Higgs, Edward. *Making Sense of the Census Revisited. Census Records for England and Wales 1801–1901. A Handbook for Historical Researchers.* London: The Institute of Historical Research/The National Archives of the UK, 2005.

Edward Higgs. *Life, Death and Statistics. Civil Registration, census and the work of the General Register Office, 1836–1952.* Hatfield: Local Population Studies, 2004.

Hutchinson, Roger. *The butcher, the baker, the candlestick maker. The story of Britain through its census, since 1801.* London: Little, Brown, 2017.

Lumas, S. "Women Enumerators." *Local Population Studies Society Newsletter*, 14 (1994): 3–5.

Mills, Dennis and Kevin Schürer, eds. *Local Communities in the Victorian Census Enumerators' Books* Oxford: Leopard's Head Press/Local Population Studies, 1996.

Szreter, Simon. *Fertility, class and gender in Britain, 1860–1940.* Cambridge: Cambridge University Press, 1996.

Thorvaldsen, Gunnar. *Censuses and census takers. A global history.* London: Routledge, 2018.

Tillott, P. "Sources of inaccuracy in the 1851 and 1861 censuses." In *Nineteenth-Century Society. Essays in the use of quantitative methods for the study of social* data, edited by E.A. Wrigley, 82–133. Cambridge: Cambridge University Press, 1972.

Wildsmith, Judith. "The 1871 Census Enumerators in the Subdistrict of Witney." *Local Population Studies Society* Newsletter, 17 (1995): 3–5.

Wrigley, E.A., ed. *Nineteenth-Century Society. Essays in the use of quantitative methods for the study of social data.* Cambridge: Cambridge University Press, 1972.

Woollings, B. "An Orsett Census Enumerator." *Local Population* Studies, 56 (1996): 54–59.

18

A Bibliography of Published Works

Professor Emeritus Tom Beaumont James, MBE

University of St Andrews: MA (1971), PhD (1977)

FSA (1980); FRHistS (1986).

Current

Completing website with Jen Best for July 2021. Biographies of 459 men from the City of Winchester who gave their lives in the First World War.

Team Leader from January 2015. English Heritage/Natural England Project Design for future conservation and maintenance of Clarendon Palace, Wiltshire (funded by Natural England and Historic England).

Publications

Books: authored and edited

[with Allan L. Merson]. *The Third Book of Remembrance of Southampton 1514–1602*, vol. 4 (1590–1602). Southampton Records Series 22. Southampton: Southampton University Press, 1979.

Southampton Sources: 1086–1900, Southampton Records Series 26. Southampton: Southampton University Press, 1983.

[with Roger C. Richardson]. *The Urban Experience: a sourcebook – English, Scottish and Welsh towns, 1450–1700*. Manchester: Manchester University Press, 1983.

[with Anne M. Robinson and Elizabeth Eames]. *Clarendon Palace: the history and archaeology of a medieval palace and hunting lodge near Salisbury, Wiltshire*, Reports of the Research Committee of the Society of Antiquaries of London 45. Society of Antiquaries of London and Thames and Hudson, 1988.

Clarendon Palace. Salisbury and South Wiltshire Museum, 1988.

[with John Simons]. *The Poems of Laurence Minot 1333–1352*. Exeter: University of Exeter Press, 1989.

[with J.E. Hewitt]. *The Port Book of Southampton, 1509–10*, vol. 1, weeks 1 to 26. Southampton Records Series 32. Southampton: Southampton University Press, 1990.

[with J.E. Hewitt]. *The Port Book of Southampton 1509–10*, vol. 2 weeks 27 to 52. Southampton Records Series 33. Southampton: Southampton University Press, 1990.

The Palaces of Medieval England c.1050–1550: royalty, nobility, the episcopate and their residences from Edward the Confessor to Henry VIII. London: Seaby, 1990.

[with Martin Doughty]. *King Alfred's College, Winchester: a pictorial record*. Winchester: King Alfred's College with Alan Sutton, 1991.

Winchester: a pictorial history. Chichester: Phillimore, 1993.

This Scepter'd Isle. London: BBC Radio 4/BBC Worldwide, 1996.

English Heritage Book of Winchester. London, Batsford, 1997.

The Black Death in Wessex. Hatcher Review 5, no. 46 (1998).

The Black Death in Hampshire, Hampshire Papers 18. Winchester: Hampshire County Council, 1999.

Clarendon: landscape, palace and mansion – a walker's guide. Salisbury: Salisbury Museum, 2010.

The Story of England (Foreword by Mick Aston). Stroud: Tempus, 2003, reprinted 2013.

[with Mark Allen]. *The 1871 Census for Winchester* (CD-ROM). Winchester: Wessex Historical Databases, 2006.

[with Christopher M. Gerrard]. *Clarendon: landscape of Kings*. Macclesfield: Windgather, 2007.

Winchester: from Prehistory to the Present. The History Press, 2006.

[with David Perry *et al.*]. *Perth High Street Archaeological Excavation 1975–1977, 1. The Excavations at 75–95 High Street and 5–10 Mill Street Perth*. Perth: Tayside and Fife Archaeological Committee, 2011.

[with Stephanie Spencer, Andrea Jacobs and Camilla Leach]. *Alumni Voices: the changing experience of higher education*. Winchester: Winchester University Press, 2015.

The University of Winchester: 175 years of values-driven higher education. London: Third Millennium, 2015.

[with Jen Best], *Debt of Honour. Winchester City's First World War Dead, incorporating notes and appendices, including a reprint of the Winchester War Service Register of those from the city who served* Gloucester: Hobnob Press, 2018.

Edited works: some contributions

[with N.A. Price]. "Measurement of the Change in Populations through Time: capture-recapture analysis of population for St Lawrence parish, Southampton, 1454–1610." *Journal of European Economic History* 3, no.5 (1976).

[with Anne M Robinson] "The Historical Context" and "Synthesis"; [with Christopher E. Blunt] "Coins, Jettons and Coronation Medallion"; [with Alison . Goodall and David A. Hinton] "Copper-alloy objects"; [with Barry Knight] "Lead and Lead-alloy objects"; [with John Ashurst] "Stonework and plasterwork." In *Clarendon Palace: the history and archaeology of a medieval palace*, edited by James and Robinson (1988).

"John Hancock: Pre-Raphaelite Sculptor?". In *Pre-Raphaelite Sculpture: nature and imagination in British sculpture 1848–1914*, edited by Benedict Read and Joanna Barnes. London: The Henry Moore Foundation with Lund Humphries, 1991.

"Introduction" and "Conclusion." In *The Black Death in Wessex*, edited by Tom Beaumont James. *Hatcher Review* 5, no. 46 (1998).

"The Black Death in Berkshire and Wiltshire." In *The Black Death in Wessex*, edited by Tom Beaumont James. *Hatcher Review* 5, no. 46 (1998).

"The Black Death: a turning point for Winchester?" In *The Black Death in Wessex*, edited by Tom Beaumont James. *Hatcher Review* 5, no. 46 (1998).

"Les palais anglais: le terme *palatium* et sa signification dans l'Angleterre médiévale, 1000–1600." In *Aux marches du Palais. Qu'est-ce qu'un palais médiéval? Données historiques et archéologiques*, edited by Annie Renoux. Actes du VIIe Congrès international d'Archéologie Médiévale (Le Mans-Mayenne, 9–11 septembre 1999). Le Mans: Publications du LHAM, Université du Maine, 2001.

"John of Eltham, History and Story: abusive international discourse in England, France and Scotland." In *Fourteenth Century England II*, edited by Chris Given-Wilson. Woodbridge: Boydell and Brewer, 2002.

[with Martin Henig, Anthony King and Nigel Ramsay]. "Martin Biddle and Birthe Kjølbye-Biddle: an appreciation." In *Intersections: the archaeology and history of Christianity in England, 400–1200. Papers in honour of Martin Biddle and Birthe Kjølbye-Biddle*, edited by Martin Henig and Nigel Ramsay, British Archaeological Reports British Series 505. Oxford: BAR Publishing, 2010.

"Colin Platt: an academic life." In *A Fresh Approach: essays presented to Colin Platt in celebration of his eightieth birthday*, edited by Claire Donovan. Bristol: Trouser Press, 2014.

"Networking Students of the Clarendon Ruins: Oxford, Southampton and the London Antiquaries." In *A Fresh Approach*, edited by Claire Donovan (2014).

"Medieval Palaces and Royal Houses." In *The Oxford Handbook of Later Medieval Archaeology in Britain*, edited by Christopher M. Gerrard and Alejandra Gutiérrez. Oxford: Oxford University Press, 2018.

Journal papers etc

"Administration and aspiration: some Southampton property owners c. 1400–1600." *Proceedings of the Hampshire Field Club & Archaeological Society* 37 (1981): 55–62.

"Medecroft: A Victorian Town House." *Hampshire Field Club and Archaeological Society section newsletter*, 3 (1985): 24–26.

"The population size of Winchester over 2,000 years: a survey." *Hampshire Field Club and Archaeological Society section newsletters*, new series 9 (1988): 1–3.

"Visitors to Coombe Bissett and Clarendon Palace, 1930–39." *Hatcher Review* 28 (1989).

[with Martin Doughty]. "Tenements and the Historical Landscape of Winchester." *News*, 13. Hampshire Field Club (1990): 16–17.

[with Ann McLellan]. "Strategies for Data Output: the Winchester History Project." In *Yesterday. Proceedings of the Sixth International Conference for History and Computing,* edited by Hans Jorgen Marker and Kirsten Pagh, 244-247. Odense: Odense University Press/ International Association for History and Computing, 1995.

"Southampton and Spain in the 16th century to the 1588 Armada: a sample of sources for ceramic study." In *Spanish Medieval Ceramics in Spain and the British Isles: Cerámica medieval española en España y en las Islas Británicas*, edited by Christopher M. Gerrard, Alejandra Gutiérrez and Alan G. Vince, 41–49. British Archaeological Reports International Series, 610. Oxford: BAR Publishing.

[with Janet Burt]. "Source-oriented data processing: the triumph of the micro over the macro?" *History and Computing* 8 (1996): 160–68.

[with Edward Roberts]. "From Palace to Pentice: Winchester and late-medieval urban development." *Medieval Archaeology* 44 (2000).

"Years of Pestilence: archaeology and the Black Death." *British Archaeology Magazine* 61 (2001).

"Les palais anglais: le terme palatium et sa signification dans l'Angleterre médiévale." In *Aux marches du Palais: Qu'est-ce qu'un palais médiéval? Données historiques et archéologiques. Actes du VIIe Congrès international d'Archéologie Médiévale (Le Mans–Mayenne 9–11 septembre 1999)* edited by Annie Renoux, 135–143. Caen: Société d'Archéologie Médiévale, 2001.

"Migration and the Southampton Melting Pot in the Fifteenth Century." *Southern History* 28 (2006).

"Lost portraits of Bodley's First Librarian and his Grandson." *Journal*. Bodleian Library (2006).

"Mary Seacole's Lost Letter: the only known handwritten letter by Mary Seacole, the 'Greatest Black Briton." *BBC History Magazine* 11, no. 10 (2010).

[with William Poole] "Thomas James (1572-1629) to Thomas James (1640-1710). From the Bodleian to the Jamesian Library. A Royalist High Anglican family promoting the Reformed Faith?" (forthcoming 2021).

Review articles

"Forgotten and Ephemeral? The palace of the kings of Majorca, Perpignan." Review of *Un palais dans la ville, vol. 1: le palais des rois de Majorque à Perpignan*, and Un palais dans la ville, vol. 2: Perpignan des Rois de Majorque, edited by O. Passarius and A. Catafau. Canet en Roussillon: Trabucaire, 2014. *Antiquity* 89, no. 347 (2015).

"The Abbey and Palace of Westminster." Review of *Westminster: the art, architecture and archaeology of the royal abbey and palace* vols. 1 and 2, edited by Tim Tatton-Brown and Warwick Rodwell, British Archaeological Association Conference Transactions 39.1 and 39.2. Leeds: Maney, 2015.

"New Light on the Cinque Ports." *Southern History* 33 (2011): 108–112

Book Reviews for journals including: *Antiquaries' Journal, Antiquity, Archaeological Journal, English Historical Review, Medieval Archaeology,* etc.

Websites

"Black Death: the lasting impact." BBC History. Last modified February 17, 2011.

http://www.bbc.co.uk/history/british/middle_ages/black_impact_01.shtml.

"Overview: the Middle Ages, 1154–1485." BBC History. Last modified June 17, 2011.

http://www.bbc.co.uk/history/british/middle_ages/overview_middleages_01.shtml.

[with Jen Best]. "Debt of Honour: Winchester's First World War dead. Short biographies of the men of Winchester who gave their lives in the Great War." Accessed July 25, 2018. http://debtofhonourwinchester.weebly.com/.

Media

Radio

This Scepter'd Isle. (Continuity texts for tapes, won Sony 'Talkies' Award). Radio scripts by Christopher Lee. London: BBC Radio 4/ BBC Worldwide, 1996.

Radio and local radio interviews and contributions: BBC 5 Live, BBC Wiltshire, BBC Radio Solent etc.

Television

Edward Windsor's *Crown and Country*. Ardent Productions: Carlton Television, 1998.

Melvyn Bragg's *2000 Years of Christianity*. ITV, 1999.

Bettany Hughes's *Seven Ages of Britain*. Channel 4, 2003; Sky Atlantic, 2012.

Sky Atlantic, *Seven Ages of Britain*, 2012.

For Bragg, Hughes and Sky Atlantic he acted as consultant on their interpretation of the Black Death, among other topics

Also

"Foreword." In *Titanic Threads*, by Mary L. South. Bishopstoke: Hamamelis Books, 2012.

Lightning Source UK Ltd.
Milton Keynes UK
UKHW050707280421
382758UK00004B/19

9 781407 357812